P9-CSV-233

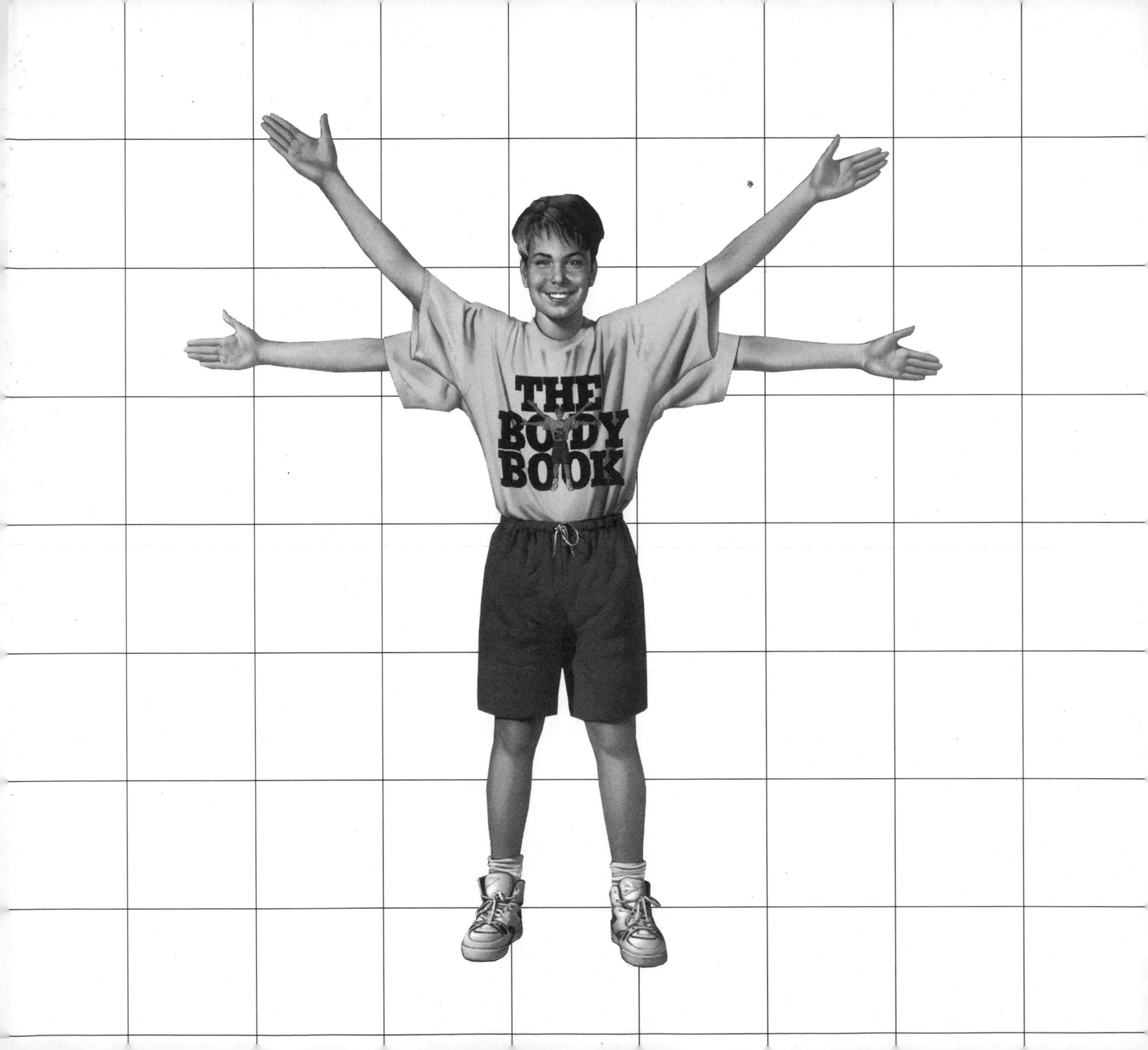
THE
BODY
BOOK

THE BODY BOOK

Written and Illustrated by

Sara Stein

Workman Publishing, New York

For Emma,
The first of the next generation

Published simultaneously in Canada by
Thomas Allen & Son Limited.

Library of Congress Cataloging-in-Publication Data

Stein, Sara Bonnett.
The body book / Sara Stein; illustrations by Sara Stein.
p. cm.
Includes index.
Summary: Facts and explanations about the various body systems, plus information on vaccines, tears, and many other relevant topics.
ISBN 0-89480-805-2 (pbk.)
1. Human anatomy—Juvenile literature. 2. Body , Human—Juvenile literature.
[1. Body, Human.] I Title.
QM27.S74 1992
612—dc20
91-50957 CIP AC

Front cover illustration: Sandra Marziali

Workman Publishing Company, Inc.
708 Broadway
New York, NY 10003

Manufactured in the United States of America

First printing May 1992
10 9 8 7 6 5 4 3 2 1

CONTENTS

STUFF

TAKING SHAPE *6*

ALL-WEATHER OUTERWEAR *28*

Marbles in a box make diffusion easier to understand (page 117).

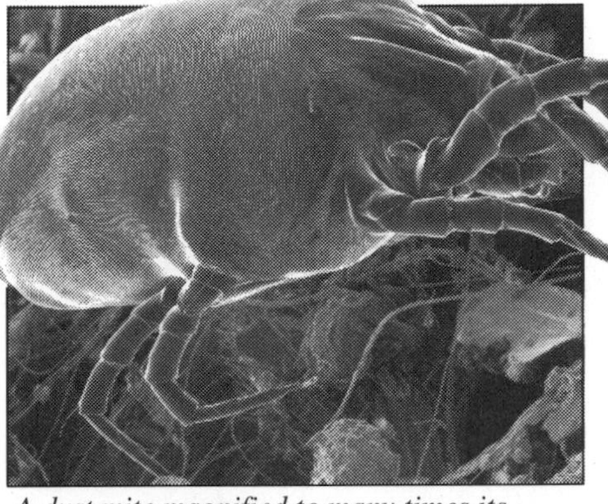

A dust mite magnified to many times its normal size looks scarier than it is (page 43).

BODY BUILDING *46*

If your friend walked by dressed in a snake, you might not "see" it immediately (page 255).

When ragweed pollen is magnified, you can see its spiky shape (page 243).

A gram of clay particles has a total surface area the size of a basketball court (page 111).

SENSES

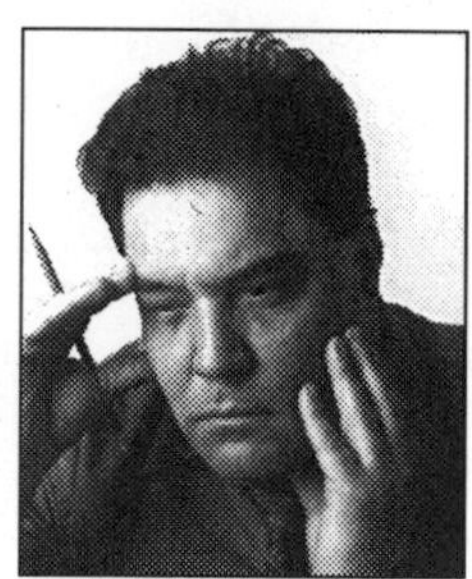
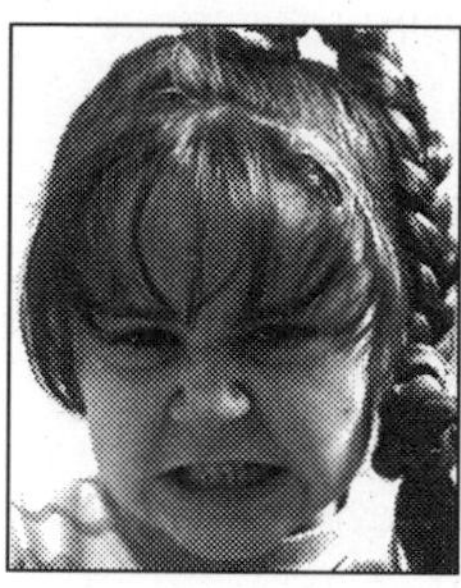
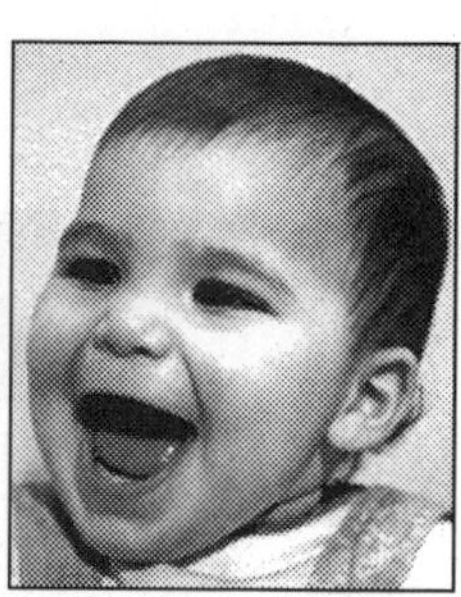

A person's expression often makes it easy to guess what he or she is thinking (page 193).

The carotene in carrots helps us to see (page 187).

Lips can detect two separate touches even if they are only 1/16 inch apart (page 176).

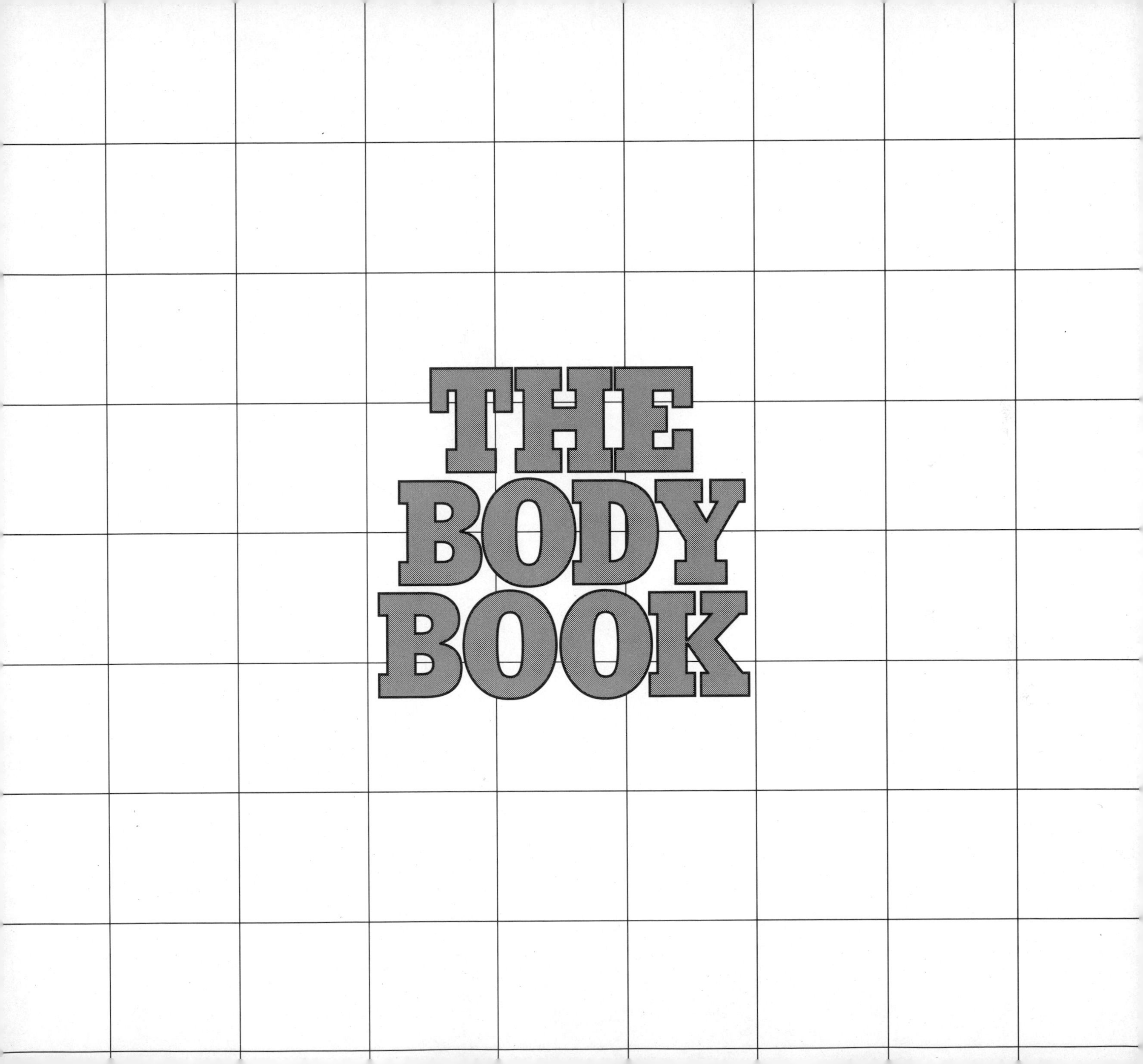
THE
BODY
BOOK

NO BEGINNING

Where did you come from? Not from cabbage leaves or storks, of course, but the straightforward answer that you grew from your mother's egg fertilized by your father's sperm doesn't completely answer the question either.

A body contains tens of trillions of cells, all descended from the one cell that results from the union of an egg and a sperm. The one cell divides, the two it divided into divide again, and the four divide; and so, division by division, the whole human is built. So you came to be.

But so, too, did your parents before you. Since each parent began as a fertilized egg, and each one's cells are all descended from it, a father's sperm are offspring of an egg, and so are a mother's eggs offspring of the egg she was to start with. Nor is that the beginning: Grandparents and great-grandparents were fertilized eggs, and so were all ancestors back to the first humans, and further back still through the mammals, reptiles, and fish from which humans are descended. And fish weren't the beginning.

The knowledge of how to be a living creature goes back much farther than the knowledge of how to be anything as complicated as the communities of cells called fish, or even worms. Before there were many-celled creatures, the knowledge of how to be alive at all was handed down generation to generation by single cells, such as bacteria. And bacteria weren't the first life, either.

Where did life come from? Life evolved among mixes of chemicals that happened to react with one another in self-perpetuating ways, some forming patterns for others' assembly, others assembling the patterns to make more of their kind. Aliveness has been inherited in an unbroken line from such chemicals for about 4 billion years, almost since the world began. Where did the chemicals come from? From Earth's rocks. And Earth? From the dust of a star that exploded somewhere in the Milky Way some 5 billion years ago. And stars?

All the stuff of which you are made has been recycled over and over again. You certainly contain minerals that were once in dinosaurs. Water in your body now was certainly in the first raindrops that fell on Earth. Oxygen you breathe into your lungs was set free by dandelions in the yard, and they'll grow and bloom by using the gas you breathe out. Hair you shed and skin you wear away may blow as dust, be taken apart in soil, rebuilt by plants, and may well come back to you as salad.

The design of your body is also nothing new. You have pairs of ribs, pairs of limbs, and backbones all in a row because ever since worms began, bodies have grown symmetrically in segments in a row, sprouting pairs left and right. At one end is a mouth, at the other an anus, with a tube between. Worms are made the same. Even your most personal possessions, the sex glands that hold the sperm or eggs of the next generation, are modeled on ancient fish kidneys that were tinkered with in the course of evolution to take care of other things than urine. Sperm themselves swim by whipping tails identical to those by which many one-celled creatures swim, and eggs are moved along by cells waving shorter whips that also originated in one-celled forms of life. And what makes the movement—of cells swimming with whipping tails, or you swimming with flailing arms? There you must go back to molecules—constructions made of atoms, the chemistry of life itself.

In the end, there may be no beginning.

On the other hand, there may be no end. A baby not only grows itself into the next generation: It takes care to keep some part of itself for the generation after. The cells that will be your eggs or sperm were set aside for future use when you were an embryo as yet no bigger than a lima bean, and when your birth was still more than half a year in the future.

Part One
STUFF
THE BODY BOOK

TAKING SHAPE

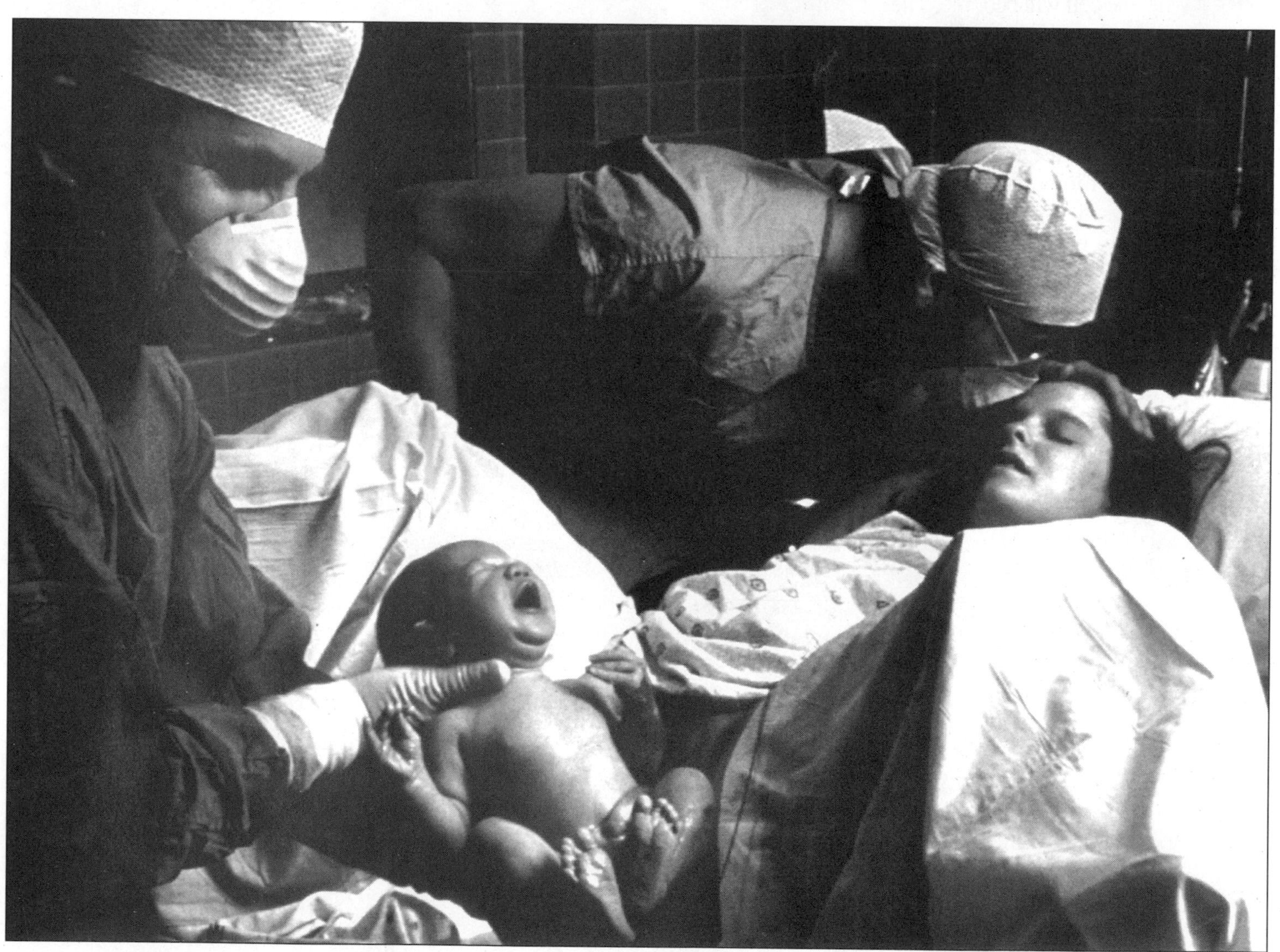

Each person begins as a single cell, a tiny sphere about the size of a period. Inside it is an even tinier sphere, the cell's nucleus, and inside that are packaged all the instructions for what the cell will become. The instructions are threads so narrow that they are invisible even under a school microscope. Were the threads straightened out and laid end to end, they would not even reach the length of your pinky. Yet in the nine months before you were born, you used the information on those slight strands to grow from a single cell into a human baby.

You will never in your life again do anything so mysterious, or so miraculous. Scientists are only beginning to understand how a small set of instructions—the equivalent of no more than 100,000 words, a book about 300 pages long—can build an organism so complicated that a complete description would fill all the libraries of the world. It is as though a cell, a mere dot, knew more than the smartest brain can know—in fact knew how to construct the brain that now puzzles over how it came to be.

Think of the dot you were. Somehow, tucked tightly into its nucleus, was the secret not only of your human shape, but of your intelligence and feeling, of the means to be aware of a world the cell itself knew nothing about. Most mystifying of all is that a cell that knew how to grow, but couldn't think about it, grew into a self that thinks about itself.

Mothers and Daughters

Life is lived inside containers. Some scientists think the first containers might have been pores (small spaces) in clay. There, protected from dashing waves and diluting rain, chemicals crucial to life might have accumulated, become organized within the microscropic layers of clay crystals, and begun to react with one another in ways on which life still depends. The earliest fossil record, however, is of cells, the containers in which all the life we know is lived today.

A cell is enclosed by a membrane that lets some substances in, and keeps others out. Its interior is therefore a select chemical environment unlike the environment of the sea, soil, or atmosphere that surrounds it. To put it simply, life is the chemical reactions that go on among this specialized collection of substances. The reactions make more of the cell: They grow it. And they also reproduce it. A cell grows to a certain size, and then divides into two smaller cells, each containing the same specialized group of chemicals and surrounded by a membrane that selects the substances with which the cell will again grow, and again divide.

Traditionally a cell before it has divided is called a mother cell; the two cells into which it divides are called daughters. This is confusing because, once there are daughters, there is no longer a mother. But that's life: Cells are mothers, then daughters, then mothers again. One cell, way back when, was the mother of us all.

Evidence that all life descended from the same ancestor is in our genes, the chemical instructions that say how to build bodies whether those bodies are one-celled blobs, or strands of seaweed, or bees, or mice, or us. Genes are sections of molecules—attached groups of atoms—that provide patterns for assembling other molecules that give a body its shape and substance. Differences in the patterns account for differences among organisms. But although a human has genes that a bacterium doesn't and a bacterium has genes that a human doesn't, each can read the other's instructions. The genetic language is life's mother tongue.

Because genes say how to be to be alive, a cell can't divide haphazardly like a drop breaking into droplets. Each daughter has to receive a full set of instructions. Your first act as a fertilized egg was to copy your genes, separate the copies into two sets, and split.

A Cell Divides

Genes are strung together and packaged within very long, twisted, threadlike structures called chromosomes. In humans, each cell has 23 pairs of chromosomes, 46 in all. The two chromosomes in a pair are similar: If one contains a certain gene, so does the other, but the genes may differ slightly. All the chromosomes are kept in the nucleus of the cell, a sphere more or less in its center.

A cell starts to copy its chromosomes hours before it divides. Small lengthwise openings appear in them, like sewing thread teased apart in the middle. The openings spread, parting larger and larger portions of each chromosome. As each portion opens, new strands, made of materials floating in the cell fluid, assemble and twist into place, so now there are two threads instead of one. Finally all 46 chromosomes that had each been one twisted thread are two threads—two identical chromosomes—held together like Siamese twins by what looks like a knot in the middle.

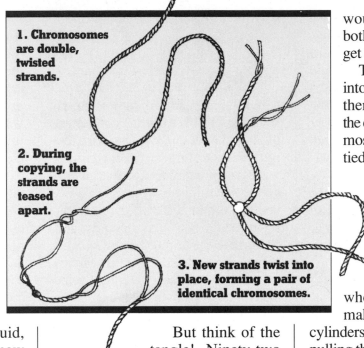

1. Chromosomes are double, twisted strands.

2. During copying, the strands are teased apart.

3. New strands twist into place, forming a pair of identical chromosomes.

But think of the tangle! Ninety-two chromosomes are now looped and snarled about one another in a nucleus that was crowded enough with half that many. If the nucleus were just to be squeezed in two, or if there were an attempt to pull the tangle apart as one does to serve spaghetti, there would be no chance at all that both daughter cells would each get a complete, unbroken set.

The long, loose strands coil up into tight ringlets, disentangling themselves as they curl. When the coiling is completed, the chromosomes are 46 pairs of ringlets tied together at their middles.

While this is happening, the cell makes other preparations for dividing. It makes extra membrane, which appears as blisters on its surface, so that it won't burst when it squeezes into two. It makes a duplicate of two small cylinders, which are its equipment for pulling the chromosomes apart. Delicate fibers grow from the cylinders, pushing them away from one another until they lie at opposite ends of the cell with the nucleus between them. At this point the nucleus comes apart, leaving the pairs of chromosomes exposed.

Now begins what looks like a tug of

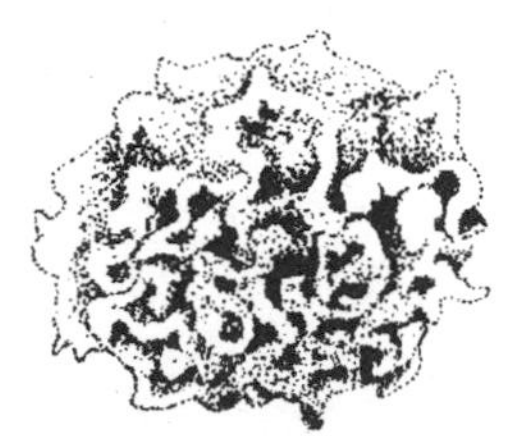

1. Cell before division

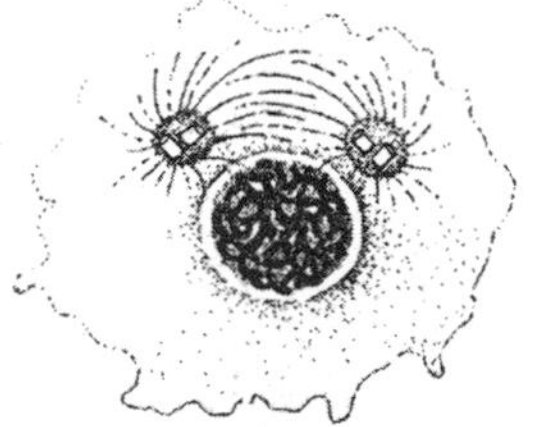

2. Pairs of cylinders forming rays

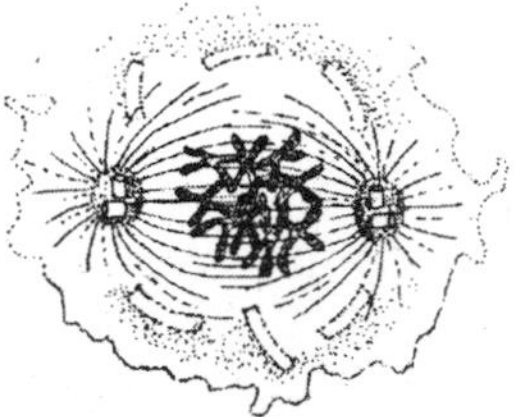

3. Nucleus coming apart

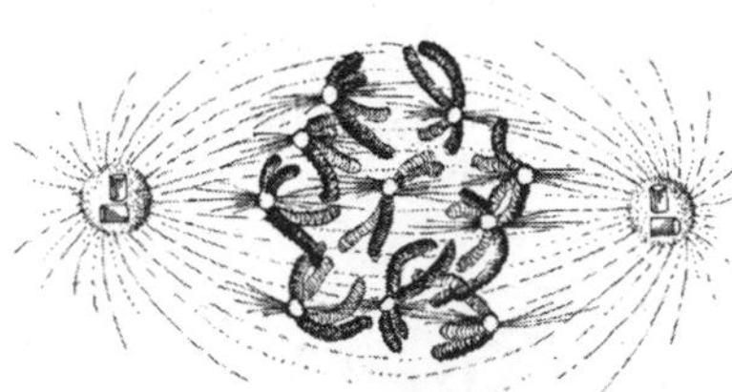

4. Chromosomes being pulled

war, the purpose of which is to pull the chromosomes apart into two separate groups. Fibers grow from the knots that hold the chromosomes together, and these fibers are pulled by those that reach out from the cylinders. Caught in the middle of this tug of war, the coupled chromosomes spin and flip, pulled now toward one end of the cell and now toward the other. Eventually the knots come undone and the copies part, pulled by the fibers to opposite ends of the cell. Fragments of the nucleus reattach around the two sets of chromosomes. There are now two nuclei in the cell, one at each end, one for each daughter.

There only remains for the cell itself to split. A belt of fibers forms around its middle, halfway between the new nuclei. It tightens. The cell's membrane begins to wrinkle like a bag cinched in by a drawstring. Finally only a narrow neck remains between the soon-to-be daughters. When the neck is pinched to nothing, the job is done: The one cell has divided into two.

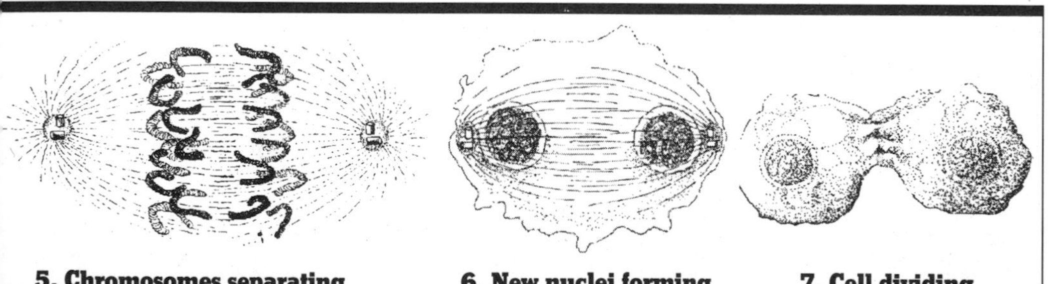

5. Chromosomes separating **6. New nuclei forming** **7. Cell dividing**

You

You performed your first division during your first day, a few hours after fertilization. Since then the number of divisions has been countless. Millions of cells in you are dividing right this minute, healing bruises, making blood, growing you. All your cells, for all these years, in all divisions, have faithfully copied the genes that were copied the first time.

Some of those genes are identical to some in bacteria, and have been copied since bacteria began. Other genes are not: Over time, the patterns of genes are occasionally miscopied, or break and are patched together in a slightly different way. Through such mistakes the chemistry of organisms changes, and so, too, does their shape and substance. Those changes are responsible for evolution, the continual creation of new forms of life.

Human genes are therefore a historical record, written in the genetic language of our species' evolution. Your genes record some changes by which fish evolved, some by which mammals evolved, some by which apes evolved, and some—perhaps a thousand novel genes out of a hundred thousand altogether—by which humans came to be. In a way, there's nothing new about you.

And yet you are unique. There's never been a person like you, and there won't ever be again. Over the millions of years of our evolution, many genetic mistakes too minor to have caused a new species have nevertheless added a great deal of variety to the human race: to nose shapes and hair texture, eye color and foot size, voice, temperament, intelligence, and strength. You share with your parents some of their variety, and so you resemble them. But you don't share *all* your parents' genes. You have just half of your mother's genes, and half of your father's. The particular combination of genes you received is what makes you unlike any other person.

Each sperm or egg is itself unique, for it bears a selection of genes chosen randomly from among those available on both sets of a parent's chromosomes, and then divided among the daughters, half to each. The unique egg you grew from was one of about 300 to 400. The unique sperm that fertilized it was one of hundreds of millions. Usually just one egg ripens per month. It will die if it is not fertilized within the next two days. The chance of that particular egg, at that particular time, being fertilized by that particular sperm is therefore nearly nil. And never mind the chance of your parents ever meeting one another, or making love just then!

Yet here you are: you.

A Sperm's Journey

Sperm are designed for one job only: to deliver genes to an egg. They are a great deal smaller than the usual body cell—they have almost none of the cell fluid by which other cells are nourished, and no equipment with which to make anything, or grow, or divide. Their shape is like a stretched-out tadpole—a head, a short neck, and a very long, very skinny tail. The head contains chromosomes, the 23 strands of genes that it brings from the father. They will be half the baby's instructions for how to become a human. The tail wiggles the sperm, swimming, to the egg.

The egg carries the other half of a baby-to-be's instructions, genes strung on 23 chromosomes donated by the mother. By comparison with average body cells, an egg is huge. At a tenth of a millimeter in diameter, it is the only body cell that can be seen with the naked eye, although it looks simply like a speck. The reason the egg is so large is that it contains grains of yolk—not as much as a bird egg, which must supply nourishment to a growing chick for weeks, but enough to keep the cell nourished for several days.

Multiplications

Identical twins are an exception to the rule that each person is genetically unique. These twins are the result of an egg whose two daughters, after the first division, failed to hold onto one another. Each then continued to develop separately. Had daughters of the first two also failed to remain attached, there might have been identical quadruplets, or, if one had not survived, identical triplets. Twins, triplets, and quadruplets that are not identical are the result of two or more eggs ripening and being fertilized in the same month. Although they have shared the same womb at the same time, they are no more alike than other brothers and sisters born at different times.

This overstuffed cell can't move. It reaches its ripe size in one of two ovaries (egg containers) that lie to either side of the womb where a baby might grow. When the egg is ripe, the ovary pops it out. The tube through which it reaches the womb sweeps it up into its funnellike entrance. Cells lining the tube move it along on waving fingers called cilia. Perhaps the egg hatched from the ovary hours ago. The egg has been pushed only an inch down the tube, and awaits sperm that have to swim to it, first through the womb, or uterus, then through the tube, upstream against the beating cilia.

Some 400 million sperm attempt this journey. They are spurted from the man's penis into the woman's vagina, which leads to the womb through a narrow opening. From there on, the sperm are on their own, still inches from the waiting egg.

The death rate among sperm is appalling. Some dive in error into pits in the wall of

the womb, and perish there. Others die of exhaustion. Only a few thousand reach the opening of a tube at the top of the womb, but there are two tubes, one for each ovary: Half the survivors reach the wrong tube by mistake and, for all their effort, find no egg in it. By the time those that have stumbled into the right tube struggle to its far end where the ripe egg lies waiting, their number is reduced to a few hundred. If the couple who launched this journey made love at bedtime, they have now been sleeping for an hour.

Six more hours must pass before a sperm can penetrate the egg. The egg is surrounded by a thick jelly coating that sperm can't swim through. They must digest a tunnel through it. Sperm come equipped with the chemicals to do that, but they can't release the chemicals until substances in the fluid they swim through have prepared them. The preparation takes seven hours altogether—nearly a full night's sleep.

A sperm's route to the egg begins at the vagina, and ends in the egg tube.

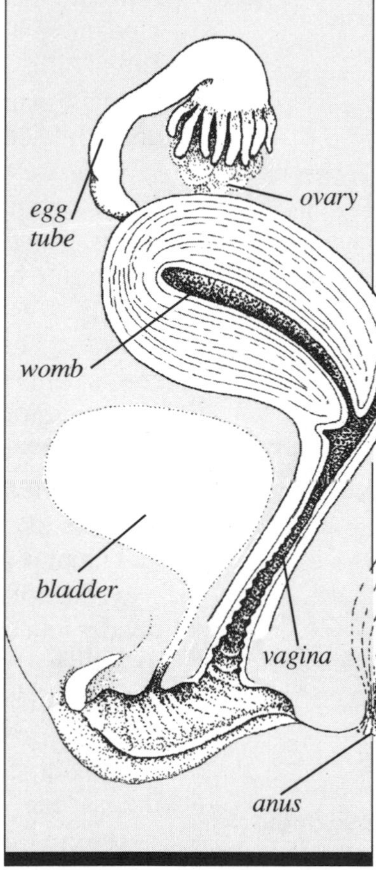

As the new day dawns, sperm are prepared for their finest moment. Embedded in the egg's thick coat are about a billion receptors shaped to grasp projections on the heads of sperm, like docking devices on space stations that lock onto arriving spaceships. As a sperm nudges against the egg, tens of thousands of receptors grip its head, and the two are firmly bound to one another. Dozens, scores, a hundred sperm lock onto the egg until it is so covered with tail-waving sperm that it looks as though it had sprouted hair. But however many sperm succeed in docking, the egg is not yet fertilized, for there is still the jelly coat to get through.

While the sky lightens each docked sperm begins to digest a tunnel through this last obstacle. The tunnel is very narrow, just wide enough for a sperm to squirm through. About the fastest a sperm can travel through the coat is a micron—a millionth of a meter—a minute. The coat is seven times that thick: The alarm clock on the bedside table ticks out another seven minutes.

The alarm rings. One sperm has made it. At a touch, the cell membranes of sperm and egg fuse together, and in that instant the egg exudes all over its surface a substance that inactivates all the receptors on its coat, and makes the jelly indigestible. Arriving sperm can no longer dock; sperm still tunneling to the egg are stopped in their tracks. Fertilization, the union of one sperm with one egg, has begun.

Strangely, the winner of this long race, the single sperm now fused to the egg, is paralyzed by the act of fusion. Having swum so far and struggled so mightily, it can't go any farther. The egg must actively haul the sperm inside. It reaches out with tiny feelers that wrap around the sperm, contract, and pull the limp suitor in.

The sperm enters the egg naked, leaving its own thin covering to blend with the egg's membrane. Once inside, its tail disintegrates. Then the nucleus containing its chromosomes falls apart. So does the nucleus containing the egg's chromosomes. Slowly—coffee brews, noon passes, night falls again—the two groups of chromosomes move toward each other.

About 24 hours after the sperm started its perilous journey, its chromo-

The Right Sperm

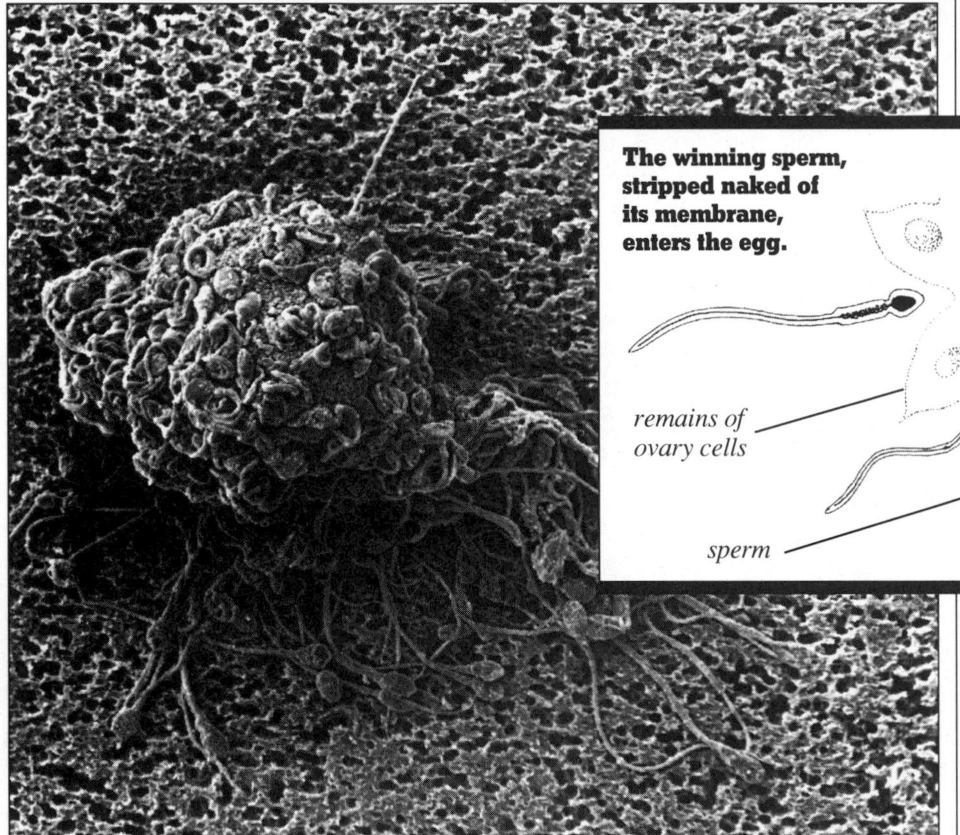

The winning sperm, stripped naked of its membrane, enters the egg.

These sperm are able to dock on this egg only because the egg has receptors with which to grasp them. Each species' sperm receptors recognize by shape only the knobs on sperm of that species. This is necessary because all sperm swim, whether in a lake, in body fluids, or in the film of moisture on damp moss. Were eggs to accept sperm of other species, they could be fertilized by the wrong kind. It is also important that the egg let only one sperm get inside. More than that would give the fertilized egg the wrong number of chromosomes.

somes meet and pair up with the egg's chromosomes, pooling information that, the day before, was the exclusive property of two separate individuals, the man and woman who, for all the drama of these events, have as yet no way of knowing that they have produced a fertilized egg, one cell, a whole new individual.

Burrowing In

The fertilized egg continues its slow roll to the womb where it will find the space and the nourishment it needs to comfortably grow into a baby, but it wastes no time along the way. It copies its chromosomes and divides four times while still in the tube: to 2, then 4, then 8, then 16 cells. The round clump of cells looks much like a raspberry. On the fourth day it rolls gently into the womb, where it at first floats free.

By the fifth day, there is a change inside the berry. The cells had so far stuck to one another solidly. Now some inside become unstuck, leaving a space that fills with fluid. This hollow capsule is made of only one layer of cells except for a thick place at the top where a solid bump of cells remains.

The bump will be the baby—or, as it is called when still so young, the embryo. The capsule will be a life-support system that will keep the embryo living and growing in an environment that, without it, would not feed it, not dispose of its wastes, not give it shelter, or even recognize its presence. It will be the baby's placenta, an organ that exchanges the embryo's waste products for nutrients and oxygen in the mother's blood, and the umbilical cord by which the placenta is connected to the embryo. The capsule will also be the beautiful, transparent balloon in which, as the baby grows, it will float and kick, sleep and drink, blink and pee, listen to the thump of its mother's heart and even, as it develops enough to do such wonderful things, look around in the dim red light that penetrates its cozy home.

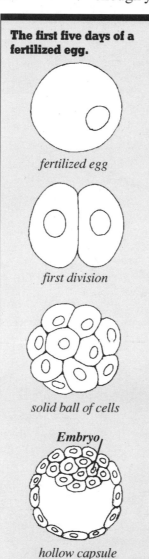

The first five days of a fertilized egg.

fertilized egg

first division

solid ball of cells

Embryo

hollow capsule

But right now, as the embryo rolls around the womb in its round container, it is in danger. There has been enough yolk to live and to divide for these few days, but not to grow. At each division, the daughter cells are only half the size their parents were, so the whole group is no bigger now than the single egg had been. And the yolk is nearly gone. The only other source of nourishment is the surrounding fluid the capsule can absorb. The bigger and thicker the embryo grows, the less fluid will reach its innards. The embryo is in danger of soon starving.

A woman's womb is a pear-sized, pear-shaped hollow muscle with a soft lining. Once a month, as an egg ripens in an ovary, the lining in the womb thickens. Blood vessels grow into it. Deep glands that make a fatty, starchy juice form in the lining—they are the pits some sperm swim into by mistake. The blood and juice in the womb lining contain the food the embryo must have. Ordinarily, this thick lining detaches and is shed during a woman's menstrual period, leaving only a thin skin from which the thicker lining will regrow as the next egg ripens. It is the embryo's responsibility to make certain that doesn't happen.

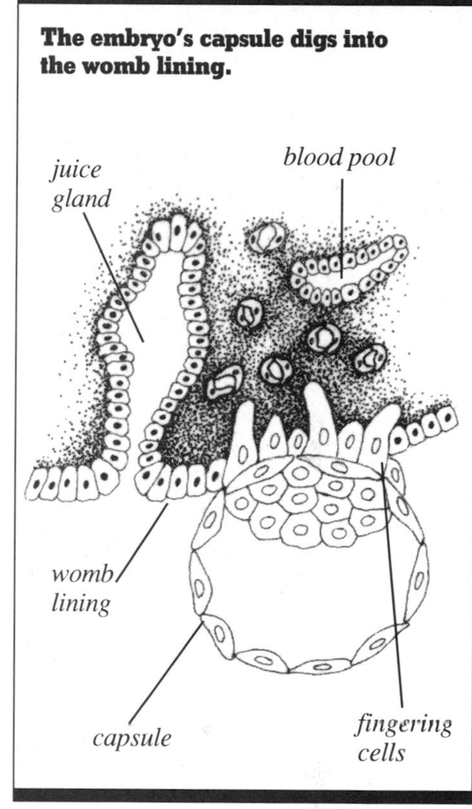

The embryo's capsule digs into the womb lining.

As soon as the berry becomes a hollow capsule, its outer cells begin to secrete a hormone—a chemical signal—that makes the womb lining stay put. On the sixth day of the embryo's life, some outer cells attach to the lining just at the place where the bump that will be the baby bulges inside. Capsule cells there divide fast, forming fingers that dig into the lining of the womb. The fingers eat their way into glands, and the gland walls disintegrate, spilling their rich juice in puddles of good food. As the fingers burrow deeper, they pull the whole capsule into the lining. By the tenth day the embryo inside its round container is completely buried in its mother's flesh, an invader now about as big as a pinhead.

Spacesuit

By two weeks after fertilization, the capsule holding the embryo has grown to about the size of a capital "O," and the place where it burrowed into the lining has closed behind it.

The embryo has hardly grown at all, but its shape has changed. The bump of cells has flattened into a pancake two cells thick. The top of the pancake will be the baby's back. Toward one end, the two layers are tightly attached to one another in a small circle, like a spot weld, that will be the mouth. Toward the other end a similar round spot will be the anus.

A blister covers the pancake like a domed ceiling. Another blister swells below it. Both blisters are attached to the embryo all around its edge. The lower blister is the same wrapper that, in a bird's egg, holds the yolk. No yolk is left by the time a human embryo's yolk sac forms, but most of the sac will

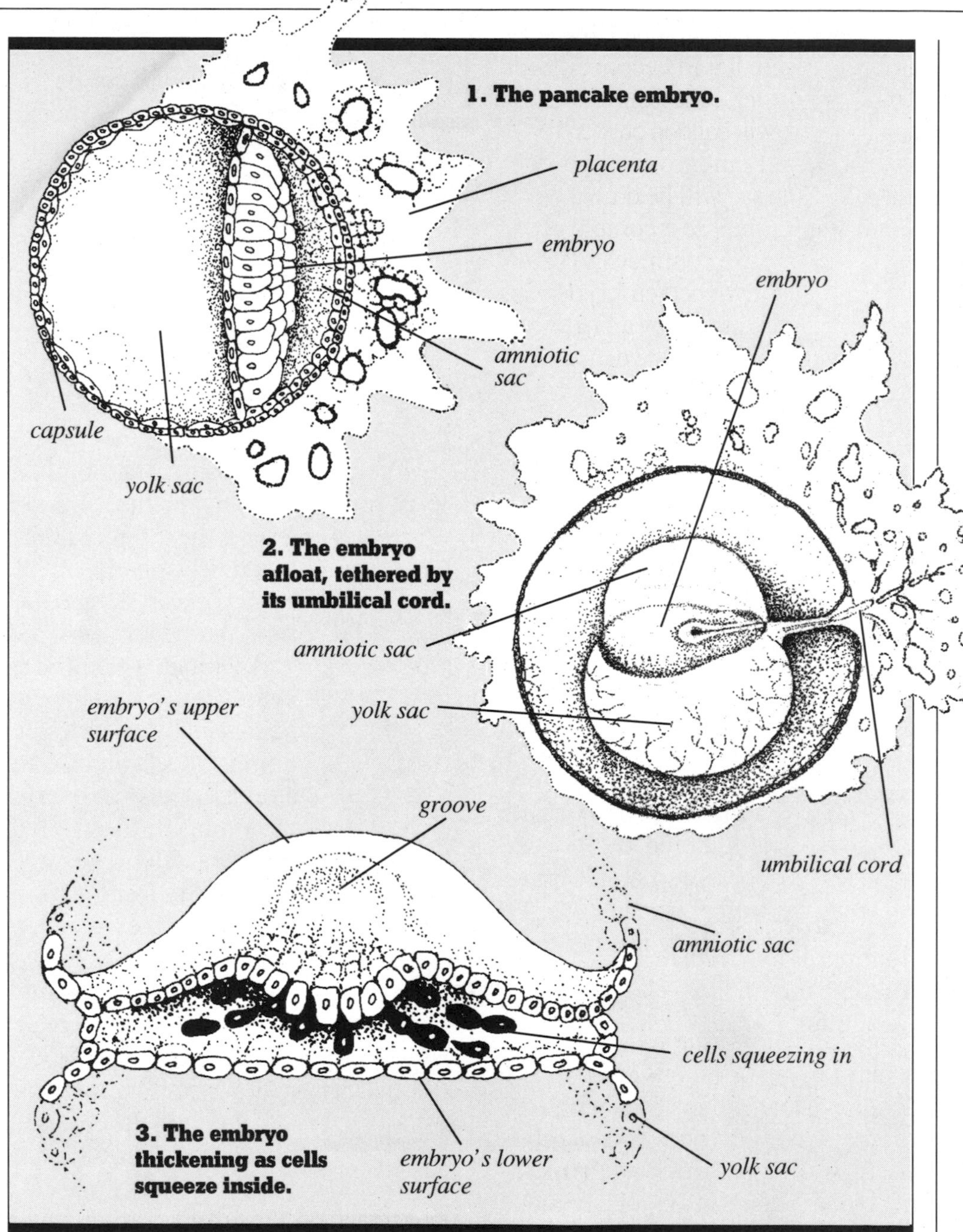

1. The pancake embryo.

2. The embryo afloat, tethered by its umbilical cord.

3. The embryo thickening as cells squeeze inside.

eventually become wrapped inside the embryo, where it will become its gut. The upper blister, called the amnion or amniotic sac, will balloon outward; and, as the pancake embryo curls under at the edges, the sac will be drawn down around it and enclose it completely.

As the capsule continues to grow, the blister-sandwiched embryo is left suspended from its wall by a single tether, its umbilical cord. The capsule has grown a good deal. The embryo suspended in this fluid-filled space has room to grow.

The capsule has also thickened. Its fingering walls now reach deep into the womb's lining in all directions. Pools of blood have formed where vessels in the lining have disintegrated. Pockets have formed in the capsule wall as well. Blood seeps from pools to pockets. The capsule and the layer of lining it has invaded is becoming the placenta.

Over the next few days this very complicated little machine in which the embryo floats tethered by its cord begins to function as a spacesuit, bringing from the mother ship her oxygen and food, and dumping into her body its wastes.

Pockets like those that have already formed in the capsule wall now form within the wall of the yolk sac, too. The pockets grow longer, join with one another, and form networks of tubes that fill with blood. This is not the mother's blood. Vessels in the yolk sac make

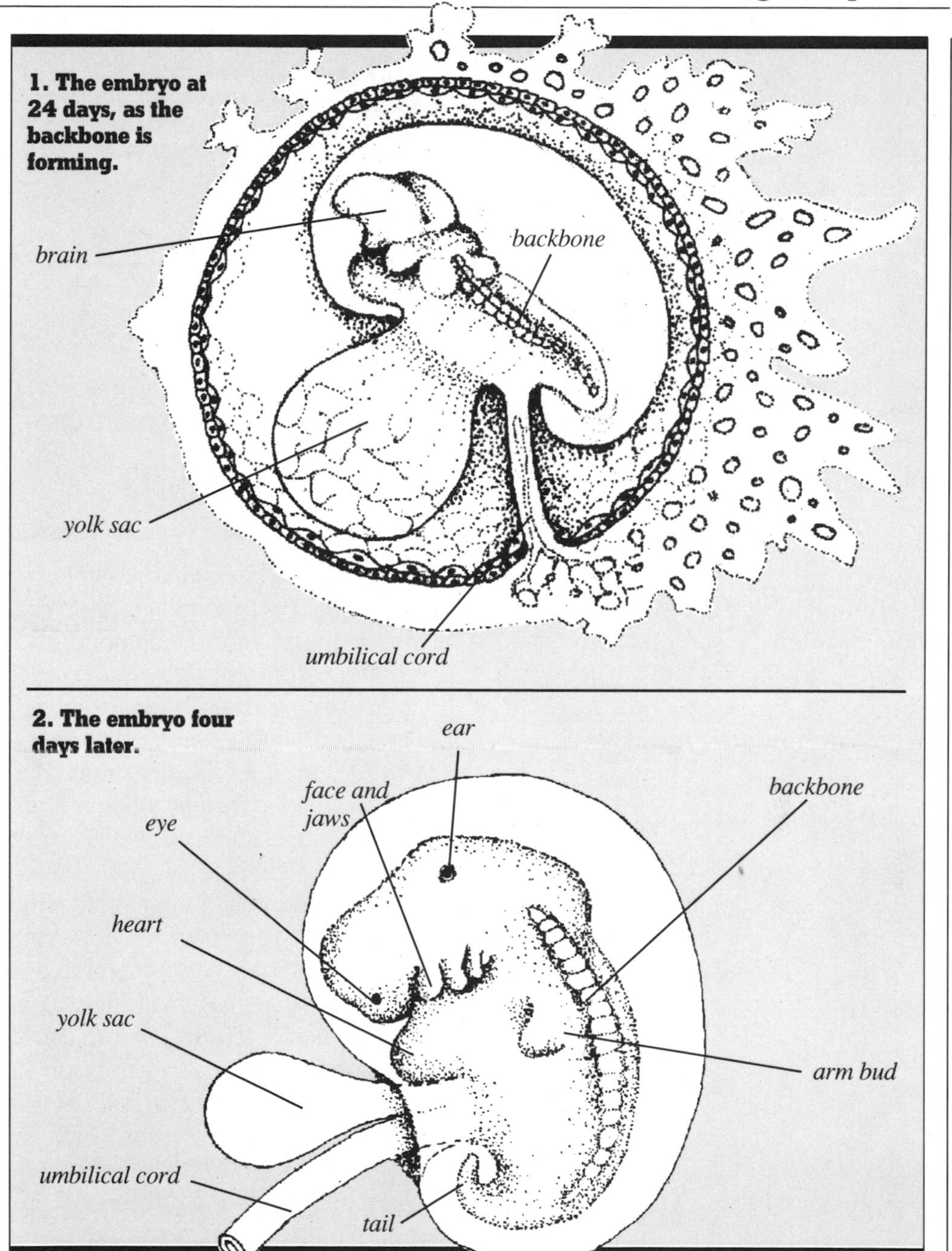

1. The embryo at 24 days, as the backbone is forming.

2. The embryo four days later.

it themselves; it is the embryo's own.

Meanwhile the embryo thickens. Cells along the midline of its back sink inward, then squeeze inside between the two pancake layers and spread, plumping the embryo up with a thick stuffing of inner cells. Pockets form within this thickness too, and lengthen into a pair of tubes that fuse together at the front end and beat like the little heart they are. By 22 days old, the embryo is pumping its own blood out through its umbilical cord into the blood vessels of its placenta, and receiving the blood back freshened up and newly stocked with food.

The embryo's mother may suspect that something's up: What else but a human being the size of a corn kernel could be holding back the womb's rich lining that, were she not pregnant, would by now have been shed?

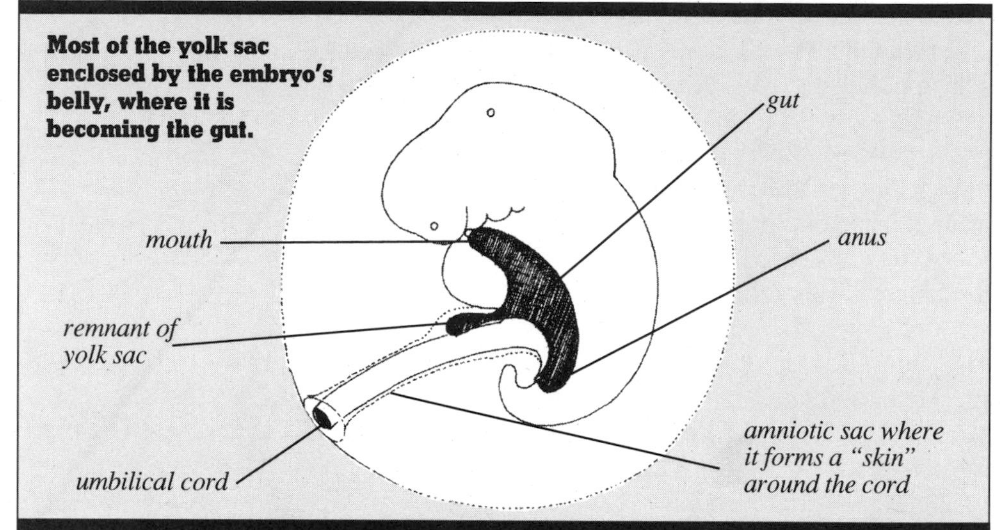

Most of the yolk sac enclosed by the embryo's belly, where it is becoming the gut.

The Little Monster

The embryo doesn't look like a pancake anymore, but it doesn't look like a baby either. For the next month, it is fair to say that the embryo looks like a little monster.

The ugly stage begins with a groove that grows forward over the embryo's back from its tail end to about its middle, where it forms a pit. The pit bottom continues to grow forward inside the embryo, forming a sort of worm hole that soon loses its hole and becomes a solid rod. The rod isn't permanent. It's a placemarker to show the spinal column, brain, backbone, and ribs where to begin.

Backbone and ribs begin as groups of inner cells that congregate into pairs of wedges to either side of the rod. The wedges show as bumps where vertebrae—the small bones that make up the backbone—will be.

Nerves begin as a thickening strip of skin along the embryo's back that creases just above the submerged rod. The crease deepens. Its top edges fuse together, making it a tube. Skin to either side of the tube closes over it, burying it inside. The tailward part is the spinal cord. The forward part—half the tube!—grows up to be a brain.

The brain makes a monster of the embryo right away. It grows like a bulbous nose drooping over the round spot that isn't yet a mouth. Then the top-heavy head bends downward, burying the mouth spot in a deep fold between the front of the brain and the heart, which bulges out in a lump nearly as big as the brain. Tucked between mouth and heart are what look like three or four chins. They are arches of cells that haven't yet moved into position as a face and jaws. The embryo is, in fact, faceless. Two spots that will be eyes stare blindly at the bulging heart. Floating in the middle of nowhere on the lumpish head are two holes that will be ears.

The rest of the body is not much prettier. Two buds of flesh to either side in its middle are the only sign of arms. Leg buds have not begun. The only charming feature is a fat tail which now,

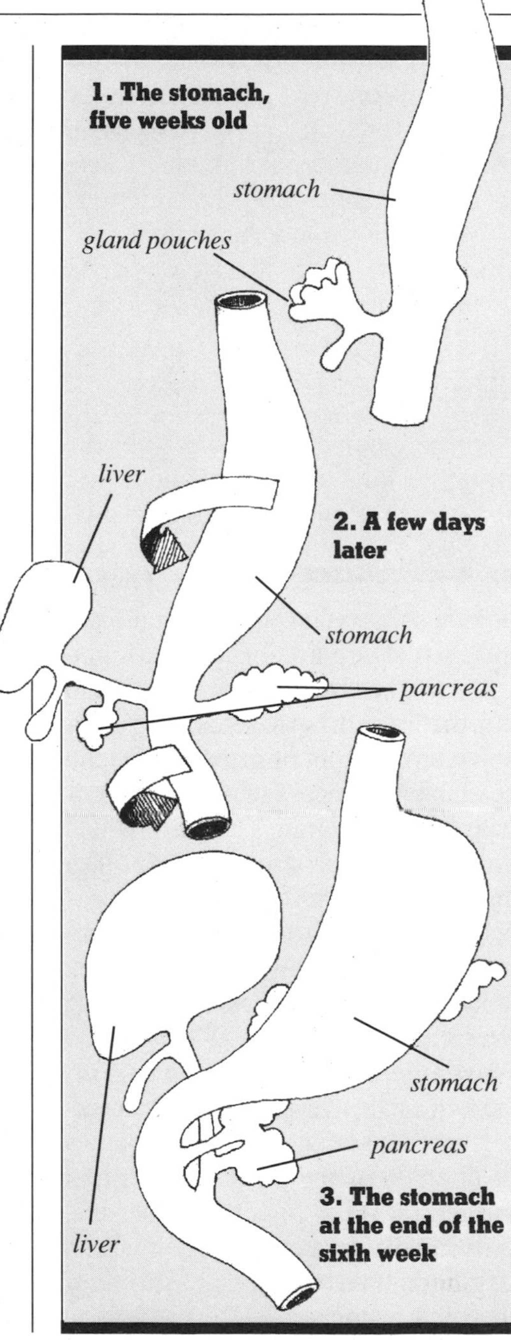

like the brain, curls downward. From the side, the embryo's body is shaped like the letter "C."

At the same time that head and tail are curling, the sides of the embryo's body, originally as flat as a pancake, begin to grow and curl down around the yolk sac. As the edges grow, meet, and fuse together, they trap part of the sac inside the embryo. (The seam shows in some people as a thin, brown line from belly button to crotch.) Because the embryo is now longer than it is wide, the sac is naturally squeezed into a sort of sausage casing that runs straight through the embryo from mouth spot to anus spot. The two spots deepen into pits, the pits fuse with the sausage, and their bottoms open. The embryo is no prettier, but at least it has a front hole, a rear hole, and a gut between.

All this curling wraps the embryo completely in its amniotic sac, for the circular edge to which the sac was originally attached is now drawn together like a pouch around the umbilical cord. The amnion fuses to the cord, and grows down around it like a skin. This frees the embryo from any attachment except the umbilical cord. It is as free to float in its water-filled balloon as an astronaut in space.

Embryonic Geometry

The geometry one learns in school stands still. Circles don't curl; cones don't grow. The geometry of an embryo is dynamic, on-the-go, pitting in and pouching out, thickening and thinning, coming open and glomming shut, curving, bending, twisting into continually changing shapes. Yet it is very simple: There are only five ways in which an embryo shapes itself. Cells divide more or less rapidly; cells move; cells attach to one another; cells let go of one another; cells die.

To curve the body, cells along the top divide more rapidly than the others. Cells move from the surface to the inside to plump the embryo up. Spaces that will be blood vessels begin when cells let go of one another. The heart starts when cells on two tubes cling to one another. The mouth opens when cells at the bottom of the mouth pit and cells at the end of the sausage casing first attach to each other, then die.

Picturing how such things as guts are shaped makes the anatomy of innards easier to understand. At four weeks, the yolk sac that was enclosed within the curling embryo is a straight tube open at both ends—the mouth and anus. By five weeks, cells in one area of the tube are dividing faster than others; that expands the tube into the beginnings of a stomach. Below the stomach, round patches of cells divide quickly, forming pouches. The pouches are the beginnings of other digestive apparatus—the liver, and a gland called

Insies, Outsies

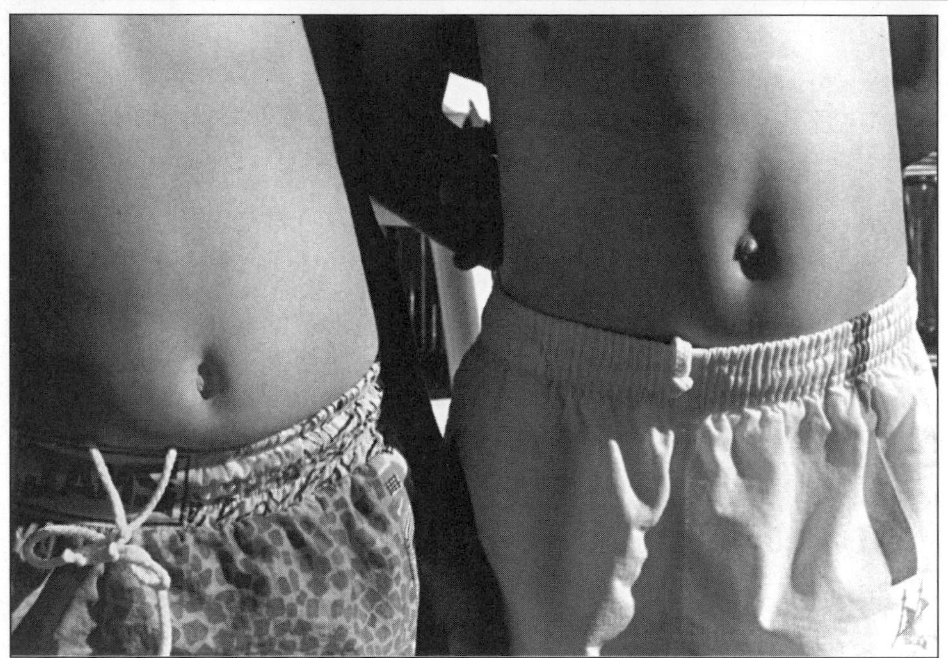

Your belly button marks the spot where your umbilical cord was attached. After birth, a baby's cord is clamped shut and cut to several inches long. It doesn't hurt: The cord has no pain nerves. The stump of the cord dries up and falls off, leaving a small scar that you can find if you look hard enough. If the stump falls off at the surface of the belly, the belly button will dent inward—an "insie." If it falls off a short distance from the belly, the belly button will stick out—an "outsie."

the pancreas. By the end of that week, the arrangement is more elaborate. Pouches are branching into new pouches, cells dividing at the ends of some of them are sticking together, making a solid lump instead of a hollow pocket.

Now the whole arrangement begins to twist in the same way that the embryo's body curled. By the sixth week the embryo's stomach has twisted and turned into its final tilted-to-one-side position, two pancreases have fused into one, the liver is in its proper place, and the portion of intestine where these two glands empty their digestive juices has bent into a sharp curve. Two weeks from tube to digestive system, compliments of embryonic geometry.

Shape Up the Old Way

At the beginning of the sixth week the embryo's lidless eyes point sideways. As for the rest of the face, hardly visible below the bulging brain, the nostrils are continuous with a slit of lipless mouth; there is no nose; the ears are holes. Just behind the ears the buds-becoming-arms are longer, but they end in paddles. There are legs; they look about the same as the arms. Curling up between the legs is a tail twice their length.

It would be hard to tell what sort of animal this embryo is going to be. Its eyes are in the right position to be a donkey's, not a human's. Its paddles might be hooves, for all anyone knows. The ears might stay holes, as they are in whales, or grow as big as bat ears. Certainly the face would look more endearing to a mother bat than to this baby's mother. And that tail! Humans just don't have them.

In fact at six weeks a donkey, whale, or bat embryo hardly looks different from a human one. A little earlier you couldn't have told this embryo from a fish, or from a bird. This is because the basics of embryonic geometry are as old as fish, which evolved more than 500 million years ago. Each kind of animal begins with old, time-tested shapes and then elaborates them in its own inventive way.

All mammals make two sets of kidneys before fashioning their final pair. The first set is of a kind used long ago by primitive fish; it is of no apparent use now. The second is of a kind still used by fish, and makes the embryo's urine for a few days. Neither kind is completely discarded: Tubes from the first are reused as tubes for the second, and then reused again for portions of the reproductive system.

In a fish, some of the arches that give a human embryo its many-chinned look become the bony arches that support its gills. Human embryos use the same arches for fashioning jaws, ears, tongue, voice box, and all the grinning, frowning muscles of the face. The seam where one pair of arches grows together to form the lower jaw shows as a chin dent in some people. Occasionally a baby is born with a small pit in the skin behind an ear; that's the remnant of a gill slit that would, in a fish, open into the mouth. Parts of the same arches in a reptile embryo become the hinge of its jaw. In us those parts of the arches become minute inner ear bones. Yolk sacs in fish, reptiles, and birds are filled with yolk, which is the embryo's only food. Ours contains no nourishment, but the sac's talent for absorbing food is not wasted, since it becomes our digestive tract.

Tails do seem a waste. All that's left of yours is a short length of fused tail bones that you can feel at the base of your spine. Although our species hasn't found a use for tails, they are apparently too fundamental to be dispensed with. Maybe they, like the temporary rod that came to us from boneless animals more ancient even than fish, tell other parts—legs or behinds—where to be.

For all this repetition of ancient history, the embryo by the end of the sixth week looks definitely human. It is as though its built-in and obligatory repertory for shaping the basic body has been run through, and now it can play uniquely human themes. Growth of the back of the head pushes the eyes forward. Nostrils separate from mouth, a snubby nose grows, and there are lips and those familiar shell-shaped ears. Paddle hands have formed finger ridges that, as they separate, will leave only tell-tale webs between the fingers as evidence that they once were joined. Toes, too, have begun. The tail has shrunk to a stub.

Obviously, the chemistry of this final shaping is no longer fishy. Whatever is happening in the butt end of the baby to make the tail self-destruct is direct-

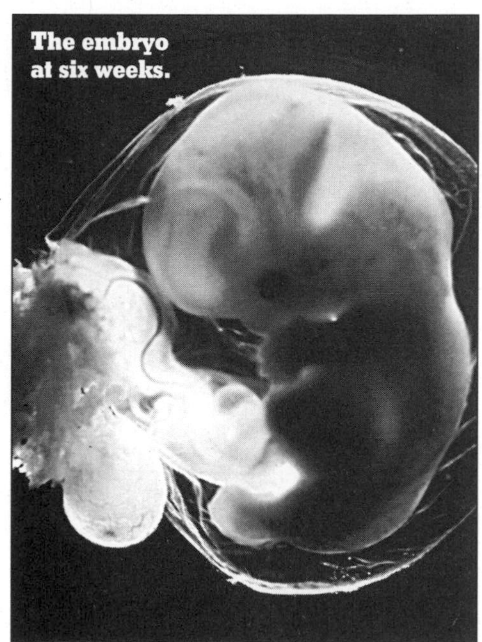

The embryo at six weeks.

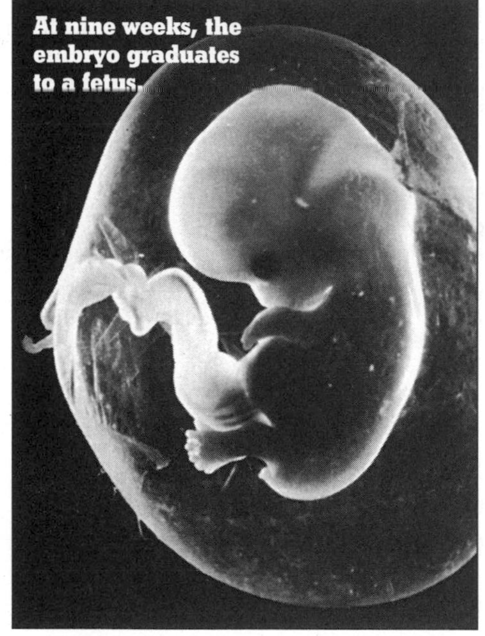

At nine weeks, the embryo graduates to a fetus.

ed by genes that won't make a monkey of him.

Him? You can't be sure yet. Two weeks' time will tell.

Male or Female

Nine weeks old is a graduation of sorts: The embryo is from now on called a fetus. This is not because any one dramatic thing has happened. But looking at the little creature now, you would be more likely to say "ooh" or "ahhh" than "ugh." True, its head is bulgy still, its arms and legs too skimpy, and its body is so ridiculously small that there isn't room inside for the rapidly lengthening intestine, which for now hangs in loops inside the umbilical cord. But the fetus has elbows and knees, toes and fingers, face and rump—now altogether tailless—and it is big enough to snuggle comfortably into a peanut shell. Even more important for people's sense that this little human deserves a higher status is that it can no longer be called "it." He, a boy, has a penis and testes, which hold sperm-making cells. She, a girl, has a vulva and ovaries, which hold eggs.

Each sex *is* that sex from the moment of fertilization, but both sexes look the same inside and out for the first two months. Sex is determined by one particular chromosome brought by the sperm. All eggs have the sex chromosome called "X." That same chromosome in a sperm may be an "X," or it may be a "Y." If the sperm brought an X chromosome to the egg, then both sex chromosomes are X's and the fertilized egg is female. If the sperm brought a Y chromosome, then the fertilized egg has one of each kind, and is male.

Only the tiniest part of the Y chromosome is responsible for producing a boy instead of a girl: less than 0.1 percent, a single gene. This gene is instructions for making a molecule that acts as a switch to open for reading a series of other genes in the chromosome. The chemicals for which those genes provide patterns do all the rest of the work. Both sexes have all these other genes. The switch is all that's necessary to make a boy.

Ovaries and testes (also called testicles) are at first identical bumps way up against the back, in the neighborhood of the kidneys. If the switch opens the crucial genes, the bumps become testes, and begin to make masculinizing hormones. These hormones are signals to surrounding tissues to change the pattern of their growth: Some cause the development of male parts, such as the penis, and some prevent the development of female parts, such as the womb and the vagina. Nothing is needed to make female parts. If there is no switch, and therefore no special chemicals to change the basic plan, the bumps become ovaries, womb and vagina grow, and genitals are female.

At six weeks old, the embryo's genitals, just in front of the anus, are a mound surrounding two lengthwise folds to either side of a central slit. There is a small swelling above the slit. From this construction both male and female genitals are shaped over the next three weeks.

In a girl, the swelling becomes her clitoris, a nubbin of flesh toward the front of her genitals. The two folds and the central slit remain, and the mound grows into a pair of soft, protective flaps. All these parts together are called the vulva.

In a boy, the swelling becomes the tip of his penis, and the central folds fuse shut to form the rest of it. The two sides of the mound also come together in the middle—they are the scrotum, the sac into which testes eventually descend.

Most extraordinary is that as these external changes begin, the future generation has already settled down in the developing ovaries or testes. The cells whose offspring become sperm and eggs are nothing like either at first. They behave like amebas, those one-celled jelly splats that ooze around in a drop of pondwater on a laboratory slide. You'd think sperm and eggs would originate right where they belong, but they don't. They come from the top of the yolk sac. When the yolk sac is enclosed within the embryo, the sperm

Shaping the Sexes

As different as male and female genitals look, they start the same: a mound, two folds, and a slit. These pictures show how they grow from that shape to their final shapes.

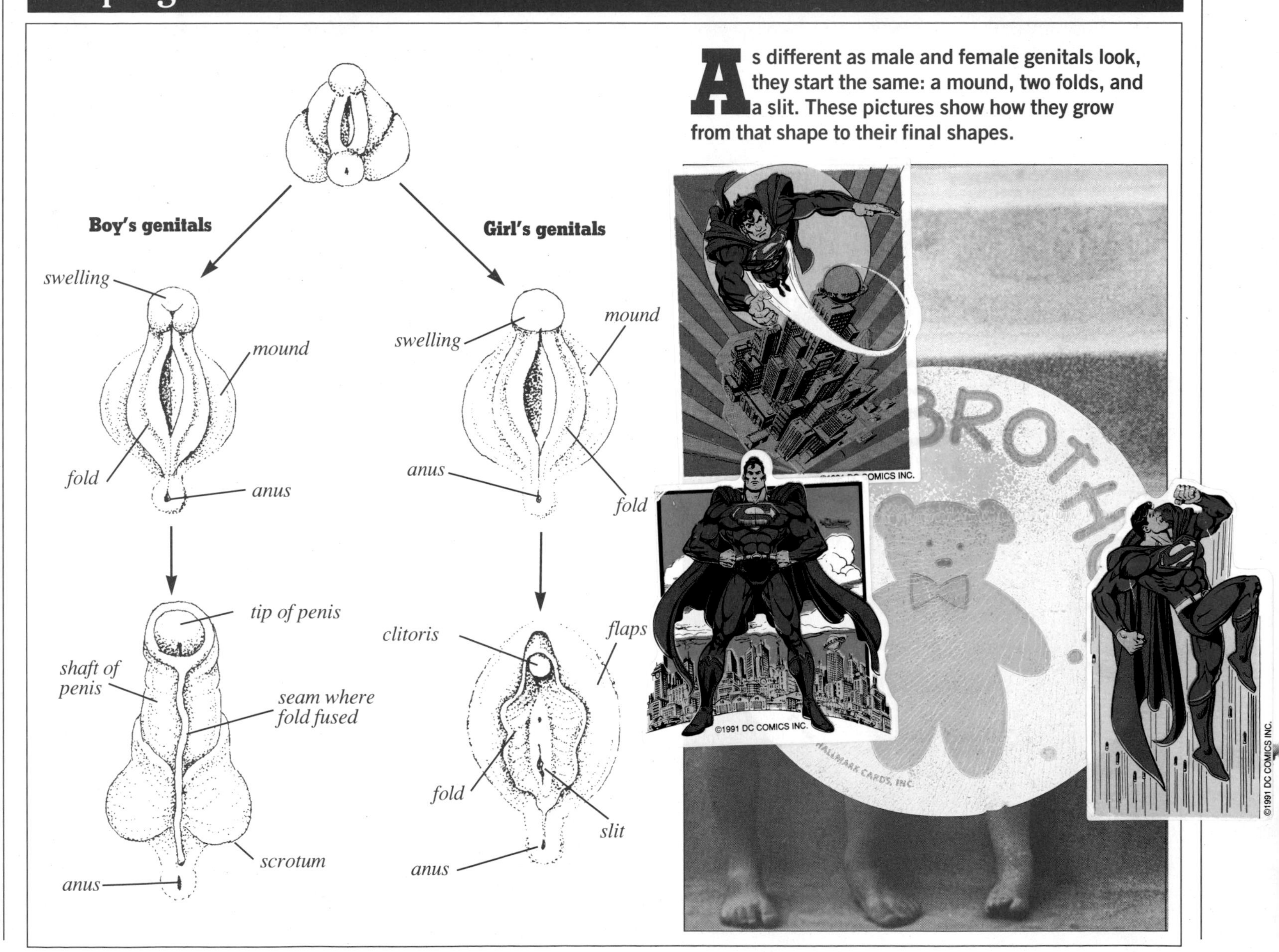

or eggs ooze off their original home and travel to their permanent one. They are snugged into place by the sixth week, before any of the sex organs have even been told which sex to be.

Suck, Pee, Kick, Blink

As busy as the fetus's cells have been for nine weeks now, he or she has done little. But over the next few weeks bones grow toward one another within the limbs, meet in elbow joints and knees, attach to muscles that move them. A four-month-old fetus begins to twitch, then learns to kick.

A fetus at 5 months.

This is only one new talent. Eyelids have grown over the eyes and, for now, have fused together, yet if the lid is touched, the fetus blinks. If its lips are brushed, it sucks. It drinks. It pees. It defecates just like a baby.

The mother is unaware of any stirrings. Although the fetus more than doubles in length between the beginning of the ninth week and the end of the twelfth week, twice the size of a peanut is still puny. The amniotic sac has grown even faster, and it is filled with fluid that continually leaks into it from the mother's blood supply outside the capsule walls. Any kicks the tiny fetus makes inside its oversized balloon sends it tumbling, now right side up, now upside down, so weightless in the water that even if it bounces it is not felt. Weightlessness allows the fetus to exercise: Its muscles are too weak so far to move against the pull of gravity.

Most of the things the fetus begins to do about halfway through its stay inside the mother seem to be for practice only. The fetus doesn't need to suck, swallow, eat, or drink. Nourishment in the mother's blood is removed by the placenta and transferred through its blood vessels down the umbilical cord directly into the fetus's circulation. Since the fetus doesn't eat, it has nothing much to defecate—some dead cells from the lining of the gut, some liver juice and such—but it defecates anyway. As ribs and chest muscles develop, the fetus makes breathing motions that bring water, not air, into its lungs. There is no need for air. Oxygen, like food, is taken out of the mother's blood at the placenta and delivered to the fetus. As its heart pumps its own restocked, refueled blood around its body, wastes are picked up and circulated back through the umbilical cord for dumping at the placenta. So the fetus doesn't need to pee either, although it does.

As it practices for the time when it will leave its spacesuit and brave the outside world stripped to a birthday suit, the fetus drinks urine, swallows feces. It can't be helped. Drinking water is necessarily toilet water too. Amniotic fluid does not, however, get dirty. Fresh fluid seeps into the sac as soiled fluid seeps out. The entire volume is completely changed every three hours. The fetus cleans up the environment too. When it breathes and swallows amniotic fluid, its lungs and intestines absorb it and deliver it to its bloodstream which, via the umbilical cord, sends any wastes to the mother for disposal. By the end of pregnancy, the fetus drinks about 12 ounces of amniotic fluid a day. You can see the point of practicing: That's how much milk a newborn baby drinks.

All this time the baby's spacesuit

Bump Goes the Baby

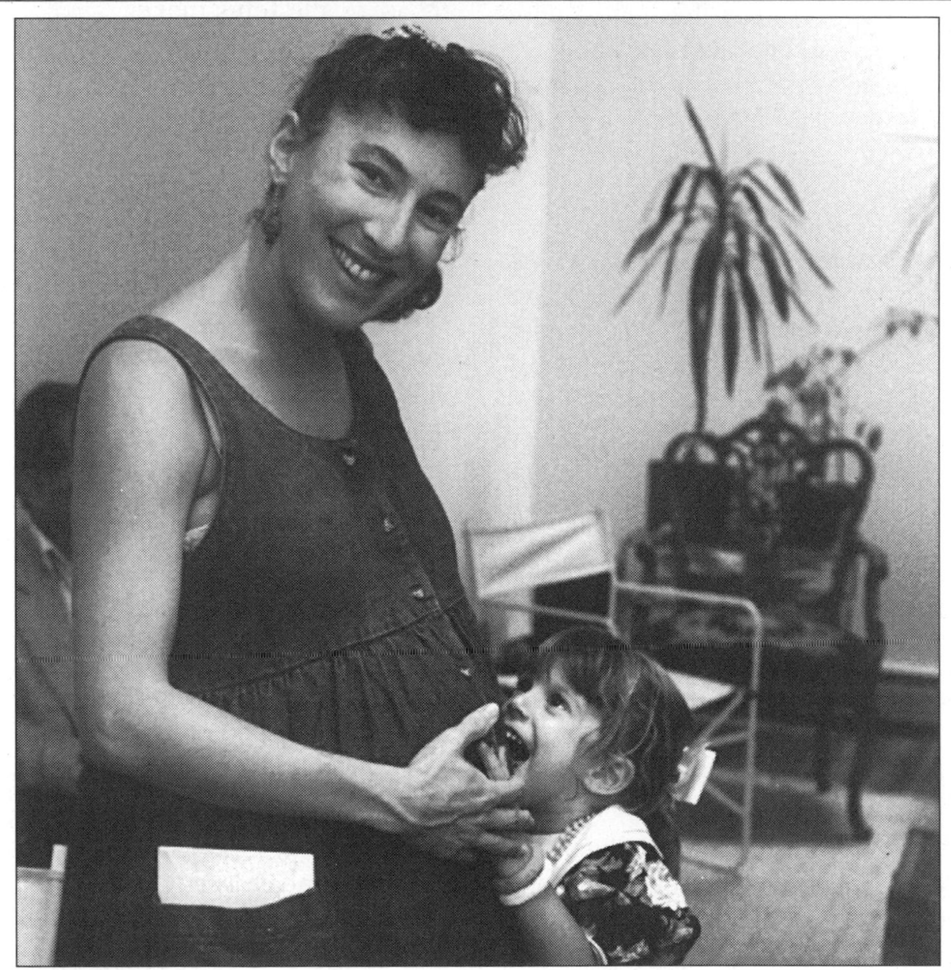

When a baby bumps against its mother's belly, people say it's kicking. The bumps aren't just feet, though. Straightening arms or legs bounces the baby around the womb, hitting its mother with its head, rump, knees, elbows, and fists, as well as feet. This woman is eight months pregnant; her fetus's movements are strong enough for others to easily feel.

grows and changes, too. The umbilical cord becomes coiled because the thick vessels inside it grow more quickly than its covering. The coils let the cord stretch like a spring so the fetus can bounce around without harming its lifeline. By the time the fetus is thumb-size, the placenta bulges out into the womb, where it begins to thin and smooth. The portion that remains buried becomes even thicker and more elaborately branched. The thinning bulge of placenta finally becomes as thin as skin, and the bulge fills the whole womb. The portion remaining deep inside the lining is like a large, wet sponge soaking up the good things, dripping out the bad.

Besides providing oxygen and nourishment, the placenta through all the months of pregnancy makes the mother cooperate. Its various hormones keep the womb muscles relaxed, the lining rich and firmly anchored. They temporarily loosen the joints between the mother's hip bones so the baby can eventually slip through. The placenta even sees to the fetus's future milk supply by secreting hormones that grow the milk glands in the mother's breasts. The placenta is so bossy, so responsible for running this whole show, that it's hard to remember that the baby made this suit itself, to control its mother through it.

When the mother is five months pregnant, the fetus has mushroomed to

10 inches (25 centimeters) long. The fetus in its cushioning spacesuit stretches the mother's womb, pushing out her belly. The place is becoming cramped. Now, when the fetus moves, it pokes its mom. If she could see the fetus now, she'd say "Oh, baby!"

Finishing Touches

The last four months of a baby's stay in the womb provide all the finishing touches that other humans will find adorable when they meet the newborn boy or girl at last. By 20 weeks there are fingernails and toenails, as well as the unique fingerprints and footprints that will stick with that baby all through life. Its ears are distinctive: They may stand out from the head like Grandpa's, or have a notch like Mom's. People will notice such resemblances as soon as the baby is born. Its skin is covered with a fine down; it has eyebrows.

By 26 weeks the eyes begin to open, and the lids have lashes. By 28 weeks the head has hair. If the hair will be dark, it is dark now. If the person will have a cowlick, the pattern of its future unruliness is already visible even if the hair is little more than fuzz.

By 36 weeks the fetus is getting plump. It pads itself out with the white, insulating fat that makes chubby cheeks and dimpled knees. Deeper inside, the fetus makes pads of a brownish kind of fat that produce heat like heating pads. It's a cold world out there.

By 38 weeks fingernails have grown so long that the fetus may scratch its fat cheeks as it moves thumb to mouth, and sucks it. The hands may hold one another; a hand may grasp the umbilical cord. Once in a while air leaks into a baby's spacesuit: It can then be heard to cry.

In two weeks more—when it is delivered into the outside world at about the age of 266 days—its plump face, wide-open eyes, loud cry, practiced sucking, strong kicks, and firm grasp will convince the audience that this baby was ready to be born.

Yet everyone will be surprised that the baby has the right number of toes and fingers, finished ears, a face that's quite complete—and that it acts so human.

Hints of a World Beyond the Womb

Few people are aware of how experienced a baby becomes while still inside its spacesuit. In fact, a baby probably learns more about the outside world from within the womb than anyone outside it learns of the baby.

A mother can't hear her unborn baby's heartbeat without the aid of a stethoscope, but the baby for months listens to the mother's thumping heart. And not only thumps, but burps, growling guts, the lilt of the mother's voice and, from farther away, drumbeats and symphonies, rock music and jazz. Cracks of thunder and booming jets make the fetus jump. Lullabies and stories read aloud soothe the fetus. A bell jingled outside the baby's hideaway causes it to turn its whole body and gaze in that direction as though trying to catch the jingle with its eyes.

In fact, there is light inside the womb. Perhaps all is blackness while the fetus's eyelids are fused tight shut, but two months before birth its eyes open on a world that, in the sun at least, is ruddy red like the glow of a candle through the hand. The baby will turn to gaze at a flashlight held against the mother's belly.

A mother notices that when she is active, her baby isn't. Walking rocks the baby right to sleep. When the mother lies down for a nap, her baby awakes, and kicks. But when the mother actually falls asleep, her baby becomes drowsy too, and when she wakes up, that rouses her son or daughter. By birth, the baby has learned from the mother the basic rhythm of night and day. The baby wakes during the night, but usually less so than during the day; it may eat a midnight snack, but eats more at noon.

Whatever a mother eats, the fetus in her womb eats too. If she takes aspirin, her fetus gets aspirin. If she drinks wine, her fetus gets tipsy. Some foods even

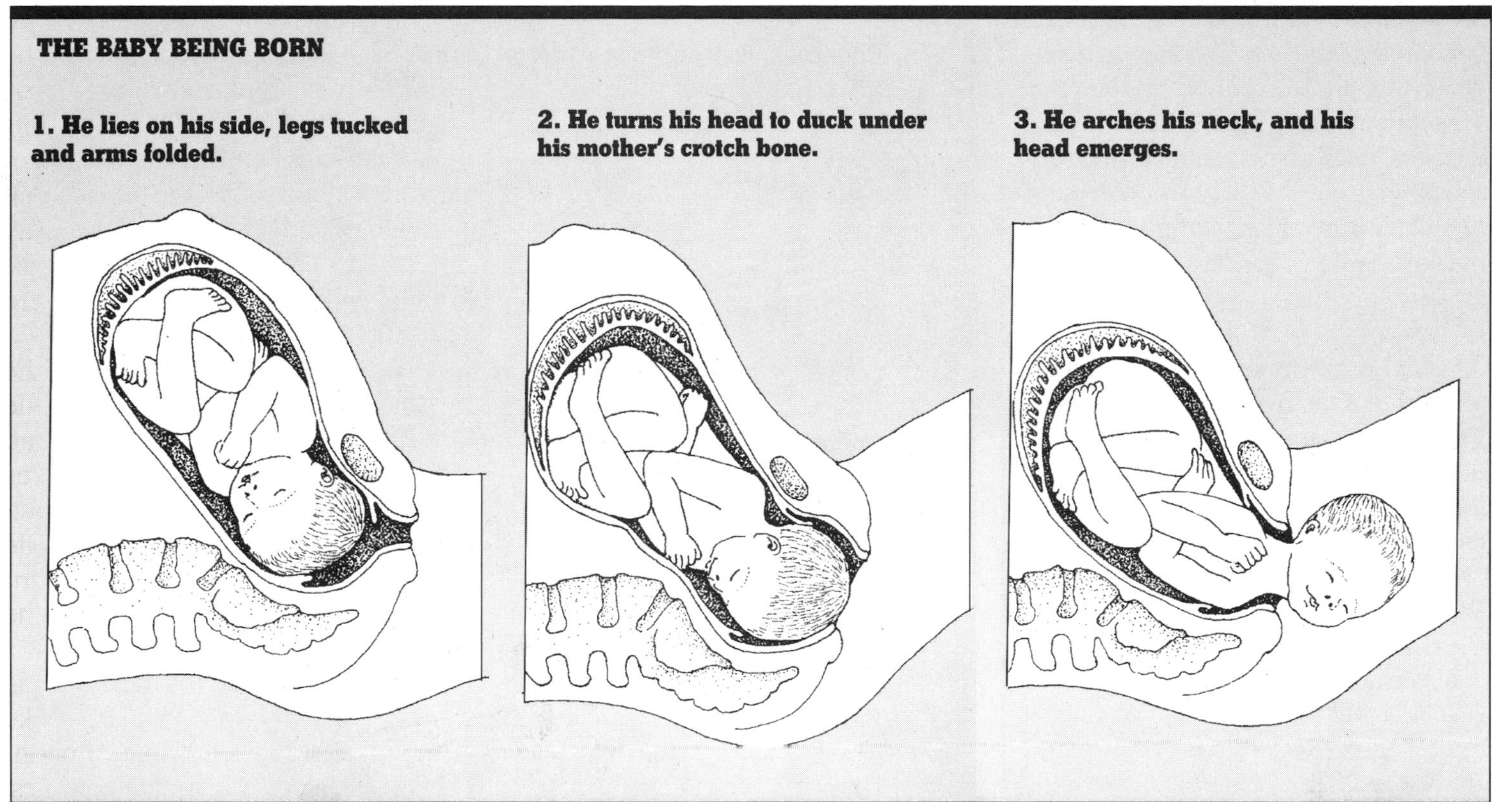

give babies hiccups. The mother feels the fetus's hiccups as a gentle jerking in her belly.

THE BABY BEING BORN
1. He lies on his side, legs tucked and arms folded.
2. He turns his head to duck under his mother's crotch bone.
3. He arches his neck, and his head emerges.

It may be that human fetuses smell their mother from inside. Certainly mice do. If lemon scent is injected into a pregnant mouse's womb, her babies will not suckle after they are born unless the mother's nipples are rubbed with lemon scent! Even without such interference, baby mice won't nurse at well-washed nipples. They have learned the smell of mother mouse from inside, and they expect the familiar smell outside as well. Although human infants probably have less talented noses, they at least are born prepared to catch on fast: A baby recognizes the smell of its mother's milk within a week after birth.

The mother's mood affects how her baby feels before birth. A fetus growing inside an unhappy woman seems overactive before birth, and more often crying, wakeful, tense, and difficult to soothe after birth. Although there is no exchange of blood itself across the placenta, many of the mother's hormones pass as freely to her fetus as aspirin and alcohol. Sadness, fear, and anger produce particular hormones, and the baby gets a dose of what the mother feels.

A mother's experience of her baby is less enlightening, but still she forms an opinion. She may decide—and she may be right—that her baby is sensitive to disturbances, or sleeps little, or is a placid sort of fellow. The details of her opinions, and whether they are right or wrong, are less important than the general sense of things the baby is giving her. Through placental hormones, she or he makes her or his mother hungry, sleepy, disinterested in the stock market, and very interested in baby clothes.

Toward the very end of pregnancy, the unborn baby does the most remarkable thing, though no one knows how: The mother quite suddenly feels the most urgent need to clean house, go through drawers, stock up on food, sort, pack, paint, knit, fuss everything into order and readiness. This is called "nesting," and it has got to be the about-to-be-born baby's most commanding achievement.

Happy Birth Day!

There is one last somersault that, for all but a handful of butt-first babies, lands the fetus head down in the womb with the top of its skull pressed against the exit. The baby lands head first for a simple reason: it is top-heavy. The baby will turn no more for just as simple a reason: There's no space left for acrobatics. It is now about two weeks to Birth Day.

The placenta steps up its hormone production, and changes their proportions. Joints between the mother's hip bones, which surround the bottom of

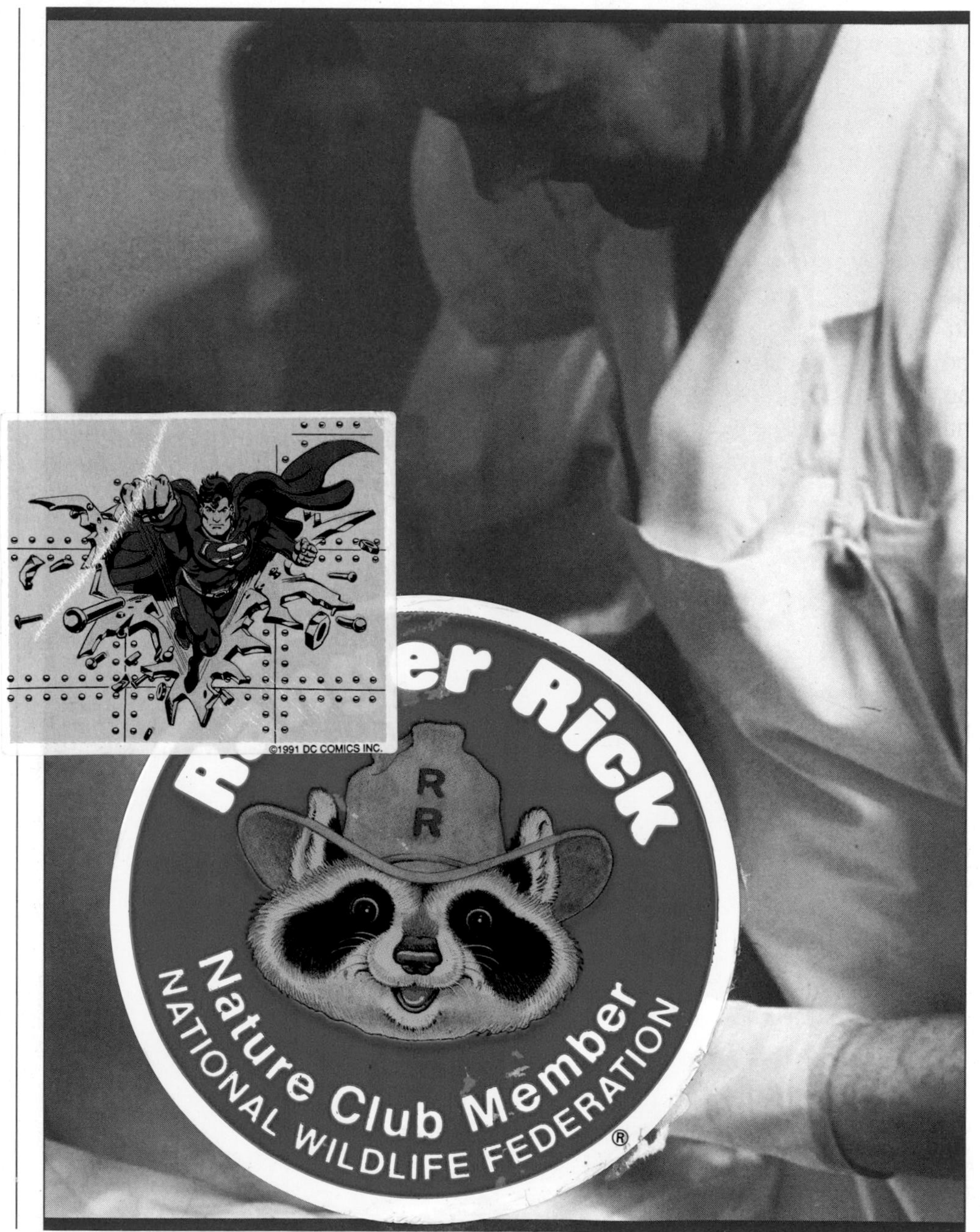

the womb like an upside-down lampshade, are now quite loose. The womb itself, once kept relaxed by its occupant, becomes irritable, like an overstrung muscle prone to cramping.

During these last days, the baby yawning and stretching, or the mother bending to refold baby clothes for the dozenth time, makes the womb contract in a wave that spreads from top to bottom. That pushes the baby's skull against the narrow exit, and two things happen: The passage widens, and the pressure on it tends to cause another contraction.

A kind of teasing "is-it-coming, is-it-not" goes on for days or even weeks, but as more powerful contractions press the baby harder, there comes a point of no return. Each squeeze of the baby against the bottom of the womb triggers another, harder squeeze: The mother is in labor; the baby is on the way out.

Getting through the exit from the womb and down the vagina is not usually a problem, for the exit has by now been wedged open by the baby's big head, and the vagina is naturally stretchy. The problem is the bones. Even loosened at their joints, they are as tight a fit as the neck of an outgrown T-shirt. But the baby is prepared to assist at its own delivery.

The baby lies on its side with arms folded and knees tucked tightly up against its belly, as neatly bundled as can be. As its head pushes through the neck of the womb, the baby turns it as though to glance over one shoulder at the mother's tailbone. That ducks the head under the mother's crotch bone above. Now the baby arches its neck. That brings its head up on the other side of the bone—and out. The rest of the body follows easily: The head always was the biggest part of this smart kid.

It is hard to imagine what the drastic changes of birth must feel like. This baby has always been a floating acrobat. Now gravity weighs it down so heavily it can't even lift its head. It is used to dim light, not fluorescent tubes; muffled croons and rumbles, not a doctor demanding scissors to cut the accustomed umbilical cord. The baby was always warm before, and always wet. Its lungs have known nothing but a gentle flow of water. Now it has only minutes to make the transition from the underwater, aquatic animal it has been so far to what it will have to be hereafter: An air breather, a terrestrial.

The moment the umbilical cord hits the air, its stuffing expands, pinching shut the blood vessels that have been the baby's lifeline for nine months. The baby gasps. A valve in its heart snaps shut; a vessel in its belly clamps closed. Blood races to its lungs. The baby breathes. It cries.

But only for a moment. Then, calmly, as though it had been expecting to arrive at an interesting place, the newborn baby looks around at what, to it, is truly outer space.

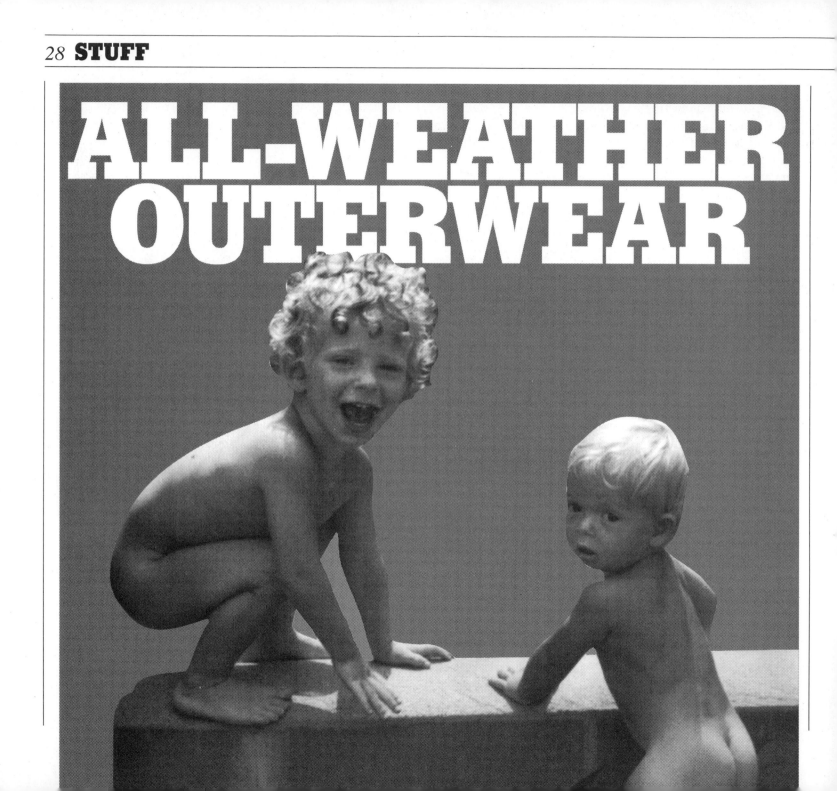

ALL-WEATHER
OUTERWEAR

You live out in the air, where the sun shines and the wind blows. It seems a healthful environment, full of life. Everywhere you look lives are being lived: Ants work, grass grows, birds sing, kids play. There's nothing like fresh air and sunshine—as long as they never really touch you.

Sun and air are deadly to the living flesh that is your body. Cells have to be wet all the time; they can't stand the drying wind. They don't work unless the temperature is just right, lukewarm. Expose them to the hot sun or the cold night air and they die. Sunlight is too strong for cells. It burns and breaks and kills them. All the life you see around you in this bright windy world of yours is living only because it is safe inside a skin, a crust that's dead already.

Born to Die

Although skin is your surface that you think you know so well, the bloodless, nerveless outer crust of you is so transparent that you are actually looking through it to brown pigments, blue veins, and rosy blood in the living flesh below. Heel blisters and sunburn peel are the dead crust itself. Injury has detached those patches, but the attached skin all over you is the same dead stuff. In most places it is thin—no more than a millimeter—but in other places it is very thick, as thick as the sole of your foot after a barefoot summer or a callus after years of hard work. It is waterproof: Blisters don't leak until they break. And even though dead skin is stretchy enough for knee bends and grins, it is surprisingly strong.

As much as a sunburn peel looks like a piece of stuff, like a sort of plastic or rubber film, it is actually layers of flat, dead cells called squames. Each squame is six-sided, a hexagon. Stacks of them overlap one another at their edges, like cards when you shuffle them. These overlapping layers form a nearly waterproof seal. Some water molecules do manage to sneak up between squames and evaporate at the surface, but the fit is so tight that your skin leaks less than a pint of water every day.

Even less water gets in than leaks

A Slice of Skin

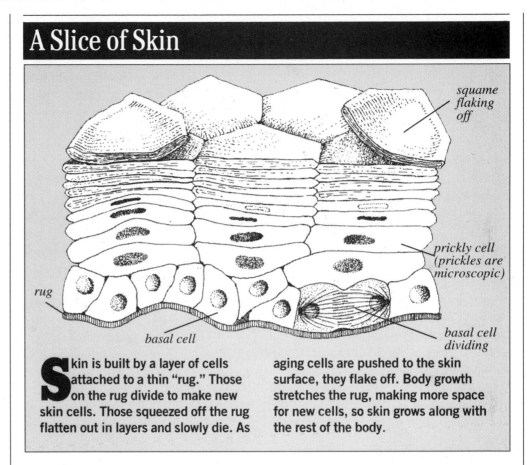

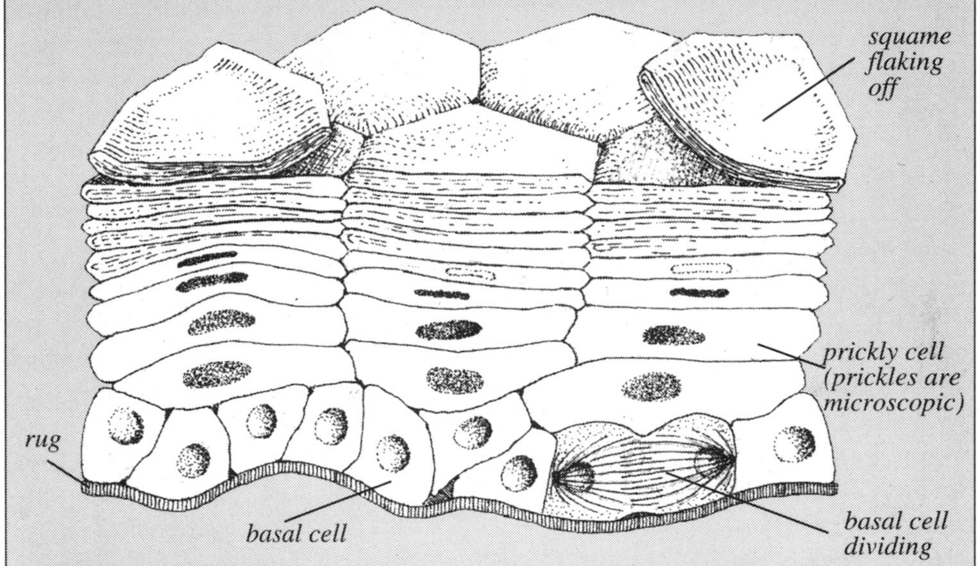

Skin is built by a layer of cells attached to a thin "rug." Those on the rug divide to make new skin cells. Those squeezed off the rug flatten out in layers and slowly die. As aging cells are pushed to the skin surface, they flake off. Body growth stretches the rug, making more space for new cells, so skin grows along with the rest of the body.

out. When you soak in a bathtub, squames swell up with water. Where there are many dead layers, as in the thick skin of fingertips and the soles of feet, skin becomes too bloated to lie flat, so it wrinkles. But water gets no deeper than that sodden surface. Bathmats work the same way. By absorbing water that drips from a wet you, none gets through to the floor.

Squames in the outermost layers of skin come loose easily: You can scrape them off with your fingernail. No other part of the body takes the abrasion and abuse skin suffers. Just the ordinary wear and tear of washing, dressing, and moving around rubs off 500 million squames a day. When you're finished with your bath, you can feel scrubbed-off squames lying in a ring around the bathtub along with that day's dirt. Those squames were born weeks ago; the skin you wear after a bath is a little newer than the one you scrubbed away.

New layers of cells are born at the bottom of skin, at the raw, living surface that you can see when a fresh blister gets torn away. There a single sheet of cells, called basal cells because they are at the base of skin, divide to form new layers of squames to replace old ones that have worn away. New skin cells push against the stacks of squames that are above them, lifting them up a bit. Your skin is always growing outward.

A Squame's Story

Basal cells are plump, not flat. They live crowded against one another on a fibrous rug they make for themselves. This rug is very important to them; in fact it is a matter of their life and death. As long as a basal cell is touching the rug, it will live and divide. If it loses touch with the rug, it will stop dividing, and die. The rug is only as big as you are, and it holds only so many basal cells, so most daughters among the dividing crowd get squeezed up off the rug and lose touch with it. These cells are doomed to become squames.

A newborn squame is round and squishy like its parent, not flat and tough like the flake it will become. But as soon as it's off the rug it starts to flatten and to toughen with fibers of a stuff called keratin. The fibers bristle out through its surface, giving it a prickly look, and lock onto the prickles of other young squames. The thousands of prickly connections by which these youthful cells hold onto one another keep skin from tearing when it is stretched.

As the days pass, the prickly cells mature, and newer, younger cells push up from below, lifting their elders closer to the surface. The elders now flatten more. Keratin accumulates inside them; they start to harden with age. And gradually their clutching prickles loose their grip on neighbors.

Pressure from below is relentless. Day after day new generations of young cells lift older cells above them farther up toward the scraping world. Now the aging cells become senile. Their innards disintegrate; their keratin-making machinery falls apart. Finally, as the cells are pushed still farther by the upcoming generations below, they die, dry, and flake away.

It seems odd that these tiny flakes, as fine as dust, can serve as the body's outer armor. Not that a squame isn't tough, but how does a shield protect a body if, at the first scratch, it falls off?

Think of squames as the front rank of a defending army. You rub the first rank off. The next rank moves up. Rub again and there's another. Each shield is meager, but there are always more, an endless horde prepared to die, to fall away, to make room for the defenders coming up. The strength of skin is in its ability to continually renew itself, to turn out 500 million fresh new cells every day.

The Skin That Fits

You grow unevenly—an inch one year, two the next—but your skin has never been too tight, or hung too loose. Sometimes feet grow faster than hands, or arms grow faster than legs. Still skin fits each part just right. Skin fits because wherever the growing body stretches it, newborn squames find extra room on the rug among the stacks already there to start new stacks of their own. Since it's the stretch that makes the space, skin can't overgrow.

When you skin a knee, you tear off not only the covering of squames but the basal cells too, right down to the bare rug. New skin, protected by a scab, grows from the edges of the scrape, where there are unharmed basal cells ready to divide. They divide over and over again, recovering the bare spot from the outside in. When the gap is covered with a solid sheet of cells, crowding begins to squeeze some off the rug. Stacks of squames pile up, and push the scab away. Of course, the patch of brand new skin fits perfectly: Neither more nor fewer cells can crowd onto the rug than crowded there before.

How to Build a Callus

New skin matches surrounding skin: knee-thick on knees, hair-free on palms. If you injure a fingertip, the original fingerprint is reproduced exactly. All the instructions are woven into the fabric of the rug. The rug is as old as you are, and although it has been enlarged by adding fibers, its original pattern has never been revised. That's why fingerprints don't change. Basal cells learn from the weave of the rug where they are to divide often in order to build the unusually high stacks of squames that form fingerprint ridges.

To keep skin a certain thickness, basal cells must produce new cells at just the same rate that old ones are lost. But although the old rug gives general guidance, it keeps no diary of a day spent lying on the couch wearing hardly any foot skin off, or of the unusual number of squames you lost while scratching your ear just now. Basal cells learn how often to divide to keep skin's proper thickness from squames themselves.

Squames near the surface of your skin leak a chemical that makes basal cells divide more slowly, so the more layers of old squames there are, the fewer new ones are made. The day you spent on the couch was a lazy day for foot-skin cells as well. When you scratch layers of old squames off, the lack of their chemical lets basal cells speed up division and so replace them. Nothing so violent as scratching is needed to speed them. The system is so sensitive that if you merely strip off a few layers of squames with a Band-Aid, basal cells below start immediately to divide.

What about the times, though, when you need thicker skin to protect bare feet rubbed for weeks by sand, or fingertips pressed daily to the strings of a guitar? Extreme wear calls for the extreme thickness of a callus, and to

White Dust

A single squame is too small to be visible, but batches of them are the flakes of dandruff, and in hospitals, where hundreds of people are shedding on the bedding around the clock, squames may powder every surface with a film of fine, white dust.

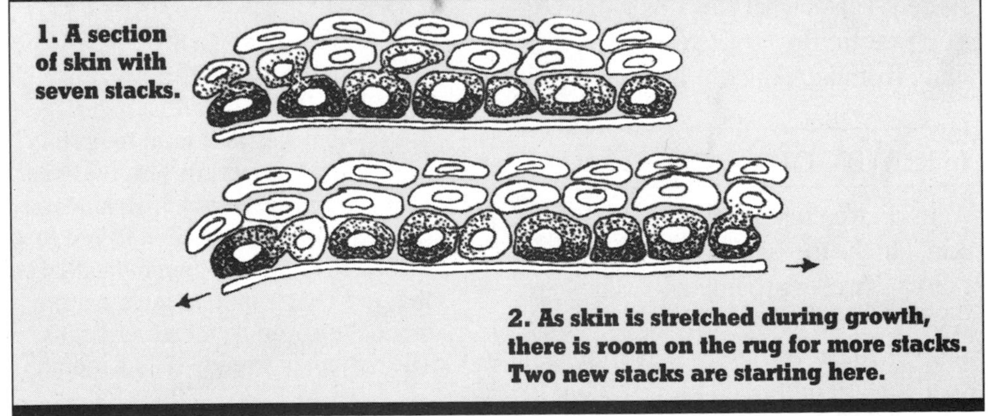
1. A section of skin with seven stacks.
2. As skin is stretched during growth, there is room on the rug for more stacks. Two new stacks are starting here.

build a callus, basal cells have to divide *more* quickly than squames are worn away.

When you first practice the guitar, your fingers hurt. That pain may be necessary, for scientists think the message to build a callus comes from injured cells. The message is a growth hormone that makes basal cells divide more quickly, and makes young squames age more slowly. Apparently living flesh battered by guitar strings sends this growth hormone message. Basal cells then divide like crazy, and keep the squame stacks rising, while the squames stay prickly for a while longer before they flake away. The result is a gradual thickening of skin in the places where it is abused.

But how can basal cells divide to keep a callus thick while hordes of squames above are screaming STOP!? Hurt cells, it seems, scream louder. The squames' chemical message will come through again when no one's getting injured. That's what happens when you stop practicing: Your fingertips thin again from lack of continual abuse.

The Way of a Wart

Warts, like calluses, are over-thickened skin, but the message to make a wart is a virus. Viruses are not cells. They are genes that escaped from cells, scraps of information that, when they get inside a cell again, can tell it what to

Five Billion Different Fingerprints

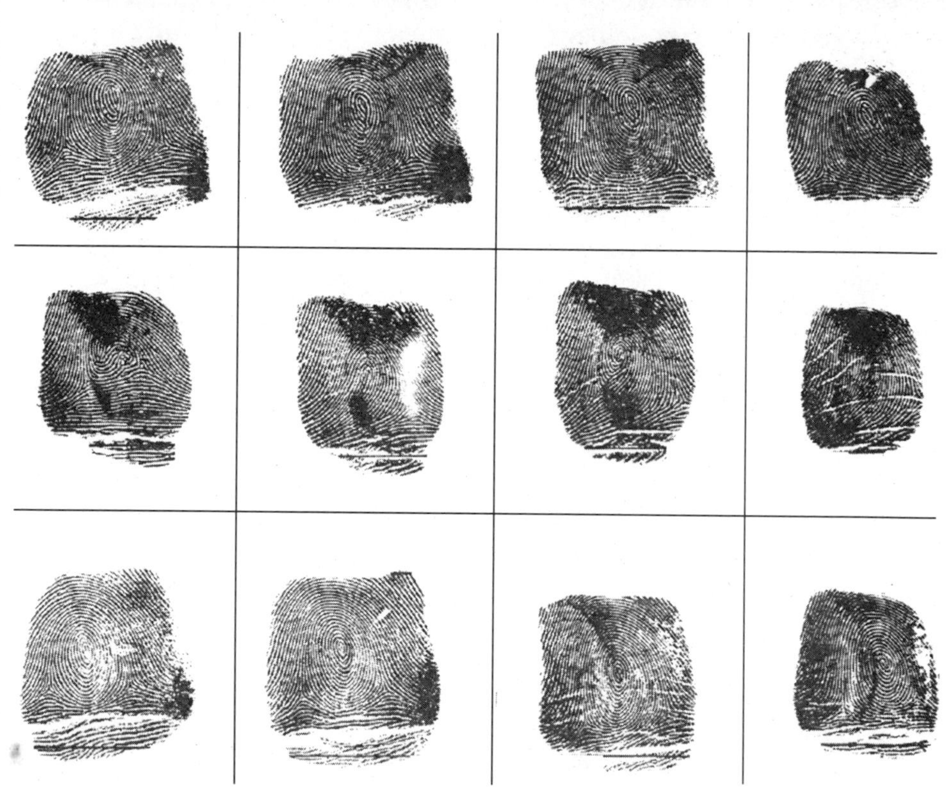

The ridges that form footprints and fingerprints give these surfaces extra friction, a kind of no-slip grip for firm fingering and footing. Each of the 5 billion individuals in the world has a unique ridge pattern originally woven by their basal cells. The pattern is already visible months before birth, and never changes. Even identical twins have unique fingerprints, although they are similar ones. Nevertheless, fingerprints can be classified according to their types of swirls—called whorls. Maybe your thumbprint is of one of the types shown here.

do. Viruses don't grow. There's no such thing as a little baby virus that will expand as it is nourished the way cells do. Viruses don't divide, either. Their reproduction is done for them by the cells that take them in. A wart is a virus's way of forcing a skin cell to make more viruses. And yes, warts are catching: The surface of a wart is covered with viruses that are shed along with the squames that made them.

A wart begins when a basal cell welcomes one of these genetic scraps through its surface and lets it into its nucleus as though it were a part of its own chromosomes (as, in fact, it might once have been). The virus tells the cell, in its own native tongue, to divide. Surrounding cells notice nothing. The victim seems perfectly normal. So do the excessive numbers of daughters it soon produces, and its daughters' daughters, and generation after generation until the too-numerous descendants of the infected basal cell have formed a horny lump. These rising squames have all inherited the full set of viral genes, and though they can't divide once they are lifted off the rug, for a while they still can make what their chromosomes tell them to, whether it is keratin or viruses.

When infected cells are middle-aged, they begin to make multiple copies of the viral genes. By the time the cells approach the surface, each has completed thousands of copies of the genes, and the genes have self-assembled into viruses. The viruses escape the wart at the top. More copies are just behind them. The basal cell, obeying what it takes to be its own instructions, keeps right on making daughters that make warts.

Kiss Away the Hurt

When dogs are injured, they lick their wound. Their saliva, and that of other mammals, contains a growth factor—a chemical that makes skin cells divide more quickly. It is probably the same substance that makes our skin thicken into calluses where it has been injured by wear. Our saliva also contains this growth factor, but only children tend to lick their wounds. In adults the only trace of that behavior may be "kissing away" the hurt. The skin growth factor mammals make seems to be understood by plants. When cows munch grass, their drool encourages their food to grow more.

Most people do eventually become immune to warts, but the immune system is made up of wandering white blood cells that don't often patrol so close to the outside world. When they do find infected basal cells, they kill them, and soon the wart wears off. Until

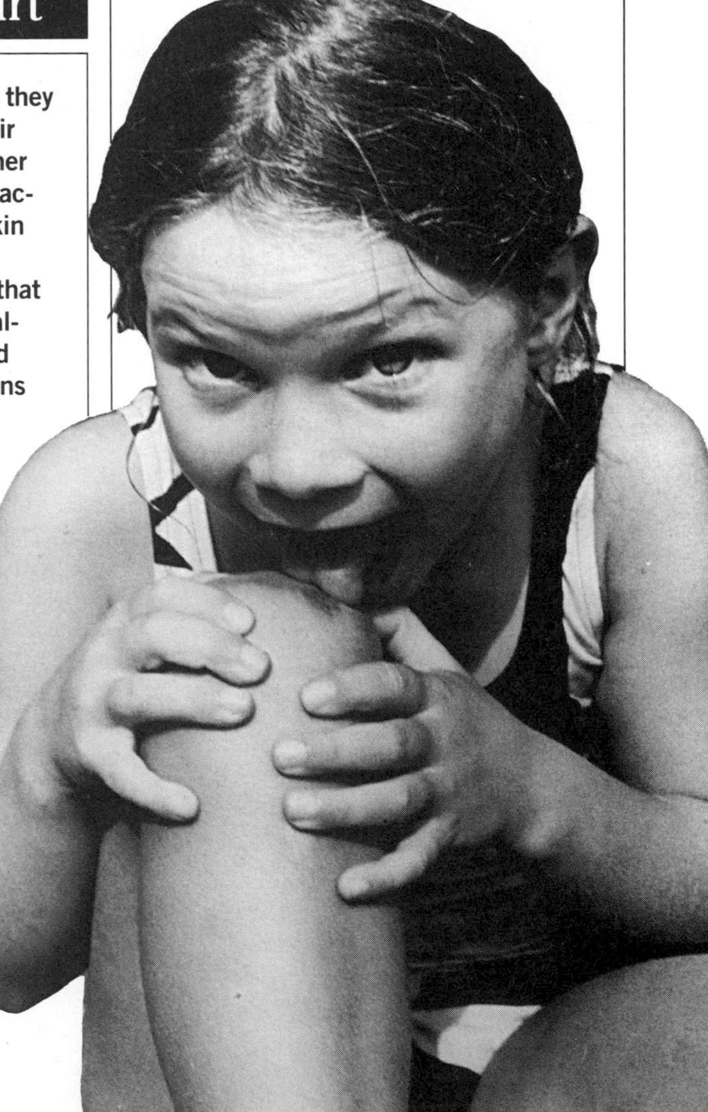

that happens, though, the wart can spread—from thumb to finger, hand to hand, wherever skin rubs skin. That's why the horny little devils tend to come in groups, and why, among we handholders, warts so often grow on fingers.

Answers in Black and White

People come in every shade from creamy white to rich black coffee. Yet the rich black coffee pigment is what shades every one of us, no matter whether we are light or dark. The pigment, called melanin, is made by melanocytes, octopus sorts of cells that snug their tentacles among basal skin cells and inject them with their pigment. The only place where you can see melanin's true color is in the darkest of dark moles. A mole is a spot where melanocytes have crowded into a group instead of living singly and spread out, and where they have climbed above basal cells instead of staying snugged among them. The darker the mole, the more melanocytes have gotten together to make it. You'd think skin color as a whole would also depend on the number of pigment cells, but it doesn't. Everybody has the same number of melanocytes; your skin shade depends on how productive your melanocytes are—how much pigment they make.

Light skins and dark skins both have advantages. Dark skins are best for protection against the sun. Outdoors, every sunlit square inch of your skin is bombarded by ultraviolet photons, particles of light so packed with energy that they can blast cells to death. Sunburn is one result of that blasting. You actually destroy skin cells that are living by staying in the sun too long. Melanin protects you because it is a light trap that catches ultraviolet photons and robs them of their energy. The less pigment you have, the more you can be damaged by too much sunlight.

On the other hand, pale skins are best for making vitamin D. Some of the energy from ultraviolet light not trapped by pigment is used by skin cells to make this "sunshine vitamin." Bones need vitamin D to harden themselves with calcium, so a child with too little of the vitamin has soft bones, and grows deformed and crippled. The more pigment you have, the more you can be damaged by too little sunlight.

These days sunscreens protect light people from too much sun, and vitamin pills and vitamin D fortified milk protect dark people from too little sun. Health doesn't depend on skin color any more. But that wasn't always so. In fact, the health of people living hundreds of thousands of years ago is the reason palefaces came to be. Certainly we are all descended from blacks. The oldest human fossils, and also the apelike fossils of earlier ancestors, are found in

Away With Warts!

A wart can be removed only by killing the basal cells that harbor the virus. There are several ways: cutting that piece of skin away, destroying it by freezing, or killing it with chemicals. The first two ways must be done by a doctor. Chemicals, available from the drugstore or by a doctor's prescription, can be used at home. They take about 10 days to work.

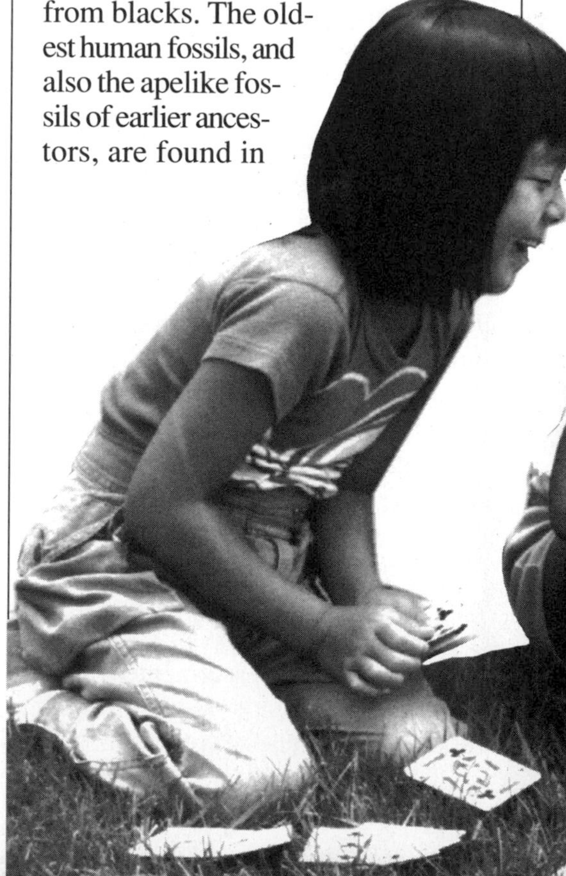

Africa in the sunburned river valleys of Ethiopia and Kenya. Naked humans evolving there could not have survived without dark skins to protect them from destructive doses of ultraviolet light. Vitamin D deficiency was not a problem. It is unknown in tropical climates, where everyone gets enough sun.

But about 2 million years ago Africans began to migrate to northern climates in Europe and Asia. Winters were cold. People covered their skins for warmth, moved into caves for shelter. The farther north they went, the longer the winters, the more feeble the summer sun, the less ultraviolet light they got—and the more they suffered from vitamin D deficiency. With sun scarce, the healthiest people were the palest ones, and the darkest were unlikely to even survive into adulthood. As the lighter people survived and the darker ones died out in those areas, there was a gradual shift from dark coffee to light cream—what we now call races.

Making a Tan

When, after a winter under wraps, you first expose your skin to sunlight, melanocytes immediately step up their pigment production. At the same time, basal cells exposed to sunlight increase their rate of division, so skin both thickens and darkens. This happens to blacks as well as to whites: Everybody tans.

Melanin pigment in varying amounts accounts for all the shades of skin color people come in.

What you see as smooth brown is made up of microscopic dots of color. Each dot is a clump of pigment molecules, and each pigment molecule is made up of many thousands of smaller molecules pieced together according to the instructions on a gene. The color is so intense that the difference in amount of pigment between a white person and a black wouldn't even fill a thimble.

Melanocytes keep stores of pigment on hand at all times so that as the cells they've colored die and their pigments disintegrate, they can color new ones coming up. The amount of pigment needed to make a tan, however, is way beyond their storage capacity. Before you can see the effects of a morning in the sun, melanocytes have a great deal of work to do. It will not be until evening that you can see they've done it.

First, they must make many copies of genes that carry the pigment's instructions. The copies will serve as patterns for assembling the complicated molecules. The pattern, however, is not for the finished product. Before pigment can be shipped, each roughed-out molecule has to be snipped here, and tucked there, given finishing touches at stops along a chemical production line.

The production line is very different from the wet slosh one might picture as the interior of a cell. It is a marvelously elaborate group of compartments that, when drawn, look as though they couldn't possibly fit into anything as minuscule as a cell. Embedded in the membrane walls of these compartments are various kinds of molecules that do the final shaping step by step. Sometimes pigments move along attached to the compartment wall as on a conveyor belt. Or they are carried in membrane tubes that snake out from one compartment to another to temporarily join them, or inside membrane bubbles that pinch off from one compartment and fuse with the other.

Such bubbles carry loads of finished pigment to the melanocyte's tentacle tips. The melanocyte sticks the tips into surrounding cells, and squirts the pigment out. That's when you look down at your arm and say, "Hey, I got a tan today!"

A Warning

Or maybe you got freckles—and a sunburn. Freckles are areas where melanocytes are more productive than those in the surrounding skin. The freckles tan, but the pale skin between them burns. Some people with very pale skin never get a tan, not even a freckle of it. Doctors warn that anyone who burns easily should stay out of the sun or use a sunscreen, a lotion that blocks ultraviolet light. This is not just because sunburn can itself be a serious injury—many cells are actually killed—but because high doses of ultraviolet light may damage genes in surviving basal cells and melanocytes. Later in life either kind of cell may begin to divide out of control, and become skin cancers. Basal cell cancers are slow growing and grow only outward, as all skin grows. They are therefore easy to remove before they have done any damage. Out-of-control melanocytes multiply extremely fast, and invade the interior of the body. Once they begin to invade, that kind of skin cancer can seldom be removed, and is very often fatal.

Pigment Production

Cells that make products for export have complicated manufacturing equipment. Copies of genes, which are patterns for making the product, emerge through holes in the cell's nucleus. They are received by large molecules, shown here as black bumps, that assemble the molecules and thread them into the interior of an elaborate series of compartments that surround the nucleus. Inside, the product receives finishing touches. At the end of the production line, the molecules are sent to a shipping department in round packages, or sometimes in tubes. There they are sorted and repackaged for export through the cell membrane.

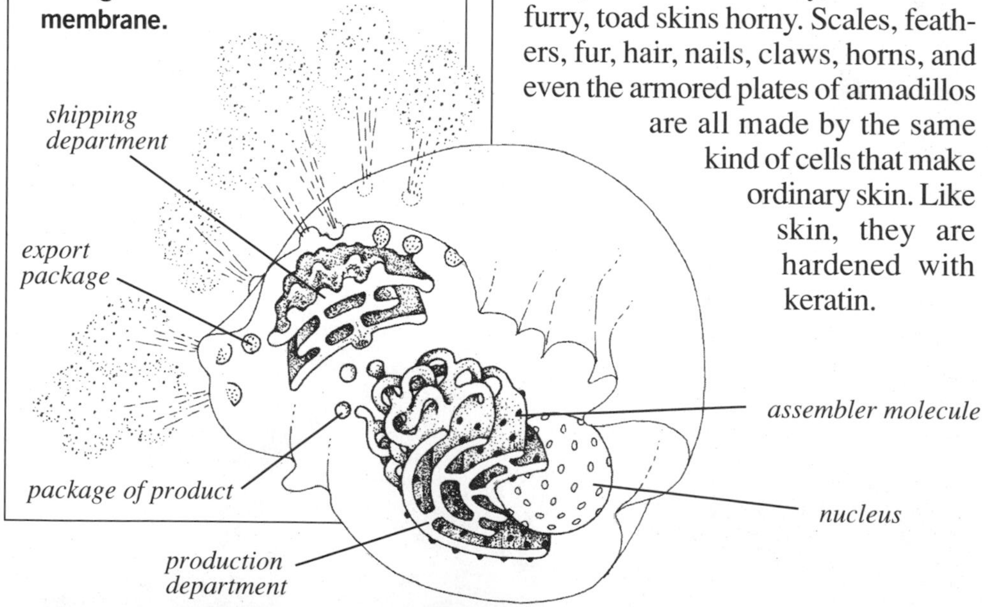

The Skin of a Hair

Darting, splashing, swooping, dashing about in our sunlit world are animals with all sorts of skins. Fish skins are scaley, chick skins downy, mouse skins furry, toad skins horny. Scales, feathers, fur, hair, nails, claws, horns, and even the armored plates of armadillos are all made by the same kind of cells that make ordinary skin. Like skin, they are hardened with keratin.

Wherever there is a hair on your body, there is a pit in your skin. The pit, called a follicle, reaches way below the rug from which skin arises. Down at the follicle's very bottom is a group of basal cells that form a sort of cup. Because these reproducers are at the bottom of a pit, their daughters have nowhere to go but up. Daughters produced around the rim of the cup age into a sheath of flat keratin scales. Those produced in the center of the cup rise up narrowly, forming a core of keratin fibers within the cylinder. The keratin of these core cells is different than that made by the outer hair scales: It is soft, not hard, more elastic than brittle. The core makes hair springy; the scales give it strength and sheen.

Shampoo and conditioner ads may claim to make your hair "alive," but hair is dead before it ever sees the light of day. The life of a hair cell is like the life of other skin cells—a gradual hardening with age until what was once plump and juicy is all dried up. The hard scales in the outer sheath overlap one another like the scales of an unopened pine cone. The overlapping is close and tight, but you can feel the scaliness. Take a few hairs between thumb and finger and pull downward along the lay of the scales. Hair feels smooth when stroked that way. Stroked in the other direction, toward the scalp, the hair feels slightly rough because now you are pushing against the free edges of the scales.

You have to see hair through the magnification of an electron microscope to appreciate the torture people put their hair through. When hair is teased, scales are actually lifted and broken, and the sheen it had when its covering lay sleek and flat is lost. Rubber bands fracture the sheath, leaving the softer fibers of the core to hang together as best they can. Even corn-row braids break hair. Curling irons can melt the tender core; it blisters and bulges from the wound. Chemicals used in bleaching, dying, permanent waving, and straightening not only damage fibers, but distort their parallel arrangement. To make a curl, for example, the fibers in the core must be squashed flat. When hair is dyed, small molecules from the various chemicals used barge between scales and join together as giant molecules wedged among the central fibers. At least the hair is dead, and can't feel what we are doing to it.

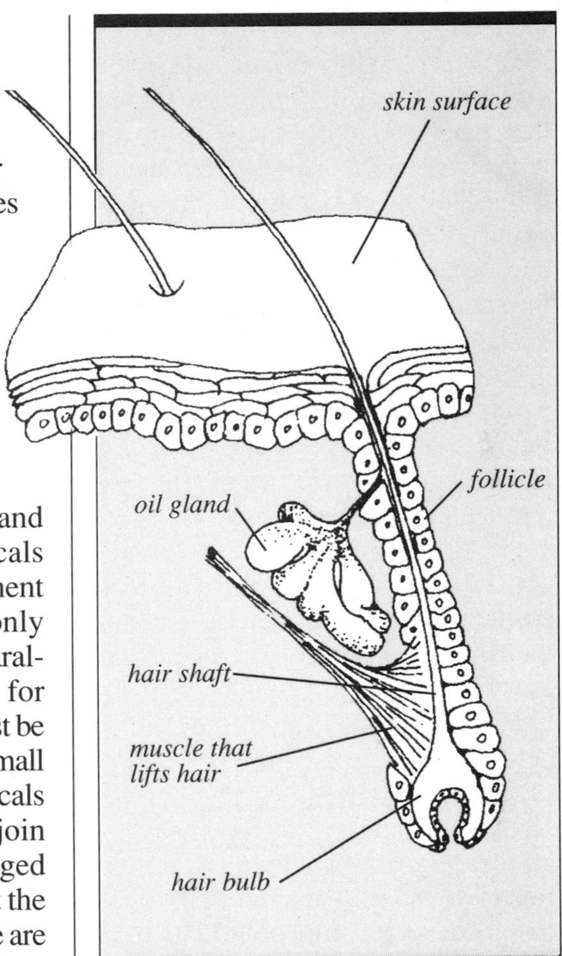

Your natural hair color is injected, as it is in skin, by a melanocyte living among the basal cells at the bottom of the hair follicle. The paler hair is, the less melanin it contains: Black hair has the most melanin; white hair has none. Red hair, however, is a real oddity. The red color is produced by a different pigment, coded for by a different gene. A person who produces this red pigment produces melanin too. With only a little melanin added, the hair is strawberry blond. The more melanin, the deeper the red until it may resemble the color of mahogany. But if there is a great deal of melanin, the red is mostly hidden, appearing only as coppery highlights. Some men produce less melanin in facial hair than in the scalp. They may have brown hair and a blond beard, or, if they have the gene for red hair, black hair and a red beard.

As people age, melanocytes in hair follicles begin to fail. The first unpigmented hairs usually appear in the mid thirties. The whole head of hair seldom turns white until very old age, when every melanocyte has died.

Not so Naked

Humans appear to be among the few bare animals in the world, as bare as an elephant or a hippopotamus, as nude as the naked molerat. But appearances are deceptive. In fact, people have about the same number of hairs on their body as a gorilla.

Five million hair follicles cover the entire body except for lips, the palms of your hands, and soles of your feet. Not all the follicles are producing hair all the time. After growing a hair for from two to six years, a follicle typically rests for six months. The hair remains attached for about half that time, and then falls out. Of the 100,000 or so hairs in your head, 50 to 100 fall out or are brushed out every day. Bodywide, about 15 percent of your hair follicles are resting at any given time, leaving you covered in a coat of a little more than 4 million hairs.

Much of this hair is nearly invisible. Unlike the hair of the scalp and, in men,

A Tortured Hair

This hair, viewed through an electron microscope, has been damaged by teasing. Its outer scales are ruffled and torn; it is holding on only by its tender, inner core. Hair that has not been tortured is smooth, elastic, and so strong that it actually takes more strength to snap a strand than to snap a strand of steel of the same diameter. The core gives hair its elasticity; wet hair can be stretched to more than 1½ times its usual length, and still spring back. The hair of Egyptian mummies 7,000 years old remains flexible and strong, if a little dull and dry.

the beard, body hair grows only to a certain length and stops. That length may be an inch or more on a man's hairy chest, but the hair on your inner arm or a baby's behind may be so fine and short and shy on pigment that you need a magnifying glass to see it. Whether hair is coarse or fine depends on the width of the follicle. A narrow follicle grows a fine hair; a thick follicle grows a coarse hair. Follicles grow wider as you grow, so your hair is coarser now than when you were a baby, and will be coarser still when you are an adult. Straightness or curliness is controlled by the shape of the follicle. If the follicle is a round tube, the hair is also round, and straight. The flatter the tube, the flatter the hair, and the curlier.

The length your head hair can grow depends on the habits of your follicles. An active follicle adds new cells to the base of its hair at a rate of about six inches (15 centimeters) a year. If it remains on the job for six years, the hair can grow a yard long. But people vary both in how quickly their hair grows, and how long their follicles remain active before stopping to recuperate. Some people can't get their hair to grow below the neck; others can grow it right to the ground. Of course, the tips of floor-length hair might be a decade old, and damaged from so many years of sunlight and shampoo. Few people can grow their hair very long without wearing the scales off the last few inches. Without armor to protect them, tender cores frazzle to split ends.

Beastly Reminders

Each hair follicle is set at an angle, so the hair that grows from it slants rather than sticks straight up. A tiny muscle is attached to one side of the follicle. When the muscle contracts, it pulls the hair erect. Nerve endings that convey the sense of touch wrap around the follicle, and it is the stimulating of millions of these nerves that you feel as a prickling sensation when your hair is on the rise.

Everyone knows what a "hair-raising" event is. It is the terror of screeching brakes, the knock on the door at midnight, the bloody hand creeping up the bed. But why should fear make hair stand on end, and why do fright wigs and spiky punk cuts make other people feel uneasy?

Watch a spooked dog and you'll get your answer. When a dog senses danger, it raises its hackles—the fur along the crest of its back. The raised fur makes it look bigger than it is. Were the danger another animal, the dog, though it feels frightened, would look threatening, and perhaps the danger would slink back into the night.

Almost every kind of animal has a way to make itself look bigger than it really is—by rearing up, puffing up, ruffling, bristling. Our head hair is too heavy, and our body hair too slight, to make much of a show when we bristle in the face of danger, but when a gorilla erects its hair, that's quite a show! Fright wigs and punk cuts have a double meaning when you think about it. They may be an attempt to intimidate others, but they likely arise from fear.

Long, curved, sharp nails are intimidating too. Witches with short fingernails are unthinkable; there is no monster that clips its nails.

Fingernails and toenails are dead cells stuffed with keratin just as hair is. Nails come out flat instead of round because they grow from a ditch rather than a pit. The ditch is called the

Okay to Shave

Is it true that shaving makes hair coarser? No, it only seems that way. Uncut body hair is tapered, and so feels softer at the tips. The bristly feeling of hair that has been shaved is the cut ends. If prickly legs are just too awful, there are waxes sold in drugstores to strip hair off, and depilatory creams that dissolve hair at the roots. Neither treatment is permanent. In both cases hair follicles simply go about their business producing a new crop of hair.

"quick" of the nail, meaning that cells there are living basal cells.

Nails never stop growing. If you didn't cut, bite, wear down, or break off your fingernails, they would grow about an inch and a half a year, but not evenly. Like the horns of antelopes—and made from the same stuff—they would curl, and twist. This is because the basal cells lining the ditch don't all divide at the same rate. Portions of nail made by fast dividers lengthen faster, bending the nail. Usually you can see the beginning of a downward bend as a nail grows beyond the fingertip. The faster dividing of the basal cells that produce the top surface of the nail is again a leftover from the very distant past, when that area curved claws.

Flaky

Some dandruff is normal: Scalp skin sheds squames at a particularly rapid rate. But overactive oil glands create a real problem by sticking squames together in patches where bacteria tend to multiply. Dandruff shampoos contain anti-bacterial pine tar, sulfur, or other chemicals that kill bacteria. They also irritate the scalp: Squames shed faster still, and take bacteria with them.

Of Tears and Earwax

People don't think of skin as an oozing organ, but just to get an idea of how oozy it is, consider this: An oil gland opens into every hair follicle, and there are as many as 650 sweat glands in a square inch of skin.

Skin makes oil, sweat, spit, tears, earwax, and milk from glands that, when they first evolved in fish, made them merely slippery. The skin inside your mouth still makes the slippery mucus that lets your tongue glide smoothly, but other oozes have newer uses that fishes never needed. Earwax keeps debris from accumulating in your ears; tears wash dust out of your eyes. Oil lubricates you. Sweat cools you. Breast milk is the perfect food for babies.

Skin glands are pouch-shaped communities of skin cells that specialize in making other products besides keratin. Their special product is exported through a pore, a hole at the top of the pouch that you can see in a piece of blister skin viewed through a magnifying glass. An oil gland is very simple. The pouch, up near the top of each hair follicle, oozes all the time, lubricating the hair as it grows outward, and spreading oil over the skin surface too. When oil-making cells are heated, they produce faster, so people tend to shine in the summer. Dry skin, on the other hand, is a winter problem.

Not too Long, Not too Sho[rt]

Left to themselves, nails grow into useless corkscrews. If bitten for years, the portion that clings to the finger becomes permanently shortened, and the fingertip is unprotected. "Normal length" in a practical sense is long enough for nails to scratch, short enough for fingertips to feel. A good test is whether you can pick up a needle from the floor!

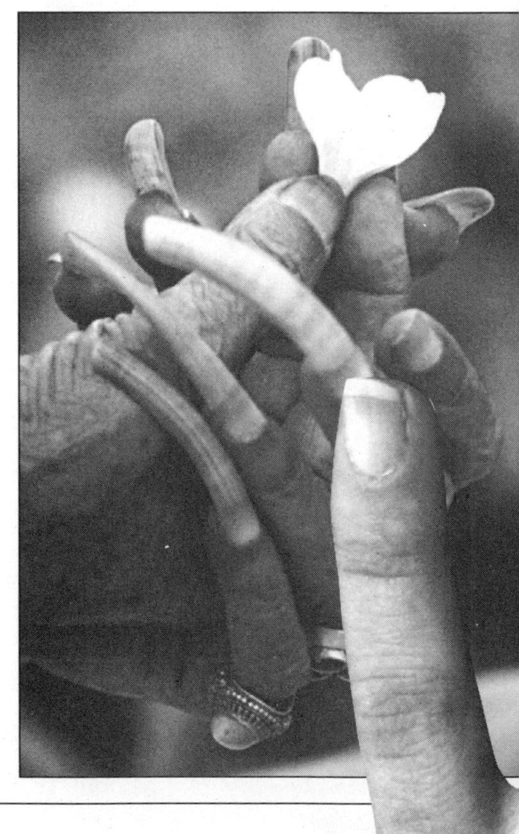

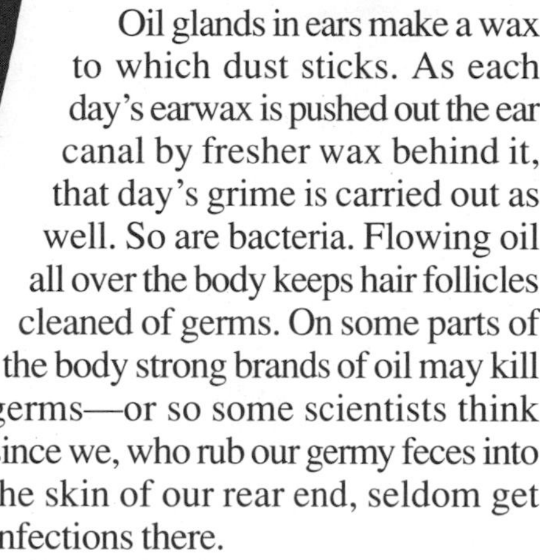

Oil glands in ears make a wax to which dust sticks. As each day's earwax is pushed out the ear canal by fresher wax behind it, that day's grime is carried out as well. So are bacteria. Flowing oil all over the body keeps hair follicles cleaned of germs. On some parts of the body strong brands of oil may kill germs—or so some scientists think since we, who rub our germy feces into the skin of our rear end, seldom get infections there.

Sweat glands are more complicated than oil glands. The pouch is coiled and deep, and it opens to the pore through a long tube. Cells that form the tube are basal cells that keep the pouch supplied with sweating daughters. Sweat accumulates in every pouch: Your skin is always full of it. A basket of muscles embraces each pouch. When they contract, the muscles squeeze the sweat up the tubc and through the pore at the skin's surface.

Sweating is one way the internal temperature of your body is controlled. When sweat evaporates, it removes heat from your body, and flies with it up into the air. A person doing hard work on a hot day can lose as much as a pint of water an hour as countless sweat glands pump body heat away. There is so much salt in sweat that on a dry, windy day, when drops dry before they drip, you may accumulate a crust of crystals on your skin.

So might you by crying. The liquid of both sweat and tears is brought to cells by blood, and blood is just a little less salty than the sea.

Tear gland pouches in each upper eyelid are joined together in a weepy group that drips tears over the eyeball through about a dozen tubes. They weep all the time. Blinking spreads the tears, and sweeps the salty water toward two holes in the inner corner of the eye. The holes drain into the nose, which runs if there's a flood of tears. Crying is too great a flood for the drains to handle, and so tears overflow.

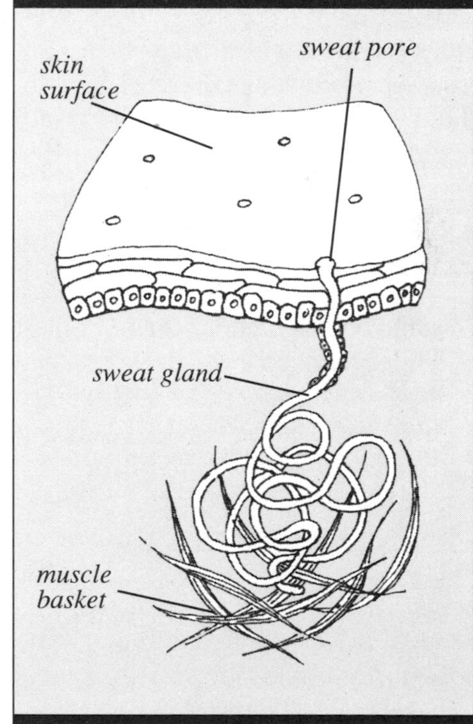

Eyeballs are self-cleaning because tears continually wash the dust that lands on them down the drain, or beaches it at the corner of the eye. Eyeballs are nearly germfree too, for tears are antiseptic. But most extraordinary is that when you cry in sorrow, tears may flush away your sadness. Researchers studying crying have noticed that tearfulness makes people feel better. Girls and women, who seem to become tearful more easily than boys and men, cheer themselves by a "good cry." Children of both sexes soothe themselves by crying themselves to sleep at night. Sobbed tears, it turns out, are chemically different from the ordinary eyeball wash that flows at other times. The researchers think that sad tears carry in them chemicals responsible for sad feelings, and so flow sorrow down the cheeks in rivers of relief.

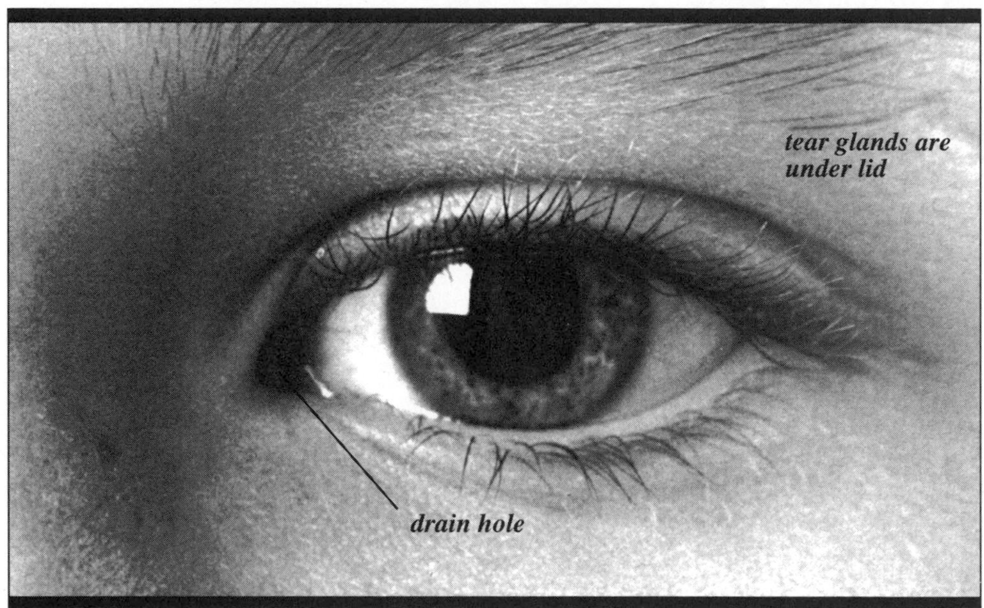

A Word From the Interior

As child bodies change into the bodies of adults, basal cells receive chemical messages that cause the skin-deep differences between the sexes. The chemicals are hormones made in testes, where males make sperm; in ovaries, where females make eggs; and in other interior glands that are the same in both sexes. The hormones circulate in blood, seep from vessels beneath the skin, soak through the fibrous rug, attach to basal cells, and move in. All kinds of things then begin to happen.

All over the body, hair follicles make thicker hairs. In some places—crotch, chin, cheek, chest, and armpit in particular—hair-making cells have an extra number of receptors to which hormones called androgens attach. Follicles in these places may flatten, curling hair that had been straight, as well as widen, and thickening hair that had been thin. They work for longer periods, lengthening hair that had been short. Melanocytes may also receive new instructions—to darken crotch hair, redden beards.

Everyone knows that hairy chests and faces are what men, not women, get. The word *androgen* means "making male," and the most powerful androgen is the hormone testosterone, made in testes, glands that men, not women, have. So how come girls nevertheless sprout bushes in crotch and armpits, and maybe a shadow of moustache? Males and females both make in other glands small amounts of androgens similar to testosterone, and although there's not enough to make girls bearded, their most sensitive hair follicles get enough to grow on.

The crotch is so unusually sensitive to androgens that it acts as an early warning system: Hair there means growing up has started, and you're in for a lot more than having curls in funny places.

Zits

While follicles follow androgen instructions to step up hair production, oil glands get the message to pour out more oil. The result is often acne. Why these hormones should have something to say to oil glands instead of minding their own business growing hair, deepening voices, changing figures, and stirring sexual feelings is a mystery, but few people get adult bodies without getting zits.

Acne starts as a stoppage. Oil is made faster than it can ooze out, and the follicle gets plugged. The cup from which hair grows is forced into a resting state; the hair falls out. Dead cells, which would normally be pushed out the pore, accumulate, and their keratin thickens the plug to a waxy stuff. Will this miniature disaster become a whitehead, a blackhead, or a pimple?

If the pore is widened by the plug, the exposed wax will darken from exposure to oxygen in the air and you'll have a blackhead. If the pore stays tiny so air can't reach the plug, you'll have a whitehead. And if bacteria happen to be living in the follicle eating oil, they might cause the swollen, red, painful, pus-filled infection called a pimple. The body tries to contain this infection by surrounding it with a fibrous bag. Popping a pimple's bag shoots bacteria out beneath the skin to all the follicles nearby.

Would You Believe...

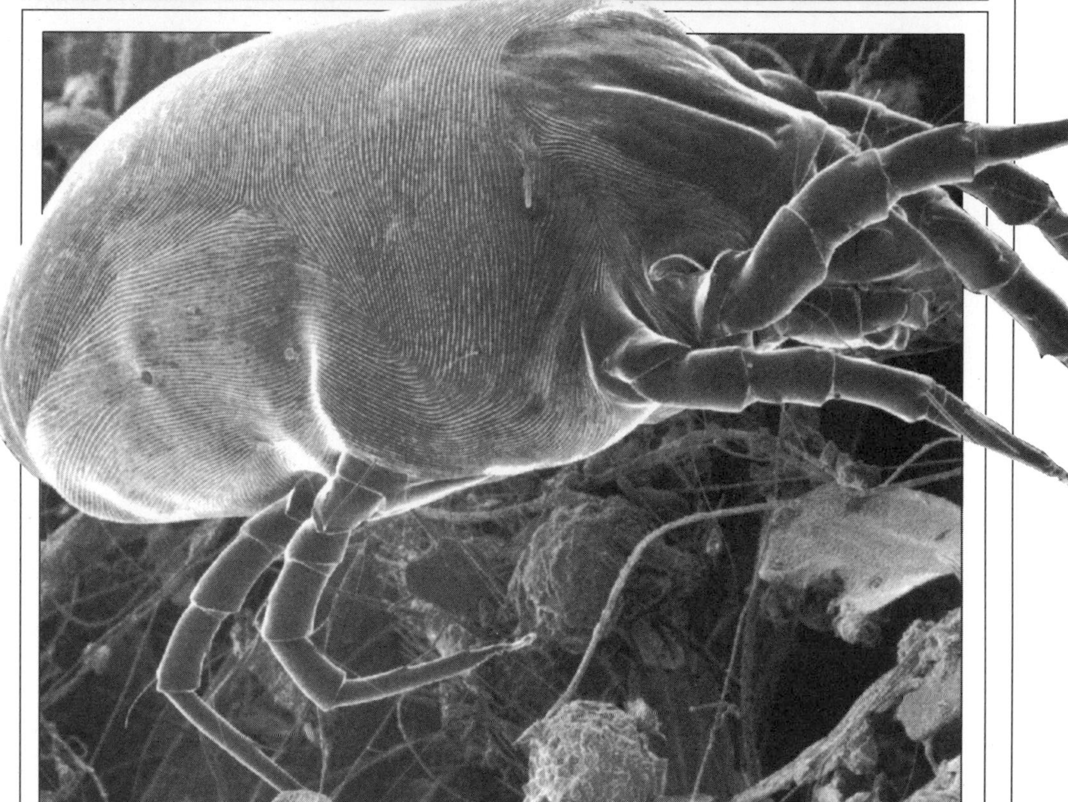

The most monstrous-looking but least harmful creature that inhabits skin is the minute mite *Demodex folliculorum*. These mites inhabit hair follicles in eyelids, eyebrows, ears, and noses, where they dine on oil. They cause no trouble at all, not even an itch. People who have them don't know it, and people who "catch" on their own hairs the dust-size eggs will never find out either. A mite that causes real trouble is one that lives off squames, but not on skin. It is called a dust mite, shown here at more than 300 times its actual size, and it feasts especially on squames shed in bed. People who think they have an allergy to feather pillows are often suffering instead from an allergy to the mites they share their pillows with.

Seventh Grade

Class pictures of seventh graders show one awful thing about growing up: It doesn't happen evenly. First, it happens to girls, then it happens to boys. And it happens to some girls years ahead of other girls. That goes for boys too. Bodies don't even grow evenly. Feet and hands may grow before anything else, or arms dangle too long, or legs get gangly. Then chins and noses start up—not just getting bigger, but changing shape. Worse, bones grow faster than muscles, so bodies for a while look gawky. The only consolation is that everything eventually catches up, limbs with trunk, muscles with bones—and boys with girls.

Adults are never more irritating than when they tell kids that if they'd just wash their face, they wouldn't have pimples. Continual scrubbing causes more harm than good because it stimulates gland cells to make even more oil. Soap anyway can't clean out the junk in a stopped-up pore, and the blackness of blackheads has nothing to do with dirt. Diet also has no effect on acne. Fatty chocolate, greasy pizza, and oily potato chips don't affect the amount of oil your skin makes, or the number of bacteria enjoying it.

Most people's acne goes away as their body makes less hormone, or as their skin glands listen to it less. But nice skin is hard to wait for, and no amount of waiting erases the scars serious pimples leave. Luckily, skin doctors now can prescribe medicines that heal acne promptly in almost everyone. The catch is that you have to see the doctor; drugstores can't sell without

prescription any other medicine that works as well.

The Scent of Sex

All sweat glands in children, and most sweat glands in grownups, produce the ordinary salty stuff that drips from pores everywhere on a steamy summer day. But in adolescence sweat glands in the armpits and the crotch begin to make a richer, thicker fluid. Fresh, ordinary sweat doesn't smell (it's bacteria living in the sweat that can make it stinky), but this rich sweat is scented. In other animals, such scents contain substances called pheromones that, like airborne hormones, convey messages. The receivers of the messages are not, however, other cells in the same body: They are other bodies.

Pheromones wafting through the neighborhood tell male dogs that a female is in heat. Pheromones drifting from male rats to female rats tell them it is time to produce some eggs. Not surprisingly, since we, too, are animals, pheromones from women's armpits attract men, and pheromones from men's armpits stimulate women to ripen eggs. This is in spite of the fact that, as far as we know, we are aware only of the stinkier smells in sweat and can't discern the scent of pheromones among the mingled odors of armpits. We may say "Ugh!" to body odor, but it has power over us nonetheless.

Budding Out

Of all the skin glands descended from the simple ones of fish, those that make milk are the most elaborate. The gland is made up of several dozen tubes, each of which branch into hundreds of pouches lined with milk-making cells. The tubes open to the nipple through pores. Each pouch is surrounded by a basket of muscles to squeeze milk out the nipple in the same way that sweat is squeezed from sweat glands.

Both sexes are born with milk glands, but they are too small in childhood to make a bump. What makes them grow in adolescent girls is the hormone estrogen, made in ovaries. Just as some girls make enough androgens elsewhere than in testes to grow a shadow of moustache, so some boys make enough estrogen elsewhere than in ovaries to grow minor bumps beneath their nipples. Bumps, however, don't grow to breasts in boys.

In girls, the small buds of milk glands, hard and sore at first, are only the beginning of breasts. The tubes gradually grow longer and more branchy, but there aren't any pouches, and the whole gland takes up very little space. Most of a girl's breasts is padding, plain old fat.

Only when a woman becomes pregnant do pouches sprout from her milk glands, and only when she is nursing do they really bulge enough to emphasize the shape fat alone had given. So what was the fat for in the first place? Probably it was just for show. When you think of the sweat, the hair, the oil of adolescence, you have to realize that whether people like it or not, their body doesn't intend the change from child to adult to be a private matter.

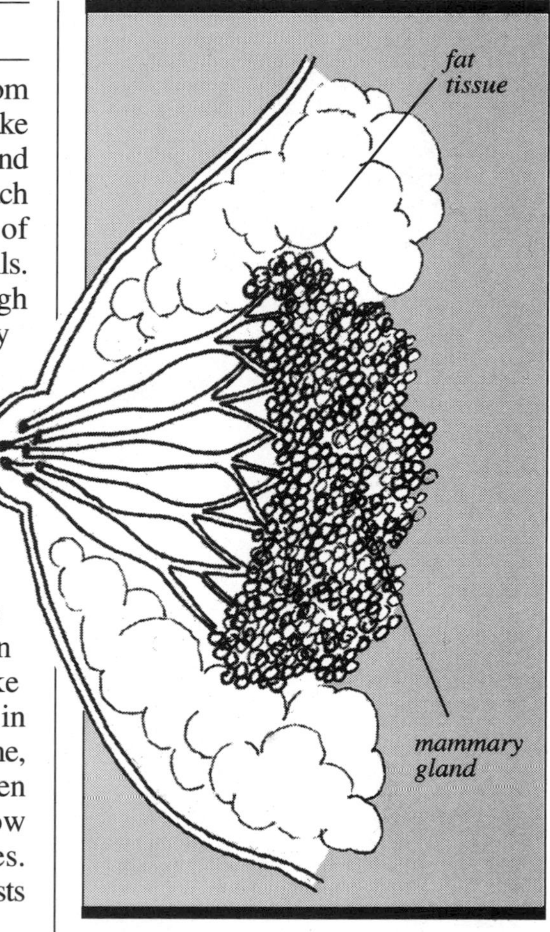

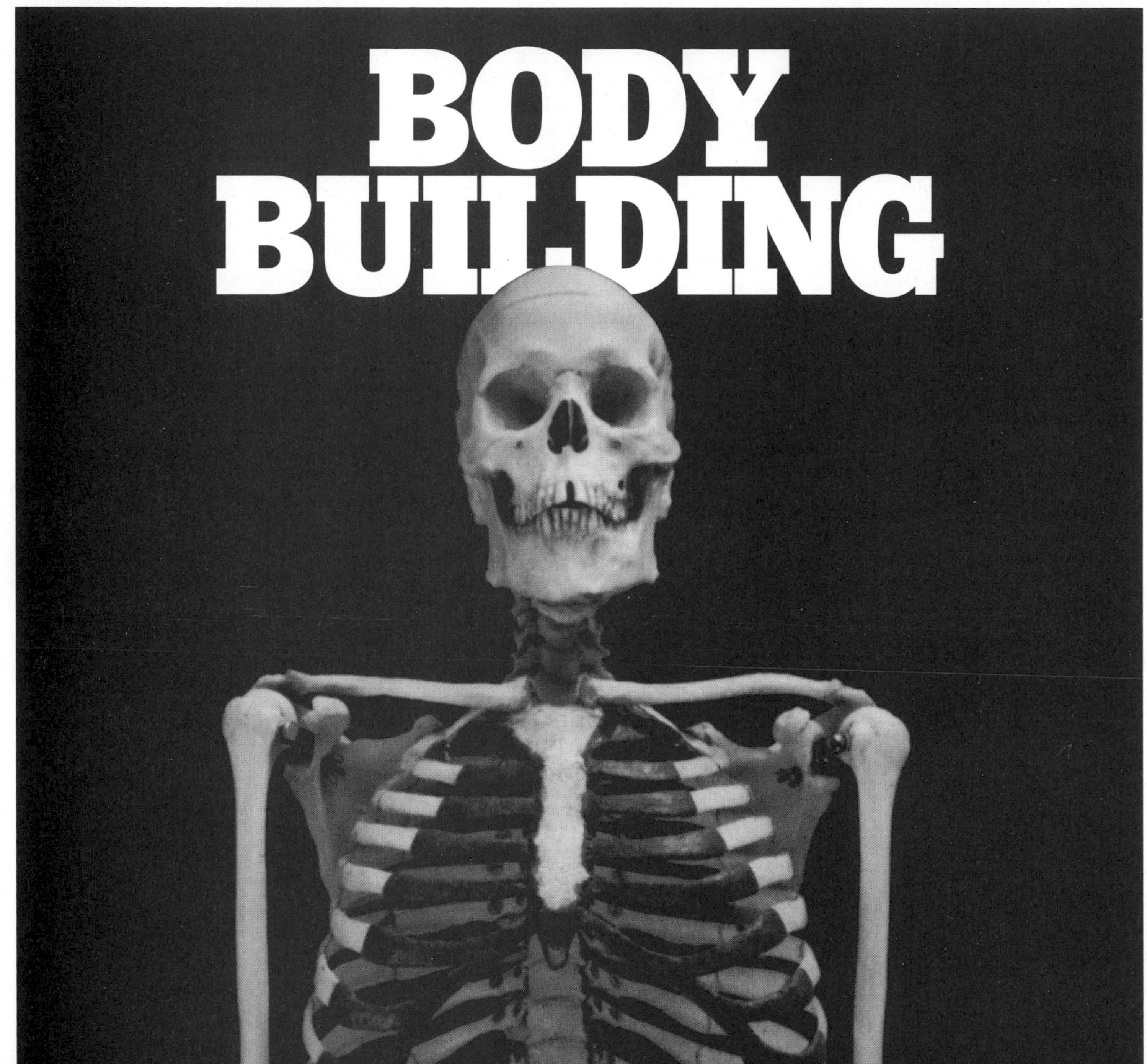
BODY
BUILDING

Underneath your outer covering of cells is an altogether different kind of skin called dermis. Pick up a fold of skin on your neck: The thickness is mostly dermis. Examine your wallet, your belt, your shoes. If they're leather, they're made of dermis. While blister skin is bloodless and nerveless, this deeper layer of you hurts when pinched, bleeds when pricked. Yet cells are as rare there as tigers in the jungle, for this stuff really is a stuff, made *by* cells, not of them.

Cells are called the building blocks of the body. That's true for plant bodies. Each cell in a plant is contained in a box of cellulose, the tough crunch of celery stems and carrot roots. Cylindrical and cubical plant cells you might have studied in vegetable slivers under a microscope are stacked like walls and towers. They really are the bricks and pillars that plant bodies are built of.

There are no such boxes around animal cells. The limp membrane that holds their wet innards is so thin that it looks like no more than a boundary line through a school microscope at highest power. If these squishy things were your construction material, you would be a heap, not a body.

Spun Together

The materials that make you firm and strong are spun by fiber-making cells into the space around them. The fibers hold you together. Your outer skin is attached to you by the woven dermis, and similar materials hang onto your muscles, cement your muscles to your bones, strap your bones to one another, and keep your organs from jiggling, or falling to the bottom of your belly. Even individual cells are held together and tied in place by webs of these materials. Your very bones are spun.

Materials made by various kinds of spinners are called connective tissues. They include bone, cartilage, ligaments, and tendons, as well as dermis. You have met some of these products outside of bodies. The casings that hold sausages together are tubes of connective tissue spun around pigs' intestines to hold them in shape. The same strong material, but from cats instead of pigs, is used for violin bows. Gristle in meat is connective tissue that joins one muscle to another. The beautiful materials of shell buttons, fish bone chopsticks, and ivory piano keys are all spun by fiber makers, and then hardened with minerals.

You can see on the rough side of leather—or better yet on suede—the actual fibers like those that cells called fibroblasts are making now inside your dermis. But leather doesn't give you a good idea of what dermis is like before it becomes shoes. For that you have to imagine yourself microscopic, the size, say, of a germ that's fallen into dermis through a scratch—a "mere" scratch, but nevertheless a tear in the rug that lets a germ fall into the wet inside of you.

A Trip into a Scratch

A bacterium, this kind a round cell only one-twentieth the size of the basal cells it's just slipped past through a tear in the rug, sinks among pits of follicles and sweat glands into a wet tangle. Among the strands lies a fibroblast—a fiber maker—spinning like a spider in its web. The cell is barely visible through the dense webbing it is making as it lies motionless, anchored by spiky arms to its handiwork, while from its surface grow fibers that are like cables, elastics, threads of glue. Watery juice, called body fluid because it fills all body spaces between cells and among fibers, flows slowly among the spider's meshes.

There are other features in the wet strangeness of the dermis. Long, thready ends of nerve cells rise upward through it. The scratch has fired them, causing pain. Close by are tiny blood vessels—capillaries—broken and bleeding slightly, their torn cells dying. Even cells of sweat glands, ragged where they were broken by the scratch, are leaking out their contents as they, too, die.

Only the one fibroblast is around at the moment. But the chemicals leaking from ruptured cells flow out through the watery neighborhood, and soon other fibroblasts, following the scent of death, creep to the scratch. Other kinds of cells also smell the injury. A phagocyte—a white blood cell that can slip out of blood vessels like a blob of flowing jelly—slithers into view. A couple of chubby cells, speckled all through with dark granules, also pick up the scent.

Each of these cells has a special job to do, and you can notice some evidence of their work over the few days it takes for a scratch to heal.

For instance, the scratch is sorer after a few minutes than it was at first, and the area around it reddens, heats, and swells. Even a fingernail scratch that doesn't break the skin will redden in less than a moment (try it on your belly for best results). This inflammation is at first the work of the chubby cells, although later the job is taken over by others. Chubby cells are called mast cells after an old German word for pig food because they look so stuffed. Mast cell granules, however, are chemicals that, when released at the site of the injury, have dramatic effects. They make the cells of blood capillaries part a bit from one another, so the vessels leak. The leaks are not large enough for the red cells that color blood to get through, but the clear liquid of blood does seep out. This is the liquid that fills a blister, and that swells the dermis around the scratch. More blood than

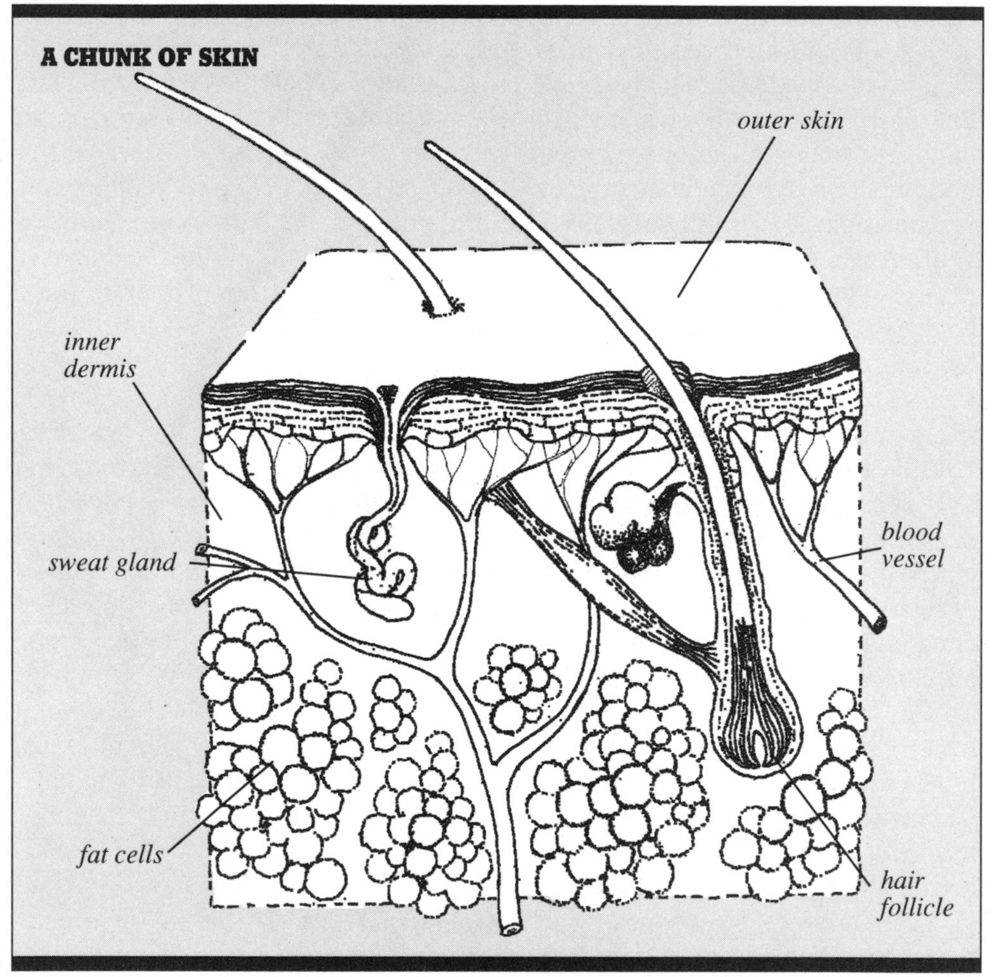

usual flows through expanded capillaries. That's what makes an injury feel hot, and heat makes every cell around work faster.

Another of the mast cells' chemicals stimulates nerve endings that convey pain. That's how you are reminded, after the hurt of the moment, to still protect the injured area. After a few days, the scratch may itch instead of hurt. That's because of another chemical, histamine, that fires itch nerves. Mast cells are responsible for the itchy bump you get after a mosquito bite.

The job of phagocytes is to clean up the mess. They are extraordinary cells. They have no shape, or, rather, they can flow themselves into any shape. Those that travel through blood vessels squeeze out through gaps like egg white slips through fingers. Whole gangs of phagocytes creep out around the scratch. Other, giant ones slither there from elsewhere in the dermis, where they are always on patrol. Phagocytes are scavengers. They clean up dead cells and broken strands of web by engulfing the debris, oozing it into their inside wrapped in a bag of membrane, and digesting it. They are also predators: They eat bacteria.

Even the largest phagocytes—the giant ones are 10 times the size of an average cell—are too small to see without a microscope, but you may see heaps of them in a scratch, for they are the bulk of pus. If germs succeed in multiplying in a wound—if the scratch becomes infected—these countless blobby bodies gobble the germs all up.

Scars and Scabs

As the scratch is cleaned of junk and germs, fibroblasts make repairs. They replace broken fibers, reweave webs, bind up torn edges of the skin's thin rug. If the scratch is deep, you may get to see in a week or so an example of their weaving right up on the surface of your skin, for if the ripped rug gapes wide

Denizens of the Dermis

Mast cell

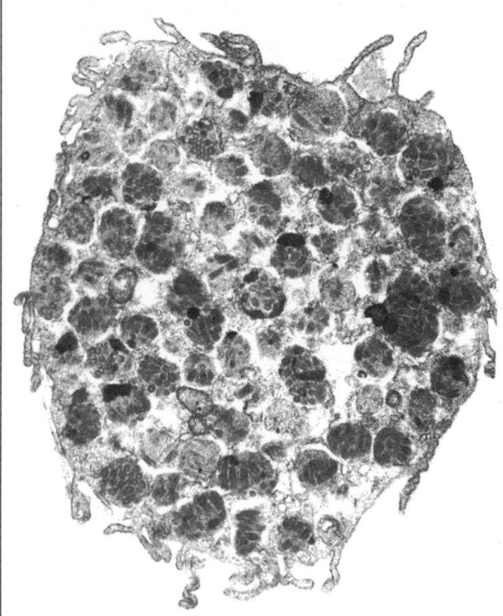

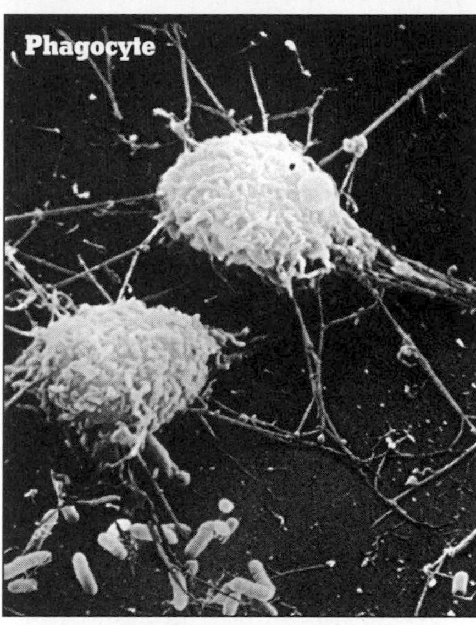

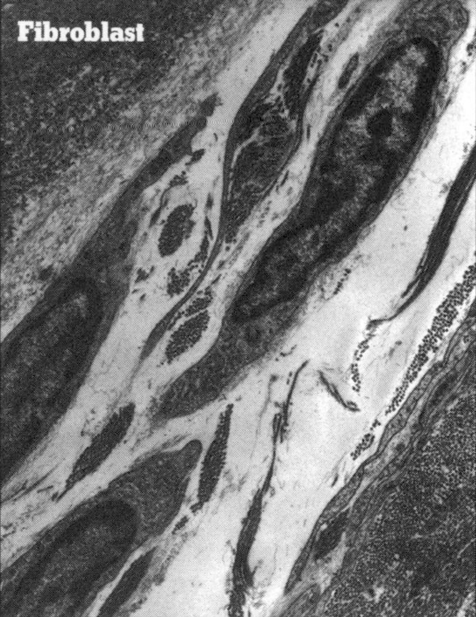

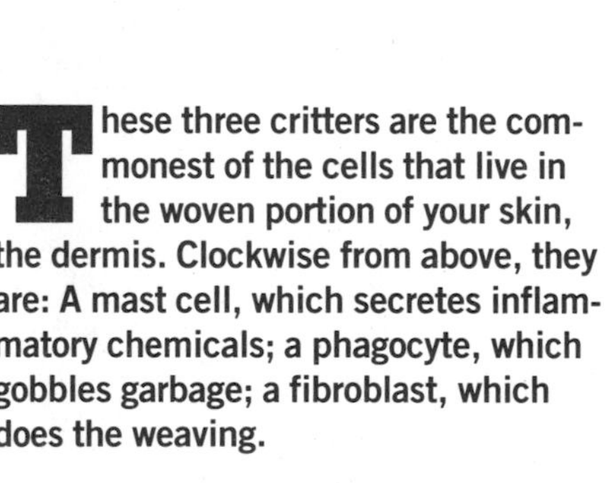

These three critters are the commonest of the cells that live in the woven portion of your skin, the dermis. Clockwise from above, they are: A mast cell, which secretes inflammatory chemicals; a phagocyte, which gobbles garbage; a fibroblast, which does the weaving.

open, or if a chunk of it is torn away, fibroblasts will fill the gap with the strong white fibers of a scar.

All of this happens underneath a scab, a temporary plug of dried, clotted blood that seals the opening of a wound while cells repair it. Clotting is so fast that if the blood circulating in your vessels were to all begin to clot at once, you would be solidified in 20 seconds. A clever system prevents that from happening inside of blood vessels. A protein needed to start blood clotting is embedded in the membranes of all sorts of body cells—except blood cells themselves, and those that line their vessels. As long as blood stays in veins and arteries, it remains a liquid. It solidifies only when it escapes through an injury and encounters the protein that turns the leak into a plug.

You can watch clotting happen to the few drops of blood that seep from a scratch. For a moment it drips, and would feel thin if you smeared it. In seconds it stops dripping, and feels thicker. Moments later it has become a solid plug made of a meshwork of fibers in which blood cells are trapped. The fibers were not there in the blood when it was liquid. But as you watch, the protein embedded in your scratch have started a chemical reaction in your blood that, for each single molecule of the clot triggerer, will produce 160 *billion* molecules of fiber!

A clot at the surface of your skin dries to a scab. As scab pickers know, the scab comes loose at the edges first. That's because new skin, as it grows in from the edges of an injury, breaks fibers that had glued the clot in place.

A bruise is a clot from bleeding beneath the skin. Bruises are bluish because that's the color of stale blood; the pigments change color as phagocytes eat the bled blood cells and chemically destroy their once-red pigments. You can understand why it takes so long for a black-and-blue mark to fade when you realize that the whole clot, fiber by fiber and cell by cell, has to be eaten up and digested by the phagocytes that keep your dermis clean.

Itching Juice

The histamine mast cells make causes the itch of poison ivy and mosquito bites. To stop the itching, hold the area under the hottest water you can stand for about half a minute. The heat will make mast cells blast out all the histamine they have stored. But the chemical is used up immediately, and it takes mast cells hours to make more of it. During those hours, your rash or bite won't itch a bit.

Making Leather

There are funny things you can notice by poking and pulling skin. You can't, for instance, separate it from your body: It's attached all over. You can stretch it only so far, and no farther. When you let it go, it snaps back. When you poke it, it bounces. The strength, stretch, bounce, and attachment of dermis come both from the way it's woven, and from the kinds of fibers used in its weaving.

Fibers are proteins, exceptionally complicated molecules that, when they form long strands, are often assembled from shorter units much as yarn is spun from a sheep's short hairs. Each kind of fiber in dermis has different physical characteristics.

The strongest one is collagen, the fiber that strengthens skin and that scars are made of. A collagen unit looks like a short length of rope made up of three strands twisted around one another. Fibroblasts manufacture just these short lengths, preassembled into twists, and push them out through their membrane. Once out of the cell, the twists of collagen self-assemble, first into long, thin bundles, then thicker ones, and finally into the cablelike bundles that are fibers. Each finished collagen cable is a long, shiny, white strand of tremendous strength.

Other molecules supplied by fibroblasts tie collagen strands into a loose web in three dimensions, something like a cobweb. That arrangement is called a matrix. A collagen matrix is equally strong in all directions, and altogether stronger than the little prickles by which squames cling together.

Although a collagen matrix is flexible, it has no elasticity. The stretchiness of skin is allowed by a second type of fiber called elastin, which is also made by fibroblasts. Each molecule of elastin is shaped like a squiggle or a loosely coiled spring. When pulled, the squiggle straightens; when let go again, the molecule recoils. These springy squiggles are spot welded to one another in a matrix that is interwoven with, but not attached to, the collagen matrix. You can stretch your skin only as far as collagen allows: When that mesh is taut, skin will stretch no further. But when you let go, the elastin matrix springs it back to shape.

Both collagen and elastin are floppy; they can't hold up the skin, give it the fullness and bounce of palms and cheeks. Without some material to fill up the spaces within the matrix, a material like skin would simply collapse like a deflated balloon. Plumpness is provided by monstrous molecules shaped like long-legged centipedes that coil their enormous length within the spaces between fibers. They themselves lack bounce, but they attract water, and hold it. The result is that the matrix inflates with water, and that's what gives your skin its waterbed consistency.

One other important fiber, called fibronectin, acts as an anchor for the fibroblasts themselves. Fibronectin adheres cells to collagen, and also attaches cells to one another. It is the universal body glue, the stickiness that keeps your skin on you, and holds the whole of you together.

Communications Networks

Fibroblasts live not just in your springy hide, but everywhere in the body where their fibers are needed to hold things in place. Fibroblasts suspend your intestines from the walls of your abdomen so that when you stand up guts don't fall down. They are the makers of sausage casings and the stringers of muscles onto bone. Fibroblasts are even the crafters of your corneas, the perfectly transparent circles that cover the colored centers of your eyes.

The fibers these spinners use to make various materials are the same, but they are used in different proportions and are arranged in different ways. In a tendon that attaches a muscle to a bone, and in a ligament that attaches

When Clotting's Not Enough

Although blood always clots as soon as it escapes a blood vessel, clotting is not always able to plug the wound. The reason is that a large would—especially one to an artery through which blood is pumped under pressure from the beating heart—releases such a flow of blood that clots are washed away as they form. For clotting to help under those circumstances, pressure has to be applied to the wound or to the artery above the wound to lessen blood flow while the clot grows large enough to do its job. If a large artery has been cut, the cut often must be stitched up to stop the bleeding.

Your Inner Weave

The dermis, shown here far greater than its actual size, is woven from several kinds of fiber that together give it strength, elasticity, and volume.

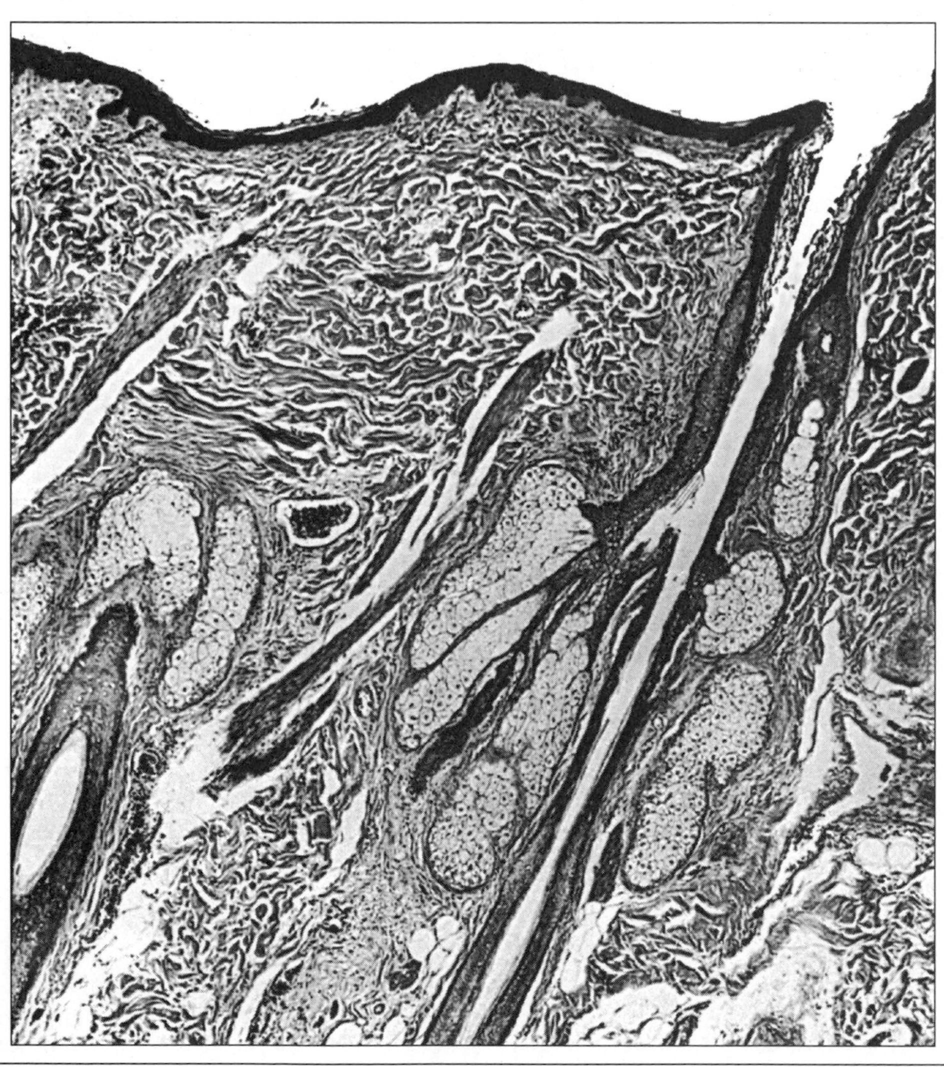

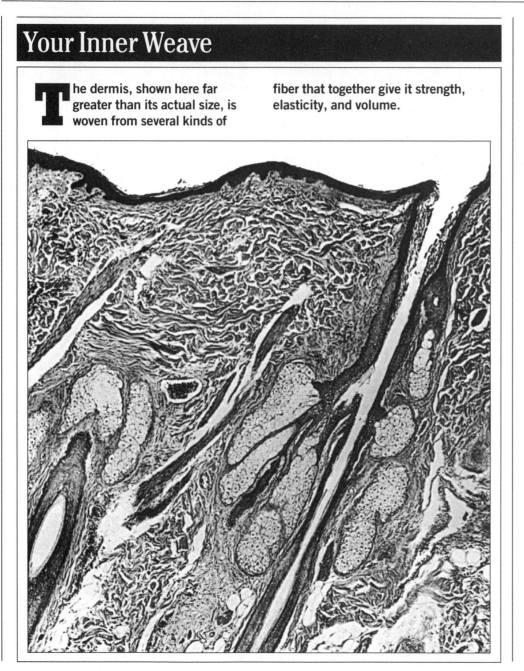

one bone to the next, collagen fibers are tied parallel to one another in thick bands for maximum strength in one direction. This is the arrangement in turkey leg tendons, which are nearly impossible to break by pulling. Tendons are only slightly stretchy: Less elastin is used to make them. Collagen fibers in the transparent cornea of your eye are laid parallel in sheets, and the sheets are stacked in layers. The grain of each layer lies at right angles to the grain of the layers above and below, giving the cornea strength in both directions, but leaving the water-filled gaps you see through.

The odd thing is that no fibroblast is a specialist in a particular kind of material. If you could move a fibroblast from a scratch into a twisted ankle, it would repair ligament as well as it had repaired dermis. A fibroblast summoned to an injury spins material to exactly match the pattern of the weave there whether or not it has ever made such stuff before. More amazing still, if a fibroblast working now on your finger dermis were moved into the cartilage of your knuckle, it would actually change its appearance: It would turn into a chondroblast, a cell that makes cartilage.

Until recently scientists assumed that connective tissues were inert construction materials—like the plastic, rubber, steel, and concrete that are a building, but that take no part in the lives that live in it. A closer look at spinners as they spun in laboratory dishes revealed a curious fact. When a fiber maker extrudes a twist of collagen, it hangs onto one end while assembly begins. Collagen is in that way forced to self-assemble in a particular direction. The direction is the same as the direction of certain filaments inside the cell. The internal filaments of a fibroblast spinning tendon lie parallel to the collagen strands it produces, whereas the internal filaments of fibroblasts in the dermis lie in various directions, like collagen strands in the mesh it makes.

When fibroblasts are moved to another material, they appear to catch hold of fibers in their new neighborhood in order to get the lay of the land. They then rearrange their internal filaments to match the direction of the fibers that surround them, and produce new fibers in the new pattern. In this way cells influence the structure of their neighborhood, and are also influenced by the structures others have built before them. Connective tissue guides its own mending and, when you grow, its own enlargement.

But who thought up these patterns in the first place? The earliest ancestors of cells now living in your body laid down the patterns of materials while you were an embryo when your body plan was still quite simple, and fiber-making cells were just beginning to settle into their permanent locations.

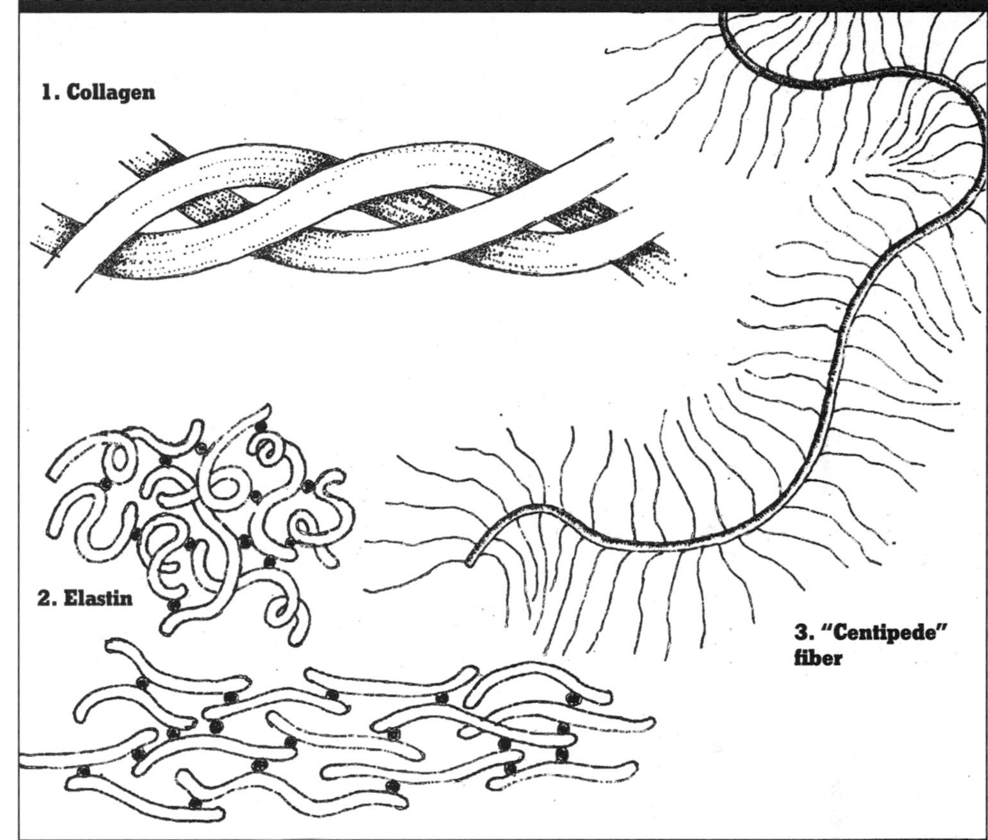

Ever since, their descendants have relied on the knowledge of that original weave. Basal cells in skin wove their rug atop the dermis then, too. Chondroblasts in the depths of you spun the shapes of your bones. Even muscle cells, which no longer spin, built around themselves during your earliest weeks cocoons that still govern the way they are to grow.

This is really something to think about when you consider that the fibrous materials cells secrete are not alive. Since they're not alive, they can't be killed. When you are injured, cells may die, but the patterns by which new cells replace the injured portions survive the way the weave of plaids and tweeds survive the ripping of a fabric.

How Bones Begin

A leg bone that will be more than two feet long and a couple of inches thick begins in an embryo's paddle-footed limb as a cartilage model only a few millimeters long. The cartilage model is made by both chondroblasts—cartilage builders—and fibroblasts. Chondroblasts inhabit the center of a growing bone model. They secrete around themselves an elastic kind of cartilage. When they divide, each daughter cell also secretes a cartilage matrix around it, and the model grows.

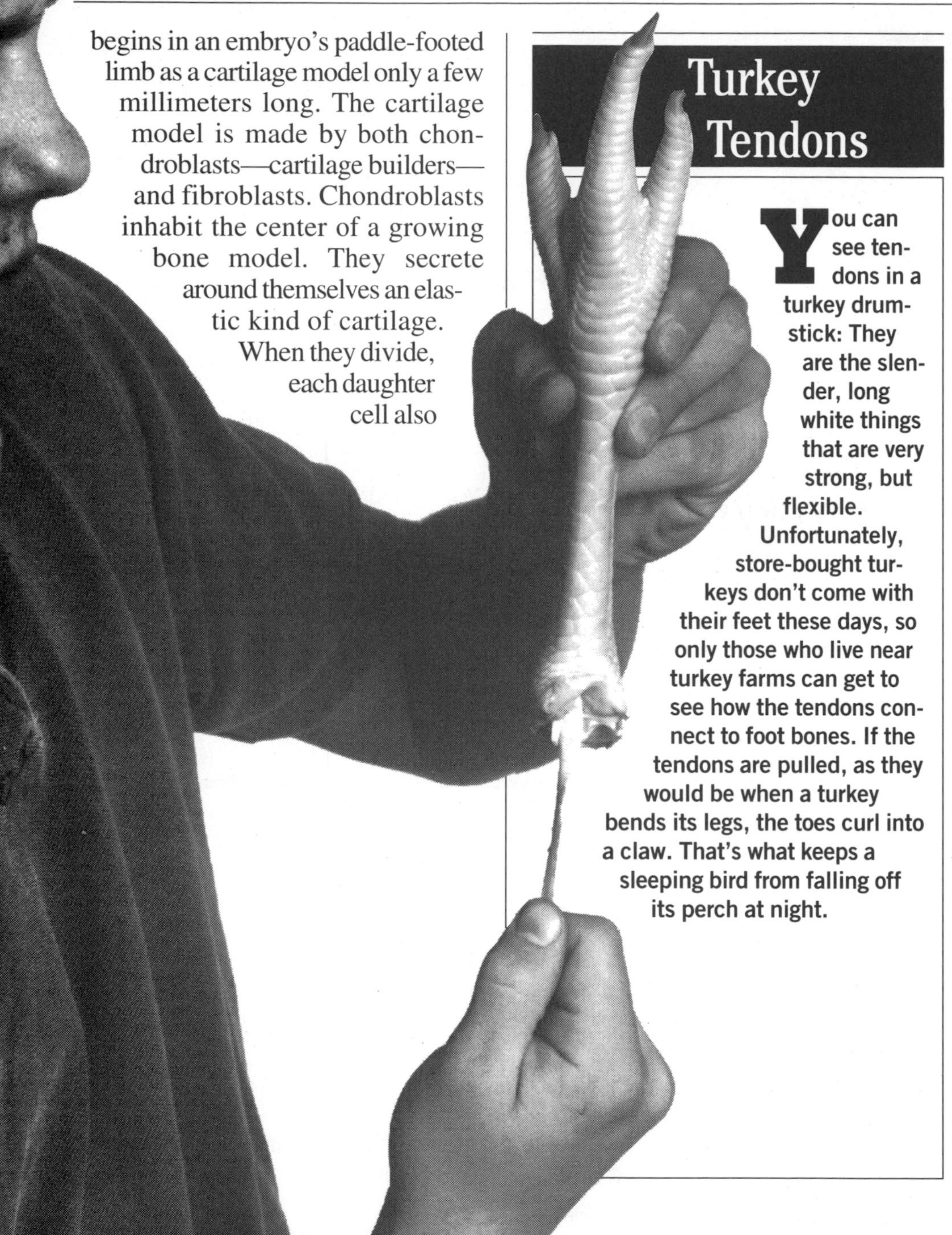

Turkey Tendons

You can see tendons in a turkey drumstick: They are the slender, long white things that are very strong, but flexible. Unfortunately, store-bought turkeys don't come with their feet these days, so only those who live near turkey farms can get to see how the tendons connect to foot bones. If the tendons are pulled, as they would be when a turkey bends its legs, the toes curl into a claw. That's what keeps a sleeping bird from falling off its perch at night.

Fibroblasts live at the surface of the model. They coat it with a firmer type of cartilage. While chondroblasts add more matrix to enlarge the bone, fibroblasts spin the corset that holds the bone in shape. The cartilage model is like a scaffolding. It won't actually be incorporated into the finished bone, but the bone will be built within the scaffolding using its shape as a guide.

Bone building begins in the middle of the cartilage scaffold, which was the first, and is therefore the oldest, portion of the bone-to-be. Chondroblasts there begin to swell up and die; holes are left where their living bodies used to be. Blood vessels invade these holes, and they are followed by a crew of excavators and builders. The excavators are called osteoclasts, "bone destroyers." They are actually communal phagocytes fused from four or five of those whose specialty is scavenging. They eat away channels in the cartilage model, including the central cavity that will become filled with marrow. They are followed by osteoblasts—"bone builders." While osteoclasts eat tunnels through the scaffolding, osteoblasts coat the tunnels with layers of collagen matrix. The matrix is at first fibrous, not hard.

Bone hardness comes from calcium phosphate, a mineral that circulates in the blood and body fluid. It is captured by a protein that anchors it to collagen in the bone matrix. An anchored molecule of calcium phosphate serves as a "seed" crystal; it grows the way rock candy grows, by binding other molecules to it in the tight pattern that gives bone its rocklike rigidity.

This replacement of the soft cartilage scaffolding with hard bone is called ossification, and it continues from before birth until the end of puberty. During all those years chondroblasts add new cartilage; it is their work that makes bone grow. Osteoclasts and osteoblasts ossify the structure, but they can't extend it; they are trapped inside the bone. Over the years of childhood, generation after generation of chondroblasts age and die, leaving daughters only at the joint ends to carry on the work of lengthening bone while older portions of the model are ossified.

An X-ray of a newborn baby's hand shows that at birth only the middle portion of finger bones are ossified. The joints are just cartilage. By one year old, two new centers of ossification have begun, one in each joint end of each finger bone. The area between the bony joint and the bony shaft is still cartilage, and this is the part that continues to grow. At puberty, these last gaps are invaded by bone. Within a couple of years, all the bones in the body are completely ossified from one end to the other except for a cushion of cartilage at either end, and growth is over.

Scars

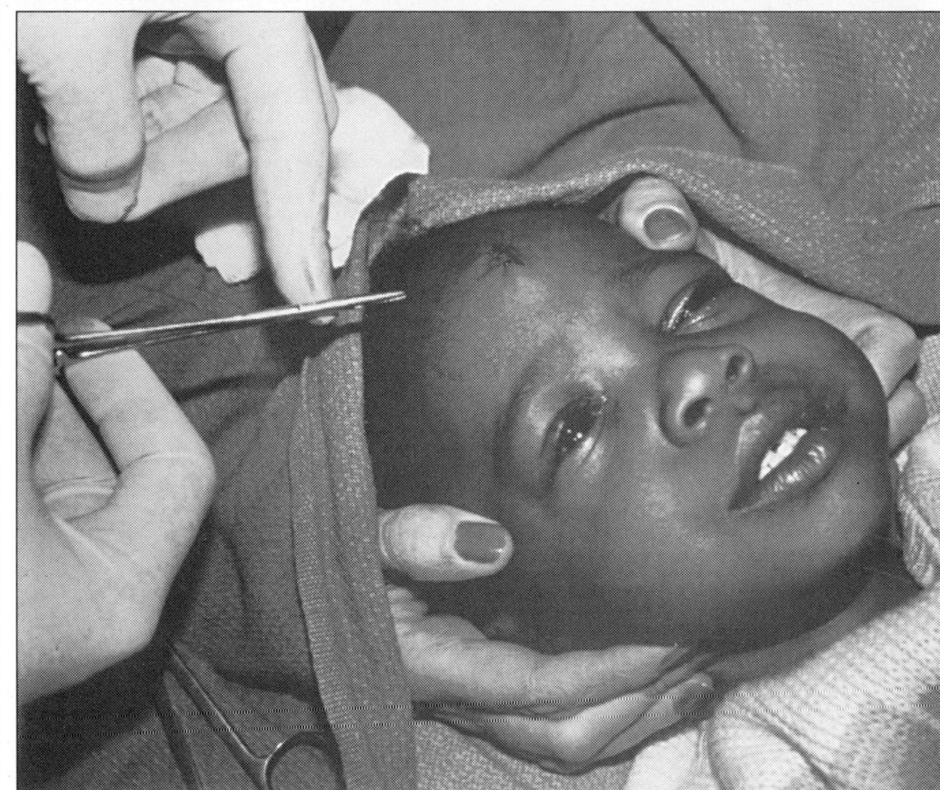

Deep cuts cut right through the rug that skin cells sit on. If the cut gapes open, skin cells can't cover up the gap. Instead, fibroblasts fill the opening with the tough, white fibers of a scar. Skin cells can't grow over a scar, and it remains white because melanocytes can't inject it with pigment. Doctors stitch gaping cuts to prevent scarring. When a doctor stitches a cut, she is simply pulling the two edges close to one another so that fibroblasts will have no gap in the rug to fill in with scar tissue. Skin cells can then rejoin, and the cut is healed within about a week. A local pain killer, given by injection, is used when putting stitches in, but taking them out hardly hurts at all.

Elastic Babies, Brittle Kids

These X-rays show hand bones in a baby, a six-year-old, and a young adolescent. The paler portion is cartilage; the darker portion is ossified bone whose minerals reflect X-rays better, and therefore expose the film more completely. The baby's finger bones have begun to ossify in the middle. The teenager's bones have nearly ossified right to their tips, indicating that she has almost completed her growth.

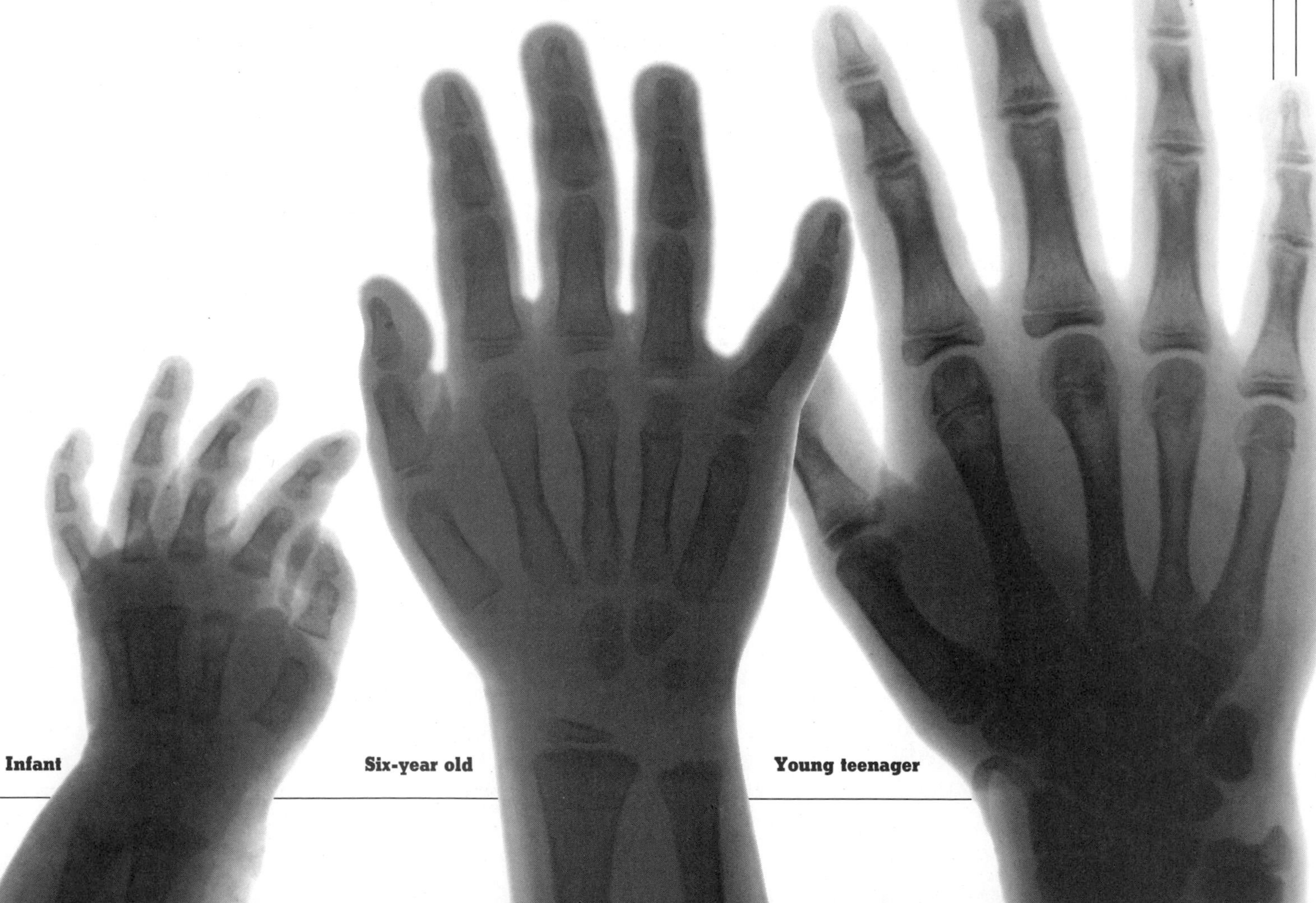

Infant **Six-year old** **Young teenager**

A skeleton crew of cartilage makers remains for maintenance and repair jobs. But the full crew of osteoclasts and osteoblasts stays on: Their job is never done.

The Renewable Skeleton

None of the bone in your body is as old as you are. Every year, as much as 10 percent of your bone is eaten away and replaced with new bone, so very little of your skeleton is more than a decade old. At every moment osteoclasts inside your bones are excavating new channels, and osteoblasts hard on their heels are building new bone.

Bone is very durable stuff. The bone that is replaced is old, but there is nothing wrong with it. Why should it be continually torn down and made anew if it could have served its purpose for decades?

Old bone is remodeled, not just rebuilt. The combined efforts of many thousands of work crews burrowing through a bone may subtly change its shape, thickening it here, thinning it there, adjusting its strength to the pressures that are placed on it.

Putting a load on bones causes them to thicken. A farmer's hands, a runner's legs become thicker than they would have been if these bones had not been loaded by pounding work. Fishermen may have a broad stance: Their hip bones have been reshaped to accommodate the rolling gait with which they keep their balance on a heaving deck. Bones respond even to local pressures. Horseback riders develop thickened bone where their buttocks bang the saddle, and students develop bone bumps where pencils press against the fingers. Everyone develops a bump behind each ear that no one had as a baby. The bump (check it out) is caused by the pulling of neck muscles against that portion of the skull.

Occupational sculpturings are sometimes used to help identify skeletons, or to discover how people lived in ancient times. The throwing arm of baseball pitchers develops a specific kind of crest; a similar crest on skeletons of Ice Age men shows that they hunted with spears. Squatting leaves telltale bumps and dents in hips, knees, and shinbones. Based on their bones, Neanderthal people squatted, not sat.

When the load is taken off bones they slim right down. A person laid up in bed for only weeks loses bone, and bone is lost from limbs while they are immobilized in casts. Saddle lumps and pencil bumps also are gradually lost if the pressure is not kept up. Yet a fin-

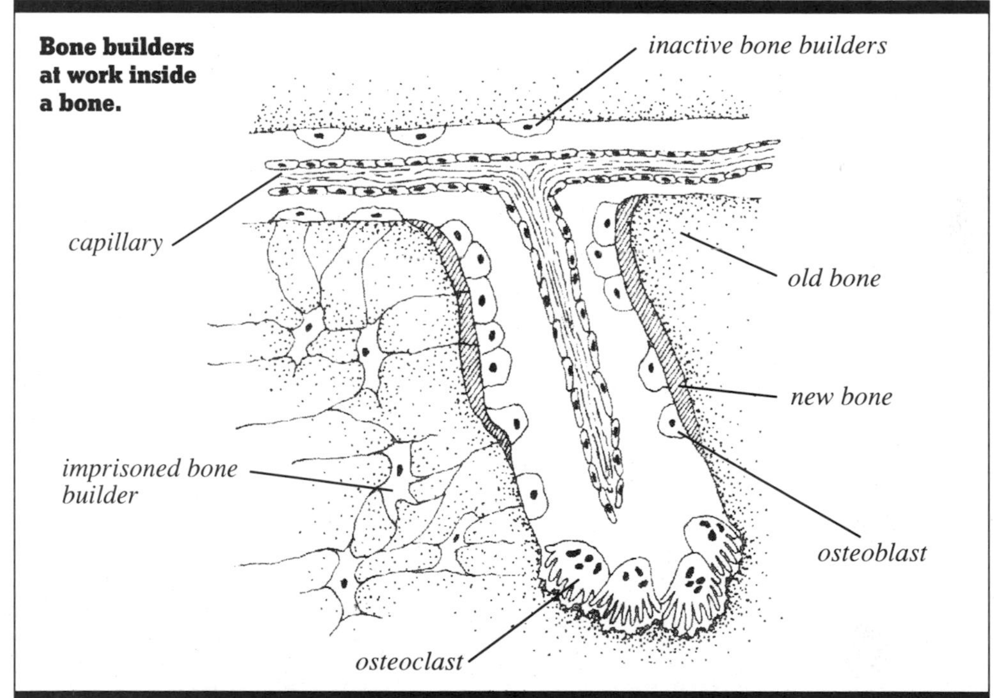

Bone builders at work inside a bone.

ger bone looks like a finger bone whether it is used for the heavy work of playing a guitar or the light work of keyboarding a computer. Through all these resculpturings bones keep the overall shape of the corset within which they were originally built.

The Point of a Plaster Cast

When a person breaks a bone, cartilage makers rebuild the scaffolding across the break. As in all healing, they start the repair at the edges of the injury where there is some record of the original to guide them. They continue to add cartilage into the gap until it is completely filled. Then, as before, osteoclasts and osteoblasts move in to dismantle the soft scaffolding and replace it with hard bone.

If the injury is just a crack, the repair may go well without outside help. But chondroblasts repairing more serious breaks may have to cope with broken ends that don't line up correctly, or with splintered edges. And, if the bone moves, they must fill in a gap that keeps changing as they work.

When doctors "set" a fracture, they are aligning the broken ends. Sometimes they have to operate to remove bone splinters so chondroblasts have neat edges to rejoin. Then they immobilize the bone in a cast so the broken ends stay put during the weeks or months of their repair.

The Better to Bite With

Antlers, tusks, and teeth are bones that, by growing, punch their way right through the skin. Although no teeth will push through the gum for months, a newborn baby's jaws are already equipped with miniature sets of both 20 baby teeth and 32 adult teeth.

Examining a shed baby tooth will give you some idea of tooth structure. The inside is hollow. That's where there were blood vessels and a nerve, and where the cells that made the inside of the tooth lived. Most of the tooth is a material called dentine, which is very much like bone, but you can see that the outside is coated with a shinier, harder layer. This is enamel, the hardest material that cells know how to make. Enamel is thickest at the top surface, where teeth get the most wear. Roots, the portion of the tooth below the gum, have no enamel. But a shed baby tooth, you'll notice, has no roots. It did have, before it loosened. As an adult tooth grows, it releases a chemical that dissolves the roots of the baby tooth it will replace. The baby tooth loosens because it is no longer rooted into a socket in the jawbone.

The kind of teeth a mammal has depends on how the mammal lives. Dogs, for instance, have tusklike fangs that stab through living hide, and overlap to lock the flesh in place. Our fangs—named canine teeth after those in dogs—don't overlap and are too short to puncture with. We bite apples, not rabbits on the run.

The front teeth in both dogs and people are incisors, so-called because they have a cutting edge. Ours are large, flat blades that overlap like scissors. They make sense as cutting tools. But dogs couldn't cut a bite of fruit with theirs. Dog incisors are small and pointy, and, when the jaws are closed, meet exactly. They are for nibbling, as at fleas.

To slice through tough things like hunks of meat or leather, dogs use teeth behind the canines that have sharp, overlapping edges. We don't have those teeth. Instead, we have two kinds of molars. The rear, flat ones grind hard things like bran and pumpkin seeds. You move your jaw sideways to do that. The forward molars are dual-purpose teeth: Their raised edges chomp through meat and their flattened middle surfaces grind. Dogs don't have any grinding teeth. They can't move their jaws sideways, anyhow. They swallow food in chunks, not mush.

What teeth tell about how an animal lives has let scientists make good guesses about how humans used to live. No fossils of even the earliest humans have large canines, so we can't ever have attacked living prey by biting. But none of the fossils have truly huge, flat grinders either, although some ape relatives did. That means we probably never lived entirely on roots and seeds.

Fixing the Break

X-rays of our relatives, the apes, show that many of them break their arms or legs in falls from trees during childhood. The bones are rejoined, but the two pieces don't meet properly. Sometimes the broken ends lie nearly side by side; they are attached together one way or another by new bone in the gap, but the arm or leg may be weak, crooked, and not move right. The purpose of setting a fractured bone is to align the broken ends so that when chondroblasts build a scaffold, they can follow the original lines of the bone. A cast keeps the ends from moving long enough for chondroblasts to complete the cartilage filler, and for bone cells to replace the temporary structure with new bone.

This x-ray shows a fracture of a right arm radius and ulna.

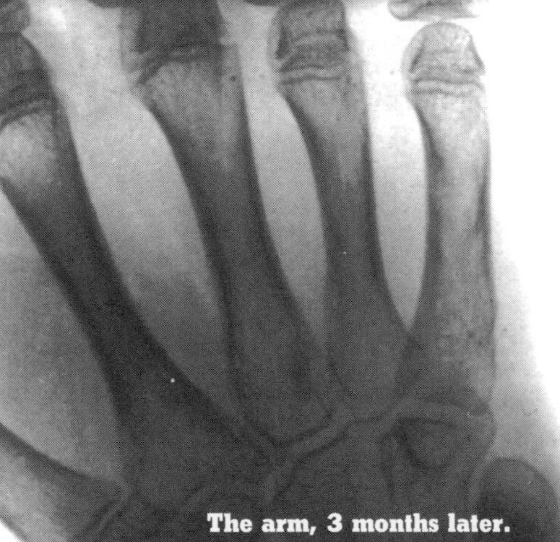

The arm, 3 months later.

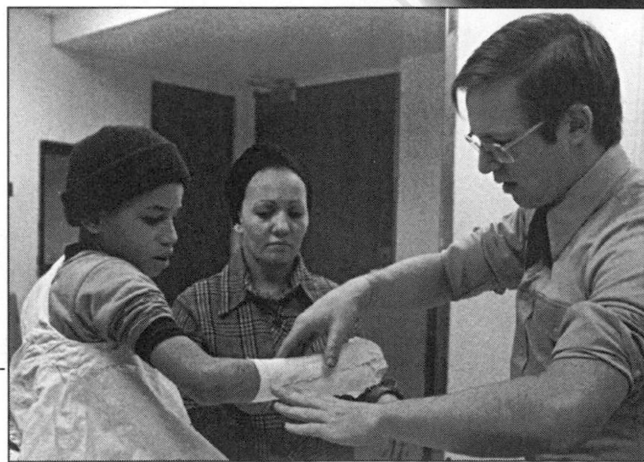

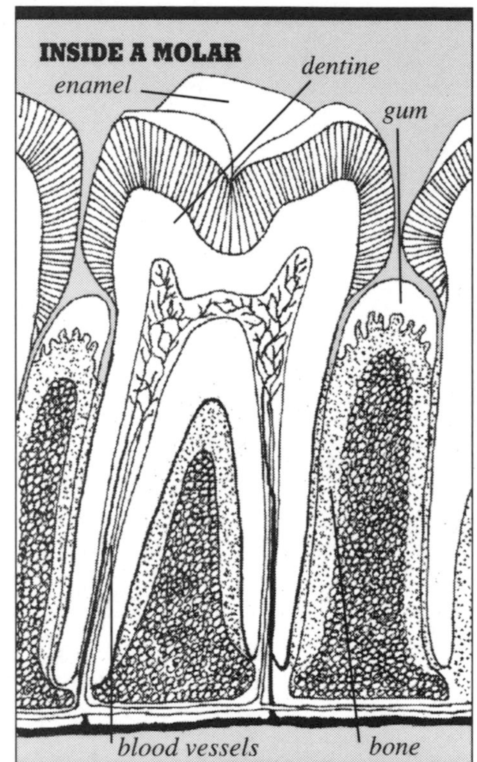

On the other hand, early human molars were larger than those of their ape ancestors. Perhaps we ate fewer juicy forest fruits, more tough cereals of the open plains. But we must also have eaten meat, for fossil humans had the same dual-purpose molars that are useful still in chewing chunks of steak.

Human teeth have been shrinking in size since before Neanderthal days, until we now have the smallest teeth our species has ever had. Jaws have gotten smaller along with the teeth they hold, and so have the face bones to which jaw muscles are attached. Scientists aren't sure what to make of this general shrinkage of our faces, but one thing is sure: If we were now to have to use our teeth to rip raw meat, gnaw wild roots, crunch unhusked grains, and break hard-shelled nuts, we'd starve. Farms and kitchens may not have caused our dinky jaws, but they couldn't have shrunk so far without them.

The Trouble Is Braces

The genes that determine jaw size are different from those that determine tooth size. A child can therefore inherit mismatched sizes. Teeth may be too large to fit the jaw without sticking out or overlapping. Teeth may be too small to fill it up completely without leaving gaps between. Upper and lower jaw may not match either, so when the person bites, the teeth don't meet correctly. Luckily, teeth are movable, jaws are expandable—and braces aren't as ugly as they used to be.

Braces work not because the wires actually pull teeth around, but because they encourange bone builders to move the sockets that hold teeth in the jaw. The orthodontist wires teeth so that they press against their sockets in the right direction. Osteoclasts in the pressed side of the socket destroy bone there, and the tooth moves. As a gap develops to the other side of the socket, osteoblasts fill it in with new bone. The socket is now in a new position, and the tooth has simply gone along for the ride.

The upper jaw can be made to grow itself wider. The device used is an expandable plate molded to fit against the roof of the mouth. The bone there is jointed in the middle. As the joint is stretched, osteoblasts fill in the gap, and the jaw widens. Sometimes orthodontists can avoid using braces by removing a few teeth before they have grown enough to crowd each other crooked. Bone builders tend to space teeth evenly if they have room enough to do so. That tendency, though, can lead to other problems. If a baby tooth is knocked out before its replacement is ready, bone builders may move sockets around to fill the present gap without accounting for the tooth that's still to come. Or, the opposite can happen: a baby tooth's roots don't dissolve, and the adult tooth comes in behind or in front of it. One reason dentists like to see you twice a year is that they can often urge bone builders to mind their places before braces are the only pressure possible.

Of course, the other reason is decay.

Tooth Rot

Tooth decay may prove to be a brief episode in the history of human ills. People got few cavities in the days when honey was a rarity, and cane

Pressure on the Bone Builders

These slim wire braces, held to the teeth by small pieces of transparent plastic, have pressured bone builders into spacing sockets evenly. The cast the girl is holding shows where her teeth were four years before.

sugar was unknown. Today, a mineral called fluoride that is added to water or toothpaste or taken as pills gives enamel makers a new strengthener to harden up tooth coatings, and decay is in decline. Kids have a good chance of growing up without any cavities at all if they have fluoride—and if they brush, and if they take it easy on the sugar.

Sugar is the food of the 10 billion bacteria, of about a hundred species, whose home is in your mouth. They come in three shapes. The commonest are round ones that cling together in clusters like bunches of luscious grapes, or form chains like strings of beads. Other bacteria are shaped like rods, and often live in patches. The most ominous-looking mouth bacteria are spiral ones that move with a screwing motion that unpleasantly resembles a corkscrew twisting through a cork. All these kinds of bacteria live together in the community called plaque—the fuzzy stuff that you're supposed to brush away.

One round kind of bacterium called *Streptococcus mutans* is responsible for holding the community together. It uses sugar you eat to make an adhesive that attaches it to teeth. The thready glue forms a network within which other species that can't themselves hold onto tooth enamel find refuge. They, too, are sugar eaters: None of the plaque residents eat teeth. Cavities are corroded into a tooth by an acid waste product of bacteria's sugar-digestion.

You can see the importance of brushing: Without sticky fuzz, few mouth bacteria can get a foothold; they are continually swallowed to their death in spit. Settled into plaque, though, they can't be swallowed, and they multiply very quickly. Some bacteria can divide as often as every 20 minutes. The population on a tooth you fail to scrub at seven may have doubled their number by the time of your first class. Think of the bacteria doubling every time the bell rings. Think of how many there could be by lunchtime, especially if they have been well fed.

So you can also see the problem with sugary foods. Every cupcake, every Coke, every candy snack feeds the multiplying crowd, and extends the sticky fuzz they're growing on your teeth.

Bacteria, by the way, smell. Their body odors are a person's bad breath.

Germ Ecology

All this sounds disagreeable and dangerous. But in fact the normal human zoo contributes to our safety as well as to our scent.

You were germfree until you were born. You picked up your first bacteria on the way out, got more from every hand that handled you, and have been generously exchanging them with other humans ever since. Besides the billions

Fuzzmakers

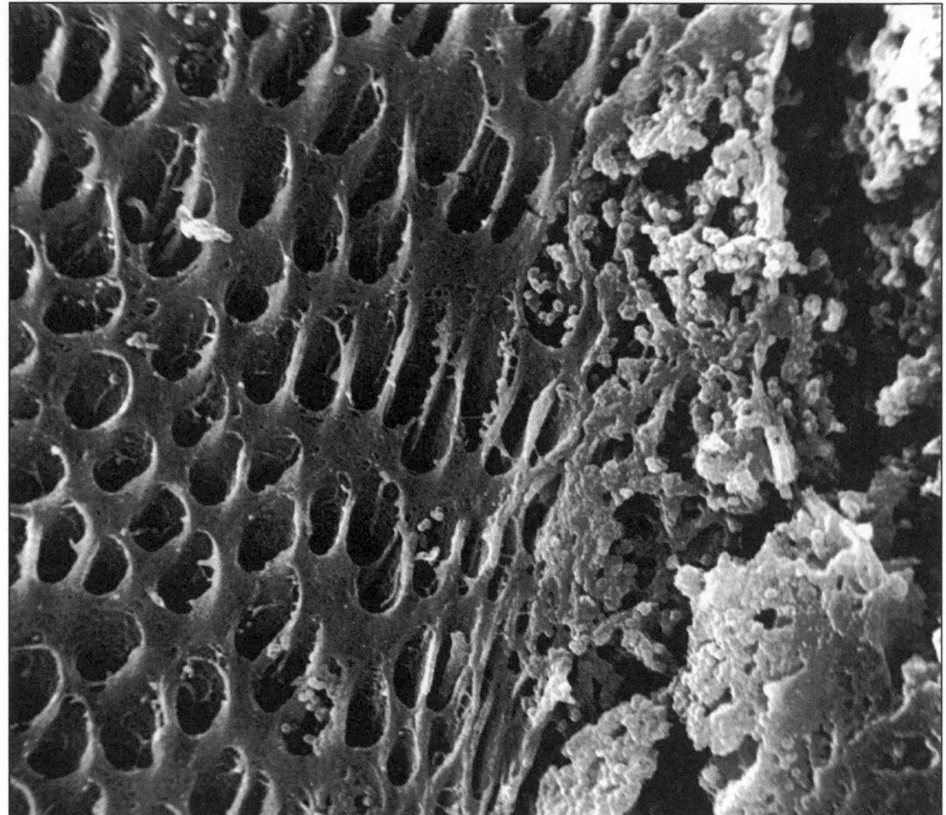

The mouth bacteria shown here at about 2,000 times larger than their actual size were raised in lab dishes among their own kind. In your mouth, they live as mixed communities in a network of plaque made by the fellows on the right, *Streptococcus mutans*. Having your teeth cleaned by a dental hygienist twice a year is important even if you scrub these guys away three times a day because hygienists clean plaque where you can't, below the gums. If you do get a cavity, it will have to be drilled before it's filled. Drilling removes the corroded surface acid has eaten away, leaving a smooth and germless hole that can then be neatly filled.

in your mouth, you harbor about a trillion bacteria—1,000,000,000,000 of them—on your skin. Yet they have seldom caused you any trouble.

These are our accustomed germs, ones we have given to our babies for countless generations, and that are usually well behaved. We suit them well. We provide moist armpits, humid feet, damp crotches, wet mouths that protect them from the drying air. We keep them warm. We have always fed them plenty of sweat and oil, and, before humans knew how to make jam and candy bars, a modest dose of sugar. Our pores ooze substances that are poisonous to dangerous bacteria, but not to our skin inhabitants. By so encouraging them, we help them to cover all available space, eat whatever food there is, multiply on us so successfully that the bad guys, the really dangerous germs, are crowded out and starve to death. Some skin bacteria make antiseptics that kill the bad guys too.

Think of yourself as a habitat in which, as in a forest, there are many ways to earn a living. Each niche—the follicle of an eyelash, the skin of an armpit, or the surface of a tooth—offers for some species the particular conditions of shelter and nutrition it requires. These species divide resources among them, some eating this, some eating that, and each behaving in ways that help or hinder others. In a forest, populations of each species control the populations of other species, so there is a balance among such creatures as birds, beetles, and mice. The balance is upset by unusual events: Kill owls and the forest becomes infected with mice.

A body is the same. Among the mouth's balanced population are fungi—microscopic relatives of mushrooms and the white strands that live in decaying wood. Ordinarily these fungi are rare in this ecology: They are kept down by the thriving crop of bacteria. Antibiotics upset that balance. They kill mouth bacteria, but not fungi. If a person has to take antibiotics for several weeks to cure infection elsewhere, so few bacteria may survive in the mouth that fungi grow like weeds, causing the white scum and open sores of a disease called thrush.

Thank your bacteria if you have never noticed there were fungi living in your mouth. But don't reward the bacteria overmuch, for that, too, upsets the balance. When too much fertilizer gets into a lake, it causes an overgrowth of scummy algae. When too much sugar gets into your mouth, it causes an overgrowth of fuzzy plaque. Looked at that way, you can see the truth of sugar treats: They pollute the environment of your mouth.

Spray 'em Dead

Bacteria that live on moist skin between toes, in armpits, crotches, and in mouths cause various body smells. The smells are different because skin glands make chemically different oils and oozes in each place, and they are eaten by different groups of bacteria whose fragrant waste products differ too. Those between toes are close relatives of bacteria that give to certain French cheeses their pleasantly cheesy reek. Babies and young children enjoy all sorts of body smells, and lovers love each other's. Biologists are pretty sure our natural odors are attractants, not repellents.

So why do we want to disguise our breath with mouthwash and deodorize our bodies? Maybe because, in this crowded world of strangers, body odors are too intimate for comfort.

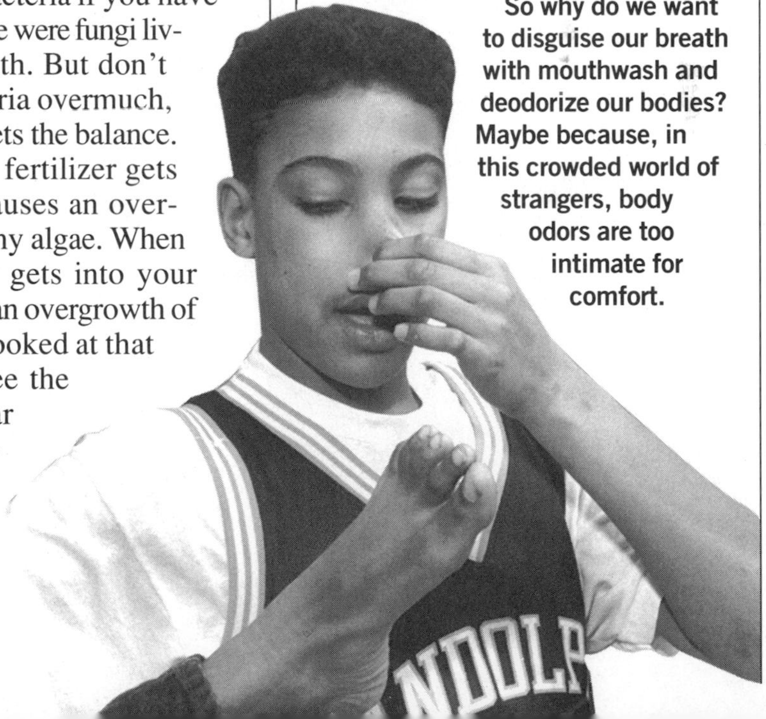

FLESH
& FAT

Skeletons have been compared to the steel framework of a building that holds it up against the pull of gravity, and to walls that protect the plumbing. Bones are strong and bones protect, but if that were all they did we could be held up by stiff rods; we could have shells, not skulls. Bones are to move with: They are pegs to hang muscles on.

Internal skeletons like ours evolved in fish, which don't need them for support. Fish are so perfectly buoyant in water that they are as weightless as an astronaut in orbit or a baby in the womb. Early fish made bones on their outsides as well as in their insides. Their outside bone was armor, not a skeleton. A skeleton is whatever a muscle exerts its force against to make a movement. It was the internal bones that fish invented that opened up to them and their descendants a world of motion unknown to worms or beetles.

Worm Motions

Motion is caused by muscles contracting (shortening). Muscles relax (and so lengthen) as well as contract and shorten, but relaxing has no force at all. Therefore all motion is a result of pulling, not pushing. A worm only appears to push itself forward by stretching its body. What it actually does is pull itself into a narrower shape by contracting muscles that circle its body. This is like a hand squeezing clay: The narrower a worm's body becomes, the longer it grows. To move forward, a worm braces itself against the ground with stiff, backward-facing hairs, and squeezes. That pulls its body narrower and, because it is braced, moves the front end forward. Then it shortens its body by pulling with muscles that run along its length. That lets the tail catch up with the head, and the whole worm is now farther along its way. These two groups of muscles, one running round and round and the other running head to tail, are the only muscles a worm has to move along with.

Worms can also curve and undulate. Curving results from contracting lengthwise muscles on only one side of the body. Undulation results from alternating contractions of lengthwise muscles on both sides of the body. While a group of muscles on one side is contracted, a group on the opposite side is relaxed. The wave of contraction proceeds down the animal from head to tail, giving it a wriggling motion.

Leeches, relatives of earthworms, use both groups of muscles to loop along a surface. They attach a rear sucker to the surface, and contract their circular muscles to reach forward. Then they attach a front sucker to the surface, detach the rear one, and contract lengthwise muscles to pull into a loop. An animal called a hydra uses such simple muscles to move end over end in an improbable somersaulting gait.

Still another kind of motion, called peristalsis, is achieved by contracting circular muscles one after another from head to tail. As the wave of lengthening passes down the body, each portion in turn moves forward. Earthworms burrow through the soil by peristalsis.

People think of squishy creatures like worms as having no skeleton at all, but if that were so, they wouldn't move. Think of a muscle floating in space, contracting and relaxing. It can't move anything because there is nothing for it to exert force against. Muscles have to exert force against something in order to cause motion; whatever that something is, it is called a skeleton.

In the case of worms, muscles exert force against the fluid that fills their bodies: They have what is called a hydrostatic skeleton. The system works because water is not compressible (it can't be squeezed smaller). Whatever the volume of a worm, that volume stays the same when muscles press against it. It grows longer but thinner, or shorter but fatter. Worm motions are shape changes.

Skeletons Outside and Inside

One obvious problem with a hydrostatic skeleton is that it is hard for the

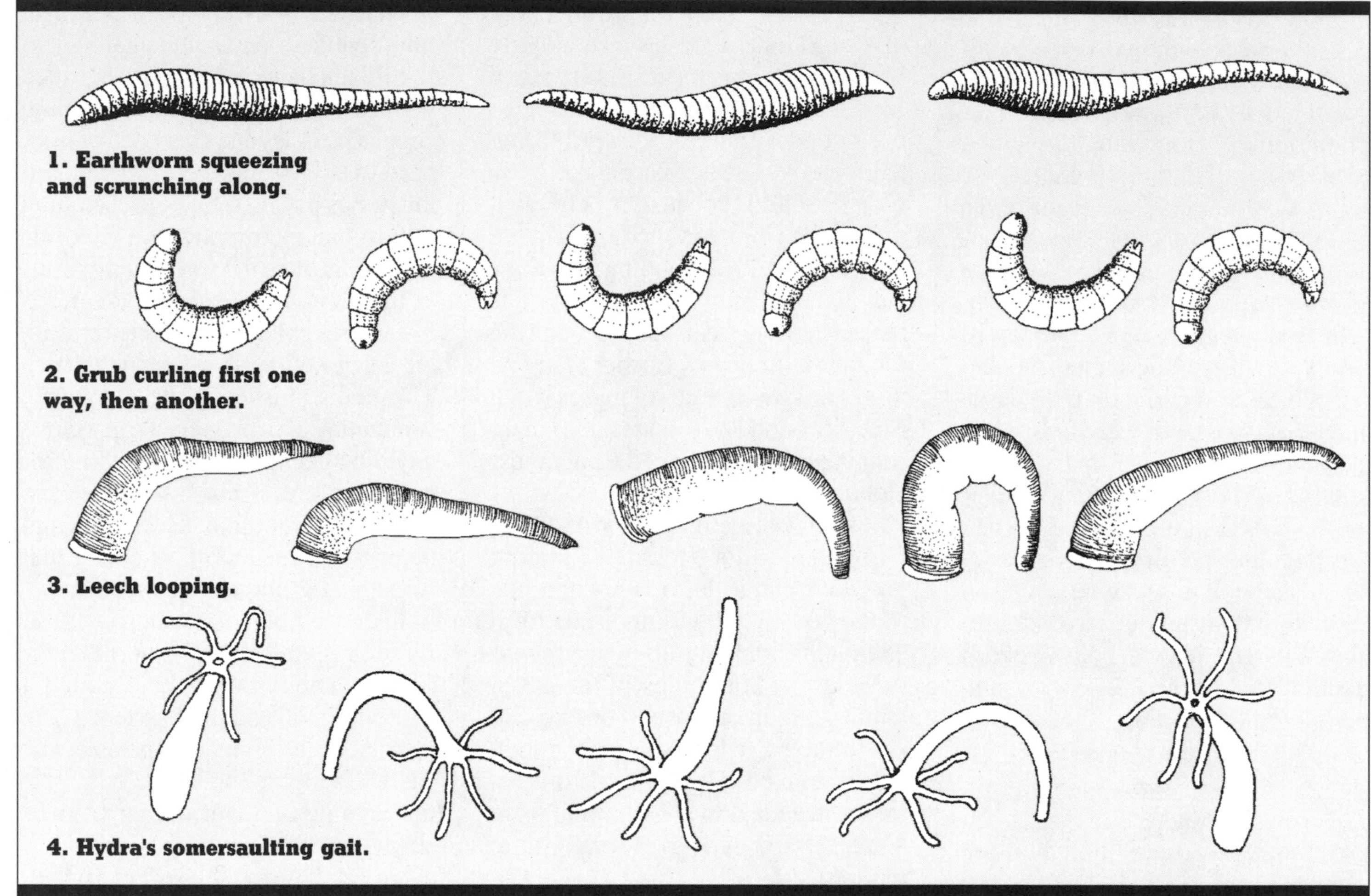
1. Earthworm squeezing and scrunching along.

2. Grub curling first one way, then another.

3. Leech looping.

4. Hydra's somersaulting gait.

animal to move one part of its body without at the same time moving another part. Earthworms have to some extent solved the problem by segmenting their body into separate, fluid-filled chambers, each with its own sets of circular and lengthwise muscle. Every segment can be shortened or lengthened independently of the others, and an earthworm can therefore wave its snout without budging its tail. Still, each segment has to be able to change its shape; worms must be squishable.

Once there are separate segments in a body, another possibility arises: Instead of running lengthwise muscles within segments, they can be run from one segment to another across a joint. This is an altogether different system from an earthworm's. It requires a stiff skin, not a flexible one. Muscles are anchored to the animal's rigid covering, and that's what they pull against. No pressure is exerted against body fluid; the segment neither lengthens nor shortens. Rather, the pull bends adjacent segments toward one another at a joint between them. And the skeleton has changed location completely. In a worm the skeleton was the whole inside of the body; now it is the whole outside.

Outside skeletons, called exoskeletons, are used by such animals as grasshoppers and crabs. Their solid skeletons have tremendous advantages over liquid, hydrostatic ones. For instance, it's hard for a worm to power limbs with muscles anchored in its squishy skin, for the force of the contraction pulls the skin as well as the limb. There are sea worms that paddle, but with little power. The great strength of a grasshopper's leg or a crab's claw comes from anchoring both ends of a muscle to a rigid exoskeleton. The whole force of contraction then goes into bending the one flexible portion of the limb, its accordion-pleated joint.

However, there are also disadvantages to exoskeletons. As much as the sculpturing of an insect's joints allows it to bend its legs, rotate its antennas, bat its wings, and close its jaws, it is a rather stiff affair. A grasshopper can't curl up, scratch its back, chase its tail. It can't even shake its head. Then, too, an exoskeleton doesn't grow. It hardens around an animal like a shell, and however big the animal is then, that's the size its exoskeleton remains. To grow, a crab has to shed its skeleton, expand, and make a new one to fit its larger size.

An endoskeleton—an inner one like ours—is a good compromise. You get the strength that comes from attaching muscles to rigid surfaces, and you get the complicated joint shapes that allow a variety of movements, and you get the suppleness of a squishably soft, stretchable covering that allows even the wormish curl of snuggling into bed or the amazing undulations of a belly dancer. And you never have to change your bones—at least not all at once.

Spurts and Spasms

Ring-shaped worm muscles are what allow you to close your exit holes—your anus and your urine tube. In a male, ring muscles in the penis are also responsible for pumping out spurts of semen, the fluid in which sperm swim. First, tubes where semen is stored contract, pushing the fluid into the penis. Then ring muscles at the base of the penis contract several times, pumping the semen out in spurts. At the same time, limb and trunk muscles also tense, and then relax. The whole spasm is called orgasm. A female's orgasm is just the same except that girls don't spurt.

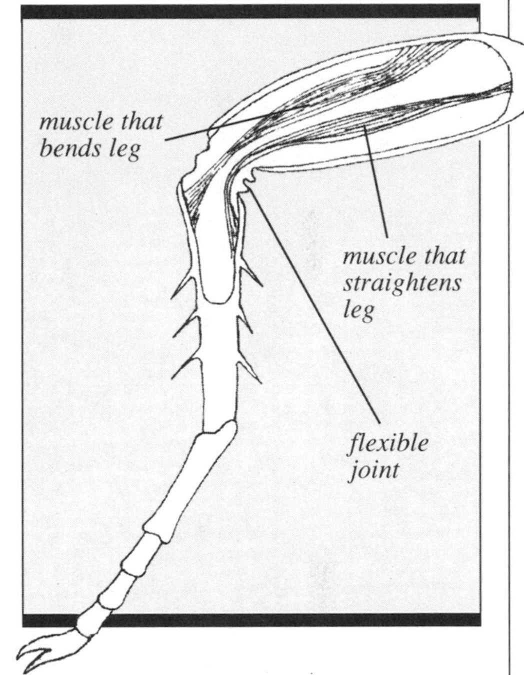

Bend, Rock, Twist, and Turn

Fish never took full advantage of their invention—streamlining requires a certain simplicity of design—but every sort of joint is possible. An elbow is a hinge joint similar to the joints in a crab's leg: It bends in only one direction. But the more complicated wrist

Bones, Bones, Bones

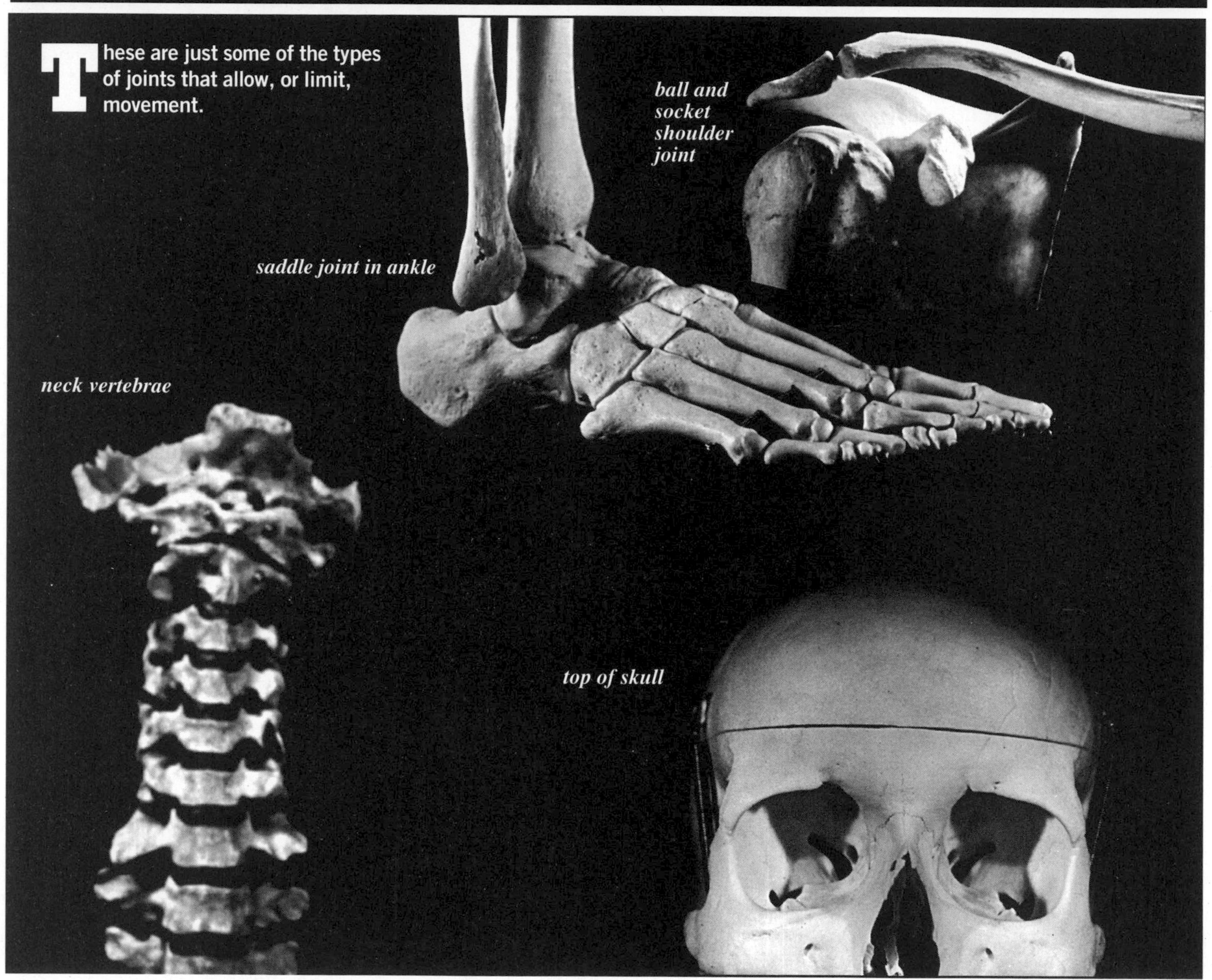

joint allows a sideways swing as well. Crabs have nothing like that. The joint between a finger and the palm of the hand is an interesting one. It lets the finger waggle in a circle, but it doesn't allow any rotation at all. The saddle joint in your ankle lets you rock back and forth on your feet, and also turn your feet outward like a duck or inward like a pigeon. Ball and socket joints in the hip and shoulder let you both twist and circle your arms and legs. The one in the shoulder is particularly flexible. You can wave your arm in a full circle. You can't circle your head; the pivot joint at the base of the skull allows rotation only. That's the one you use to shake your head "No." To nod "Yes," you use the neck joint below it.

You also have joints that prevent any movement at all. Skull bones are designed not to move: They are fused together along interlocking zig-zag joints. Your face is made of many bones fused together, and so is your lower jaw. Parts of your wrists and ankles are also fused bones. A baby is born with 350 separate bones, 144 of which fuse together to give the usual adult number of 206. That number isn't accurate for everyone. Some people have an extra vertebra or an extra rib.

In spite of all these bones, your innards are boneless. And yet they move: Throats swallow, stomachs churn, guts push meals down and out. What is the skeleton of the heart?

All these soft parts have hydrostatic skeletons. Heart muscles pump against the hydrostatic skeleton of blood. Stomach muscles work against the hydrostatic skeleton of a meal. The whole movement of mush from mouth to anus through the intestine is done by peristalsis, like a worm. If an intestine had a way of holding onto a surface it, too, would burrow. You have an exoskeleton, too. Each muscle that raises hair in horror uses the hairshaft as an exoskeleton to exert its force against.

All Strung Up

A crab skeleton stands up by itself; ours clatters to the floor. Our loose bones

Slow Fusion

Some people dislike eating fish because they have so many tiny bones, and so many of them seem just stuck into the flesh instead of being firmly jointed to each other as in our own, more simple skeleton. Since fish are buoyant in the water, their skeleton need not be designed for structural strength. Land animals need fewer but larger bones, firmly jointed to one another. Yet because we are descended from fish, we, too, start out with many bones.

Bones begin to form within the embryo at many scattered sites, for instance as numerous small plates of bone within the skull, jaws, and face. These bone centers then grow toward one another, and fuse to form the jaws, cheek bones, eye sockets, and the case of the skull. However, if fusion were completed before birth, a baby could not be born. We are such big-headed creatures that we must be born somewhat prematurely, before our skull becomes too large and rigid to squeeze through our mother's hip bones, and when we are still, compared to other mammal relatives at birth, more like a fetus than a baby. A newborn chimpanzee can cling to its mother while she takes a stroll, while a newborn human can't even lift its head.

Even born so early in development, a baby's skull plates are squeezed together during birth so that they actually overlap, a sight that worries many first-time parents as they see their child emerge looking like an alien from Mars. Fusion of the skull bones proceeds only very slowly after birth, too. A human brain triples in size over the first few years of childhood, and skull plates must leave it room to grow before encasing the brain entirely in bone.

are held together by nothing but connective tissue: Ligaments connect bone to bone; tendons connect muscle to bone. We are strung together like marionettes.

Ligaments are like the tapes that hold a marionette's hand to its arm. They allow movement, but don't cause it. They also prevent excessive movement. All the separate vertebrae of the backbone are strapped by ligaments that let the back bend in every direction, but only so far and no farther. Ligaments are therefore necessarily more strong than stretchy. When a baby prepares for birth by loosening its mother's hip joints, it does so by making the ligaments more elastic. This is good for the baby, but uncomfortable for the mother: Her gait may become waddling—even wobbly—when she is loosened so.

Holding muscles onto bones is more complicated than strapping one bone to another. Bones are hard objects, whereas muscles are soft meat that tears and crushes. Meat is cells, or rather groups of them that have fused into long, thin cylinders. Biologists prefer to call such groups "fibers," although that's confusing. A muscle fiber is larger than fibers like collagen and, what's more, is alive. A single

Wow!

Skeletons have no trouble bending into these extreme positions. What prevents most people from doing such acrobatics is not their bones and joints, but their tight ligaments. If you stretch gently for a while each day, bending a little further than is comfortable, fibroblasts will lengthen your ligaments for you so you can bend more.

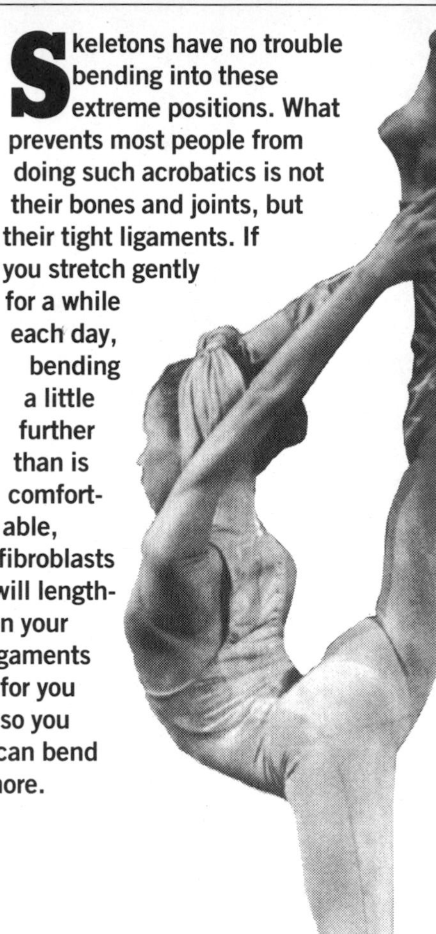

These young contortionists perform with the Cirque du Soleil.

muscle fiber is too thin to see with the naked eye, but you can see bundles of them as the "grain" in meat. A shred of meat stuck between your teeth is a single bundle of muscle fibers. The covering that holds the bundle together is part of that muscle's tendon.

The whole tendon is a continuous web of connective tissue that binds a muscle's separate fibers into bundles, wraps the bundles in a sheath, and attaches the sheath to the skeleton. You can see the sheathing clearly around each of the muscles in a raw, skinned chicken leg. At either end of a muscle the sheath forms a thick rope or broad fan that connects that muscle to a bone. An easy connection to feel in your own body is the Achilles tendon, the thick, tough, rope that fastens your calf muscle to your heel bone. You can feel another on the inside of your elbow, where one fastens your big biceps muscle to your forearm, and other tendons on the underside of your knee joint, where several thigh muscles attach to your lower leg.

A joint bends because muscles are attached from one bone to another across the hinge. To close your elbow hinge, you contract the big biceps muscle on the upper surface of your upper arm. To open your elbow again, you contract the triceps muscle on the lower surface of your upper arm. Both of these muscles are connected by tendons to your shoulder, as well as to one of the two forearm bones below the elbow.

When you contract your biceps to bend your arm, the triceps muscle doesn't relax completely. Instead, it slightly pulls against the biceps' pull to fine-tune the movement.

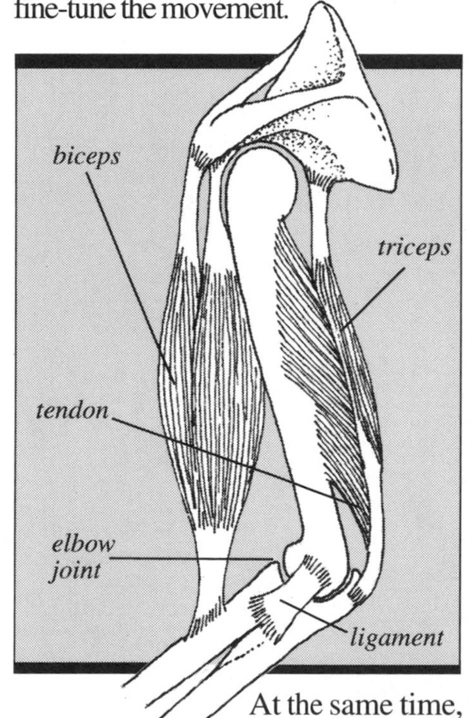

At the same time, muscles attached to upper arm and shoulder blade across the shoulder joint tense too. That stabilizes the limb: Nothing moves but the forearm. There's not a move you can make that doesn't involve coordinated contractions of whole groups of different muscles.

Where muscles span boneless places, they pull against one another. That's how you tighten your belly or curl your tongue. In such places the attachments that muscles pull against are the sheets of tendon you know as gristle. The gristle that lets tongue muscles pull against one another gives cow tongue its rubbery texture.

Cocoons, in Case...

Fibroblasts—the spinners that make your dermis—shaped your muscles just as they shaped the bones to which muscles are attached. More than that, fibroblasts guided muscle cells to their proper places. Muscle cells originated in wedges on both sides of your spine when you were an embryo. Then, following fiber trails laid down by fibroblasts, the muscle cells migrated outward as your limb buds grew. Once at the proper spot, fibroblasts guided the direction in which the muscle cells were to lie, and bundled and sheathed them into shapely calves and bulging biceps. But each group of muscle cells that is now a muscle fiber spun its own cocoon around itself. Each of your muscle fibers still lives inside its original cocoon. Although the individual cells of each muscle fiber are now fused together—there are no membranes separating them—they are made up of the original cells that traveled from your spine.

Most of your muscle fibers will live as long as you do. They haven't much choice because, once fused, they can't divide. But what if an accident should happen and a fiber is crushed or cut to death?

Snugged just inside of each cocoon is one (or a few) embryonic muscle cell that remained aloof from the fusing crowd. This tiny cell has a better chance of escaping injury than the large fiber it inhabits. When the fiber dies, the surviving cell divides again and again until its fusing daughters refill the cocoon. The new fiber is a perfect replica of the one that it replaces, right down to the one daughter that waits separate from the rest, just in case.

A cocoon serves as a memory not only for a muscle fiber, but for the nerve cell that makes it contract on a signal from the brain. When an injury disconnects the nerve, its severed end regrows toward a spot marked for it on the cocoon, and it reconnects precisely.

Dark and White

A chicken has white wing meat and dark leg meat, but a rabbit's leg meat is white, and beef is dark all over. In case you've ever wondered about your own meat, you're like a chicken: Your leg muscles are dark; your arm muscles are white.

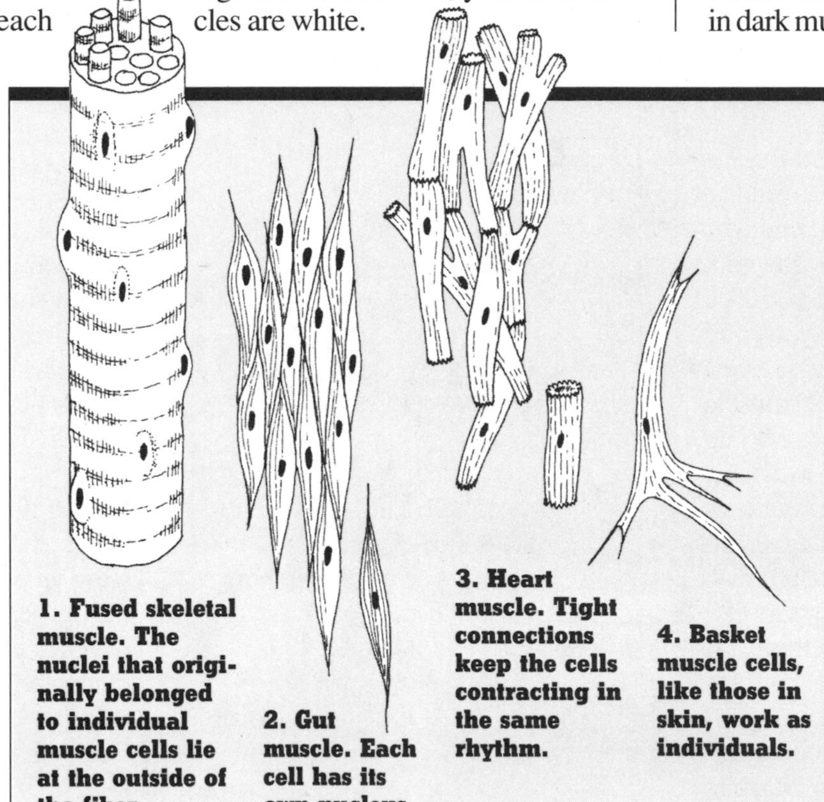

1. Fused skeletal muscle. The nuclei that originally belonged to individual muscle cells lie at the outside of the fiber.

2. Gut muscle. Each cell has its own nucleus.

3. Heart muscle. Tight connections keep the cells contracting in the same rhythm.

4. Basket muscle cells, like those in skin, work as individuals.

These differences have to do with what demands are placed on limbs. Dark muscle is specialized for endurance, for trotting with the herd or hiking through the woods. Its color comes from a rich blood supply—dark meat is red before it's cooked—that brings it large supplies of oxygen. Dark muscle uses fat for energy. That's why doctors concerned about too much fat advise against "red meat," the dark muscle of all long-distance trotters. Fat in dark muscle is conveniently located within it, among the fiber bundles, through and through, even when it lies in streaks too small to see.

Endurance in dark muscle is at the expense of speed. Your legs can carry you all day, but they can't move with the flash of a magician's hand. White muscle specializes in very fast contractions: flurries of beating chicken wings, spasms of leaping rabbit legs, outbreaks of wildly clapping hands. But white muscle tires quickly. It is white because it is less well supplied with blood. Such meat is lean because these muscles use for energy sugar delivered by the blood, not local fat. Sugar is stored in only small amounts in the muscle fibers, and when that is exhausted, so is the muscle. Arms subjected to thunderous applause soon fall limply to the lap, while feet stamp on.

Skeletal muscle, the dark or light muscle that moves our bony skeleton, is quite different from the kind of muscle that squeezes sweat or swallows food. Internal muscle fibers aren't fused communities: Each is a separate muscle cell. These cells aren't bundled up by fibroblasts either. They interlace into baskets like the ones that encircle sweat glands, or into the squeezing tubes of guts.

Nerve connections in internal muscles are different too. You can tell your finger to bend; you can't tell your stomach to churn. Each skeletal muscle fiber has a single nerve connection that is its electrical switch. When the nerve fires the fiber contracts; when the nerve stops firing the fiber relaxes. Muscles that move internal organs have connections with two kinds of nerve, one that excites them to contraction and another that dampens their spasms. The two together work in the gut like a volume knob, modulating movement from easy squeezes to nasty cramps. Many of these muscle cells make electrical connections with one another: If one contracts, so do its interlaced neighbors. The gut can perform its wormlike peristalsis without any nervous commands at all.

Limbs rest, guts relax, but hearts beat on and on. Muscles that contract the heart are separate cells tightly connected to one another in a 3-D mesh. The heart has nerve connections from the brain, whose signals speed or slow its beat. But the brain doesn't set the heart's basic rate. Hearts beat according to their own, built-in rhythm, even when removed from the body. The steady *lub-dup, lub-dup, lub-dup* is set by a small area of muscle that, each time it contracts, emits an electrical signal. The signal spreads through the meshwork of interconnected cells setting off the wave of contraction that, as blood pounds first through the heart's upper, then its lower chambers, is the *lub*, then *dup* you hear.

Make a Motion

Just now, when you turned a page, you made the movement by contracting muscles. But think about that: If your biceps contracts, then so must the muscle fibers of which it is made, and if muscle fibers shorten, something inside them must make the motion.

Although a muscle fiber in your biceps may be no wider than 10 microns (10 millionths of a meter), it may be 10 centimeters long. The whole length is filled with thick and thin rods arranged in such a way that the thin ones form tubes around the thick ones. They shorten the muscle by telescoping, something like the way in which the segments of a television antenna shorten it by sliding into one another.

Each telescoping unit in a muscle is a rod that slides into two tubes, one at either end. Now, while your biceps is at rest, the two tubes of each unit stick out beyond the rod, leaving a gap in the middle. When you turn the page, the tubes will slide toward one another over the gap, and the telescoping unit will

Heart Stats

An adult heart pumps 1½ gallons of blood per minute, for a total of more than 56 million gallons in an average lifespan. To fuel all this pumping, the heart routes about 5 percent of the total blood supply into arteries that feed its own muscles; that's about a hundred gallons of blood a day. Want to know the number of heartbeats in a lifetime? The resting rate for a man is 72 beats a minute, for a woman 75. Walking raises the rate to at least 94, but hard exercise can raise it to 200. Athletes' hearts grow so large that their resting rate can get as low as 35 beats a minute, and still pump out enough blood. Fear and anger raise heart rates by as much as 50 more beats per minute; sleep lowers the rate by 20 beats or so. Before birth, a fetus's heart rate is as high as 150, after birth it subsides to somewhere between 60 and 100. So, if a person lives to be 75 years old, and there are 525,600 minutes in a year, his or her heart will have beaten a total of...you figure it out! *(Hint: A conservative estimate is over 2 billion beats in a lifetime.)*

shorten. These individual units are tiny: The tubes, for instance, are only 50 millimicrons (50 billionths of a meter) wide. The power of a muscle comes from the combined effort of countless telescoping units assembled lengthwise from one end of the muscle fiber to the other, and stuffing it completely.

But what pulls the tubes over the gap? The thick rod is the puller. It is made up of several hundred molecules that look something like two-headed golf clubs. When assembling into a rod, the molecules at one end point their heads in one direction; the ones at the other end point their heads in the opposite direction. Their shafts form the middle of the finished rod, where there is a gap between the tubes. The head ends of the rod lie within the tubes. Each head can assume two positions: upright, touching the tube and holding onto it, and flexed, bent toward the gap. As you begin to tighten a muscle, the heads move from the upright to the flexed position, pulling the tube a little over the gap. Then they momentarily let go, reattach further down the tube, and pull again. They repeat this stroke five times a second, telescoping their unit completely in the blink of an eye. At your command, all the rod-heads in all of the telescoping machines begin to stroke: The biceps shortens, the page is turned.

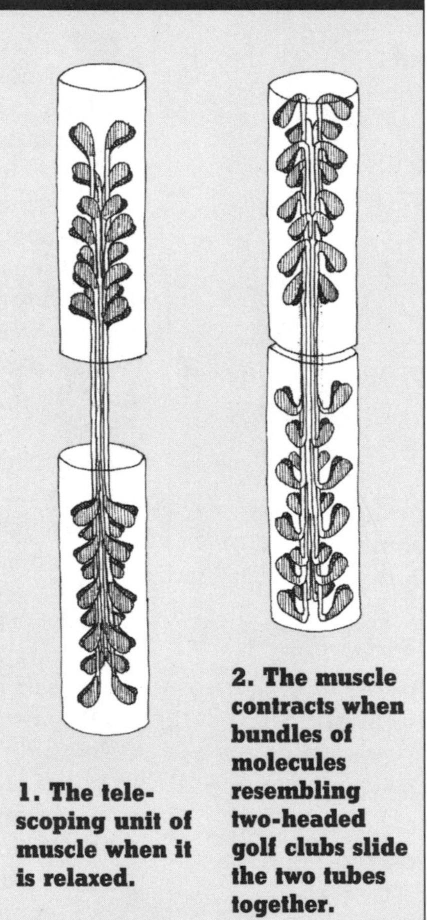

1. The telescoping unit of muscle when it is relaxed.

2. The muscle contracts when bundles of molecules resembling two-headed golf clubs slide the two tubes together.

Muscle Building

Your muscles now are enormously larger than they were when you were born, yet you have no more muscle fibers now than then. Muscle fibers grow by adding to their length and bulk, not to their number. The size of a muscle really depends on how much machinery is stuffed inside it.

As your bones grow longer, your muscle fibers keep up by adding more units to the length of their telescoping strands. At the same time, they thicken by packing in more strands.

Thickness, not length, is what makes you strong. Bone thickens where it is loaded, skin thickens where it is worn, and muscle thickens where it is made to work. Muscle fibers in a newborn baby's neck are too thin to hold its head up because, in the underwater environment of the womb, the head floated. The fibers thicken—and strengthen—quickly once the baby's heavy

Minimotions

The same kinds of molecules that telescope muscle fibers to shorten them are responsible also for other kinds of cell motion. The motions differ according to the ways the thick and thin rods are arranged. They can be arranged as a sort of conveyor belt to move pigment granules into a melanocyte's long tentacles. Phagocytes use the same molecules to ooze along a surface, gathering garbage, and to pull in their prey. Every sort of cell arranges these molecules into a tightening belt to pinch themselves in two during division.

head has to be held up against the pull of gravity. Just as bone bumps and skin calluses thin again when those areas are no longer stressed, muscles thin from lack of work. Astronauts exercise extra hard to keep their muscles (and their bones) from thinning in the weightlessness of space. Wearing a cast on a limb leaves bones skinny, and muscles weak.

Ordinary play, work, and two-footed transportation are probably enough strain to keep muscles strong enough for most things. But in these couch-potato days of TV instead of tag, and wheels instead of legs—not to mention meals that you don't have to cook, much less to hunt or grow—people tend to be less strong than they once were. So we have entered the Age of Exercise when, to counteract the lazy life our inventions have made possible, we have to work out, lift weights, jog miles in order to be as muscular as our great-grandparents were.

There is a limit to how thick muscles will grow regardless of the strain that's placed on them. Girls are born with fewer muscle fibers than boys have, so even thickened to their limit, girls' muscles don't grow as big. And the growth limit of their muscles is less than that in boys. Muscle fibers produce extra amounts of machinery in response to the androgen hormones, the most powerful of which is testosterone. In adolescence, when males'

Working Out

Working out is not like working. Almost any kind of labor you can think of—lifting and hauling, hammering and sawing, hoeing and raking, hiking and climbing—uses some muscles more than others. The muscles used the most bulge; the others don't. In working out, each piece of equipment is designed to stress a certain group of muscles, such as those on the back that would ordinarily be stressed only on the rare occasion of ripping a telephone book in half. The result of using *all* the equipment is that *all* muscles eventually stand out, even the usually itsy bitsy ones between ribs whose work would otherwise be no harder than breathing. A peculiarity of bodybuilders is their small, smooth faces compared to their bulging bodies. There's no equipment for exercising the hundred muscles of the face.

muscles get a hefty dose of testosterone, they thicken dramatically. The instruction delivered to muscle fibers by testosterone is, what's more, indelible. It switches on genes that for the rest of the boy's life raise the rate of rod and tube production, even if he is a couch potato.

The steroid drugs that cheating athletes illegally take to grow their muscles stronger are synthetic forms of testosterone. Such unnaturally high doses do other things besides enlarging muscles. They work in the brain, making the person anything from psyched up to fighting mad. The hormones deepen voices, coarsen skin, grow body hair, and turn on the genes that eventually cause baldness. A female athlete taking steroids is masculinized—hairy-chested, small-breasted, with a future that, if she continues to take them, very probably includes a balding head and no babies.

Some male athletes seem to think that because testosterone is natural to them, they can't be injured by it. No such luck. When their own glands discover that the body is already awash in testosterone, the testes stop making it themselves. Loss of his own hormone can make a man unable to make sperm. Testosterone is also a signal—in both sexes—for cartilage-makers to finish up their work. The bones of young athletes, male or female, taking steroids before they have reached adult size stop growing, ossify, and stunt their height forever.

Wrinkling Up

The only workout for the face is expression. This woman's facial muscles and crinkly creases show that she has been a longtime smiler.

Have a Happy Face

Kids used to be told not to make ugly faces for fear they might freeze in that position. That's not true, but there is a relationship between what people look like and what they are like.

More than a hundred facial muscles are involved in "making faces." Those muscles that are used most often grow larger, and those that are used less often shrink. If you are a person who always smiles, the muscles that pull the lips outward and upward become more pronounced; if you are a person who always frowns, the muscles that pull the corners of the mouth downward become bigger. Even an expectation that circumstances will often call for a particular facial expression keeps the appropriate facial muscles tensed for action, thereby expanding their bulk. Over the years, sheer readiness to lift an eyebrow in contempt, widen the eyes with delight, scrunch the forehead with worry, or purse the lips in disapproval subtly alters the way you look as you age.

Over several decades, muscle size sculptures the contours of the face. A smiler will by middle age have noticeably plumper cheeks than a frowner, whose cheeks gradually slacken. Even bone is affected. It thickens where it is most stressed by the pull of muscles, so a smiler will develop larger cheekbones, and an altogether broader, fuller face.

And the skin changes. Face skin is attached to face muscles, so it creases when you make a face. Crinkles fork the eyes with a smile, wrinkles crease the forehead with a frown. As skin becomes less elastic with age, the temporary creases of facial expression become permanent lines. So the old warning is really true in a sense: Your attitude toward life freezes in your face.

Cushions and Quilts

Pinch your cheek—gently, of course. You are holding between your fingers not only the thin covering of squames, the thick dermis below it, and the cheek muscles below that, but also a plump pad of fat. Fat is white lumps of beef suet, yellow gobs of chicken fat, solid hunks of salt pork. When you heat these lumps and chunks the clear liquid that forms in the pan is the real stuff, the fat itself; the crispy crust remaining is burst fat cells and the fibers that in the living animal weave them into quilts and cushions. Most fat in other animals is deep inside them, packed around beef kidneys, layered between pig belly muscles, lumped inside the tail end of roasting chickens. A lot of human fat is close to the surface, plumped between the muscles and the dermis.

Fat cells look just like they ought to—fat. They are perfectly rotund individuals plumped up sometimes to quite enormous size by a single glob of fat that is liquid at body temperature. They are so round they would roll if they were not held in place by strands of collagen. It is fat tissue's webbing that crackles as raw suet is pulled apart to feed the birds, and that crunches when you eat bacon fried to a crisp.

The weave of the webbing where fat meets muscle determines how tightly or loosely hide is held to the body. The sole of your foot is held tightly by dense webbing; the skin of your throat is looser because its fat is not attached by as many strands. The weave among fat cells determines how firm the fat itself feels. Cheeks are firm, but buttocks may jiggle.

No one these days admits to being fond of fat, but sitting on skinny buttocks is no fun. Animals that don't sit on their bottoms are bony there. If you had to walk on feet unprotected by fat pads you would bruise in minutes. Toddlers certainly enjoy sitting on well-padded laps: Fat is much more comfy than taut muscles and rocky bones.

Fat also keeps you warm. Not as warm as a walrus, whose unusually heavy insulation may be eight inches thick, but warm enough. If your ancestors are from beyond the Arctic Circle, you are likely to have a good layer of fat all over; and if you don't have good padding, you're likely to suffer from the cold in Alaska. Like skin color, fat thickness evolved in response to climate, and can be inherited. The thicker the layer of fat between dermis and muscle, the better the insulation, and the less heat you lose on a cold day. The thinner the layer, the poorer the insulation, but the less you are likely to suffer in summer.

Fat is what makes skin smooth to touch and nice to look at. If you have ever felt the uncushioned flesh of a starving dog, you know the awful feel of sharp spine, jutting ribs, the stringy muscles of the limbs. Even the remarkable detail in which bodybuilders display their muscular development is best viewed through a smoothing quilt of fat lest they look like lab lessons in anatomy. We don't really want to see our skeletons. However interesting joints may be, we want babies to have dimpled knees, not knobby ones. We love a child's fat cheeks, not the bare sculpture of the skull. Without fat, a woman's breasts are just small lumps of gland.

The sexes are not born equal in fat. Girls are born with more fat cells than boys. An adult woman's weight is 28 percent fat, while a man's is 18 percent. Why should that be?

Fat is the body's major way of storing food. The body manufactures fat from carbohydrates—sugar and starch—as well as from plant oils, other animals' fat, and even parts of proteins. Fat can be used "as is" by guts and muscles, but it can also be converted back into sugar to fuel the sugar-hungry brain, which can't use fat for fuel. Fat is what you live on between meals and overnight. A good store of fat sees people through times when there is too little food, or for short periods when there is none at all. Even with three good meals a day, half of what you eat is shuffled in and out of fat cells as gluts are followed by shortages of fuel.

So think of a baby: Its mother's fat is insurance that, come feast or famine, she has stored enough food to feed herself and feed baby too. Females are born with that insurance, just as they are born with the eggs that make insurance necessary. When a dancer or a runner loses so much weight that her percentage of body fat approaches that of a man, her eggs refuse to ripen until she puts more fat into her insurance fund.

While men tend to accumulate belly fat, women tend to fatten hips and thighs, as well as breasts. It's always been that way: The very first sculptures of the female body, which date from the Stone Age, are shaped like an hourglass, big in the bust and big in the hips. The female figure may originally have served as an advertisement, not of sexiness so much as of the ability to bear babies. Large hips suggest a spaciousness between the bones through which a baby's born. Large breasts suggest a copious supply of milk. Like most advertisements, though, these are exaggerated. The amount of fat that rounds a woman's hips says nothing about how much space there is between her hip bones for a baby to be born through, nor does the amount of fat padding her breasts say anything about how much milk her mammary glands can make. Still, such a shape might well have fooled a cave man.

As for men with bellies, where else could the storehouse go? Pillowed arms and legs get in the way of movement, and to resemble the opposite sex is certainly confusing. Fat, love it or loathe it, has to be kept somewhere.

To Diet, or Not to Diet

Much advice on dieting claims that losing weight is a matter of simple arithmetic: You have to eat less food than your body uses up. When the body isn't fed enough to meet its energy needs, it raids its fat stores, and so slims down.

But here's the first complication in this simple formula: Some skinny people get rid of excess food without moving a muscle; they burn it up and emit extra heat instead of storing the excess as fat. Some fat people do just the opposite: They waste little as heat, store much as fat. Those two kinds of people can eat the same dinner, yet while one radiates the apple pie away, the other stashes it in fat.

Another complication is that people who have been fat during childhood may have twice, or four times, the normal number of fat cells. Even if each cell stores no more than the usual drop of fat, their padding is pretty plump. How can a person tell fat cells to stop doing what they're supposed to do? In fact, fat cells deprived of food to fill their stores behave as though they're starving. The brain, getting word of their distress, jacks up the appetite, fills thoughts with food images and cravings, and—worse yet—increases the rate at which fat cells grab at every scrap to stuff

Death by Dieting

Among the strangest diseases is one that most often strikes young women. It is called anorexia nervosa, which roughly means "lack of appetite for psychological reasons": A person with anorexia looks in the mirror, and sees the fat lady, no matter that to others she is slim. So she won't eat, or makes herself vomit if she does. She loses fat; she loses all the fat she has. Then her body begins to use its own proteins as fuel, beginning with skeletal muscles. She still looks fat to herself, but to others she looks like bare bones. It doesn't end there. A body that has used up its outer muscles begins to use up its inner ones, right to its central pump, the heart. Unless treated, anorexia is a fatal disease.

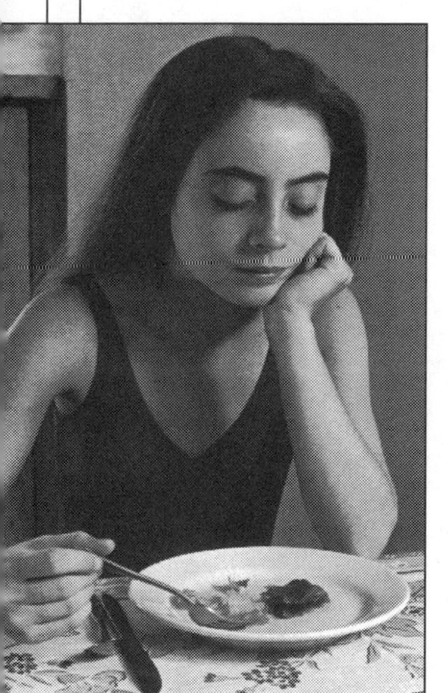

Yet it is not a disease caused by germs or poisons; it arises in the person's own mind, where appetite is controlled. Why would a person starve herself to death over worries about her figure? Most likely—but not consciously—because the additional padding girls get as they grow to be women signals maturity, and these girls are terrified of that. Maybe even ordinary dieting arises from this meaning: In our society, to be girlish is to be thin. The cure for anorexia is a lot of help to bear the scariness of growing into womanhood.

themselves up fuller. The body chemistry of a fat person on a crash diet is very like the chemistry of starvation.

Worst of all, the body seems to learn a permanent lesson by dieting. It assumes that one starving time will be followed by another, regardless of the months of plenty in between. With each crash diet, a person's body learns to more efficiently store food as fat.

The mechanism probably evolved as a safeguard against recurrent famines long ago. Maybe it was responsible for your own descent from ancestors whose numerous and greedy fat cells saved their starving owners' lives. Here and now, however, excellence in fat storage doesn't do anyone any good. So what does one do about it?

Rule number one is to use up more of the food you eat—and more of the fat you've stored—through exercise. Exercise doesn't alarm fat cells. Rule number two is to deprive fat cells of the best food with which to make fat: fat itself. Rule number three is to not let your fat cells think you're starving. That means no crash diets of any sort, ever. The last rule is to eat a little less. Every day, always, all the rest of your life. There is no other way to control cells that, obeying the instructions of genes inherited from ancient times, will never learn not to make the most of any food they get.

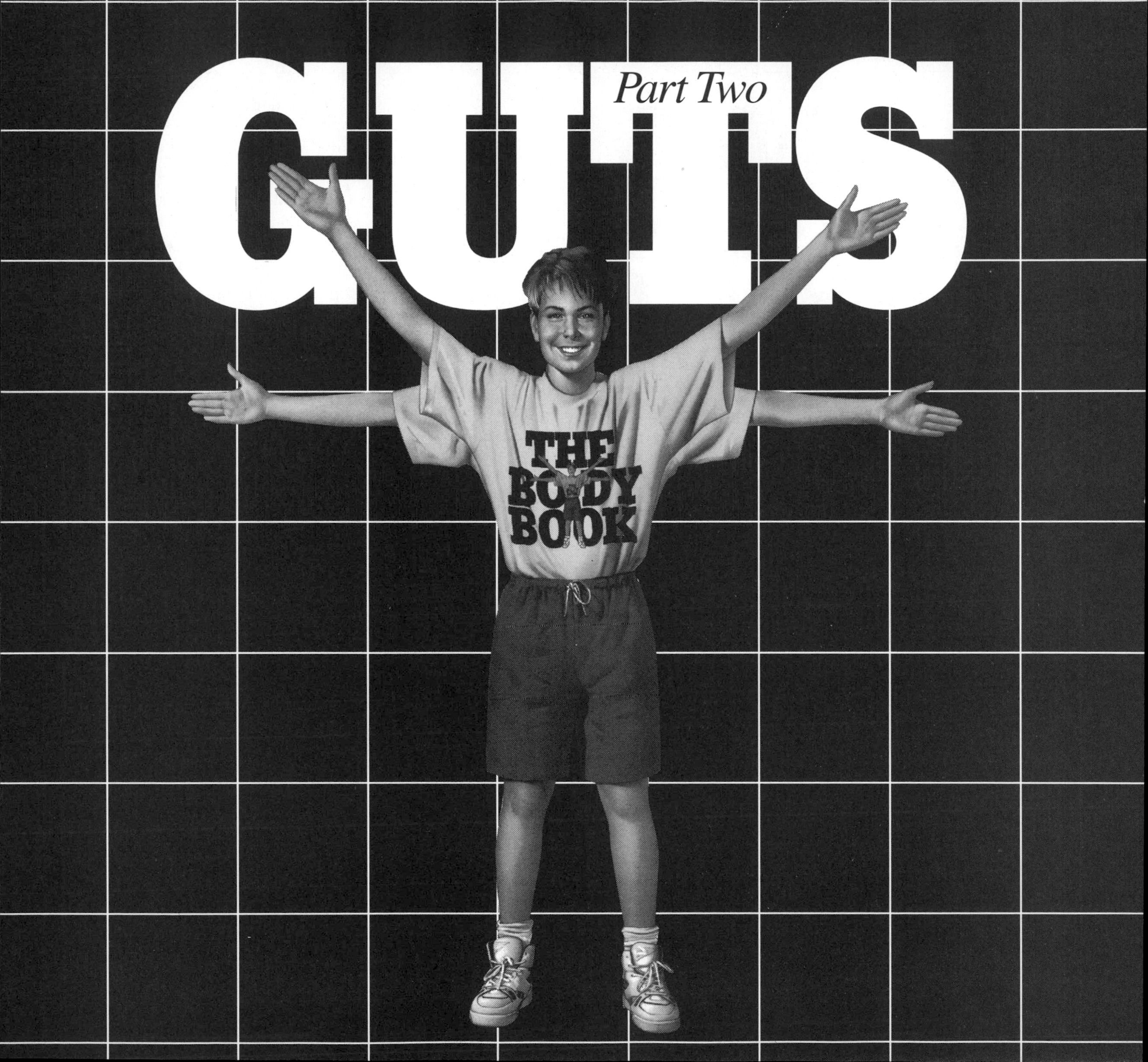
GUTS
Part Two
THE
BODY
BOOK

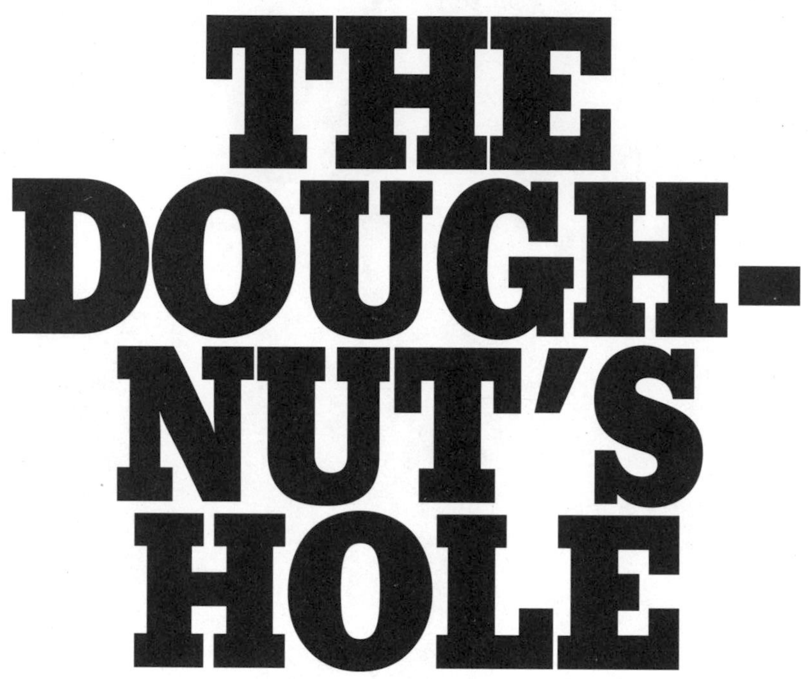

Where does your outside end and your inside begin? Not, as people think, at the mouth. And not deeper either. Not in the throat, or stomach, or even in the bowels.

Geometrically speaking, you are a doughnut. The skin that covers your outside continues right through you from mouth to anus, just as the crust that covers a doughnut continues through the hole. In all the labyrinth of looping tube that people call their guts there is no opening anywhere through which even a grain of rice or speck of dust might get inside. This is reassuring: Your true inner flesh, like the doughnut's dough, is protected on all sides by skin. But it is also mystifying: How is flesh to be fed if there's no way in for meals?

The answer to that question is very strange. Food gets inside, *really* inside. in only one way: A gulp of milk or bite of meat has to pass *through* gut cells, in one side and out the other. The skin cells that line your intestine have the amazing job of transporting at every meal enough to feed the whole of you by gobbling food at one end, and spitting it out the other.

Dissolving and Digesting

Nothing you eat is small enough to get inside a gut cell. Fragments of chewed-up raw carrot are still whole cells, still attached to one another. Well-cooked food, in which cells have been broken, is still glommed-together chunks of protein fibers, globs of fat, masses of starch. Not even mushed-up bits of baby food, not even the minute particles that make milk white or cider brown are small enough for a gut cell to take in. For them to bring your dinner in to you, food must be taken apart into separate molecules, and even smaller, into the units of which molecules are made. That's what digestion is: a molecular disassembly line.

Molecules are disassembled by digestive juices, which are mostly water. You've seen water alone disassembling such substances as salt and sugar by dissolving them. When sugar is dry, its separate molecules hang onto one another in crystals large enough for you to see. When sugar is wet, water molecules surround each individual molecule, barging between neighbors, shoving them apart from one another, breaking the crystal to bits. Separate sugar molecules are too small to see, so the sugar disappears. That's dissolving.

Small as ordinary sugar molecules are—45 atoms altogether—each is made of two even smaller molecules joined end to end. It's those smaller bits of sweet that cells can eat. But the bits are attached to one another too firmly for water alone to pry apart. Digestive juices contain proteins called enzymes that help water take molecules apart into truly tiny snippets. That's digestion.

An Experiment With Spit and Starch

The digestive juice you know the best is spit. Spit is made in salivary glands behind your jaw and under it. They are similar to sweat glands, but with many pouches that open through tubes under your tongue and in your cheeks. Their juice is 99 percent water, thickened with a little slippery mucus, laccd with a trace of an enzyme.

Parents who, for convenience, feed babies baby food straight from the jar, and then save the leftovers for another meal, find out how powerful spit is. Just the bit of spit on the spoon will have digested bananas or sweet potatoes to liquid by the next meal. The same won't be true of chicken or spinach. Each enzyme digests only one kind of molecule, and spit is a starch digester. That's why a starchy cracker held in the mouth liquefies to mush; protein foods like meat get wet, but not digested.

A Molecule of Water

To see dissolving and digesting as chemistry instead of magic disappearing acts, you have to picture the action at a smaller scale than even that of cells.

Picture an atom. Atoms are made of smaller particles, two kinds of which have an electric charge. Protons in the nucleus of an atom have a positive charge. Electrons that swarm around the nucleus have a negative charge. Opposite charges attract, and the attraction between protons and electrons is what holds an atom together. Like charges repel. Since atoms are all aswarm with negatively charged electrons on their outside, they repel each

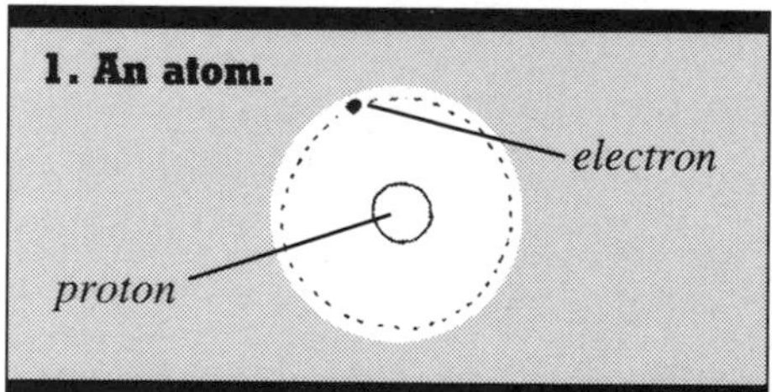

1. An atom.

other. Only when atoms are forced very close together can they overcome their mutual repulsion by sharing one or more electrons. That's how atoms come together into molecules.

Now picture a water molecule. It is made of only three atoms—one big oxygen (with eight electrons), and two little hydrogens (with only one apiece). Both oxygen and hydrogen share their electrons, which buzz now to oxygen, now to hydrogen, keeping the three atoms together in a Y-shaped molecule.

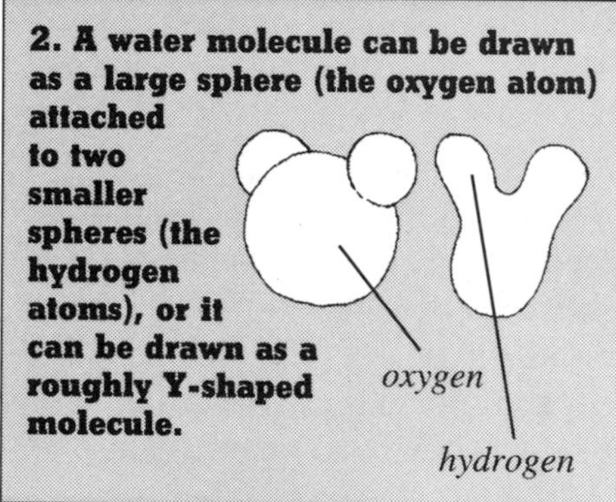

2. A water molecule can be drawn as a large sphere (the oxygen atom) attached to two smaller spheres (the hydrogen atoms), or it can be drawn as a roughly Y-shaped molecule.

But the sharing is not equal. Oxygen's pull is greater than hydrogen's. At any instant, shared electrons are more likely to be buzzing around the oxygen stem of the Y than around the hydrogen arms; in fact, the pull is so strong that much of the time hydrogen can't even hold onto the one electron it had originally. The oxygen stem of a water molecule therefore has a slightly negative charge, and the hydrogen arms are left slightly positive. Molecules like that, in which electric charge is unevenly distributed, are called polar molecules.

Picture a group of these polar molecules—in a jar lid, for instance. Molecules are always in motion: The hotter they are, the faster they move. Even at room temperature, water molecules jiggle and spin; and dash, collide, and ricochet off one another at over 1,000 miles an hour. But because they are polar, like little magnets, they momentarily cling to one another when they collide, oxygen stem to hydrogen arm, in a pattern that is repeated throughout

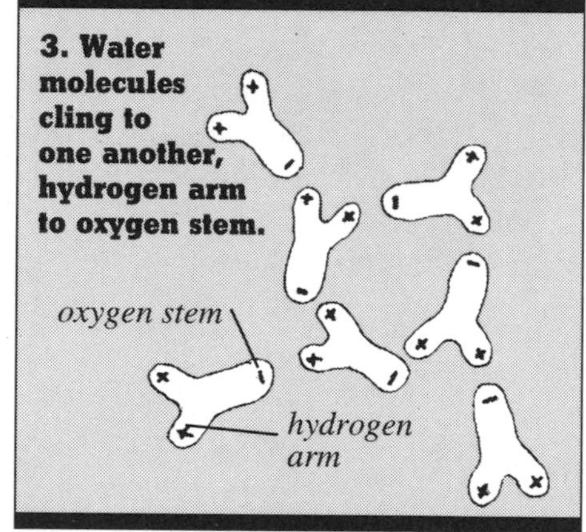

3. Water molecules cling to one another, hydrogen arm to oxygen stem.

a body of water, whether it is drop or an ocean. Each joining is brief: Within just millionths of a second, they shake free of one another, then in an instant grab new partners, and again jiggle loose and dash away. Water molecules sometimes shake themselves to pieces, and pieces rejoin. The slippery, flowing quality of water is this continual shifting of molecules and pieces of molecules as they bounce from partner to partner.

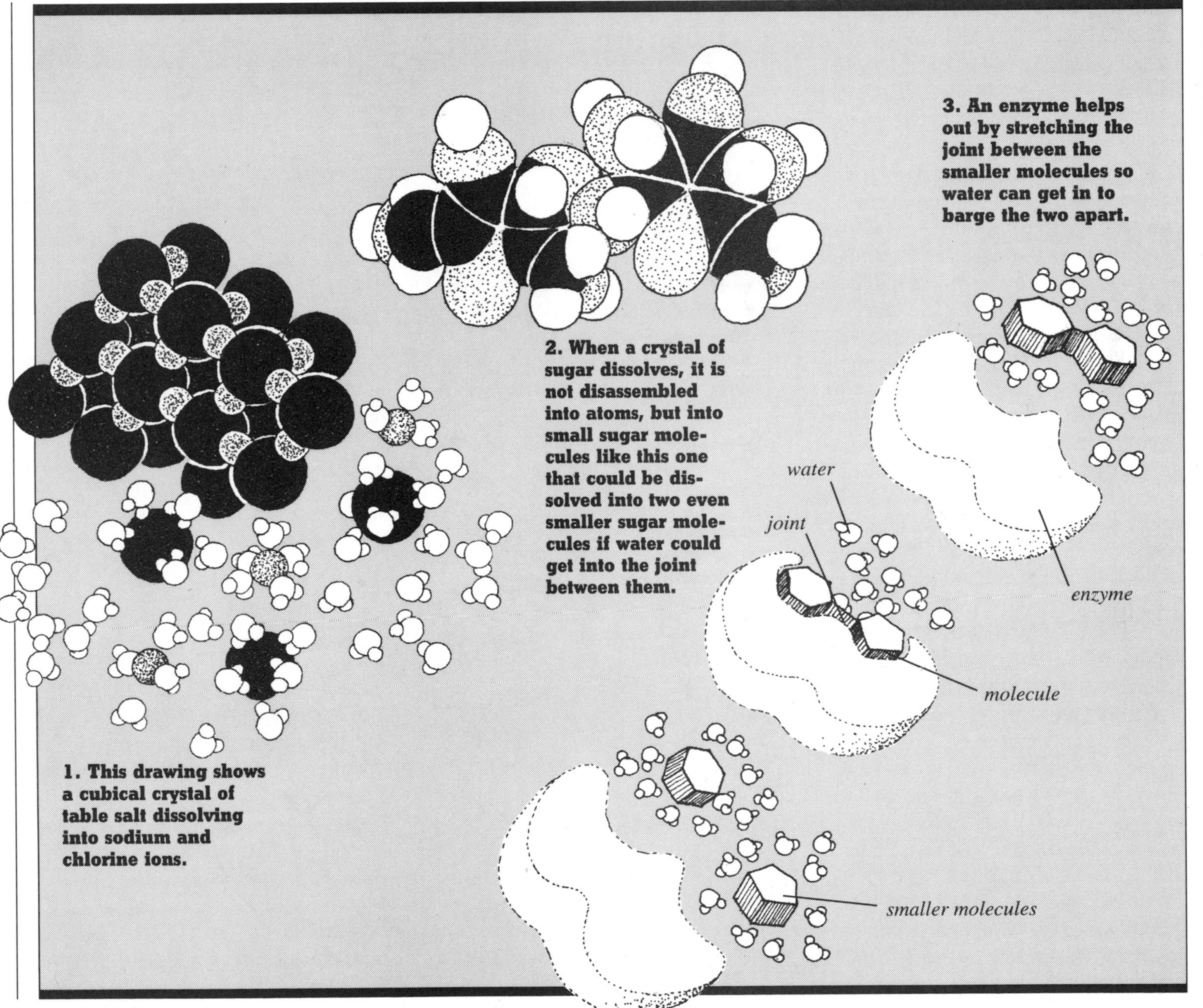
1. This drawing shows a cubical crystal of table salt dissolving into sodium and chlorine ions.
2. When a crystal of sugar dissolves, it is not disassembled into atoms, but into small sugar molecules like this one that could be dissolved into two even smaller sugar molecules if water could get into the joint between them.
3. An enzyme helps out by stretching the joint between the smaller molecules so water can get in to barge the two apart.
water
joint
enzyme
molecule
smaller molecules

Spit and Starch, Magnified

Imagine putting a sugar crystal into this hyperactive water. Sugar molecules are polar, too. The attraction between their positive and negative spots is what holds them together into a crystal. But in water, these charged spots powerfully attract water molecules, which barge between the sugars and surround each one of them completely. They become separated from one another by cushions of water: They become dissolved.

A few of the sugar molecules will also be broken into the two smaller units of which they are made, but these are lucky breaks: The charged places where the units join are at a narrow neck between them where water molecules seldom penetrate. Starch is made of the same units, but the molecule is much larger, and the joints are twisted in such a way that they are even harder for water to get into. This is where enzymes come in—literally.

An enzyme is a large molecule with a slot or bump shaped to fit a particular kind of joint to which it attaches by means of its own electric charges. The enzyme in spit attaches to the joint between starch units. As it fits itself into place, it stretches the joint, bends it out of whack, and holds it still. Water can then get into the weakened joint and sever it. That releases the enzyme, which bounces on to open up another

From Mouth to Anus

The digestive system is essentially a tube, open at both ends. The stomach is an enlarged portion of the tube. Two digestive glands, the pancreas and the liver, begin as small pouches growing from the tube in the embryo. They gradually fill out with cells that make digestive juices.

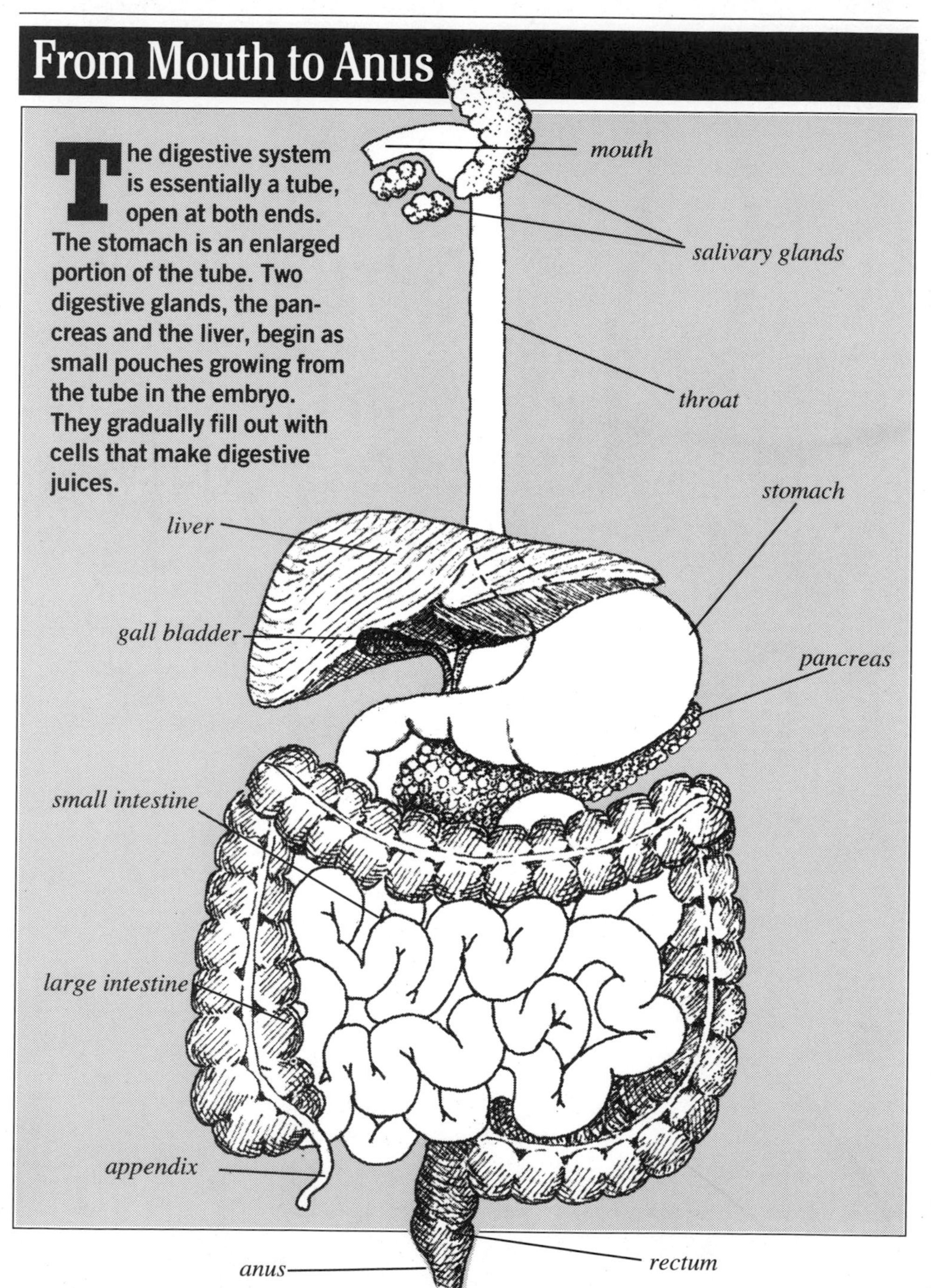

joint. A single molecule of enzyme may do its job 20,000 times a second without wearing out.

So stop reading for a moment. Get yourself a snack. Feel your mouth water. Take a bite. From this moment, and continuing for the next few hours, several liters of digestive juice laced with several dozen different kinds of enzymes will be severing your snack into the multitude of molecules it's made of.

Interrupted Swallows

The digestive system is a 30-foot-long tube open at both ends, at the mouth and at the anus. Along that route, each portion of the tube does its own thing. The front end disassembles food, the middle eats it, and the rear end reabsorbs the juices that the rest released. The entire process, from the time a meal enters to the time leftovers leave, takes about 24 hours. During all that time—sometimes quickly, sometimes slowly—worm-type muscles that, in earthworms, burrow them through the soil, swallow food through your digestive tract from one end to the other.

The first swallow is the familiar one that moves a meal from mouth to stomach. As food is chewed to moist mush, the tongue curls around it, collecting it from the teeth and molding it into a ball. Then the tongue humps against the roof of the mouth to push the ball of food toward the throat. The mouthful bulges the throat, causing rings of muscle to tighten one after another, each ring in turn squeezing shut behind the bulge to force the food down like toothpaste from a tube. The final ring of muscles at the entrance to the stomach is normally shut tight. It relaxes when food hits it, lets the mouthful through, then shuts again to keep the food ball down.

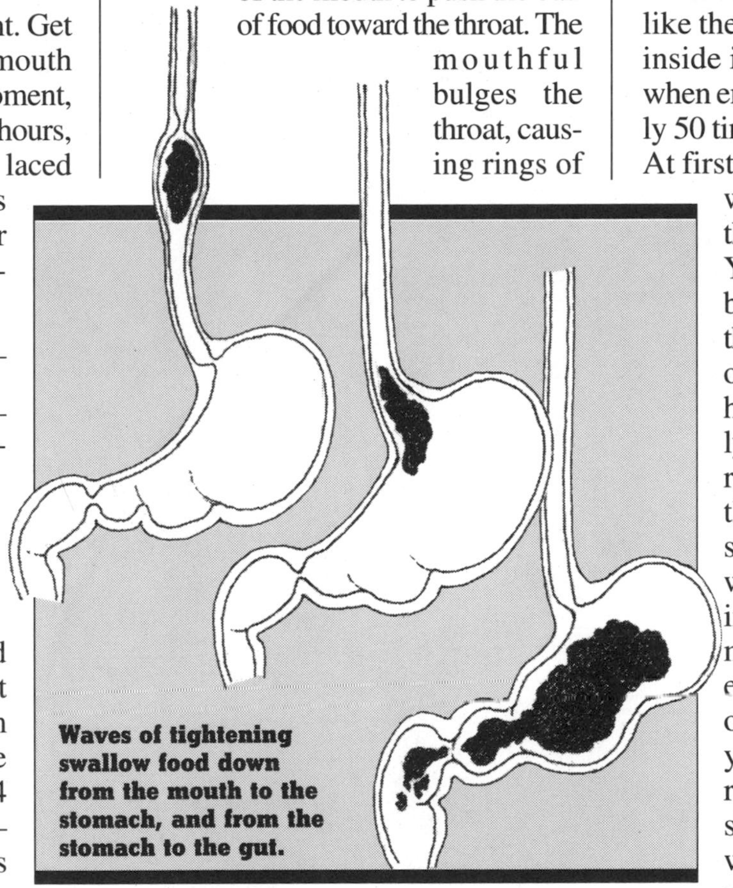

Waves of tightening swallow food down from the mouth to the stomach, and from the stomach to the gut.

The stomach is a widened portion of the digestive tube shaped something like the bag of a bagpipe. The space inside it is only about 50 milliliters when empty, but it can stretch to nearly 50 times that big, up to 4 liters full. At first, your meal sits in a heap just where it landed, about level with the bottom of your breastbone. You can feel the fullness as it balloons out the stomach wall in this bulgy, flabby, upper portion of the bag. Over the next half hour, the mass of food gradually slips downward into the narrower, more muscular bottom of the bag. There powerfully squeezing muscles continue the work the mouth began, kneading and churning your meal to mush. Stomach lining cells soften the mush further with oozes of their own digestive juice. As your meal becomes about as runny as thick soup, it begins to slosh against the stomach's exit where it joins the narrow tube of your intestine. And now the stomach swallows.

You can't feel your stomach swallowing, although you may be aware of a certain lightening as the bulge of fullness is squeezed on down the tube. The squeezes come in waves one after another, but each squeeze squirts out much less food than the mouthfuls

A Closer Look at Food

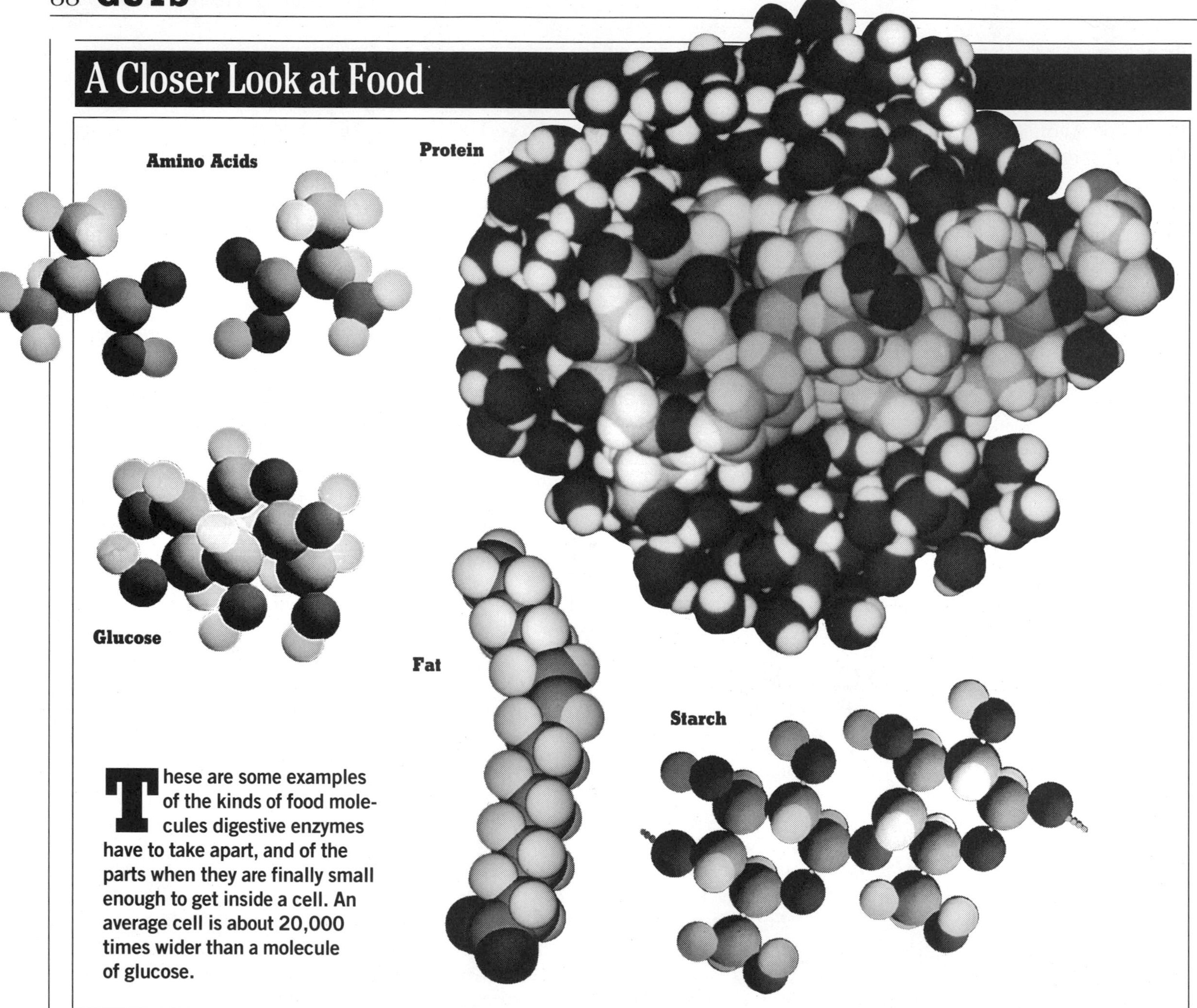

These are some examples of the kinds of food molecules digestive enzymes have to take apart, and of the parts when they are finally small enough to get inside a cell. An average cell is about 20,000 times wider than a molecule of glucose.

throats can swallow. This is because of the perverse behavior of the ring of muscles that guards the stomach's exit. Instead of relaxing to open up and let the food on through, this ring tightens as each wave of contraction reaches it, and shuts the exit off. The spurt of soupy food from stomach to intestine is like a swallow cut short by a gag: Some soup gets through, but most of it is splashed back into the stomach.

Gagging at every swallow is a slow way to move a meal along, but that is just the point: The most important purpose of a stomach is to slow food down, to keep it from getting into your intestine as quickly as you got it down your throat.

The Difference Between Knots and Noodles

What's in a meal? Take a look at a turkey sandwich.

The bread has cane sugar or some other sweetener in it, and starch from rye or wheat. Sweets and starches are both carbohydrates, molecules made of various kinds of sugars. All carbohydrates have charged spots on them.

Turkey and every sort of meat are mostly proteins. Proteins, too, have charged spots on them, but protein molecules are made up of 20 uniquely shaped units called amino acids.

Butter is fat; mayonnaise is mostly oil. Fats (which are solid at room temperature) and oils (which are liquid at room temperature) have large areas without charged spots on them. They don't dissolve in water.

Each of these substances presents a different digestive problem. Carbohydrates are the least difficult to take apart. They are always chains of sugar units linked end to end, and the joints between the links are much alike. However long the longest carbohydrates may be—and some are hundreds of sugar units long—their simple spaghetti shape usually makes them a cinch to snip to smaller noodles. Still, the enzyme in spit doesn't fit every carbohydrate joint.

Proteins are knottier problems. They are enormously large molecules; some contain hundreds of thousands of atoms. The joint—or bond—between any 2 of the 20 different amino acids has its own particular shape and its own particular arrangement of charge: No one enzyme fits more than a few kinds of joints. What's more, protein molecules are coiled and bent and folded and wrapped into 3-D puzzles that can only be undone bit by bit, working from exposed bonds to those buried inside. A single steak muscle fiber contains at least 10,000 different kinds of proteins—billions of protein molecules altogether—and meat arrives at the stomach still glommed together, masses of muscle bundled in sheaths and webbed in threads which are also proteins, and which must be painstakingly undone from one another before there are even separate molecules to work on.

Fats are more troublesome still. This is not because their shapes are torturous—most fats and oils are straight chains or, at most, branched ones—nor is it because their joints are difficult. Fat and oil molecules are hard to take apart because they have few charges. Enzymes can't cling to them; neither can water.

All food molecules are taken apart in steps by relay teams of chemicals supplied by specialized cells or glands stationed along the digestive tube in the order in which their services are needed. Saliva and stomach juice do only the preliminary work. When a turkey sandwich leaves your stomach, bread starch has been cut into segments several units long, but very little has been cut up entirely. Proteins have been

Bulletin!

Your stomach has just replaced half a million damaged lining cells! It does this every minute—a complete relining job every three days, 122 new linings per year.

The Mark of the Meat-Eater

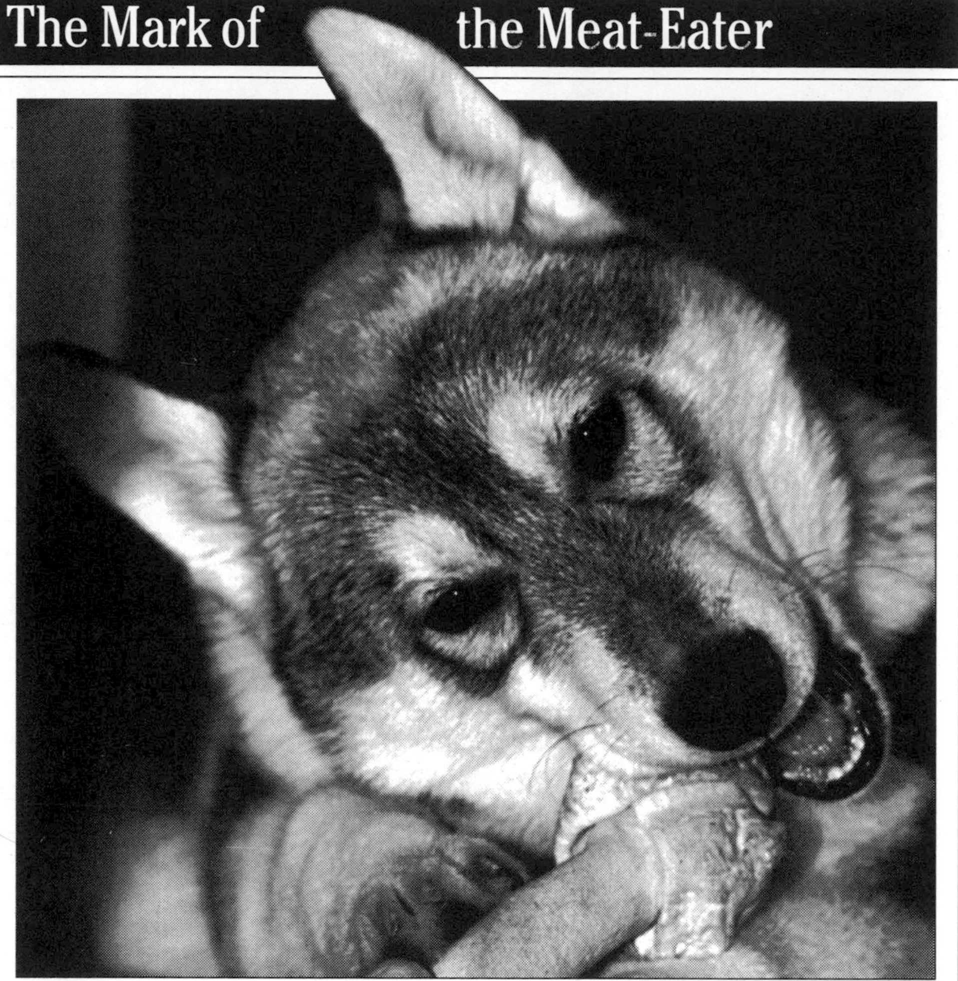

Every kind of animal makes digestive enzymes, but only vertebrates—animals with backbones—make protein-digesting enzymes that can survive in acid, and only vertebrates have acid stomachs. Wonder why? Because only vertebrates eat other vertebrates. Hydrochloric acid dissolves bone, and as bony vertebrates began to eat other bony vertebrates, an acid stomach helped to soften the splinters while a new protein-digester that worked in acid nibbled, so to speak, between the ribs.

untangled from one another and the molecules have been shortened, but none have been disassembled into separate amino acids. Pools of fat have just been splashed to drops; they aren't a bit digested.

You have seen a meal in this preliminary state: It is vomit, a partially digested meal that has come back up instead of continuing on down. The stomach's major job is to dole out vomit the right way, into the gut, and slowly, spurt by spurt, no faster than the rest of the chemical disassembly line can finish the work that the stomach has just begun.

A Nibbling Thought

What if there were no stomach? You'd have to chew more thoroughly, and digestion would be very slow, but it would not be impossible, for stomach juice contains no absolutely necessary ingredients. But a sandwich you may have swallowed in a minute takes hours to take apart into morsels small enough for cells to eat, and more hours still for cells to haul inside your body. Without a stomach, you would have to pace your eating to suit your intestine. That would mean continual nibbling, without time for any other business in life but feeding tidbits to intestines. As it is, you need to fill up only three times a day: You supply your stomach, your stomach supplies your gut.

Overstuffed

An adult's stomach when empty is like a deflated balloon. The 4 liters (about 4¼ quarts) of food an adult can eat stretches the stomach to about the size of this water-filled balloon.

Puke

Throw-up doesn't smell like dinner smelled. Its stink shows that food has undergone some chemical changes: The milky, meaty molecules that, sniffed at mealtime, made your mouth water and your stomach juices flow, have been cut by just those juices into vomit's cheesy reek.

Stomach juice has a flavor all its own: sour. The sourness of vomit is hydrochloric acid made by stomach cells. If your throat hurts after vomiting, that's because stomach acid has burned it. "Heartburn" is pain from just above the stomach, where acid sometimes leaks through the ring of muscles and hurts the lower portion of the throat. Burps may bring up stinging spurts of acid, too. Stomachs are rarely injured by their own acid because mucus glands coat the surface with thick goo. You can see that in vomit, too: It's slimy.

The longer your meal has been worked on in the stomach, the smaller chewed lumps of food are, and the mushier. Hydrochloric acid loosens fiber bundles, softens gristle sheaths, untangles collagen webs, dismantles muscle machinery, unwinds, unsnarls, unravels, teases open the twisted, knotted shapes of protein molecules. Then a team of seven protein-digesting enzymes made by stomach cells begins the first steps of disassembly. Lumpy puke is food that acid and enzymes

UGH!

Vomiting is controlled by a vomiting center in the brain that is switched on automatically by various events. An overstuffed stomach, for instance. Or twirling around and getting dizzy. Or smelling something vile. Or certain drugs or poisons, many kinds of germs, and fear, or pain. Or just touching the gagging spot at the back of the tongue also switches on the brain's vomiting center, and starts the programmed sequence of a stomach dump.

After some sweating, salivating, and nausea, the stomach dump itself begins with a giant breath. Your breathing tube then shuts off, while the soft flesh at the roof of the mouth lifts up, as when you say "ugh." Although you can't feel it, the ring of muscles at the top of your stomach loosens. Now your chest and belly muscles contract in a mighty spasm that squashes the stomach, and heaves the puke right out. Spasm after spasm can completely empty not only the stomach, but the first foot or so of intestine, too.

Hmmmmmmm…

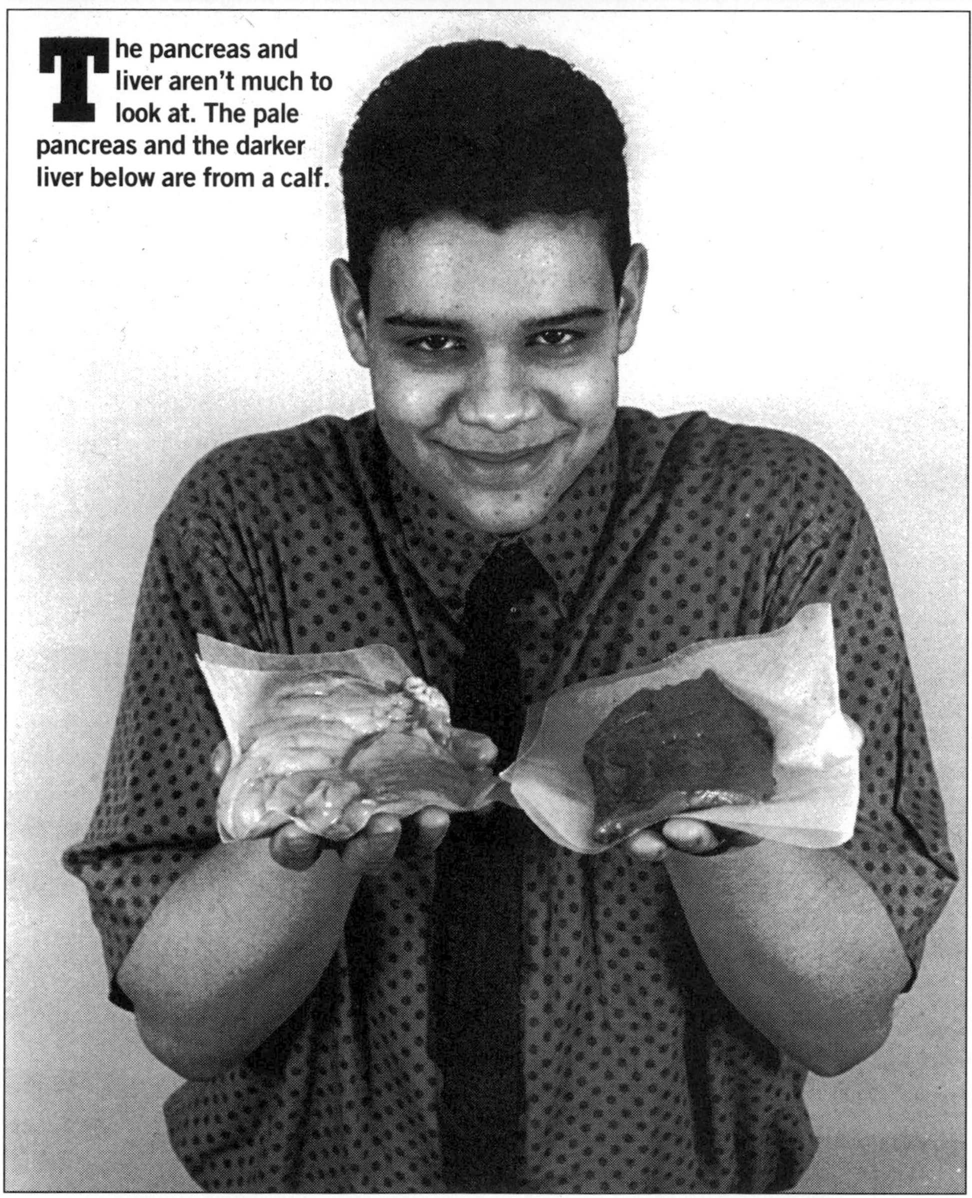

The pancreas and liver aren't much to look at. The pale pancreas and the darker liver below are from a calf.

haven't changed much yet. Pasty puke is ready to be spurted onward. And soupy puke has been upchucked not only from your stomach, but from the loop of intestine just beyond, where, little by little, it is digested to clear broth. By then it is beyond the point of vomiting.

Through the Loop

Most of digestion takes place in a short loop of gut, just past the stomach and only 25 centimeters long, called the duodenum. The duodenum includes cells that make various enzymes, and also receives enzymes and fat-processing chemicals from two large digestive glands, the pancreas and the liver. The pancreas of a calf is sold in meat departments under the name "sweet breads"; liver is just called liver. Both glands start in the embryo as small pouches, similar to other skin glands, that open into the gut. But by birth the pouches have grown so elaborately folded that no amount of picking at them with a knife and fork would suggest their original pocket shape. Nevertheless, their lining is continuous with the gut lining, part of the doughnut's hole, not the dough itself.

Digestive juice poured into the duodenum by the pancreas contains a starch-digester that completes the job started by saliva, teams of protein-digesters that give proteins their final pruning, a group of enzymes with the special task of taking genes apart, and one that—with the help of liver juice—tackles fat. Most of these chemicals are destroyed by acid. That problem is taken care of by the body's own version of Tums and Rolaids: a dose of acid-neutralizer poured out by the pancreas along with its other products.

These chemicals aren't dished out between meals when the stomach's empty. Nor are they mixed haphazardly—a dash of this, a squirt of that, some gushes of the others. Amounts of juice, the mix of their ingredients, the turning on and off of the cells that make them, and even the rate at which the stomach delivers food to be digested, are controlled by devices that analyze your meal. Pressure sensors measure fullness. Chemical sensors test for acid, and gauge the concentration of fat, and of partly digested carbohydrates and proteins.

When these devices detect that the duodenum is full, or holds a large amount of fat, or a lot of acid or protein fragments indicating a big digestive job is coming its way, it sends the stomach signals that calm its muscle waves to ripples. You have felt the results of such duodenal decisions: Hard-to-digest greasy meals stay put for hours, while simple Chinese fare rushes right on through.

What you can't feel is that, whatever you have eaten, the duodenum doles out just the right kinds and quantities of enzymes to digest it.

Degreasing Dinner

The liver's juice contains no enzymes and digests nothing. The liver secretes bile, a dark, bitter fluid made of oils and colored by pigments left over from used red blood cells. Bile acts like a detergent: It washes fat.

Fat doesn't dissolve in water (or in stomach juice) because its molecules have no negative or positive charges to which water could cling. In fact, fat molecules come together in water into tiny droplets, and the droplets join into larger drops, and the drops combine into greasy puddles. You've seen that happening to the oil in salad dressing that's been shaken. Yet fat molecules have no attraction for one another. They gather into groups because water pushes them out of its way.

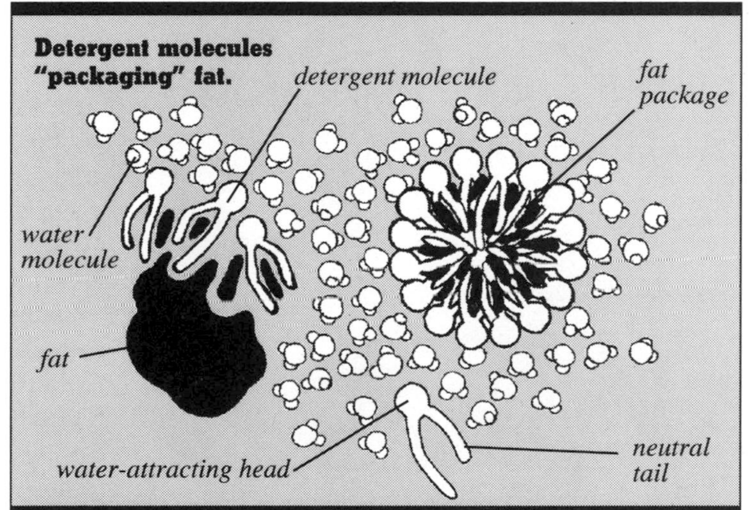

Fat molecules shaken among water molecules tear through their pattern of clinging stems and arms, breaking their hold on one another. In the course of repairing this tear by hooking up with one another again, water molecules push oil molecules aside. By the time the water molecules are again clinging to one another arm to stem, the oil has been herded all together, out of water's way. This is the condition in which a meal leaves your stomach. Droplets of fat released from fat cells in meat, or from salad oil or butter, have been pushed together into greasy masses, as they would be if you tried to wash fat from dishes with water alone.

When you add detergent to greasy dishwater, the fat disappears. It is not dissolved. It is instead packaged into tiny spheres surrounded by detergent. The spheres, of a few thousand molecules each, are too small to see.

The "head" end of a detergent molecule has charged spots on it to which water clings, but the "tail" is a neutral fat. Water molecules reassembling around such molecules cling to the head

Dishpan Hands

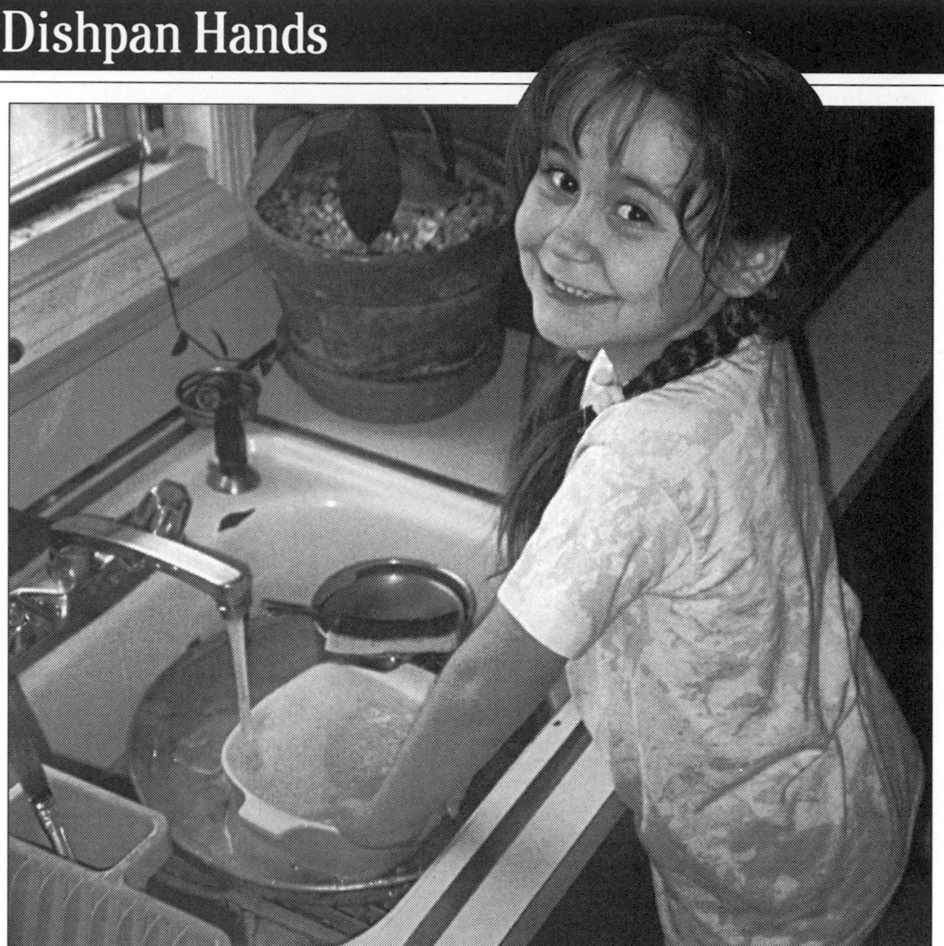

Detergents remove oil from the skin surface just as they do from pot surfaces, but the dissolving goes deeper in skin than it does on pots. Cell membranes are oily. When dish detergent gets to them, it separates the molecules, injuring the cell. Doing the dishes every night won't harm your hands, but people who scrub many times a day—including surgeons and house cleaners—may be injured. The response is the same as from other injuries: Histamines are released, and hands get red, swollen, and itchy.

ends, but push the tails aside. The result is solid balls of detergent molecules whose heads face outward attached to water, and whose tails are buried inside well away from it. When detergent and oil meet in water, the oil gets pushed into the same container, packaged among the fatty tails.

Bile does the same job on fats in your intestine as detergents do on grease in the kitchen sink. Then fat-digesting enzymes are able to grip the surface of the package to expose the fat inside, and break it up a little. Any fat fragments released this way are promptly repackaged by bile into even smaller balls. Yet no fats are completely digested. Fat gets into cells only because cell membranes are made of molecules that are themselves detergents.

Gurgling Along

Food emerging from the duodenum into the next 18 feet ($5^1/_2$ meters) of coiled tube is nothing like the food you ate. It is clear: Nearly everything in it has been digested, and dissolved. There is enormously more of this clear fluid than there had been food. In the course of a day, salivary glands alone pour 1,500 milliliters of water into the digestive system. The stomach and intestine together secrete another 3,500, and the liver and pancreas add 2,000 milliliters more. That outpouring, plus about

1,200 milliliters of fluid that you drink, amounts to a total of over 8,000 milliliters of water gushing through your gut each day. That's the equivalent of eight one-liter bottles of soda—or, per meal, somewhere between two and three liters, plus the meal itself.

Clear as the fluid is, it is not calm. At the lukewarm temperature of the intestine, water molecules careen around at 1,500 miles per hour, each one colliding at the insane rate of millions of collisions per second. Dissolved food molecules move slower because of their greater size, but even they are no slowpokes. Sugar units, for example, dash at about 500 miles per hour in the gut. Added to this molecular turmoil are powerful currents and eddies. The intestine here is wrinkled, almost entirely filled with lining uplifted into folds through which fluid floods in gushes with every new contraction. No wonder that, when bubbles of swallowed air gurgle through this turmoil, their noise is heard across the room!

For the next several hours, the surface of the gut's rough landscape will pluck from the buffeting tide enough nutritious molecules to feed all the body's cells. That's a job almost beyond belief: Your body has 40 trillion cells to feed.

Your Daily Dose

This is the amount of water that gushes through your gut each day.

Eating for 40 Trillion

If the lining of the gut were as smooth as your outer skin, the area of its surface wouldn't be nearly large enough to take in that huge load. Surface area is enormously

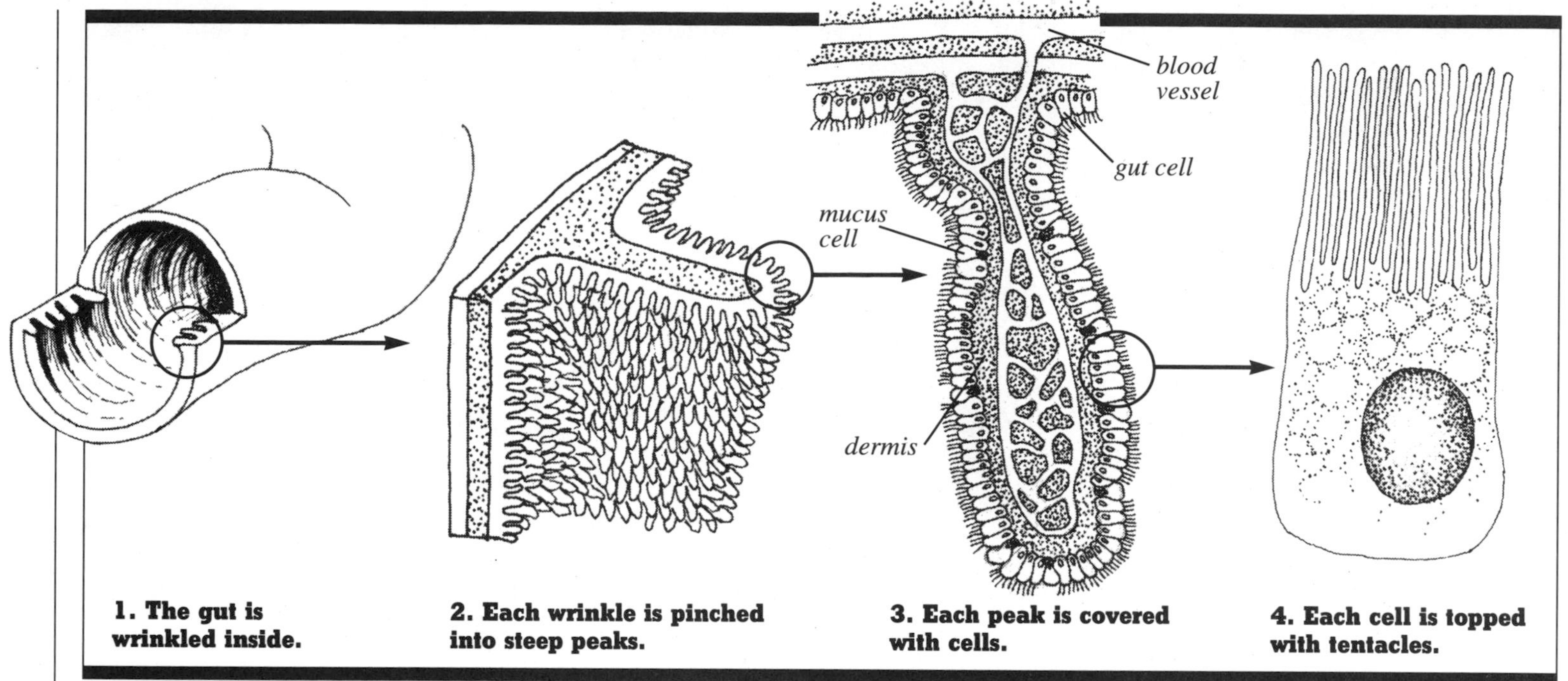

1. The gut is wrinkled inside. **2. Each wrinkle is pinched into steep peaks.** **3. Each peak is covered with cells.** **4. Each cell is topped with tentacles.**

increased in the small intestine by its mountainous topography—lining uplifted into folds, folds pinched into steep peaks and valleys. The central cavity of the small intestine is almost filled with nubbly lining. Even the individual cells have a greater surface area than those in skin. Their tops are covered with hundreds of short tentacles; they are bushy, not smooth. In all, the surface of the gut is 2,000 square feet, the size of a baseball diamond. Compare this to the skin's 25 square feet: The doughnut's hole, in the case of a human, is 80 times larger than the rest of the surface!

The gut lining is also more alive than dead. Basal cells in gut skin live in the valley bottoms. As they divide, new daughters push against older daughters, driving them uphill toward the peaks. Every valley supplies the mountainsides with fresh new bushytops all alive and greedy. They die only as they reach the summit, from which they are rubbed off by passing meals.

This vast and very lively lining of the gut can eat almost as much as you can swallow. Of all the solid food and watery juices swallowed down into your stomach and squirted out into your small intestine, 94 percent is removed by the cells that line it.

But where is it then put? Think of the tube of skin that covers your finger: The outer layer faces the outer world; the dermis is inside. The tube of the gut is like finger skin turned outside in. The cells that line its wrinkled surface face the cavity that runs through you. That layer is encircled by a layer of dermis, woven by fibroblasts and networked with blood vessels. The dermis layer of the gut is the immediate destination of food molecules.

The trip is short—in through the top of a lining cell, out through its bottom. For a water molecule, that distance is about 800,000 times its own length. No detours are possible: Gut cells are welded to one another by collars that completely seal the cracks between them. The whole bulk of you, all the blood, fat, bone, and muscle between your inner tube and outer skin, has entered through gut cells' tiny tentacles.

Mealtime for a Gut Cell

Gut cells engulf large molecules of food the way garbage-eating phagocytes swallow broken fibers and living germs. You could call that method eating, but whereas a body has a permanent mouth, stomach, and anus, a cell makes a new mouth for every bite it takes, and uses that mouth as stomach and anus, too.

Say that one of a bushy cell's tentacles has been hit by an exceptionally large molecule, such as one of vitamin B_{12}. Immediately the tentacle forms a mouth to swallow the morsel. The mouth begins as a dimple in the membrane that encloses the cell. With the big vitamin molecule attached, the dimple sinks inward, forming a pocket. The pocket holding the vitamin pinches off from the tentacle's surface. Now it is a round stomach carrying its bulky load through the cell. At the bottom of the cell, the stomach rejoins the membrane, opens into a pocket again, and dumps the molecule out into the dermis. No membrane has been lost.

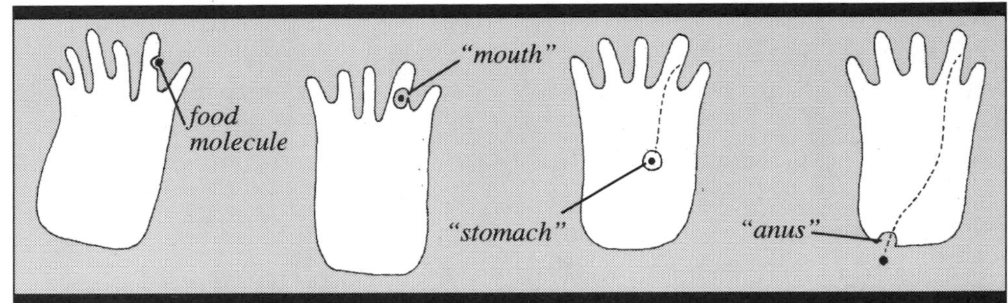

The patch that detached at one end of the cell is reinserted at the other end, and the vitamin is now loose in the wet jungle of your interior. And, strictly speaking, the vitamin hasn't entered the cell: It has been ferried through it without coming into contact with the fluid inside the cell itself.

Smaller molecules are not packed up in pockets and ferried through the way large ones are. They actually get through the cell's membrane, into its inner fluid.

The material of the membrane that encloses a cell is an oily film, only two molecules thick, that flows like the sur-

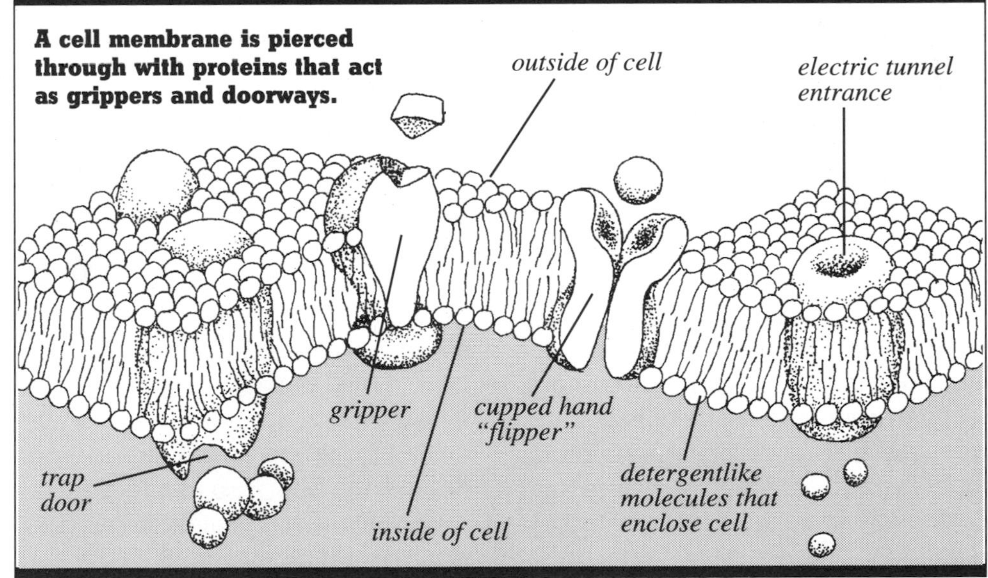

A cell membrane is pierced through with proteins that act as grippers and doorways.

face of a soap bubble. The molecules are similar to other detergents: Water-attracting heads with fatty, water-repellent tails. These molecules are arranged around the cell in a double layer. The heads in the outer layer face the liquid that surrounds the cell, the heads in the inside layer face the liquid that fills the cell, and the tails of both layers are sandwiched in between.

Water molecules are so small that they enter cells simply by slipping between these membrane molecules. Fat molecules, continually knocked from their ball by all the commotion in the intestine, find refuge in the oily innards of the membrane, and regather on the other side. Everything else gets in (and out) through channels or doorways specially designed for them.

These entrances and exits are made of proteins that pierce the membrane. Some form electric tunnels that pull molecules of a certain size and charge through the membrane. Others are trap doors that pop open when triggered by a specific kind of molecule, and shut when the molecule has reached the other side. The fanciest doorways are groups of proteins that, like a pair of cupped hands, capture their molecule at the outer surface, and flip to dump it in. Five different sorts of doorways are required just to escort amino acids through the membrane. To even use the pocketing technique of swallowing big mouthfuls, a gut cell must first grip that kind of morsel with a protein in its membrane. Altogether, a gut cell's surface is studded with several hundred thousand proteins involved one way or another with escorting your meals into the interior of your body.

Down to the Bowels

What's left of a meal as it reaches the end of the small intestine is mostly water made slimy by cells that have secreted mucus all along the route. Slimy water doesn't seem worth saving until one remembers how much of it there is: If you were to lose each day the eight liters of water you supply for food digestion, you would soon dry up. The job of the last portion of the gut is to reabsorb the water that the rest of it poured out.

The last four feet of the digestive tract is variously called the large intestine, colon, large bowel, or simply bowel. It begins at the right side of your belly, below the level of your hip. Contractions in the bowel are normally slow, only about two an hour, so the river runs slow down there. The tube through which it runs is broad—several inches in inside diameter compared to the wrinkled narrowness of the small intestine. That, too, slows the flow, as when a rushing mountain stream empties into the calm meanders of a broad river. And the course of the bowel does meander: At first it climbs straight up nearly to the level of the stomach, then it turns and leisurely crosses from the right side of the belly to the left, and only then bends downward toward the exit at the anus.

As the river runs its slow, winding course, it is reduced to a stream, then to a trickle. By the time it has reached the end of the course, bowel cells have recovered all but 100 grams of the water that flowed over them. This small amount—only enough to fill half a cup—remains to soften feces to their usual consistency.

But what is left to make feces of? If the small intestine absorbs nearly all the solid material you ate, and if what arrives at the bowel is mostly mucus, what accounts for the large lumps of solid stuff that come out the other end? And why are they brown?

The color of feces is leftover bits of bile; feces would otherwise be ashy white. The only food in it is cellulose, the stiff boxes of plant cells which animals can't digest. But even if you have eaten lots of popcorn, with its tough cellulose husks, or celery, with its crunchy cellulose fibers, or oat bran, which is nothing but cellulose, undigested leftovers account for very little of the solid stuff in feces. Feces are mostly dead gut cells—hundreds of millions of them scraped off by the average passing meal—and bacteria, alive and dead. Bacteria account for a full quarter of the volume of a bowel

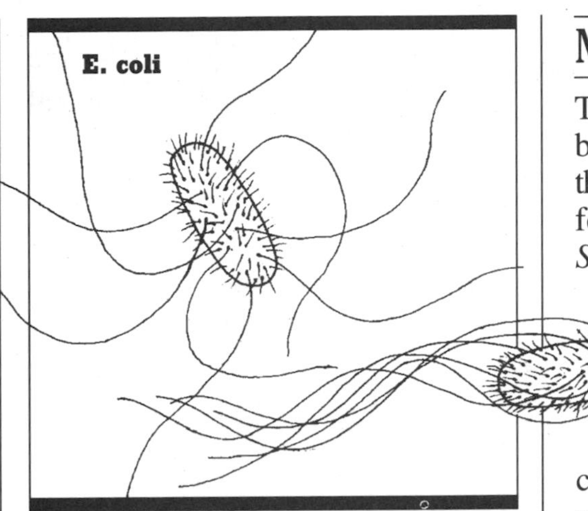

movement, or half of it in dry weight. Your bowel is inhabited by about 10^{14} bacteria—100,000,000,000,000, or 100 trillion. They outnumber the cells of your body five to two.

As much food as might seem necessary to feed such a horde of microbes, gut bacteria don't compete with gut cells for the food you provide. Few even live in the small intestine where your cells bring in the meal. Most bacteria you swallow with food or spit are killed by stomach acid. Those that survive can't gain a foothold in the small intestine, what with its continual gush and push and flood of juice that flushes them along. Only as they emerge into the bowel, where the waves calm down and there is room to grow, can bacteria settle down to stay. There they eat what you have not: cellulose from bean skins and radish roots, discarded enzymes, and, of course, dead gut cells.

Meet Your Guests

To some extent, your guest list of bowel bacteria depends on the menu you offer them, for different microbes prefer different diets. One bacterium called *Sarcina ventriculi* lives almost exclusively in the bowels of vegetarians. The largest population of intestinal bacteria in breast-fed babies is a species that fails to thrive in babies fed cow's milk. But everyone, no matter what they eat, nourishes the bacterium *Escherichia coli*, called *E. coli* for short.

E. coli swims. Superficially, its swimming looks like that of a sperm, but the mechanism and the motion are both entirely different. Instead of one tail, *E. coli*'s tail is many very long hairs, called flagella, twisted into a bundle. Instead of wiggling like a sperm's flagellum, this tail twirls. When it twirls counterclockwise, the bacterium is pushed forward. But when it rotates clockwise, the bundle flies apart, and the bacterium tumbles. Tumbles alternate with swims, so the critter appears to dash a ways, then fall into confusion, then dash off again in another direction. That's how it finds food in the slow river of your bowel.

Besides flagella, *E. coli* grows shorter hairs that give it a wild and woolly look. It is with these hairs that the bacterium anchors to your gut cells when it isn't going anywhere. On occasion it forms a thick, hollow hair that it sticks into a neighbor like a doctor's injection needle. This is a mating tube. Bacteria

Oh Bellyache, Where Art Thou?

When you have a bellyache, such as gas pains from a bloated gut, the pain always seems to be located somewhere along the midline of the belly and toward the front, even though there's intestine to the right, the left, and the back as well, and every inch of it is well equipped with pain receptors that respond to pressure. The reason people can't localize gut pain accurately is because the intestine isn't well mapped in the brain. The map's representation is more like the original gut, the one that was taken into the embryo's body at its front, where the belly closed over it at the midline. The map was not revised to represent the coiling and folding that later distributed intestines, so pain anywhere seems to come from its original location. Doctors know that a patient complaining of any pain in the abdomen is not likely to give a helpful answer to the question, "Where does it hurt?"

don't make sperm and eggs as animals do, but they once in a while pass genes around. The bacterium copies a section of its genes, sends the copy down its tube and into a mate, then severs the connection and tumbles away. Mates stuck with new genes distribute them to daughters during each division.

Among the most frequently injected genes are ones for resistance to antibiotics. Mating is, in this case, very like inoculations you've been stuck with to protect you from disease, for a bacterium with such a gene is protected from antibiotics that, in germs, cause fatal illness.

Very likely your present population of *E. coli* is descended in part from ones swallowed in infancy, and very likely, since children are often given antibiotics to kill the germs that ail them, some few who happened to have the gene for resistance have by now spread it by injection and by division among the others. No matter. Your harmless gut bugs compete against the bad bugs that cause intestinal ills, and you should celebrate their health.

Bloat

Even though your normal population of gut bacteria—*E. coli* and some others—rarely makes its presence known by causing illness, it's a noisy lot. Many belly rumbles and most puffs and

Why Once a Day?

Why indeed? There's no particular reason why a person should defecate daily. Some people normally go every other day, or every several days, or even once a week without the hard lumps of constipation. Their bowel just naturally has a laid-back pace. There's nothing wrong with week-old feces—no rot, no poisons, and no unusual germs.

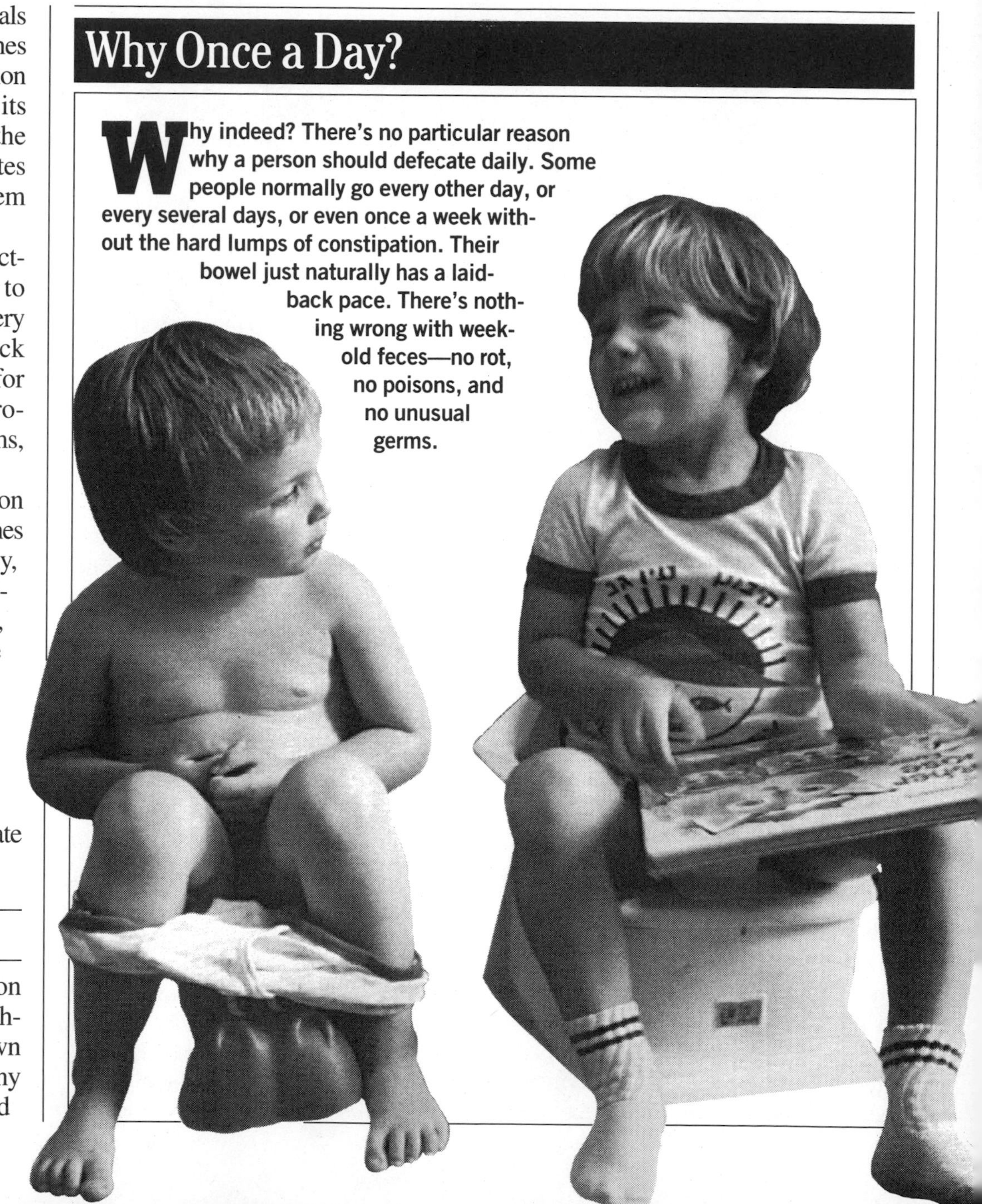

blasts of gas out the anus are vapors bacteria release as waste products of their own dining. The gases include nitrogen, carbon dioxide, methane, hydrogen sulfide, and hydrogen. The last three are flammable. Methane is the gas used in stoves and furnaces. Hydrogen sulfide is the stinky stuff added in small quantities to warn you of gas leaks. Hydrogen is what made the Hindenberg zeppelin blow up.

Sometimes you're so gassy your belly's bloated. And sometimes the bloat's so bad your belly aches. The steady pain of a bellyache is from gas that overfills the gut, and stretches it. One reason for excess gas is excess food—not the food you digest, but the food you don't, like cellulose bean skins and cabbage veins that feast the gas-makers of the gut. Well-fed bacteria not only make more gas: They make more bacteria. Given enough leftovers, the inhabitants of your bowel can double their number several times over in the time it takes to move them and their gas on out.

Hard Lumps, Soft Messes

The bowel doesn't always move the flow along at its usual, lazy rate. Sometimes it contracts violently and the river rushes. Sometimes it slows, and the river stills. When it speeds up, bowel cells haven't time enough to absorb the usual amount of water. Then feces are runny; you have diarrhea. When it slows, bowel cells have time to absorb nearly all the water. Then feces are hard lumps; you're constipated. Both conditions hurt. Diarrhea cramps are from gas pressed hard against the bowel by strong contractions. Constipation ache is pressure from accumulating feces as well as gas.

The bowel's speed is controlled by nerves within its walls that receive messages from gut cells. If these nerves detect injury within the tube, they speed its movements. That way whatever's causing damage is rushed out fast. It could be gritty sand a toddler's eaten, or scratchy bran a person's overeaten. It could be any of many "stomach flu" viruses that enter gut cells, multiply inside, and burst them. It could be toxic chemicals from one of the several kinds of bacteria that cause food poisoning. Messages of fear and worry come to the bowel from far and wide—via the bloodstream, and from the brain—and they, too, can make it cramp and dump.

Like the duodenum, the bowel has pressure sensors that measure fullness. A sense of emptiness quite reasonably slows it down—and causes constipation. Fiber—the undigestible cellulose of bran and beans, fruit skins and salad greens—makes feces bulky, and so informs the bowel to keep on truckin'. Without fiber, feces are so pitifully small that the bowel, supposing itself empty, takes a snooze. Of course, too little water also causes constipation: A dried out body makes dry lumps.

Pushin' On Out

During sleep and even during most of the day, the bowel hardly moves at all. Fecal material accumulating like silt may therefore take as long as 24 hours to reach the exit. But as a new meal enters the digestive tract, the bowel tends to wake up. Contractions come faster and stronger, and large sections of the tube may contract simultaneously, pushing feces three-quarters of the entire length of the bowel in seconds. Feces then hit bottom hard, and stretch the last portion, the rectum. The rectum instantly contracts, so does the bowel above it, and rings of muscle around the anus relax. Like it or not, you've got to go.

People usually assist their feces out by pushing. A push out the rear end works the same as a heave out the front end: You take a big breath, and squeeze.

With this last conscious act, you have finally disposed of meals eaten yesterday when, just as consciously, you swallowed them down. Every other act of eating has been done without your knowledge, without you even feeling it, by cells whose needs you must somehow meet by choosing from among the world's enormous delicatessen the particular selection of nutrients they need to keep on living.

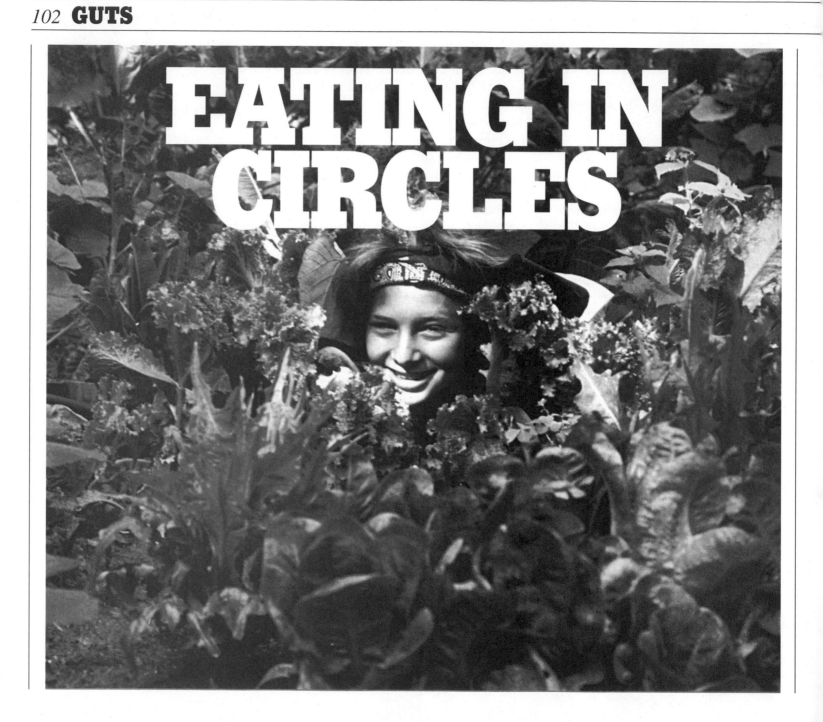

EATING IN
CIRCLES

People are told to eat cereals for energy, meat to build muscles, milk to strengthen bones, and vegetables for any number of specific nutrients that enrich blood, harden teeth, improve eyesight. It's never explained why energetic cows, which have perfectly fine muscles, bones, blood, and eyes, don't have to eat any of those things. Among all the sturdy, healthy animals remarkably few eat what we call a "balanced diet." Some eat only meat, or only grain, or only grass. No matter what they eat, they are all made of the same materials you are made of: The composition of the human body can't be what determines human diet.

Then there are plants. Plants don't eat, yet they contain the vitamins, minerals, oils, carbohydrates, and proteins for which humans eat them. They can provide us with a balanced diet without having a diet of their own.

Plants don't need to eat because they can use air, water, and simple minerals in soil to make their own sugars, their own oils, and all their own amino acids. Animals can't do that; they must eat the basics they can't make. If you need to eat nine kinds of amino acids, but a cow needs to eat none, that is because you can't make those kinds, and cows can. But all we mammals have to eat something. Tracing back that something to its source, it is inevitably plants: We are the eaters; plants are the eaten.

People Versus Peas

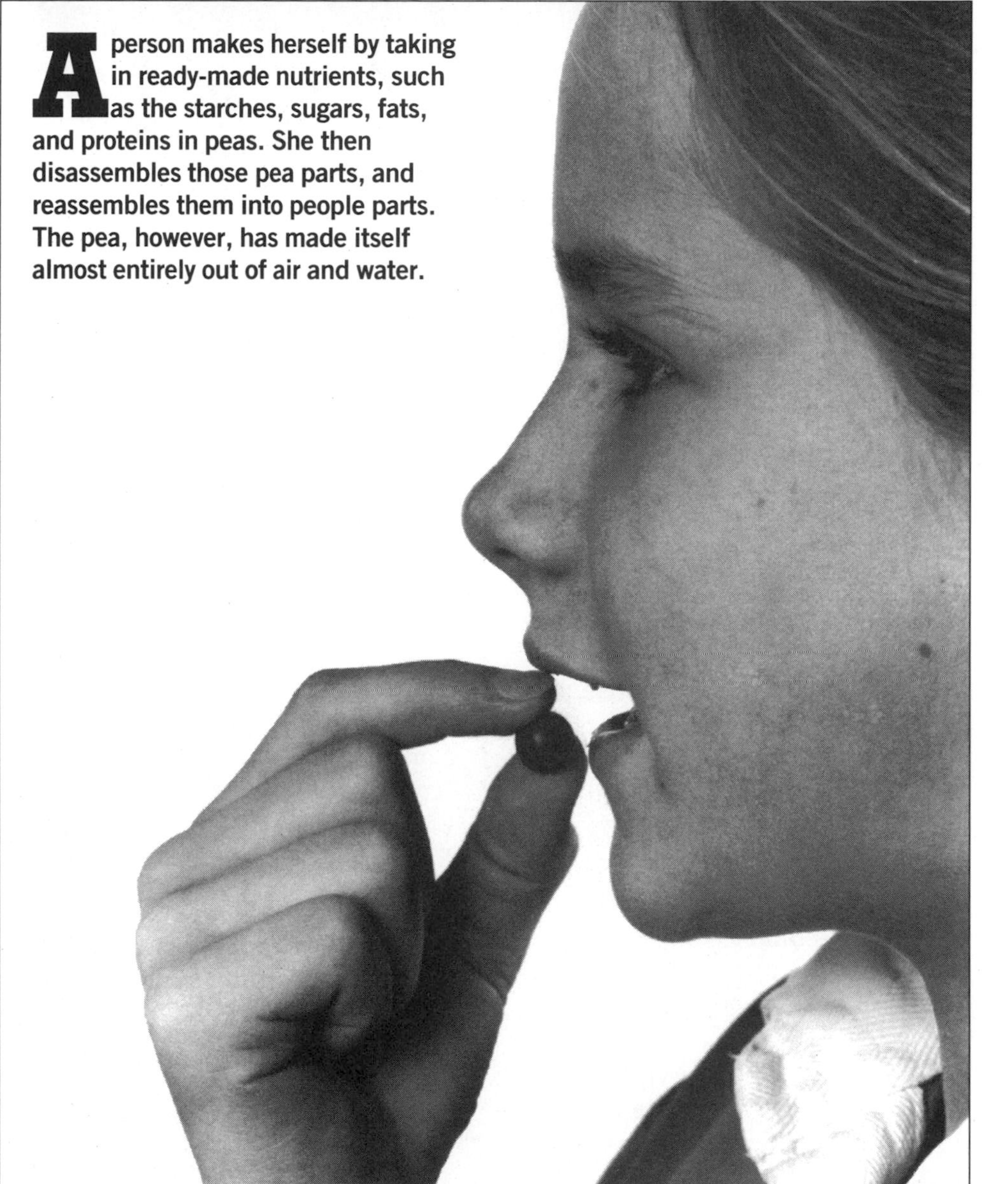

A person makes herself by taking in ready-made nutrients, such as the starches, sugars, fats, and proteins in peas. She then disassembles those pea parts, and reassembles them into people parts. The pea, however, has made itself almost entirely out of air and water.

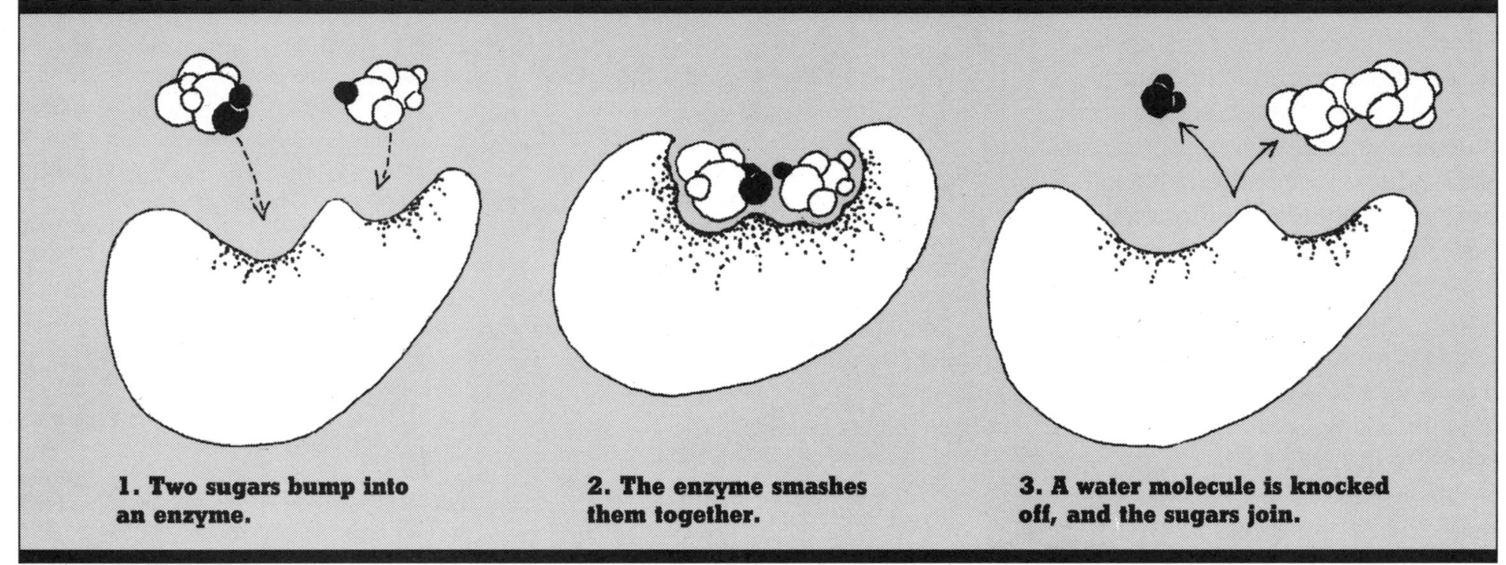
1. Two sugars bump into an enzyme.

2. The enzyme smashes them together.

3. A water molecule is knocked off, and the sugars join.

A Short History of Eating

Which came first, the eaters or the eaten? The answer seems obvious: First life could not have been an eater, for whom would it have eaten? But on second thought, the answer's not so clear. To make from scratch—from atoms of carbon, oxygen, hydrogen, nitrogen, sulfur—all the different building blocks needed to make a body is surely more complicated than to eat them ready-made, and surely first life was too simple to have done it. Scientists suppose that, at first, life was nourished in a chemical environment rich in such basic items as sugars, amino acids, and the molecules from which genes are assembled. So first life was an eater.

That nutritious environment, however, could not have lasted very long. Organic molecules—molecules made mostly by living organisms—self-assemble only rarely outside of bodies. Whatever had accumulated on early Earth before there was life would soon have been eaten up after there was life, and that should have been the end of living. Since, in fact, it wasn't, life must have become able to survive without eating. Let's say sugar became scarce. Then any individual that, by chance, was able to make its own sugar out of air and water would survive. Finally, as all nutrients ran out, those still alive would be those that could use the plentiful materials found in air, water, and soil to make everything they needed. So that was the end of eating.

But not for long. If others are taking the chemical trouble to make everything you need, why bother doing it yourself? It's easier to eat them. That's the way life has been for billions of years now: Plants make everything for themselves, and every other body eats them, or eats their eaters.

The Littlest Construction Sets

The various nutrients that now, some hours after dinner, are finally inside your body, will not stay in their present shapes for long. Well before the next meal, the molecules so painstakingly cut to tidbits in the gut will either be taken apart entirely or rebuilt into other molecules. Those that are rebuilt will not necessarily be rebuilt into molecules resembling the ones they came from. Oils may be incorporated into hormones, not fat. Amino acids may be rebuilt into sugars, not proteins. Sugars may end up as carbon dioxide and water. The body uses the molecules it eats as so many Tinkertoys that can be reduced to sticks and knobs, or assembled into bones, moles, sweat, fat, scabs, or toenails.

Molecules are assembled into new materials by undoing the damage that made them fall apart. A protein taken apart by shoving water between neighboring amino acids can be reassembled by removing intruding water, allowing units to reattach. Long carbohydrates can be built the same way: The ends of two sugars to be joined are brought together; a hydrogen is removed from one and a hydrogen and an oxygen are removed from the other to form a molecule of water. The "dry" ends of the sugars now stick to one another.

Such assembly jobs are done by enzymes. Just as one kind of enzyme can yank a starch into position to receive a molecule of water, another kind of enzyme can jog sugars into position to release a molecule of water. Often a molecule is entirely rebuilt: Portions of it are removed and replaced with different parts. Then disassembling enzymes are also needed. Disassemblers are just as common as assemblers inside the body, and between them they shove water in and out of joints to ply their tinkerer's trade.

Enzymes, however, are precision tools. Each is shaped for a specific job, and a whole set is needed to complete each kind of product. That you build animal starch, not plant starch, or human flesh, not hamburger meat, is because your enzyme tool set is different from that of a plant or a cow. In fact, the very reason you were born a baby instead of a potato or a calf was because your uniquely human enzymes controlled the chemistry by which your body took shape. The vast majority of genes are instructions for enzymes: Enzymes, in turn, are responsible for assembling the rest of you—using, of course, the Tinkertoys in digested food. A fundamental difference between you and a tree is that a tree has enzymes for manufacturing itself out of almost nothing but thin air.

Trees From Thin Air

Most people assume that most of the substance of plants comes from the soil they grow in. That makes sense: Soil has substance, but water has little to it, and air has less. But more than two centuries ago a curious doctor wondered if that assumption was right. He planted a willow branch in a pot containing 200 pounds of soil which he had carefully dried before weighing it. The 5-pound willow branch had grown into a 169-pound tree after five years, yet when the doctor uprooted it and again dried and weighed the pot of soil, the dirt was only 2 ounces lighter than it had been before. He concluded that the tree's bulk had come from atoms in the water he had given it over the years.

As it happens, he was wrong. Of the three possible sources for a plant's substance, a tree is almost entirely made from the atoms in air. The weight of even an immense oak tree is mostly carbohydrate (and products made from it). Carbohydrate, in turn, is made from the sugar unit called glucose. Each molecule of glucose is composed of 12 hydrogen atoms, and a half dozen each of oxygen and carbon. The carbon and oxygen, both heavier than hydrogen, come from carbon dioxide gas in the atmosphere, and this accounts for 93 percent of a tree's weight. Its hydrogen, the lightest element of all, comes from water. That accounts for nearly all the remaining 7 percent of a plant's weight, leaving the contribution of soil measured in fractions of percentages, or, in the case of the doctor's willow tree, 7/10,000 of the plant's weight.

Making It With Minerals

The materials from which a plant makes itself are very simple. Carbon

Milk Haters

Milk contains its own sort of sugar, lactose, for which mammals make a special digestive enzyme, lactase. Or at least they do while they are milk-drinking infants—adult mammals normally lose the ability to make lactase. Some humans, however, are abnormal: Peoples from northern, milk-drinking cultures evolved the ability to make lactase even as adults, and so can drink milk all their lives. Others are not so lucky. Where milk soured quickly, it never became part of the human diet, and those whose ancestors lived in tropical climates are more normal mammals who make the enzyme for a few years only. After that time, drinking milk bloats them, nauseates them, or gives them diarrhea. Milk sugar is not directly to blame. *E. coli* and other intestinal bacteria gorge on the undigested lactose; their acid wastes irritate the gut and their gassy wastes bloat it. That's a pretty good reason to hate milk.

Children, however, need twice as much calcium to supply their growing bones than adults need, and milk is our best calcium source. What to do?

Eat milk products like yogurt and cheeses whose lactose has been predigested by bacteria. There is also now low-lactose milk, and lactase enzyme in tablet form.

Cats, like some people, can digest milk as adults.

dioxide and water are both molecules of only three atoms apiece. Soil minerals are typically just single atoms, such as calcium or chlorine. By comparison even glucose contains 24 atoms. Protein molecules may contain hundreds of thousands of atoms, and a chromosome—a strand of genes—is a giant molecule containing as many as 50 billion atoms.

To assemble tiny parts into such immense constructions requires many steps. There are, for instance, 13 steps in the assembly of glucose from carbon dioxide and water. Each step requires a separate enzyme to either pry atoms apart or hold them together while they attach. The total number of enzymes needed to build a plant from scratch is enormous, and each one must be coded for by a separate gene. Given the numbers, the feat of self-assembly seems impossible, yet the bulk of living stuff on this planet is plants. With air, water, and soil minerals alone, plants grow as big as redwoods, as numerous as weeds. They are able to make the most various and complicated products that exist in any form of life: lemon juice and lemon oil; linen and wax; peach fuzz, cactus spines, nutshells, tree bark, corn husks, and hemp twine; caffeine, cola, aspirin, cocaine; and herbicides, insecticides, vitamins, and the colors of every flower, and their perfumes, and the flavors of cinnamon, vanilla, pepper, and sage. All these materials are made of a short list of simple substances, only 16 in all.

As mammals, we can't begin to match this chemical virtuosity; we are, by comparison with plants, enzyme-deficient.

A Very Long List

The billion-year history of nutritional evolution in animals is one of increasing enzyme deficiencies. Our ancestors made vitamin C from glucose using an enzyme whose gene, 25 million years ago, went kaput. Since those ancestors got vitamin C from plants anyway, it was goodbye and good riddance to the tedious process of manufacturing it. Whereas plants can make all the amino acids they need for protein construction, our evolution has dropped so many enzymes from our repertoire that we must eat nearly half the 22 amino acids we need. That's the catch to enzyme streamlining: The more deficient an animal's manufacturing skills, the greater its dependence on diet.

Our menu is nearly three times longer than the 16 items plants require. Among the essentials are seven major minerals (and as many as a dozen others needed in trace amounts), 13 vitamins, and a handful of fatty acids (the units fats are made of). Of the 22 amino acids from which we build our proteins, we must eat nine. Altogether, nutritionists know of 45 different nutrients that we absolutely have to eat to stay healthy.

Major minerals are the easiest nutrients to come by even though we can't, like plants, go to their source in soil. Sodium and chlorine come to us as salt. Potassium, magnesium, and phosphorus are incorporated into the molecules of so many kinds of foods that you'd have to go to all sorts of trouble to *not* get them. Sulfur automatically arrives attached to many animal proteins, and some plant proteins, too. Calcium can be a problem for people who don't drink milk or eat cheese, but there's plenty of it in dried peas and beans, in oranges, and—if you eat the bones—in sardines.

As for trace minerals, which include such oddities as selenium, molybdenum, chromium, and cobalt, the only one that Americans frequently run short of is iron. The problem is not that iron isn't plentiful in ordinary foods; it's that our gut cells don't consume very much of it, especially from vegetables. As little as 2 percent of the iron in vegetables—even spinach, which is famous for it—actually gets into you. You absorb nearly 20 percent of the iron in meat. In some parts of the country, soil is deficient in iodine, and therefore so are the plants that grow there, and the herds that eat the plants. That's the reason for iodized salt, although only people who eat food grown in iodine-deficient places really need it. Fluorine,

None of This Is Necessary

All young children—and all too many adults—think that vitamins and minerals make them stronger, more vigorous, healthier. Vitamins and minerals can't *add* anything to muscles, energy, disease resistance, or growth rate. The vitamin A in carrots doesn't make you see better; the calcium in milk doesn't make your bones stronger; the iron in spinach doesn't give you extra get-up-and-go. These substances can only restore normal health to those whose health has been damaged by lack of them. There is therefore no reason to pop "health" pills unless a doctor has diagnosed an actual deficiency, or thinks you'll get one because you eat an awful diet. The bigger worry than deficiency is overdose. The toxic dose of chromium, for example, is only a couple of times the amount you normally get in food. Because such dangerous substances are nevertheless nutrients, they are officially "food" by law. No prescription is needed for people to foolishly poison themselves with pills.

which hardens tooth enamel, these days arrives in fluoridated water, toothpaste, and mouthwash, and vitamin pills.

The need for vitamins in the human diet is truly humbling: They are enzyme parts that we have lost the ability to manufacture. Vitamin C is part of an enzyme needed to manufacture collagen. Therefore a deficiency of vitamin C, the disease called scurvy, weakens such tissues as skin and blood vessels. An early sign is mushy, bleeding gums. Lack of vitamin K causes bleeding for a different reason: It is needed in the manufacture of a blood clotting protein. The B vitamins play various roles in energy exchanges when, for example, sugar or fat is used to power muscles. Red blood cells can't be made without vitamin B_{12}, and another B vitamin assists in assembling materials needed to duplicate chromosomes when cells divide.

These jobs that involve vitamins are so fundamental to the workings of all the organs, or even to all the cells of the body, that vitamin deficiencies often cause a bewildering array of symptoms. Vitamin A deficiency retards growth, hardens skin inside and out, and causes blindness. Too little vitamin B_1 (thiamine) results in a disease called beriberi in which the person weakens, becomes confused, paralyzed, and finally dies of heart failure.

Yet for all this, too much is made of vitamins. They are needed in only minute amounts because each molecule of a vitamin is used over and over again, billions of times a day. They aren't needed in the diet on a daily basis because they are small, simple, strong molecules that last a long time. And vitamins are so common in ordinary food that unless your diet is mighty peculiar it's hard to run short of them.

Some vitamins have to be eaten only under abnormal circumstances. You don't need to eat vitamin K. It is made by bacteria living in your bowel, and cells there absorb enough of it to supply the body. Bowel bacteria also make vitamin E, vitamin B_{12}, and several others in sufficient quantity that you can go without eating them for quite a while. Vitamin D is added to milk and other foods only as insurance: Most people get enough sunlight to prevent the softened bones of rickets.

Vitamin D has been given the healthy name "sunshine vitamin." Don't let names fool you. However necessary vitamins are in small doses, they can be toxic in large doses, and none more darkly than the sunshine vitamin. Megadosing on vitamin D can slow growth, damage the liver, inflame joints, make hair fall out, and cause mental retardation.

The Trouble With Vegetables

If plants are wonder-bodies able to synthesize every nutrient animals need, why aren't all animals vegetarians? The work of rearing or snaring—and the cruelty of killing—creatures as warm and lively as ourselves seems unnecessary when unmoving, unfeeling vegetables are there for the plucking.

Strict vegetarian diets made up of only beans, greens, grains, fruits, and nuts are possible for humans, but our particular deficiencies make them difficult. Although plants contain protein in ample quantities, each kind of plant has too little or none of one or more of the amino acids

Minimum Daily Allowance

This is an example of the minimum daily allowance of vegetables needed to nourish a 140-pound male adolescent vegetarian if he eats no milk products, and no eggs.

humans need. We can't store amino acids: All those we can't make for ourselves have to be on hand while a cell is building proteins. If any one is missing, the protein can't be built, and the other amino acids that would have been used in that construction project are wasted. Corn lacks two needed amino acids; beans lack a different pair; wheat is very low in one amino acid, and leafy greens have none of still another. It doesn't help to eat salad one meal and beans the next because by the time the beans deliver the amino acid the salad lacked, the amino acid the salad offered isn't around anymore. To feed cells all their Tinkertoys simultaneously, you have to eat them simultaneously—wheat or rice or corn with peas or beans, for instance. The mix also has to be in the right proportion, because if any one amino acid is used up before the others, construction comes to a halt and, again, the rest are wasted.

Another problem with strict vegetarian diets is bulk. Whereas an egg has all nine essential amino acids, you have to eat two kinds of vegetables to get the full number. The servings might have to be pretty big, too, because so much of vegetables is undigestible cellulose. A typical balanced vegetarian meal is a cupful of brown rice with beans, a big baked potato with margarine, a full cup of vegetables as well as a salad, and, for dessert, a banana, an apple, and an orange, plus a handful of nuts and

The Little Worm

Just where the small intestine opens into the bowel is a worm-sized, worm-shaped pouch called the appendix. Our appendix is all that remains of a storage pouch where helpful bacteria once digested for our ancestors the otherwise undigestible fibers of a leafy diet. Unhappily, bacteria still live there, occasionally causing the infection called appendicitis.

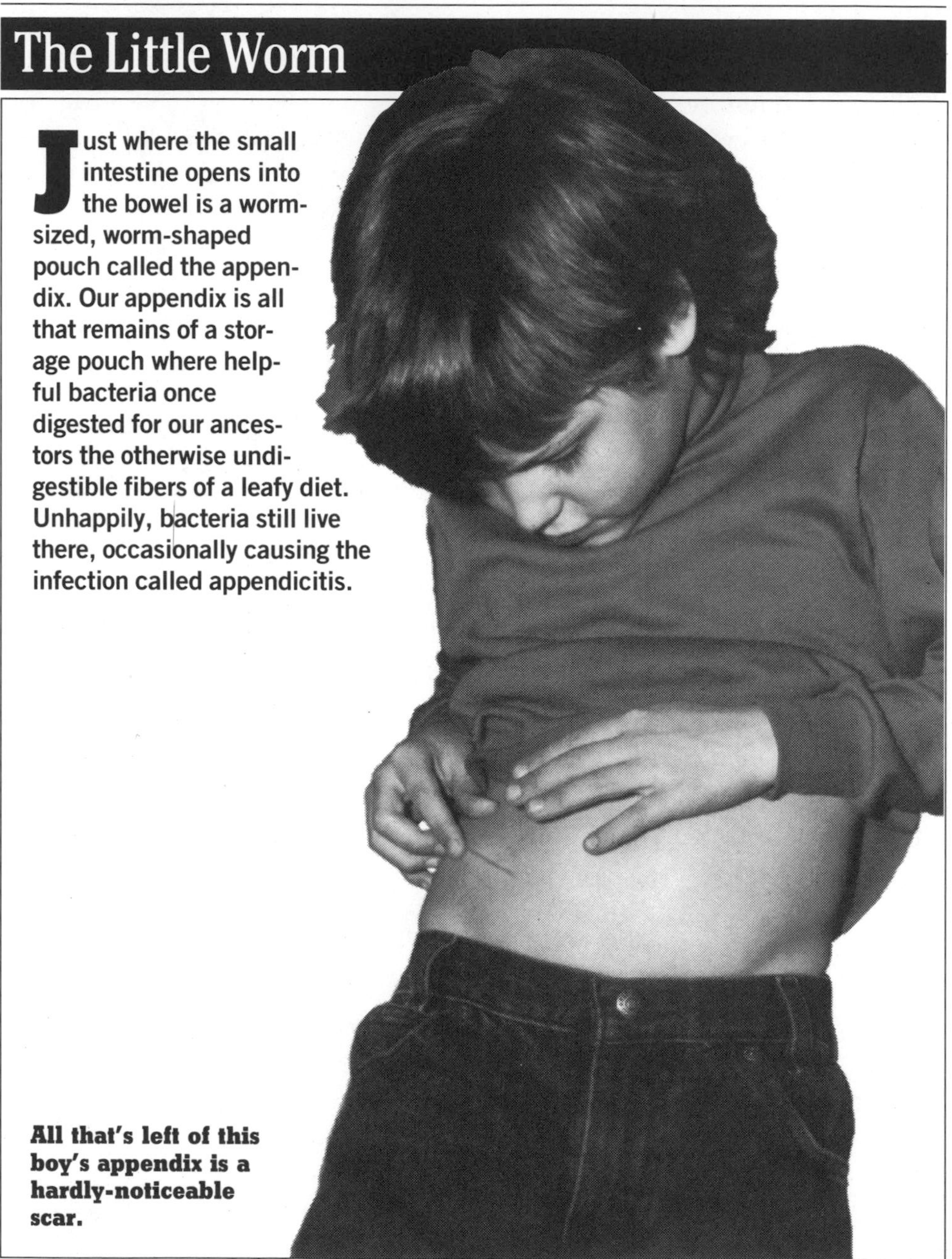

All that's left of this boy's appendix is a hardly-noticeable scar.

raisins. Talk about stuffing!

And that meal adds up to only 900 calories. A 15-year-old boy needs about 20 calories a day for each pound of body weight. If he weighs 140 pounds, he has to tuck into a meal that size for breakfast, lunch, and supper. Children raised on strict vegetarian diets are often undersized for their age. They just can't eat enough to grow.

Adding eggs and dairy products to an otherwise vegetarian diet simplifies matters. A boiled egg or a chunk of cheese contains all the essential amino acids in much less bulk than a head of cabbage or a heap of beans. Easiest of all is to eat everything, just as humans always have.

What You Eat When You Eat a Cow

Meat, whether it is from a chicken, a carp, or a cow, has every one of the amino acids people need. Yet chickens eat grain, carp eat pond weeds, and cows eat nothing but grass. Part of the explanation for how a vegetarian animal can supply amino acids that vegetables don't have lies in their enzymes. Chickens and carp are not so degenerate as we are; they make more of their amino acids for themselves. Cows are a different story. They depend on ancient do-it-yourselfers to manufacture for them.

Eight Hundred Square Meters of Clay

Water, along with dissolved minerals, clings to clay by electric charges. The more surface there is to cling to, the more water can be held. Clay particles are so small that if you measured the surface of all the particles in this gram of it, the total surface area would be 800 square meters, the size of a basketball court.

A large particle has a small surface area...

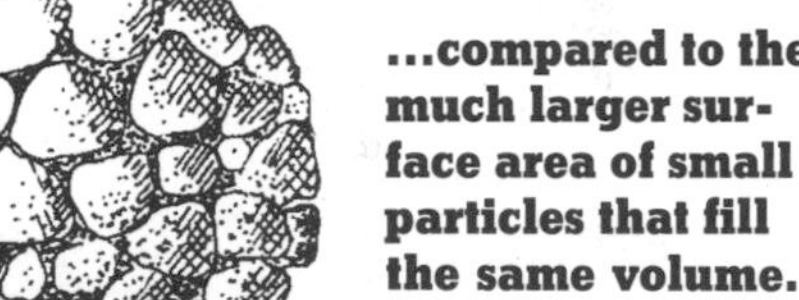

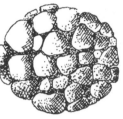

...compared to the much larger surface area of small particles that fill the same volume.

Cows need no amino acids at all. Of all the vitamins we eat, cows need only two, and those in nearly undetectable amounts. Cows eat grass, which is mostly cellulose, but that is not what a cow digests and, in a way, grass is not really a cow's diet.

No animal has ever evolved the enzymes that take cellulose apart. Only bacteria can do that. Cows grow cellulose-digesting bacteria in a huge chamber near the front end of their digestive system. There countless bacteria digest the grass swallowed down to them, and convert it into various nutrients, some of which are their bodies, and some of which are their wastes. When the job is done, the refuse of this microbial feast, including bacteria and bacterial wastes, passes along the length of the cow's absorbing intestine. A cow's diet, strictly speaking, is bacteria and bacterial waste products. The bacteria's diet is grass.

The fact that beefsteak and cream cheese are made of bacteria, and that bacteria are made of grass, and that grass is made of air, water, and dirt, gives pause for thought. The nutrients in meat you eat are at least third-hand by the time you use them, and you wouldn't have their use at all without the plants that made them in the first place. But it doesn't all stop there: What you are made of is very likely to reappear someday on someone else's plate.

R.I.P.

Sad as it is to bury a dead animal, burial is necessary to restore its nutrients to the soil, from which they will be absorbed by plants and made available again to animals.

Back to the Soil

Think, for a moment, about soil minerals, those itty bitty portions of plant bodies from which comes the iron of red blood and the calcium of strong bones. Such minerals come originally from rock, the crust continents are made of. Rain falling over the surface gradually dissolves iron and calcium from sand and stone, and makes them available for plant roots to absorb. But what is dissolved in water flows with water, and minerals freed from rock flow toward the oceans as fast as rain falls and rivers run. Life's nutrition depends on trapping them before they flow away.

None are trapped deep where bedrock has eroded to a soil coarse with stones and grit. A small reservoir of minerals is trapped near the surface, where grit is mixed with velvety clay to which water clings. But now come the grass roots, poking among clay particles, tapping the reservoir, soaking up its store of mineral water. The trouble is that grass roots in a meadow soak up minerals faster than minerals dissolve from rock. Although rock continents are what iron and calcium come from, they don't come fast enough to feed a field of grass, much less your blood and bones.

For a field of grass to get enough to live on, it must retrieve what has been lived on before. It must gather up nutrients from lives finished, from fallen sparrows, drifting leaves, the corpses of bacteria, and its own discarded straw. The mineral reservoir in soil is nothing, really, but a recycling center. The real reservoir, so vast that it is awesome to contemplate, is all the living bodies on the earth. More awesome still is that the entire stockpile of minerals now safely banked in bodies is what has been mined, bit by bit, by plants over their whole history of life.

With the Help of Microbes

If plants are able to soak up continents as they dissolve and, by being eaten, invest them in the living world's total stock of minerals, they are helpless to turn their eaters' dead bodies back into the minerals from which they came. Plants, noneaters all, digest no foods. Even the powerful digestive enzymes in an animal's gut can't disassemble organic molecules into their mineral ingredients. Certainly no body falls to pieces by itself.

The disassembly of previous lives back to mineral currency is done by soil organisms, digesters of wastes and corpses. The top foot of a one-acre field may contain more than three tons of bacteria, fungi, protozoa, algae, worms, and insects, all of which have some part in unlocking from organic refuse the elements of which new lives are made.

An earthworm eats dirt at its front end, digests organic material in it, and excretes it out the other end, freeing in the process 5 times more nitrogen, 7 times more phosphorus, and 11 times more potassium than had been available before. Those are the three ingredients of fertilizer, what people call plant "food."

That's just the beginning. Five billion bacteria and 21 million other microorganisms inhabit a single teaspoon of garden soil. They are like teams of digestive enzymes that patiently, one after another, unknot and chop a protein up. Leftovers in the earthworm's droppings are reprocessed by another creature, then by another, and another, until all is minerals. A meadow is one huge digestive system.

Among the countless soil microbes are bacteria that are responsible for all the nitrogen in every protein in every organism in the world. Nitrogen is among the most plentiful elements on earth—the atmosphere above an acre of land contains 75 million pounds of it—but atmospheric nitrogen isn't usable to plants. The gas molecule is a pair of atoms that can be pried apart only by certain bacteria that, in the course of running their own lives, make nitrogen available for ours. Other nitrogen-providers retrieve used nitrogen from amino acids, recombine it with hydrogen or oxygen in forms that roots can absorb, and dish it up to plants, which recombine it with sugar to make amino acids and dish it up to you, who take it apart again and, one way or another, dish it up to bacteria.

So who feeds whom?

We all, living and dead, feed one another. What's entering your body now has been in bodies before—not just in a potato, but in birds and fleas and germs and salamanders, and not just recently, but once upon a time when your rust-red iron colored the blood of a dinosaur, or way back on some sunshiny day, when, just then dissolved, the iron first entered into the life of an alga sprawled upon an ancient rock.

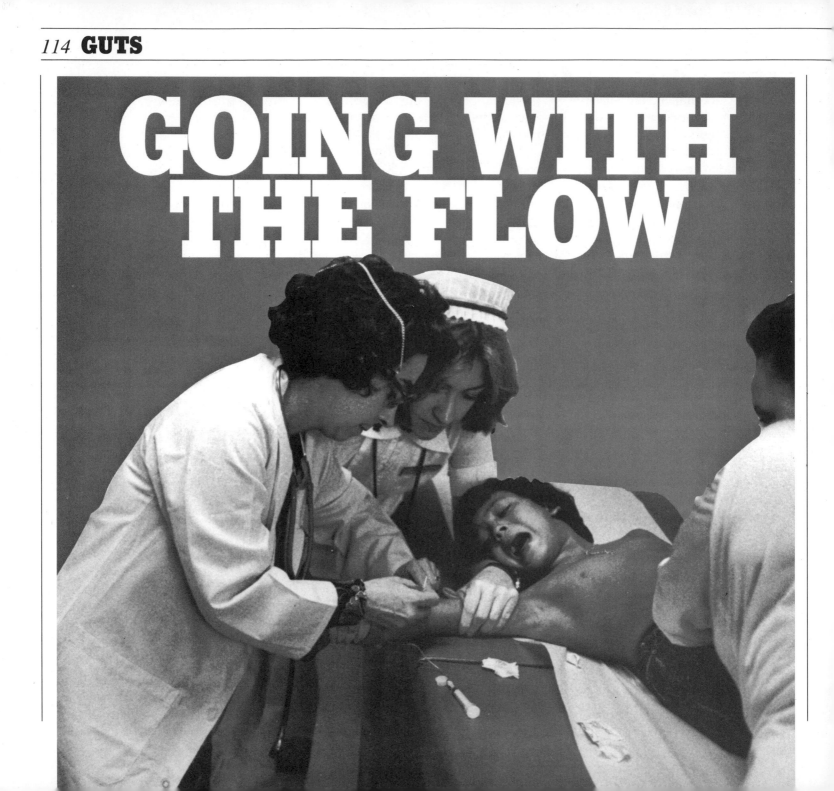

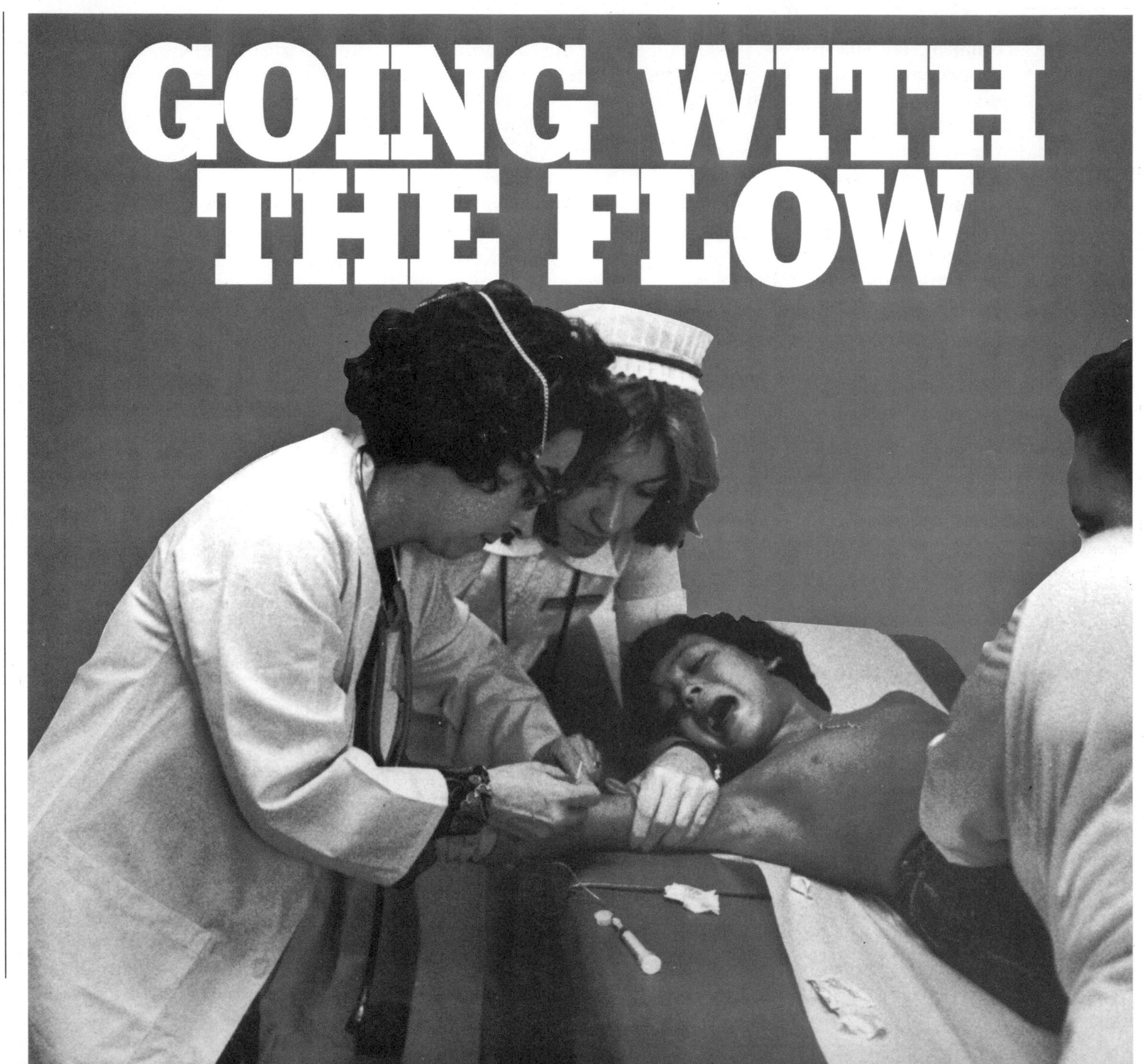
GOING WITH THE FLOW

There is direction in this flow of nutrients from soil through grass, bacteria, cows, and us. This is very strange when you stop to think about it. Why should iron choose to move into a root instead of sticking with a particle of clay? Why should a cellulose molecule climb through a bacterium if it could just as well go past it and out the cow's back door? How come nearly everything you eat—countless molecules in rapid transit through the hollow of your gut—goes into you?

It is no more obvious what pushes food molecules out of a gut cell again, much less out of the end opposite to where the food entered. And once out into the connective tissue of the gut, floating in body fluid among webs of collagen, there seems to be no particular reason why a glucose or an amino acid should promptly do what it does next: make its way into the nearest blood vessel.

At human scale, of course, the distance isn't very far. The interior of the small intestine is so stuffed with blood vessels that even to the microscope's eye every lining cell seems almost to touch one. But at the scale of molecules the distance to be traveled from the hollow of the gut to the closest vessel within it is a mind-boggling trip, equivalent, at our size, to a 400-mile run. The way materials are guided to their distant destinations depends on the fact that molecules really take no particular direction at all.

Going Places Randomly

Food molecules move from gut to blood entirely under their own steam. Their speed depends on their weight: The 1,500-mile-per-hour dashes of a water molecule at body temperature are over three times faster than a jet plane; glucose moves at the less breakneck speed of 500 miles per hour. Molecular motion, however, is random, an expression of how hot the molecule is, not of an intention to get anywhere. Molecules in a liquid are close enough together so that none can go far without colliding with another. At each collision, they ricochet off one another like marbles, abruptly changing direction. The course of any one particular molecule is therefore a random zig-zag as it ricochets from collision to collision millions of times a second.

The more crowded molecules are, the more often they collide. That tends to spread them out from one another. If there is a bunched-up group among more spread-out molecules, they naturally bump themselves about until they are as spread out as all the others. By then they are thoroughly mixed up with the others, too. Nor can they bunch up again: Every collision bounces them away from one another.

This molecular behavior is no mystery. It's the way pool balls behave on pool tables, or marbles in a box. But it has been given the solemn name "diffusion." As molecules diffuse, they move from areas where they are most concentrated to areas where they are least concentrated until their concen-

Think Small

How big is small when one considers a meal reduced to molecules? Measuring objects as tiny as atoms and molecules in inches or centimeters would involve ridiculous fractions. Hydrogen, for instance, has a diameter of .000000004 inch. These small objects are therefore measured in small units called millimicrons. One millimicron is one billionth of a meter. A hydrogen atom is .1 millimicron wide; a water molecule is about .3 millimicron wide. The distance a water molecule has to travel through a cell's membrane to reach the interior of the cell is about 7.5 millimicrons, or 25 times its own length. An average human cell measures 10,000 millimicrons in diameter, or about 33,000 water molecules wide. The distance between a gut cell and the nearest blood vessel is another 20 millimicrons, or about 66 water molecules away.

tration is everywhere the same. No individual molecule takes any specific route in order to get out of a bunch and into the open. It's just that as it dashes in its random way, most hits will bounce it out of bunches.

Food molecules moving in and out of cells have to go through various holes in the cell membrane, but that doesn't change the way they behave. If glucose molecules, for instance, are more crowded outside a cell than in it, more of them will be bounced into the holes than out of them. Again, no molecule knows where it is going: At any moment some sugars are bouncing in and others are bouncing out. But on the average, more enter than leave until they are all equally spread, and there is no bunchiness to either side of the cell membrane.

You can now imagine one way in which diffusion could be used to get molecules flowing in a particular direction in spite of their random ways. If you could remove molecules as they enter a cell—thin them out, so to speak—the more bunched up ones outside would have to keep bumbling on in.

This method of directing the flow of molecules is called a concentration gradient, and it is how the body contrives to move a meal along. Between meals, gut cells (and other cells too) use up most of their stock of nutrients: Their food molecules are thinned out. After a meal, the fluid in the gut is filled with nutrients, which naturally move from stream to cell. Then the gut cell is crowded with nutrients compared to the body fluid in the dermis beyond, so food molecules move on out. Then the body fluid is more concentrated in nutrients than the blood, which arrives emptied of goodies delivered elsewhere in the body. So nutrients now bounce into blood vessels, and flow away. The entire space between the coursing river of a meal and the trickling stream of a blood vessel is one long concentration gradient along which food just naturally moves inward into you.

Rapid Transit

Theoretically, food could move by diffusion alone throughout your body until such incoming items as sugar were distributed evenly everywhere. The trouble is that by the time that happened, you would have died of starvation. In spite of the reckless speed with which glucose molecules ricochet around, diffusion is too slow for the speed of life. It takes 3.5 seconds to equalize the concentration of glucose over just the distance of a cell. At this rate it would take a dozen years for glucose to diffuse across four inches, perhaps a century and a half to make it from the belly to the toes. Diffusion is fine for moving molecules around inside a cell, and for a distance of a couple of cells beyond it. But there is no way any of the molecules more distant cells need could diffuse to them fast enough to keep them alive.

The materials cells need are delivered instead by the much faster method of pumping them through the circulatory system.

The circulatory system is often misunderstood because it is impossible to draw it. Pictures show blood vessels called arteries, which carry blood away from the heart along branching routes to everywhere in the body, and blood vessels called veins, which return blood to the heart along similar routes. But pictures show no connections between the branch tips of arteries and the branch tips of veins, so that blood would seem to exit from the system at the end of an artery in the thumb, for example, and there, in the flesh, find its own way back into a vein. Experience also gives the impression that blood somehow sloshes about among the body's cells. Wherever one is cut, one bleeds.

In fact, blood vessels branch so many times and into such increasingly narrow vessels that no artist could draw the circulatory system in its real complexity. And, at the branch tips, arteries and veins are linked by networks of the invisibly small blood vessels called capillaries. There is no opening anywhere from which blood can escape. The circulatory system is entirely closed.

The heart pumps blood round and

Marbles Games

Diffusion is easier to understand if you do it as well as read about it. Jiggle two colors of marbles in an open box. Start with one of the groups of marbles in a bunch. As you jiggle the box to make the marbles collide randomly as molecules do, the bunch will spread out until marbles of that color are evenly distributed among the others.

A "cell membrane"—a partition with marble-sized holes in it—will slow the game, but not change the result. Put all the marbles of one color on one side of the partition, and all the marbles of the other color on the other side of the partition. The marbles will take longer to distribute themselves evenly when you jiggle the partitioned box, but they still obey the law of diffusion: Each color of marble moves from where it is most crowded to where it is least crowded until its "concentration" is everywhere the same.

You can eventually force all the marbles of one color to move from one side of the partition to the other by removing those that get through. This is what happens when a cell, by using up the glucose that gets into it, creates a concentration gradient that keeps the glucose coming.

Marbles have been grouped by color in a box.

The marbles distribute themselves evenly as the box is shaken.

round in this closed system through two great circuits, one from the heart to the lungs and back again, the other to everywhere else in the body and back again. The blood now being loaded with food at capillaries in your gut arrived there through an artery from the heart, and will leave through a vein to the heart. Then it will make a circuit through the lungs, and only upon its second return to the heart will it be pumped out again fully loaded with everything cells need to stay alive.

The Squeezer

The walls of arteries are elastic: At each heartbeat they swell with blood; between beats they shrink back again. This swelling and shrinking is the pulse you feel when you place a finger on the large artery in your wrist.

1. Pictures of the circulatory system are misleading because arteries and veins don't seem to join at their branch tips.
vein carrying blood to heart
artery carrying blood from heart
network of capillaries
vein
2. This blowup shows how circulation actually works: The branch tips of arteries join the branch tips of veins through a network of capillaries.
artery

The force of blood pushing against the elastic walls of arteries is called blood pressure, and blood pressure is what moves blood into capillaries. Although the heart creates the pressure by forcefully squeezing blood into the main artery, pressure is also controlled by arteries themselves. A ring of muscles at each branch tip, just where an artery divides into capillaries, tightens at each pulse of blood. That momentarily increases blood pressure against the bulging artery wall, but decreases the amount of blood that can get through into the capillaries beyond. By

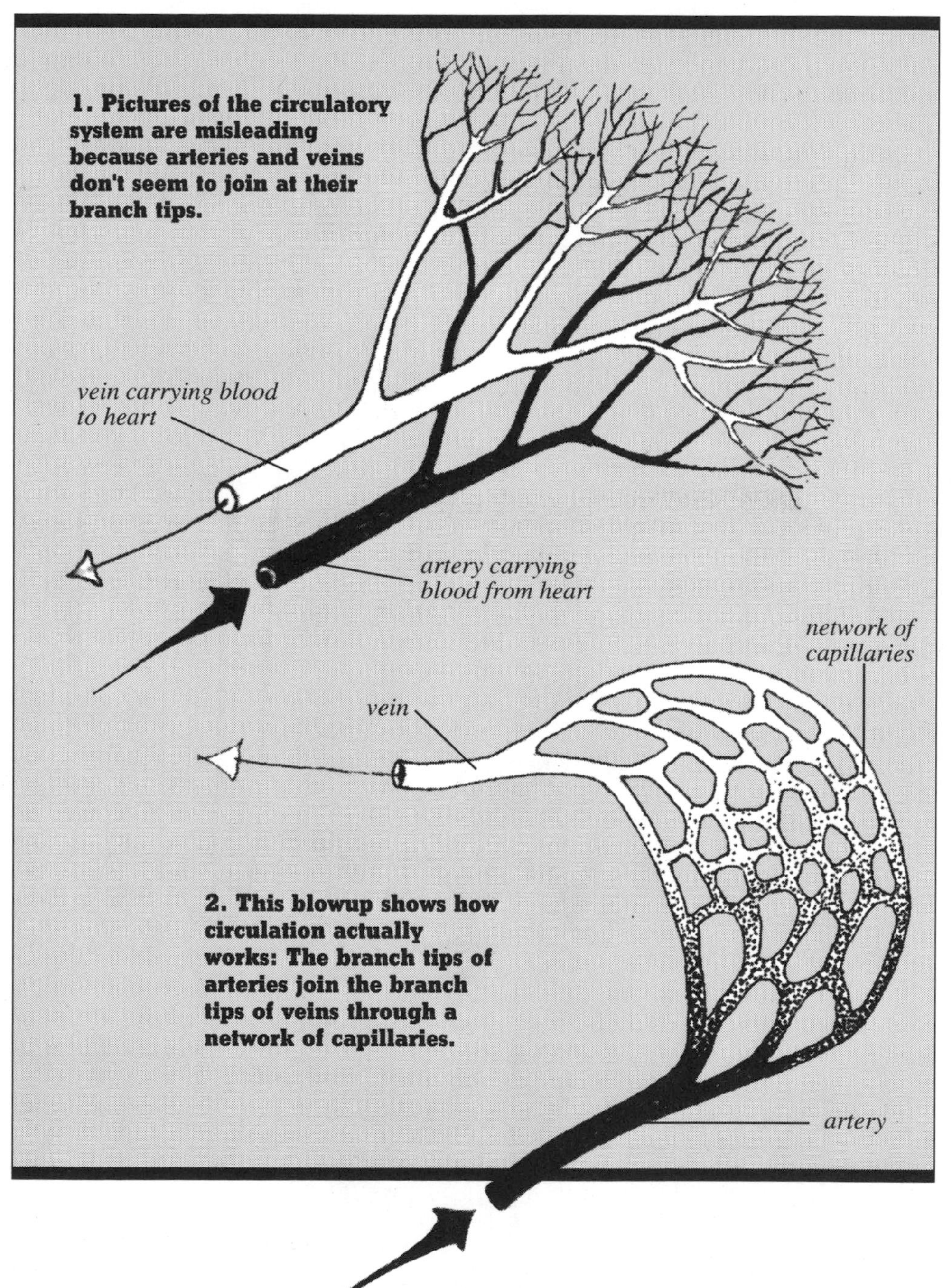

tightening at each beat and relaxing between beats, these muscles keep blood flow even.

"High" blood pressure results from arteries squeezing too tight both during and between beats, cutting off blood supply and forcing the heart to beat harder to make up for it. High blood pressure can damage the heart, arteries, and other organs. That's why doctors measure your pressure. You can wow your doctor by mentioning the tongue-twisting name of the blood pressure measurer—it's called a sphygmomanometer cuff. This is how it works:

The rubber cuff wrapped around your upper arm is inflated until it squeezes with a pressure greater than your own blood pressure. That cuts off all blood supply through the large arteries of your arm.

The doctor or nurse can tell when that has happened by listening with a stethoscope to blood coursing through your arm. When the noise stops, so has the blood.

Then air is let out of the sphygmomanometer cuff until blood flow can be heard again. At that point, air pressure in the cuff is the same as your highest blood pressure—that during a heartbeat.

The cuff is deflated a little more to get the lower reading between beats. Readings are in millimeters of mercury—how high a column of mercury the pressure could support. Adult blood pressure could normally support about 120 millimeters of mercury during a beat and 80 between beats for a blood pressure of 120/80, but at your age your blood pressure is more likely 120/60.

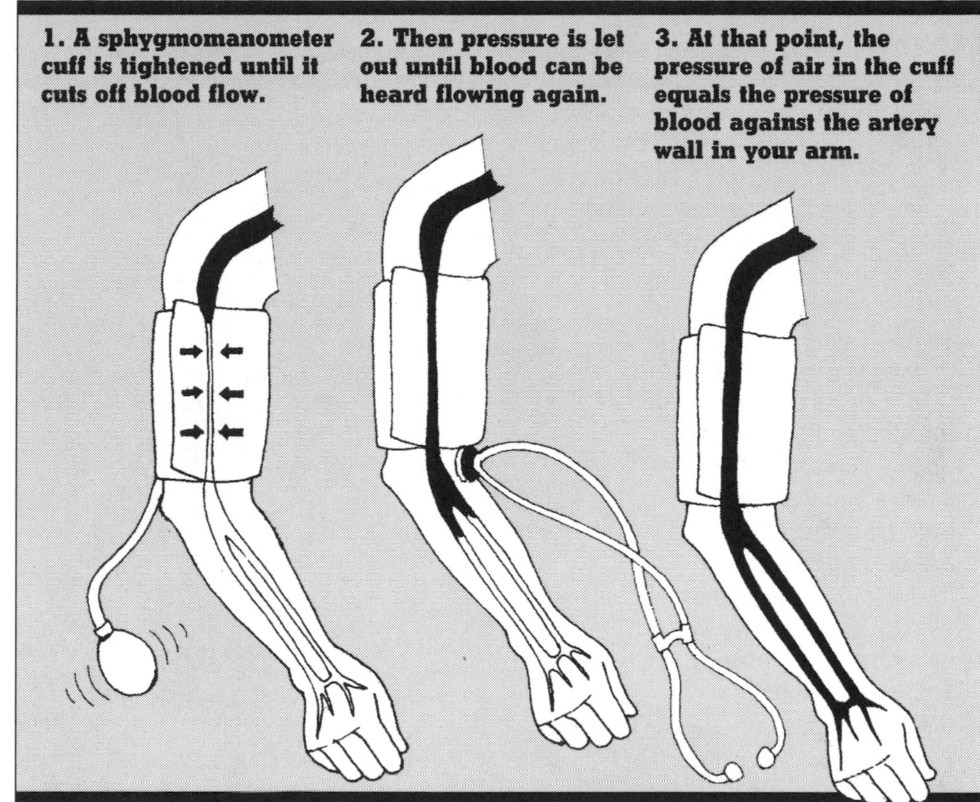

1. A sphygmomanometer cuff is tightened until it cuts off blood flow.
2. Then pressure is let out until blood can be heard flowing again.
3. At that point, the pressure of air in the cuff equals the pressure of blood against the artery wall in your arm.

What's Blood?

Among the nastier things done at medical checkups is the jab for blood to test. Sometimes just a drop is taken from a finger prick. This is smeared onto glass slides to do a "blood count"—a count of the number of blood cells within a small area of the slide. Based on the count, the doctor can tell whether you have the normal number of cells per cubic millimeter of blood.

The normal number is enormous. Each cubic millimeter of blood—one good-sized drop from a finger prick—contains between 5 and 6 million red blood cells. They are the cells that give blood its color, and that carry oxygen.

Pulses

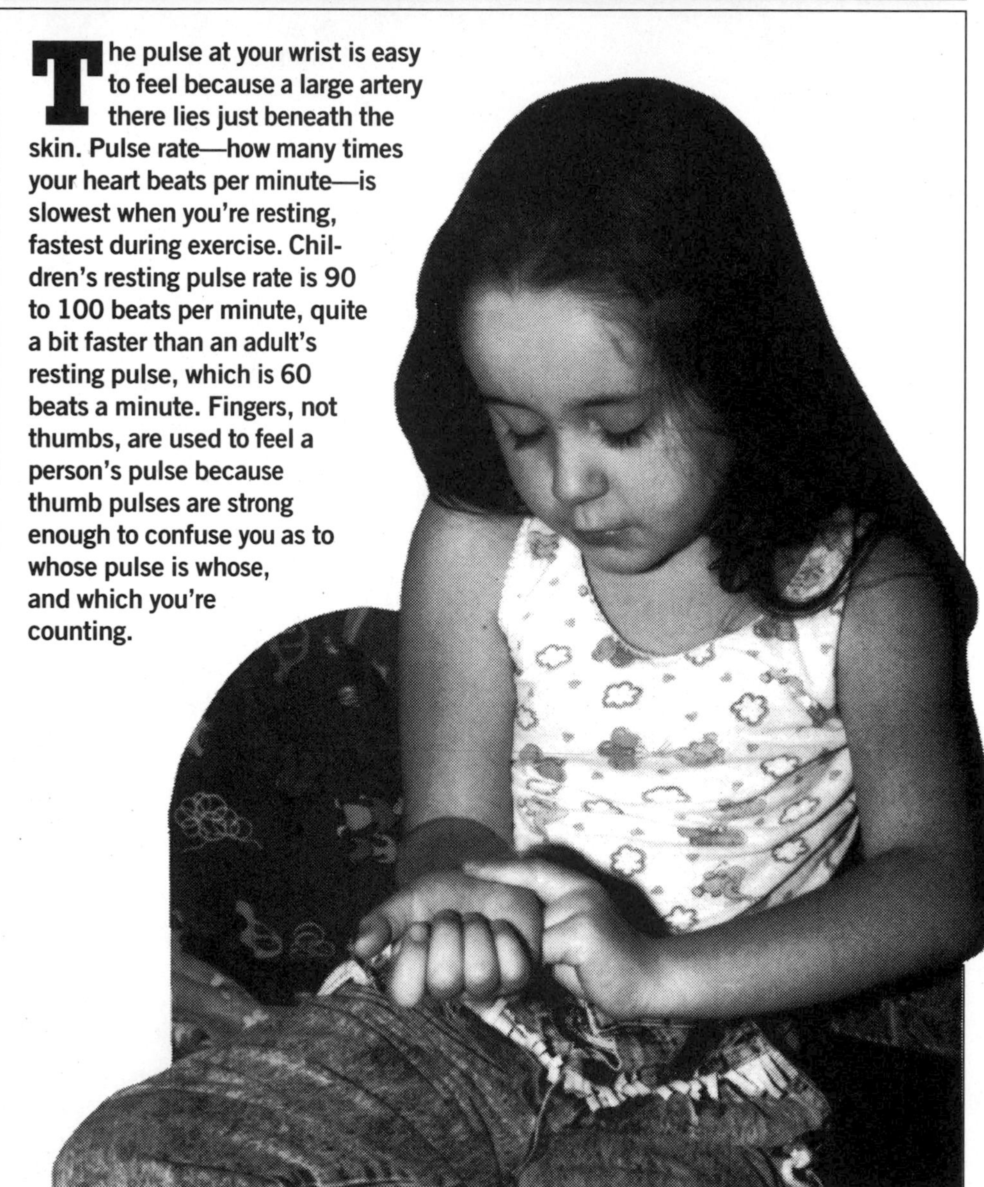

The pulse at your wrist is easy to feel because a large artery there lies just beneath the skin. Pulse rate—how many times your heart beats per minute—is slowest when you're resting, fastest during exercise. Children's resting pulse rate is 90 to 100 beats per minute, quite a bit faster than an adult's resting pulse, which is 60 beats a minute. Fingers, not thumbs, are used to feel a person's pulse because thumb pulses are strong enough to confuse you as to whose pulse is whose, and which you're counting.

The same drop of blood also contains between 5,000 and 10,000 white blood cells of five different kinds. All of them are larger than red cells, some as much as quadruple their size. Some white cells are similar to the chubby, speckled mast cells (the ones named after an old word for pig food because they look so stuffed) that release chemicals at the site of an injury, and that make mosquito bites itch. Other white blood cells are "baby" phagocytes that, when they slip out of blood vessels, grow up to be the garbage and germ eaters of the body. Still others are immune cells whose job is to recognize germs or foreign substances and mark them for disposal. All white blood cells are involved in one way or another with defense against disease.

Besides red and white blood cells, there are up to 400,000 cell fragments, called platelets ("little plates"), per cubic millimeter of blood. Platelets help blood clotting, both by releasing some of the chemicals involved and by stuffing the fiber network of a clot with their own bodies.

All these cells and cell fragments are made by mother cells in bone marrow, the fatty filling in the hollows of your bones. You don't have to worry about those millions of red blood cells lost in the pricking of your finger: Red cell mothers produce about 8 million new red blood cells every second. White cell mothers don't produce that fast, but when you're infected with viruses or bacteria, they divide more quickly. A blood count then will show many more than the usual number of white blood cells. Although platelets aren't whole cells, they have mothers that make them by continually pinching off small pieces of themselves.

And That Ain't All!

Altogether, the solid cells and cell fragments in blood make up less than half the total volume. The rest is a clear liquid called plasma.

Plasma is similar to the body fluid that surrounds cells everywhere in the body, except that it has in it some large proteins that give blood extra volume, and that are used to keep capillaries from collapsing. Besides blood proteins, plasma contains a long list of ingredients that are also found in body fluid: hormones that serve as chemical messengers; antibodies that attach to germs and mark them for destruction; gases such as carbon dioxide and oxygen; minerals like sodium and calcium; all the other nutrients, of course; and water, in which everything else is dissolved.

It is no coincidence that this long list of ingredients is the same as that in body fluid: Blood plasma is what delivers everything everywhere by mixing with the body fluid that surrounds cells. As far as body cells are concerned, plas-

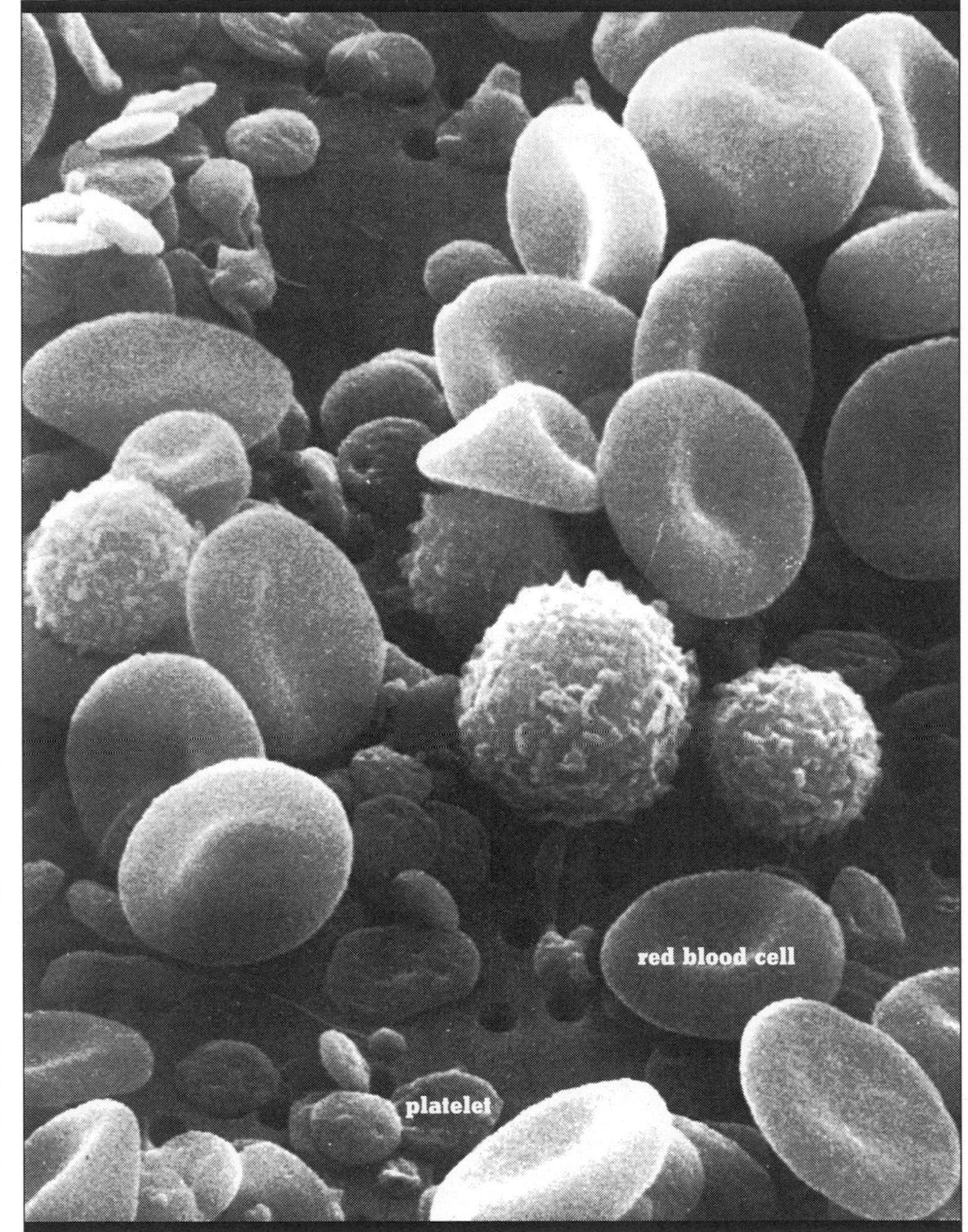

ma, not the solid part of blood, is the juice they need to live on. But how does plasma get out of the closed circulatory system into the wet meshwork of the body?

Leaks in the System

At each trip around, blood leaves the heart through a large artery. The large artery branches into smaller ones, and these in turn branch into still smaller vessels, which branch still again into capillaries. Capillaries are the smallest vessels of all; each is about 1/300 the thickness of a human hair, and only about a millimeter long. At the end of that distance, groups of capillaries rejoin into larger and larger tubes, the veins through which blood flows back to the heart for its next go-around.

Arteries and veins are thick-walled tubes: Not even gases pass through their muscled, fibrous walls. But capillaries are different. Their walls are a single layer of naked cells, not woven with fibers or girdled in muscle. The cells are flat. They curve around and meet one another edge to edge to form the capillary tube. It takes only two wall cells to encircle the interior space, which in some places is so narrow that blood cells must squeeze through in single file.

But the cell edges don't meet exactly. Capillaries have gaps between their cells: They leak.

They don't, however, bleed. Most blood cells and the chunkier proteins are too large to slip through the gaps in capillaries. Only plasma leaks, and only plasma, as it trickles out into the watery jungle that surrounds your cells, feeds them the meal you've eaten.

Every cell has to be extremely close to a capillary if it is to be served a meal. None of the 40 trillion cells in the body is farther than 50 microns (.002 inch) from a capillary, and there are some 10 billion capillaries in the body, or thousands of miles altogether. If you were to cut through a cube of meat measuring only one centimeter on a side, you would slice through 60,000 capillaries, just as you do when you cut your thumb.

Plasma is forced out of each capillary by pressure from the beating heart, although the pressure is just barely enough to do the job. Think of the circulatory system as a river flowing into the branches of a delta. As the number of branches increases, the pressure of water flowing from the river is spread over a greater and greater area, so in any particular rivulet the pressure is less than in the river itself. As arteries branch and rebranch toward capillaries, blood pressure decreases. Pressure at the beginning of a capillary is only just enough to push plasma through the vessel's leaky walls, and then it drops to nearly nothing.

At this point blood is a sluggish stuff, for it has lost a good deal of its watery plasma and is now thick with cells and proteins too large to leak away. There would be no hope of flowing such sludge all the way back to the heart unless the water it lost could be returned to it. Yet there is no tide to force water in again from the surrounding body fluid.

Luckily, there is also nothing to keep water out. Water molecules diffuse back into capillaries until they are as crowded inside as outside, and the vessels are refilled. The amount of water gained at the end of a capillary is about the same as the amount of water pushed out at the beginning, so blood is about as wet when it turns back toward the heart as it was when it left.

No System Is Perfect

This all sounds pretty neat, but it never works out quite right. Some blood proteins do escape from capillaries. Slightly more fluid leaks out than returns. Small as such mistakes might be, they would end in disaster if there weren't a way to correct them. The more proteins escape from capillaries, the more collapsed they become, and the less water can get back in. Little by little blood would thicken, slow down, and stick. Meanwhile excess water accumulating outside of blood vessels would have waterlogged the body to a soggy mush.

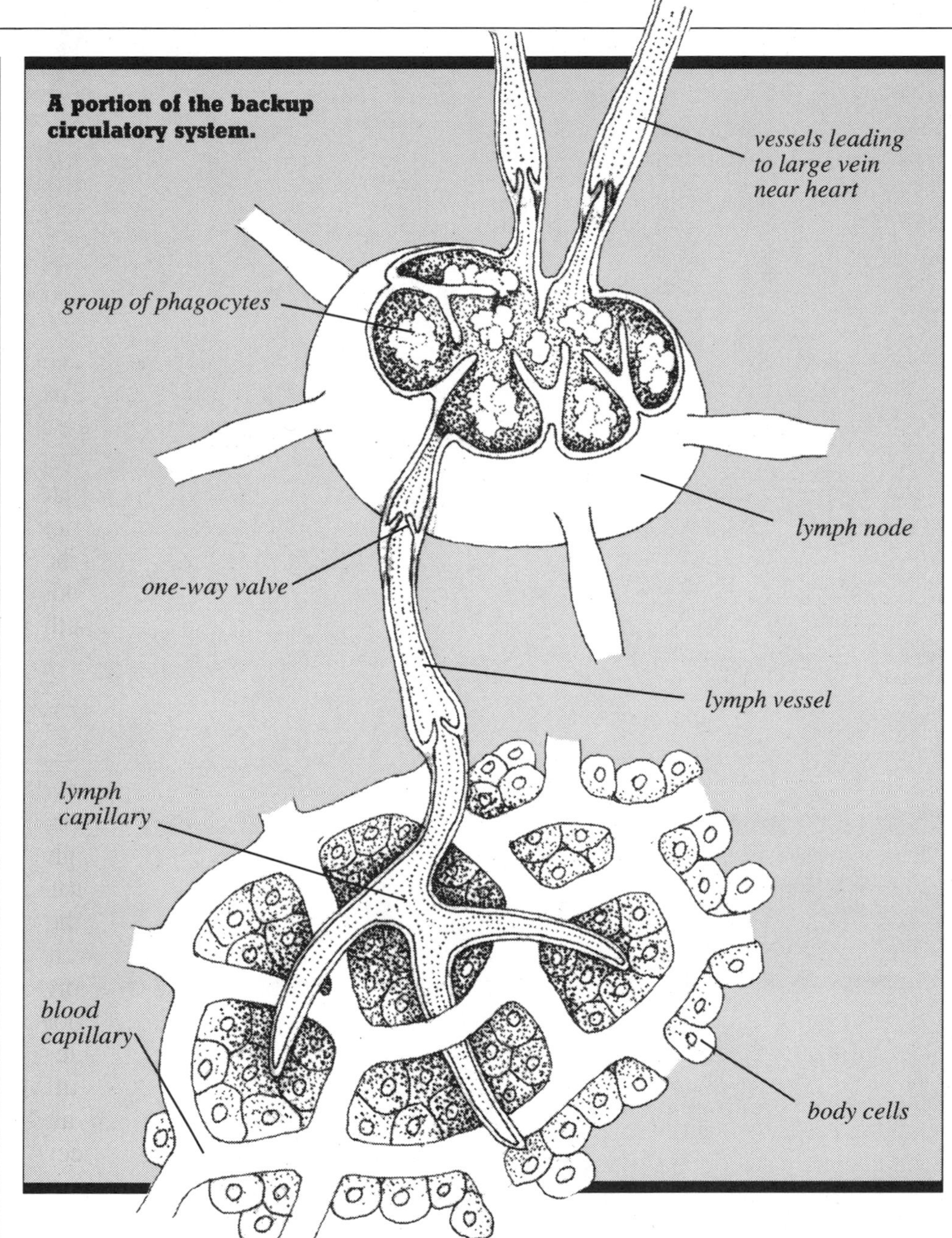

A portion of the backup circulatory system.

Your body has a whole backup circulatory system, the lymphatic system, whose vessels deliver back to the blood circulation system fluid and proteins lost at capillaries. The lymphatic system has neither a heart nor arteries, but it does have capillaries and vessels as numerous as those that carry blood.

Lymph capillaries are dead ends, but they are very leaky, with gaps so big that proteins can enter them. Lymph capillaries picking up such cargo widen into lymph vessels; the vessels enlarge here and there into large chambers called lymph nodes; and the whole system eventually trickles body fluid and blood proteins picked up in tissues throughout the body to a large blood vein near the heart.

You can feel lymph nodes in your groin, armpits, and just inside your lower jaw. They are cleanup stations occupied by phagocytes and immune cells that cooperate to dispose of unwanted articles like dead cells and germs. The blood circulation system has no such sanitary facilities, and it relies on lymph nodes for much of its protection against infection.

Since lymph is not pumped heartwards, there has to be another way to move it in the right direction. The same is true of blood that has passed through capillaries and entered a vein returning to the heart, for blood pressure has fallen too low at that point to push blood along at all.

Both fluids are squeezed uphill by ordinary muscles as you walk, wiggle, squirm, kick, wave your arms around—or simply tense your muscles. Lymph vessels and blood veins are collapsible, like canvas fire hoses. At intervals along their length are one-way valves that open when fluid is squeezed heartwards, and then close so no liquid can flow back. The technology here is not impressive. When people stand still for a long time, blood and lymph pools in their feet, swelling them and causing an aching discomfort. But then, no system is perfect.

Tradeoffs

Circulation is surprisingly fast. Any particular speck of blood makes the complete circuit of your body in only 20 seconds. Each second, about a gallon of fluid leaves and reenters capillaries. During that one second—and every moment of your life—nutrient molecules dissolved in plasma are exchanged for waste molecules dissolved in body fluid.

1. Crosswise section of capillary. Just two cells enclose the interior space.
flat cell of capillary wall
space inside capillary
2. Lengthwise section of capillary. A new branch is growing upward to the right.

Good stuff can be traded for bad stuff because, as cells use food and make garbage, they create a concentration gradient between body fluid and blood. Think of skin cells in your thumb. They are continually using up amino acids to build the keratin protein that stiffens them, and to replace the squames you're rubbing off every time you turn a page. So amino acids supplied by plasma continually diffuse out of body fluid, into cells. As cells take apart and rebuild nutrients, they end up with leftover bits and pieces—waste products such as ammonia and carbon dioxide. These waste molecules become crowded, and so they diffuse in the other direction—out of the cells, into body fluid, and on into the cleaner rivulet of a capillary. There is therefore a two-way traffic of molecules, a trade of goods for wastes; and what turns back toward the heart at every circuit is more

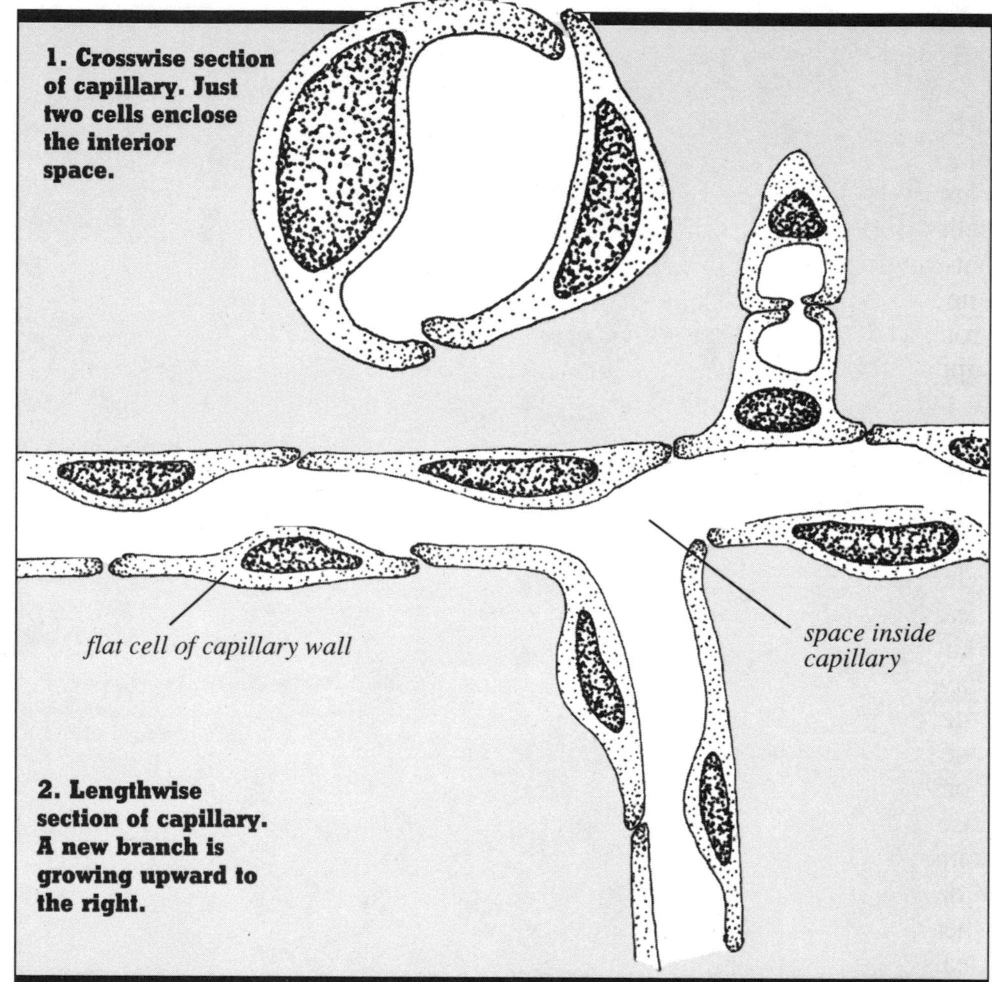

sewage than it is stew.

Except the stew that leaves the gut. It is mixed with wastes, of course—gut cells make garbage of their own. But in each trip through the body, blood plasma loses nutrients to all the other cells it feeds, so diffusion from nutrient-rich body fluid in the small intestine after a meal works the other way around, reloading plasma with a fresh supply of food.

Neither Feast nor Famine

When you think of the hours between meals, you can appreciate a problem: Skin grows, hearts beat, phagocytes scavenge around the clock, yet food enters the blood stream only three times a day. A brain cell can't survive more than a few minutes without glucose, yet, when you have an upset stomach, you may not eat for several days. If all your body cells ate only when you did, you would die between meals.

And there's another problem: The gluts of food you absorb can be an overdose for cells. Several amino acids are toxic in large quantities. Too much sugar sends brain cells into coma. And "too much" can mean what is, to you, no more than stuffing on Thanksgiving turkey or eating the whole bag of Halloween treats.

And another problem still: When you race around or take a test, muscle or brain cells need extra nutrients that they don't need when you rest or sleep, yet you eat at a rate that takes no account of special events.

And more problems: Such plant products as peanut oil and apple-skin wax have dissolved into you without being digested at all. No matter how useful they were to the nut or fruit, they are still nothing like animal fat, and can't be used by your cells in their present shape.

And more: You can't at any meal eat just the nine essential amino acids; your gut cells take in willy-nilly a host of other amino acids that you have the enzymes to make for yourself. There are still other substances that you need even less, or not at all: Plant pigment and plant odor molecules are taken in along with sugars and amino acids, yet you have little use for large amounts of carrot yellow and none for asparagus smell.

And that's not all: The meal may have contained the brown crust of fried meat, or caramel. These brown molecules of fats and sugars get their color from burning. When molecules are burned, hydrogens come off them. That leaves bare charged spots where unwanted bonds can form. These particular burned molecules form mischievous bonds with all sorts of other body molecules. In the dermis, they bind collagen to elastin so that skin loses its spring. Inside cells they bind to protein equipment, clogging the works, sabotaging cell machinery. Worse yet are actual poisons, such as insecticides and bacterial toxins that may get into food in small amounts by accident; or the much larger amounts of poison people take on purpose, like alcohol and drugs.

The upshot is that what's a fine meal for you is not, as it enters the bloodstream at the gut, fit for cells to eat. And that explains why blood leaving the gut stuffed with an ill-assorted mix of helpful, harmful, and useless mealtime molecules takes a detour through the liver before proceeding to the heart.

Little Trickles Add Up

Since a capillary may be only wide enough for blood cells to pass through in single file, and since the gaps blood plasma leaks through are many times smaller, you'd think the amount of water leaving and reentering a capillary must be the merest trickle. True. But trickles add up to rivers. The amount of water going back and forth, out of and into your thousands of miles of capillaries adds up to a total of 62 gallons *per minute!*

Say "Ahhhhhhh"

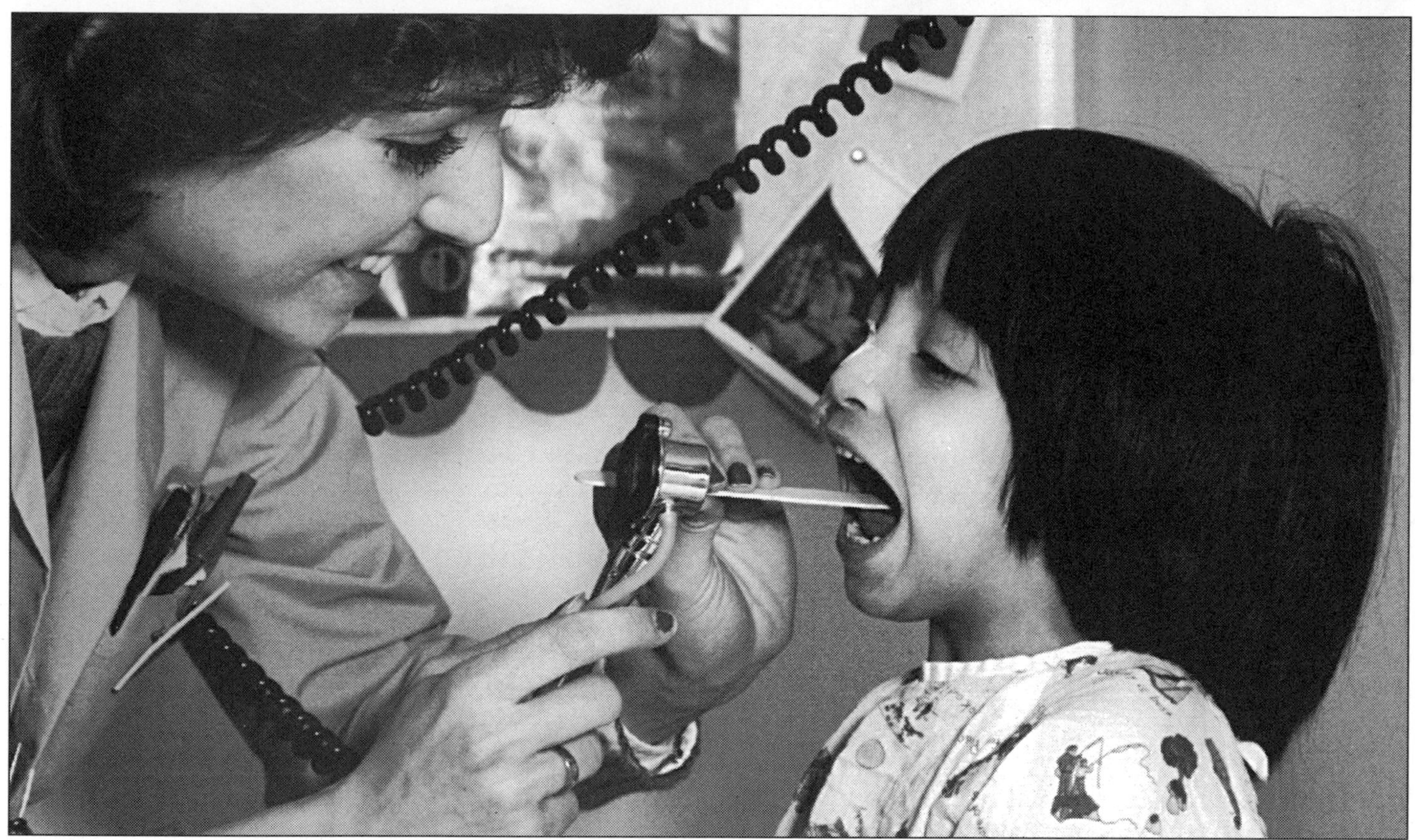

When the doctor holds your tongue down with a tongue depressor, shines a flashlight into your mouth, and says "say ahhhh," she is checking your throat for signs of infection. An infected throat is fiery red. Tonsils, bumps of lymph tissue at the back of the throat, also become inflamed with infection, swollen, and flecked with patches of pus. At one time doctors thought that tonsils were nothing but trouble, and were therefore best removed. Your grandparents' generation is largely tonsil-less. Now doctors realize that, although tonsils do tend to get infected, they are home to hordes of phagocytes and other white blood cells that learn from such infections which germs to guard against. These days most children get to keep their tonsils. You can see your own by looking in a mirror while saying "ahhhhhhh."

So You Think You Don't Like Liver

Most kids don't like liver. It's mushier than muscle, and has a suspicious smell. Yet parents are forever trying to cajole kids into eating it. Liver is notoriously "healthy." There was a time—and an awful time it must have been—when people suffering from iron-deficiency were forced to drink minced liver, raw. What is so good about liver, and why must its goodness come in such a mushy, smelly form?

The liver is a warehouse and a shipping company, a toxic waste disposal system, a recycling plant, a vast chemical industry: It is the primary environmental protection agency of the body. The stink of liver is the odor of a laboratory, of cells that smell of their work. And it is nourishing because what can't be eaten now the liver stores for later, for emergencies, for a sudden need of sweets, a midnight raid, and snacks around the clock.

Although the number of products reprocessed in the liver is enormous, its cells are all alike, all chemists that, by mixing this with that, make something altogether different. The organ is soft partly because these cells are not hardened by such things as the keratin in skin or the fibers in muscle, and partly because the liver is built like a sponge. There's no particular anatomy that you can make out by looking at chicken liver, or by slicing through it.

The liver's microscopic structure is layers of chemist cells sandwiched between layers of blood vessels that here expand into great sluices through which blood washes freely. The gaps between cells in these blood sluices are so large that the chemists to either side actually touch blood, pore through its contents, taste and swallow it and spit it out again. Much of a meal actually goes through liver cells before it gets to the rest of you, for these chemists take all sorts of things into them in membrane packages, mix the molecules there with enzymes of all sorts (most of them not made anywhere else in the body), and expel nutrients newly tailored to the body's needs, and in just the right amounts.

The liver's chemists can store only a few excess amino acids for later use; the rest they take apart and rebuild. First they remove the nitrogen portion that is typical of all amino acids. Then they use the remaining carbon "spine" of the molecule to make glucose, fat, and the animal starch called glycogen. They also link excess glucose units to make fat and starch, and rebuild alien vegetable oils into human fats. They strip down the yellow pigment that colors butter, yams, and carrots to its essential portion, vitamin A. The chemists then export the needed quantities of these products out again into the bloodstream. They keep the rest in storage—not only fat and starch, but iron and vitamins.

That's what's so healthy about liver: It is stockpiled with more nutrients than any other part of the body.

Detox and Cleanup Jobs

At the same time, liver cells detoxify—make nonpoisonous—pollutants in the blood. Some they knock to bits and rebuild into useful things, like fats or sugars; others they alter enough so that even if they aren't useful, they're at least not harmful.

Then there is junk to clean up. In every circuit through the body, blood proteins are damaged or broken, and their debris makes a mess. Blood cells and cells lining the blood vessels die; their corpses clutter the blood. Phagocyte relatives that live among liver cells eat this junk and digest it. They recycle usable portions. Many blood proteins, including those that support capillaries when they are emptied of plasma, are made in the liver, and remade when they break. The liver returns such rebuilt proteins to the blood.

Pigments from old red blood cells are discarded into bile for ultimate disposal in feces, but bile's active detergent ingredients make round trips,

Two Hearts, Not One

The pictures here show two ways of illustrating blood circulation through the heart. In both drawings, the thick black arrows show the flow of oxygenated blood. The picture on the far right seems realistic: If you sliced a heart in half, it would look something like this—that is, pretty complicated! The second, simpler picture makes circulation easier to understand. It shows the heart as two separate pumping organs. One receives blood from the body and pumps it to the lungs. The other receives blood from the lungs and pumps it to the body. In a way, the simplified diagram is as realistic as the more complicated drawing. The heart begins in the embryo as two separate, muscular swellings in a pair of blood vessels. The two swollen portions fuse to form the heart. Although the two pumps beat in unison, each remains a separate organ whose blood never mixes with the other pump's blood.

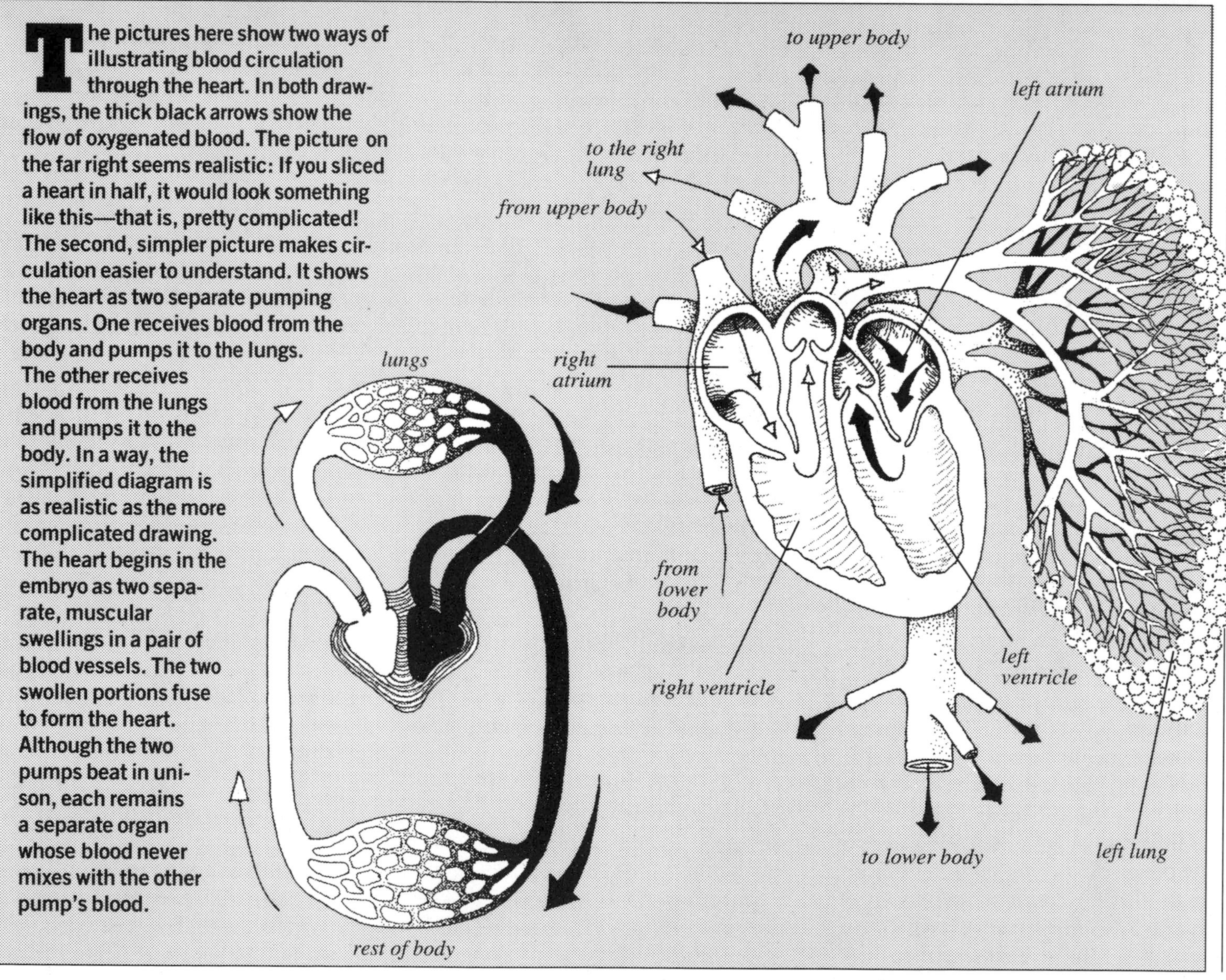

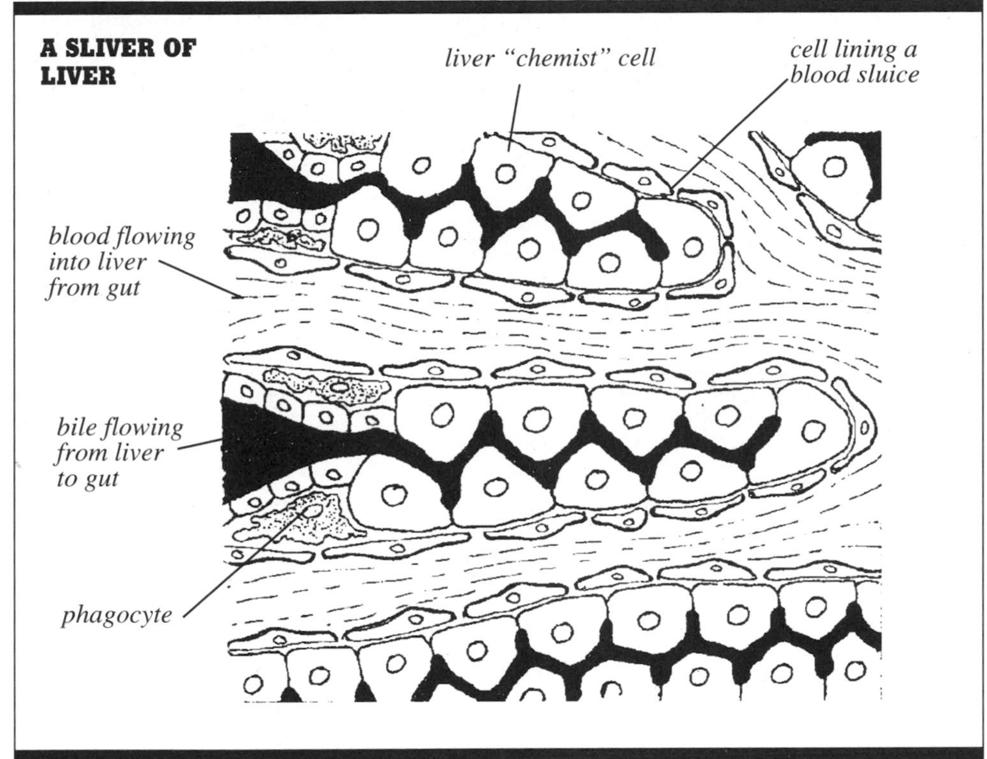

packaging fat in the gut, and delivering it to the liver. Sooner or later—reprocessed, repackaged—fat will be sent on its way around through the body, in measured doses, according to your needs.

No dietician could feed you with such precision as your liver does, with so little waste, and with such care for the purity of your food. Some people hate liver like poison, but their own liver is what keeps them from being poisoned by their meals.

Keep on Truckin'

Cleaned-up blood leaving the liver freshly supplied with a selection of nutrients joins blood arriving from feet and hands and limbs and head. The whole stream, flowing in from veins all over your body, pours into the heart, but it does not immediately circle back toward hands and feet again. The heart is a central traffic control station whose interior partitions, valves, entrances, and exits determine the route of all substances blood trafficks in.

This batch of blood enters the heart into a thin-walled chamber called the right atrium. From there it flows through a valve into a muscular pumping chamber, the right ventricle. Blood at this point is rich in nutrients because it has just been loaded with reprocessed food by the liver; but blood carries oxygen to cells too, and cells in those hands and feet and limbs and head have taken oxygen from it as it passed. If the heart were to pump this blood directly out through the body again, cells would have enough to eat, but they would suffocate.

The right ventricle therefore pumps this batch of nutritious blood to the lungs to load up with oxygen as well as food. Not until after your meal-filled blood circulates through the lungs refreshing its oxygen supply does it reenter the heart, this time on the other side, into the left atrium. Then it flows through a valve into the final muscular chamber, the left ventricle, from which it is pumped out at a speed of 50 centimeters a second to the zillion cells awaiting dinner.

Maybe you picked up a hamburger and french fries at lunch, and gave them to your body; a lot has happened since then. Only now, beyond the gut, on past the liver, once through the lungs and twice through the heart, the body at last delivers those molecules of meat and potatoes to the hand that fed it.

A BREATH OF FRESH AIR

You take a breath of air 20 times a minute, over 10 million times a year. In your lifetime, you will probably breathe in 700 million lungsful of air. Breathing is one of those automatic motions you don't have to bother your head about. Air goes in, and air goes out; lungs fill and empty. But what happens to the air in those few seconds? What is all this huffing and puffing for? When you hold your breath, it is your lungs that seem to scream for air, as if they were the only place where it was needed.

The oxygen in air is needed by every cell inside you, for it is used to take apart food molecules in order to capture and reuse their energy. The process by which this is done is called respiration. Respiration provides energy for building fibers, enzymes, pigments; and energy for phagocytes to creep, or sperm to swim, or hearts to beat; and energy to keep you warm; and energy for breathing.

Oxygen is distributed bodywide in blood, as food is; and blood is loaded up with oxygen in lungs, as blood is loaded up with nutrients in the gut. The digestive and respiratory systems have much in common. Both provide vast, thin surfaces through which molecules from the outside world diffuse into the inner river of the bloodstream. Both share the same opening at the mouth, and even the same tube for a few inches. In fact, lungs evolved as simple pouches sprouted from the guts of fish that, trapped in stagnant water where oxygen was scarce, gulped air as well as food to keep their bodies energized.

Crisscross

You can gulp air down to your stomach, or breathe it down to your lungs. You can swallow food the right way, or inhale it down the wrong way. You can sneeze food into your nose. Obviously food and air travel along the same passage for a while before going their separate ways.

A clever engineer would probably not design a tube system in which stomachs can get bloated with air, and windpipes choked with food. But in the makeshift ways of evolution, such mistakes can happen. This mistake happened because fish in stagnant water

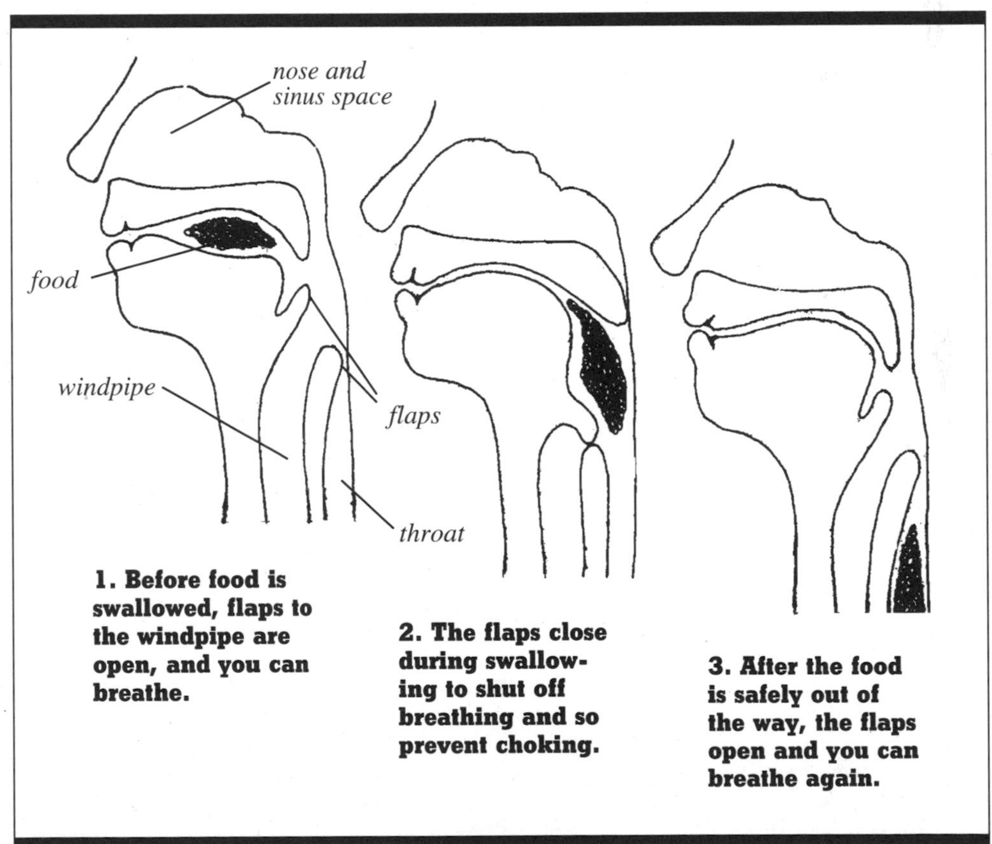

1. Before food is swallowed, flaps to the windpipe are open, and you can breathe.

2. The flaps close during swallowing to shut off breathing and so prevent choking.

3. After the food is safely out of the way, the flaps open and you can breathe again.

already had a digestive tube richly supplied with capillaries that could take up oxygen through the gut's large, thin surface. What could be easier than to elaborate that surface for a specialized job in the gut's usual way, by adding pouches such as those that are digestive glands, or the appendix? If we had two completely separate tubes for eating and for breathing, we could swallow and inhale at the same time. As it is, we are stuck with doing the one or the other, but never both at once.

Air comes in through the nose to the back of the throat, but the windpipe that carries air to the lungs opens at the front of the throat. Food comes in from the front of the mouth, but goes down to the stomach through the back of the throat. Therefore the routes of air and food crisscross one another. During swallowing, a flap flops down over the entrance to the windpipe to close it off, and another flap flips upward to keep food from getting up the nose. Choking can happen when food is sucked into the windpipe before it has been swallowed out of the way. A gasp of surprise can pull a bit of food into the windpipe, just as an explosive burst of laughter can spurt food out the mouth.

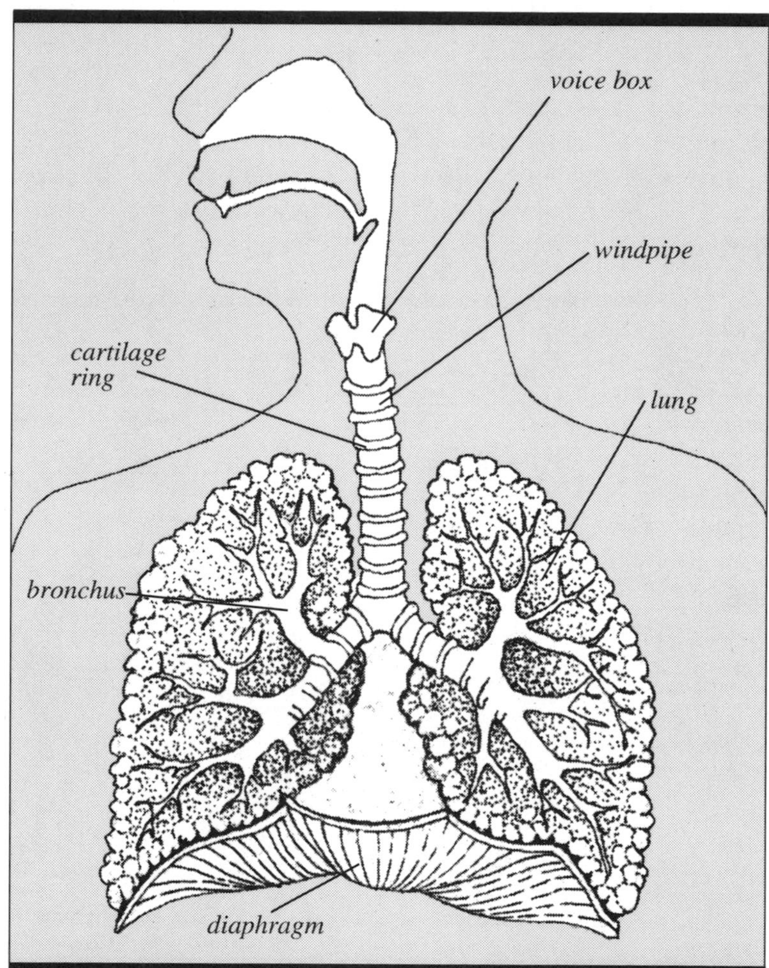

If it were not for a special safety mechanism, hiccups would often make people choke on food. A hiccup is a muscle spasm in the chest that sucks in a sudden rush of air. But before the air can reach the windpipe, the spasm triggers an automatic reflex to cut off the rush, and block the passage of any food that might accompany it. The reflex snaps down the dangling flap over the windpipe. That closes it—and makes a noise. The noise is air slapping the flap.

Oddly, hiccups are most often caused by a complaining stomach overstuffed with food, or irritated by such things as alcohol, hot peppers, or raw onions. How the stomach communicates its annoyance to breathing muscles—or why—isn't known. Maybe hiccups are just another mistake.

Spreading Thin

The windpipe that carries air to lungs is quite long. You can feel the first part of it at the front of your throat; you'll notice the rings of cartilage that keep it from collapsing. About midway to the collar bone the windpipe enlarges into the voice box that contains the vibrating muscles of the vocal cords. Past the voice box the pipe continues on past the collar bone, past ribs, all the way to where the lowermost ribs meet at the center of the chest, and still another inch beyond. There the windpipe divides into two tubes called bronchi, each leading more or less sideways toward a lung. The bronchi in turn branch into numerous smaller pipes, and the smaller pipes, too, branch again and again into smaller and smaller tubes, each of which opens into a separate air chamber. These air chambers are the lungs. When inflated, they fill the chest entirely all the way to the shoulders.

People tend to think of lungs as empty bags that fill, then shrivel, with each breath. A simple bag could never be large enough to accommodate our gaseous traffic, for a huge surface is needed if enough oxygen is to diffuse into an animal of our bulk. Although your lungs may take up less space than two footballs when inflated, their surface is increased by partitioning the volume into many smaller spaces. Lungs are so partitioned that they resemble heaps of bubbles, foam pink-tinted with capillaries. Each bubble is a separate air chamber, and each one is inflated through its own tiny pipe. In addition, each air chamber is frothed with minute pockets, called alveoli, which again increase the surface area. The total bubbly surface of a single lung is 100 square meters, or enough to carpet two average living rooms.

This surface is exceedingly thin. An alveolus is no more than two cells thick; usually it is only one. Each alveolus is held in a nest of capillaries; they, too, are one cell thick. Oxygen molecules you breathe in through your windpipe have to diffuse across no more than a couple of cells to reach the bloodstream.

Blood entering lung capillaries has traveled the body from head to toe and is now at the very end of its oxygen delivery route. Since it is therefore very low on oxygen compared to the rich air you breathe, the gas molecules diffuse into it. The trip is short, and so fast that blood is fully reloaded within one second of its arrival at the lungs.

Climate Control

Although a respiratory surface has to be open to the environment so oxygen can diffuse across it, it can't be open to the harsh environment your skin has to face every day. The lung's delicate bubbles are easily torn, infected, or dried to a crisp. The environment inside lungs is more like that inside a hothouse than like the raging world outside. It is heated and humidified; the air is filtered, the floors are swept, and germs are sprayed away or killed.

None of these things are attended to by the lungs themselves. Like hothouse orchids, they are helpless to take care of their own environmental needs. Lungs depend for their health on crews of caretakers, from nose hairs to rib muscles, and slippery little sweepers that line the breathing tubes, as well as giant garbage eaters that crawl down in their depths.

Lungs have no muscles; they can't inflate themselves. And unlike stomachs, which can vomit powerfully, a lung can't spit out something that has entered it in error.

Breathing is run by muscles between the ribs, and by a thick, flat muscle called the diaphragm that separates chest from belly just above the stomach. When your chest is relaxed, your ribs droop downward and your diaphragm arches upward. When you inhale, muscles pull ribs upward at the same time that the diaphragm arches downward. The slouched space inside your chest expands and sucks air in. Just relaxing again shrinks the space and forces air out. Normal breathing, the kind you are so accustomed to that you rarely notice it, neither fills the lungs completely, nor empties them completely. There is always some reserve of air, although it is not altogether fresh. If necessary, you can inhale more deeply to fill the lungs to capacity, and exhale forcibly to empty them out. Panting is forcible breathing, and so is sighing.

Coughing is done by suddenly reducing the space inside your chest while holding your throat shut. Air pressure mounts, and, when you open your throat, air shoots out explosively.

Sneezing is much the same, except that the mouth, too, is closed long enough to force most of the air out the nose—sometimes at over 100 miles per hour!

Coughing and sneezing rid you of stray items that have gotten into your breathing tubes. You cough when crumbs get down your windpipe by mistake; you sneeze when pepper gets up your nose. When infectious microbes irritate the mucous membrane that lines your nose and bronchial tubes, you cough and sneeze out great quantities of mucus along with great quantities of germs.

Germs and junk rarely get as far as the lungs before they are blasted out. Some are trapped before there is even a need to cough or sneeze by hairs in the nose, which seem to have no other purpose than to catch dust. A lot of intruders are simply swallowed: Dust is an indifferent matter to the intestine, and the kinds of germs that are able to infect the lungs might as well descend to hell as into stomach acid.

The whole system of tubes, from the great big windpipe to the tiny pipettes that feed air into alveoli, is lined with weepers and sweepers. The weepers are mucus cells that keep the ductwork slippery wet. The sweepers are covered with the short tentacles called cilia. As breathed-in debris sticks to mucus on them, ciliated cells wave the whole mess back up for swallowing.

This warm, wet carpeting of a lining controls the climate. Air flowing over the inner surface of the nose and on down the long descent to the lungs gets warmer and moister along the way until at the end of the pipe air is as steamy as the tropics. The carpeting keeps breath moist in a desert and warm in a frost. Cold, dry air breathed in only a moment before on even the driest and bitterest winter day puffs out as a cloud of warm, wet steam. As the inner atmosphere is heated and humidified, particles of soot and sawdust, cat hair and pillow feather, and influenza viruses, pneumonia bacteria, and a multitude of sore throat germs are caught and pushed right back where they came from by the ciliated sweepers. If, by any chance, sweepers miss a menace, phagocytes haunt the lungs to swallow bad things up.

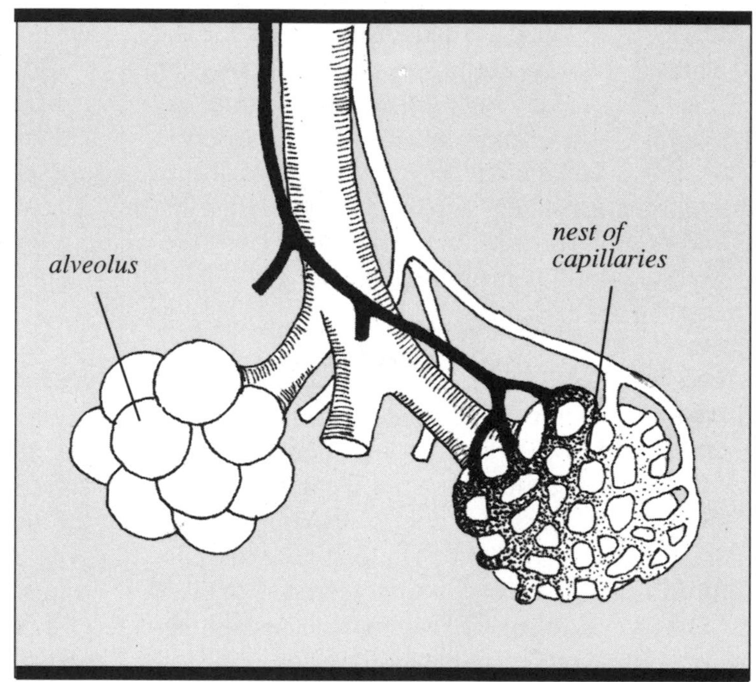

Blue Blood, Red Blood

Lungs need to be wet not only for the sake of tender membranes, but because without moisture, oxygen can't diffuse into the body. To get into a cell (or out of it to enter a capillary beyond), an oxygen molecule must be surrounded by an escort of water molecules which, diffusing through the cell membrane, carry it along. There needn't be a lot of water; just a film like that which wets your lungs is plenty.

But there is a problem: Oxygen is not very soluble (it doesn't dissolve easily). Whereas a fifth of the air you breathe into your lungs is oxygen, the proportion that dissolves in lung moisture is only about .004 percent. The same is true in blood plasma and body fluid. The bottom line in the arithmetic of oxygen supply inside thick, watery bodies is that even with bubbly lungs and speedy delivery the suffocatingly small amount of oxygen that can be dissolved in blood plasma and body fluid is used up too fast to keep a body living. We big animals can live only because we have a way to package and dole out as needed much more oxygen than all our water holds.

The package is a pigment molecule containing an atom of metal that greedily bonds to oxygen. By using such pigments an organism can circulate as much oxygen as it has molecules to carry it. The metal atom may be copper, or it may be iron. If the pigment molecule has copper, it is called hemocyanin, and it turns blue when it is oxygenated. Many mollusks use hemocyanin, and their blood is blue. If the pigment molecule has iron, it is called hemoglobin, and it turns red when it is oxygenated. We are red-blooded hemoglobin users.

Vertebrates carry their red hemoglobin in red blood cells made by blood mother cells in bone marrow. Just before new daughters leave a bone to enter the bloodstream, they do a strange thing. They spit out their nucleus, and leave it behind in the bone for a phagocyte to dispose of. Without a nucleus to round them out, they collapse: That's why red blood cells look like pita breads. Within a few days of entering

Take a Deep Breath

What are doctors listening for when they thump your back, or ask you to breathe evenly? Thumps have a hollow sound when there is nothing but air inside your lungs. A dull sound means there's fluid in your lungs—a sign of infection such as pneumonia. Normal breathing heard through a stethoscope has a clear, windy sound. Rasping, rattling, or wheezing noises indicate some blocking of bronchial tubes, either because there is mucus clogging them, as in the infection called bronchitis, or because tensed muscles surrounding the tubes are constricting the flow of air, as in the wheezy disease called asthma.

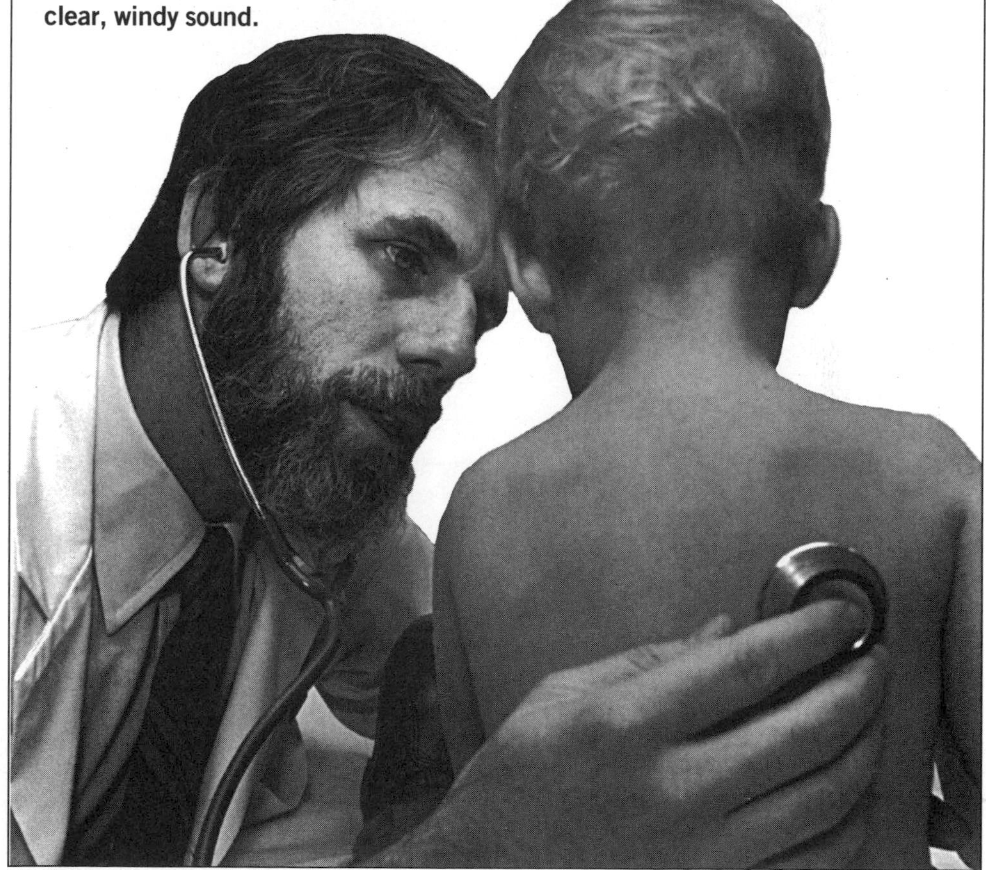

Smoke in the Hothouse

There's only so much abuse a lung cell can take and cigarette smoke's the limit. It's not just that cigarette smoke has too much soot and tar for sweepers to handle, so pink lungs turn inky black. It's that the chemicals in smoke get inside cells, and hurt them. Damaged weepers make a thick, sticky mucus that balls up inside the lung's tiny pipes, and plugs them. The mucus is too gummy for sweepers to sweep, and their tentacles anyway get paralyzed by smoke. The result is clogged alveoli that can be cleared only by the smoker's hacking cough—if they can be cleared at all. Smokers' lungs are usually too clogged with gunk for them to get enough air, and a short run to get the bus or catch a ball leaves them panting.

The long run is worse: Chronic lack of oxygen forces the heart to pump too hard to circulate blood faster, and that raises blood pressure, and overpressured veins can burst, and overworked hearts can get exhausted. That's not to mention what happens to the lungs themselves, which become too stiff to fill, or get filled up with cancer caused by the tar in cigarette smoke.

Then there's the suffocation smokers suffer by breathing the wrong gas. Smoke contains a gas called carbon monoxide (it has one oxygen compared to carbon dioxide's two). It just so happens that carbon monoxide binds to hemoglobin even more easily than oxygen does, and yet the body can't use the gas to meet its oxygen needs. While smokers puff, red blood cells that would ordinarily be loading up with oxygen pile in carbon monoxide instead. There's not enough that they will die for lack of oxygen right on the spot, but smokers suffer a degree of suffocation with every puff.

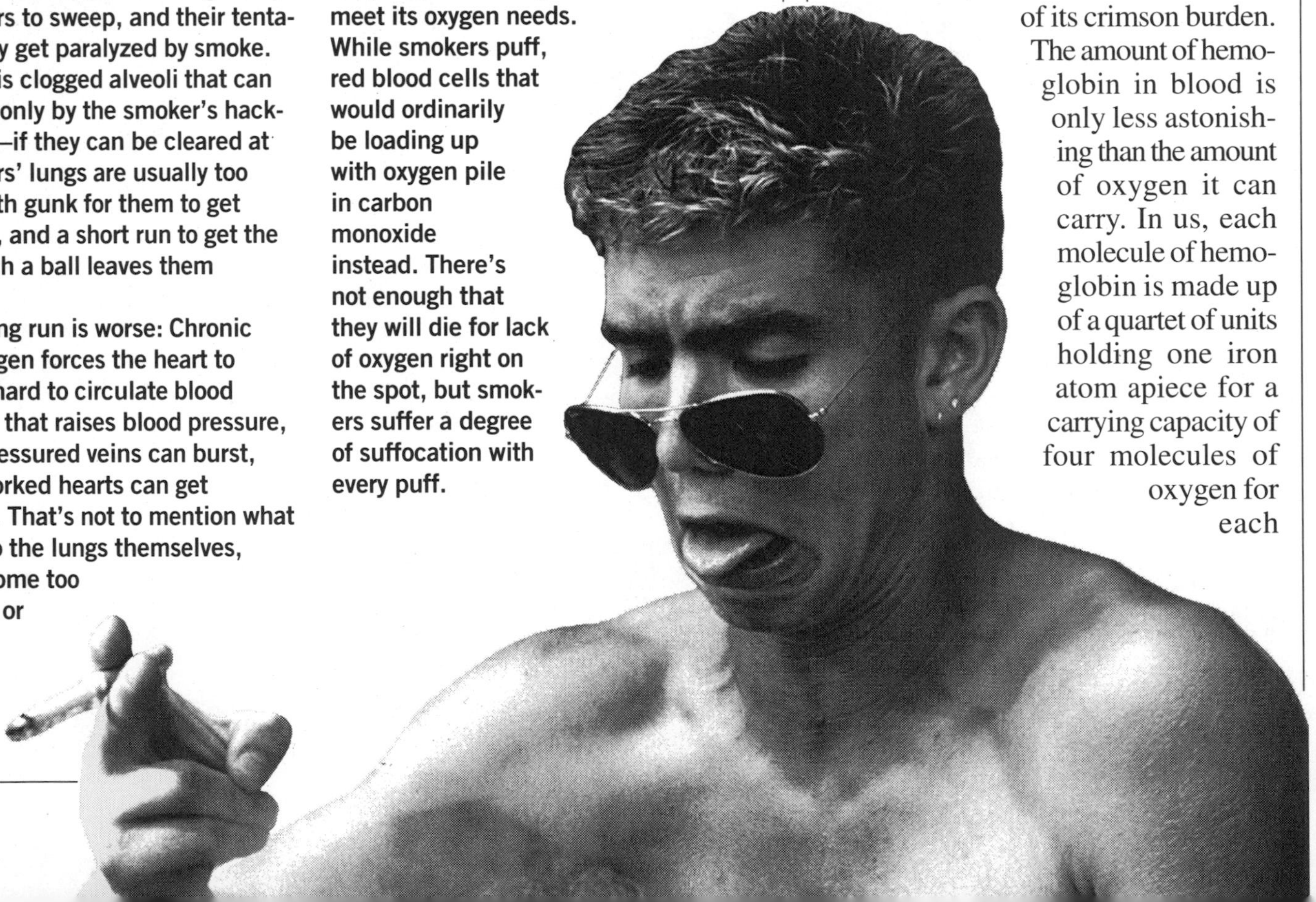

the bloodstream they also get rid of all their other innards.

As you can imagine, these gutless wonders don't live to a ripe old age: The oldest ones in your body may have left the marrow nest only a couple of months ago, and, after about a quarter of a million round trips through the body, will be gobbled by a garbage eater or disassembled in the liver.

Each of these otherwise empty cells is simply stuffed with hemoglobin. A single red blood cell hauls 280 million molecules of its crimson burden. The amount of hemoglobin in blood is only less astonishing than the amount of oxygen it can carry. In us, each molecule of hemoglobin is made up of a quartet of units holding one iron atom apiece for a carrying capacity of four molecules of oxygen for each

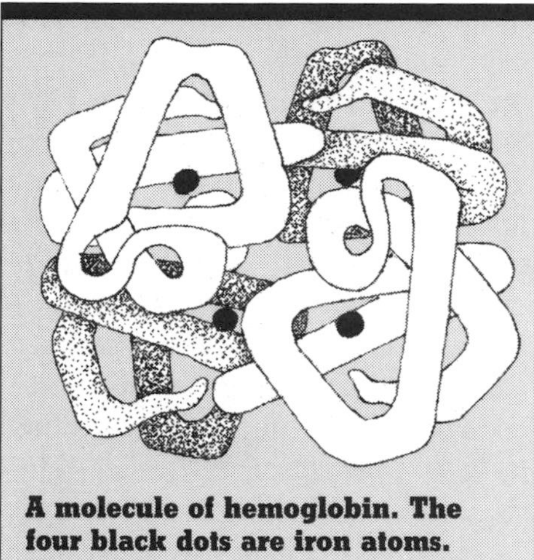

A molecule of hemoglobin. The four black dots are iron atoms.

molecule of hemoglobin. A single red blood cell can therefore carry over a billion oxygen molecules. There are roughly 5 million red blood cells in each cubic millimeter of blood, so each cubic millimeter can be loaded with 5 million billion O_2 molecules. The final piece of multiplication—the number of oxygen molecules in a single cubic millimeter times the number of cubic millimeters of blood in your body (3,300,000)—will run you right off the calculator. By comparison, a cubic millimeter of water carries about 1 percent as much oxygen.

Supply and Demand

Red blood cells' greed for oxygen is what keeps O_2 moving from the air you breathe into the damp film of your lungs, and on through lung cells into

The Beating of the Cilia

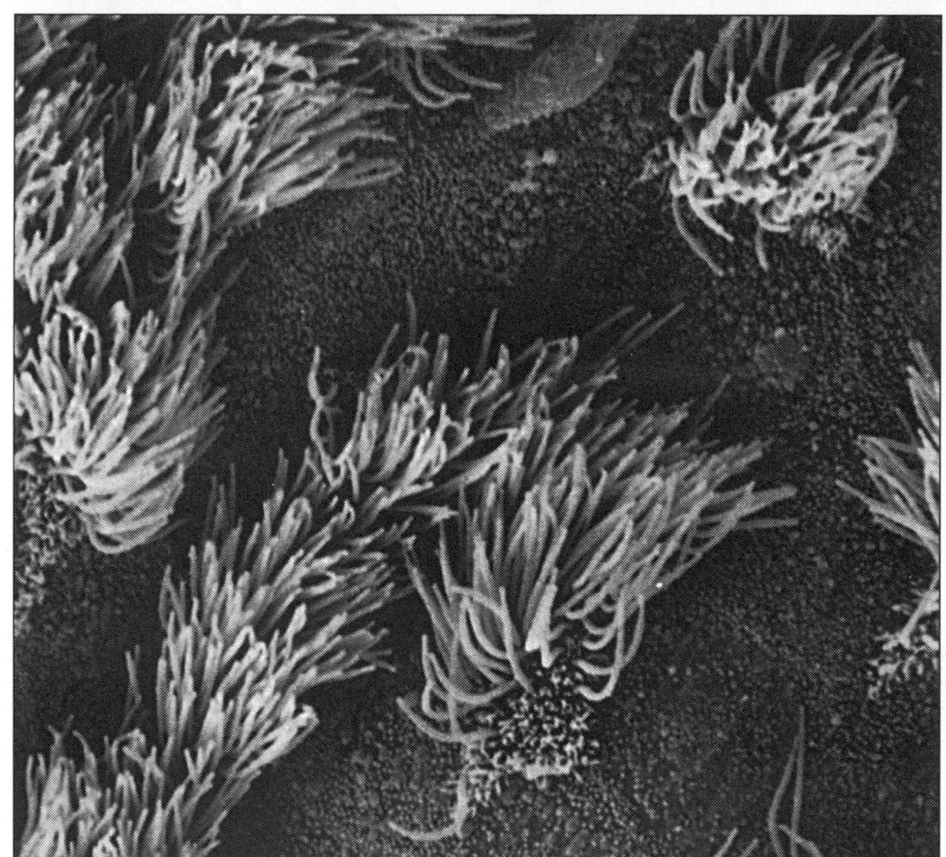

The cilia with which sweepers wave debris away are simply shorter versions of the tail with which a sperm swims. The stroke of all the cilia on a cell is always in the same direction. In a single cell free to move around, the combined action of all the cilia swim it through the water. In the respiratory system, where cells are tied to one another, the same strokes create a current of mucus. The current is quite powerful: There are at least a billion cilia per square centimeter beating back the incoming tide of flotsam in your windpipe.

Metal Colors

When iron atoms bond with oxygen, the metal reddens to rust. When copper atoms bond with oxygen, the metal turns to greenish blue. Rusty old cars and beautiful blue copper roofs are colored the same way blood is.

capillaries beyond. The more oxygen molecules are captured, the rarer they become in blood plasma, in lung cells, and in the damp film. That leaves room for more of the oxygen you breathe to dissolve, move, and in turn be captured. Before you have finished reading this sentence, red blood cells arriving emptied out and dreary dark will leave your lungs cheery red and fully loaded.

What happens then? Hemoglobin would not work if it held tightly to oxygen, and wouldn't let it go. The bond, however, is a weak one. Hemoglobin at every instant is both capturing and releasing oxygen molecules, so blood has some free oxygen dissolved in it all the time. When blood pumped out into the body reaches capillaries, free oxygen diffuses from plasma into body cells, leaving less to stumble into red blood cells and collide with hemoglobin. There is therefore less chance that an oxygen molecule dropped by its carrier will bump into another carrier and be recaptured. The whole business of oxygen pick-up and drop-off is run by supply and demand: The greater the supply, the more is loaded; the greater the demand, the more is unloaded. You, by breathing, create the supply. Your cells, by respiring, create the demand.

To call the organs that pull air into the body a respiratory system is therefore deceptive: Lung cells respire for themselves, not for other cells, and they respire neither more nor less than does a skin cell or a phagocyte. The facts would have been better served if the lungs and air pipes were named "air supply system," but anatomists figuring out the body's ductwork centuries ago didn't know what really goes on in cells, the bodies *in* your body. Even less did they suspect what we now know: Respiration is actually performed by a body in the body of a cell, and *that* body was once upon a time a bacterium.

Enter the Mitochondrion

At some time in the history of cells, long before there were either animals or plants or anything that was more than one cell big, certain bacteria evolved the chemical ability to extract enormous amounts of energy from food molecules by burning them with oxygen in the chemical process called respiration. In the course of time, other cells without this special talent ate respiring bacteria, but were unable to digest them. The respirers lived on inside their hosts' bodies quite normally. They shared whatever food came into the cell, reproduced there, and handed down to their daughters their extraordinary chemical ability.

Eventually a real partnership developed between the undigested prey and its would-be eater: The host cell supported the invader in return for the energy it provided. These invaders are today called mitochondria, cell organelles ("little organs") that provide 95 percent of all the energy your cells use to build themselves, manufacture their products, and move.

Mitochondria have evolved a good deal since they first moved in. Over the ages, some of their genes have gotten into their host's nucleus, and their host does the work of manufacturing the products that they code for. Mitochondria appear also to have given over to their host control of their number and of their location within the cell. Liver cells, which need a great deal of energy to run the laboratory, may have as many as 2,000 mitochondria apiece; heart muscles are peppered through and through with mitochondria; a sperm cell keeps a single long, snakelike one coiled tightly around its flagellum, where the energy it provides is used for swimming.

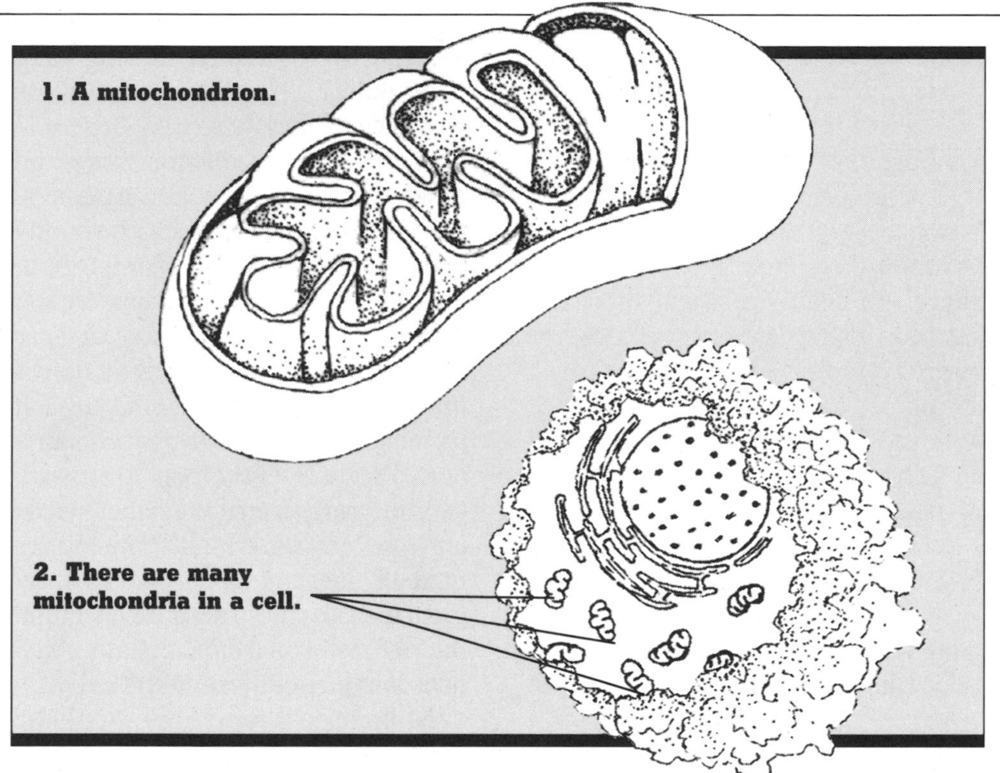
1. A mitochondrion.
2. There are many mitochondria in a cell.

Was There an Eve?

When a sperm enters an egg, it leaves its tail behind, along with the mitochondria wound around it. You therefore inherit your mitochondria from your mother's egg, not from your father. Some scientists studying small changes that have occurred in mitochondrial genes over history have concluded that all members of the human race can trace their ancestry to one woman, from whose mitochondria all ours are descended. She lived somewhere between 100,000 and 200,000 years ago—probably in Africa.

But mitochondria reproduce by themselves, without help from their cell. They have kept some of their original genes, and unlike ours, which are bundled up in proteins, theirs are naked. These naked genes aren't coiled and kept in a nucleus either: Like the chromosomes of bacteria, they are a bare loop on the loose. The enzymes mitochondria use to duplicate their genes when they divide are not like any enzymes we animals have ever made, but they are very much like enzymes bacteria still make.

A mitochondrion lives in a sac similar to those in which phagocytes digest bacteria. The sac is its outer membrane. It is full of very large pores that accommodate a busy traffic of most of the sorts of molecules common in the fluid that fills your cells. Inside that outer membrane is a much more discriminating inner one studded with many more than the usual population of membrane proteins, and very unusual ones at that. Many of these proteins are found in only two other types of membrane: The one that surrounds little green bodies in plant cells that capture energy from sunlight in the process called photosynthesis (and that were also originally undigestible prey) and the one that encloses respiring and photosynthesizing bacteria.

This inside mitochondrial membrane is pleated—it may have five times as much surface area as the outer one—and it encloses an inner sanctum in which are made enzymes found nowhere else in the cell. The inner sanctums of the hundreds or thousands of mitochondria in each of your body's cells are also the destination of nearly all the oxygen you breathe.

The truth of a body is this: All you

contribute to getting energy from the "energy foods" you eat is breathing, the gross sucking in of raw atmosphere. Your cells themselves don't contribute nearly enough to keep them cooking, crawling, or even living. Nearly all the energy to be warm, strong, growing, thinking is donated to your cells and you by respiring mitochondria.

But What Is Energy?

Nothing is more slippery than the idea of energy. You can feel it: It is heat. You can see it: It is light. You can inflict it on someone else, because it is the motion of a slap on the back, or of a fastball. But as commonplace as energy is, it can be described only in terms of its actions. You can't say much about energy when it isn't doing anything, because it's neither a thing nor a stuff.

You use this frustratingly indescribable energy all the time to run machines. When you stretch, compress, or wind a spring you are storing energy in an indescribable form. The amount of energy stored is the amount of energy it took to put the spring in a tense position. If the spring is let loose, that is the amount of energy that will be released as it snaps back to its resting position.

Not all of that energy will be in a useful form. Some will sweep air molecules into the bunches we hear as noise. Some will jiggle molecules in the vibrations we feel as heat. But if the spring was in a contraption such as a rat trap, some of the energy will do the work of bashing a rat.

Energy is stashed away in a cell in much the same way as it is in a rat trap. A molecule is forced into a tense position by the addition of a kind of wedge. As long as the device is in place, the energy it took to force it in is stored in the altered molecule. When the wedge is removed, the molecule springs back to its original position, and the energy it releases can be used to power muscle machinery, or slam amino acids together to build a protein.

The particular molecule most often used for ready energy by cells is called adenosine triphosphate, or ATP. Adenosine is a molecule similar to those of which genes are made. Phosphates are like the little heads on detergents or cell membrane molecules, and this adenosine has three of them—thus *tri*phosphate. One of the three phosphates is the "wedge."

Before the wedge is added, the molecule has only two phosphates; it is therefore called adenosine diphosphate, or ADP. It takes a lot of work to force the third phosphate into place on an ADP molecule but—again like a rat trap—very little effort to release it. In fact, to spring loose the stored energy of ATP requires only that a weak little water molecule, with the help of an enzyme, nudge the phosphate off. The much harder job of recharging ADP with phosphate to make ATP is done almost entirely by mitochondria.

ATP is used in cells for every kind of work. It is in such constant demand that each molecule typically lasts only a second or two before it is sprung back to ADP. This must be done at the site where energy is needed—you can't use a rat trap's energy to bash a rat unless the rat is in the trap at the time it springs—and this is why mitochondria are so conveniently located at work sites in a cell. Even though there are at any moment countless ATP molecules in a cell, they can supply enough energy to meet the cell's need for no longer than a fraction of a minute. Since ADP is about as much use to the cell as a dead battery, it must continually be recharged with an extra phosphate to restore its energy. Mitochondria "energize" ADP to ATP by respiration.

The Art of Burning Sugar

Respiration is similar to burning (though without the flame): A fuel is taken apart and the energy that originally held it together is released. The fuel can be sugar, fat, or amino acids. Fat molecules can slip whole into a mitochondrion for respiration, but the sugar glucose and amino acids must first be chopped up like kindling. Chopping is done by the cell itself, and a little energy is captured in the process.

Sugar is chopped by a procedure called glycolysis, "sugar destroying." The glucose molecule, whose oxygen and hydrogen atoms are attached to a spine of six carbon atoms, is first bent, then broken in half using energy from two ATPs. But while it has cost the cell those two ATPs to break the glucose, the energy that held those two pieces together is released, and is used to recharge four ADPs right on the spot. At the end of glycolysis, the six-carbon sugar has been reduced to a pair of three-carbon molecules, and the cell has gained two more ATPs than it invested.

Glycolysis is the only way a cell is able to get energy from food without the help of mitochondria. The amount of energy released from the sugar is very small: less than 2 percent of what it took to build it, and what was therefore stored within it. The remaining 98 percent is still trapped in the pair of three-carbon molecules. These molecules are now imported into a nearby mitochondrion for respiring.

Respiring is a form of oxidizing, in which oxygen pulls electrons from a substance, causing it to fall apart and release its energy. When gasoline burns, the release of energy is explosive: The fuel bursts apart in a flash of heat and light. Because exploding food would destroy a cell, mitochondria can't oxidize fuels in such a sudden way.

Trapping Energy

When you set a rat trap, you are stretching bonds between metal atoms in the trap's spring. The atoms, pulled somewhat away from one another, attract each other all the more. That additional attraction is the energy you have stored in the trap, and that will be released when it snaps. Energy is stored in a molecule in the same way: Bonds between atoms within the molecule are stretched; energy is released when the molecule snaps back into its original shape.

Instead, enzymes in their inner sanctum disassemble the three-carbon molecules gradually. They remove the hydrogen atoms one by one, take off each one's electron and, by slowing down the electrons, rob them of their energy before passing them to oxygen.

The process is something like a ball game: Each electron, whizzing very fast, is gradually robbed of energy by a row of proteins which, each in turn, catch the electron briefly before passing it to the next. At each catch, some of the electron's energy is used to recharge ADP. Only at the end of the line are slowed-down, de-energized electrons passed to the final receiver, oxygen.

By then, each three-carbon molecule has been reduced to three molecules of carbon dioxide, CO_2. Each oxygen molecule, which has received four electrons, now attracts the hydrogen atoms from which the electrons came originally, and becomes two molecules of water, H_2O. Along the line energy removed from electrons has been used to recharge 36 molecules of ADP, or 18 times the number recharged by glycolysis.

This stepwise form of oxidizing, in which oxygen is not allowed to steal electrons until a great deal of their energy has been safely stashed in ATP, is more efficient than the explosive engines devised by humankind. Nearly half the energy of the fuel is recovered for the cell's own work, compared to the 15 or 20 percent typical of combustion in the family car. Most of the rest is "wasted" as heat, but of course that's a lot of the heat that keeps a body warm. Only a very little energy is left in the waste products, carbon dioxide and water.

The Receiving Line

Proteins that receive electrons in a mitochondrion are arranged in rows in its inner membrane. Three of them are very large, and both ends poke through the membrane. The two smaller oval proteins actually carry electrons from one large protein to the next. The first moves within the oily center of the membrane. The second moves across its surface.

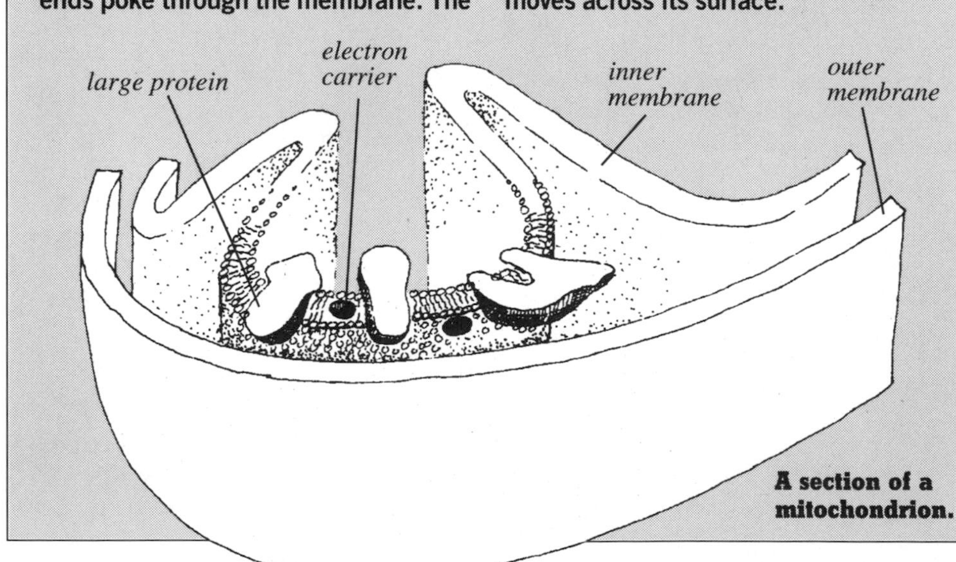

A section of a mitochondrion.

Any Food for Fuel

There is never a moment when a cell doesn't need energy. Every molecule of ADP shuttles into a mitochondrion for recharging thousands of times a day. To meet the cell's energy needs, mitochondria will burn anything the cell provides. When they run short of sugar, they burn fat, breaking it first into two-carbon pieces. When fat runs out, the cell chops up its own proteins for its mitochondria to burn. The proteins are broken into amino acids, the amino acids' nitrogen ends are taken off, the

Rah! Rah!

These cheerleaders are spending energy in their yells and acrobatics, and in the heat they are losing, the sweat they are producing, and the skin they are shedding. Their total energy loss could be expressed in calories. Calories are units of heat energy: One calorie is the amount of heat needed to raise the temperature of a gram of water 1°C. The dietician's "calorie" is actually a kilocalorie—a thousand times the amount of heat a scientist means when using the word.

High-energy fat molecules release a good deal of heat when they are burned, and so are said to "contain" more calories than lower-energy proteins and carbohydrates. Fat is a tremendous source of energy. With each fat molecule respired, mitochondria recharge a total of 450 ATP molecules, compared to the 38 ATP molecules recharged with a molecule of glucose. Of course, the fat molecule is bigger, but pound for pound fat yields three times the energy of glucose. To lose a pound of fat a person has to expend energy equivalent to 40 hours of cheerleading.

remaining pieces are chopped up into the same three-carbon or two-carbon bits as a sugar or a fat is, and finally they are shipped to mitochondria for burning. No matter what a molecule was when you ate it, it is nothing but carbon dioxide and water after it is respired.

That is, of course, all the molecule was to begin with, when a plant first began to build it out of air and water. If we are so good at tearing these things apart, how come we can't put them back together again like plants can?

We just don't have the energy. For every bit of energy we recover from a molecule of sugar, fat, or protein, we lose an equal amount as heat. At every transfer of energy from ATP to a bit of brown pigment or a scrap of gristle, a little more leaks away. Great quantities of energy are lost in sound and motion: Every kick and scream spends energy. Some we simply shed: as dead skin and gut and red blood cells, and as hair, fingernails, sweat, and tears that have taken hoards of energy to make. The tremendous amount of energy needed to put together a glucose molecule out of carbon dioxide and water is not within any animal's budget.

Most forms of energy that we lose aren't reusable. Shouts die out, kicks are over in an instant, heat escapes not only from us, but from our planet, our atmosphere, our solar system, and out into the universe. Even if our intestinal bacteria or those that live in soil reuse power stored in shed gut cells or in dead bodies to recharge their own ADP, half, again, is lost. Energy is not like nutrients, which are recycled through so many bodies so many times over so very many lifetimes. By the time a body is reduced to minerals for recycling, nearly every scrap of energy it had has slipped away, gone forever.

If all the world were animals, our energy would soon run out. What keeps that from happening is another kind of bacterium, the green one that was also eaten by cells in ancient days, and stayed.

These critters, now known as chloroplasts, were engulfed by cells from which all green plants are descended. Chloroplasts are what supply vegetables—and, through them, animals—with the only renewable source of energy we have, our sun.

Like mitochondria, chloroplasts have genes of their own, but these genes direct the process of photosynthesis, which is almost the opposite of respiration. Again, they contain rows of electron catchers. And again, each catcher in turn slows a whizzing electron, robbing it of a bit of energy with which to recharge a molecule of ADP.

But the electron passed along the receiving line inside a chloroplast has been energized by a photon (the smallest quantity of light energy) that the chloroplast has caught in its green pigment as light zoomed in from the sun. The ATPs charged with the electron's energy are used to build glucose, not to take it apart. A plant making glucose ends up with more energy than was in its parts, whereas animals unmaking glucose end up with less energy than the whole contained. The carbon dioxide and water that are waste products of glucose destruction in a mitochondrion are the raw materials of glucose construction in a chloroplast. The waste product of photosynthesis is oxygen, the essential element for respiration.

That the sun's energy flows through all life copiously, continuously, in an abundance that grows the hair and pumps the heart and warms the skin and speeds the legs and gives the brain the power to even think about it all is thanks to the likes of cabbages and salad—or, rather, to their chloroplasts. That there is oxygen to breathe at all is also thanks to them. That the oxygen can be used by either plants or animals is thanks to mitochondria that respire in all of us, whether we are leaf-green or browning in the sun. So here's a toast to tiny partners: Triple thanks to ancient meals, whose indigestibility made our living possible!

Exhalations

Whatever can't be used by a body is a waste product, and if it is not to foul up the works, it must be excreted. People have vivid imaginations: Mention excretion, and they think of "excrement," by which they mean feces. Feces are not excretions. To be excreted, something has to have been inside a body, and what goes out the anus never really came in and was never a part of you. What you excrete are waste products left over from the constructions and destructions of molecules that take place inside your cells.

Compared to our view of the dirtiness of feces, excretions are quite clean: They are the water and carbon dioxide that are the waste products of respiration, the nitrogen ends that are taken off amino acids before they are respired or rebuilt into other kinds of molecules, excess vitamins, salt, and minerals that have come in as food, and whatever potential pollutants the liver has done its best to render harmless before they are excreted.

Of all excretions, the easiest to elim-

CO_2 Sensors

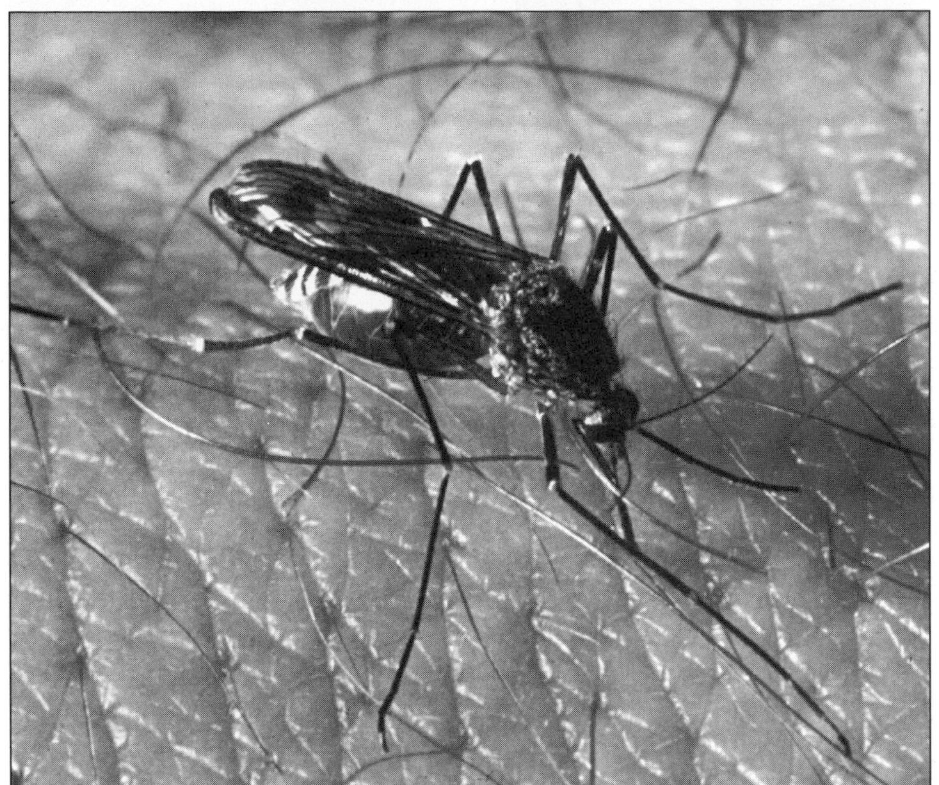

Ever wonder how mosquitoes find you in the dark night? By your breath. Mosquitoes have carbon dioxide sensors with which they measure the concentration of CO_2 in the air. They locate a breather by following the concentration gradient to where the gas is most abundant. Once mosquitoes are close, they use heat sensors to zero in on skin that is thin and well-supplied with capillaries. The tube with which they pierce is so narrow that they may not hit a capillary on the first try, and so may be seen to putter around a bit before actually getting down to business. It takes several minutes for them to fill up. So that blood doesn't solidify before they are finished, they drool a bit of anticoagulant into the hole.

inate is carbon dioxide. Air has little carbon dioxide—only 0.03 percent compared to the 21 percent of oxygen. Cells respiring produce CO_2 in a richer mix than that. The gas dissolves very easily (it is the bubbles dissolved in soda pop), and the excess can easily escape the body by diffusion in a direction opposite to the route of oxygen. The gas diffuses from cells into surrounding body fluid, and from there to capillaries. It is carried in blood to the lungs. Freshly inhaled air in lungs has little carbon dioxide, blood flowing through lung capillaries has lots, and so the gas diffuses out. Lungs therefore are crisscrossed by a two-way traffic in gases—oxygen in, carbon dioxide out.

Which crisscrosser is the one that makes your inner sensors scream for air when you hold your breath? Theoretically, either gas would do, for as oxygen is used up, carbon dioxide piles up. Oxygen sensors in your brain do kick in when the brain is suffocating, but well before that happens CO_2 sensors cause that feeling of lungs longing to be filled. The message is a translation of its opposite: a body longing to be emptied.

Bodies empty out quite a few excretions in sweat—waste water, salt, and sulfur compounds such as fragrance of garlic. But the great dumpsters of the body are kidneys, excreters of mellow yellow urine.

THE INSIDE SEA

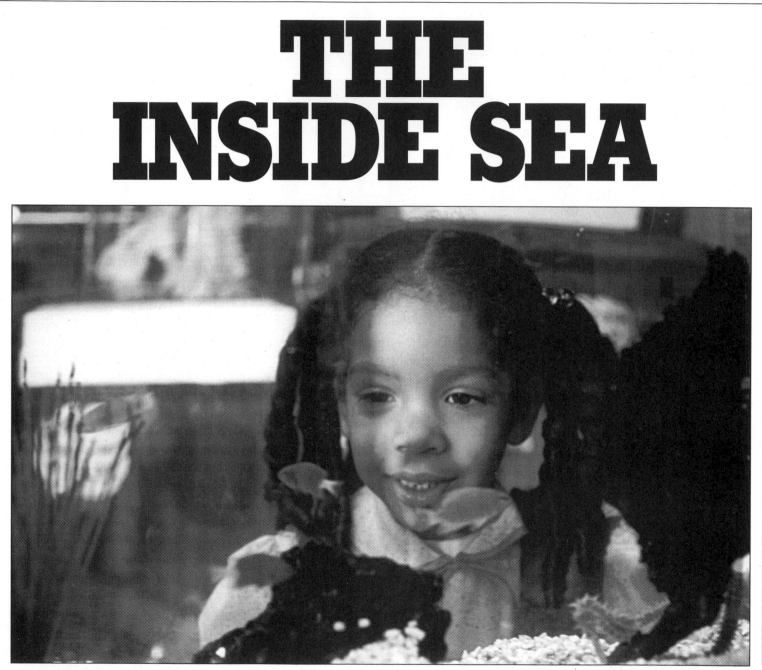

Your kidneys are right in the small of your back, at about the level where a poke makes you jump. They're simple-looking things—kidneys are shaped like the kidney beans that were named after them, and are about the same red-brown color. Their rich color comes from an enormous blood supply: Although the weight of both kidneys together is only about 1 percent of your total weight, a quarter of all the blood in your body passes through your kidneys every minute. Altogether, 700 liters of blood flow through capillaries in kidneys every day. Since your body holds only about three and a half liters of blood, that means the entire contents of the circulatory system runs through the kidneys 200 times a day.

The job of kidneys is to keep blood just right: not too salty, not too bland; not too thick, not too thin; balanced with the right mix of minerals, and cleansed of wastes. Everything in blood that oughtn't to be there when it enters the kidneys is trickled away as urine.

Inside a Bean

The work of excreting is done by microscopic funnels, about a million of them per kidney. If you split a lamb or veal kidney in half (like a bean), you can see where these funnels converge into collecting tubes, which empty into a cavity in the center of the kidney. The

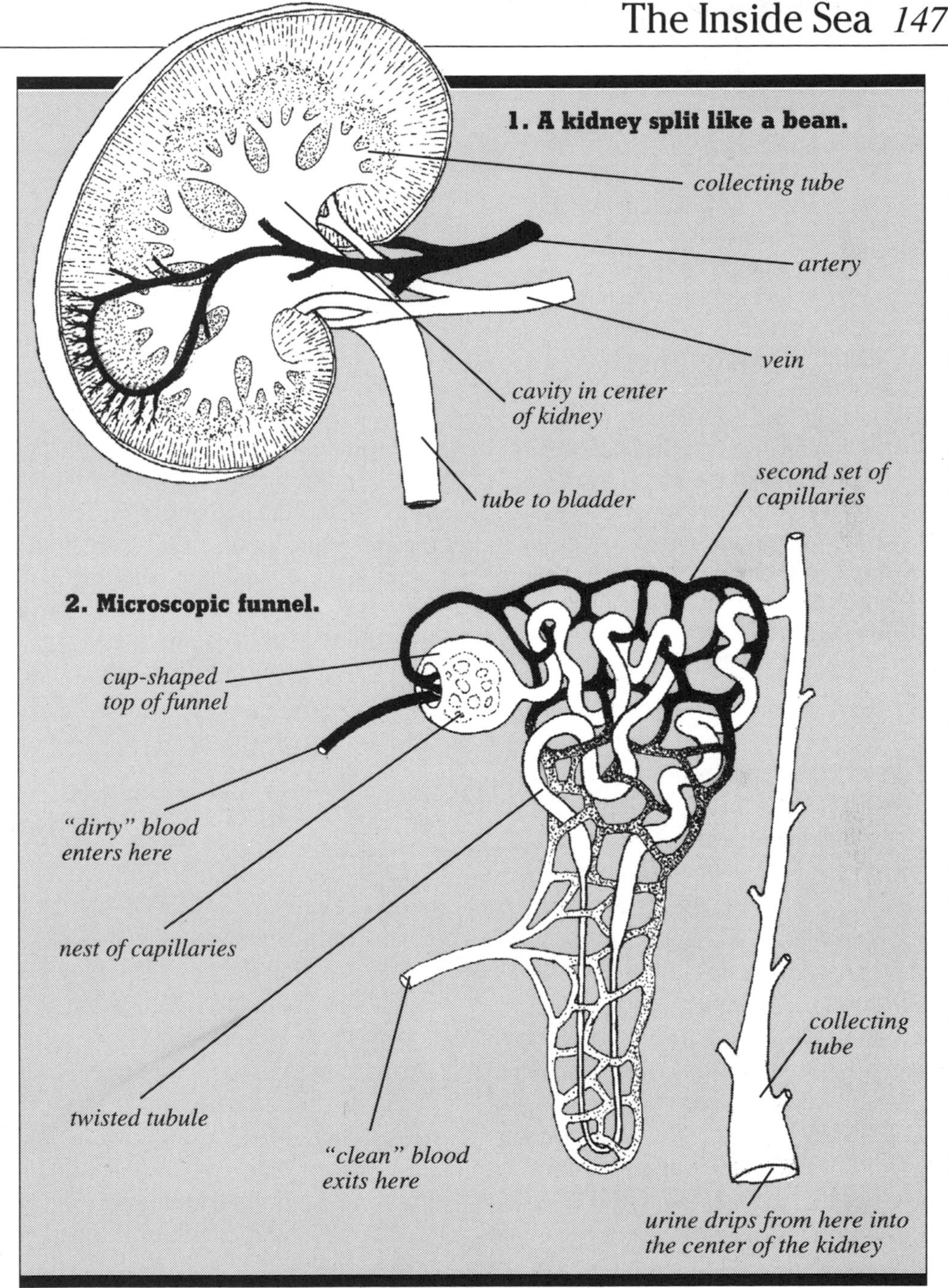

Why Two?

There's no practical reason for having a pair of kidneys; one could do the job as well. It's just that we're symmetrical: Our whole body develops things in pairs. We have two mirror-image sets of ribs, two eyes, two ears, two nostrils, two lungs, two hands, two feet, two hearts fused into one. We don't have a pair of stomachs. That's because the gut develops in the very middle, like our one nose, one mouth, one anus. Pouches that become the pancreas start out, however, as a pair, and the liver has two lobes.

funnels themselves are microscopic; they, and the capillaries that surround them, are the "meat" of a kidney. Liquid entering these funnels is blood plasma; liquid leaving them is urine.

The top of each funnel is shaped like a cup, and holds a nest of capillaries through which blood plasma filters into it. The rest of the funnel is a long, looped, twisted tubule ("little tube"). Tubule cells act something like gut cells: They remove valuable molecules from blood plasma as it passes through the tubule, and spit them out the other side, into body fluid. There a second set of capillaries picks up the "good" fluid, and returns it to the bloodstream. "Bad" stuff goes right on through the tubules, collects in the hollow interior of the kidney, and flows from there through a larger tube into the bladder.

Groups of cells that form a kidney's tiny funnels are specialized in various ways. Those at the neck of the funnel speed plasma along by beating their cilia. Cells just below them nibble tidbits of glucose and amino acids to regurgitate outside the tubule. Further along, other tubule cells do the same with needed salt and minerals. Toward the end of the tubule, just before liquid trickles into the kidney's hollow center, cells recover most of the water running past them. From all the plasma filtered into a kidney's million funnels every minute, only a drop of urine drips on into the bladder.

The Rest of the Plumbing

Your two kidneys make urine continuously. The drip, drop, dribble, trickle never stops. Hours go by. Urine accumulates in the bladder as in a bucket below a leak. Finally, when stretch sensors in its wall report its fullness, you are made aware that your bladder needs emptying once again.

Although bladders are stretchy and thin, they are very strong. Bladders from large animals used to be used to carry water, and even our less-than-horse-size bladder holds at least a pint.

The bladder signals well before it is completely full, so there is time for a body to decide where and when to drain it. Urine drains out of the bladder through a tube, the urethra. The tube is opened and shut by rings of muscle similar to those that work the anus.

Because the urethra in a male runs all the way to the end of his penis, it is quite a bit longer than the urethra of a female. A grown man's urethra is about 8 inches (20 centimeters) long; a woman's is just 2 inches (5 centimeters). Bacteria from skin may inhabit the first few centimeters, but germs have a hard time holding on against frequent floods of urine, so the remainder of the urethra is usually germ-free. So is the bladder. And so is urine. Urine is therefore not the "dirty" excretion it is often thought to be. In fact, it is largely salty water.

How Not to Burst or Shrivel

When you eat a lot of salt, you drink a lot of water. When you drink a lot of water, you pee a lot of pee. Why? Why not just get saltier on pretzels, or diluted on soda pop?

The answer can be simply put: Cells evolved in water of a certain saltiness, and they can't get their protein machinery to work in a fluid that is much more salty or much more dilute than they were originally accustomed to.

Salt is very highly charged, so it sticks to the charged spots on protein molecules. In the right amounts, it helps to stiffen their shape. But too much or too little salt can crumple them to useless knots or loosen them to useless strands. Cells are therefore extra fussy about keeping their salt concentration just right.

They do this by preventing salt from getting through their membrane except through pumps which they operate according to their needs, into the cell or out of it. This wouldn't be necessary if cells could control the amount of water that enters or leaves them, but water is an uncontrolled substance. It flows through the membrane freely in both directions.

Water is powerfully attracted to salt because of salt's high electric charge, so water follows salt wherever it goes. This puts cells in a predicament every time you eat a salty snack, or drink a glass of water.

Let's say you just ate a slice of pepperoni pizza. The salt is absorbed at the gut into body fluid, and into the bloodstream. The fluid surrounding cells is now saltier than their own fluid, and so some water in them, attracted to the salt outside, flows out of cells, leaving them slightly shriveled, and too salty. To correct their saltiness, cells all over the body now pump out excess salt. The result is that, although cells are now in balance, their volume is smaller, and the volume of blood and body fluid has increased by the amount of water the cells lost. If you continued to eat salt and there were no way to get rid of it, the increased volume of blood would swell veins and arteries, and body fluid would waterlog every other space with-

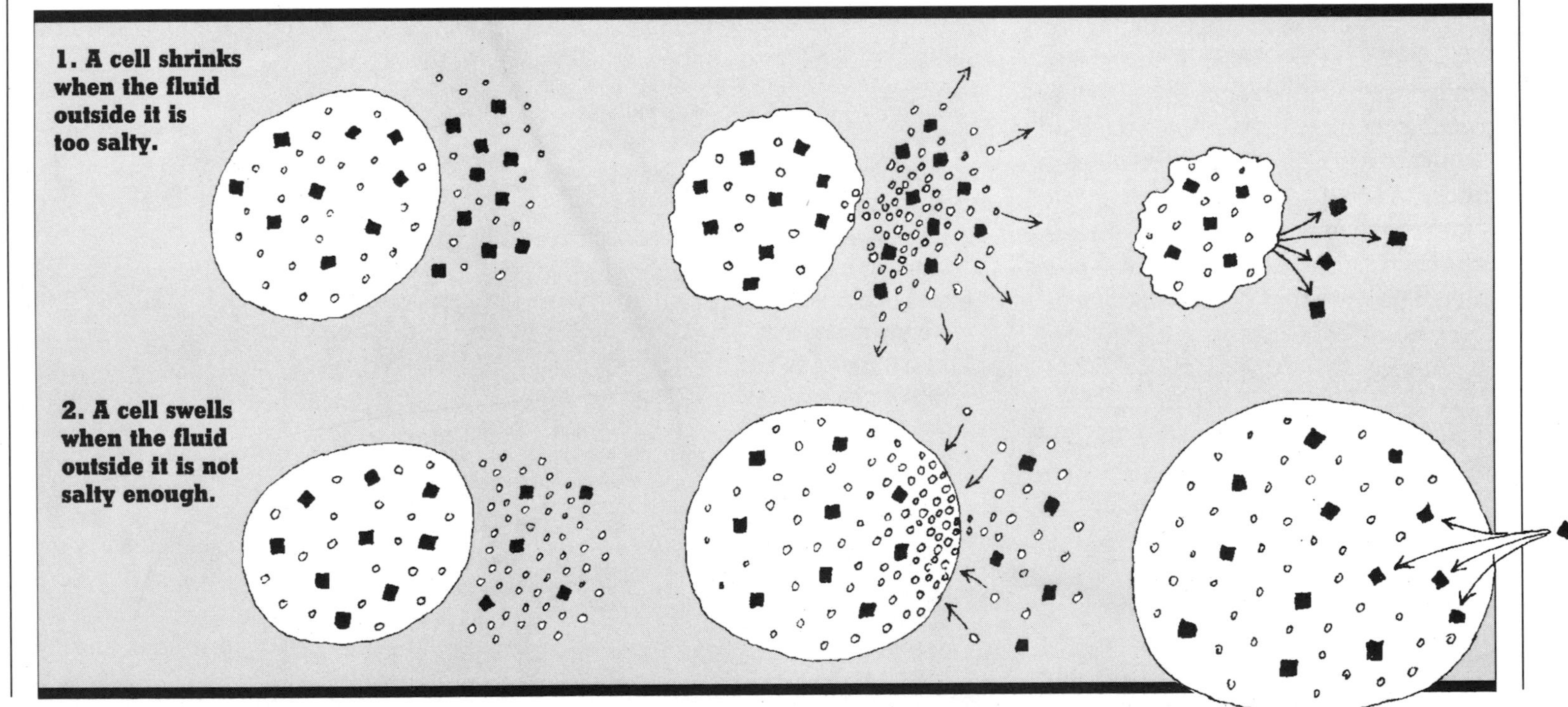
1. A cell shrinks when the fluid outside it is too salty.
2. A cell swells when the fluid outside it is not salty enough.

in the body. Meanwhile, cells would shrivel to death.

Water causes an opposite crisis. Let's say you drink a quart of it. The water, absorbed at the gut, dilutes blood and body fluid. The fluid inside cells is now saltier than surrounding fluid, and so some water, attracted to the salt inside, flows into cells, swelling them somewhat and making them too watery. Again, cells all over the body correct their saltiness, this time by pumping extra salt into them. Now the result is lowered volume of blood and body fluid, and cells that, if you kept on drinking without getting rid of the excess water, would burst to death.

The original, and still essential, job of kidneys is to spare cells these constant crises by removing excess salt or water from blood, and so keep the fluid surrounding cells of the same saltiness as cells keep the fluid inside them. But the problem of regulating a body's inner sea has changed considerably over time, and therefore so have kidneys.

As Steady as the Sea

The sea where life began is a "body" incomparably larger than the bodies our cells live in now. Because it is so immense in volume, and because it is continually in motion, a fresh shower is swamped in its vastness, salt dissolved from its rocky bed is lost in its waves. Sip the Pacific, gulp the

Pickles and Jerky

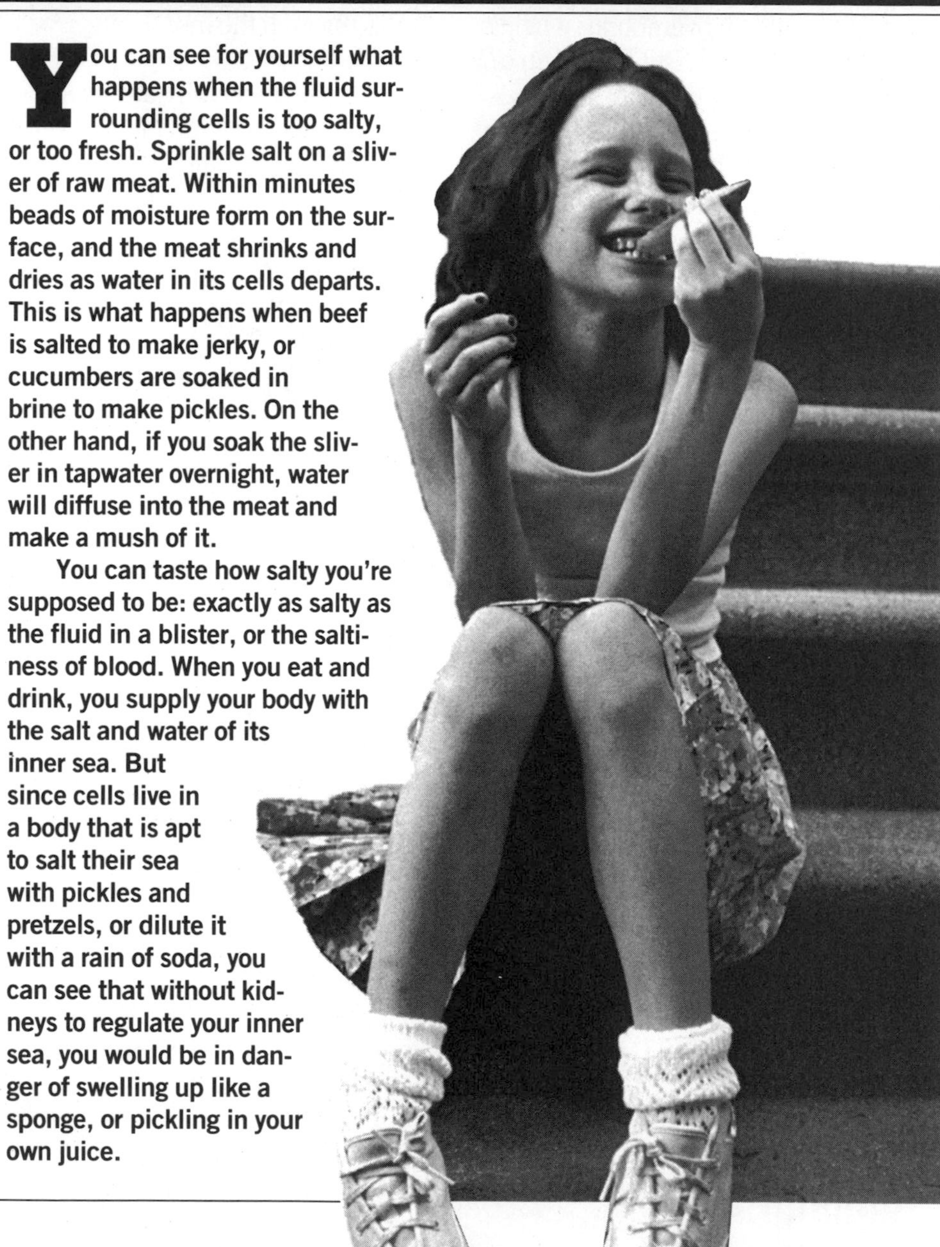

You can see for yourself what happens when the fluid surrounding cells is too salty, or too fresh. Sprinkle salt on a sliver of raw meat. Within minutes beads of moisture form on the surface, and the meat shrinks and dries as water in its cells departs. This is what happens when beef is salted to make jerky, or cucumbers are soaked in brine to make pickles. On the other hand, if you soak the sliver in tapwater overnight, water will diffuse into the meat and make a mush of it.

You can taste how salty you're supposed to be: exactly as salty as the fluid in a blister, or the saltiness of blood. When you eat and drink, you supply your body with the salt and water of its inner sea. But since cells live in a body that is apt to salt their sea with pickles and pretzels, or dilute it with a rain of soda, you can see that without kidneys to regulate your inner sea, you would be in danger of swelling up like a sponge, or pickling in your own juice.

Atlantic: Each is as salty as the other.

A clam living in the sea has no bursting-shrinking problem, and no need to regulate its juices. Its body fluid is essentially continuous with the whole ocean, and of the same saltiness as the fluid inside clam cells. Should a clam suffer some momentary imbalance, the steady composition of seawater flowing over its flesh and among its cells instantly returns its juices to the Atlantic and Pacific salt standard.

Our fish ancestors, however, did not evolve in the salty sea. They evolved at the mouths of rivers, where salt concentration varies daily with the tide. When the tide comes in, the water is salty, but as the tide goes out, fresh water floods out from the river. Kidneys arose in these first vertebrates as devices for conserving salt, and excreting excess water.

Cells in such kidney tubules take up salt from blood plasma, pump it back into body fluid, and let the water drain on out as very watery urine. In addition to these salt-conserving kidneys, fish moving upriver into even fresher water evolved other devices to keep their body juices from becoming too diluted. Gills pumped extra brine from water to salt their blood. Skin grew waterproofing armor. The fish stopped drinking. They even adjusted the fluid in their cells: Freshwater fish cells are somewhat more watery inside than clam cells, and so their body fluid need not be quite as salty as the sea. This is a difference you can easily taste: You might want to sprinkle a little salt on a sunfish or a trout, but no one salts their clams.

Now consider the problem when fish that had gone to all this evolution to thrive at below the Atlantic and Pacific salt standard began to move offshore into the ocean, where so many fish live today. Just the opposite of their original predicament, they were by then less salty than the sea. Out in the saltier-than-a-fish ocean, water tended to diffuse out of them. Yet their kidneys excreted huge amounts of nearly fresh water, and their salt pumps worked in the wrong direction. Evolution had to shift gears.

Saltwater fish pump salt out through their gills instead of in. They drink water constantly instead of spurning it. And their kidneys, instead of conserving salt, conserve water by excreting salty urine.

Over the next millions of years, as vertebrates gradually grew flippers and feet, and lungs to breathe the air, kidneys evolved that could custom-make an inside sea whether their body lived in an ocean, a pond, a desert, or the city of San Francisco.

The Real Stuff

Here in the air, where fish-becoming-amphibians first ventured some 225 million years ago, an overwhelming problem is how not to dry up. Part of that problem had already been solved by the first freshwater fish when they evolved waterproof skins, for although that invention was to keep water out, it serves as well to keep water in. Nothing, however, can be done to waterproof respiratory surfaces: They have to let water through them to get gases in and out. We lose water with every breath, and also with our sweat, and feces, and, of course, our urine. The loss can be made up in only two ways: by respiration, in which new water is produced, and by swallowing wet food and drink.

But it's not possible to provide enough water to keep your sea filled up without the kidney's water conservation. If the amount of fluid circulating through your kidneys were to be excreted without being concentrated, you would have to make up the loss by drinking 45 gallons of water a day. That's 30 glasses an hour around the clock, one glass every two minutes. If you couldn't keep up, you would pee out all your blood plasma in half an hour. Fortunately, kidneys can reabsorb up to 99 percent of the fluid passing through them, leaving as urine only a liter or two per day.

Your body is about 70 percent water by weight, and 90 percent of the molecules dissolved in your fluids are ordinary table salt, the salt of the sea. You'd expect, then, that urine is salty too, and so it is. But, compared to the salt sea where fibroblasts and phagocytes live their moist life, urine is at times nearly as fresh as rain, and at times as salty as brine. Our modern kidneys can do both the jobs that early versions did—get rid of excess water, and get rid of excess salt.

Kidneys usually excrete some 3 grams of salt a day, or about the amount a person eats. People who oversalt their food, however, can excrete as much as 20 grams a day, or about a teaspoonful of table salt, yet they need produce no more urine than people who never salt their food. Kidneys can excrete small or huge amounts of very salty water, or small or huge amounts of quite fresh water.

Yellow Observations

Maybe everyone won't admit it, but everyone is a urine watcher. Who has failed to notice that sometimes urine is richly golden, and sometimes it is pale? Salty water's clear: There must be something else to urine than plain old seawater.

Dry Fish and Drinkers

The mackerel (top) and the trout (bottom) don't look so very different on the surface, but mackerel live in the sea, and trout live in streams. That makes them very different inside. Saltwater fish get rid of excess salt by excreting it through their gills and in their urine. They drink all the time. Freshwater fish don't drink. They get extra salt by pumping it in through gills, and conserve it by not excreting it in urine. For all that trouble, a trout is still less salty than a mackerel.

Urine's yellow color comes from bile pigments that, during digestion, have been taken in by gut cells. Just as feces would be ashy white if they were not colored by bile pigments, urine without these leftovers would be as clear as water. The pigments absorbed into the blood are chemically a little different, making urine yellow instead of brown.

The intensity of urine's color is related to the time of a meal—when the liver last provided spurts of bile—and to how much water dilutes the pigment's vivid gold. The amount of water, in turn, has to do with the water volume in your body. The more you drink, the more you pee, and the paler your urine is. The less you drink—or the more you sweat your juice away—the less you pee, and the yellower your urine is.

What's All the Stink About?

Fresh human urine has little odor, yet the ammonia reek of a baby's diapers in the morning is enough to make your eyes smart, and the baby's bottom rashy. The ammonia has been made by skin bacteria out of one of urine's main ingredients, a waste product called urea. The bacteria haven't had to work much to make the stink: Urea is made of ammonia in the first place.

Bacteria have been working with ammonia for a long time: They were the first cells, and ammonia gas was plentiful in Earth's atmosphere when cells began. It was the original source for the nitrogen end of amino acid molecules, for ammonia is nitrogen with three hydrogens attached, NH_3, and the nitrogen end of an amino acid is just one hydrogen atom less, NH_2. Plants still use ammonia when they build amino acids out of glucose. Ammonia is therefore a handy little molecule for plants: By removing hydrogen from it, they can make amino acids; by adding hydrogen to remake ammonia, they can break them. Given that cells evolved in an ammonia atmosphere, its use seems elementary.

The strange thing is, no animal can use any of it. We humans pee all of ours away.

Ammonia, the same fuming stuff in bottles of household ammonia, is poisonous to every sort of animal. Ammonia stings the eyes and burns the skin. Breathing the fumes can knock you cold. Drinking it can kill you.

We animals therefore have a problem. Like plants, we take apart amino acids by adding hydrogen to their nitrogen end to release molecules of ammonia, but we have lost the enzymes for transferring these poisonous pieces to glucose molecules to make new amino acids. The dozen amino acids that humans can make for themselves are not made from scratch, but by altering other, unneeded amino acids. The rest of the great excess of protein many people eat is willy-nilly taken apart in the plant way in order to rebuild it into glycogen or fat, or to burn it up for energy. The more is processed, the more poisonous ammonia is made.

All our cells make some ammonia. It diffuses from them into the bloodstream, and there is always a little

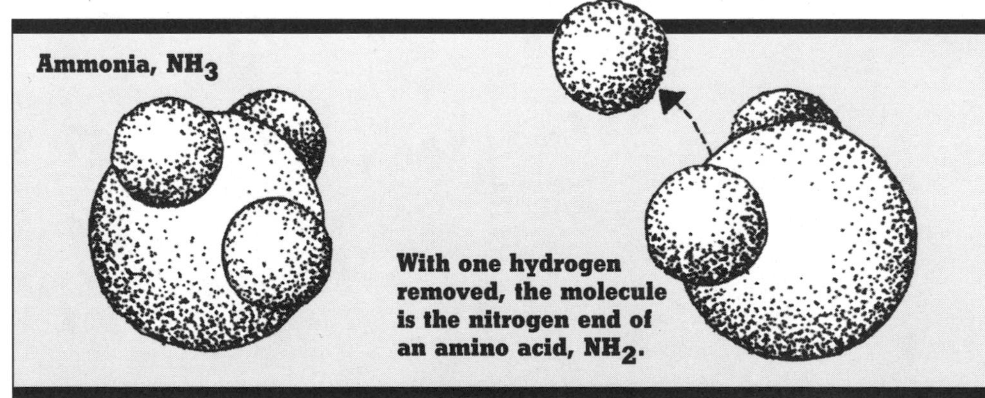

Ammonia, NH_3
With one hydrogen removed, the molecule is the nitrogen end of an amino acid, NH_2.

Satisfying Sprinkles

Researchers have just discovered an odd but helpful fact. Food cooked with salt tastes less salty than saltless food sprinkled with a little salt on the surface. In other words, first impressions—the tongue's sampling taste as it meets a morsel—count more than chewed-over ones. If the tongue is so superficial in its judgments, then it can easily be tricked: Cook food with no added salt at all; satisfy your appetite with a mere surface sprinkling. The total amount of salt a person takes in with this method is much less than if the food were cooked with it.

ammonia in the blood. But most amino acid processing goes on in the liver after meals. If all the liver's ammonia were also to be dumped into the bloodstream, we would be poisoned by our own waste product.

Before dumping, the liver's chemists perform a neat operation: They combine ammonia with the gaseous waste, carbon dioxide, to make a less toxic substance called urea. Urea is excreted in urine, and urinating is an occupation peculiar to animals.

Varieties of Urine

Sea-keeping for landlubbers is no simple job. Think of camels, who go weeks without a drink. Think of seals, landlubbers gone back to sea where every drink is salty. And think of all the meat-eaters who must, with all that protein in their diet, make great quantities of urea. Yet the body fluids of mammals as unlike each other as camels and seals are all about the same, and so is the juice of reptiles and of birds. It is their urine that is not alike.

The most obviously peculiar urine, at least to us, is that of birds. Bird feces are the greenish stuff in pigeon poop; the white part is their urine. This solid form of urine became necessary when egg-layers invented waterproof shells that keep their embryo's egg-white sea from drying out the way fish roe or frogs' eggs dry out in the air.

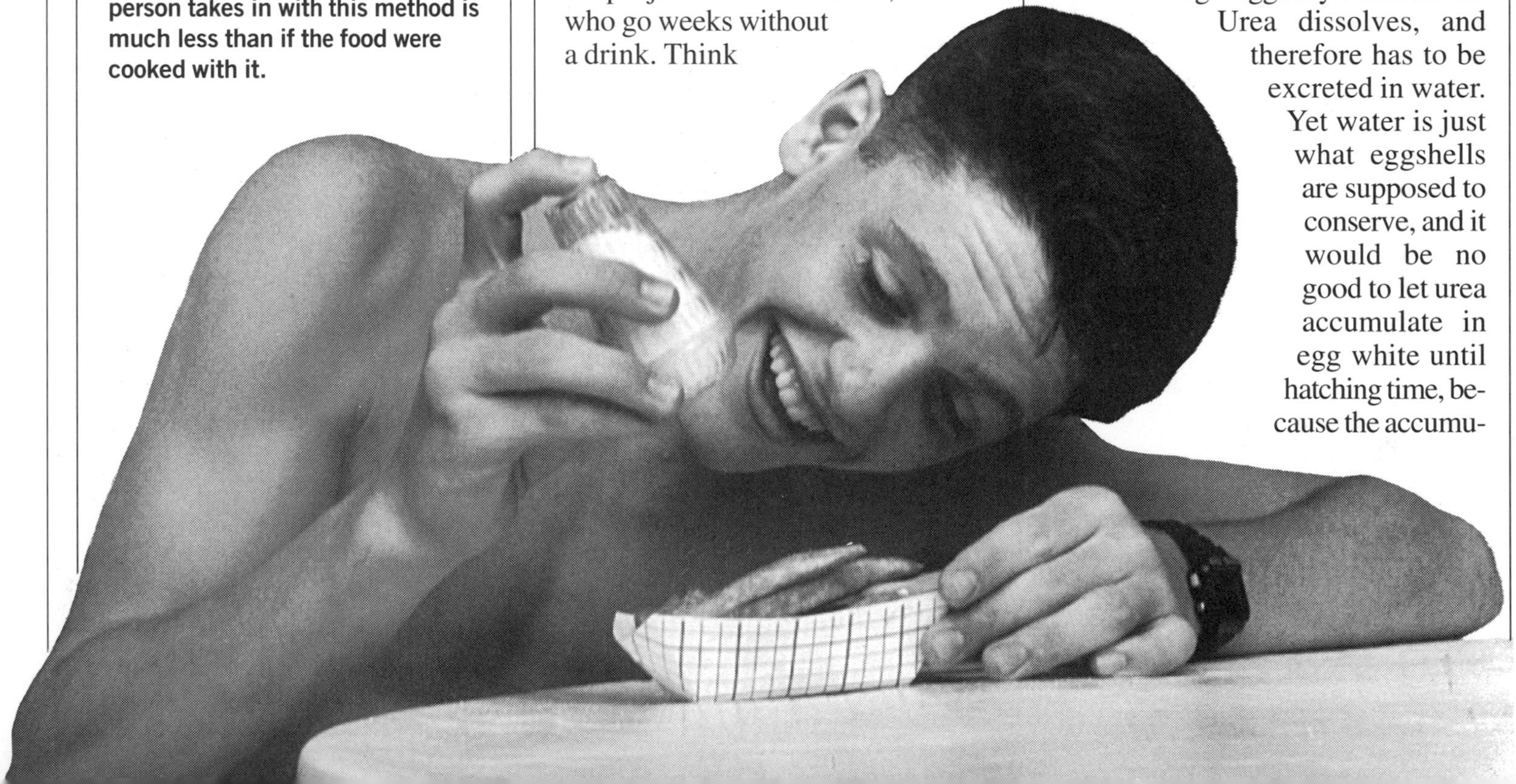

Urea dissolves, and therefore has to be excreted in water. Yet water is just what eggshells are supposed to conserve, and it would be no good to let urea accumulate in egg white until hatching time, because the accumulation would by then have killed the little pigeon.

Egg-layers—reptiles as well as birds—instead convert ammonia to uric acid, white crystals that, because they don't dissolve, can't reenter cells. The urine that bird and lizard kidneys excrete is therefore nearly solid.

Other varieties of urine may look like ours, but are quite different. Seals seldom drink; they get their water from the fish they eat, and so they benefit from the saltwater fish's ability to pump salt out. But to use fish for both meat and drink is to consume enormous amounts of protein, and therefore to produce staggering amounts of urea. Seal kidneys excrete urine with much higher concentrations of urea than ours. Some whales eat nothing but such salty foods as clams and crabs, the equivalent of drinking ocean water. Their urine is saltier than the saltiest stuff we can make. Kangaroo rats living in the desert eat only dry seeds, and drink nothing at all. The only water they get is H_2O from their own respiration. Their urine is the strongest stuff of all, and just a drop a day.

Such Interesting Stuff!

Finger pricks and back thumps are bad enough. Why do you have to pee into a bottle too? What doctors are mostly checking for is sugar. Sweet urine is a symptom of diabetes, a disease in which the amount of glucose in the blood is not properly controlled, and an excess shows up in urine.

The doctor may also be checking for white blood cells, which would be in urine if the bladder were infected. Bladder infections are uncommon in men. Their urethra is 20 centimeters long, and bacteria that get into the first third of the tube are flushed out frequently by a flow of urine. Women get bladder infections more easily than men because their urethra is only 5 centimeters (about 2 inches) long, but in both sexes the environment of bladder and kidneys is usually as clean as clean can be, and so is their urine. The bacteria that make stale urine stink in unwashed toilets arrive after pee has left the body. That bad smell is the waste products bacteria produce as they digest urea, which doesn't stink until they meddle with it.

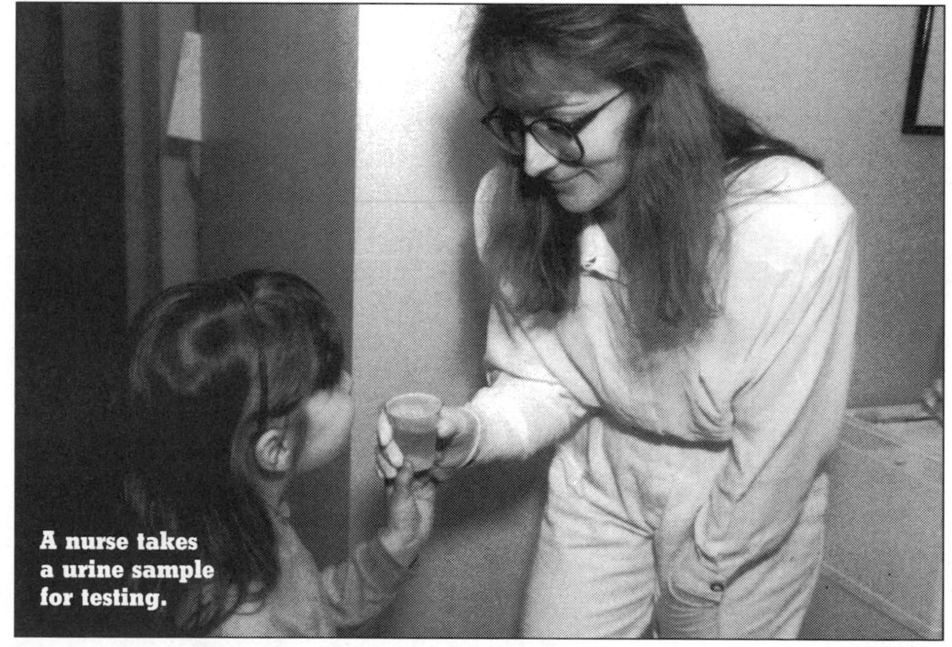

A nurse takes a urine sample for testing.

A Thirst for Water, an Appetite for Salt

No organ in the body can do its job without bodywide cooperation. Kidneys, for instance, rely on pressure detectors in arteries that signal high pressure caused by too large a volume of blood, and low pressure caused by too small a volume of blood. Arteries also contain salt sensors that report the blood's salt concentration. When the kidneys learn of such imbalances, they adjust the quality and quantity of urine to solve the problem. But when the situation is too much for kidneys to handle, the brain is called on to tell you to alter your behavior, too: You suddenly feel thirsty, or you crave a salty snack.

The same signals of low blood pressure that conserve water at the kidney make you feel thirsty. The signals that report a high concentration of salt to the kidney also reach the brain, and make you thirsty as well. Dryness of the mouth and throat is reported only to the brain, and causes an urgent thirst which, strangely, is satisfied by a mere wetting.

What's Coming Down the Tube?

After any kind of surgery, the body rightly assumes a crisis. In times of crisis, it reasons, it's more important to supply blood to brain and muscles than to guts, for the body can get along awhile without food, whereas strength and smarts might get an injured person out of trouble. So the gut shuts down. If, while the gut is sluggish and nearly bloodless, the person eats and drinks, bacteria feast. The result is awful, painful bloat. For that reason, patients who have had surgery are always connected up to an intravenous ("into vein") tube. The bottle that drips fluid into the vein through the tube and a hollow needle contains a mix of ingredients—water, salt, a little glucose—that amount to sea-in-a-bottle synthetic body fluid.

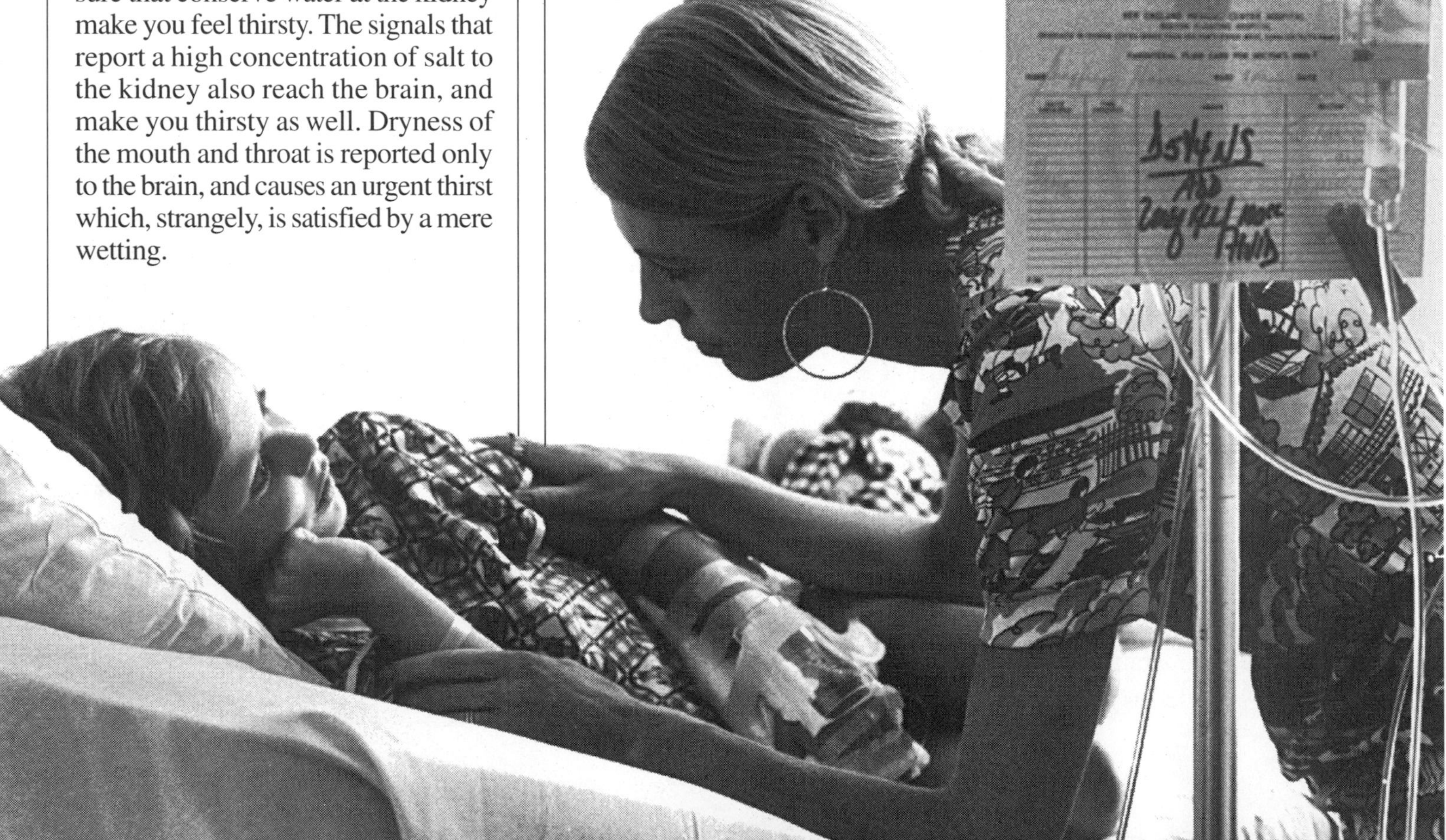

That's not all that's strange about thirst. When a camel has become dried out from days without water, it drinks exactly the amount its body lacks, then stops, even though at that point the gut has not yet had time to absorb the water into the body. Dehydrated people also seem to know how much to drink to make up just the amount of water they have lost. Scientists suppose there must be some "water meter" in the intestinal tract, but they have not yet found it.

Most of what we drink, we drink before we get thirsty—that is, before we need it. That kind of drinking, mostly with meals, is thought to be a learned behavior. We find out by experience what amount of fluid will prevent our getting thirsty later, and drink enough for the hours to come.

Craving for salt arises in two ways. When you are actually short of salt, salt sensors tell your brain, and you begin to hunger mightily for a salty snack. But even when the sea inside is absolutely perfect, people enjoy the taste of salt, and so sprinkle it without needing it. Since large amounts of salt seem to tax the kidneys and lead to various diseases, one would think that such an unhealthy appetite for it would have been wiped out in the course of evolution. But, in the course of evolution, salt was quite scarce. Very little is in grains and vegetables; there is no more salt in meat than in our own flesh; and there were no salt mines in the days of ancient ancestors. The human body seems to be wired to want what salt it can get, never mind the need.

The Fate of Fishy Kidneys

The kidneys that regulate salt and water are only the last pair of three that develop one after the other as an embryo grows. The other two resemble old fish kidneys. The first pair isn't used, and soon disappears except for some tubes that are incorporated into the second pair. The second pair may actually make urine for a few days, but then the plumbing is altered for an entirely different job: the care of the next generation. It is to these fishy kidneys that cells destined to become sperm and eggs migrate from the yolk sac before the yolk sac has become the gut; sex cells are already settled into their kidneyish homes as the old plumbing is modernized into a reproductive system.

Sex hormones shape the system. In males, the kidneys become testes where sperm mature, and tubes for storing and transporting them. In females they become ovaries where eggs mature, and the womb, and tubes for carrying sperm to eggs and eggs to womb.

Testes remain rather kidneyish. Inside them is a system of coiled, looping tubules. The tubules are lined with cells that, as a boy grows up, begin to make sperm. The sperm tubules drain into collecting tubes, the collecting tubes drain into the original old kidney tube, and the old kidney tube drains into the modern urethra. Along the way are sperm storage tubes, and small glands that make semen, the fluid in which sperm swim. Although a valve prevents pee from getting mixed with semen and sperm, boys have only the one exit hole for both sexual and excretory products.

All these connections are made in the embryo, when testes (or testicles, which means "little testes") are still inside the body more or less where the early kidneys first grew. Shortly before birth—sometimes shortly after—testes take a trip: They move down along the inside of the belly, through a gap in muscles, into the scrotum.

The scrotum is just a sac, but it has an important job. Sperm-making cells are sensitive to temperature: They can't get too hot; they can't get too cold. The scrotum is equipped with muscles that tighten with cold, pulling the scrotum closer to the body for warmth. The muscles relax when warm. That lets the testes hang further away from the body, and cool off.

A More Radical Renovation

Female reproductive plumbing undergoes a more radical reshaping. A pair of tubes that isn't used (and shrivels away) in boys becomes the oviducts ("egg leaders") through which eggs travel to the womb, and the lower portions of these tubes fuse to form the womb itself, as well as most of the vagina. There is no connection to the urethra. Sperm enter women and babies exit them through the vagina, which is behind the urethra and entirely separate from it. Girls therefore have two holes, one for peeing and one for sex.

Ovaries become less kidneyish than testes. The tubules that nearly fill testes in boys disintegrate in the ovaries of girls. The space is filled with egg cells. Ovaries themselves resemble eggs. They are completely enclosed ovals held in place to either side of the womb by a rope of connective tissue, with no tube for eggs to exit through.

Eggs "hatch" from an ovary by breaking through its surface. They are transported into the womb by the oviducts. Oviducts look like sea anenomes but they work like vacuum cleaners. Their open end is a funnel fringed with tentacles. As eggs begin to ripen in the maturing girl, these funnels sweep softly over ovaries feeling for an egg to hatch. The tube beyond the funnel pulses with waves of sucking contractions. As sweeping tentacles dislodge a ripe egg from the ovary surface, it is sucked into the tube. Inside, cilia beat the egg gently toward the oviduct's outlet in the womb.

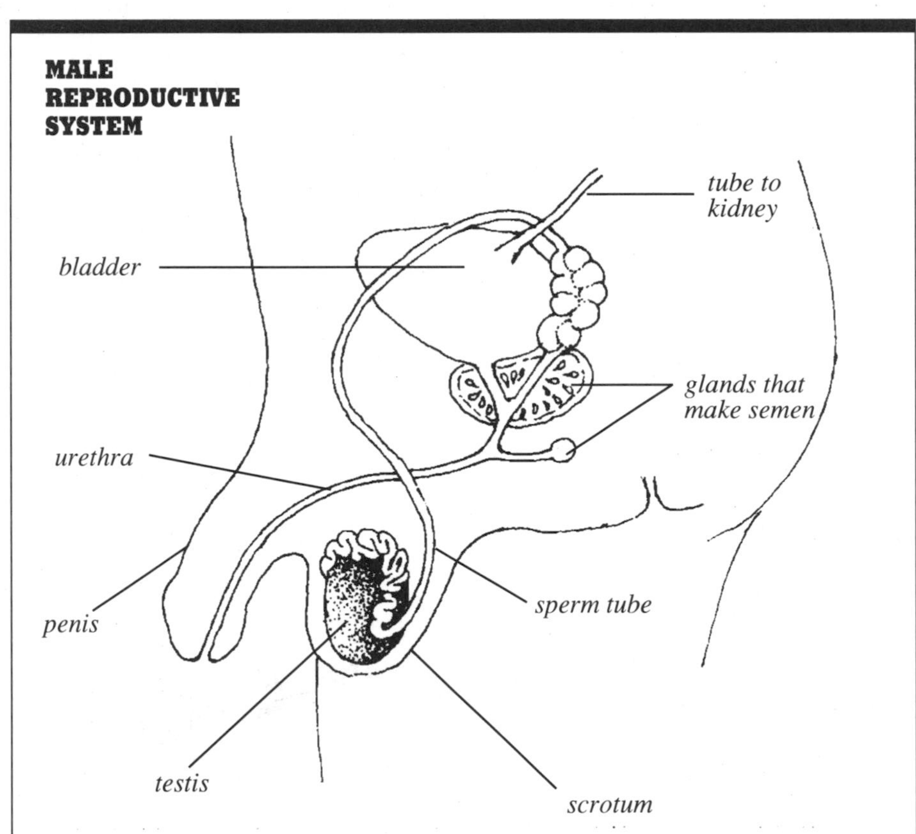

Getting Ready

People tend to think that ovaries and testes have nothing to do during the years of childhood. It's true that they don't yet make sperm, ripen eggs, or secrete the large amounts of sex hormones that make men of boys and women of girls. But even in childhood sex glands in both sexes have the important job of caring for the cells of the next generation.

The work is done by nurse cells. In a boy, nurses are scattered among the spermmakers that line the tubules of his testes. In a girl, a group of nurses surrounds each of the eggs in her ovaries. In both sexes, the nurse cells are connected to their charges. Spermmakers are connected to their nurses by membrane bridges; eggs are connected to their nurses by ring-shaped rivets. Through these connections nurses deliver such foodstuffs as fats and amino acids. Most important for the safety of the next generation, nurses feed the youngsters a substance that prevents them from maturing until their owner begins to grow up.

The cells nurses care for in the testes seem quite ordinary. They are plump and tailless. Like other body cells, they have the full number of 46 chromosomes, half from the boy's father, half from his mother. There are quite a few of them, but their number is nothing compared to the number of sperm they will one day produce: At maturity, spermmakers can turn out several hundred million sperm a day!

Sperm production begins when a boy is about 14 or 15 years old. At that time cells that surround sperm tubules in the testes begin to secrete the hormone testosterone. Aroused to action by the hormone, spermmakers begin to multiply. They do so very much like skin cells: The tubule wall is like the rug that skin cells sit on; those spermmakers that remain in touch with it continue to divide all through a man's life. Daughters squeezed off the tube wall divide a few more times in the ordinary way, and then divide twice more in a different way called reduction division. Reduction division results in daughter cells that instead of having 46 chromosomes like other body cells, have only 23 apiece—one of each kind instead of a pair. These are the cells that become sperm.

It's not hard to see why sex cells—eggs as well as sperm—must contain only half the usual number of chromosomes, for when they come together to start a new individual their two half-libraries will combine to give the baby the complete set. But how should the half be chosen?

Certainly not haphazardly. Each of the 23 kinds of chromosome contains genes that are unique to it. The next generation must receive a pair of each—not three or four of one kind, one or none of another.

For each kind of chromosome, one of the pair was originally from a child's mother, the other from the father. Perhaps some sex cells could get the whole maternal set, and others the whole paternal set. But then there would be only two kinds of sperm a man could make, two kinds of egg a woman could make, and, when they joined, only four possible kinds of children that could result. That would be strange—each kid would have one chance in four of being identical to a sibling!

Obviously that is not what happens.

FEMALE REPRODUCTIVE SYSTEM

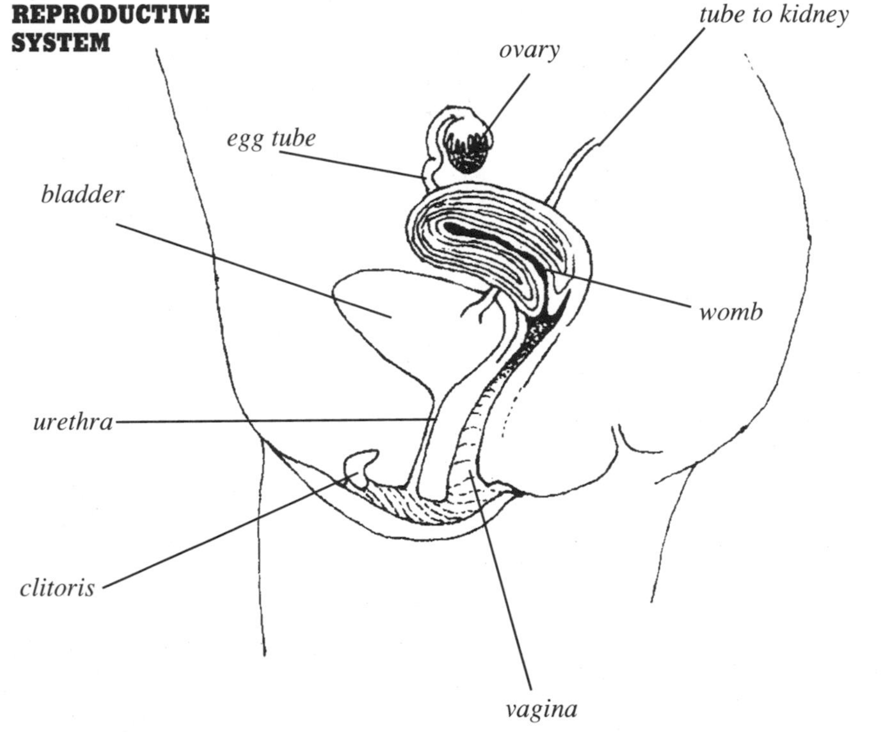

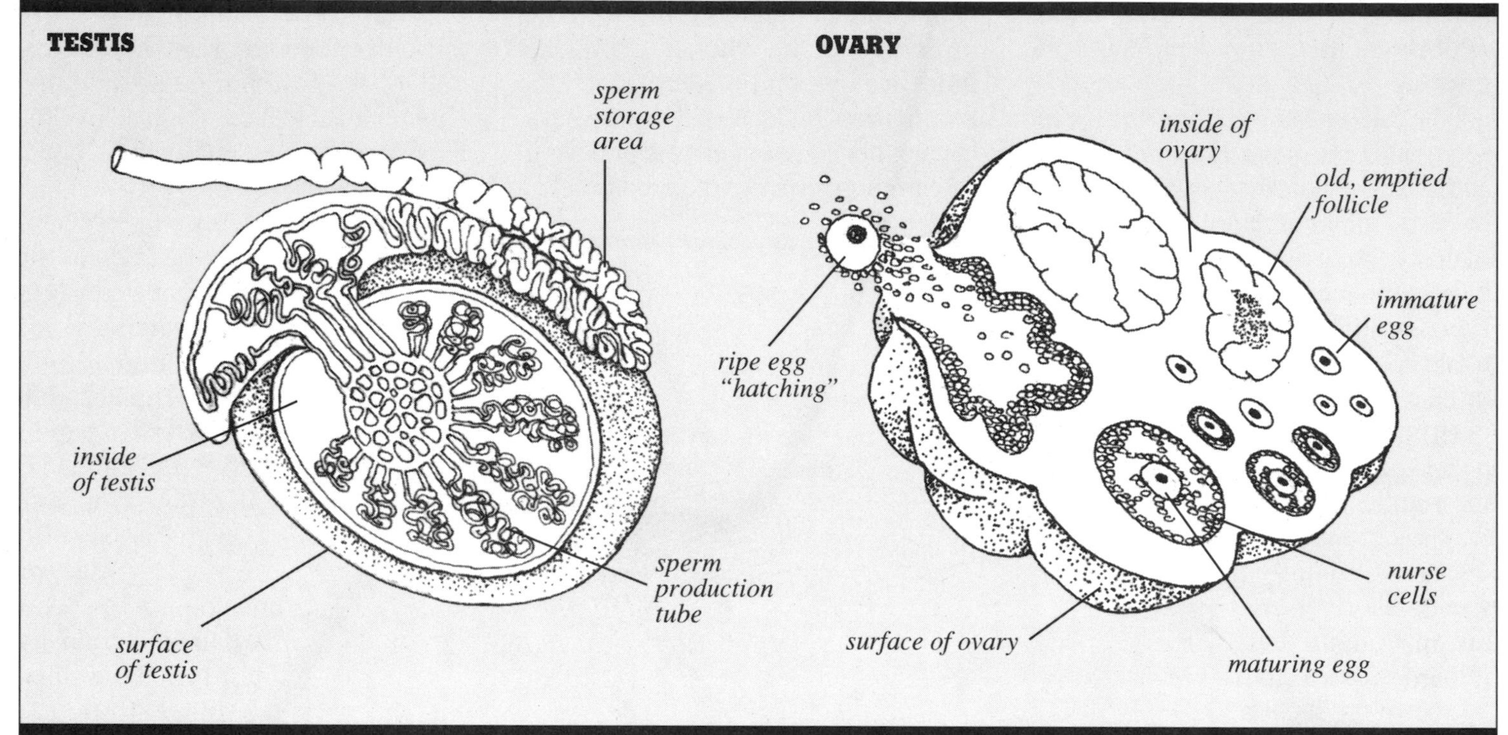

The reduction divisions by which spermmakers halve the number of their offsprings' chromosomes mix up the libraries entirely by a process of gene exchange.

Reduction division begins in the usual way: The cell duplicates its chromosomes (now there are 92), and two copies of each, held together at the middle, coil into tight ringlets. In ordinary division the copies are soon pulled apart as the cell divides, and each daughter gets an identical set of 23 maternal chromosomes and 23 paternal ones—46 in all. In reduction division, there is an additional step before the cell divides. Each pair of maternal copies joins the matching pair of paternal copies. While joined, each foursome swaps pieces: these genes for those, this batch for that. When the swap is done and the foursome breaks into couples again, each chromosome is a hybrid of both maternal and paternal genes.

The cell now divides twice. In the first division, each of the two daughters gets a pair of hybrids—still attached—of each of the 23 kinds of chromosome. In the second division, the pairs come apart, and each of the four daughters gets one of each kind. And each one of each kind is truly one-of-a-kind, for no chromosome belonging to these four cells is the same as any in the original maternal or paternal libraries. Nor are their libraries the same as one another's. Nor will other sex cells undergoing reduction division swap just the same genes. Sperm and eggs are as unique as people are: No two are alike.

Arm in Arm in Arm in Arm

One set of genes is not enough to survive on. Such a cell can make only half the usual amount of ordinary "housekeeping" proteins, or, if a gene is defective, none at all. Most people carry a few defective genes. Usually this is no problem. Because they have two sets of chromosomes, each cell has two of each kind of gene. If one's no good, the other serves instead. Sex cells, with their single set, don't have that choice.

Sperm have an additional problem. Of the two sex chromosomes that are divided between them, half of the sperm get the X, and half the Y. But the Y chromosome, the mighty mite that makes a male, is a defective chromosome that lacks a bunch of genes X chromosomes carry, and that are necessary to life. If sperm that have Ys were to die, then all eggs would be fertilized by X-sperm, all babies would be girls, and that would be the end of reproduction.

These problems are solved by sharing. When a spermmaker divides, the two daughters remain attached to one another by a membrane bridge through which they share their products. That pair's 4 granddaughters, their 8 great-granddaughters, their 16 great-great-granddaughters do the same: All descendants remain connected through all their doublings. They still hold onto one another as they double and redouble during their reduction divisions. Half are finally deprived of the X chromosome they need to mature into sperm, but whatever they can't make themselves flows to them from their sisters. In addition, the whole arm-in-arm group remains plugged into a nurse cell, which grows longer and longer to accommodate her multiplying charges.

One might expect that after the final reduction division, these plump sex cells would gradually slim down, grow tails, and swim away as sperm. That is not what happens. Each cell instead grows a tiny sperm that dangles from it like a tadpole on a stalk. The large cell bodies and the nurse that feeds them nourish the sperm while they are developing, using the combined product lines of the whole group. As each sperm's body is finished, the cell

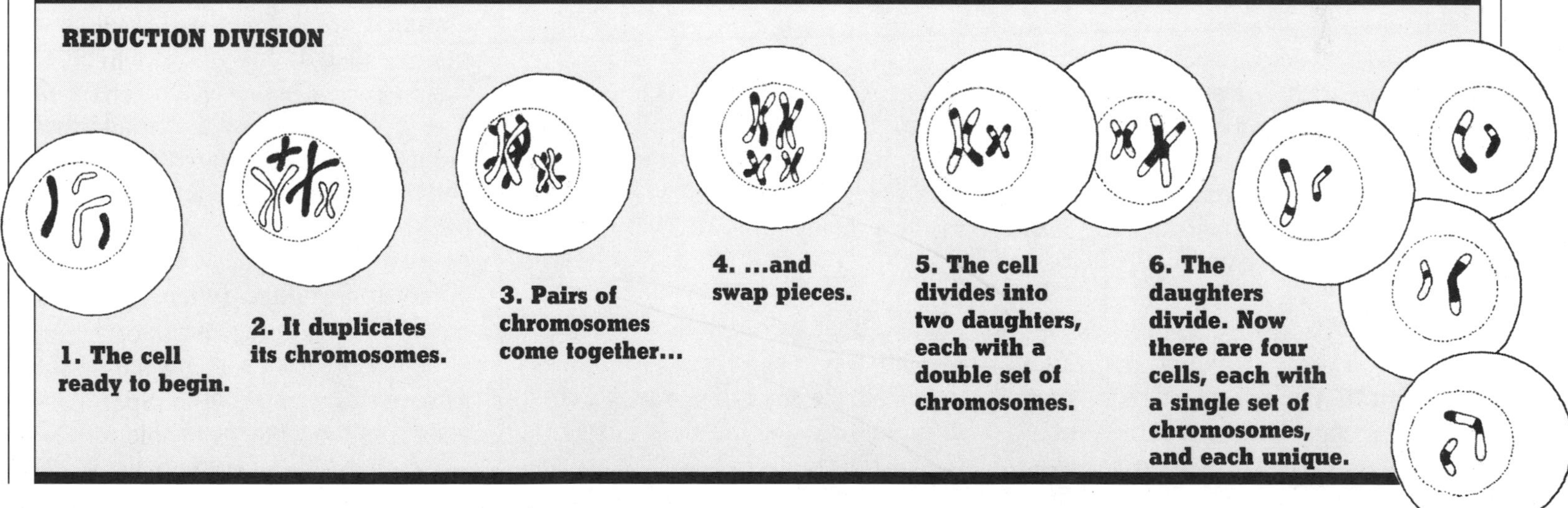

REDUCTION DIVISION
1. The cell ready to begin.
2. It duplicates its chromosomes.
3. Pairs of chromosomes come together...
4. ...and swap pieces.
5. The cell divides into two daughters, each with a double set of chromosomes.
6. The daughters divide. Now there are four cells, each with a single set of chromosomes, and each unique.

An Unusual Use of Blood Pressure

Usually the amount of blood outward-bound through arteries is the same as the amount of blood returning to the heart through veins. But there is one kind of tissue especially designed to swell with blood. Genitals—a male's penis or a female's vulva—contain erectile tissue that can swell and harden because more blood is coming in than going out. The effect is more dramatic in a male, whose penis is nearly filled with spongy erectile tissue that can fill with blood. Normally, muscles around the arteries leading into the penis are tightened. Little blood is pumped in, and the penis is small and floppy. During erection, those muscles relax. Much more blood now enters the penis, and it fills up. The pressure, in turn, flattens veins, so less blood can leave. The penis expands to a couple of times its usual size, and becomes hard. When the muscles relax again, the penis empties, shrinks, and softens.

The biological purpose of erection is to stiffen a man's penis so that it can deliver sperm into the woman's vagina, and to give sexual pleasure to both sexes. But children, girls and boys, experience erection and enjoy it many years before it will serve a reproductive purpose. There is no harm in this; in fact it's unavoidable. People are born with the sexual organs they will need as adults, and that offer from the outset a mild form of pleasures yet to come.

scrunches its chromosomes into a tight package, and exports its shrunken nucleus into the sperm's head. The sperm then detaches, and swims away. What is left of parent cells disintegrates, and the nurse is free to nourish the next batch.

The divisions by which spermmakers produce a batch of sperm take a total of 16 weeks. That seems too slow by far to supply hundreds of millions of sperm a day. However, there are altogether 750 feet of tubules lined with spermmakers in the testes, and everywhere along them sperm-making goes on all the time, week in week out, to assure a steady supply of swimmers.

Big Eggs

The life story of eggs from the time they travel into the embryo's ovaries is very different from the life story of sperm. About 1,700 cells originally make the trip. For the next few months they divide exuberantly until they number 7 million. Then, before the baby girl is born, they begin their first reduction division—and abruptly stop. Their nurses have dosed them with anti-ripener.

At this point eggs have doubled all 46 of their chromosomes. But the maternal and paternal libraries are not yet mixed, and the 92 chromosomes are not yet tightly coiled. Eggs stay in this state of arrested development until a girl's puberty, when they resume the division they began some dozen years before.

Arrested development must be hard on eggs, for most do not survive it. By birth, 5 million would-be eggs have already died. Of the 2 million remaining, only 300,000 will live the dozen years to puberty. More will die in the succeeding years. In all, 99.9 percent of cells that might have ripened fail. During her reproductive life, a woman ripens a total of only 300 to 400 eggs.

These eggs, however, are enormous. The bulk of each is a thousand times greater than that of the average body cell. Such growth is possible because each egg has a whole crew of nurses to nourish it, and it can use its extra set of genes to produce twice the usual amount of anything it needs.

As an egg grows, its nurses divide. Toward the end of childhood nurses caring for the most mature eggs multiply to form a thick capsule, called a follicle, around it. A hollow forms at one side of the follicle. As the hollow enlarges, the egg bulges at the surface of the ovary. Nurses lose their grip. They can no longer dose the egg with anti-ripener, and now the egg picks up where it left off so long ago: It completes its first reduction division.

Yet it doesn't become two eggs. The division is an unfair one in which one daughter gets all the cell fluid, and all the cell machinery. The other remains as a mere bump inside its sister: The egg has got it all.

At this point a sperm cell would divide again to dole out one of each kind of hybrid chromosome to each of two offspring. Eggs don't—not yet. In fact, few ever do. The bulge on the ovary where an egg has ripened thins to a blister, and breaks. The egg is swept up into the oviduct, is moved down it toward the womb. It will complete its last division only if, during that brief trip, it meets a sperm, and is fertilized.

A fertilized egg again divides, and again unequally. One daughter gets nothing but the surplus set of chromosomes; it will eventually disintegrate. The other gets all the nourishment, and all the equipment, to grow into an embryo.

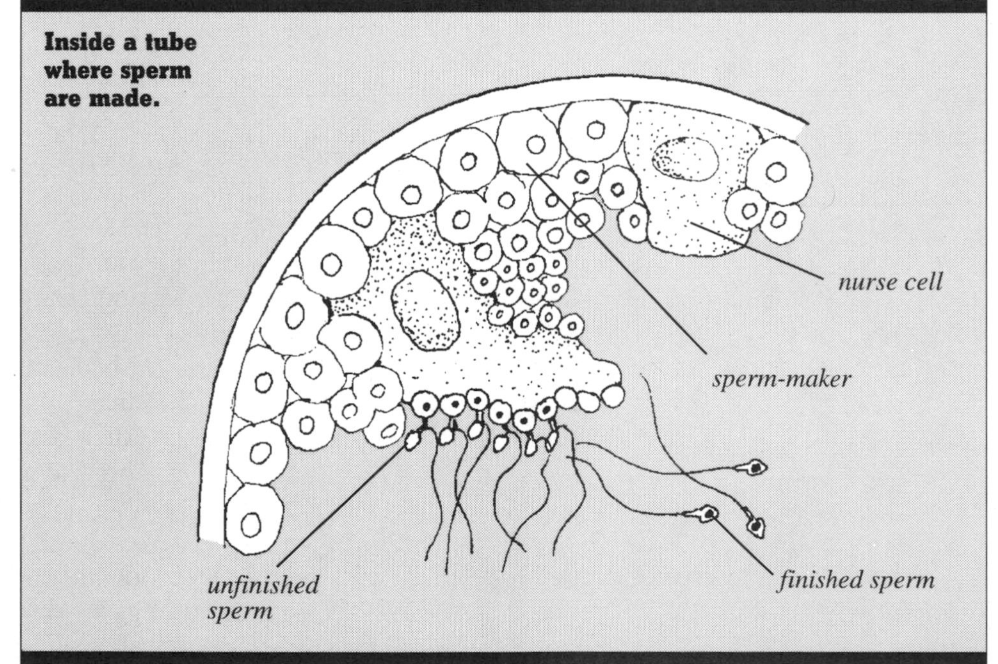

A Vital Link

Reproduction is not just the business of the reproductive system. Your whole body—by eating, growing, breathing, peeing—serves the sex cells that depend on it for their own continuance. No other cells in you contain genes that will express themselves beyond your own, individual lifetime. From the point of view of sex cells, your body is an environment in which they can survive until, by pairing with another sex cell, they can make a body of their own. In this sense, you have been a parent of the next generation since long before you yourself were born. Your sugar treats give them energy; your fresh air is what they respire; your kidneys care for their sea, too. And you are their vital link with the outside world from which comes the salt and sweet and wet and breath of life.

But how is that connection made? How do you know salt when you find it? How do you recognize, from behind your dead skin, any of the ingredients that—absorbed by the gut, processed by the liver, pumped by the heart, cleansed by the kidneys—make up the juice that keeps all your cells alive? Ultimately, through all the thickness of its 40 trillion cells, a body's got to know what's out there in the world.

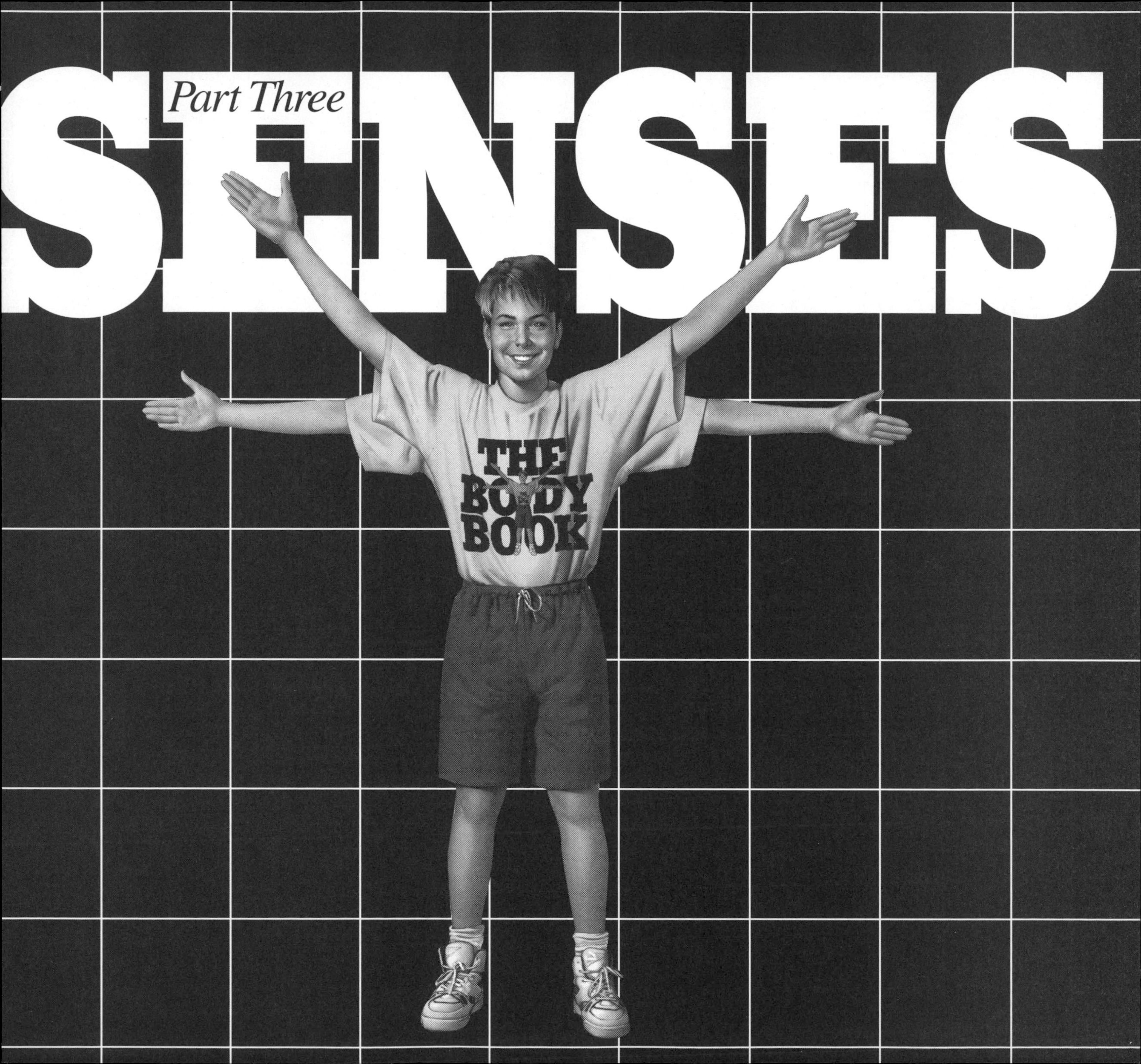
Part Three
SENSES
THE BODY BOOK

THE WORLD THROUGH CRUST

The inside of a body is not at all like the "natural" world outside, for the environment in which your cells live is climate controlled, with piped-in food, and air, and water. Yet everything needed to maintain a body's cells must be selected from the outside world, fresh air instead of smoke, food, not poison. Air is there for the breathing, but food is walked to, reached for, cut and cooked. Cells are in jeopardy every moment. If their body fails to eat, they perish of starvation. Their body, not them, must dress for a blizzard, steer clear of poisonous snakes, hide from lightning, pull back from burning irons, choose to drink water instead of ammonia.

All this is not so easily done since, in order to live at all, the body has had to seal itself inside dead crust. The crust itself, the only part exposed to the outside world, can't make a move, can't raise a hair or sweat a drop or lift a finger to eat a bite without muscles, which live in darkness and in ignorance. Within the body, the lame lead the blind, and the blind lead the lame, and nevertheless you manage to come in out of the cold.

The Smallest Motor in the World

The twirling flagella that propel *E. coli* are driven by the world's smallest electric motors. The electrical current is a flow of protons pumped through the cell's membrane. The current spins a rotor connected by an axle to the flagellum through a stationary bearing. Although each motor draws only one thousand-trillionth of an ampere of current, it can twirl the flagellum at a speed of 200 revolutions per second.

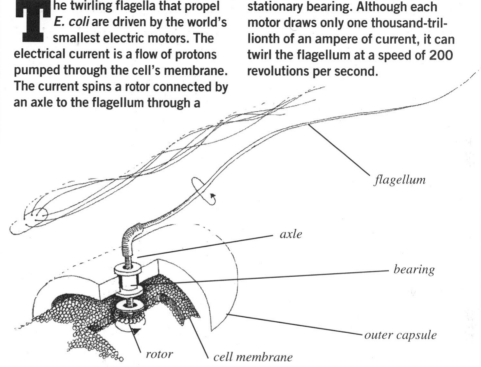

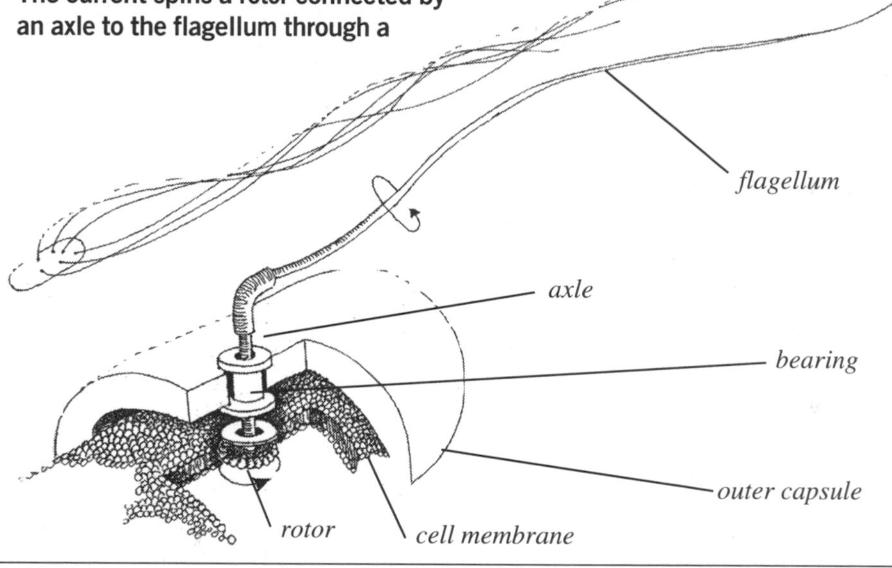

Nosing Along

Keeping in touch with its environment is much easier for a one-celled organism, which has no thickness to speak of. *E. coli*, your common intestinal bacterium, has a perfectly simple way to find a meal, while avoiding danger. Sugar is among the bacterium's favorite foods; too much acid injures it. These two substances exist in varying proportions in the bacterium's environment, plentiful sugar here, too much acid there. *E. coli* therefore has to direct its movements toward where its environment is more sweet than sour.

The bacterium is able to sample water by means of receptors in its coat. Some receptors respond to sugar, others to sour, and both register a "hit" by releasing a messenger substance to the interior of the cell. The number of these messenger molecules that are released correspond exactly to the number of hits, and so relay an accurate count of the amount of sugar and acid bumping into the cell in the outside world. As *E. coli* swims along, the count changes as the proportion of the two substances changes. The microbe in this way monitors its surroundings, learns whether it is swimming into sweeter or more sour water.

Let's say the water becomes more sour. The greater number of sour messages inside the bacterium reverses its flagella for an instant. The bacterium tumbles, then takes off in another direction, still sampling. Now the number of sweet messages increases. Its flagella twirl steadily. They will keep it swimming in sugar until, again, its little world goes sour, and it turns to taste anew.

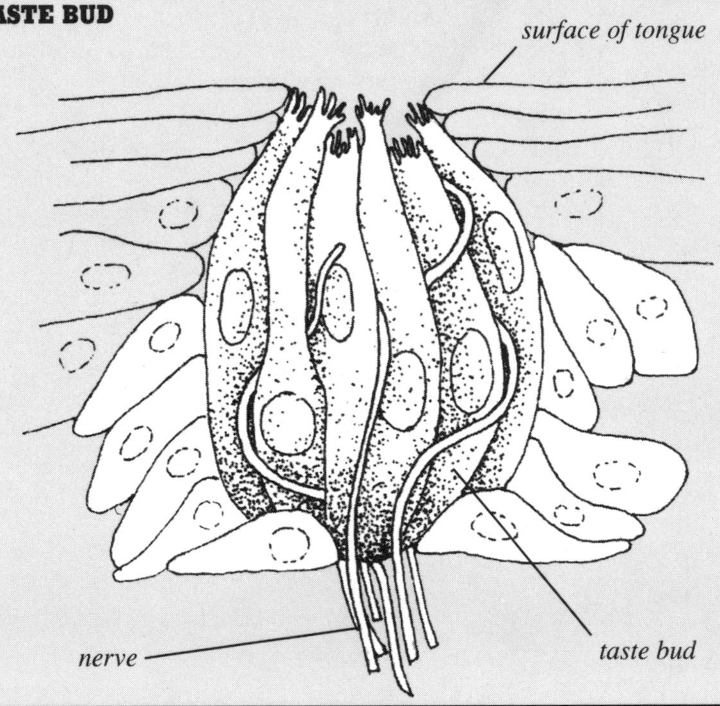

Now imagine that this bacterium loses its twirling flagella. It can taste, but can't move. Were it able to team up with a swimming buddy, and signal to it the results of its environmental survey, the buddy could propel it—be its "muscle"—even if it had no sense of taste itself. One could even insert between sensor and mover a third cell that had neither nose nor tail. As long as this chain of cells were able to convey signals from the cell in front to the cell in the rear, this invented creature would get to where the sugar was.

This is how all bigger bodies work: Some cells sense, others move, and the two kinds communicate by signals along nerve cells that connect them.

The receptors with which a bacterium samples water are similar to chemical sensors on other organisms. They are like the receptors with which a phagocyte tracks its prey, and the ones with which you follow a nasty smell to find out where a puppy has made a mess, or sample the flavor of liver to decide whether to spit or swallow. Such chemical receptors work only with molecules dissolved in water, and therefore are in wet places. If an organism is to know what's ahead of it, the receptors must also be placed in front, in the direction of travel which, in animals, is the head. Our chemical receptors are in moistened skin of nose and mouth that, with every lick and sniff, sample the outside world.

TASTE BUD

surface of tongue

nerve

taste bud

Free Samples

Both smelling and tasting are done with protein molecules studded through cell membranes like cufflinks through a shirt. Each receptor protein is shaped to fit one or a group of chemicals. In *E. coli*, a filled receptor snaps into a different shape that releases the messenger molecule from the bacterium's inner surface. In other one-celled organisms, the shape change triggers an electrical charge that travels along its cell membrane. That is the signal used by our taste and smell cells, and with good reason. Chemicals travel in cells by diffusion, and if your feet are to find out you've smelled a skunk,

Born Knowing

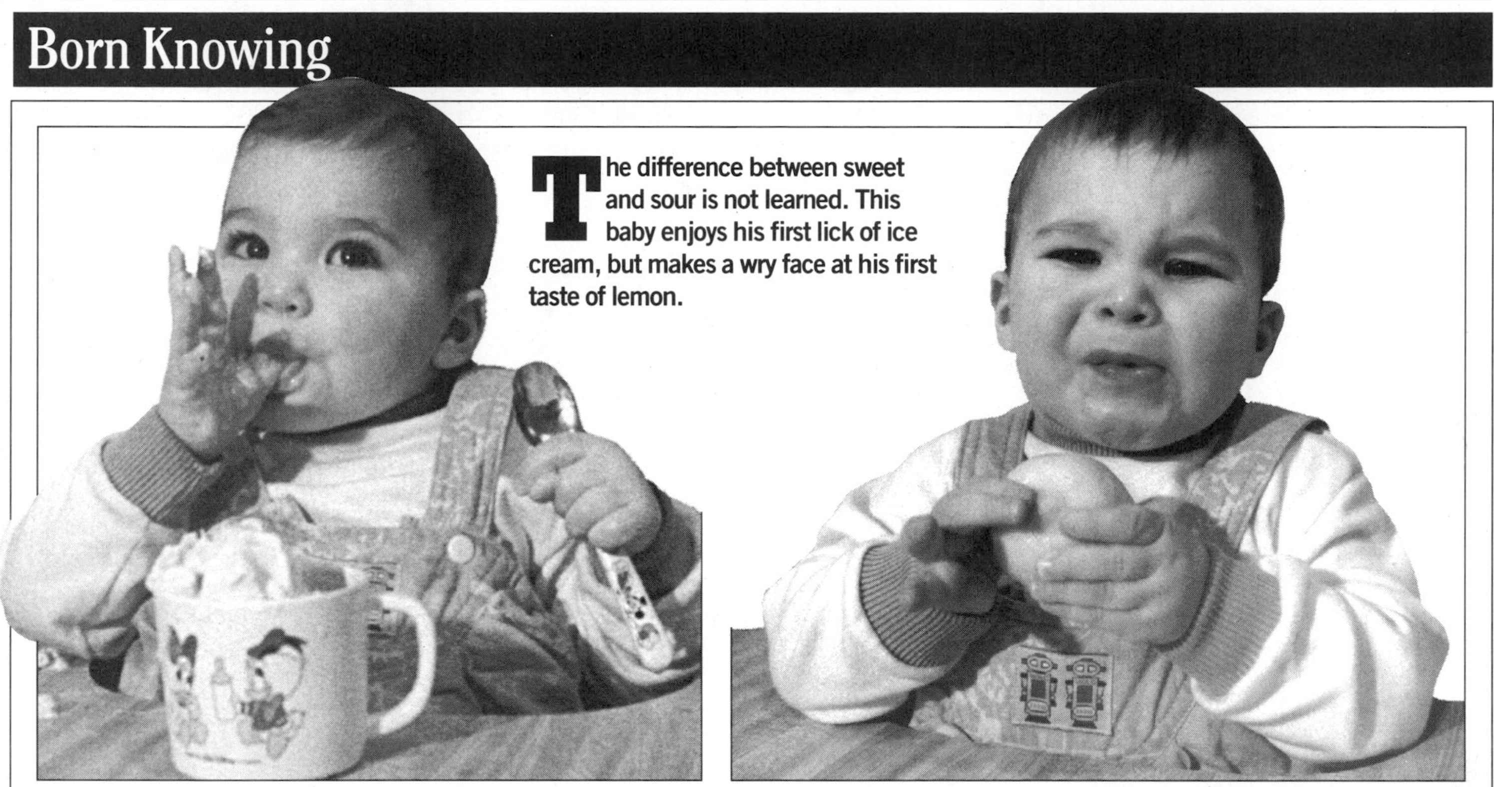

The difference between sweet and sour is not learned. This baby enjoys his first lick of ice cream, but makes a wry face at his first taste of lemon.

diffusion is too slow by a couple of centuries. Electrical signals travel fast, as fast as 90 meters (about 295 feet) per second.

You taste food mostly on the upper surface of your tongue, where there are deep pits much larger than pores elsewhere in the skin. Each pit is lined with dozens of taste buds, groups of cells that really do look like flower buds. The tips of the cells are fringed; taste receptors stud the fringes.

It was once thought that there were four kinds of taste buds, one whose receptors responded only to sugar, another only to salt, a third exclusively to sour acid, and the last to nothing but bitterness. It turns out that each taste bud tastes one of the four best, but that it can detect the others too. Many substances that are not sugar taste sweet, and there is quite a range of chemicals that all taste salty, or bitter, or sour. Some chemicals that taste one way to one person taste different to another: Saccharin is very sweet, unless you are one of those people to whom it tastes bitter. Most substances are picked up to different degrees by several kinds of receptors. The result is the unique blend of flavors that helps to identify what in the world you've gotten into your mouth.

Smell receptors are way up the nose, along the roof of the nasal cavity, less than a finger's width below the brain.

This space opens into the back of the mouth, where fragrant vapors rise from food you're eating. The "taste" of food is therefore really a mix of scent and flavor that gives much more detailed information than does the tongue alone. Without that additional detail, it's hard to tell a clam from a cantaloupe. Food is "tasteless" when you have a cold because your scent receptors get covered with thick mucus. With a clear nose, there's a clear difference between a bite of white bread and a bite of rye; with a clogged nose they taste about the same. Yet how, exactly, scent receptors discriminate between skunk spray and skunk cabbage, or between cabbage and kale, is still a mystery.

The Smell Biz

By analyzing the structure of natural scent molecules, scientists are able to construct similar ones that smell about the same. This knowledge has been used not only to make artificial flavorings, such as chocolate and vanilla, but also canned odors. Among the smells made by Aroma Tech in New Jersey are "Fish," "Pickles," "Rose," and "Chocolate." They smell bad or good, but because they don't contain a great variety of molecules, they don't smell as bad or as good as the real thing.

Many attempts have been made to classify smells, without much success. One smell expert identified seven categories: floral, musky, minty, pungent, putrid, ethereal (like ether), and camphoraceous (like camphor) that differed in construction. He found, for example, that substances identified as minty by trained sniffers are wedge-shaped molecules of a particular size, those that smell like camphor are spherical, and those that smell like flowers are discs with a flexible tail. He figured that for each category there would turn out to be a receptor shaped in such a way that only those molecules would fit into it, as a key fits into a lock. And he predicted that he would be able to manufacture molecules that, to his sniffers, would be indistinguishable from the real thing even if they were chemically very different substances. He was right, according to his sniffers. But the problem was not solved.

The very same molecule may have a wedge-shaped bump in one place and a flexible tail in another. Like molecules that are tasted, it might fit two or more kinds of receptors, depending on

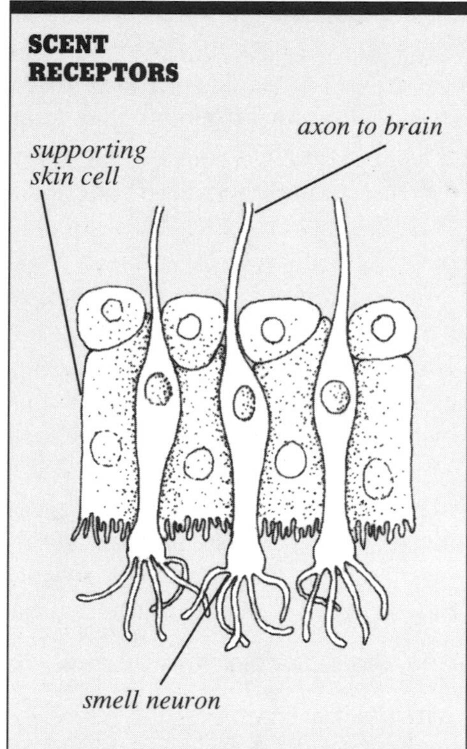

which part of it settled on the cell surface. You probably wouldn't have much trouble deciding that thyme is minty, or that bad breath is putrid, but try fitting toast, chocolate, mowed lawn, burnt rubber, Swiss cheese, or newborn baby into such categories. How would you classify the smell of spring? The problem isn't clarified by getting the tongue's opinion: Describe the smell/taste of chicken soup.

Smells are typically made up of numerous kinds of molecules stimulating several kinds of receptors, or

Skunk Anosia

An anosia is an inability to smell a certain odor; among the most common anosias is an inability to smell the stink of skunk. Those with skunk anosia aren't missing much, but they should be careful not to show off by sniffing skunks a lot. The cause of an anosia is a lack of one or some kinds of receptor necessary to smell a certain smell. The lack, however, is not complete. When cells that have a few of the proper receptors find them often filled with fitting scent molecules, they begin to make more of those receptors. Soon there are enough of them: The stink of skunk is smelled.

This fact was more or less stumbled upon by researchers, and it excited them very much, for it is similar to the way in which immune cells intensify the body's sensitivity to germs. At first, the body has an "anosia" to a germ that it has not met before: Those immune cells (kinds of white blood cells) that have receptors to fit the germ are very few, and rather scantily equipped with receptors. But if those few should find their receptors filled by fitting germs, they multiply, and manufacture many more receptors. In this way the body becomes "sensitized" to that germ, and launches an attack against it. So, too, a body becomes sensitized to skunk smell, and runs the other way.

stimulating all of them in varying proportions, and so they are blends that defy classification. Vanilla, for example, is made up of over 150 different kinds of odiferous molecules. Artificial vanilla flavoring is a poor substitute for the real thing: It contains only one of those ingredients.

A scent molecule is held only for an instant, and then let go, freeing that receptor to sniff again. How strong a smell smells depends on how many molecules of it are being sampled by receptors at that moment. This is why you are able to find out where a smell is coming from. Notice how you behave when you try to discover the source of an odor. You lift your head. That puts your nostrils straight out in front of you. You close your mouth; air comes only through your nose. You turn your head from side to side. You don't breathe normally: You sniff short, fast breaths, in, not out. You may, like *E. coli*, take steps in different directions to discover where in the air the scent is strongest. At each sniff you are doing what bacteria do, counting the number of molecules arriving from that direction.

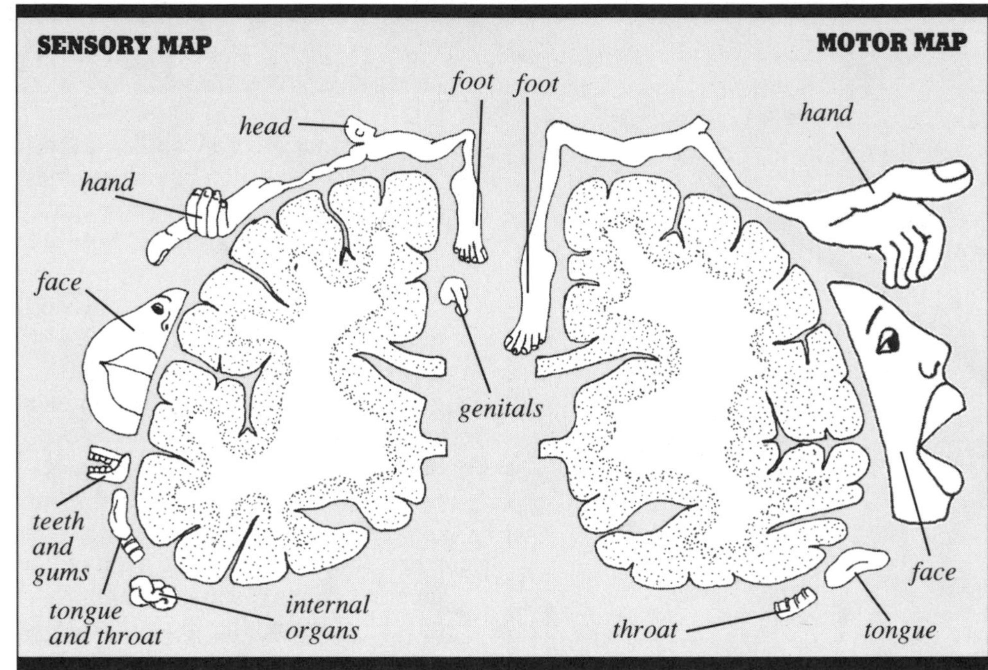

Messages of Plain Vanilla

Smell cells are neurons, individual nerve cells that go straight from nose to brain. Those in the nose are short. They have little blunt arms that wave around in the watery mucus that coats nostrils, sweeping up samples of the chemicals you sniff. Their narrow bodies are squeezed between tall skin cells, which support them. Just at the level of the basal cells, each neuron body narrows even further into a single, wire-like stem, called an axon. The axon is the cell's transmitter, the path along which its traveling charge speeds upward toward the brain just above the bony basement of the skull.

Filled receptors in a smell neuron trigger its charge, firing a momentary message along the axon like a flash in the night. Each flash from every neuron is identical. None is stronger, or lasts longer. Messages sent from the tongue are just the same. So are messages fired from neurons in touch with the world anywhere, in eye or hand or ear, all like identical flashes in the dark. So there is a mystery here: How do you know what the nose knows when what reaches the brain is just a burst of charges, and not the real vanilla?

Each smell neuron has thousands of receptors. It may fire when only a few of these are filled; others don't fire unless many are filled; none fires unless fitting molecules land on it; and all fire more frequently the more frequently they are filled. Each flash may be identical, but when vanilla hits the nose, the pattern of which neurons fire, and how often, encodes some pretty particular information. The pattern, not the smell, is what the brain calls vanilla.

As for the smell, that is, in a way, imagined. Axons from nose neurons terminate in their own, exclusive portion of the brain. Were nose neurons instead to terminate in the vision area, the brain would make an image of the message. Were they to flash in hearing centers, the brain would make a plain vanilla sound.

The Men in the Mind

When a gnat gets up your nose, you know where it is. If it tickles an ear instead, that's where you slap. Even though there are parts of your back that your hands can't reach, and that you have not been able to closely study in a mirror, you know exactly that an itch is located up a little higher and to the left of a helping scratcher's hand.

Signals from neurons that carry touch information from the body surface arrive at a map of the body that is a narrow strip along the top of the brain, roughly from ear to ear. The map isn't a picture, but it can be drawn as one by enlarging or shrinking a drawing of a person according to how much space is represented by each body part in the strip of brain.

The resulting image is far from the appealing shape you see in the mirror. It is a dismembered monstrosity split down the middle. Each half, one to either side of the brain, includes a huge-thumbed hand connected to a foot by a wormlike stretch of limb and trunk; a nearly skull-less half-head with gigantic lips; a tiny, separate set of teeth lying next to a tongue three times its size. If you lick an ice-cream cone, the sensation of cold arrives at this disconnected tongue. If you prick your thumb, the pain signal arrives at just that point on the gruesome map's body. If you pick your nose, you pick its nostril.

The distortion of the mental map represents how the outside world actually strikes your body. The hands are oversized because huge numbers of neurons signal from their surface; the top of the skull is disappointingly small because the skin there has fewer neurons, and therefore little to report, and not much brain space on which to say it. Yet the relationships are preserved: Each finger is in its proper place; neurons lying next to one another in a thumb signal to neurons lying next to one another in the brain.

This man in the mind is what feels pricks and itches, the coarse rub of wool, the silky slip of ribbon, raindrops, snowflakes, sharp corners, round curves, hot cheeks, cold toes, and wind. Sensations occur at the surface where the charge in a sensory neuron begins its travels, but they are not felt until they reach their destination in the map. Skin itself does not feel the sensations it transmits. Its fundamental numbness is apparent when its signals to the map have been interrupted, as happens when a doctor injects an anesthetic to painlessly stitch a cut, or when you sit on your foot until its sensory neurons have "gone to sleep."

Lying alongside the sensory man of the mind is a second map, the motor man. It, too, if drawn in the shape of a person, is split in two, dismembered, and distorted. But the proportions are different. On the motor map, sizes of

All the Way to the Pencil Tip

As a child learns to use tools, they must in some way become represented on the sensory map, for when you write, such sensations as the sharpness of the pencil or the roughness of the paper seem to arise from the end of the pencil, not from the fingers that are holding it. Gardeners have a similar experience when using much larger tools, such as hoes and pruners. What feels the texture of the pavement when you ride a bike?

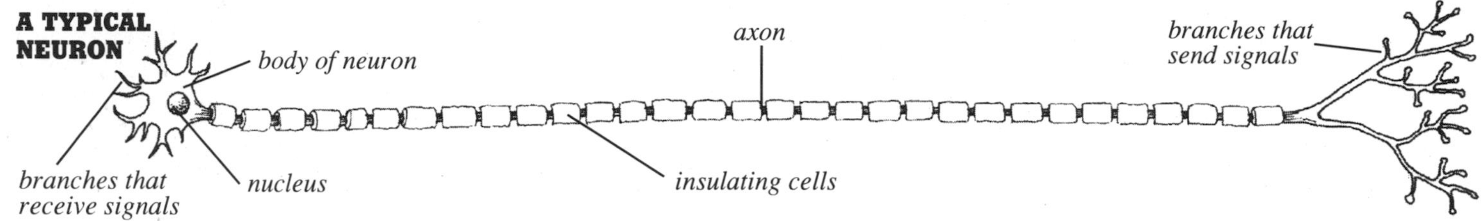

body parts represent the number of neurons that signal to muscles: Those parts of the body capable of delicate and precise movement require more neurons to signal their more numerous muscles, and so are exaggerated. The forehead, hardly there on the sensory map, is large on this one, and so are the eyes and eyebrows. The hand is as large as the head.

This second map is where signals to make purposeful moves arise. If you wiggle a toe to test the fit of a shoe, run your finger along a groove in a desk to detect the shape, turn your head to feel which way the wind is blowing, the signal to move is fired off from toe, finger, or neck of the motor man in the mind.

Gushy Gray Stuff

Neurons on the sensory map that receive information from the outside world, and neurons on the motor map that tell muscles what to do about it, make connections with one another, but not direct ones. The substance of the brain, a gushy gray and white stuff, is billions of interneurons that relay messages within the skull, and to and from the nerves of the spinal cord. The branching ends of each interneuron's axon may communicate with a thousand other nerve cells, and a single nerve cell may receive messages from as many as 10,000 other neurons.

A signal received at the sensory map spreads through the brain among these connections before heading back again along various routes to neurons at the motor map. On the way, uncounted other interneurons are tapped for information—an elbow itch, a commotion in the hallway, thunder, nausea, a memory of chewing gum stuck to the bottom of the desk. Some of these interneurons, when they fire, fire up their contacts. Others do the opposite: They stop the firing of other interneurons with which they come in contact. So the myriad messages wending their way through the brain from the sensory to the motor map contradict one another, like messages of sweet and sour in a bacterium.

E. coli "decides" to move when the positive message of sweet is stronger than the negative message of sour. So does a motor neuron in the motor map. If more of the interneurons in touch with it say "no" than "yes," it fails to fire, and nothing happens. If more interneurons say "yes" than "no," it fires. Then, and only then, you make your move.

No Democracy for Jerks

There is good sense behind skin's inability to feel for itself, for who would want skin to make decisions? If finger skin could decide for itself that its finger should shake off an offending fly, it might give the order just as the hand was poised to deflect a falling brick.

Skin is prevented from making such decisions by its isolation from the rest of the body. No neurons connect skin receptors with one another, or with finger muscles. Every sensory neuron in a finger stretches all the way to the spinal column within a nerve, which is a bundle of individual neurons whose paths lie next to one another. Each of the individual cells within a nerve is insulated all along its axon by special cells that coil around it. Like an electrician's insulating tape, this sheath of cells keeps charge from escaping. There is no cross talk among neurons as they carry their signals headward. They don't know, and will never learn, any gossip from anywhere else in the body.

But the way in which a multitude of gossips in the brain make the eventual decision is not always the best way either, for it is slow. The system by which many neurons contribute to each decision is like a democracy in which each person has a vote. Sometimes you can almost feel the votes being cast. Perhaps you are running a finger beneath the edge of a desk when it hits a lump. One part of your brain votes to investigate further, and you dig in a fingernail. But then other circuits receive a smell, retrieve a memory, create an image, register disgust. You change your mind about investigating: This is a wad of chewing gum. But you have already gotten it under your fingernail. Votes take time to count.

Even the best democracy writes into its laws ways to circumvent voting when decisions must be made in a hurry. The President doesn't have to consult the opinions of 250 million citizens to launch a defense in time of war, and the body doesn't have to count the votes of its brain population to jerk a finger from a flame.

Emergency decisions are made at the spinal cord through a neural short circuit. Pain receptors in a fingertip flash their hurt to where their axons terminate alongside the spinal cord. Many interneurons pick up the news, but while some carry the signal upward toward the brain, others signal to motor neurons only a fraction of an inch away. These motor neurons in the spine are fast-wired, hair-triggered ones. Without waiting for a decision from on high, they fire. Your hand jerks back immediately.

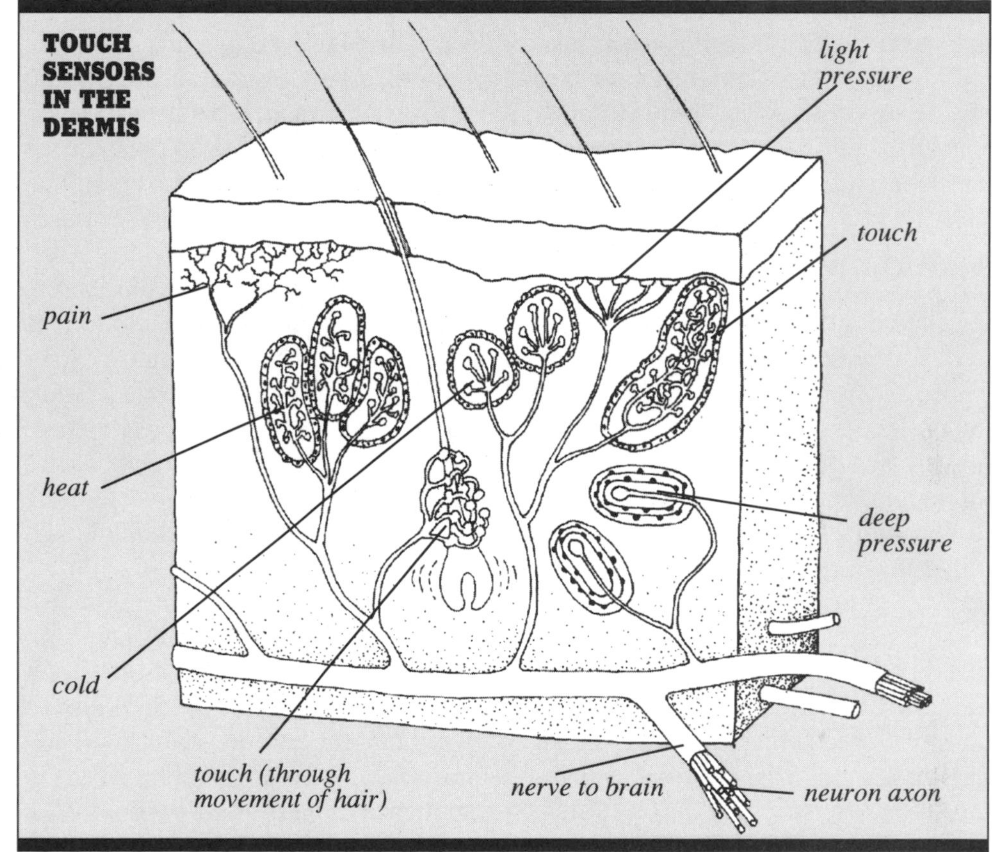

Such jerks happen so fast that signals traveling up the spinal cord to the surface of the brain haven't nearly gotten to the sensory map yet, much less meandered through the brain and, so much the wiser, pricked the neurons in the motor map. You pull your hand from heat before you know anything about it, before you have issued instructions to your muscles, and even before you feel the burning pain.

Not that the clamorous democracy of the brain doesn't soon find out. You may then mutter about your stupidity, or fetch a potholder. But those body jerks that catch you when you trip, take your breath away when freezing water hits, or startle you when the door bangs shut all happen before you know what's happening.

Mixed Messages

People have the darndest time trying to describe sensations from the skin. There are itches, burns, and burning itches. There are tickles: the kind that make you gasp for breath and want to kill the tickler; the kind that make you look for ants or ticks; the kind that is only the wind at play. Pinpricks don't feel the same as blackberry prickles, and neither feels like prickly heat. Sun feels hot, but does a burn? Sunburn sort of does; the burn of a hot iron sort of doesn't. A bee-stung finger feels unlike salt-stung eyes, which in turn feel nothing like those stung by onion fumes. What the dentist may call the "pinch" of an injection is not like a pinch on the arm. A breeze feels cool, snow feels cold, but whether freezing toes feel cold, or hot, or just plain painful is hard to say. What is the sensation of a thunk on the head? A charlie horse? An electric shock? They all hurt, but words can't say the ways.

Everything that happens to skin fires off a combination of sensory neurons unique to that event. Some fire when they are heated, others when they are cooled. The ones that signal pain fire when they are disturbed, and also when they receive chemical messages that cells around them have been injured. Neurons that signal deep pressure, as when you push your thumb against an object, are encased in capsules made of layers of springy connective tissue. Squashing the capsule fires the neuron. Those that signal surface friction, as when you brush a finger against something, fire when they are jostled. Every hair on your body is monitored by these touch sensors: When a breeze blows hairs out of their usual position, the motion causes neurons around each jerked follicle to fire.

The "sense" of touch is therefore five different senses—heat, cold, pain, and pressure, as well as touch itself. Think about a moment at the beach. A gust of wind lifts the hair on your arm, firing movement-sensitive touch neurons in sequence as hairs along your arm rise and fall. At the same time, neurons sensitive to cooling signal the change in temperature as sweat evaporates, pain sensors are zinged by blowing sand, pressure sensors dented by it, and all the while heat sensors blast away in the noonday sun. No other event turns on just that combination of sensors in just that pattern and proportion: There is no feeling quite like that gust of wind at the beach.

The various kinds of sensors are not equally distributed over the skin. When

One or Two?

To find out how closely spaced touch receptors are on various parts of your body, open out a paper clip so the two ends are pointed in the same direction. Close your eyes, and have someone else touch your skin lightly with the tips held at various distances from one another. On your back, the two tips will feel like one if they are less than an inch apart, but lips and fingers detect both tips only 1/16 inch apart. These differences are also reflected in the sensory map in your brain: wherever touch receptors are sparsely scattered, the man in the mind is shrunken; wherever they are densely packed, the man in the mind is swollen.

your feet are so cold they hurt, they may no longer feel cold. There are 30 times more pain receptors than cold sensors: Their message is overwhelming. On the other hand, feet feel cold when their surface temperature drops only a little; they are far less sensitive to rising temperature because they have only a tenth as many heat receptors as cold receptors. If you lightly touch your lip with a fingertip, you'll feel the touch on the lip but not on the finger: Lips are better equipped with touch detectors than any other part of the body. Touch your back the same way: Your finger will feel your back, but your back won't feel your finger.

A point dragged across the skin fires one neuron after another. Neurons in the map receive signals in the same order, so the sense of touch detects movement and direction as well as location. A flat stick leaves a broader trail of signals than a pin. A fast scratch whizzes across the brain; a slow drag drags.

How do you know the strength of a poke or jab? A single touch neuron may have dozens of short branches sprouting from its body. Some fire the neuron when they are jostled only slightly; others have to be nudged harder, or really knocked about. Although any single firing of a neuron is no stronger than any other, the more branches are stimulated, the more frequently the cell fires. Like the alarming *wow-wow-wow* of an ambulance in a hurry compared to the occasional beep of a car in traffic, the frequency of flashes signifies to the brain the severity of the event.

You sense texture through a combination of the number of neurons fired, how they are grouped, and how frequently they fire. When you run your hand through sand, the number of neurons fired depends on how far apart the grains are; the size of each group of neurons fired depends on the size of each grain; how frequently they fire depends on how hard they pull on the skin. Even the minifeet on your man-map can tell coarse sand from fine sand.

Heat Control

All through the hours at poolside or beach, skin sensors flash to the brain the latest surface temperature—the heat of concrete, sand, and sun; the cold of wind, cloud, and water. Air at ground level may be 120° F, ocean water only 60° F, and the change from hot to cold can be as quick as a dive. You feel broiling, you feel freezing, yet all the time, the temperature inside your body hovers within a degree or so of 99° F, the same comfortable lukewarm you've always been. What you feel is not what you are.

Nevertheless, your skin makes quite a fuss about these rises and falls in surface temperature. You lie in the sun, sweating. Those baskets of tiny muscle cells surrounding sweat glands

Heat Stroke

Unlike fever, in which the body gets hotter because its thermostat setting has been raised, the rising heat of heat stroke is due to the thermostat breaking down. Heat stroke happens when the body, for all its sweating, can't get rid of heat fast enough to prevent temperature from rising. The rising heat causes a breakdown in the thermostat, as well as in the circuits that direct sweating. Unless cooled down, a person with heat stroke can heat to death.

Luckily, there is usually a warning: heat exhaustion. A person with heat exhaustion collapses because extreme sweating has depleted the volume of blood in the body, and so the person's blood pressure drops. Without enough blood flow to supply muscles and brain, the person feels sick, dizzy, and may faint. Fainting accomplishes two things. It lets more blood flow to the brain, and it stops the person from getting hotter still by moving. Heat exhaustion is the body's attempt to avoid heat stroke.

Fever

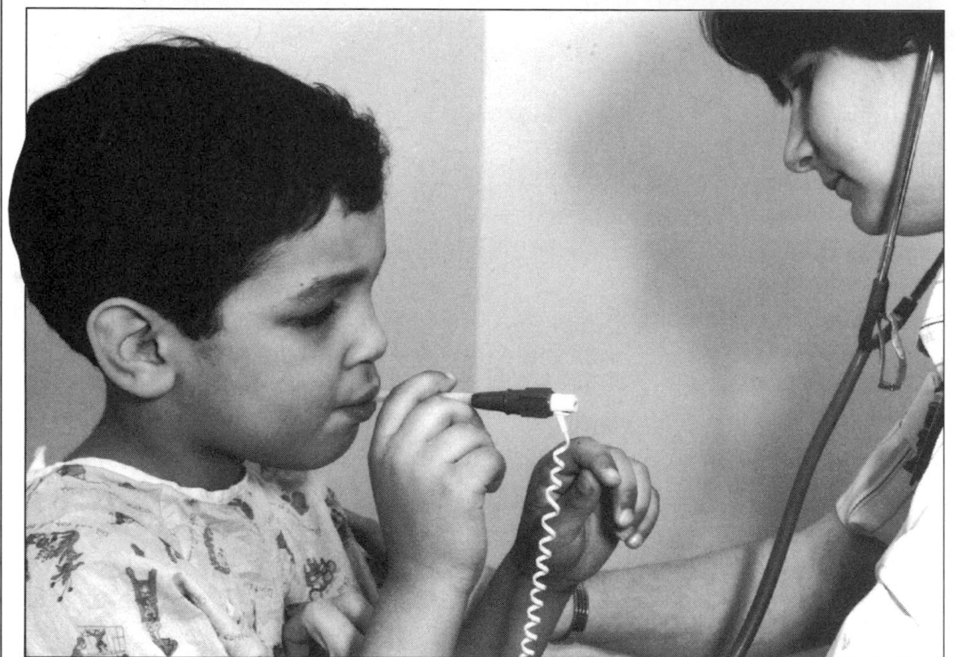

How can it be that when you get a fever, you feel chilled? Fever is a resetting of the body's thermostat. Let's say the thermostat has just been reset from its normal 98° F to 102° F. Your internal temperature is still normal, but that's cold compared to the new setting, so your hypothalamus turns on your heat-conserving mechanisms. You pull another blanket over you and lie there shivering with chills. The chill will stop only when your internal temperature has reached 102° F.

Fever has a purpose: to make cells that fight disease more active, and to make things uncomfortable for bacteria. It is started up by a chemical released from cells that are actually experiencing infection. These chemicals, reaching the brain in the bloodstream, raise the thermostat setting. A second chemical, released locally in the brain, alerts the heat-conserving circuits. Aspirin reduces fever by blocking the manufacture of that second chemical.

squeeze sweat out of pores, cooling your crust by evaporation. Arteries in the dermis dilate. The extra blood blushes you pink but, as it flows beneath your cooling skin, it, too, is cooled.

Clouds cover the sun, wind blows. Sweating stops. You are all goose bumps now. Human goose bumps are pathetic, not much good for anything. The bumps are caused when the muscle attached to each hair follicle pulls the hair erect, pushing skin on one side into a bump. If we were downy or furry, that stand-up plush would trap an insulating layer of air next to the skin, hold heat in, keep wind out. All we get are bumps.

But other things happen. You shiver. Shivering is muscles jiggling; as they jiggle they heat. Arteries constrict, keeping blood back from the dermis, conserving heat. Skin is pale now, not blushed, and lips may look blue with the darker blood of veins.

With all this sweating, flushing, paling, bumping, and jiggling, the temperature inside your body is still the same, and this is strange, for what seems to happen is that the body takes actions to cool or warm itself before its temperature has changed at all. That can only be done by a clever sort of thermostat.

The body's thermostat is within a tiny lump of brain called the hypothalamus. Like a household thermostat, this one is set to a particular temperature. Like one that controls both furnace and air conditioner, it switches on mechanisms both to raise and to lower temperature. But it has another feature that household thermostats don't have. Besides its own internal thermometer that tells it how hot or cold it is, it receives readings from all over the skin surface. A thermostat like that would be nice to have in a house: Instead of waiting until the internal thermometer dips, it would switch on for rising winds and passing clouds before the chill to come was felt. The hypothalamus *predicts* what is going to happen inside the body, and takes steps to prevent it.

To do that requires weighing all the evidence. For example, you might test the water with your toes, and find it freezing. Cold sensors in your feet flash the dip in skin temperature to your brain, but you don't shiver. Messages are being received simultaneously from all over your body all over the sensory map, and all of these are sent via interneurons toward the hypothalamus. Of all the messages, only those from toes say cold. Again, like the bacterium with its sweet and sour decisions, interneurons fire or don't fire according to the proportions of the two kinds of signals, and this automatic calculation sums the result: There is not enough coldness to switch the heat on.

You may, however, pull your foot out of the water, turn around, walk up the beach, and plunk right back down on your nice warm blanket. A different set of interneurons connects incoming temperature messages with the motor map which may, based on any number of inputs, decide you didn't really want to swim today. These same connections help the hypothalamus in its work. It is they that throw off covers and sprawl you in the cooling air, or hug a towel around you and huddle you hunched into a ball. It takes a lot of nerves to come in out of the cold.

Red Drums

Doctors examine ears for two things: accumulated wax, which can interfere with hearing; and a bulging, red eardrum, which is a sign of infection. They may also give two simple hearing tests. In one, they ask if you can hear a ticking watch. In the other, they bang a tuning fork, and, while it's still vibrating, touch it to your skull to test whether you can hear your own bones vibrate.

Hearing Hairs

If air can lift a hair and scuttle sand across a beach, it must be more substantial than its transparency suggests. Molecules of such stuff as oxygen and nitrogen are no more transparent or soft than other molecules, but in air they are separated from one another, each free to move in its own way like dust dancing in a sunbeam. Space between molecules is what makes air invisible, and gives it the feel of nothingness.

Air molecules in a blown-up balloon are jammed together by the pressure of the rubber against them: A balloon feels hard. The hardness is air molecules hitting the rubber. Just as in a liquid, the more crowded air molecules are, the more often they collide with one another and also with the wall of a

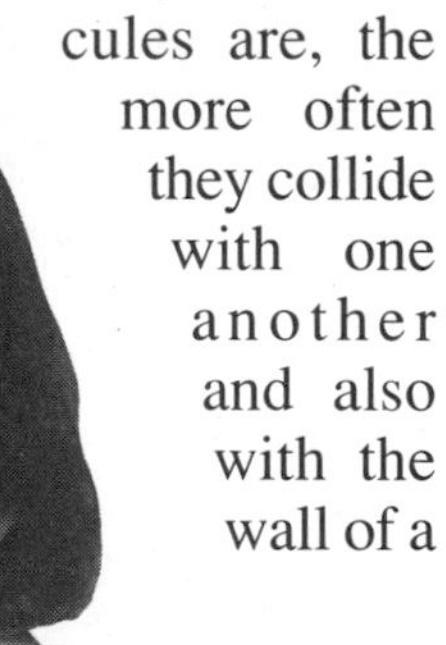

1. Air molecules before clapping are evenly spaced.

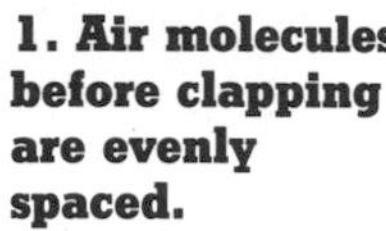

2. The clap sweeps them into a crowd that is roughly spherical in shape.

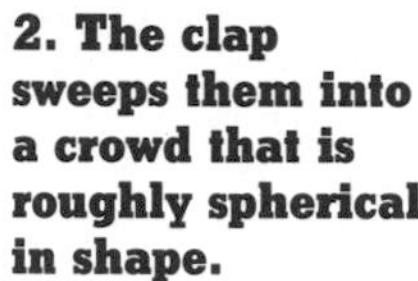

3. The crowded sphere of molecules spreads out, pushing molecules all around into waves of crowdedness like ripples in water when you throw a pebble into it, but in air the ripples are spherical instead of flat.

Clap Hands

When you clap your hands, you shove the air molecules between them closer together. As they rebound from one another, they shove the air molecules surrounding them into a crowd. A wave of crowdedness spreads through the air, and hits your ear. That hit is the sound of the clap.

container. The combined strength of countless colliding air molecules is what keeps a balloon blown up.

Air molecules are what you hear. Bang a drum, twang a guitar string, clash a cymbal. The object vibrates, moves back and forth. Each vibration is like the sweep of a broom, swooshing out air molecules behind and scuttling them into a crowd in front. As the crowded molecules mill around, banging into one another until they bounce themselves apart again, they push molecules to either side of them into a crowd. These crowds do the same, and ripples of crowdedness spread outward through the air.

The air itself doesn't go anywhere. What travels is the energy of each crowd's push against the next molecules it bumps. That's the energy that finally hits your ear.

Ears are like megaphones that funnel each ripple of crowdedness down the narrow tube of the ear canal to the eardrum. The eardrum is the "shore" against which the ripple breaks, and to which it transfers its energy. Because the eardrum is thin, elastic, and stretched tight as a drum, it vibrates when it is hit.

The vibration is slight, but it is amplified by three tiny bones that work something like an arm. When you strike a drum with your hand, your arm at the elbow moves very little, but your hand gives a real smack. In the same way, the flexing of the first ear-bone joint is slight, like the vibration that sets it in motion; the push of the last bone is hard, like a shove.

This last bone shoves against a fluid-filled coil that resembles a snail. Each shove ripples the fluid inside the coil. The coil contains a ribbon covered with cells, called hair cells, whose stiff bristles bend with the ripples. Each bend fires a neuron clasping that cell, and CLANG! goes the cymbal.

Of course, the cymbal has not made a sound.

Like the taste of plain vanilla, the sensation of sound is not a property of the molecules that cause it. An explosion can be felt as well as heard. It is felt because the energy in a scrunched-up bunch of air is strong enough to move hairs when it breaks against the skin, as well as bristles as it ripples through the ear.

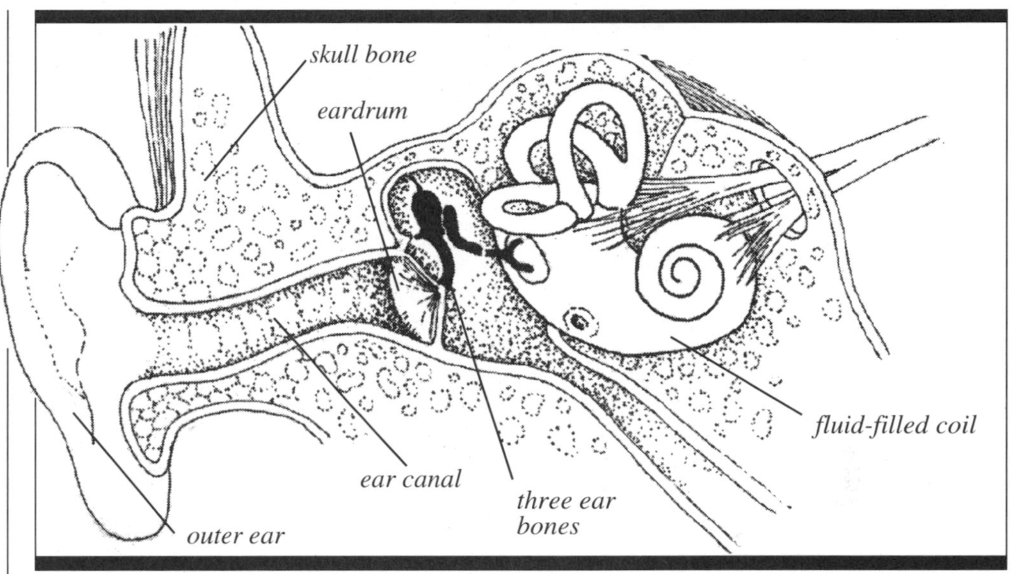

Tuning In

If you could see sound waves, they would look like bands of densely crowded dots separated by bands of sparse dots. The denseness of the dots—how crowded the molecules are—depends on the force of the blow that smashed them close together. The more crowded the molecules, the more force the compression carries, and the louder the sound you hear.

Bands of crowded dots might be separated from each other by broad areas of spread-out dots, or by narrow ones. The distance between dense bands depends on how frequently the molecules were swept—how fast the object vibrated. A narrow guitar string vibrates quickly, and so creates compressions one after another in quick succession. A thick guitar string vibrates slowly; the bands of dense air are more widely separated. We hear closely-spaced—or high frequency—compressions as high pitches, and more distantly spaced, low-frequency compressions as low pitches.

The sounds of your voice are made by forcing air through your vocal cords. Vocal cords are a pair of muscles in the windpipe that work like vibrating reeds in wind instruments, except that they are tunable. When completely relaxed, air passing between vocal cords doesn't vibrate them at all: You breathe, but make no sound. Slightly contracted, they vibrate at low frequency; the more they are contracted, the higher their pitch. As with guitar strings, pitch depends on thickness as well as tightness. Children's vocal cords thicken during adolescence, lowering their voices, and boys' vocal cords thicken more than girls' vocal cords. But no matter what these muscles' thickness, and no matter how you purposely tune their pitch, they are also controlled by emotions that you can't do much about. Anger tenses vocal cords, turning shouts to shrieks. Fear does the same, making giggles rise to nervous titters. Voice pitch is one of the ways in which we can gauge one another's emotions.

Voices and music bring to your ear many frequencies at once, and each at a different loudness. Although the ripples within the coil's fluid in your inner ear therefore form a very complicated pattern, the different frequencies and loudnesses are sorted out as they pass along the hair-cell covered ribbon. The ribbon begins thin and narrow, and gradually broadens and thickens along the length of the coil. Each portion vibrates especially well to a particular frequency. The narrower, thinner portions vibrate best to high-frequency compressions, to high-pitched sounds. The wider and thicker the ribbon becomes, the better it vibrates to low-frequency compressions, to low-pitched sounds. Hair-cell bristles bend and fire a neuron when a sound vibrates the particular portion of the ribbon on which they stand.

Bristles, too, differ. On each cell, they are as varied in height as a pipe organ, and as varied in stiffness as brush bristles. How many bend depends on how forceful the push is—how loud the sound. The more are bent, the more often the neuron fires.

As with other skin signals, what the brain receives from the ear is a mixed message from varying numbers of hair cells in various locations. Again, the message arrives at a map. The map is arranged by pitch. You can think of the pitch map as a synthesizer, for it is here in the electric brain that at last the soundless sweeping of such stuff as nitrogen is translated into symphonies.

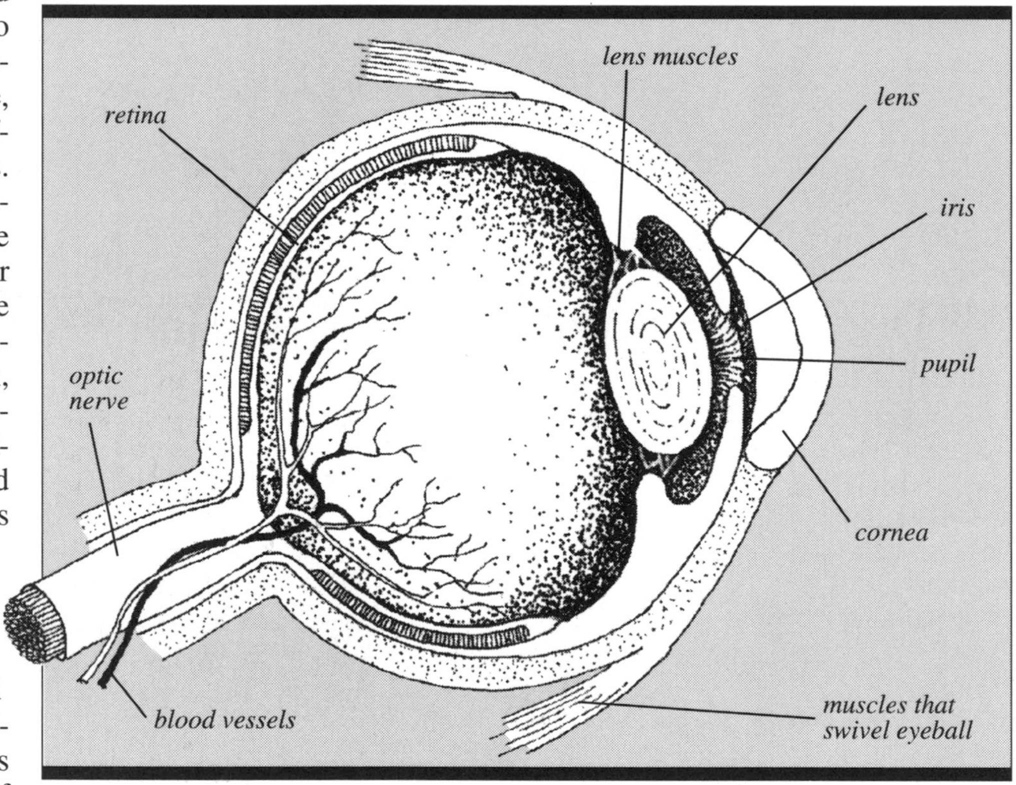

The Camera Eye

Close an eye and press it with your finger: You'll see stars. Receptors in your eye have fired, and so your brain sparkles. Receptors fire when disturbed enough regardless of the cause of the disturbance. Chemicals will do it; so will an electric shock. A loud enough explosion lights up the brain.

Because of this tendency of nerve cells to flash false messages, they must be tuned to the particular sort of sensation they're supposed to get fired up about. Nerve cells in the eyes are hair-triggered to fire when hit by photons—particles of light.

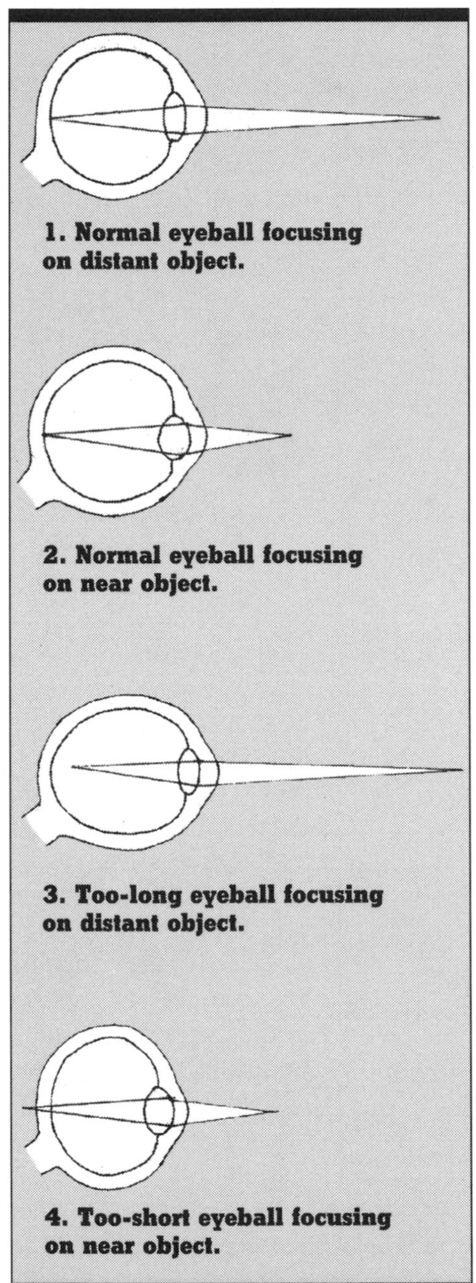

1. Normal eyeball focusing on distant object.

2. Normal eyeball focusing on near object.

3. Too-long eyeball focusing on distant object.

4. Too-short eyeball focusing on near object.

Four-Eyes

Nearsightedness and farsightedness are not caused by defects in eye lenses, but by eyeballs that are the wrong size for them. If an eyeball is too long from front to back, images of nearby objects fall on the retina, but images of distant objects fall short of it. The result is blurry distance vision, or nearsightedness. Farsightedness is the opposite: The eyeball is too short from front to back. Images of distant objects fall on the retina, but those of nearby objects fall beyond it, so they look blurry. Eyeball shape can't be changed, but additional lenses—glasses—can be added to focus images correctly on the retina.

Astigmatism, in which vision is distorted, is caused either by defects of the lens, or by defects of the transparent cornea in front of the lens. In both cases, the surface is uneven instead of smoothly curved. While some parts of an image are focused correctly, other parts are not. Glasses in this case are shaped to compensate for the unevenness so that images are no longer distorted.

The apparatus of the eye resembles a camera. The camera "box" is the eyeball. The front portion of the eyeball is the transparent cornea you see through; it corresponds to a glass lens cover. A camera is painted dull black inside to keep reflected light from bouncing around inside it. So is the inside of the eyeball covered with a layer of dark pigment everywhere except the cornea.

Inside the eyeball, toward the front, is a lens through which light passes before hitting the rear wall—the retina—whose pigmented light receptors act as film.

You adjust focus in a camera by moving the lens closer to or farther from the film behind it. This is the way fish and frogs change their eye focus. Mammals change focus by changing the shape of their lens. The shape is controlled through the tension of tiny muscles attached to the lens edge. A fat lens is for close-ups; stretching the lens thinner brings distant objects into focus.

Between the cornea and the lens is the iris, the colored circle that, like a camera's diaphragm, adjusts the amount of light reaching the retina. Light enters the lens through the pupil, a circular opening in the middle of the iris. Muscles that circle the iris, and muscles that extend from it like spokes on a bicycle wheel, widen the pupil up to ⅓ inch to allow more light to enter, or narrow the pupil to as little as ¹⁄₁₆ inch to cut down on light.

This whole apparatus, mounted on a stalk of nerves and surrounded by rays of muscle, swivels freely in the eye socket.

Rods and Cones

Although the apparatus of the eye resembles a camera, the retina is different from film. It is a layer of tall cells packed tightly together. There are two kinds, named for their shapes: cone cells and rod cells. Cones contain three pigments that are responsible for color vision in bright light. Rods function even in very dim light; their single pigment is responsible for black and white vision. The retina of each of your eyes is packed with 3 million cones and 100 million rods.

Most of the color-coding cones are in the center of the retina, and they are more densely packed than receptors toward the edges. When you are in bright sun, the narrowed pupil beams light especially to the central cones. Because cones are so closely spaced, color images in bright light are exceptionally sharp. And because they are most crowded in the middle of the retina, the middle portion of your visual field is the clearest.

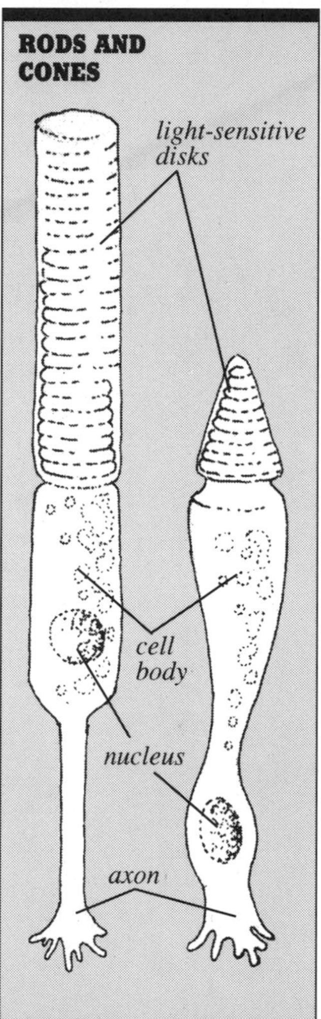

Rods are more widely spaced, and most are toward the edges of the retina. When you are in dim light, the widened pupil allows light to fall equally over the whole retina. Because of their spacing, rods convey a fuzzy image. As night falls, too few photons hit to fire cones, and only rods are activated. You then see in black and white alone, and never as clearly as when cones are helping out. But there is a trick you can use to see an object better in the dark. Look at a star the way you look at things in daylight, through the center of your eye. Then look at the star again out of the corner of your eye. The star is clearer that way because its image is falling to the edge of your retina, where rods are more closely spaced.

The retina's light receptor cells are specialized neurons whose rod-shaped or cone-shaped portion is stacked with disks studded with light-sensitive pigment molecules. A single rod cell contains about 2,000 disks, each studded with millions of pigment molecules. A photon entering a rod cell has little chance of getting through the stack without hitting a pigment molecule. When that happens, a loop in the molecule springs open: The cell fires; you see light.

When you first walk off a bright street into a dark movie theater, you can hardly see because many pigment molecules have been sprung by sunlight. After a few minutes, you can see quite well. Darkness gives eye pigments a chance to refold their open loop, and so be available again for seeing. After 40 minutes of total darkness, all pigment molecules have refolded, and your eyes are then 25,000 times more sensitive to light than they are out on the sunny sidewalk. Of course, you see better in daylight than at night: Less pigment is available, but 30,000 times more photons hit.

Minicomputers

Signals that light has hit rods and cones do not go directly to the brain. First, they are relayed through interneurons at the back of the eye. These interneurons are minicomputers that process visual information before sending it onward. Each minicomputer receives information from a roughly circular

A View to the Brain

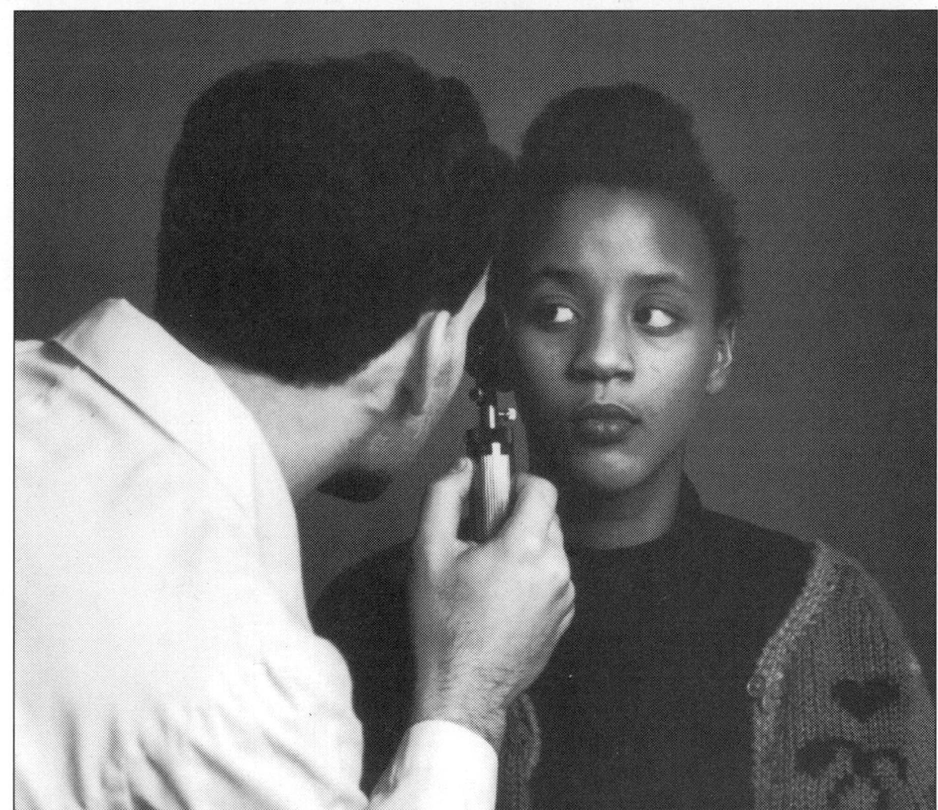

No matter whether your iris is heavily pigmented, and therefore brown, or lightly pigmented, and therefore hazel or gray, or not pigmented at all, and therefore reflects blue light like the sky, pupils are always black. They are black because they are holes through which can be seen the dark retina. When a doctor shines a penlight into your eye, he or she sees your retina, and can check such things as its blood supply. The rods and cones of the retina are neurons that, in the embryo, grew directly from the brain, and are properly a part of it. Pupils can therefore be thought of as windows to the mind.

group of several dozen rods and cones, and transmits to the brain through its own, private neuron. Many thousands of such neurons, each reporting from a mere spot on the retina, are bundled together in the optic nerve.

Retinal processing is like computer enhancement of a foggy photographic image. The minicomputers exaggerate dark and bright areas, and ignore "gray" areas. What is sent to the brain is a high-contrast version of the pattern of photons that have actually struck the eye.

Photons are energy, and some are more energetic than others: Their different energies strike us as different colors. Those that are most energetic we see as blue, those that are least energetic we see as red, and the colors green and yellow have energies somewhere in between. Sunlight and light bulbs emit photons of all these energies, and rods will spring to any of them. The reason we can see in color is that cones contain fussier pigments that, by springing most easily to photons of a certain energy, distinguish among all the colors of the rainbow.

There are three kinds of cones, each of which contains a slightly different pigment. One is most sensitive to high-energy blue light, another to low-energy red light, and the third to medium-energy green light. We might easily have evolved a pigment that springs best to yellow, but that's not necessary. Although each kind of pigment is most apt to spring when hit by a photon of a certain energy, each also springs somewhat to photons that are a little more or a little less energetic than its "favorite" color. So let's say you are looking at yellow, photons whose energy level is midway between red and green. Enough pigment molecules spring that some of your red cones, and some of your green cones signal. But yellow is not energetic enough to fire any blue cones. Each minicomputer serving a group of cones computes the color by subtraction: It can't be red, because not all red cones are reporting; it can't be green because not all green cones are reporting; and certainly it can't be blue—so it must be yellow.

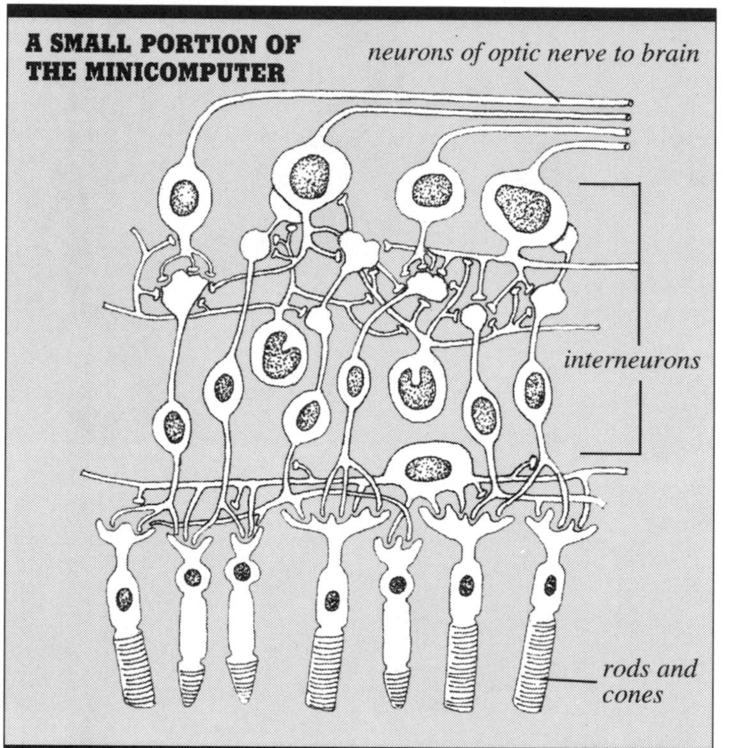

Banana, orange, raspberry, olive, plum—any color is arrived at in the eye's minicomputers by subtracting from incoming signals colors that are *not* being signaled: What remains must be the color.

However, these computer games make us see colors that aren't there. Every color of the rainbow is right now bouncing off this page into your eyes. What do you see? White. White is the made-up color the retina reports when all three kinds of cone are signaling equally. The black print is places where no cones are signaling. Black is no light at all.

To see a color that certainly isn't there, put an orange on a piece of white paper and stare at it for a minute. Then roll the orange away and stare at the paper. You'll see a circle of green. The green ghost is, again, the result of computation. Orange light is captured mostly by the pigment in red cones. After a minute of staring, lots of pigment in those cones is sprung, and they can't catch much red. When you then look at white paper, minicomputers subtract the missing red from all the reported colors, and you see green.

From Spots to Stripes

Each set of interneurons computes only the color and contrast hitting its particular group of cones and rods. What the brain receives is a million or so high-contrast polka dots in black and white and various colors. But the spots themselves are not what you see. You see the result of still more interpretation, this time by feature detectors in the brain.

At the brain, neurons in the optic nerve divide into groups. Each group carries spot messages from a particular portion of the retina, and each is hooked up to many feature detectors. Each kind of feature detector fires only when spot signals from that group are in a particular pattern. Line detectors fire when spots are in a row, and others will fire only if the row is horizontal, vertical, or slanted, or when dots lie in stripes of a certain width, or form curves, or corners. Spots that represent the edge of a pear would fire curve detectors, but not stripe detectors. Spots representing the top left of the letter "P" would fire line detectors, corner detectors, and stripe detectors.

Thanks to Carrots

Although plants can't see, they, too, use pigments to capture light energy from photons. Chlorophyll, which colors leaves green, captures light energy for use in building glucose, and a yellow pigment called carotene, which colors carrots, yams, and banana skins, also captures light for photosynthesis. Our light-sensitive pigment is purple, but it's not all ours. One portion of the molecule is vitamin A, and vitamin A is, in turn, a portion of a molecule of carotene.

There are also motion detectors that fire when the same dots are signaled over and over again, each time by a neuron at a different location in the group. Again, they are very specific: Each motion detector fires only for dots moving at a particular speed, and in a certain direction.

But for all this analysis, each group of feature detectors reports only on a small portion of the total view that is out there in front of your eyes—bits of shape, parts of lines, fractions of motion. Now, in the visual center at the back of the brain, all these fractured parts must be put together into the whole we see: a 3-D, full-color, motion picture of our world. Yet the whole process of seeing, from the time photons bouncing from this page spring pigments in your eyes to the time you see the words, takes just 1/500 of a second.

Imagining the World

There is more to seeing than simply making pictures, as you can appreciate by imagining what you would see if these words were written in Arabic or Chinese. Somewhere along the pathways through the brain, images are given meaning: What you see is not just the geometry of our alphabet, but also words, and you even see the images those words stand for, such as oranges and pears.

The visual center is wired every which way, plugged into the emotional base of the brain where fear may make a snake look worse than just a slither in the grass, into memories that may make the diamonds on its back more sinister than speckles would have been, into sound areas that anticipate a rattle. You don't "just see." You create images that are colored as much by emotion, knowledge, and experience as they are by photons.

In fact, you don't even see most of what's out there. These words you're reading take up only the center of your visual field. Beyond them are the edges of the book, and beyond the book a roomful of detail that—you now realize—is within sight without moving your eyeballs. Nothing stops photons from this whole area from entering your eyes, and nothing stops spot and feature detectors from conveying their computerized versions of what's hitting. But, while the brain assembles the entire view, you see only those parts that interest you at the moment.

How real is such an image? Since a camera records the arrival of photons on film without computer processing, and without emotion, knowledge, experience, or interest, perhaps we could compare our mental images with the faithful ones of photos. But no, how could we? We have no idea what a "faithful" photo looks like because, in seeing it, we break it into spots, make up colors for them, rebuild them into lines and curves and corners, stir them up with memories and feelings, and recreate the scene into still another of those peculiarly personal pictures by which we think we know our world.

Need to Know

If green might be a ghost, if stars you see aren't there, if real vanilla is a rendition of 150 different molecules, and a melody the music of a silent synthesizer, then what is reality, really? Even the squeeze of your mother's hand is a figment of your imagination, constructed from some millions of identical flashes that were meaningless until you made a meaning for them.

Philosophers have struggled for thousands of years with the question of whether our perception of the world accords with what is out there. In one sense, the answer is clearly "No." Our version of the nature of a sugar molecule may be its sweet taste, of the nature of photons their sparkling light, but these characteristics don't exist without lickers and lookers to taste and see them. Reality includes an absolute bombardment of photons we don't see, forces we don't feel, molecules we can't detect. You don't notice gamma rays zipping right through you at the beach. You're not spun around by your planet's powerful magnetic field. You don't sense the electric field surrounding every living body, in spite of the popularity of such notions as personal "wavelengths" and ESP.

In another sense, the question of whether our perception of the world accords with reality can be answered "Yes." Because it works. When you hear thunder, there is a storm. When you feel pain, there is an injury. Sensory input appears to be doled out to creatures on a "need to know" basis: No kind of body needs to include gamma rays in its world view because they go right through the world, as well as through the bodies on it, without affecting anything. If you need to eat sugar, you taste it. If you don't, you don't.

Each kind of animal earns its living in a different way, and may need to know something you don't know. Other animals' realities are therefore likely to be unique, although each is sliced from the same whole from which humans also take their slice.

Take a snake that hunts at night. When the sun sets, the photons of a moonless night arrive only from distant stars or, under clouded skies, hardly arrive at all. They may be real, but they are not very helpful at that rarity. Visible photons are not the only kinds, though. Less energetic than photons that can spring apart a pigment are the infrared photons we feel as heat when they hit our skin. Sun-warmed landscapes radiate infrared light back to the

Colorblindness

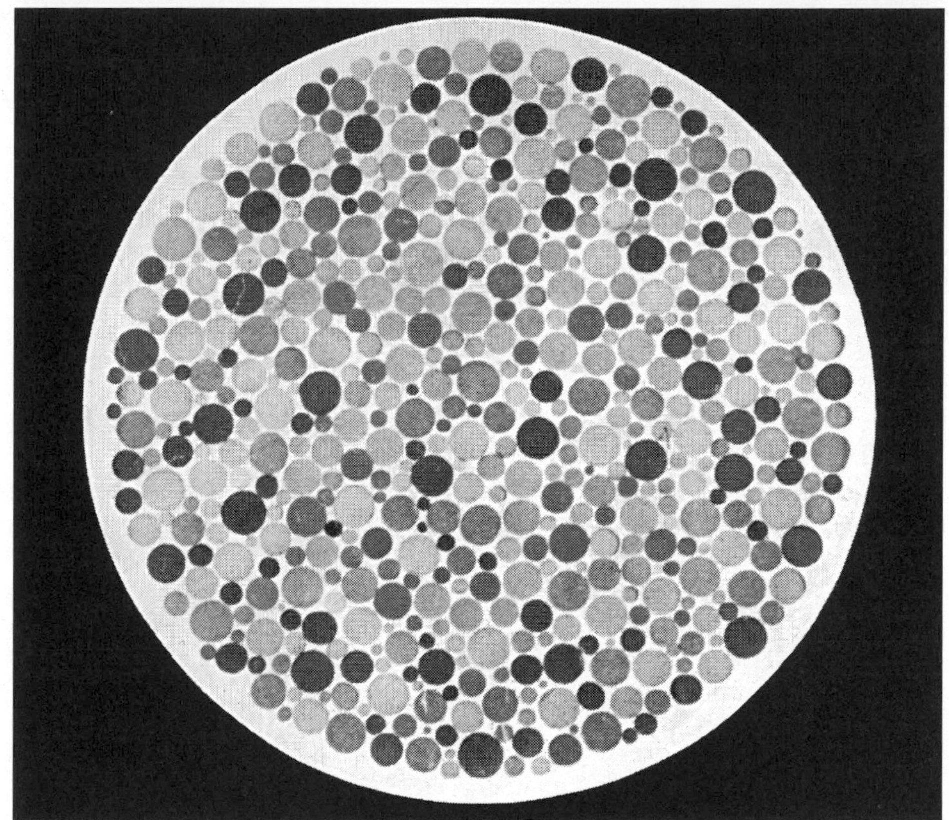

People who are colorblind fail to distinguish some colors because they lack one or two of the specialized cone pigments. Depending on which pigment is missing, they may see red and green, but not blue or yellow; or they may see blue and yellow, but not red and green. Eye doctors use pictures composed of colored polka dots to detect colorblindness. The one reproduced here in black and white is actually printed in shades of green, blue, orange, and magenta, and contains the numeral 29. To a person with red/green colorblindness, the numeral would be invisible as it is here.

More Than Eyes Can See

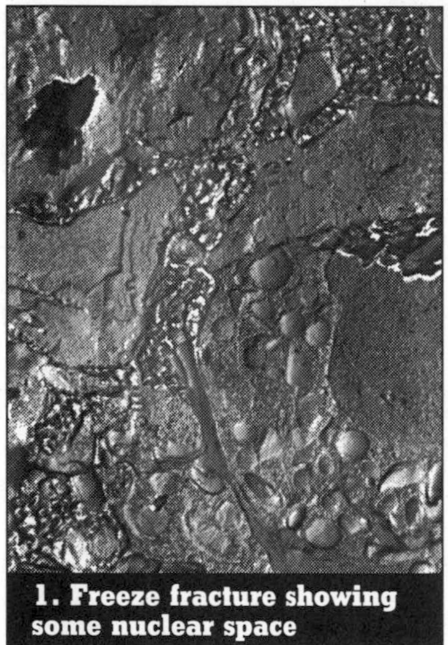

1. Freeze fracture showing some nuclear space

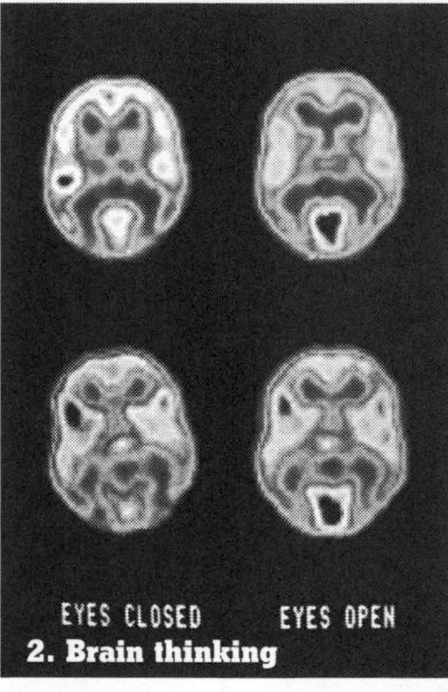

2. Brain thinking

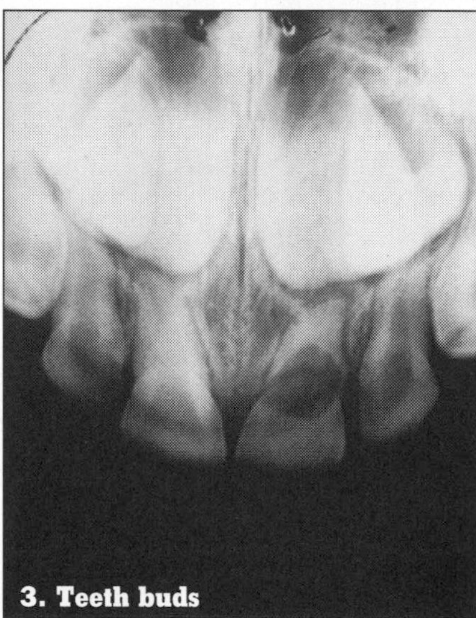

3. Teeth buds

4. Landscape

5. Images of same flower

1. The nucleus of a cell photographed in a beam of electrons instead of light

2. A brain thinking, captured by a computerized scanner that records burst of energy released by a harmless radioactive substance taken with a brain nutrient such as glucose.

3. Buds of adult teeth in a toddler's jaw revealed through film sensitive to X-rays

4. A photograph taken at night using film sensitive to infrared light.

5. Left: A silverweed photographed in white light, as seen by a human. Right: The same flower photographed by ultraviolet, as seen by a bee.

Using different chemicals on photographic film has let people make images from types of photons (and even from electrons) that eyes themselves can't see. Even more advanced are techniques that use computerized scanners to record radioactive emissions.

atmosphere at night, and busy little bodies also radiate their body heat into the dark.

Dark to us: to a rattlesnake, who knows? Using a pair of heat-sensitive pits that are in front of its daylight eyes, a rattlesnake can detect a mouse two yards away. The sensors in these pits fire at changes of temperature as little as 3/1000 of a degree Celsius, forming images in delicate shades of warmth. There's no telling what warm rocks, cool leaves, and hot mice "look" like to a snake in the dark.

To a bee, a meadow of flowers is certainly not what it is to us. Bees see ultraviolet, the energetic light that gives us sunburn, but they are blind to red. Where we see red poppies, they see black gaps. Their view of white or yellow blossoms is splashed with stripes and splotches of ultraviolet where, to us, is nothing. What color is ultraviolet? Only bees, who need to know their flowers well, know that.

Color vision of any sort is rare because it is, for the most part, useless. Cows don't need to see that grass is green because its color doesn't distinguish it from the green of other greenery. Cats don't need to see the color of their prey because fur and feather colors say nothing about the flesh inside. Fruits do advertise in color: green when unripe (and unwilling to let animals eat and release seeds unready for planting), and yellow, red, or blue when ripe (and eager for eaters to spit and defecate their seeds around). Two groups of fruit-eaters share identical color vision: birds, and primates, including us. We get the nourishment of fully ripened fruit, the fruit gets its seed-spreaders every time.

On the other hand, birds and humans have a dull sense of smell. Flies smell water. *E. coli* distinguishes among no fewer than four different sugars. Salmon smell their home stream from miles away in the ocean. Male moths find mates by the thinnest trail of female scent wafted on the breeze. Your own dog knows you and everyone in your family, its own pups and every other dog, and squirrels, cats, rabbits, and deer by scent alone, in the flesh or in the footprint. It remembers in images of odor; perhaps it thinks in smell.

If smell-thought strikes you as strange, try this: underwater ripple images, soundscapes, magnetic maps, landscapes of electric fields.

Magnetic sense is pretty common, and can be very simple. Stagnant ponds and swamps are filled with mud-dwelling bacteria that keep themselves headed toward the bottom by following Earth's magnetic field as though they were compass needles. A compass needle suspended from a string points poleward and tilts downward. Magnetic bacteria make chains of magnetic crystals that automatically tilt them toward the mud. Pigeons accumulate similar magnetic crystals under their skulls. They use them to find their way home. The same crystals have been found in many migratory birds and fish, but not in humans, who did not evolve while traveling such distances by wing and fin in the reality of airy or watery worlds devoid of landmarks.

Words are clumsy when describing strangeness. Fish "hear," or "feel," or somehow tune into ripples of underwater reality along their sides. You've seen the patterns of ripples that spread outward from where water laps at docks and boulders. Such ripples spread also within a body of water as it bounces against rocks, weeds, and other fish. Fish detect the crisscrossing ripple patterns in fluid-filled, hair-cell-lined canals that run along their sides. Since fish don't bang into boats, don't stray from schools of their companions, do find their proper food, and the places where their species lays eggs, they must know where they are going even in the deep, dark sea. Presumably fish form images of waving weeds, sloping sands, darting companions, lurking predators, and fleeing prey from the ripple pattern as it is mapped in their brain.

More familiar, but no less mysterious, are the soundscapes by which bats enlighten their inky reality. As the ultrasonic squeaks of bats echo back to them from branches, bushes, buildings, they "see" sound images of their whereabouts. Echos of insects are as clear to bats as visual images are to us.

We are as deaf—or is it blind?—to such high-pitched echoes in the air as we are to bouncing patterns under water. They are the sound of silence, the black of night, the blank of the abyss to humans.

But we keep hoping that we have some sense by which we make contact with others of our kind by tuning in to their frequency, feeling their vibrations, getting on the same wavelength. It is quite true that the brain leaks electric current, and that rhythms, called brain waves, that result from this current change with intense thought, mere musing, sleep, dreams, and emotions. In fact the whole body emits an electric field just from flexing muscles.

Some fish do have the electric sense we long for. Sharks pick up the electrical profile of flounders invisibly floundering in mud. Other fish monitor their own amplified electric field for the typical distortions caused by nearby prey, which they then track down and swallow as bats chase and gobble moths.

Using "vibes" to find dinner isn't exactly what people have in mind when they hope to tune in to one another. We think more of soul mates than of food. We are not alone. The most exquisitely tuned senses of every kind of creature are reserved for what it needs most of all to know: its kind, its kin, its mate.

Our Kind

Electric fish—species that stun their prey with an electric shock—live in water so murky that they will never clearly see their love. They seek mates electrically, by sending out hopeful profiles of themselves, the unique electric field that identifies their species. The answer is a matching signal: an electric snapshot of another of their kind.

The sensations that electrify a creature's recognition circuits are suited to its circumstances. Spiders tap out their identity on strands of web, fireflies flash a catchy rhythm from the sky, moths signal with long-distance smells. Whatever the medium, the message has a special significance unlike the yanks of a struggling fly, moonlight twinkling through treetops, or any flower's perfume. Among all the molecules a moth might smell, the one emitted by a female of its species stands out as something special. Of all the cricks and croaks pulsing through a summer night, one crick attracts one species of cricket, one croak attracts one frog.

Not all messages are reserved for lovers. A new-hatched gull will peck at its parent's beak to receive a meal of fish only if it sees a red spot at the tip of the approaching beak. An antelope lost among strangers on the African plains recognizes its own kind by a stripe of white or a curve of horn that ornaments no species but its own. Schools of fish stay together within a mesh of familiar ripples.

Species recognition is hard-wired, built into the brain's circuitry long before birth. It may become sharpened by experience, but the basic patterns that make the animal pay attention, sense familiarity, say "here is something important" are there from the start.

Of all the sounds humans can hear, those within the frequency range of the human voice are heard the clearest, as though they are more vivid, loud, and interesting than any other. Newborn babies have an even narrower range of appreciation. Their favorite sound is that of a woman's voice. They arrive with a mental dictionary of sorts. The sound *shhh*, which means "Be quiet!" to us, soothes and quiets a newborn, too. Clicking sounds alert her. It turns out that mothers, without realizing that they do it, click and cluck to their babies to get their attention.

Some sensory circuitry seems at birth to be poised, ready to make particular connections as soon as experience provides the means. That must be how a newborn comes so quickly to recognize her mother's milk, for of all the smells available, she selects within a week that one to which she turns to suckle, and rejects a stranger's milk.

An Easy Test

Is the woman:

a) Enjoying a chocolate
b) Excited that the Mets won
c) About to kick her dog
d) Noticing bugs in her breakfast cereal

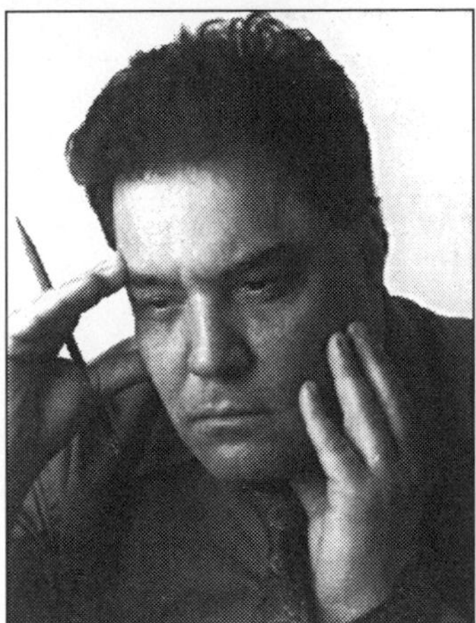

Is the man:

a) Delighted that dinner's ready
b) Furious that the newspaper didn't come
c) Worried about his income tax return
d) Sad that his dog died

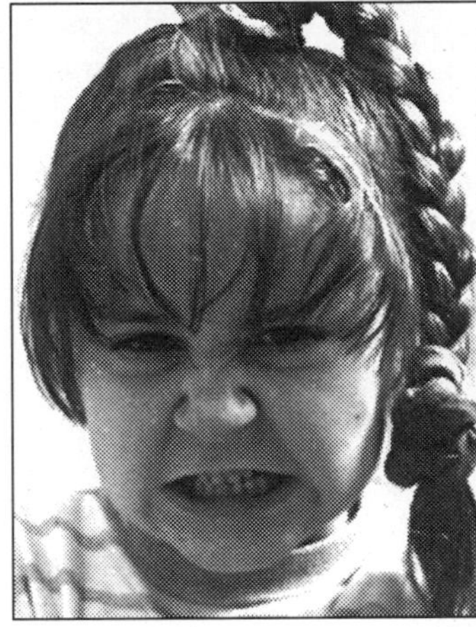

Is the child:

a) About to hug her mother
b) About to punch her brother
c) Watching cartoons
d) Looking forward to her birthday

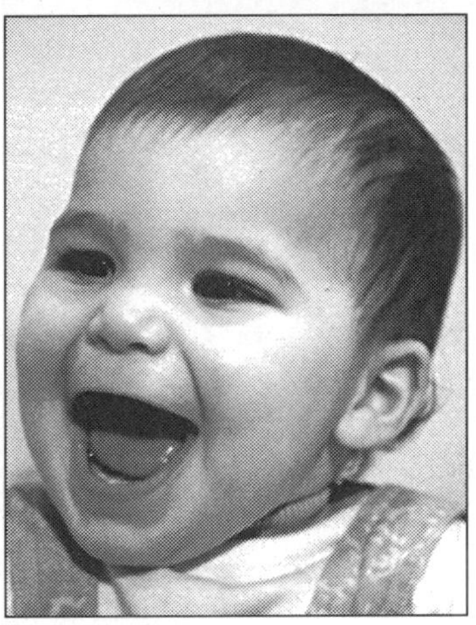

Is the baby:

a) Playing peek-a-boo
b) Getting a shot
c) Itchy all over
d) About to fall asleep

There are many visual patterns that newborn babies find entertaining—landscapes, op art, the headlines of *The New York Times*. But show a baby a picture of a human face and she will gaze at it in preference to all others. The picture need not be a photograph. An oval with two eyes and a mouth will do: That seems to be the basic picture written on the brain. The baby will not only gaze; her heart will beat faster and, if the oval is made to nod, she will smile. Only one other sight will delight her even more: A real face, bobbing and smiling back.

Smiling is one of those short-circuit movements, like jerking a hand from the jab of a needle. Instead of just one circuit, though, there are a series of circuits, as in a computer program that performs a sequence of operations. The result is the very complicated pattern of face muscle contractions that is to humans the very picture of delight. The corners of the mouth lift; cheeks bulge upward; eyes crinkle; eyebrows droop. Within a few weeks of birth, babies become able to display this automatically wonderful smile.

And, they expect their smile to be returned. People find it very difficult not to smile back to a smiling baby, but if they can manage to keep a straight face, they find that it upsets the baby. The circuitry of a baby's outgoing grin is mirrored in her brain by circuitry that receives an incoming smile. The two circuits are linked, so the act of smiling arouses an expectation of a smile returned. And both are connected to emotions: When smiles are exchanged, there is a burst of joy; when they're not, there's gloom.

There must be matching sensory and motor patterns for other expressions as well. In every human, disgust lifts the upper lip and widens nostrils. Anger lowers eyebrows, disbelief raises them, anxiety draws them together. Since you have learned from your own experience how you feel when you make these faces, you can also guess how others feel when they make them. All you have with which to gain knowledge of another is sensors on your outside; messages the other displays are on his outside, too. Yet crust to crust, from one skin to another, people see into each other's minds.

Outside-In Skin

The nervous system was skin to begin with—first a groove in the skin of an

The Longest Neurons

The cell bodies of neurons reporting water temperature to this girl's brain are in the dermis of her toe. Their axons, however, reach all the way to her spine, at the level of her waist. Much shorter interneurons pick up the message at the spine, and pass it to the brain, where, via other interneurons, it is delivered to the sensory map. For the girl to pull her toe from the water, the coldness report must also be sent to her motor map and then, via interneurons in the spine, to the long motor neurons that reach from her spine to her toe.

embryo's back, then, as the groove closed, a tube that became the spinal cord. Every neuron in you, including sensory receptors, motor nerves, and even your brain, grew from this outside-in tube of skin.

Motor nerves send their signals outward, from the spine to muscles in arms or legs or head. The cell bodies of such neurons remain beside the spinal cord where they were born. But during the early weeks of an embryo's development, each grows an axon outward, feeling its way into rib and limb wedges, groping for a muscle to attach to. By now such axons are very long: The neurons that signal your toes to wiggle have axons that reach from your lower spine the whole length of your legs and feet.

Sensory nerves send signals in the opposite direction, inward from skin to spine, or inward from eyes and ears to brain. The cell bodies of these neurons are very close to the outside world, just under your skin or no deeper than your retina or inner ear. To get to these locations in the embryo, they had to travel. Those in skin traveled there all the way from the spinal cord, moving along by oozing like phagocytes. When they reached their destination, they grew axons back to the spine they came from. They are now the receptors that bring you hot itches and cold aches, the many touches of the outside world.

The link between these incoming and outgoing groups of neurons satisfies a basic requirement of a large body—that its blind muscles be connected to its lame senses. You can see a pear, sniff a pear, pick it up, and eat it. But how do you know that you're hungry?

Big bodies have not only to link the world outside with the movements by which they deal with it. They must also link their movements and their sensations to the condition of their inner environment. You know more than pokes of sticks and blasts of air, the rough reality that rubs and bangs against your surface. Neurons descended from skin cells probe your inside everywhere, measuring muscle stretch, joint position, head tilt, blood pressure, and, like inner noses, the very chemistry of your body.

Beyond the Sixth Sense

Muscles and tendons are threaded everywhere with coils of neurons that fire when the coil is stretched. Point your toes and a zillion stretch receptors in your shin muscles measure the pull. Bend your knee and stretch receptors in the tendons report the knee's position. Close your eyes and concentrate: Although it's hard to say just what you feel or how you feel it, you know your posture, and where each finger is.

According to the traditional count of touch, smell, taste, vision, and hearing, there are only five senses. This one, the sense of position, is the sixth.

The distance of a step, the reach of an arm, the turn of a glance all depend on knowing where the foot, hand, or eyeball is both before the move is made, and at every moment during it. Position sense guides even programmed motions. Smiling, walking, running, coughing, blinking, chewing, swallowing are all run by groups of circuits that coordinate contractions of the many muscles involved. During the movement, stretch receptors feed back position changes as they occur, instantly triggering the next change in the series. It's left to you to start the circuits up if you want to, but even knowing exactly the starting position of your legs and feet, you would stand there paralyzed if you had to think out the moves to move you one step farther.

You wouldn't know if you were right side up, upside down, standing still, falling over, speeding up, slowing down, or even in which direction you were headed without still other senses located in the ear.

Above the snail-shell coil in the inner ear where sound waves are detected lie three looped tubes. The three are arranged at right angles to one another, like three adjacent sides of a box, and are filled with fluid. As you move, the fluid drags at tufts of sensory hairs. These tufts report to the brain when you accelerate or slow, and also the turns

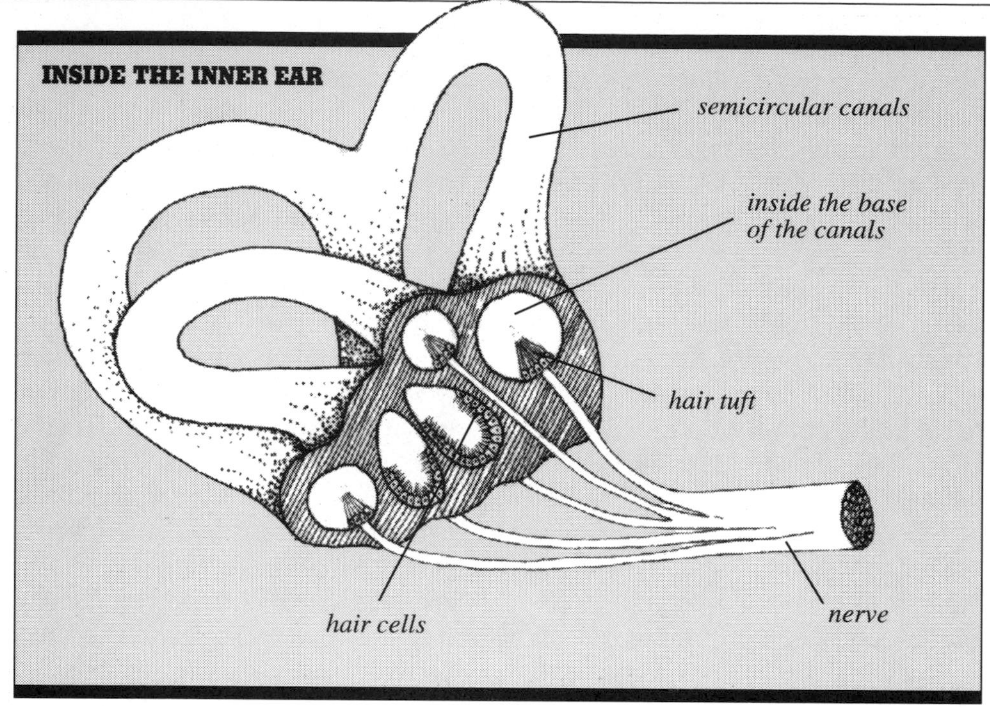

you take, and the direction you are headed. Tilt is reported by hair cells whose bristles are buried in jelly almost to their tips. On their tips rest minute mineral crystals. If you tilt your head, gravity tumbles the crystals into a new position just as it does with sand grains in a tilted jar. Crystals tumbling over sensors bend their bristle tips, and they fire their position to the brain. Because the loops are oriented in different directions, tilt reports from all three of them accurately pinpoint the position of your head with respect to gravity, or "down."

Now imagine the complexity of reportage it takes for you to do the simplest thing imaginable: stand still.

A knee begins to buckle. In a flash, stretch receptors inform an automatic circuit, and muscle tensions are retuned. Your head begins to droop. Hair tufts and hair cells in the ear send warnings of acceleration and tilt; circuits check their sensor readings, and correct the droop. Your whole body sways a trifle. All sorts of circuitry is mobilized by alert sensors everywhere. Skeletal muscles are checked again and readjusted just to keep you standing for a moment more.

In fact, you are never still, not even for a moment. To stand requires constant quivering as strings all through your marionette body are loosened and tightened by nervous circuits whose job it is to keep their home from tumbling down.

The Last Laugh

It is extraordinary how little people really do themselves—consciously and on purpose. Think of helpless laughter. Remember when it overcame you so suddenly that you exploded soda pop all over? Even up your nose? Remember when you laughed so hard you wet your pants?

You can't turn on at will the paroxysms of laughter that weaken knees, squeeze tears out of your eyes, make you clutch your belly, collapse, and gasp. Once something too outrageously funny has thrown your laugh switch, you can't turn it off again, either. You get reports, but you can't do anything about them. Chemical sensors tasting your blood warn that you are running out of air, but still you can't speak or breathe. The flavor of suffocation makes your heart thump hard and fast, and you can't slow it. Blood drains from internal organs, floods your wildly firing brain, races to convulsing muscles, pools in flushing skin. Pain sensors in the gut complain of deprivation: You get a stitch in your side. Tough luck. Nothing you can do. You are rolling on the floor.

The Jerk

You wobble on your two legs all the time because muscles never stay at exactly the same tension. They tighten, then relax a bit, then tighten again. Stretch gauges in your tendons report these tightenings and loosenings to nerves in the spine, which then send a message back to the leg to correct the tilt, and keep you upright. These automatic corrections are reflexes. When a doctor raps your knee with a rubber hammer, he or she is testing a reflex. The rap stretches the tendon below your knee cap, as though the shin muscle had suddenly gone limp. The stretch gauge there reports to the spine, and the nerve reflex instantly makes the correction: Your leg kicks up as the shin muscle tightens.

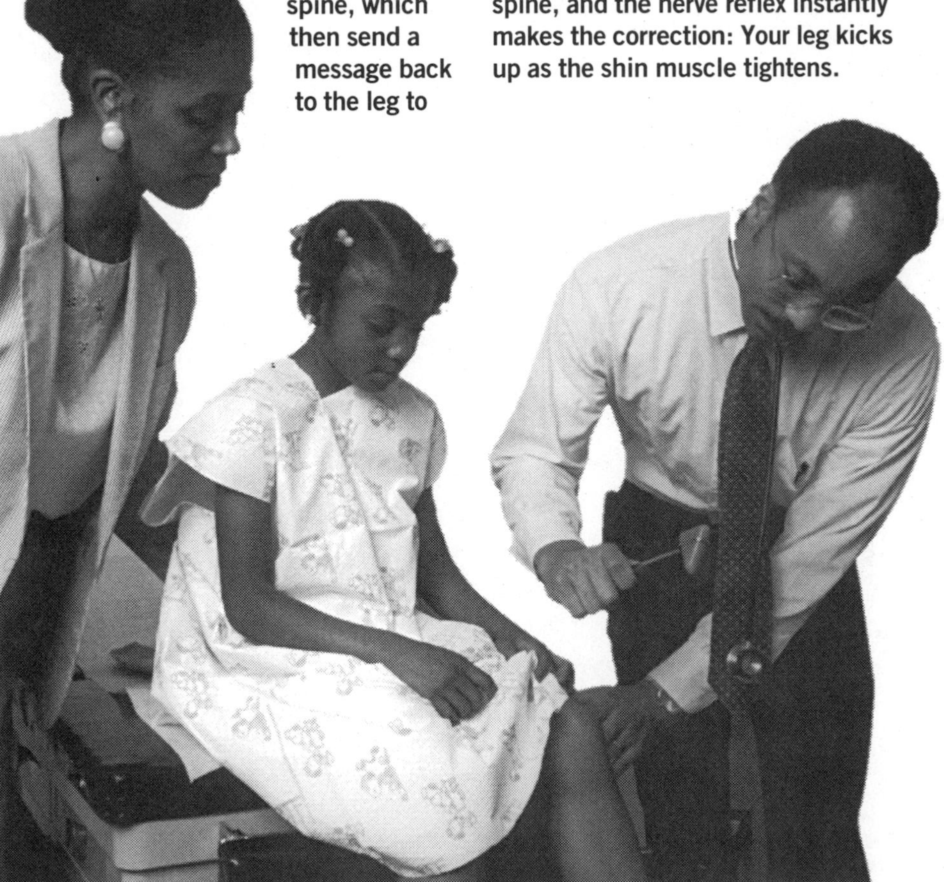

When at last the paroxysm subsides, you feel limp with pleasure. That, too, is out of your control. Laughter resounding through your body, touching sensors, triggering feedback, looping through the brain, has fired certain neurons that say: "Ahhh, that was good!" Never mind that you've forgotten what it was that flipped your switch.

Inner senses and automated circuitry are what let you mostly lead your life without giving it any thought at all. Not only do they stiffen the failing knee, straighten the tilting head, and send you into peals of laughter; they speed the slowing heart, squeeze the filling gut, make you thirsty, make you hungry, make you feel like throwing up. That's just as well: The "you" that you know is a stranger to itself. You have never met your stomach. You have never touched your bones, admired your lungs' pink bubbles, appreciated your muscles' glistening sheaths. You don't know how to run such things yourself.

Every body, never mind the grades it gets at school, has forms of intelligence of which the conscious mind is only dimly aware, or cannot sense at all. Remember the molecule by which the front end of *E. coli* informs the rear end that sugar has been found, and makes it move? You, too, have information systems that rely on molecules carrying messages among cells throughout your body.

ORGANIC GOVERNMENT

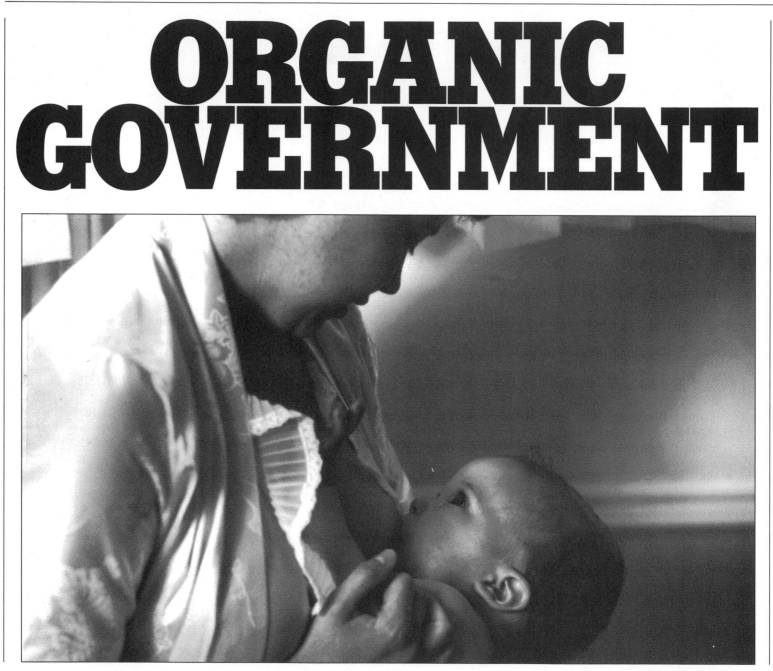

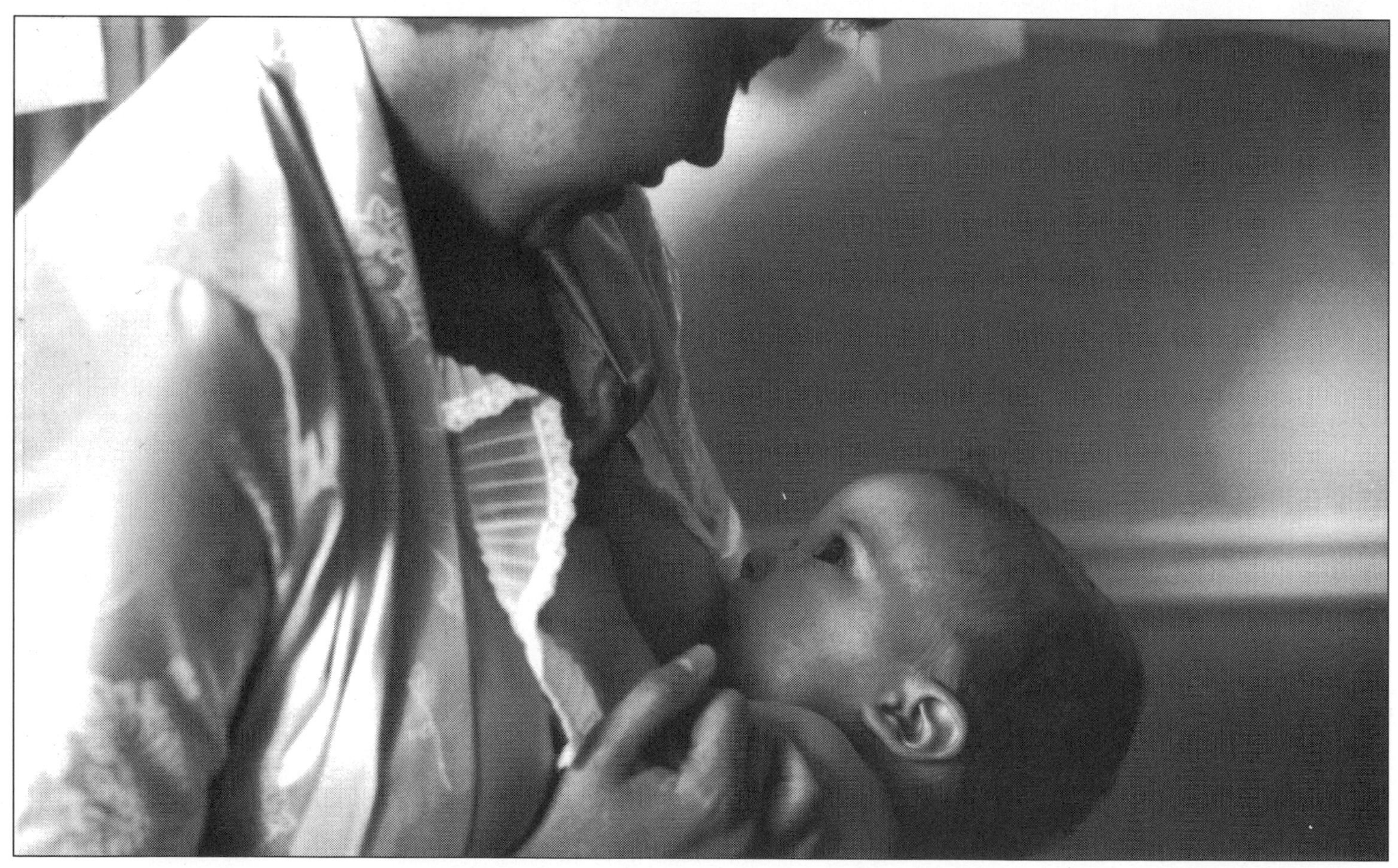

You'd think that being born would exhaust a baby. He is pressed so hard his ears are flattened against his skull, his nose is squashed against his face, and his whole head is squeezed out of shape. Yet naturally delivered newborns remain awake, wide-eyed and interested in their surroundings for hours after birth.

Babies delivered from the womb surgically are by comparison drowsy and disinterested, although the local anesthetic given to their mothers does not affect them, and it has taken only minutes to lift them out.

The difference between newborns who have been squeezed out and newborns who have been lifted out is chemical: Squeezed babies are high on their own hormones.

A hormone is a chemical released into the bloodstream that influences cells at a distance from those that secreted it. Many hormonal effects are very dramatic. Hormones thump hearts, tremble hands, fill you with the butterflies of fear. They make you grow. They make you sleep. They wake you up again next morning. Hormones shape embryos into boys and girls, and boys and girls into men and women. Certainly they are all that stood between your early demise while still an egg and the whole phenomenon of pregnancy by which, instead, you were born a baby. And, if you were allowed to fully feel the squeeze of birth so that your chemical information system was alerted, hormones heated you against the coming cold, opened your airways for your first breath of air, toned your muscles in preparation for the weight of gravity, decreased your need for oxygen, increased your tolerance of stress, alerted your brain, and altogether prepared you to face the world with open eyes, and with considerable curiosity.

Common Chemicals

Judging by what hormones do, they seem to be more powerful by far than ordinary body chemicals. Yet they are small, plain things whose great effects have nothing at all to do with any special magic of their own.

No hormone is a fabulous molecule like those that contract muscles, or form the special doorways into cells. Only a very few are even proteins. Most are short strings of amino acids, or just a single amino acid tinkered with a bit. Some are made from cholesterol, a firm fat that is necessary to strengthen cell membranes.

Whole groups of hormones don't even differ from one another much. Those that are made of cholesterol all resemble cholesterol; they may differ from one another by as little as a single atom. Yet that group includes sex hormones whose effects are wildly different; the steroids that some bodybuilders illegally use to make their muscles massive; and cortisone that, in ointment, pill, or shot, halts raging poison ivy rashes, relaxes asthma spasms, and cures the tennis player's throbbing elbow joint.

Hormones are as common as they are ordinary. Over a hundred are known in mammals, others are suspected, new ones are identified every year. No doubt the final list will double or even triple the number known today.

Special as our hormones seem to us, they are not even exclusive. Insulin, a hormone that controls the amount of glucose available to cells, has been found in insects, protozoans, fungi, and bacteria. *E. coli*'s insulin is nearly iden-

The Sugar Sickness

Failure of the pancreas to make enough insulin results in the disease called diabetes. Without enough of the hormone, cells can't take in sufficient food, and are forced to respire their own substance, including their proteins. In other words, the body starves, in spite of the fact that the person feels hungry all the time, and eats enormously. The form of diabetes that begins in childhood isn't curable, but by taking insulin diabetics can lead a normal life.

tical to ours. Protozoans—amebas, paramecia, and such—make an opiate indistinguishable from one that, in us, calms, soothes, and deadens pain. They make adrenalin, too, which, as it happens, is the hormone that keeps a newborn baby so surprisingly awake.

Hormones in Disguise

When insulin was discovered more than half a century ago, it was found to be made by specialized cells of the pancreas, the same gland in which other cells make digestive enzymes. Gradually hormones made by other glands—adrenals atop the kidneys, thyroid in the neck, pituitary in the brain—were also discovered. Skin glands and the digestive portion of the pancreas secrete their products to the outside through ducts, but hormone glands are ductless; they secrete directly into body fluid, from which their products diffuse into the bloodstream. They were given the group name of endocrine glands, and were considered a system of their own, the endocrine system. Those were the good old days, before anyone knew that the brain, too, makes insulin, and uses it for its own devices.

It turned out that besides being ordinary, common, and found in many different forms of life, hormones aren't necessarily made by endocrine glands. The stomach secretes a hormone that turns on its own digestive juices. Two other hormones secreted by the duodenum—the loop of intestine just below the stomach—trigger the release of pancreatic enzymes and the liver's bile. A hormone form of vitamin D is secreted by skin, not glands.

The target of a hormone is not even necessarily within the body that made it. A fetus's placental hormones are intended for *a* body, but the body is the mother's, not the baby's.

The definition of what a hormone is was complicated further by the discovery of "factors." Skin growth factor is the chemical secreted by salivary glands that dogs use to heal their wounds, and cows use to grow their grass. Besides skin growth factor, we make a nerve growth factor, a fibroblast growth factor, and a batch of others. They are short strings of amino acids just like many hormones are. They circulate in the blood like hormones. They influence targets at a distance like hormones. If something looks like a hormone and acts like a hormone, why insult it by calling it a factor?

Consider pheromones, those odors of armpit and mouse urine that have such fundamental sexual effects. They are secreted, act at a distance, and are certainly influential. Although they reach their targets through the air, not blood, they are at least hormonal in their action.

The question of distance is a problem: How far must far be to call a chemical a hormone? What about histamine, that swelling, red-hot-itcher that mast cells secrete to their own neighborhood after an injury? Or the factors (or pheromones!) by which phagocytes sniff their way to an injury? It can't be that insulin secreted by the brain for local use only is for that reason not a hormone. Insulin made by bacteria may not even be secreted, but being confined inside a cell doesn't change its chemistry.

Ultimately scientists studying how nerve signals travel realized that, while neurons carry electrical signals throughout their length, that is not how they communicate with one another. They secrete across the gap that separates them: They speak in chemicals. These short-distance chemicals are called neurotransmitters, but they are close cousins to long-distance hormones. Some are identical; one is made both by brain cells and adrenal glands.

On closer inspection, researchers discovered there was less difference between nerve and gland than they had at first supposed. Some of the very glands that in innocence had been plunked among the endocrines were later found to be made of neurons. Half the pituitary gland that lies behind your eyes just below the brain is drippy neurons. A portion of each adrenal gland—way down at the kidneys—grows from neurons in the embryo. The brain's

Not Just Glands

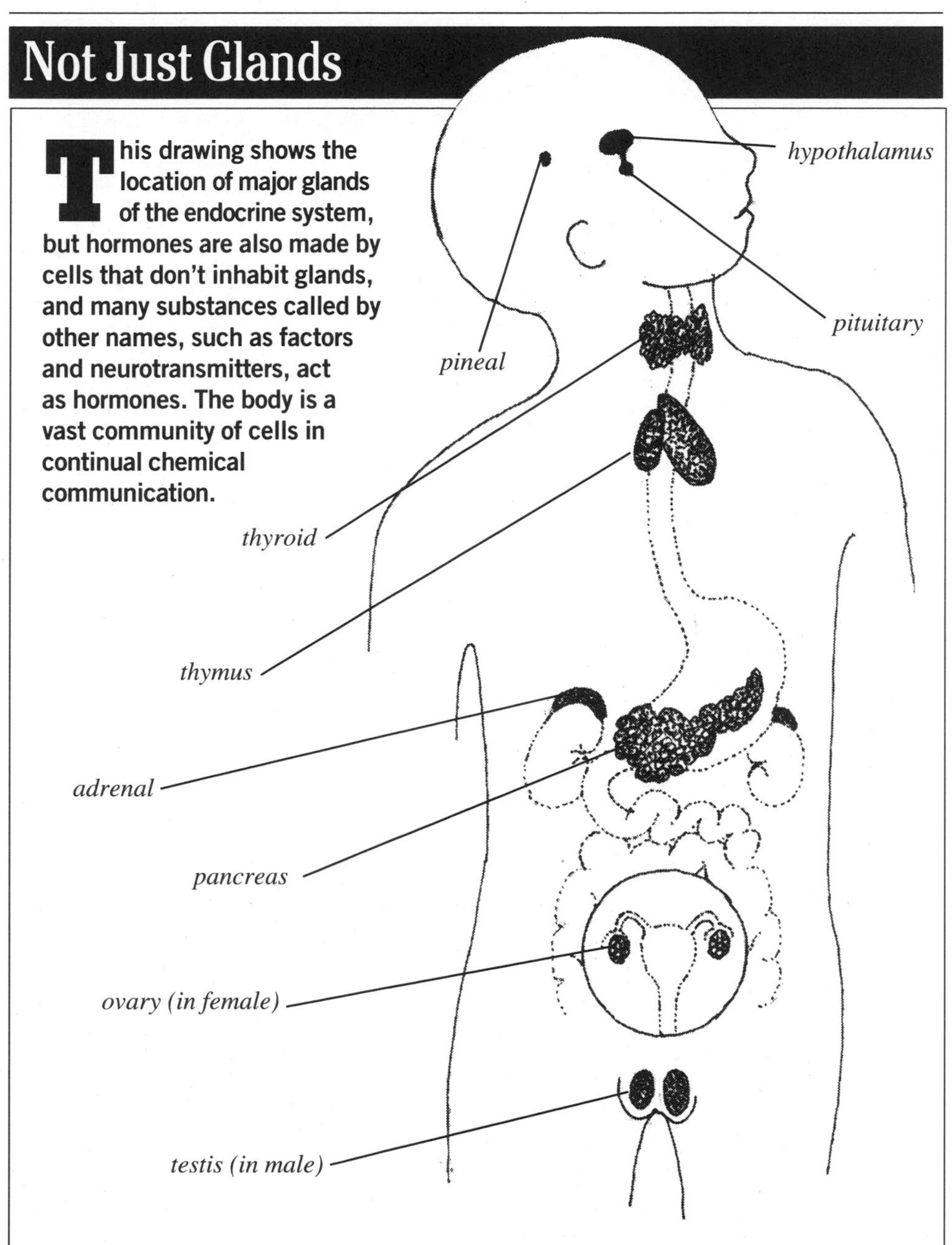

This drawing shows the location of major glands of the endocrine system, but hormones are also made by cells that don't inhabit glands, and many substances called by other names, such as factors and neurotransmitters, act as hormones. The body is a vast community of cells in continual chemical communication.

hypothalamus, which sets your thermostat and receives temperature readings from your skin, secretes hormones that direct some of the touchiest glandular affairs of all, such as the sexual revolution of growing up.

What is more, all the gossipy interneurons in the brain are forever butting into the affairs of glands. Worrying about a test may make your belly feel fluttery inside. Adrenal glands give you these "butterflies," but they don't know to spurt until the brain, listening in on your conscious thoughts, tells them to spurt worry juice. The substances that regulate your inner environment may have different names, and the cells that secrete them may belong to different systems, but organic government is achieved only because all cells everywhere communicate with chemicals.

Eavesdropping

Chemical information systems are never simple, but neither are the problems that they solve. Take the problem of providing breast milk to a baby—just when she wants it, in just the quantity she needs.

This information system is triggered by the baby's probing for the nipple. Her probe is intercepted by her mother's hypothalamus, which, like a nosey operator, listens in on every sensory message transmitted through its switchboard. At once this bit of brain secretes a hormone that, descending in a blood vessel to the pituitary gland just below, releases that gland's store of still another hormone, one that causes muscles surrounding milk glands to contract. Within the moments it takes for this hormone to diffuse into capillaries and circulate through the mother's breasts, all the little baskets of muscle around her milk pouches begin to squeeze milk through her nipples. Nosey or not, the hypothalamus has answered the baby's probe correctly: Out flows her meal.

The operator is by no means finished with this call. Indeed, the hypothalamus times it. As long as suckling continues, it drips down another pituitary releaser, this one for a hormone necessary for milk production. The longer the baby suckles, the more milk her mother will make for her next meal. The mother's hypothalamus acts, in effect, as the baby's hunger gauge.

Perhaps most extraordinary, the baby's suckling sees to it that there will be no competing sucklers for some time to come: At her hungry command, her mother's hypothalamus secretes chemical inhibitors of two pituitary hormones that, were there no baby saying otherwise, would soon cause another of her eggs to ripen.

Regardless of this last word on pregnancy, the baby must listen to her mother, too. It is her mother's secretion that, as its sweet taste and milky fragrance hits her nose and tongue, tells her brain

Growing the Baby

Breast-fed babies rarely get ear infections: Human milk contains hormones that boost resistance to disease. They seldom get diarrhea infections either. Mother's milk supplies them with antibodies that make gut germs harmless, as well as with a factor that helps gut cells to seal themselves together tightly. They don't get constipated. Breast milk is a mild laxative, too. They sleep well. Their food contains a tranquilizer. And they don't need any other food. Mother's milk contains an exact balance of proteins, fats, sugars, vitamins, and minerals suited to infant nutrition, and only to infant nutrition (the mother herself eats an altogether different diet!).

Therefore no one can feed a baby as well as his own mom, but anyone can help him grow. Gently stoking a baby's skin has a complicated hormonal effect that enables his cells to take in more nutrients, and to divide more rapidly. So stroke your brother, stroke your sister, make the baby grow!

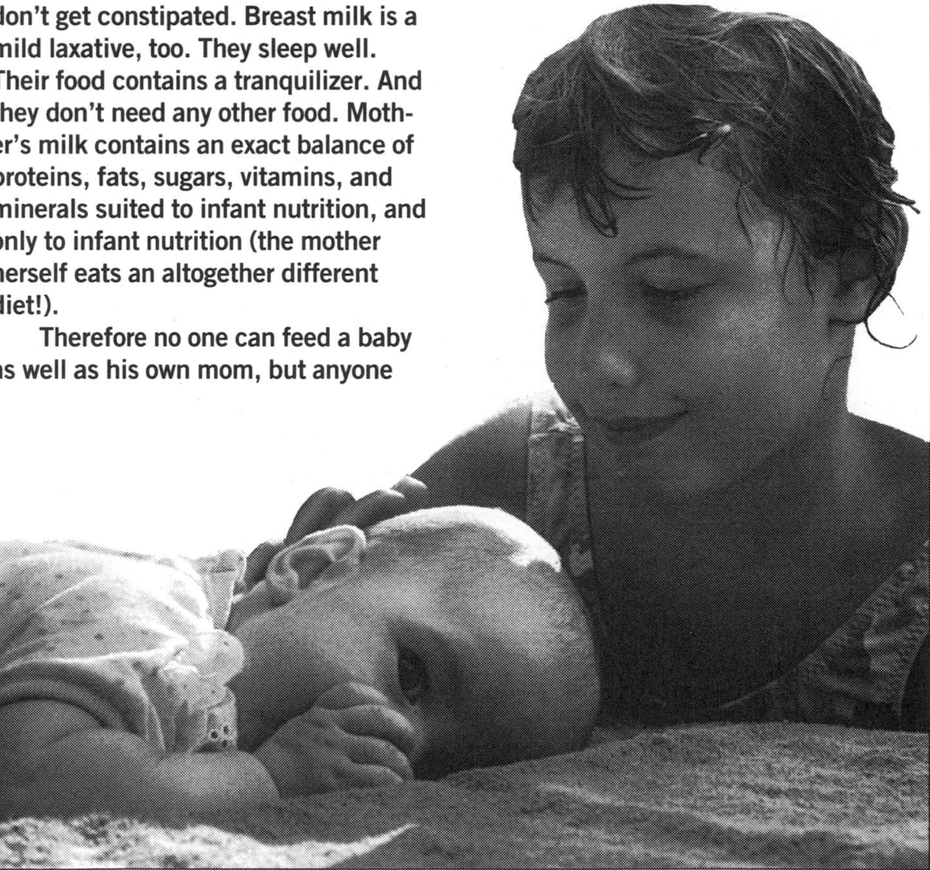

to tell her stomach to tell her glands to make digestive juices. That's a lot of telling, but it's the way these chemical conversations go. Stomachs don't recognize food. They have to be told by nerves in the brain that food is on the way. Cells that make digestive juices don't recognize food either. They have to be told by stomach hormones that it's time to go to work.

As these messages make their way from mouth to brain to tummy, Mom strokes Baby's back. Talk about complicated! Stroking an infant's skin turns on her secretion of a hormone that inhibits another hormone that would otherwise inhibit insulin and growth hormone. What in the world could this be all about?

Insulin helps the body to get the most out of a meal. It makes muscles and fat cells grab up more glucose. It tells fat cells to build more of that sugar into fat. It tells muscles and liver cells to store more of it as starchy glycogen. Insulin also makes muscles and liver cells take in more amino acids, and forces them to step up their protein assembly lines so that, clued in by growth hormone, the baby grows while the growing's good.

This is really neat: While enjoying her meal and massage, the baby takes in more food, uses it more productively, and grows more than when she is left alone. Alone, who can be sure when the next meal will arrive? So, after awhile by herself, the baby's hormone situation reverses. Insulin and growth hormone are inhibited. The baby, slowed down in all respects, now conserves her resources until her next meeting with her mother.

Food alone won't work to switch the baby's growing on. No matter how well they are fed, infants who are not handled fail to thrive. The close presence of good people is not good enough. The brain insists on touching. Substitute touches also will not do—bundling blankets, snuggly sleepsuits, cuddly bunnies are all considered counterfeit. This system says that only skin is proof, and the system is too old and too wise to fool.

What's Wrong With Old and Wise

Such systems evolved in mammals leading wilder lives than babies in a nursery. If a lion cub doesn't feel its mother's touch, then very likely she is off getting food for herself. Since there is no corner grocery in the wilderness, there's no telling when she might return. Conservation is the cub's only insurance against unforeseen delays. Self protection is also the logic of the birth-control system by which infants keep their mothers for themselves as long as they are suckling.

Yet just because hormonal wisdom is so very old, it is stubborn, conservative, will not see that times have changed. The birth-alert system believes in childbirth the old, hard way, and refuses to acknowledge modern methods. Or take the new-fangled business of baby foods. Babies on snacks don't suck for all their food. They therefore nurse less frequently, and for shorter periods of time than babies did in olden times. The birth-control system obstinately misinterprets this modernity. It assumes that the baby hasn't the strength to suckle properly, will no doubt die, and had better be replaced. The system in this way fails a good many mothers who, nursing little, are soon pregnant again.

Ancient know-it-alls often exaggerate rumors they overhear. Adrenal glands, which are responsible for getting babies through the stress of birth with such flair and heroism, are particular offenders.

The outer layer of each adrenal is true gland. The inner core develops from neurons. Because of their different origins, the inner core and outer bark hear from the brain in different ways. The neuron core gets news directly through nerves. The bark finds things out third-hand: In the brain, the hypothalamus tells the pituitary gland below it, and the pituitary drips its message into the bloodstream, which carries it to the adrenals. Both portions of the gland keep reserve hormones on

The Superman Hormone

When you're very excited, you can hear your heart thumping. That's one of the effects of adrenalin. Adrenalin widens arteries supplying blood to the heart muscle, and makes the muscle contract both harder and faster. At each thump, more than the usual amount of blood is pumped, and there may be twice as many thumps per minute. The blood is also richer. Adrenalin enriches blood by stepping up breathing to supply more oxygen, by making fat cells pour their fat fuel into it, and making liver cells add sugar. What's more, this sweet, fat, oxygen-rich, and copious flow of blood gets to where it counts: Adrenalin constricts the flow of blood through skin and internal organs, shunting an extra flow to the brain and skeletal muscles. Strength is increased almost to that of Superman: In an emergency, an average man can carry someone much heavier than himself out of a burning building. One wouldn't want to live at such intensity for long, but it's reassuring to know that in an emergency, hormones can make heroes of us all.

hand awaiting a call to action.

A call to the core comes whenever the brain considers anything an emergency. It may be pain, fear, anger, effort, a BANG!, a pang of love. No matter what, the brain's motto is: Be prepared.

The brain sends many organs a first alert. The gut shuts down. The heart speeds up. Blood shunts from narrowing vessels in the belly and the skin to widening ones in muscles of the heart and limbs. Stores of fresh red blood cells are released to carry extra oxygen. The liver contributes glucose to the cause. Pupils dilate to let in more light. Hair erects (just in case). And the cores of the adrenal glands pour forth their store of adrenalin.

Adrenalin is more a drill sergeant than a commander: It keeps the organs marching to the beat the brain has set. The brain's jolting alert is what you feel when the car skids. Adrenalin's drill is the thrill of a winning team or the excitement of a fight, as well as dread of a math exam, stagefright shakes, roller coaster pallor, and late night horror show heebie-jeebies.

The hypothalamus listens in on rumors of distress, and starts a flow of cortisone from the bark of adrenal glands. Cortisone's effects aren't felt the way adrenalin's are, and the hormone is more designed to help the body withstand long hardship than brief crisis. The hormone forces the body to break down its own proteins for food on the assumption that there will be no opportunity to eat, and that an extra supply of amino acids may be needed to repair wounds. It improves the body's ability to withstand cold and pain as well as starvation, to get rid of poisons more efficiently, and to suppress inflammation. Cortisone even asks the brain to search for novel solutions to problems it may never have encountered before: It makes you more creative.

You can see why a baby primed with adrenalin and cortisone is ready for anything. But the circuits that call these hormones into action are as alarmist as Chicken Little. When you hit them with an acorn of worry, they think the sky is falling.

The alarmist system's misunderstandings can be incredibly stupid. We report a doctor's needle, it imagines a lion's fangs. We say P.S.A.T.s are just a week away, it says "Run away right now." The alarmist system prepares us to fight the doctor and flee the test no matter that doing so can only make the problem worse.

If hitting and running were answers to our worries, no doubt we would feel much better. The brain circuits that set off alarms care more about the form of our behavior than its substance. They are calmed by aggression, soothed by exhaustion because, in their unimaginative view, that's how things ought to go in a crisis. That's why, when you're

Who Lives to be a Hundred?

Longevity is to some degree inherited: Scientists joke that if you want to live to a ripe old age, choose your parents wisely! But when people who have lived to be a hundred are questioned closely about their lives, they are found to be similar in one way: They have been happy. Pleasant relationships with others, contentment with one's work, and an ability to take events in stride are among the best predictors of longevity. The reason may be in the effects stress hormones have on immunity. Cortisone suppresses the various mechanisms by which people fight disease. Adrenalin raises blood pressure, and puts an extra burden on the heart. The less stressful one's life, the less strain on the body, and the better it is able to defend its health.

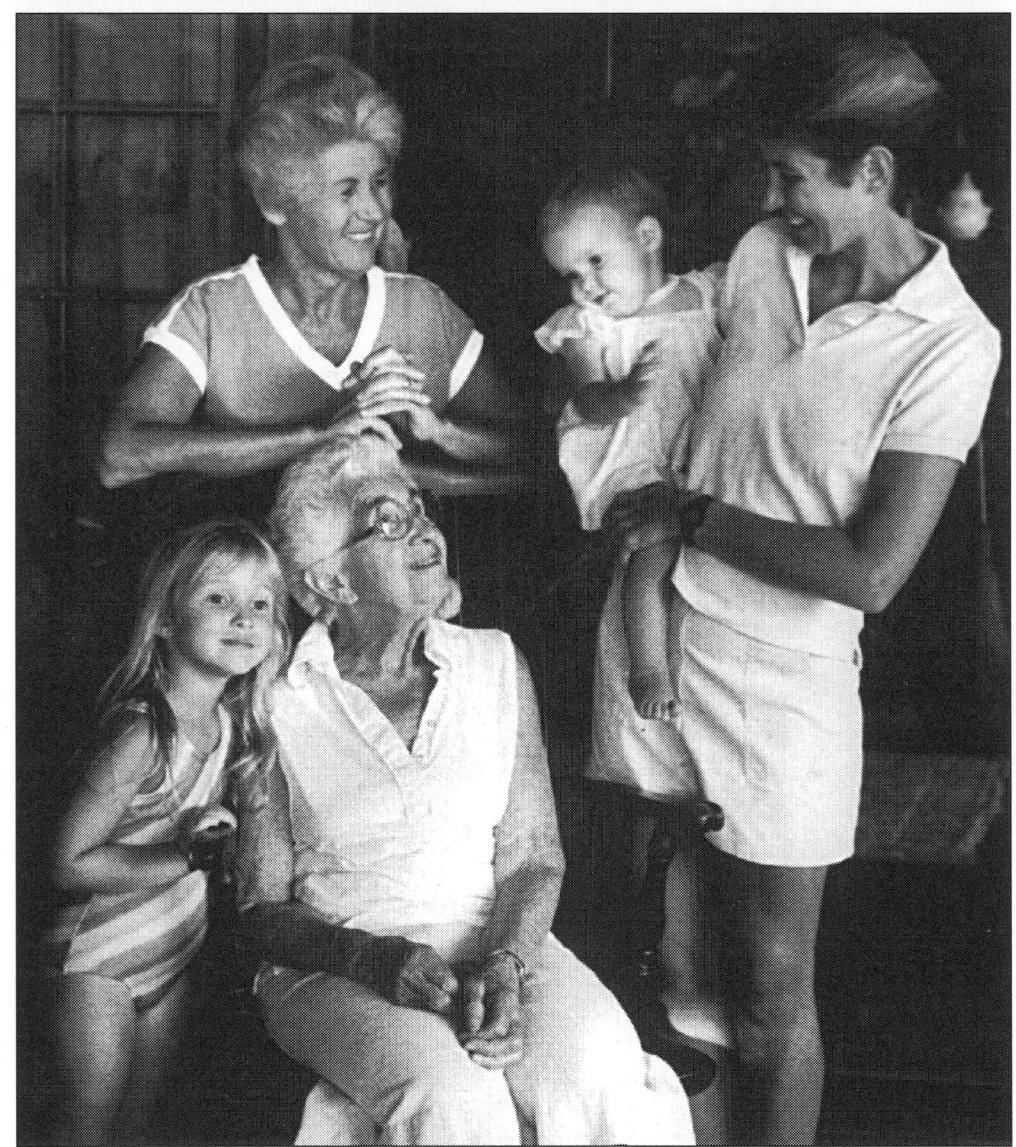

Four generations of a family get together for a memorable photo.

upset and can't do something sensible about it, dumb things like punching pillows or running around the block can calm you down. But if the call to action is ignored, adrenalin and cortisone keep hassling you, and won't stop. Our ancient alert has become our modern ailment: Stress hormones can stress us more than stress itself.

Quiet Whispers, Loud Alarms

For all their power to upset, hormones have only one ability: to bind to a receptor. That's all they ever do. They bind: Their job is done.

Cortisone and its kin are cholesterol-based hormones that, like other fats, diffuse into cells through their oily membrane. Inside, they bump into their receptor. As the two bond, the receptor slips into a new shape. That's it for the hormone. The rest is up to the receptor, which now carries the message into the nucleus of the cell.

Within the nucleus the reshaped receptor binds to a particular gene on a chromosome. The binding is the beginning of a series of chemical events by which that gene is copied, and its instructions used to build a protein. The gene is copied over and over again as long as the receptor is attached, and each gene copy is used again and again to make multiple copies of the protein. One molecule of hormone can start a production run of thousands of protein molecules.

Possibly this one protein is the point of the hormone, but just as possibly it is not. The gene whose reading the hormone made possible may code for an enzyme that is only the first link in a chain of chemical events by which a multitude of different products are assembled. These products might be for the cell's own use, or they might be for export. If they are exported, they may be messengers in their own right, which, in turn, tell cells in the neighborhood to switch production lines.

You can see one advantage of hormones. Each single hormone molecule arriving in a cell results in hundreds of thousands, maybe millions of molecules of product. It is as though the hormone message arrives as a barely audible whisper that is amplified into a mighty roar whose echoes may be heard beyond that cell, arousing the whole neighborhood to action. Sometimes the whole body hears the call.

Another advantage is also obvious: Hormone messages save a lot of words. They are like the fire bell in school. A clang is all it takes to propel monitors to their stations, raise students from their desks, line them up, march them out, bring fire fighters in a hurry.

How is the fire put out, the alarm turned off?

Sometimes the reaction just runs down by itself. Most hormones have a short life; some fall apart in minutes. Then the receptor snaps back to its original, inactive shape, and falls off the gene it had attached to. The gene can no longer be copied; the first link in the chain reaction becomes the missing link, and the whole turmoil subsides.

Or, the reaction may be self-limiting because the last link in the chain is an enzyme that sabotages the first one. Self-limiting reactions can be useful measuring devices: There may be enough saboteurs to stop production in two minutes, at which time there will be just the needed amount of a substance that was wanted.

But a third, and common, way to stop the alarm is to send another hormone to turn it off.

Contradictions

Hormones work as antagonists to one another. The message sent by one is contradicted by another, whose effects are just the opposite. The cell is then caught in an argument, one hormone saying "Do this," the other saying "Do that." How the cell resolves the conflict depends on who shouts the loudest—how many nay-sayers compared to how many yea-sayers.

This is similar to how neurons decide whether to fire or not fire by comparing the number of "no" and "yes" signals arriving from other neurons, but there is an important difference. Electrical decisions are all or nothing, fire or shut up. Chemical decisions are compromises. A cell may do a little more of this, a little less of that, and so satisfy both parties.

Continual compromise is, in fact, the essence of most hormone communication. Wherever hormones are made, they are all secreted in some small amount all the time. Target cells therefore always hear numerous murmurings, and always do a little of this, a little of that. This is like your everyday routine in which, listening to your teachers, you do some homework, and, listening to your parents, you do some housework. When somebody raises his voice, you shift: Bang out an A+ assignment but leave some pots to soak; scrub the pots until they shine but write a shorter paper. An increased number of hormone molecules doesn't ask the cell to do anything that it is unaccustomed to doing, just to do more of one job, less of another.

That makes the whole bodywide system of chemical communication a very sensitive one: Cells are poised at every moment to meet the occasion. Suppose the occasion is a candy snack. As the candy is absorbed from the gut, the amount of glucose in the blood rises. Glucose receptors on cells in the pancreas measure the rise in sugar, and respond by releasing insulin. Insulin reaching liver cells makes them store more sugar in the form of starch. So the amount of sugar in your blood drops. Now cells in the pancreas, measuring the fall in blood sugar, secrete an insulin antagonist. The antagonist, reaching liver cells, makes them break down their stored starch into sugar again. So the amount of sugar in your blood rises. What's so wonderful about this hormone information system is not only that it keeps your

How to Start a Chemical Event

Go ahead, have a piece of cake. Sugar in the icing will begin to enter your gut in minutes, and reach the pancreas seconds later. The pancreas will measure the amount of glucose, and secrete insulin accordingly. Insulin will immediately reach your liver, which will then string glucose into starches. As glucose levels fall, the pancreas will secrete another hormone to block insulin instructions. The liver then will undo the starches into glucose again, and resupply the blood. You can glut on birthday cake, but your cells will get their sugar bit by bit, and hour after hour.

blood just sweet enough, but that it's controlled by the controlled substance: sugar itself.

It's About Time

There is a time to be born: The number of human births peaks between three and four in the morning. There's a time to grow: The level of growth hormone rises about an hour after you fall asleep at night, and falls again toward dawn. And there's a time to die: The hour in which most deaths occur is the same as the hour in which most babies are born.

Life's chemistry is conducted according to rhythms called *circadian*—"about a day." Circadian rhythms may be built into cells themselves, for even one-celled algae and bacteria live by the clock, making more of this at one time of day, more of that at another. The timing is affected by day length. When researchers artificially lengthen or shorten the day by turning lights on and off at 22-hour or 26-hour intervals, lab animals adjust their daily rhythms accordingly. But even when there are no clues to time of day—the lights are always on, or always off—animals still run their lives by an internal clock that turns full cycle in about a day.

Circadian rhythms guide every sort of body function. People feel pain the most late in the afternoon, at the same time that alcohol affects them least. Body temperature is about 2° F higher at 4:00 P.M. than it is at 4:00 A.M. Heart rate fluctuates daily by as much as 20 beats a minute, and the number of white blood cells varies by as much as half. People produce the most cortisone, the stress hormone, in the hours before dawn. Men make the most testosterone at 9 o'clock in the morning.

When a person who works a day shift is reassigned to the night shift, or when a person flies through several time zones, these daily rhythms get out of whack. But they don't get out of whack in synchrony—all by the same amount of time. The distressing symptoms of jet lag—dull thinking, clumsy moving—are due not only to a general lag in timing, but to cells not keeping time with one another. To reset their clocks to run in synch requires that all learn at what time "day" begins. That information may come from an ancient little gland, the pineal.

The pineal gland originally was situated close to the surface of the skull, and had light-sensitive cells—a sort of third eye that some reptiles still have. In the course of evolution, it became buried under new thicknesses of brain, so in us it is in the center of our skull. Although our pineal gland no longer "sees" light, neurons connect it to the eyes. Light turns it off and darkness turns it on.

As night falls, the pineal gland begins to secrete a hormone called melatonin. Melatonin was discovered so recently that scientists aren't sure yet of everything it does, but they do know it makes birds go to roost. It probably makes us go to bed. And because secretion of the hormone is controlled by sunrise and sunset, it could reset cell clocks all over the body.

If for every thing there is a time, for many things there is also a season: winter to sleep through, spring to breed. The pineal gland keeps the body's sea-

Natural Rhythms

A woman who volunteered to live alone in a room without clocks or cues to day and night proved just how much we depend on sunrise and sunset to adjust our circadian rhythms. Using only her own built-in clock, her "days" became waking periods of 20 to 25 hours, followed by "nights" during which she slept for 10 hours. Her menstrual periods stopped, her muscles weakened, and her bones lost calcium, but her ability to concentrate improved. Time passed fast: When she emerged from isolation after more than four months, she felt sure she had been gone only half that time.

sonal calendar. Night length varies during the year from the shortest midsummer night to the longest night at the winter solstice. The more hours of darkness, the greater the dose of melatonin the pineal provides; the fewer hours of darkness, the less it makes. Seasonally increasing doses of melatonin are involved in hibernation. Even some humans begin to sleep longer, crave more carbohydrates (which fatten them), and feel duller as nights get longer in the fall. As for breeding, melatonin inhibits the production of sex hormones. Most animals are unable to breed during the winter. This makes sense because the weather is anyhow too cold and food too scarce for babies. With the coming of shorter nights in spring, inhibition is lifted, and the breeding season begins. We are not seasonal breeders like most other vertebrates, but, as the saying goes, "In spring a young man's fancy turns to love."

If the pineal gland tells the time of day and the season of the year, might it also measure the passage of years? That question hasn't been answered, but there is a clue: People produce the most melatonin during childhood; the amount gradually falls off toward adolescence. That is, of course, just when the sex glands, peacefully nursing their charges for the last 12 years, begin to juice up for action.

Millions a Day, One a Month

Testosterone, the hormone made by gland cells in the testes, is basically a growth hormone. Besides growing beards, bones, and muscles, it grows the penis and the testes. It also makes spermmakers grow and multiply. But another hormone is needed to get gland cells to make testosterone in the first place, and still another to get multiplying spermmakers to fashion little sperm. Both these other hormones are produced in the brain, by the pituitary gland, under instructions from the hypothalamus, possibly according to the timing of the pineal. Nothing is ever simple about hormone systems.

At least in a man all the hormones needed to make sperm are supplied in about the same quantities all the time, and so sperm are turned loose continually, millions every day. The hormone system in a woman is more complicated. The eggs she was born with can no longer multiply as spermmakers do, and the few hundred that survive into adulthood must last her for 40 years or so. They are conserved by a hormone system that ripens just one egg at a time, just once a month.

The two brain hormones men need for sperm production are identical in women, and work in similar ways. The one that, in a man, makes spermmakers fashion sperm, in a woman makes a ripe egg hatch from the ovary. The one that, in a man, tells gland cells to produce testosterone, in a woman tells nurse cells to make the "female" hormones that ripen eggs. These female hormones, called estrogen and progesterone, control the output of both brain hormones in such a way that hormone levels climb up and down in monthly cycles. Each cycle hatches one ripe egg.

At the beginning of a cycle, the two brain hormones are produced at a medium, steady rate just as they are in men. They affect the largest, most mature eggs, and the crowd of nurses caring for them. The nurses respond by producing large quantities of estrogen, and the eggs begin to ripen. At the same time, estrogen circulates to the brain in the bloodstream, where it steps up the production of both brain hormones. This surge lets one of the ripe eggs hatch from an ovary. But it also stimulates nurses to secrete the other female hormone, progesterone, and progesterone turns down the secretion of brain hormones. The nurses gradually calm down, and everything returns to normal. Then a new cycle begins.

Crampers

During egg ripening and hatching, estrogen prepares the womb for the possibility that the egg will be fertil-

Different Shapes

As long as growth is controlled by growth hormones alone, the figures of the sexes are the same. But from the age of about 10 years, sex hormones begin to control the body's shaping. There are two groups of sex hormones, androgens and estrogens. Androgens are responsible for accelerating bone growth in general, and they especially broaden shoulders. Estrogens influence growth patterns. They make hipbones grow especially large, and encourage fat cells to supply extra padding to hips and breasts. The funny thing is, both sexes manufacture both androgens and estrogens, and their bonemakers and fat cells have receptors for both groups of hormones. So why do boys and girls grow into such different shapes?

The difference is a matter of proportion. Although both sexes make estrogens, only females' ovaries make large quantities. Although both sexes make androgens, only males' testes make the most potent one, testosterone.

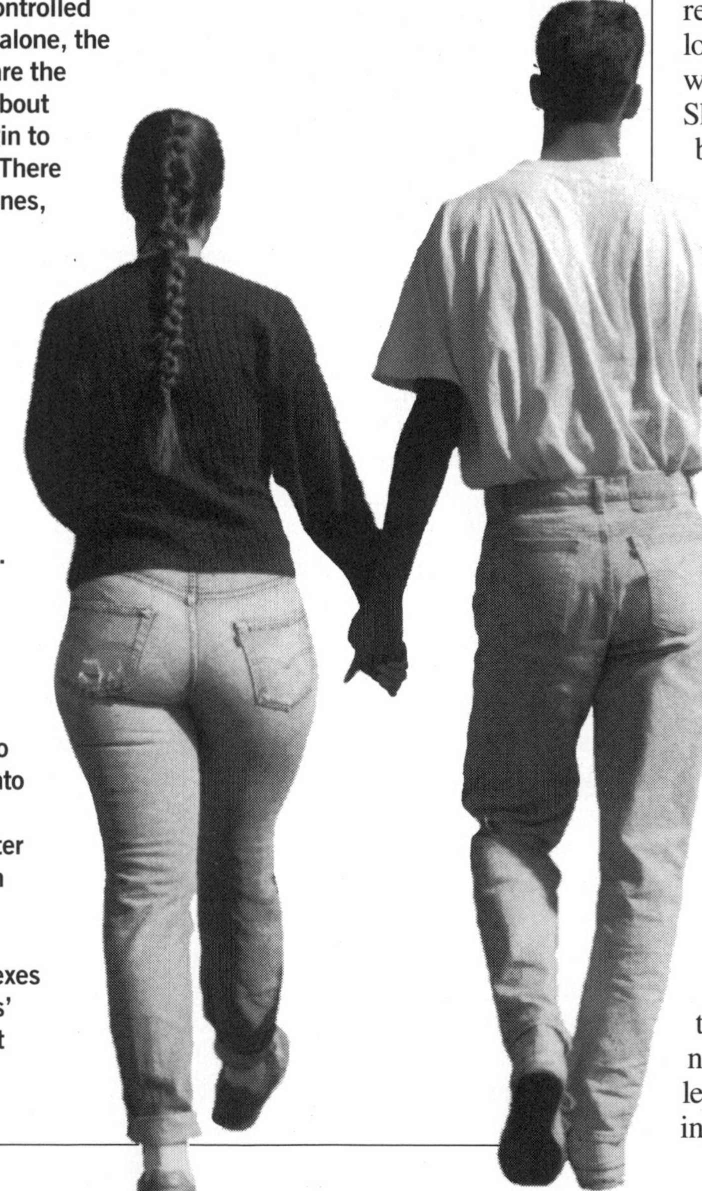

ized by a sperm, and need a place to grow into a baby. The hormone makes the womb lining thicken, and become rich with blood capillaries. The lining remains in place for 10 days or so—long enough for an embryo to enter the womb, and embed itself in the lining. Should that happen, a hormone made by the embryo's placenta will keep the original nurse cells that cared for the egg actively secreting estrogen and progesterone for the next nine months. That will prevent brain hormones from hatching any other eggs, and will keep the womb lining thick and rich for the baby's nourishment.

An unfertilized egg does not have such power. Without high doses of female hormones, capillaries in the womb lining pinch off, the thick portion of the lining detaches, and is shed through the vagina. The shedding is called menstruation after *mensis*, the Latin word for month. Menstruation takes as little as three days in some women, but a week or more in others.

Sometimes menstruation hurts for the first couple of days. The pain is not the lining detaching—that's painless. It's the womb contracting, squeezing itself free of the lining. The one in three women who get menstrual cramps are experiencing an extreme of how the womb normally behaves during menstruation, for contractions are caused by hormones called prostaglandins that wombs make to dose themselves into action. The trouble is that their womb makes too much of the potent stuff, and so it cramps harder than is necessary. Aspirin—and some of the stronger painkillers that are aspirinlike—blocks the manufacture of prostaglandins, and so helps to ease these over-vigorous cramps.

Prostaglandins were first discovered in semen, the fluid males make to protect their sperm, and which is a mixture of two fluids. One fluid, made along sperm's route to the urethra, nourishes them with fructose—fruit sugar. The other, a milky fluid, is an acid neutralizer that safeguards sperm from acidic mucus in the vagina. This portion of semen is made in a gland called the prostate. Scientists, guessing that cramping hormones were made there too, named the substances prostaglandins. As it happens, their guess was wrong; prostaglandins are supplied with the fruit-sugar juice. But what are these cramp-makers doing in semen?

Just that: making cramps. But not in the man, and not strongly enough in the women to even be felt. When semen is spurted into a woman, it causes mild contractions of her womb and tubes that seem to help sperm along toward their meeting with the egg. How's that for communication between the sexes!

Minds of Their Own

You can imagine the craziness that would result if all sorts of cells got excited whenever any hormone came their way. Were digestive glands to be roused by hormones intended to be heard by the adrenals, they would pour out digestive juices at just the time when adrenalin was supposed to be shutting down the gut. If a woman's womb responded to digestive hormones, it would cramp at every meal. If histamine were welcomed at such places, a mosquito bite might send her simultaneously into itches, digestion, labor, and panic.

Vice versa, any of the above would make her itch all over.

Some control is exercised by the fact that prostaglandins in the womb, histamines in the skin, and digestive hormones in the gut are used up locally before they can stray out of the neighborhood. But even bodywide hormones like adrenalin can affect only those cells that have receptors to receive them. Hair follicles have receptors for androgens—"male" hormones, including testosterone—and so make beards from face fuzz, but pigment makers in skin, fiber makers in joints, and gut cells in the intestine can't hear a word sex hormones say. They have no receptors for them: The hormones of adolescence don't change a person's color, cartilage, or digestion.

On the other hand, many kinds of cells do have receptors for the same hormone. Muscles have androgen receptors, and they are identical to those in the cells of hair follicles. Yet they interpret the message differently: When, in adolescence, muscles hear these hormones' call, they thicken with bundles of fibers, not hair. How can that be if the message and messenger are the same?

The idea that hormones are chemical messengers fudges the fact that they themselves are much too simple to say a lot. Most are not even able to get inside a cell, and must rely instead on surface receptors cooking up a batch of second messengers to spread word of their arrival within the interior. For all the hundred hormones known, there are only a handful of these second messengers. The second messenger for adrenalin, itchy histamine, two digestive hormones, several pituitary hormones, a couple of hypothalamus hormones, and a bunch of others are all the same, a sort of Johnny-One-Note molecule that can't possibly even say to the cell which of all these hormones has arrived. It would seem impossible to achieve the symphony of a living body with just a few monotonous refrains.

But here is the trick to it: Not only does each kind of cell differ in the selection of hormone receptors it produces, but also in which genes are available for reading, and therefore in which enzymes inhabit its cell fluid, and so which products can be made. A muscle cell receiving an androgen can't make hair because its hair genes are shut up tight, a permanently closed book. Second messengers needn't even bind to genes to transform their one-note message into a melody. They work by hooking up with any of many specific enzymes floating around in that particular type of cell, crippling some and activating others. Some production lines are therefore hampered while others are off and running, cranking up the beat of that cell's special music. No matter the simplicity of the messenger, or the monotony of its message: Each kind of cell has a mind of its own. The mind, not the messenger, composes the symphony.

Lessons in Ignorance

A body's organic government rests ultimately on the intelligence of common cells. Each kind must know which genes to read. If it did not, it would make unsuitable receptors and wrong enzymes, or fail to make the right ones. Either way it would be ungovernable.

Yet every one of the 200 different types of cells in a body is descended from just one, the fertilized egg, and the genetic library is the same in all the 40 trillion descendants that now inhabit your body. A dumb melanocyte turning out tan skin contains in its chromosomes instructions for sex hormones. Testes and ovaries contain instructions for tanning. Every nuclear library has a book on growing toenail and sperm tail. How is a cell kept in ignorance of all but a small fraction of the hundred thousand products its genes encode?

The genetic library of a cell is kept in its chromosomes. Each chromosome contains a single molecule of DNA (for deoxyribonucleic acid) that looks like a very long, very twisted ladder. The rails of the ladder hold it together; the rungs are the genetic instructions. The rungs are made of pairs of four different molecules, formally called adenine, guanine, cytosine, and thymine, but fondly called by the initial letters, A, G,C, and T. In fact, they really are an alphabet of sorts, for any three together—AGC, ATG, GGC, and so on—stand for a specific amino acid, just as the three-letter words DOG, CAT, and COW in our alphabet stand for specific animals. A gene is a portion of a DNA molecule whose sequence of three-letter words corresponds to the sequence of amino acids in a protein. There are estimated to be about 100,000 genes, each spelling out in three-letter words the sequence of from a few hundred to many thousands of amino acids in a specific protein.

Proteins are assembled by cell machinery out in the body of the cell, not inside the nucleus, and using copies of genes, not the genes themselves. The copies are made by enzymes inside the nucleus that move along a gene, assembling a duplicate of it one rung—one letter—at a time.

A gene is like a story. It can be read in only one direction, from the beginning to the end. The beginning of the story is a start mark, a short sequence of DNA to which the copying enzyme must bind before it can move along the gene to copy it. The gene ends with a stop mark, another short sequence that releases the enzyme to continue its work elsewhere. Copiers move from stop to start, copying every gene they bind to.

The only way to prevent a cell from making things it shouldn't is to hide those genes so copiers can't find them.

Hidden Genes

Copying is controlled by regulator proteins that you can think of as librarians who select which genes to look up (and which to display enticingly) within a cell's vast storehouse of knowledge. Some regulators are repressors that block start marks on the genes they regulate, so that they can't be read. Other regulators are activators that help, rather than hinder, the binding of copiers to start sequences. Regulators can also

Rungs in the Ladder

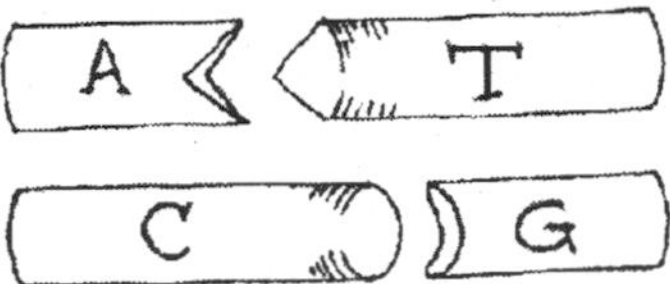

1. A molecule of DNA is shaped like a twisted ladder. Each rung is made up of a pair of molecules, of which there are four kinds—A, G, C, and T. Although rungs are all the same size, each of the molecules that forms a half a rung is a different length, and its end is a different shape. A and T fit together to make a rung; so do C and G. These fits are what make it possible to copy a gene.

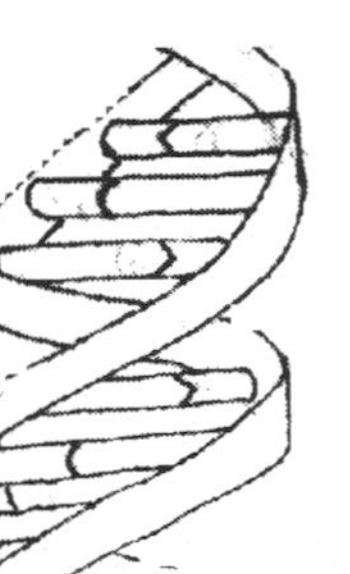

2. A gene, a portion of DNA that contains instructions for making a protein, is shown here (left) in black. It is made up of a sequence of half-rungs of the ladder. Its matching half-rungs are shown shaded. To make a copy, the gene is "unzipped" down the middle, separating the black from the shaded half-rungs.

3. Copier enzymes walk along an unzipped edge. They match rung pieces floating free in the neighborhood to the shaded halves of the rungs, and attach them to one another. The result is a copy of the black half-rungs—the sequence of "letters" that codes for the protein.

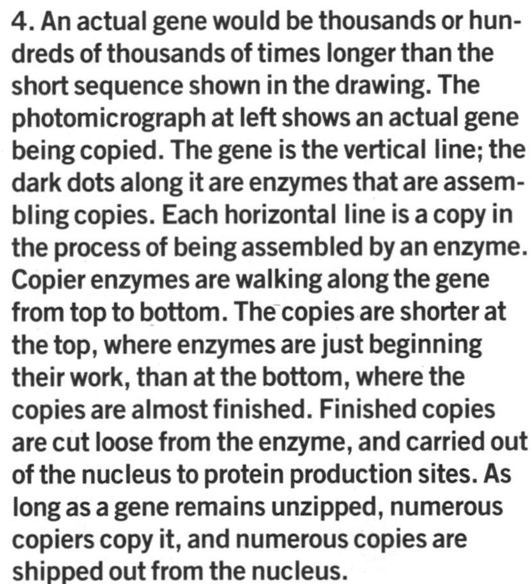

4. An actual gene would be thousands or hundreds of thousands of times longer than the short sequence shown in the drawing. The photomicrograph at left shows an actual gene being copied. The gene is the vertical line; the dark dots along it are enzymes that are assembling copies. Each horizontal line is a copy in the process of being assembled by an enzyme. Copier enzymes are walking along the gene from top to bottom. The copies are shorter at the top, where enzymes are just beginning their work, than at the bottom, where the copies are almost finished. Finished copies are cut loose from the enzyme, and carried out of the nucleus to protein production sites. As long as a gene remains unzipped, numerous copiers copy it, and numerous copies are shipped out from the nucleus.

interact with one another to lift censorship, or reimpose it; and a regulator may control a few or hundreds of genes. Of course each regulator protein is made according to instructions on a gene, and so, in a sense, copiers are forced to impose regulation on themselves: The copier copies the regulator gene, the cell then makes the regulator protein, and the regulator protein then prevents or encourages the copier's reading of the genes under its control. Copiers are never able to run rampant through the library. Their reading is at all times directed by a crew of librarians shoving books at them, slamming them shut, and on occasion stashing them away in such thicknesses of protein that copiers will never stumble across them at all.

The differences among cells depend on which regulator genes are available for copiers to read. In the beginning, when the fertilized egg is undergoing its first divisions, cells are totipotent: They might become any type of cell. However, it wouldn't do for this small cluster of cells to experiment so early in its development with teeth or stomach acid, so genes for most specialized products are temporarily censored by the regulators a fertilized egg starts out with. They also have (and you still have) some mystery genes too thickly packaged in proteins to ever be read. These probably code for products our ancestors once made: Chickens have a gene for tooth enamel that has similarly been stashed away for good. Genes that cells are able to use during their earliest divisions include those for ordinary household goods—membranes, doorways, the apparatus to divide.

In order for a totipotent cell to become a specific type, it must make decisions both as to which genes to release from censorship, and which to put into permanent storage. But the efficiency of the regulatory system makes learning to be gut or gland much simpler than if, for each of its hundred thousand instructions, it had to make a separate decision. To be gut instead of gland, an embryonic cell must learn only which of a smallish number of regulator genes to read. The regulators do the rest.

These decisions aren't made all at once. The education of embryonic cells is accomplished stepwise, one regulator at a time, until, weeks or even months after the egg was fertilized, each descendent's mind is made up by the unique selection of regulators that specify its type.

The Education of a Cell

Embryonic cells make their most drastic decision before they have even reached the womb, when there are only 16 of them. They decide which "basic book" they will read, one provided by the sperm, or one provided by the egg. In the sperm, those genes that control the development of the embryo during its first weeks are as locked up as any mystery gene. In an egg, those that control the development of the placenta cannot be read. Whether a particular cell at this point selects the regulator to read its basic instructions from the maternal library, or from the paternal library determines whether, in nine months, its lineage will be born as a baby or discarded as a placenta.

By the time the ball of cells rolls into the womb, the decision has been made. Cells around the outside of the ball consult father's how-to library on placentas; those in the inside of the ball read mother's make-a-baby book. Each cell has been forced by the accident of its position to switch on a fateful regulator: Education has begun.

The education of a cell is entirely positional. Its regulator genes are regulated by its chemical environment. For example, cells on the outside of the ball receive more of whatever chemicals are in the juices produced by the mother's oviduct through which the ball is rolling, whereas those on the inside receive less. Imagine a cell dividing along the midline of the embryo a little later in development, when the embryo is shaped like a pancake. The daughters are identical, but their position is not. One is inevitably budged edgewards of the other. Slight as this difference seems, the edgeward one receives more of any chemical diffusing inward from cells along the pancake's edge, whereas the central one receives more of chemicals made by cells along the midline. Each cell, sampling the environment with receptors in its membrane, gets a taste of its place in the world. The special flavor of its location is what turns on a specific regulatory gene, and that change might, in turn, cause the cell to produce chemicals that influence other cells in its neighborhood. In the case of the cell along the midline, its switched on regulator opens a whole bank of genes. It promptly crawls inside the pancake.

These flavors are strictly local. Their influence is also very brief: The embryo grows so quickly that a gene nudged by a whiff of the pancake's edge is within a day or so too far away to feel

The Making of a Protein

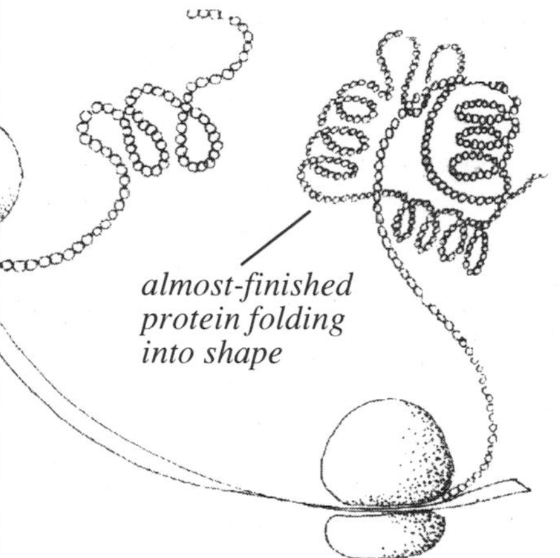

Cells make proteins according to gene copies provided to them by copiers in their nucleus. Carrier enzymes deliver their ribbonlike copies of instructions to areas outside the nucleus where protein-assemblers called ribosomes are stationed. A ribosome has two parts; the slim ribbon of instructions fits into a slot between the parts.

The ribosome feeds the ribbon through its slot, one triplet—three half-rungs or "letters"—at a time. Each triplet is like a template that fits a particular amino acid. Carrier enzymes deliver the fitting amino acid as each triplet comes through the slot. The ribosome attaches the amino acid to the previous one, and the protein grows.

Even before the first ribosome has finished running the ribbon through its slot, another has begun to also assemble a protein. Each ribbon can be used over and over again, and by dozens of ribosomes at once, and there may be thousands of identical ribbons in use simultaneously. The result is a great number of copies of the protein, all made according to instructions on a single gene. As they come off the production line, proteins fold themselves into complicated shapes according to the distribution of charges among their particular sequence of amino acids. Tiny "chaperone" molecules (not shown here) help to hold the various coils and pleats in place until folding is complete.

Small Difference

Chimpanzees are our closest living relatives, so one would expect that many of our genes—our store of inherited knowledge—are at least similar. What comes as a surprise is that they are more than just similar: 99 percent of human and chimpanzee genes are identical. That leaves only one percent to spell the difference between a human and an ape.

it. Therefore the chemical message that starts a midline cell's migration inward had better cause a permanent change of regulation so that it doesn't forget, halt, and never make a move to be a muscle. A permanent change in regulation is a form of memory: Cells learn.

On the other hand, the cell can't learn a lot at once. Were it to learn the manual of muscle machinery so soon, it would become a muscle fiber unable to creep to its proper place, or to reproduce. For now, it learns only that its fate is inward. It does not even know whether it will be muscle; it might instead make bone or gristle.

What the cell next learns again depends on where it is. It wanders randomly, creeping in the manner of an ameba or a phagocyte, not yet connected to other cells. Perhaps it ends up among a wedge of fellows, again stuck in the middle. The chemistry of its position now adds other regulators to its growing vocabulary: It's not a muscle after all; it's reading up on cartilage.

What shall it make a model of? Rib or limb? Arm or leg? Thigh or foot? Right or left? All these questions are answered by the chemical environment of its position, as though it were consulting its location in a 3-D game of tic-tac-toe. Each spot the cell might occupy is higher or lower, further forward or further backward, more to the right or more to the left. It tastes its place, refines its regulation, and models the cartilage framework for a bone in the left big toe.

A cell that, by the accident of its central position, was forced to crawl inside during those early pancake days could never learn how to be a skin cell even if were lifted out fast, before any other decisions had been made. Remaining surface cells, which have never tasted the flavor of that particular regulation, can never become fibroblast or chondroblast or osteoclast or muscle, although they might, if they are at the right place at the right time, learn how to make a toenail, or become a neuron that reports when the toe is stubbed. Those that lie along the spine when the spinal cord first forms might go forward to an exciting future as adrenal alarmists or hypothalamus snoops, but never backward to plain old skin.

What each generation of cells learns as its history unfolds can't be relearned by its descendants. By the time there is such a thing as a toe, there are no longer anywhere in the fetus the particular chemical addresses by which cells in that location learned, in previous generations, the details of their identity. So there must also be an inherited memory, for each cell continually divides into daughters that, were they born in ignorance, could no longer get a clue to what they are from where they live. An educated cell hands down its regulatory knowledge at every division to the whole lineage of cells that follows it. Your toe has inherited the knowledge its ancestors learned.

That's as far as toes can go, and that's far enough for them. But inherited knowledge is rooted in the past—not only in the history of that lineage of cells, but in know-how stumbled upon by that lineage of organisms during the history of its evolution. What if the future is not like the past?

Two kinds of cells, brain cells and immune cells, remain ready to begin an education for which there is, at birth, no lesson plan. Genes can't say how to recognize a fly; inheritance can't predict a bout of flu.

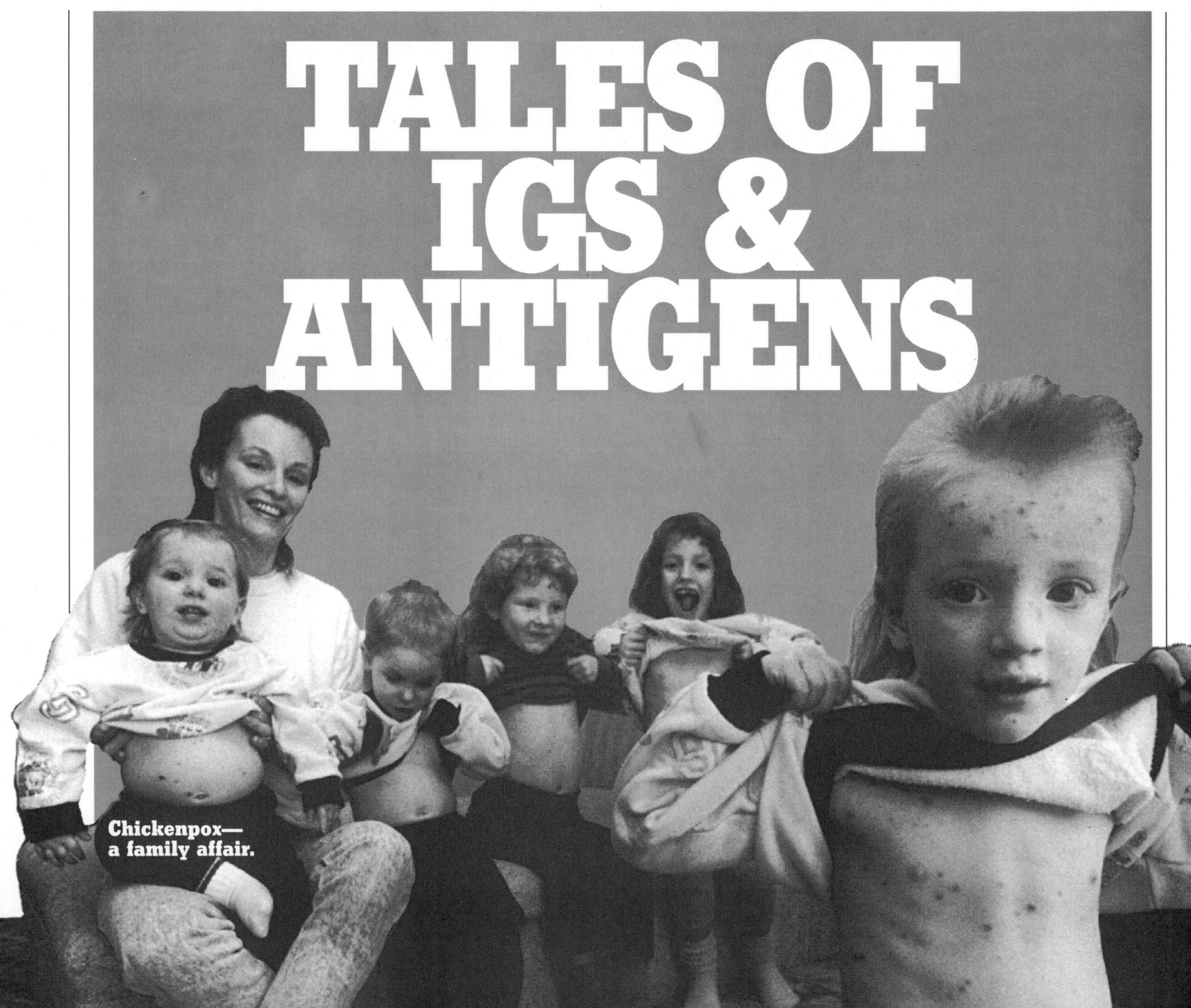

TALES OF IGS & ANTIGENS

Chickenpox—a family affair.

Ever had an earache? Strep throat? Tonsillitis? No doubt you have. But maybe you've noticed that your doctor, who breathes in sick kids' germs all day, doesn't get these diseases. Your parents seldom do either. Their bodies have been educated to recognize and kill most common germs. Yours is still learning.

The cells that recognize germs and organize the attack against them are a kind of white blood cell. When they are not circulating in blood, and when they are not on duty at the site of an infection, they live in lymph nodes, and so they are called lymphocytes. Lymphocytes are helped in their attack on germs by other kinds of white blood cells, but they're the ones that recognize what is to be attacked.

Germs—whether one-celled bacteria or those protein-coated scraps of DNA called viruses—are recognizable because the molecules that stud their surface are not the same as those that stud the surface of our own cells, or that our cells secrete. Recognition is similar to the sense of smell: Lymphocytes have receptors shaped to grasp alien molecules. But each species of bacterium, and even different breeds of the same species, has a different array of molecules on its surface. Each virus is coated with its own kind of protein jacket. Toxins bacteria produce may also cause damage, so those molecules must be recognized too. The process

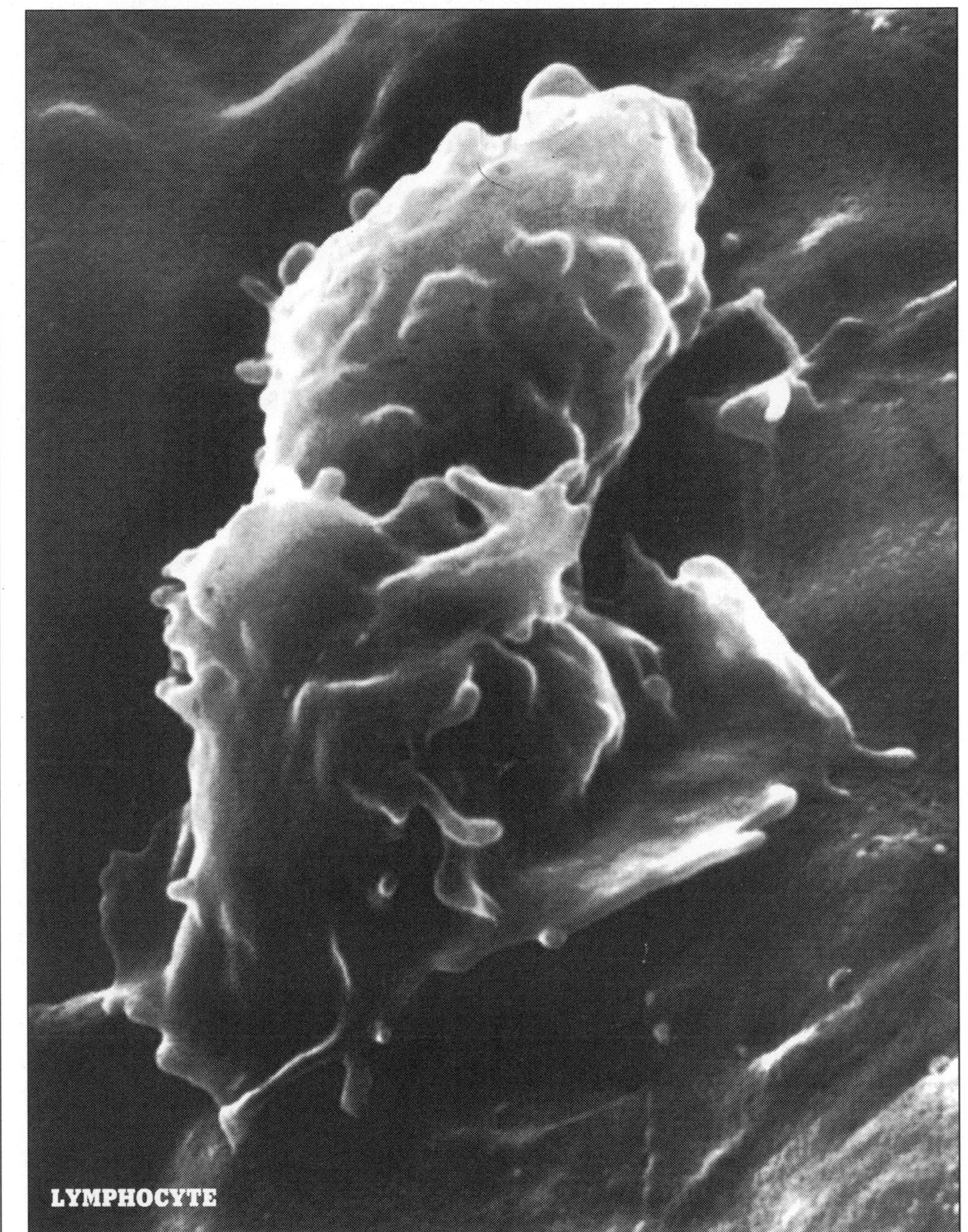
LYMPHOCYTE

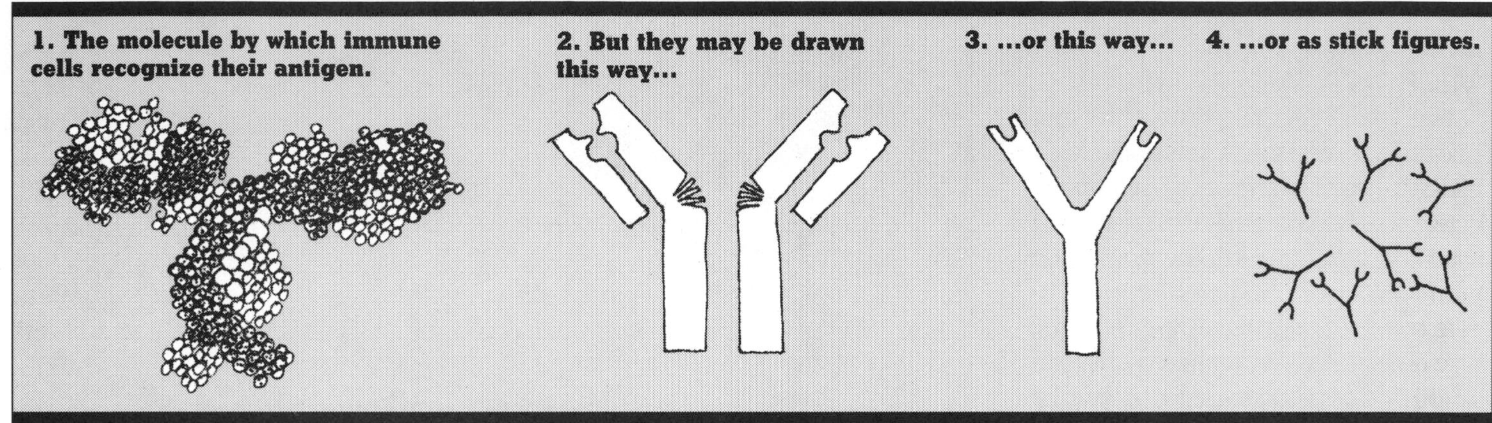

of getting sick is a learning experience in which a few lymphocytes whose receptors happen to fit that particular enemy multiply into a horde of daughters which, next time that invader gets inside your body, will destroy it before you feel any symptoms of disease. First, you have to get sick. Then you can become immune to that sickness.

1. The molecule by which immune cells recognize their antigen.
2. But they may be drawn this way...
3. ...or this way...
4. ...or as stick figures.

The Enemy Is Legion

You have about 2 trillion lymphocytes. Altogether, they are equipped to recognize every large molecule of any type that was not present in your body when you were an embryo. But for any particular alien molecule, there are at first only a smallish group of lymphocytes able to grasp it. Each group is a clone: They are identical sisters descended from the same mother. Their recognition device is receptors—or you might call them detectors—carried on their surface, that lock on to a particular portion of the alien molecule. Each clone produces its own unique enemy detectors that recognize only one or a few similar molecules. There are billions of clones because there are billions of enemies.

Enemies are anything that's "them," not "us." They are recognized as aliens by the peculiarities of molecules they wear, or make, or are—molecules whose knobby projections are unlike the ones immune cells bump into on the cells of their own bodies. Any molecule recognizable to an immune cell is called an antigen. An antigen may be any large molecule—a carbohydrate, a protein—so long as some knob on it fits a slot in some clone's unique detectors. As far as anyone knows, that is every kind of large molecule there is, for to be big in the Tinkertoy world of molecules is to be a conglomeration of knobs.

No organism can avoid presenting antigens for inspection to the immune system. Any sensor, receptor, pump, or lid studding a bacterium's cell wall is an antigen. So are any large molecules that it secretes. Proteins that jacket viruses are antigens. Human cells, too, bear antigens; if a cell is not from a lymphocyte's own body, its strange antigens mark it for attack. And—since knobs, not intentions, are all that lymphocytes can grasp—cat squames, dust mites, mosquito spit, ragweed pollen, tattoo dye, and penicillin also invite their clutch. For each of these, for each disease, for every poison, for every person, there is a clone of lymphocytes that takes it for a stranger, and knows that it has met its special enemy.

A Not-So-Simple Little Molecule

There are several kinds of lymphocytes, and although all of them carry antigen detectors, the detectors differ, and are used in different ways. The most common lymphocyte, called a B-lymphocyte (or just B-cell) uses them as surface detectors to recognize an antigen by touch, but it can also ship the devices out into the bloodstream as missiles to seek the enemy at a distance. The less common T-lymphocyte (or T-cell) uses similar devices as surface detectors to recognize by touch alien antigens that are displayed by infected cells. Lymphocytes are named for where they originated before moving into lymph nodes. B-cells originate in bone marrow. T-cells originate in a gland called the thymus.

The main difference between these two groups of immune cells is that while T-cells fight the battle at close quarters on the front lines, where cells are already sick with an infection, B-cells can fight germs at any distance, and sometimes before any cells have been injured. The two work together to orchestrate an attack that also involves phagocytes and mast cells, and a host of the most ferocious chemicals the body is capable of making.

All this is possible because the deceptively simple-looking antigen-detecting molecules lymphocytes wear on their surface are actually very complicated, and extraordinarily versatile. They are shaped like a T. The two arms of the T are hinged to the stem, so they are flexible. Each arm ends in a slot shaped to fit a knob on another molecule as a glove fits a hand. Both slots on the devices carried or shipped out by B-cells are shaped to fit an alien antigen. The slots on the devices carried by T-cells are of two different kinds: One that fits an alien antigen, another that fits a self-marker protein, a sort of passport molecule that cells carry on their surface to identify them as the body's own. A T-cell knows it has found an infected cell of its own body when both slots of its detectors—those that fit an antigen and those that fit a self-marker—are filled. A B-cell knows it should begin to ship out missiles when slots on its surface detectors are filled with antigen alone. For every alien antigen, there is a clone of missile shippers and a clone of passport checkers.

But how does filling slots on molecules make any cell know anything? The tip of the stem on these T-shaped devices is an enzyme. It is inactive until the slots in the arms are filled; then it snaps into an active shape that triggers a chemical reaction. Thousands of these tiny T's stud the surface of both kinds of lymphocyte. When they are activated, they trigger chemical actions within the cell itself, some that gear it up to fight, others that are secreted to engage the help of other cells. Detectors sent out as missiles by B-cells work the same way, but when their arm slots are filled by antigen, the stem triggers a chemical reaction either out in the surrounding body fluid, or inside the body of another cell that has grabbed the device by its enzyme stem. In these ways a fierce antagonism toward the enemy is spread to mast cells and to phagocytes, and the very environment of body fluid at the site of an infection becomes poisonous to germs.

Clone 9-633-254-001

A few days ago a B-lymphocyte was born in the marrow of a rib. It belongs to clone number 9-633-254-001, which has never been of any use at all. It's settled now in a lymph node in your neck, with nothing to do but display samples of the one uniquely slotted antigen detector it can make, and that has been displayed by former members of its clone year after year. Such a lymphocyte is called a virgin: one that has never come across an antigen that fits.

But let's say you woke up this morning with a sore throat—a strep throat, an invasion of streptococcus bacteria. Your throat is already red, swollen, and painful. That's the work of mast cells hanging around in the dermis secreting their inflammatory chemicals, as

An antibody "knows" it has found its antigen when the fit is good.

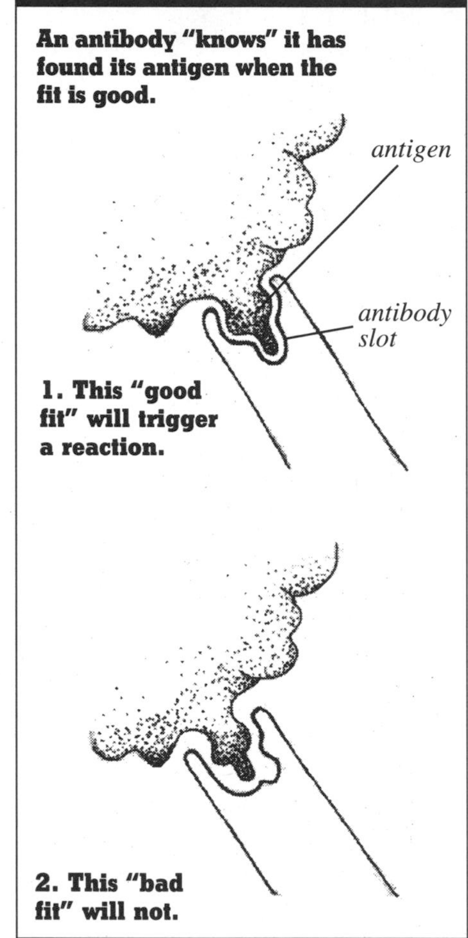
antigen
antibody slot
1. This "good fit" will trigger a reaction.
2. This "bad fit" will not.

they would with any injury, however slight. Phagocytes are at work too, cleaning up dead cells, eating up live germs. Still, the streptococci multiply. A few spill into the lymph capillaries that drain excess body fluid into lymph nodes.

They are swept into the node in your neck, followed by phagocytes bearing antigen from bacteria they swallowed only minutes before within the dermis of your throat. A hurried conference is held. T-cells paw over phagocytes, check their passports, note the stamp of antigen. Both phagocytes and T-cells crowd against the B-cell as it examines a bacterium.

Such conferences are the way in which immune cells reach decisions, and coordinate their activities. The giant phagocytes that advertise what they have eaten are specialists that remove antigen from their prey, and insert it into their own membrane. It is by touching them that T-cells learn whether the antigen is theirs to grasp. B-cells learn directly, by touching the germ itself, and they, too, nibble, and display their trophy. Together in chemical conference, the immune cells inform each other that this germ is it: It fits.

As slots in its detectors become filled with antigen, chemical changes within the B-cell begin. The B-cell now grows larger, and divides. Within a few days it has produced a horde of daughters, some large like it is now, some small like it was before.

The small ones leave the node, flow into the bloodstream, slip out at capillaries, and display the special germ detector of their now numerous clan at lymph stations everywhere in the body. They don't join this first battle: They act, instead, as their mother's memory, and your immunity. They will wander your body restlessly from blood to lymph and from lymph to blood all the rest of their long, long lives in wait for this particular enemy's return. The next time these streptococci get inside you, they will be met by an army of B-cells in position to launch an immediate attack. The present war is entered by their much larger sisters.

The B-mom's big kids produce the same detector that peppers their sisters' surface. But they also cut loose and ship out these little T-shaped molecules at the rate of 2,000 molecules a second, 60 loads a minute, around the clock, day after day. (Their wartime effort is so great that they will die of overproduction, as their mother will die of over-reproduction.) These missiles go by a special name you may have heard before: antibodies. Antibodies are empty antigen detectors secreted by B-cells into the bloodstream to seek out and mark the enemy wherever it is found.

To realize the cleverness of this strategy, picture a germ stuck all over with these tiny missiles clinging by their arms to its surface. In what direction are the enzyme-tipped stems facing? The stems of detectors on a lymphocyte stick inwards, where their enzyme tips can control the cell's internal chemistry, such as the reactions that make it grow, multiply, and ship out antibody. But the stems of antibodies clinging to antigens on a germ stick outwards. The germ is, in effect, coated with enzymes set to trigger chemical reactions that will be the death of it.

The words antigen and antibody are confusing because both begin with *anti*—"against." It's hard to remember who's against whom, which are us and which are them. Luckily, antibodies also go by the name "immunoglobulin," which at least identifies them as the product of immune cells. Luckier still, "immunoglobulin" is usually abbreviated "Ig." Igs come in brands, each of which is tipped with a different enzyme. Ig brand names are not catchy: B-cells may specialize in making any of five brands of immunoglobulins called by letters of the Greek alphabet *alpha*, *delta*, *epsilon*, *gamma*, *mu*—or IgA, IgD, IgE, IgG, and IgM. Gamma and Mu are tipped with the enzymes that are most destructive to bacteria.

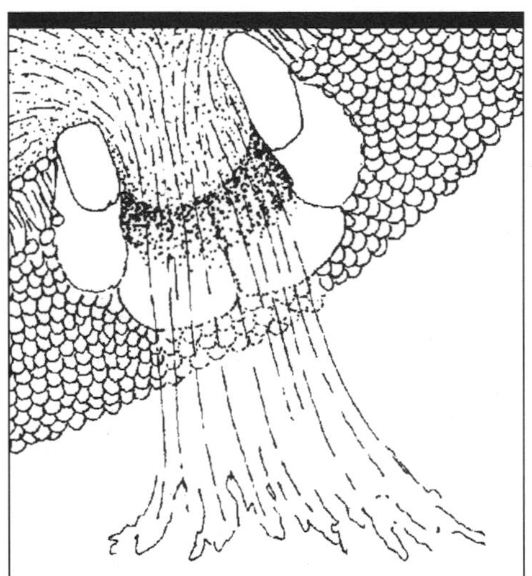

Five ingredients in IgM "sauce" cooperate to form this hole in a bacterium through which it will leak to death.

Sauce for the Goose

It takes several days for a virgin lymphocyte to multiply, and for her large daughters to begin producing antibody. During that time, germs spread beyond the original site of invasion—probably to tonsils, maybe into ears. Anywhere they can go, Igs can go too. Floating through lymph, washing through blood, pumped out at capillaries, umpteen IgM and IgG molecules spill over every battlefield. They attach to germ antigens slot to knob, with one arm or both. They pepper the streptococci with themselves.

IgM antibodies then prepare a sauce. As they grasp antigens on the surface of a bacterium, their enzyme-tipped stems trigger a chain reaction among proteins leaked from swollen capillaries. The reaction takes place right on the surface of the germ, slathering it with a sauce containing some 20 different ingredients.

It's an evil sauce: Five ingredients in it cooperate to form a gaping hole through the bacterium's wall, bursting it to death.

And it's a fragrant, tasty sauce. Mast cells getting a whiff of it step up their secretion of inflammatory chemicals. That opens the gaps in capillaries wider, letting more phagocytes out. Phagocytes are attracted to the smell. Their appetite is whetted by the taste. And gummy ingredients in the sauce make it easier for them to get hold of germs and swallow them.

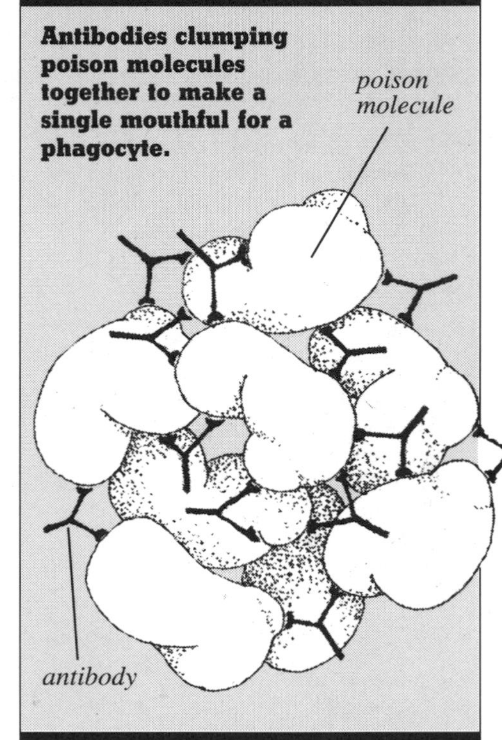

Antibodies clumping poison molecules together to make a single mouthful for a phagocyte.

While IgMs sauce the germs, IgGs also attach to them. The stem tip of IgG, however, fits a phagocyte receptor and so influences its chemistry. Phagocytes eating IgG-spiced bacteria digest their prey more quickly. They stud their

Zip, Slurp

1. This phagocyte is swallowing a bacterium. It locks onto its prey using receptors that "zipper" its meal to its membrane.

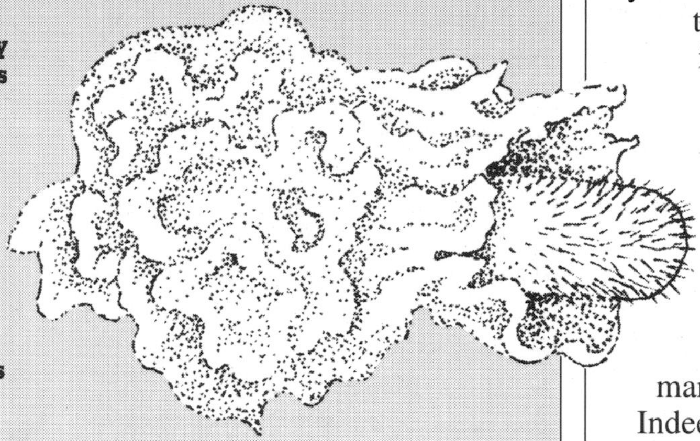

2. When the bacterium is completely zipped up, that portion of the phagocyte's membrane is pinched off, carrying the bacterium inside. Enzymes delivered to this temporary stomach digest the contents, which are used as food by the phagocyte. The empty sac of membrane is recycled to the cell surface.

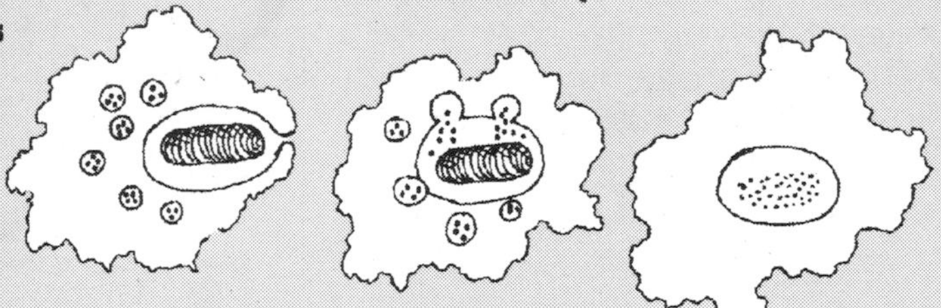

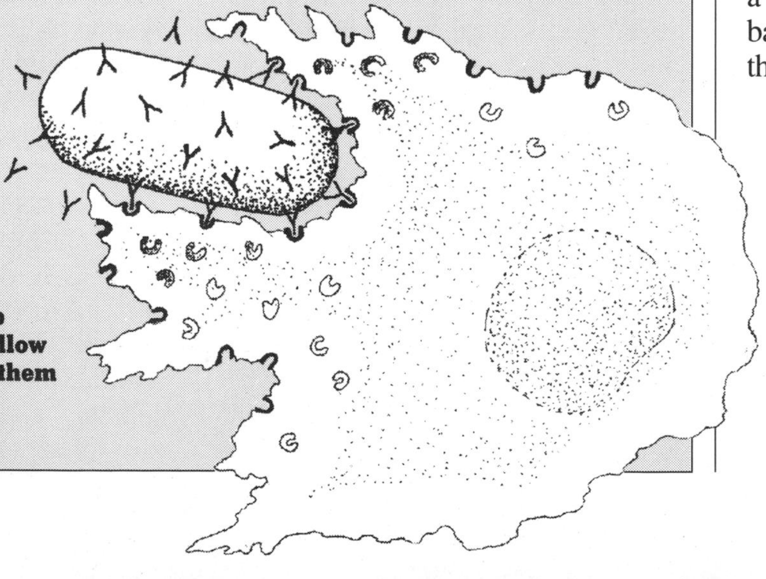

3. Immune cells help phagocytes to swallow germs by coating them with easy-zip Igs.

membrane with more IgG receptors, the better to eat spicy meals to come.

While the eaters go about their grisly business, IgG prevents germs' further spread. Although antibodies are very much smaller than streptococci, their hinged arms can spread to hold two bacteria at once. In this way many IgGs clump microbes, or the poisons they may make, together like prisoners in chains, unable to multiply, unable to escape, and every one marked for eventual execution. Indeed, they may become a single mouthful for a group of giant phagocytes that, fusing for the job, take the whole clump in a gulp.

Meanwhile, the T-Cells

All this B-cells have accomplished at a distance by shipping antibodies into battle. What about the clone of T-cells, the passport checkers whose detectors also fit this germ's antigen?

The fitting clone of T-cells behaves at first much like B-cells do. They divide, and produce some daughters to be their memory. But they produce several kinds of large daughters: Helpers, Suppressors, and a kind called, simply, Killers. They work within the lymph nodes to which germs have spread, and ride the bloodstream to any other site of infection.

Killers have a straightforward job: to kill infected cells. They check every cell they touch for passports stamped with antigen. If one arm of their detectors fits a passport, and the other fits the stamp of infection, the cell is killed. Killers are also mightily attracted to the germs themselves if they have been marked by IgGs. Killers smear IgG-marked germs with a protein that riddles them with holes, leaving them leaking out their innards. They don't bother to remove the corpses; phagocytes do that.

Helpers incite full-scale war. Their receptor arm that checks for whether a cell belongs to their body does not recognize the self-marker of ordinary cells. It recognizes an ID card that identifies only other lymphocytes, and antigen-advertising phagocytes. A fellow germ fighter that displays both the ID card and the antigen is surely engaging the enemy, and needs a Helper's help.

Helper T-cells secrete blasts of chemicals that make everyone engaged in battle fight the more fiercely. Some make phagocytes ravenous. Others fan the fires of inflammation to a blaze. Still others rev up B-lymphocytes to pour out more Igs to attract more Killers, make more sauce, sprinkle more spice, trigger more mast cells to spray more histamine to fuel the blaze still higher.

Such ferocity is destructive. The exhaustion of sickness, the soreness, swelling, fever, chill, rash, headache, joint pain—and the actual damage to tissues—is caused as much by defense against the enemy as by enemy attack. This is like a real war. The trampled battlefield becomes a scorched and cratered wasteland strewn with innocents as well as enemies. Sometimes the invaders do real harm; sometimes they threaten nothing but competition for our body goods, and we could live with them as dogs can live with fleas. Sometimes, there hasn't even been an invasion: Diseases such as juvenile diabetes, rheumatic fever, rheumatoid arthritis, and muscular dystrophy are caused when lymphocytes mistakenly take a self-marker to be an alien antigen, and so do battle against their body's own cells. Then the disease involves no germs at all. But even when germs have invaded, it's mostly the war that hurts.

Suppressor T-cells keep the war in check. They do the opposite of everything that Helpers do. Suppressors secrete a soothing potion that relaxes the whole hyperactive crew—including their own exciting sisters—and altogether dampens the fires of war.

The balance between exciting and soothing forces varies with the germ, but not because immune cells think worse of one than of another. Immune cells know only antigens, and can't judge the danger of an alien. The level of attack is determined by how many different clones find some portion of the germ that fits them, and on the goodness of the fit. A bacterium may have an antigen that fits the slots of a clone's detectors as a key fits its lock. Then more Ig is bound, more sauce is made, more Helpers help. Sometimes the fit is loose, and the key falls easily from the lock. The battle then is just a skirmish. Slots in T-cell and B-cell antigen detectors aren't necessarily identical, so there may be more sauce than fire for one germ, more fire than sauce for another. Or, a half dozen different clones of each might all find some knob of their own to grasp. Then who knows what will happen in the throat!

In the end, the war is stopped by victory. The germs are eaten. The battle halts. There is no antigen to fuel it.

The Alien Returns

So you recover from your sore throat, and forget about it.

Not so the restless children of war, who never forget. Memory T-cells and memory B-cells of any clones involved in that infection are much more numerous than their virgin mothers were, more widespread in the body, long-lived, and quick to multiply in time of need. In addition, IgG antibody molecules may circulate in the bloodstream for years.

Veterans of the first infection have also set a special trap: the alpha brand

The Killer at its Grisly Task

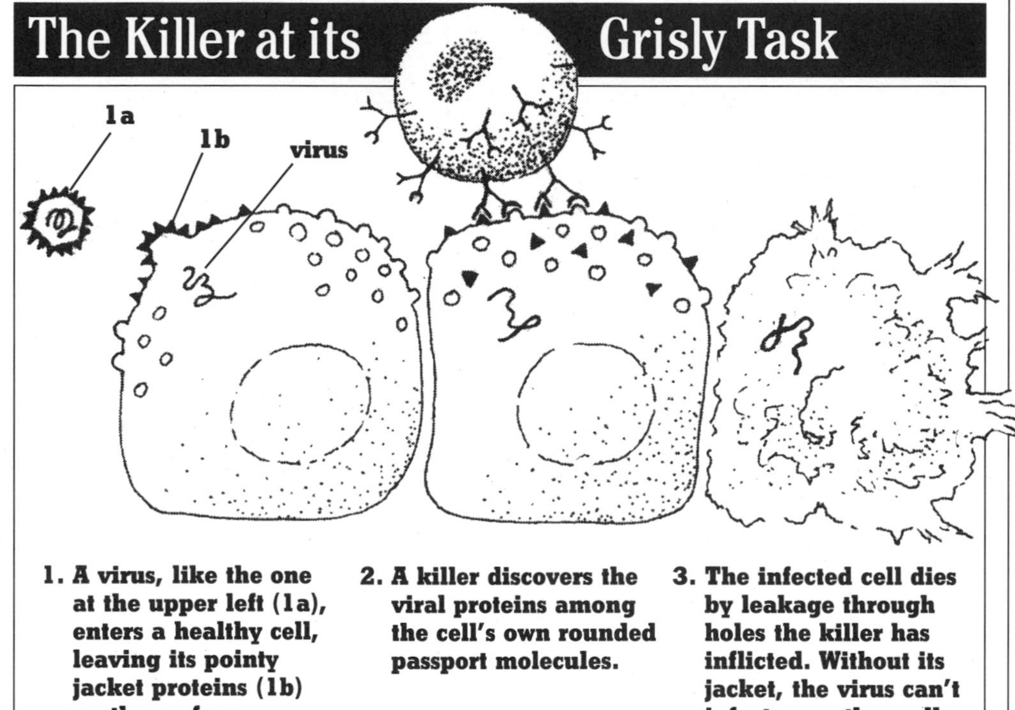

1. A virus, like the one at the upper left (1a), enters a healthy cell, leaving its pointy jacket proteins (1b) on the surface.

2. A killer discovers the viral proteins among the cell's own rounded passport molecules.

3. The infected cell dies by leakage through holes the killer has inflicted. Without its jacket, the virus can't infect any other cells.

of B-cells that specialize in making IgA migrate to secreting centers. They nestle among mucus cells, settle in salivary glands, and give their neighbors Ig to sip and mix with spit invading germs must wade through.

When, next fall, the same streptococci try to get a foothold on a tonsil, spit slobbers them all over with IgA. It covers up the receptors by which they cling to throat cells. They can't even hang on. And if some do, they are anyhow marked for death. This time there is no delay while virgins lose their innocence. Marked germs are done for before they have begun.

And so you don't get sick.

You don't get sick because victory is quick. The enemy hasn't a chance to multiply. Scant quantities of chemicals suffice to wipe them out. If there is a battle at all, it is too slight to hurt you.

This is what immunity is: Such excellent preparation that whenever the enemy returns, it's gone before you can feel it.

An Exercise in Exons

The experience of combat by which a clone of lymphocytes prepares for future invasions is a graduation for cells that already, in the embryo, had completed their elementary education in enemy recognition. The newborn baby has all its clones—and not only ones that bye and bye will grasp strep, staph, flu, and chickenpox. Not knowing what in the world their body might come upon, clones have slots for antigens on germs that have been extinct for centuries, ones that will not evolve until the year 3000, and for antigens that can't exist unless they are made by people.

Since each clone's antigen detector has uniquely shaped slots, each is a somewhat different protein, which must be coded for by a different gene. But that seems impossible. Human chromosomes contain perhaps 100,000 genes. Only a small fraction of them specify antibodies (or the surface detectors immune cells carry). How can B-cells make millions more Igs than there are genes for?

The fertilized egg does not come with a gene that codes for a complete detector or antibody molecule. It does not even have genes for the molecule's arms or stem. The only information the embryo possesses is a kit of DNA segments, called exons, from which such genes might be assembled. Each ancestral lymphocyte selects parts at random, assembling for itself the unique genes that its clone will inherit.

Kits of exons are strung like beads on long necklaces. To make a gene, a cutting enzyme snips out portions of the necklace, and rejoins the severed ends. The final gene will have many fewer exons than did the original kit.

For instance, there are several hundred exons to choose from just to determine the shape of each side of an antibody's slot—and only the upper portion of the slot at that. The shape of the rest of the slot is chosen from among still other exons. After snipping and rejoining, only one exon from each selection of slot parts remains in the finished gene.

Enzymes snipping out portions of these necklaces of choices have no preference for one exon over another. Their randomness is what makes each clone's slot a different shape. Altogether, there are 12 million different slot shapes an enzyme might piece together.

Once the selection is made, all daughters abide by it: Each clone makes its mother's, and no other's, Ig. It has no choice, since excess exons are discarded. However, a clone can improve its antibody's fit once it has met its antigen. Antibody genes are more likely than most to suffer minor errors in copying. When lymphocytes are rapidly dividing in preparation for a battle, some daughters receive miscopied genes for arms with slightly altered slots which, by chance, fit their antigen more snugly. In this way each new invasion tends to sharpen recognition of the enemy—and multiplies by mutation the original 12 million Igs to billions. All this is true also of the detectors that clones of T-cells make, and alter, and hone to fit the enemy more exactly.

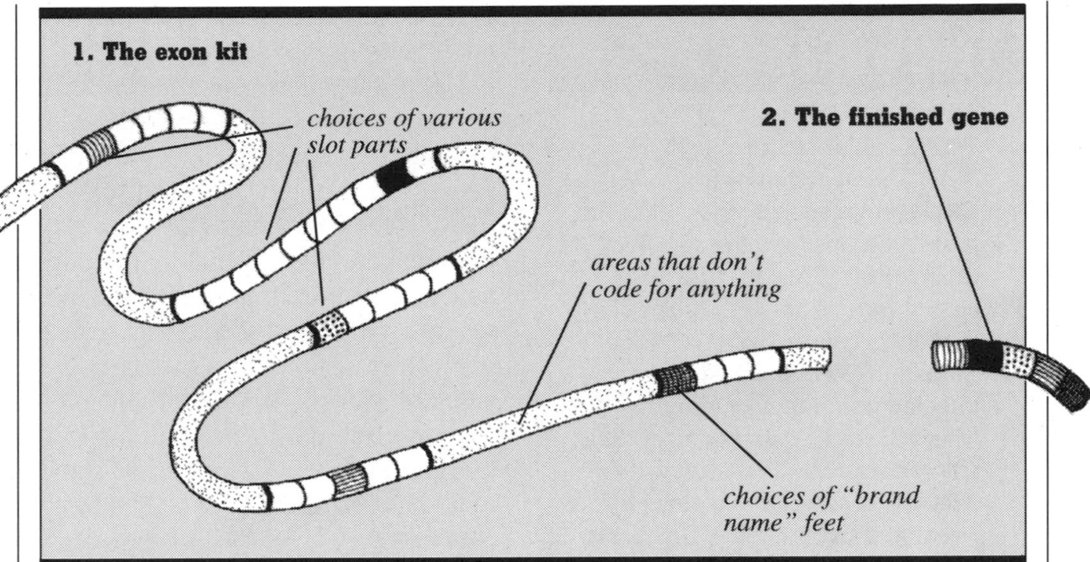

Sticking Stuff

Before vaccines were invented, children's immune cells had to hone their skills in many a bitter battle. Vaccines avoid that. You've gotten shots for typhoid, tetanus, diptheria, whooping cough, measles, and mumps, and have swallowed several doses of polio vaccine too. Vaccines contain antigens that your body would otherwise learn of only in the course of infection with diseases more dangerous than lessons ought to be. Most vaccines are the germs themselves—sometimes dead, but sometimes not.

Typhoid and whooping cough vaccines are ground-up bacteria, antigen hamburgers from which to learn the taste of microbes before they enter on the hoof. They can't give you the disease because they are dead. Immune cells don't know that, and may inflame

TB Tine Test

Regular health checkups often include a four-pronged skin prick, called a tuberculin tine test, to check for tuberculosis. The four tines are coated with an antigen, tuberculin, from tuberculosis bacteria. If you were infected in the past or are infected now, memory immune cells will start a commotion at the site of the prick. The result will be a telltale red swelling in about a week. Another version of the test is an injection just below the skin. It works the same way.

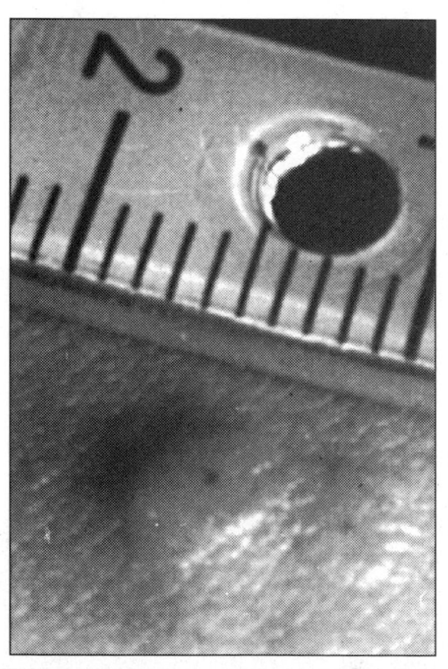

the body to a fever. That's sick, but it's not infection.

On the other hand, polio and influenza vaccines are whole viruses, dressed in their protein jackets, and with their genes intact. They can—and do—cause infection. They are, however, domesticated germs that evolved in unaccustomed cells and under unkind treatment in glass dishes in a laboratory; the disease they cause is tame compared to what the wild types can do.

Flu viruses during their taming in a laboratory are kept too cold. They would like to multiply in cells at lung temperature, where wild influenza does its damage. Instead they are forced to manage as best they can in cells kept at nose temperature. Most fail; some few succeed. Success is due to accidental changes, but the catch is that those able to stand nose cold can no longer bear lung heat. Mutant flu viruses invade nostril cells, multiply nicely, and totally alarm the immune system. But they can't reproduce anywhere deeper than the surface, or any lower in the respiratory tract. The person who was vaccinated becomes immune without so much as a cough.

Polio viruses used for vaccine have been tamed by passing them from dish to dish for generations until some strain evolved that thrived in cells in laboratories, but not in cells in bodies. The live vaccine is swallowed, and the mutant viruses infect the gut. The infection is too feeble to be felt, but enough viruses are released to train a clone of lymphocytes.

Tetanus shots don't contain tetanus bacteria, don't teach anything about germs, and don't even protect against infection. Tetanus is caused not by what the microbes do, but by what they make: a toxin that destroys receptors on muscle fibers that receive messages from nerves. The vaccine is that toxin. The molecules are crippled to make them harmless, but their identifying knobs are left intact. When you get a tetanus shot, B-cells that recognize the knob flood the body with a fitting IgG. You may get the infection, but IgG mops up the poison that is the only nasty feature of this otherwise gentle germ.

Smallpox vaccine isn't given to kids anymore because the disease has been wiped out, but it was an interesting critter, and it wasn't smallpox. It was cowpox, a close relative that, dripped into pricks in the skin, caused a local infection, a single pox. Cowpox trained immune cells to recognize smallpox because the two had antigens in common.

A Shot for Extinction

By sitting still for cowpox pricks, your parents' generation drove smallpox to extinction. You are now part of a worldwide effort to do the same to measles.

Measles is a creepy disease. Viruses enter the body through mouth and nose, and sit waiting in the throat, not multiplying, not harming anything, not giving the body reason for alarm. They are eaten there by phagocytes, but they turn the tables: They infect them.

The infection is invisible to lymphocytes. Measles viruses don't strew antigen around while multiplying inside scavengers. So they're not noticed, so there's no battle, so you don't get sick.

But within about 10 days measles has multiplied into masses of viruses which, bursting from their hosts, pour into the bloodstream. From capillaries everywhere they invade skin inside and out, scalp to sole, lungs to nose, on eyeballs, in mouths, and even up the ear. Caught by surprise, lymphocytes belatedly flash a rash—while measles leaves on coughs of air to launch on others its vicious sneak attack.

The pounding headache, burning eyes, prickly rash, high fever, and hacking cough of measles are not in themselves reasons to be frightened of it. But bacteria easily enter the body through surfaces damaged by eruptions of viruses, and by the inflammation of war. Blindness and deafness can result, and pneumonia, brain infection, and death. In 1963, the year before the vaccine was available, more than 500,000 people in America had measles; 500 of them died. Worldwide, measles is the

Boosters

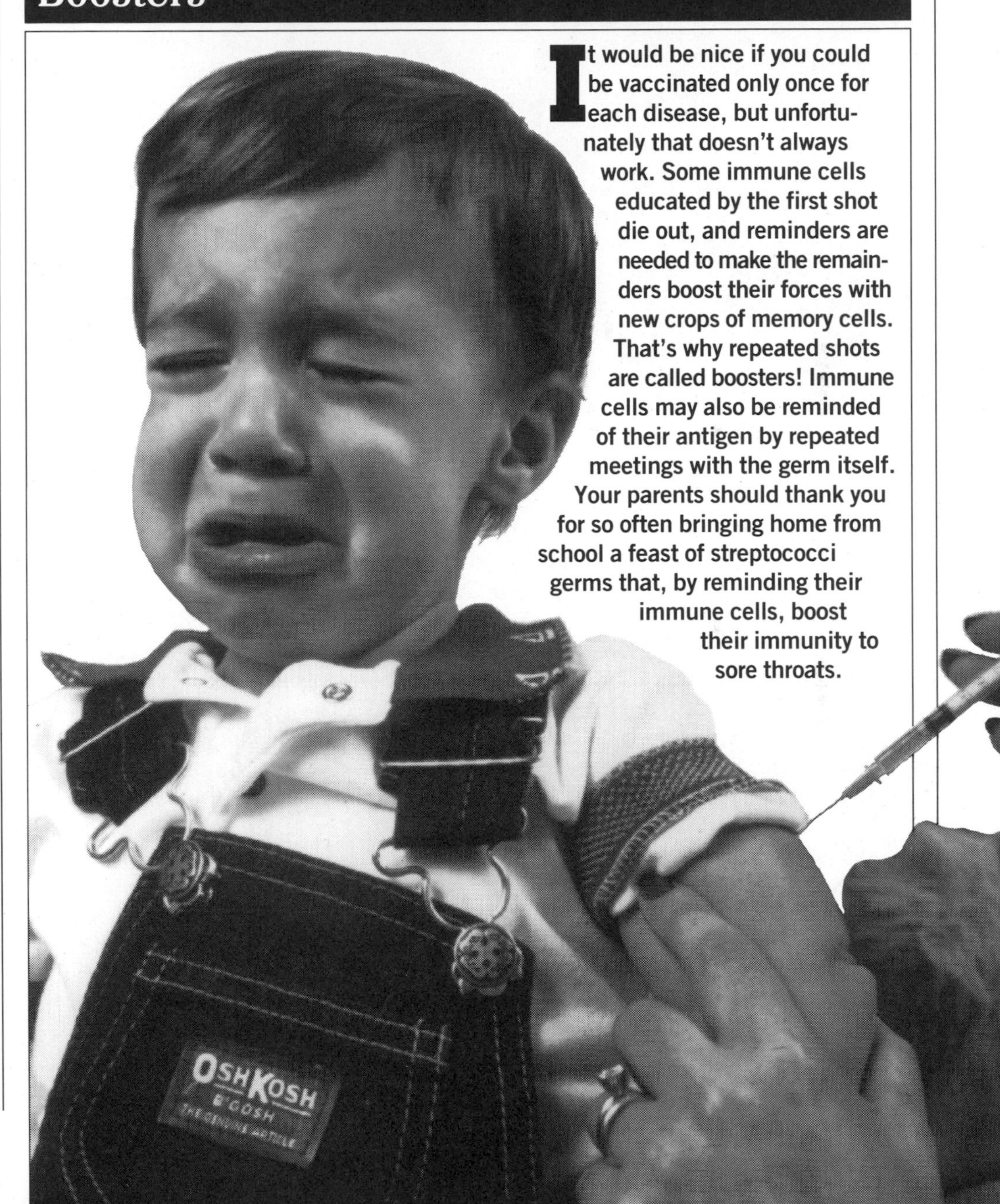

It would be nice if you could be vaccinated only once for each disease, but unfortunately that doesn't always work. Some immune cells educated by the first shot die out, and reminders are needed to make the remainders boost their forces with new crops of memory cells. That's why repeated shots are called boosters! Immune cells may also be reminded of their antigen by repeated meetings with the germ itself. Your parents should thank you for so often bringing home from school a feast of streptococci germs that, by reminding their immune cells, boost their immunity to sore throats.

Swabbing Streptococci

When you have a bad sore throat, the doctor will usually wipe a little mucus from the infected area, and send the sample to a lab for identification of the germ. If it's streptococcus, you're asked to take an antibiotic for a week or so. The reason is not that your throat wouldn't recover without drugs. It is to avoid what is called an auto-immune disease, in which lymphocytes mistake self-makers for alien antigens. Each kind of cell—nerve, muscle, gland—has self-markers that specify its type, as well as those that serve as general passports. Some strep germs carry an antigen that is similar in shape to a self-marker on heart muscle. After your throat has healed, leftover immune cells may mistake the muscle cells for germs, and attack them. The result—the serious disease called rheumatic fever—is injury to the heart. Fear of rheumatic fever prompts doctors to kill off streptococci with antibiotics before too many immune cells learn the antigen they ought not to know.

Under the microscope, streptococci look like long strings of beads. Looks alone are not enough, however, to identify bacteria. Bad ones look about the same as harmless or helpful species, such as the streptococci we use to make cheese from milk. The bacteria from your throat are grown in lab dishes. Identifying them is a complicated business of finding out which environmental conditions they prefer, what shape the colony takes after several days of growth, or how the germs react to certain chemicals.

leading cause of death in childhood.

Obviously, measles is high on the list of most wanted microbial murderers, and happily, it is among the few diseases that can, by vaccination, be driven to extinction.

Measles viruses can't live outside of bodies. They can't multiply in any other animal. Once they are noticed, they arouse fierce, lifelong immunity that gets rid of them down to the last virus, and will never again let them sneak in to multiply and spread. Therefore the only way measles viruses can persist is by infecting, one after another in an endless chain of infection, bodies that have never had the disease before. When measles has infected everyone in a community, the virus dies out, only to return with some sick visitor someday to infect children born since the last epidemic. Measles has in this way circled the globe for centuries.

Vaccination breaks the chain by depriving the virus of bodies to spread into. When the disease runs out of victims everywhere, it will be extinct. Adults may say that measles needles are for your own good, but they are much more than that: They are shots for extinction, shots that will save the lives of children everywhere.

Why Not the Rest of Them?

Since there seem to be many ways to make germs commit suicide as vaccines, you might wonder why there's no shot for strep throat, chickenpox, cold sores, or the common cold. Why is there no way to put an end to dread diseases—to gonorrhea, leprosy, or plague? There are a lot of reasons.

There is no shot for leprosy because it has no talent for living in glass dishes. How is one to harvest enough germs to kill and make a vaccine of if they grow only in humans, or—the only alternative with leprosy bacteria—in armadillo embryos? There is no shot for plague because it is not, these days, a plague. The disease is too rare—only a few or no cases in the United States in recent years—to prick millions of kids about.

There is no shot for gonorrhea because the immune system doesn't learn much from a live invasion, never mind a shot of corpses. Gonorrhea's sneaky. It changes its antigens over and over, and so people can get it over and over, too.

There is no vaccine for cold sores because the virus, one of a family of viruses called herpes, comes in many varieties. A vaccine would have to contain antigens from each to provide protection from all.

Permanent Pox

Herpes cold sore viruses spread from person to person in saliva, on kisses. The sore they cause lasts a week or so,

Measles Magnified

This is what a measles virus looks like magnified thousands of times by an electron microscope. Each child vaccinated against measles is one less person in the world who can give this virus a home. When the virus can no longer find unvaccinated humans, it will become extinct.

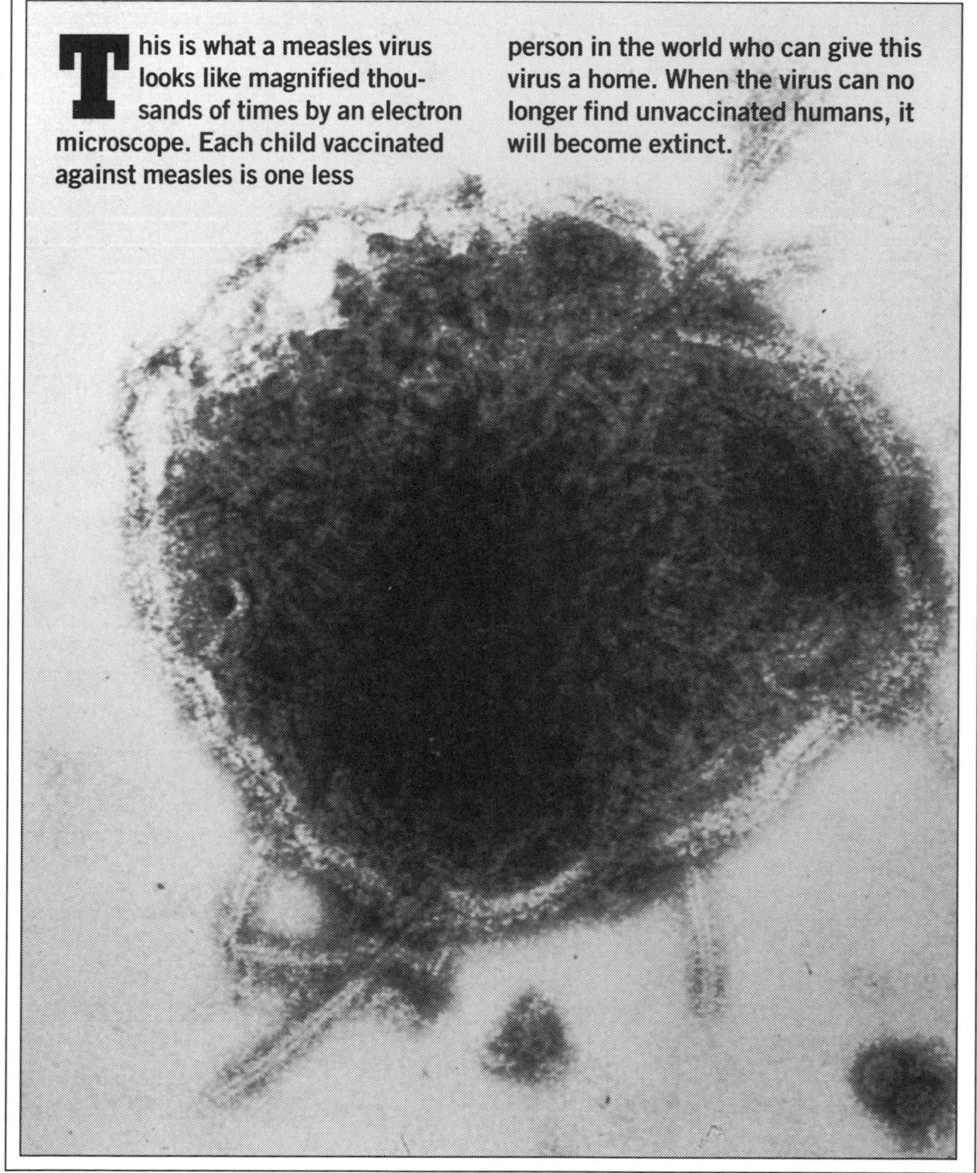

and then is gone. But the herpes viruses are not.

Herpes leaves the skin by entering sensory neurons. Within a few days the viruses have traveled the length of the axon to where it terminates at the spine. There, well hidden from immune cells, they remain uncopied, unfelt, and safe for months or years until the nerve they inhabit becomes, for some reason, upset. The upset may be sunburn, a fever, an uproar of emotion. Then the neurons containing these eruptive viruses copy a slew of them, and out the herpes go to make another sore, infect another host. A person who has herpes harbors viruses for life.

Chickenpox is another herpes virus that lives forever in hiding at the spine. It infects more than 3 million people a year. Many decades after a child was sick, when he may no longer even remember the itch and scabs of chickenpox—and when few lymphocytes are left that remember either—some stress may cause neurons to make fresh copies of the viruses they harbor. The new viruses travel the return route back to the skin, where they cause a painful blister. Luckily, only a small percentage of people infected with chickenpox ever suffer this sore reminder that their disease lives with them always.

There is a vaccine for chicken-pox which has been given to 10,000 children—but no more will get it in this generation.

The trial vaccine is a tamed virus, and tamed viruses are tricky. If they are not tame enough, they cause the disease they were supposed to prevent. But if they are too tame, they fail to multiply enough to arm immunity for life. Perhaps this trial vaccine will immunize for 20 years, perhaps for 40; no one can be sure. And while chickenpox is a disease kids tend to joke about, it is no laughing matter when it strikes adults. If all schoolchildren were vaccinated now, and their immunity failed when they were 35, a whole generation could be hit with a massive epidemic of a serious adult disease. Time will tell whether, when your own children face the needle, they will be punctured for the pox.

The Golden Age of the Common Cold

As for sore throats and runny noses, you wouldn't want shots for them. There are so many kinds of both that to protect you would be to jab you as often as a pincushion.

You have had many sore throats, many of them caused by streptococci. But not the same ones. *Streptococcus pyrogenes*, the germ behind strep throat and tonsillitis, comes in various breeds, each of which presents a different set of antigens for inspection. Invasion by a novel breed is a new learning experience for the immune system, and another sickness for you. By adulthood, lymphocytes have learned their streptococci, and, lest early lessons eventually fade from memory, receive from germy kids continual refresher courses.

Lymphocytes never learn about the common cold. "The" common cold is not a single disease; it is a group of similar symptoms that can be caused by any one of at least 400 viruses belonging to five unrelated groups. Not only is a lifetime not long enough to memorize so many, but none sticks around long enough to be memorized at all.

Cold viruses enter a nose or throat cell, multiply, burst the cell, and spread to the next like locusts over fields of grass. Mast cells in the dermis scent the warning chemicals burst cells release, but their irritating chemicals cause floods of mucus that spread the viruses over fresh, uninfected fields. Within days, the viruses have spread to nearly every cell there is to infect, have burst them, and gone their way—on just the floods that spread them.

Cold viruses depend on the watery symptoms they cause to spread from person to person. A violent sneeze produces 20,000 virus-laden droplets. Even the largest droplet can travel 4 meters before falling to the ground. The smallest ones remain suspended in the

The Kissing Disease

You don't have to kiss to get "mono," but it sure helps. The nickname is short for mononucleosis, a viral disease that infects a type of phagocyte. Because so many phagocytes live in the lymph system, mononucleosis gives people swollen nodes—popularly known as swollen "glands"—as well as swollen tonsils, which are another phagocyte hangout. Fever may last for weeks, and the person feels exhausted for that long or longer. You hardly ever hear of a little kid getting mono. You hardly ever hear of grown-ups getting it either. It hits people most frequently from junior high school through college—the kissing years when more spit is exchanged among more couples than at any other time of life.

air until they evaporate, which may be as long as an hour. Merely talking sprays viruses: Puffy consonants such as P and T carry bursts of them; a hearty laugh is loaded. Spit and sniffle linger on hands and hankies, cups and spoons, desks, books, pencils, playing cards. These viruses are onto a good way to get around.

Colds get around best in winter not because people who get cold catch cold, but because cold weather crowds people into buses, classrooms, cafeterias, and homes. None of these viruses can live for long out in the open, indoors or outdoors, winter or summer. Like measles, they must go nose to nose, or perish. Modern life has therefore suited their lifestyle very well, for compared to former centuries, when people lived isolated from one another on farms or in small villages, it is common now to brush against a hundred people a day, and to inhale the moist breath of perhaps a thousand more. In fact, by so cozily slobbering viruses at one another, we have furthered the evolution of the common cold in this, its Golden Age.

Germs by Chance

Evolution is a chance event. It happens by small accidents to genes that, just as accidentally, better suit the organism to its former life, or to a better one. The accident most often is like a sloppy typist's error: a letter of the genetic alphabet transposed, left out, miscopied; or whole genes typed twice, misplaced, dropped altogether. Sometimes the mistake instead is caused by a break in a chromosome. Breaks are mended by enzymes, but enzymes can err.

Few errors benefit the organism—many kill it—but progress is impossible without them. Accident alone makes germs of microbes that once had lived another way.

For a microbe to infect, it must at least be able to hold onto the cell it's infecting. Once upon a time, a strep bacterium by accident composed the genetic sequence for the protein receptor by which it catches onto throat cells. These receptors let it hold on against the flow of spit that would have otherwise washed it down to the stomach, and the push of cilia that would have otherwise walked it out the nose. That was only one "mistake."

Another time, another error resulted in slimy hairs by which strep often slips from the grasp of phagocytes; and, again, the tough capsule by which, cornered and eaten anyway, it delays digestion; and, finally, the chemical with which it bores holes in the phagocyte's stomach, turning the stomach into a suicide bag whose leaking enzymes digest the eater from the inside, liquefying it in three minutes flat. Shigella and salmonella bacteria, both responsible for food poisoning, lucked onto a way to enter gut cells by digesting tiny holes in the membrane, which neatly close behind them.

If there is anything one can think of to disarm phagocytes, some germ is likely already to have chanced on it. Some secrete substances that paralyze phagocytes, or ruin their sense of smell. One germ raises its antigens high like flags on poles, where IgM's sauce can't coat it. A strain of *Staphylococcus aureus*, when peppered with IgG, secretes a protein that clogs the antibody stems so phagocytes can't grip them. One indigestible microbe asks to be swallowed by coating itself with its own replica of IgG, and then infects the swallower.

Chance has also rewarded germs with ways to hide from lymphocytes. Some viral litter doesn't mingle with cell passports, and so the infected cells seem normal, and are not marked for execution. Some microbes are counterfeiters whose most outstanding antigens are copies of our own. Some parasites keep a step ahead of lymphocytes by continually changing their surface antigens. Wart viruses escape the notice of lymphocytes by not demanding their

Achooo!

This photo, taken with a strobe light, shows just how explosive a sneeze can be.

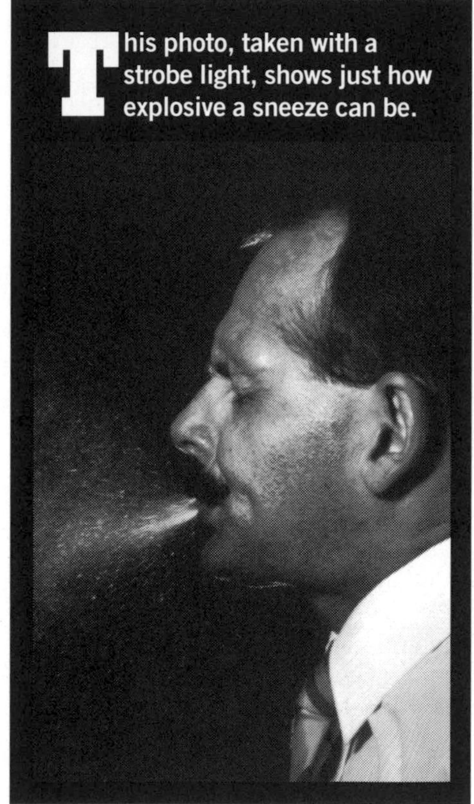

telltale protein jackets until the skin cell that carries them has risen nearly to the surface. There they hastily switch on their jacket gene, dress themselves, and leave.

The survival of a germ may depend on it evolving a way to cause symptoms of disease. What use is it for cold viruses to multiply if they can't tickle the nose to drip and sneeze them to the next guy? Measles may multiply in skin everywhere, but those measles viruses that cause a cough get out. Chickenpox irritates its host to erupt in sores from whose scabs it sheds. Mumps was lucky to find a way to infect salivary glands, from which it leaves in drool. Cholera bacteria chanced on a toxin that forces gut cells to provide them with watery diarrhea for rapid rear-end exits. Soiled hands and contaminated water then spread them to others through the mouth.

The host may favor such evolutionary accidents, or not. Cholera is done for here because of toilets, clean water, and washed hands. Spit-spread ills do well with babies, who have a wet way with the world, and among kissing adolescents. Such diseases would do better still if we licked each other, but tough luck for them.

Evolving colds are favored by being sneezed clear round the world. If a sneeze-making mutation happened to a virus in some hermit's nose, the accident would get it nowhere. As it is, the next cold you get may have originated in a businessman who sneezed it to a dozen others at a conference, and they, by jet plane before a week was out, had sneezed it to a hundred more in London, Rome, and Tokyo. Somewhere on its way back over the Pacific the virus may have mutated again, causing now the wettest, most violent explosions. It then spread all the better, and multiplied at the expense of less irritating relatives. When this newly evolved virus reaches you, you may realize the awful truth: Colds in the late twentieth century are becoming not only more numerous, but worse.

VD

Everybody jokes about it because everyone's afraid of it: VD, venereal disease. Venereal diseases are caused by microbes that flourish in the mucous lining of the penis and vagina, and are spread by having sex. They could all be exterminated. If everybody on Earth, from this moment on and for the rest of their lives, were faithful to one partner, everyone who presently carries a VD germ could spread it only to one person. Trapped that way, VD could never spread beyond those couples. Within a generation sex-spread diseases would become extinct among our species.

Just the opposite is happening. The idea that it's okay to have sex with more than one partner has caused a VD epidemic.

Herpes virus, the same one that causes cold sores, can also be spread sexually, and then the painful sores it causes erupt on the penis or in the vagina.

Designer Molecules

Dogs don't catch colds. Neither do cats or cows. Viruses can't get into a cell to infect it unless they can first get a grip on some protein embedded in the cell surface. Cells in our throats and noses have handholds to which our cold viruses can cling. Other species have differently shaped proteins, and those in dogs and cats and cows are not the right shape for our cold viruses to grab hold of.

Understanding how viruses get in may give scientists new ways to keep them out. One way would be to design a molecule that plugs the handholds by which they enter, leaving them nothing to grasp. Another way would be to design copies of the handholds themselves, and let viruses grab them instead of cells. Researchers are now working on a designer molecule to sabotage a major group of cold viruses. Success would mean fewer colds—but more shots!

It's no more curable there than on the mouth. It can't survive outside of bodies, and it can't spread to others from its home base near the spine. It spreads only from the sores. So the virus has to be lucky enough to have a host foolish enough to have sex while suffering from sores. There must be an epidemic of foolishness around, because genital herpes is spreading fast.

Gonorrhea is spreading even faster because people don't necessarily know they have it when they spread it. In men, early symptoms or a mild case may cause nothing more than a slight increase of mucus from the penis. In women, gonococcus bacteria may infect the whole reproductive tract, from vagina to ovaries, without causing any noticeable symptoms at all. But the damage is awful. Gonorrhea can leave a woman's tubes so blocked with scar tissue that sperm can't swim up or eggs roll down, and the two can never get together in her body.

Just as people sneezing around speed the evolution of the common cold, people sleeping around speed the evolution of venereal diseases. Gonococcus bacteria are rapidly evolving resistance to drugs that used to kill them. AIDS is a brand new disease, a virus that once was harmless, and now is lethal.

AIDS seems to have evolved in West Africa from a virus that had not previously caused illness sometime before the early 1970s, and has since

What a Way to Live!

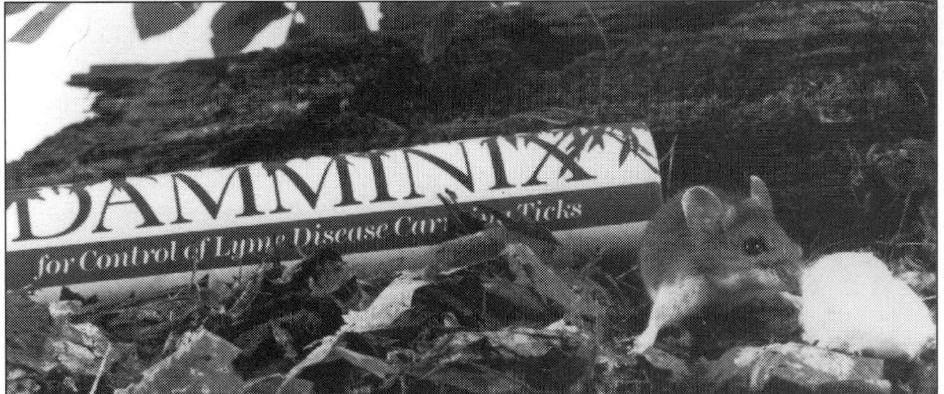

One popular way for germs to spread is via insects and other biting pests. The germ may spend part of its life inside, say, a mosquito's salivary glands. When the mosquito bites, the germ moves from bug spit to human blood. When another mosquito bites the infected person, germs move back from human blood to bug spit, and from there to the blood of the next human victim. However, the pesky bug may itself spend part of its life dining on one kind of animal, and part of its life dining on another. That complicates life for the germ, and sometimes offers humans a way to control its spread.

Consider, for instance, the life of the nasty, spiralled bacterium that causes the feverish and sometimes serious illness called Lyme disease that is spread through the bite of a tick. The disease can't go straight from person to person because the bacteria have to multiply first in tick guts, and its tick, *Ixodes dammini*, can't live on people alone: It eats mostly mouse blood as an infant, and needs deer blood to reproduce as an adult. So for the bacteria to survive, they must have their ticks, and their ticks must have their mice and deer.

Lyme disease could be controlled by wiping out these pleasant mammals, but that's an unpleasant thought. A nicer way is to supply mice with cotton for their nests treated with a chemical that kills ticks, but doesn't hurt mouse babies. Tubes filled with this cotton are available at many kinds of stores, and they are likely to complicate to death the lives of Lyme bacteria.

been spread to every continent. The initials stand for Acquired Immune Deficiency Syndrome: The virus damages the immune system by attacking T-cells and phagocytes. T-cells that harbor multiplying AIDS viruses burst, spreading the viral copies to other T-cells and to phagocytes within the same body. Phagocytes harboring multiplying AIDS viruses are harmed, but don't burst. They carry the virus from one body to another.

Phagocytes scavenge among the mucus cells in penises. They haunt vaginas too. They travel in the bloodstream. Phagocytes infected with AIDS get from one person to another in semen, in vaginal mucus, or in blood. There are free viruses in the body fluids of people infected with AIDS, too, because they escape from T-cells when they burst, but there aren't enough of them to spread the disease. That's why just being around AIDS patients—even kissing, or sharing meals and toothbrushes—is safe. Sharing needles or genitals is not.

When someone else's infected phagocytes get into a person, they are attacked by that person's own, healthy immune cells. That releases the viruses. They then spread to phagocytes, which spread them to T-cells by touching them. The T-cells make more viruses, then burst and die. The phagocytes make more viruses, and secrete them through their membrane, spreading them more. They spread them to mother cells in bone marrow, destroying the source of new immune cells. The phagocytes themselves are crippled. When some ordinary germ comes along, they just sit around, not gobbling, not telling immune cells the news. AIDS patients don't die from AIDS: They die from infections that, if their immune system were working, wouldn't even make a person sick.

Maybe AIDS will become curable

Safe Sex?

There's only one way to be absolutely safe from venereal disease: No sex.

Second best is to be protected by a condom. Condoms are thin rubber pouches that fit over the penis. They are available without prescription at drugstores. Because condoms cover the penis, the man is protected from germs the woman might have, and because they catch semen in the tip of the pouch, the woman is protected from germs the man might have. They also protect the couple from pregnancy by preventing sperm from reaching eggs. But they can fail.

A condom put on too tight, without leaving room at the tip to hold semen, bursts. A condom left on too long, after the penis gets floppy, leaks or falls off. "Ultra-thin," "natural membrane" condoms leak and break most easily. No condom can help if the person forgets to bring it, or neglects to put it on.

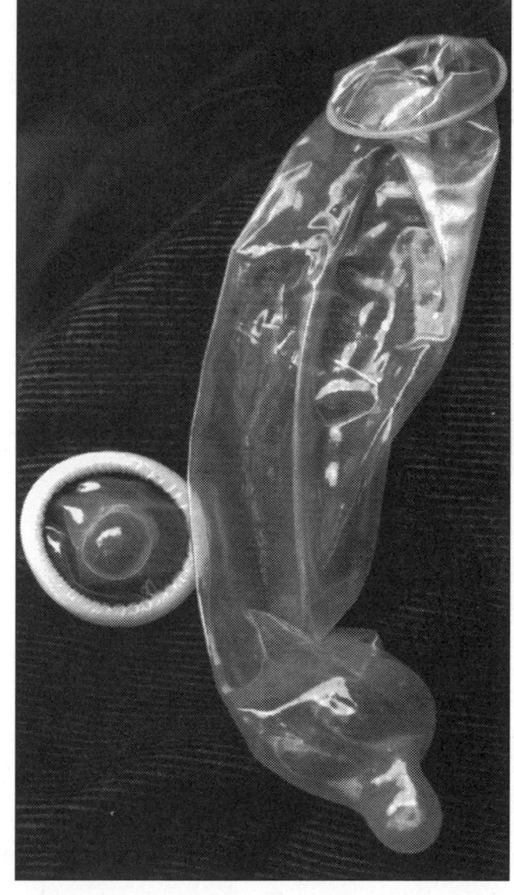

as new drugs are developed to fight it, but right now it is 100 percent fatal. And here's the worst part: There may be no symptoms for months, or years; you can't tell who has it.

Flu Today, Flown Tomorrow

We, like germs, continually evolve. Like them, we miscopy, misplace, misspell a gene from time to time, and pass our little accidents to our children. The kit of bits and pieces from which you chose your Igs is not identical to anybody else's, nor are your Igs. You may have an antibody so suited to grab a particular antigen that the germ that bears it won't have a chance in you. You won't get sick with it, or if you do you won't get as sick as others do. For every new germ that arises, there will always be some lucky people who are "not susceptible"—meaning that they or their family once made a mistake in gene copying that made possible a better defense against that germ. If the disease is deadly in the first generation, it will kill fewer in the next, and fewer still in each generation that follows, as those who can resist it multiply and spread. In this way the human population gradually becomes adapted to its germs.

But there will always be diseases. The rate of evolution within a species is limited by the length of time it takes to produce each new generation, and by the number of individuals in the population. The more individuals there are, the greater the possibility that some will produce a favorable change, and the more quickly they reproduce, the faster the change can spread among descending generations. There may be 5 billion people in the world, but trillions of microbes inhabit every one of them. Each generation of humans takes about 20 years to produce children, but bacteria can divide every 20 minutes. We have never kept up with new diseases, and we never will.

Yet deadly diseases are rare. They are rare because they are as disastrous for the germs as for their victims.

Look at the problem from the germ's point of view. By making its host too sick, it risks killing its livelihood before it has had time to multiply and escape. Even if the germ escapes in time, the more people are killed, the fewer are left for its offspring to infect. Certainly germs that use their host as permanent home bases want that home to live a long life. Both those which come and go like colds, and those which come and stay like cold sores, benefit by keeping their host well enough to socialize with others, and so spread them generously.

Over time, most bad human diseases get better, or they run out of victims and disappear. A savage form of leprosy that swept through Europe in the thirteenth and fourteenth centuries abruptly disappeared. So did a mysterious disease called "sweating sickness" that raged through England five times between 1485 and 1551, and then became extinct. During the early years of this century, tuberculosis became much tamer than the killer it had been. There are signs now that cholera, a scourge that so drains its victims of water that they may die of dehydration in a day, has found a way to be a better germ: The diarrhea it causes is less violent than it used to be, but the bacteria live longer on bedding and utensils, and so meet more bodies to infect. The terrible 1918 influenza epidemic that killed millions worldwide killed off the

A Germ's Luck

There are altogether billions of species of microbes that might, with the right combination of mutations, infect humans. But the chance of hitting on a workable combination is much less than a person's chance of choosing the right combination of numbers to win the California lottery. Of the billions, fewer than 500 germs have been lucky enough to have won the prize of infecting humans.

lethal breed that caused it. The various breeds of flu people cough around these days cause a milder illness.

If the measure of success for germs is to cause the least damage necessary for their own spread, then a germ that could spread without causing any ills at all would be the most successful. You're full of them. All the common microbes that were spread to you at birth are infections without symptoms.

A Simpler Way

Every body's got its germs. Clams get clam diseases. Spinach gets spinach sicknesses. Even bacteria get infected with viruses that are their special germs. Yet no organisms but vertebrates make Igs to fight their ills. Others have a simpler way: They poison their infectors.

The poisons that fungi and bacteria use to fight their ills are the drugs we call antibiotics. Penicillin, an antibiotic made by a common mold, was the first to be discovered. It was hailed as a miracle, and it was—at first. It poisoned bacteria that cause pneumonia, and bacteria that infect wounds. It cured a host of infections that together had been the leading cause of death.

But then, only a few years into the miracle, new breeds of staphylococcus evolved that were not harmed by penicillin. Soon other bacteria showed resistance to the drug. The poison had, by killing all the weaklings, selected just those individuals it could not hurt.

By now about a hundred antibiotics are on the market. Each new one at first kills well. Then resistance again appears, and spreads. Resistant populations move from one human to another. The mutated gene whose protein blocks the action of the drug is also passed around by bacteria inserting pieces of DNA into others during mating. The gene can be picked up by live bacteria from dead ones. It can be carried from one to another by viruses. Resistance is as contagious as disease.

Scientists discover new antibiotics pretty fast, but so far their best efforts have not kept up with either the rate of bacterial evolution, or resistance's racing spread. The problem has been made worse by lavish use of antibiotics—for minor bacterial infections, for viral infections like colds and flu that aren't affected by such drugs, and even as preventive medicine for cattle, whose drugged meat we eat. By using antibiotics against germs indiscriminately, we kill the weak and save the strong and spread resistance further.

There's another problem. Just because an antibiotic is a poison made by microbes for microbes doesn't mean it can't injure other organisms.

Many antibiotics kill bacteria by jamming their energy-producing mitochondria, or by gumming up their protein manufacturing equip-

Infectors of Infectors

Bacteria are surrounded by a tough, protective capsule. Some of their infectors, viruses called bacteriophages, have devised a devilish way of getting through it. Their jacket attaches to a bacterium by jointed legs that, bending suddenly, inject their viral genes. Some viruses kill bacteria, but others give them resistance to antibiotics much as injections give you resistance to bacterial toxins.

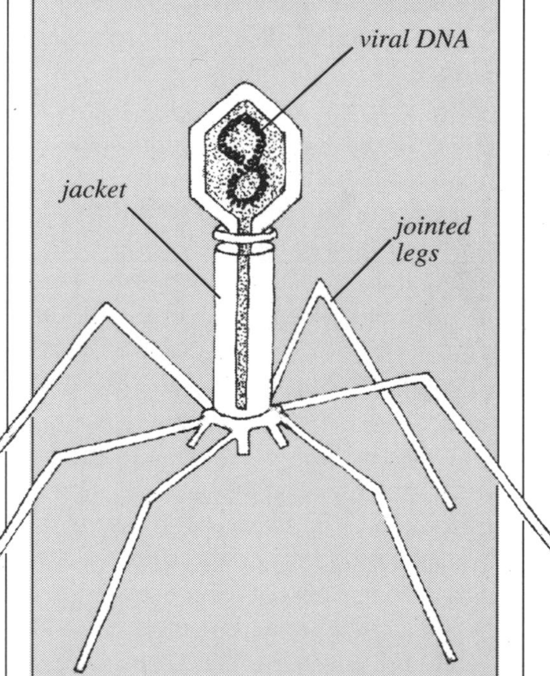

ment. Our own cell machinery is not so different; our cells die too. That's why doctors are so careful to prescribe just the small doses, and for just the short time needed to kill bacterial cells without killing too many of our own.

Finally, there is this risk: IgE may take the drug to be the enemy.

IgE, as in Error

In the Greek alphabet of Igs, only the epsilon brand of antibody routinely causes more illness than it cures. IgE causes allergy. It directs asthma wheezes, hay-fever sneezes, strawberry hives, and even the itch of insect bites. These ailments, like others, are occasioned by alien antigens, but why should the body mind an invasion of strawberries? There is some mistake here: IgE has erred.

Every breath of air or mouthful of food presents to the body for inspection a delicatessen of antigens. You breathe in feather fragments, pollen grains, perfume molecules, and dust, all marked as strangers to the self. Every food bears stranger antigens too. But none of these substances are infective. They make no toxins. They don't injure tissues. They can't compete with body cells, for they don't multiply. Yet nearly 10 percent of the population gets hay fever or asthma from airborne antigens, and quite a few get rashes, hives, vomiting, diarrhea, sores, swellings, and assorted other allergic symptoms from certain foods and drugs.

There's nothing wrong with recognizing pollen grains as foreign. It's fine for mucus, spit, and tears to slather them with IgA so that they slip on out. One is pleased to know that fly drool is marked for removal by IgG. What's wrong is getting all inflamed about such things. That's what IgE does. Its stem in even its inactive form attaches directly to mast cells, both those that inhabit the dermis of skin, gut, and respiratory system, and ones that circulate in blood. This amounts to arming mast cells with antigen detectors of their own. Mast cells coated with IgE erupt with inflammatory chemicals whenever they meet the antigen they fit.

There are not nearly as many different B-lymphocytes that specialize in manufacturing brand E antibody as there are of common IgG-makers. In fact, IgE accounts for only .001 percent of all the antibody circulating in a nonallergic person's blood. Even if you happen to have a clone whose IgE recognizes ragweed pollen, you don't necessarily sneeze. Normally, some clone of Suppressor T-cells will control the fuss. It's when they don't that people get hay fever.

Nobody gets hay fever the first time they meet their pollen. All that happens, if they happen to have a fitting clone of IgE-makers in the first place, is that the clone multiplies and begins to ship out IgE. That takes days. By the time the antibody has spread through the body and coated mast cells, the pollen has long since been blown out the nose, washed from the eyes, or eaten up by phagocytes.

With each new exposure, though, more IgE is made. In time, mast cells encountering pollen in the nose or eyes are covered with as many as 500,000 IgE detectors for recognizing it. When pollen antigen attaches to these detectors, the cells immediately secrete the chemicals that send you running for a tissue.

Substances that cause allergies are called allergens. Doctors can find out to which airborne allergens a person is sensitive by pricking the skin with a delicatessen of needles each coated with a different possible culprit. The skin around a prick reddens and swells if the person's mast cells are coated with IgE for that allergen.

Sometimes the doctor will then attempt to "desensitize" the person. The idea behind desensitization is clever: to get a clone of immune cells to coat the allergen with ordinary IgG antibody. That would make a feast for phagocytes, keep mast cells from attaching, and put an end to sneezes. To that end, doctors inject small amounts of the allergen as a probe for activating a suitable clone of IgG makers. Often they succeed: Sure enough, the patient is found after several months of shots to have many circulating antibodies that can coat the allergen. And, sure enough, some patients do stop sneezing.

But others don't. The amount of IgG a person mobilizes against an allergen seems to have no relation to the success or failure of the treatment. In fact, science has no good explanation for allergies.

They run in families, and those families are distinguished by certain types of self-markers on their cells. But one family member may get asthma from tree pollen, while another gets hay fever from the same material. Or, one gets sick on shellfish while another gets hives from bee stings. Their allergies come and go; the substances that cause them change; so do the symptoms; and many in the family might have no allergies at all.

There is one clue for how a system of sneezing without reason might have come about. Given half a chance, IgE-makers stir up cauldrons of chemicals to control parasites, especially parasitic worms. That is what their antibodies mostly recognize, and in parts of the world where parasites abound, IgE makers seems to be kept too busy to bother with trivial pursuits. Researchers have not yet been able to compare, knob by knob, common allergens with common antigens on parasitic worms, but should they prove to be similar, the mystery of allergy would be resolved

A Frog's Way

The immune system doesn't attack our usual skin and gut bacteria as long as they multiply outside the body, on its inner and outer surfaces. When they do get inside through an injury, they are attacked as any other invader might be. You might have had, for instance, an infected hangnail caused by your most ordinary skin bacterium, *Staphylococcus aureus.* But here's a mystery: Gums are often cut by such rough stuff as popcorn hulls, and skin around the anus is easily hurt by hard feces. Bacteria are abundant in both these places, yet neither gets infected, and healing proceeds without a sign that immune cells are in battle. That's just like a frog.

Frogs, who may live in murky ponds teeming with bacteria, never get skin infections. Their skin exudes antibiotics magainins, after the Hebrew word for shield. Magainins are more powerful, act faster, and kill more kinds of microbes than any antibiotics now used by doctors. They kill strep throat germs, staphylococcal hangnail infectors, a host of microbes that cause diarrhea, and infecting funguses, and protozoans. So far, few chemicals have been found in frogs which don't also exist in humans. Maybe skin of our entrance and exit holes make magainins too.

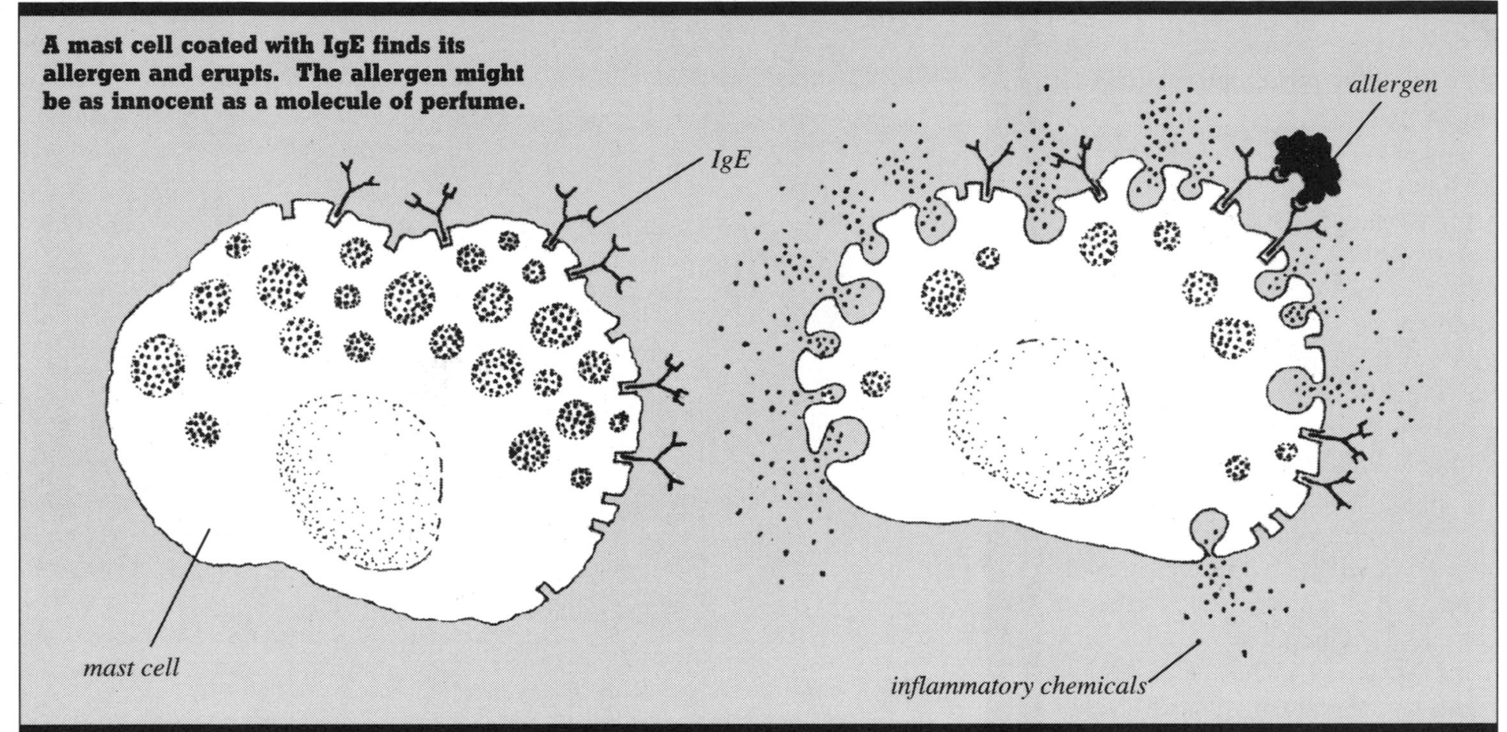

A mast cell coated with IgE finds its allergen and erupts. The allergen might be as innocent as a molecule of perfume.

into a clear case of mistaken identity.

Poison Ivy

Poison ivy and other itchy rashes that erupt when allergens are rubbed into the skin are caused by wayward T-cells, not by makers of IgE. These passport checkers detect foreign molecules attached to cell surfaces, and that is why the oil in poison ivy leaves so easily infuriates them.

Poison ivy oil contains a substance called urushiol that bonds to skin proteins on contact. Scrubbing with soap and water after touching the ivy helps to rid the skin of urushiol that has not yet bound to cells, but you have to be quick about it. Five minutes after contact so much is bound that scrubbing isn't likely to help at all.

Even scrubbing right away does less than people think to remove urushiol. The molecules don't dissolve in water. They are not destroyed by soap. Heat—even burning—doesn't injure them a bit. They don't fall apart with age. Researchers studying the oil took a glove used to collect poison ivy, stored it for months, washed it thoroughly in hot soap and water, ironed it with a hot iron, and got a rash for all their trouble.

Because T-cells release their irritating chemicals only where they find alien molecules attached to cells, you get poison ivy only where urushiol has actually touched skin. The more molecules have bonded, the more T-cells go to work, and the faster the rash appears. Skin bonded to fewer urushiol molecules breaks out more slowly. By the time it does, the first areas to

Stickers

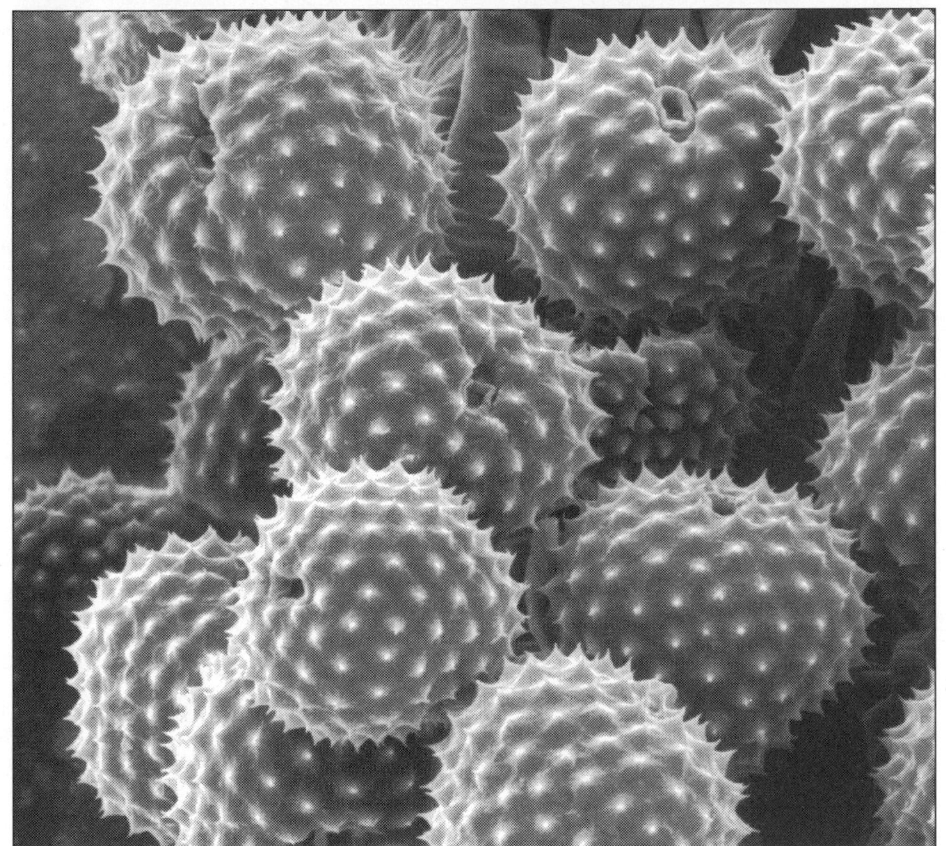

In a photograph showing ragweed pollen magnified about 1,700 times, each grain looks something like the spiny seed of the horse-chestnut tree. The spikes help it hold onto the flower it is fertilizing, to which it is blown by the wind. Only pollen small enough to be carried by the wind can cause hay fever. Plants whose larger pollen grains are carried by insects don't blow around, and so aren't troublesome. Such plants include roses and goldenrod, both of which are often blamed for allergies actually caused by wind-borne pollen from trees or grasses that bloom at the same time.

erupt have become blistered and oozing, leading people to believe that the ooze is spreading the rash. The ooze is just plasma leaked from dilated capillaries; it is no different from the ooze of any blister. Poison ivy is spread only by spreading its oil. That happened days before the rash appeared, when the person picked his nose, scratched his neck, rubbed his belly with his urushiol-oiled hands—or when he took off his urushiol-coated clothes, or patted his urushiol-smeared dog.

Perhaps it is the clinginess of the molecule that makes poison ivy such an oddity among allergies, for nearly three quarters of the population get a rash from it. That doesn't, however, make the oily stuff a poison. For those whose T-cells ignore the molecule—for those who *don't* have an immune response to it—urushiol is as harmless as peanut oil or maple juice. Misguided immune cells, not the oil, make the itch.

Unlearning

One thing that everybody is immune to is other people. Unless you have an identical twin, there is no other person in the world whose cells carry exactly the same collection of self-markers as your cells do. Even brothers and sisters, even your own parents, have only some self-markers that are the same as yours. You are unique right down to the molecules by which your lymphocytes know you for yourself.

Self-markers (including passports and ID cards, but many other proteins that stud cell membranes too, such as those that identify the type of cell) are large molecules, antigens like any other. If another person's cells were to get into you, they would be considered "infected" with alien antigens, and so they would be destroyed. That's why it's so hard to transplant organs from one person to another. The fewer self-markers two people share in common, the more clones of lymphocytes attack transplanted tissue; even when the two match quite well, the immune system must be crippled with drugs if the transplant is to work.

If your immune cells have made Igs for every antigen, even human ones, even your mom's self-markers, it seems likely that they must also have made Igs that fit your own antigens—Igs for your self-markers, Igs for self-rejection. After all, enzymes that assemble antibody genes from those kits of so many possible parts work randomly, without any special knowledge to guide their choice. The enzymes could as easily piece together a gene for an antibody that fits a self-marker or, for that matter, any other protein that studs a cell membrane, such as a hormone receptor, or a cell doorway. How is a body to know which antigens are itself? Or—a better question—how is the immune system to become self-ignorant?

Before you were born, the slots of all antibodies that fit your own antigens were plugged by, of all things, anti-antibodies. The arms of an anti-antibody are shaped like keys, not slots. They fit inside the slots of antibodies, and so plug them up. During the months before birth, whenever a clone of self-recognizing B-cells was aroused, its Igs aroused a clone of lymphocytes that made a fitting anti-Ig. Self-knowing clones were not destroyed—they are alive in you still, bound and gagged by anti-Igs.

This is dizzying to think about, for the two can only fit each other if the arm tips of anti-Igs resemble the very receptors, doorways, and self-markers that the Igs would otherwise grab hold of. Your body's immune system contains within it both the negative and the positive image of itself; the glove, and the hand that fits it.

Urushiol Everywhere

This is a poison ivy plant. The urushiol oil to which so many people are allergic is not only in its lush leaves, but in its roots, stems, bark, and berries. You can get poison ivy in the winter when it sheds its leaves. When the plant is burned, you can get it from urushiol droplets in the smoke. You can also get it from anything that has touched the plant, including tools, clothes, and dogs.

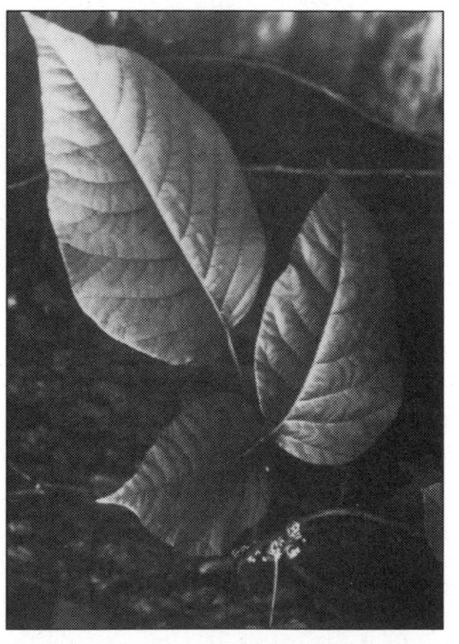

The Self, and the Whole World Too

If your immune cells can mimic your own antigens, can they also mimic alien ones? There's evidence that they can. Temporary gagging by anti-antibodies may be part of the control system by which the inflammation of disease is quieted. The immune system seems to mimic self-antigens *and* alien ones—the self and the world as well.

Then what's the distinction between self and other? There may not be any permanent, clear-cut boundary. Had you harbored an alien antigen all your life, it would have been considered part of you. Had one of your own self-markers been removed for a time, and then returned, it would have been taken for a stranger. The difference between self and other turns out to be mostly a matter of commonness, and continuity: "Other" is those antigens that appear from time to time. "You" are those antigens that are always to be found, week after week and year after year, in the embryo, the child, the adult, in large numbers, and anywhere that lymphocytes may wander.

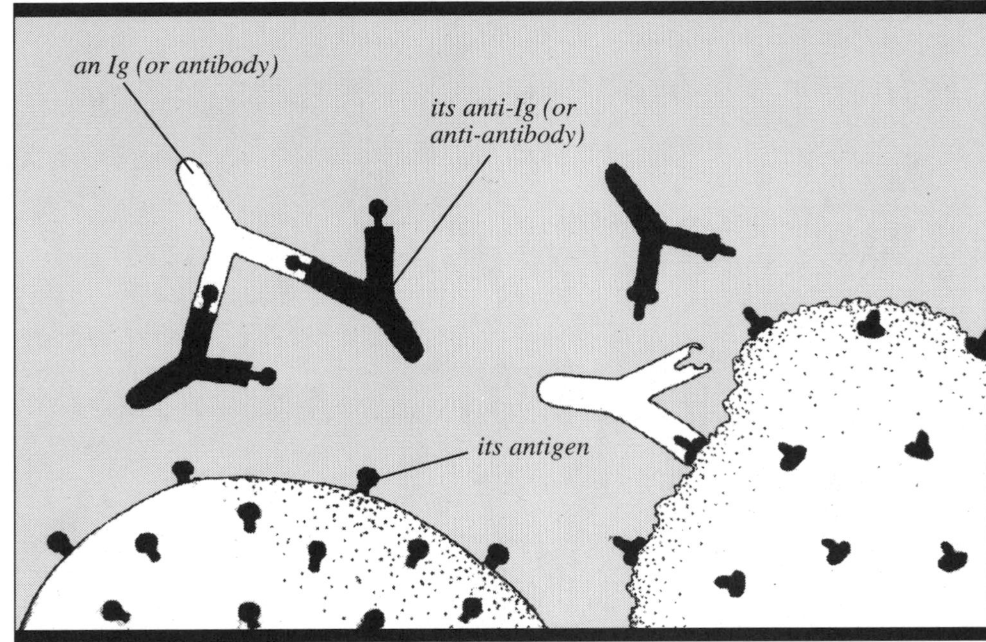

So here's one last dizzying thought: The various active clones of the immune system, aroused by experience of their suitable fit, create over time an image of both the inner and the outer world. They do so by randomly piecing together knobs and slots, and then selecting from among them those which fit, those which match the molecules they actually encounter. The result is a representation of reality.

One would have thought only the brain did that.

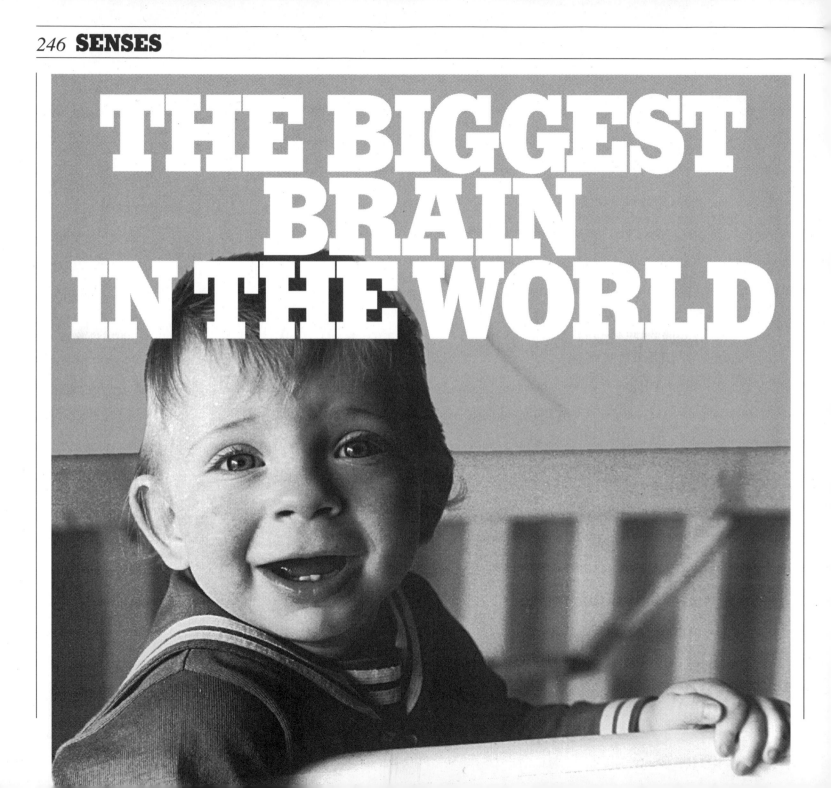

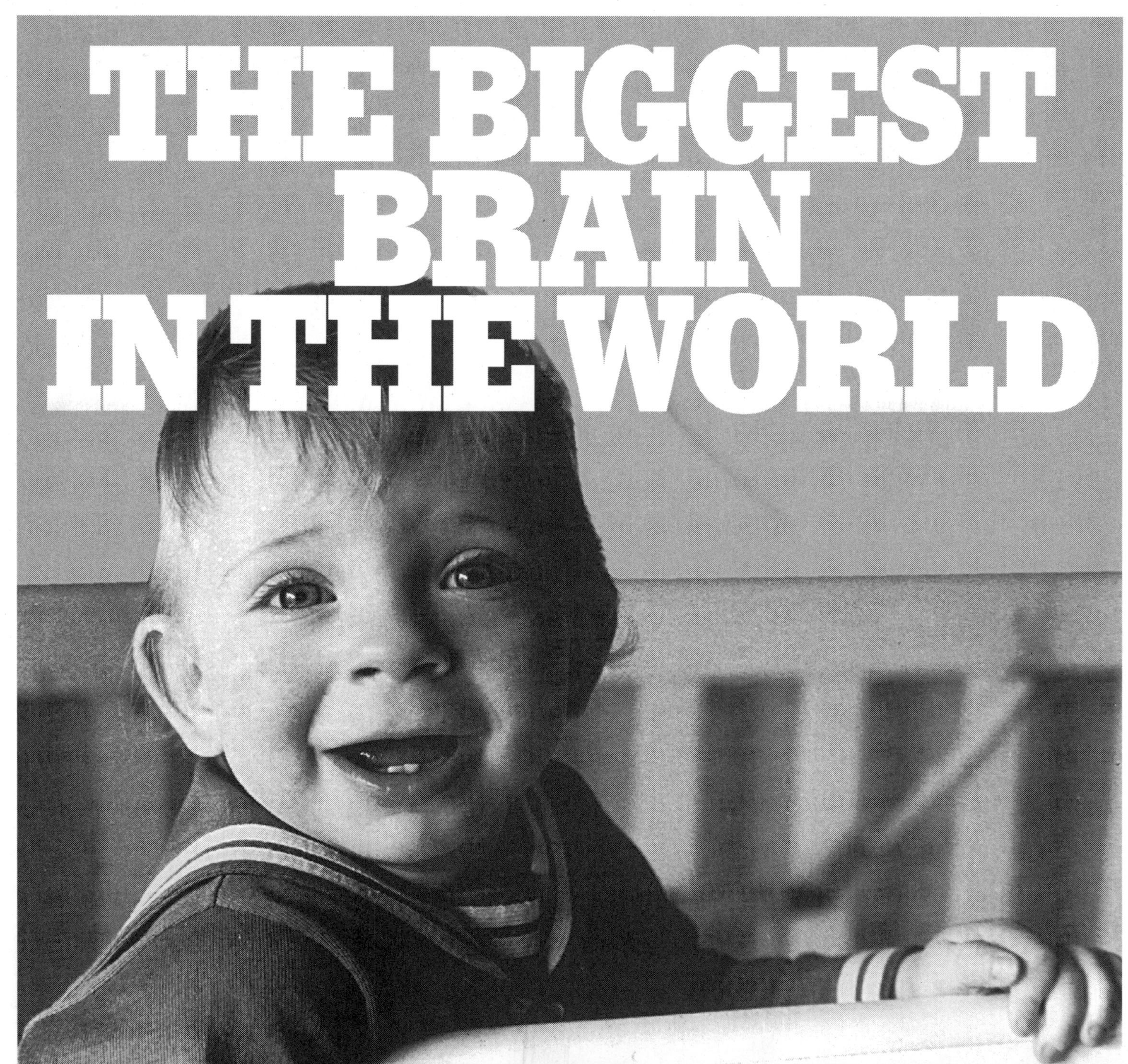
THE BIGGEST
BRAIN
IN THE WORLD

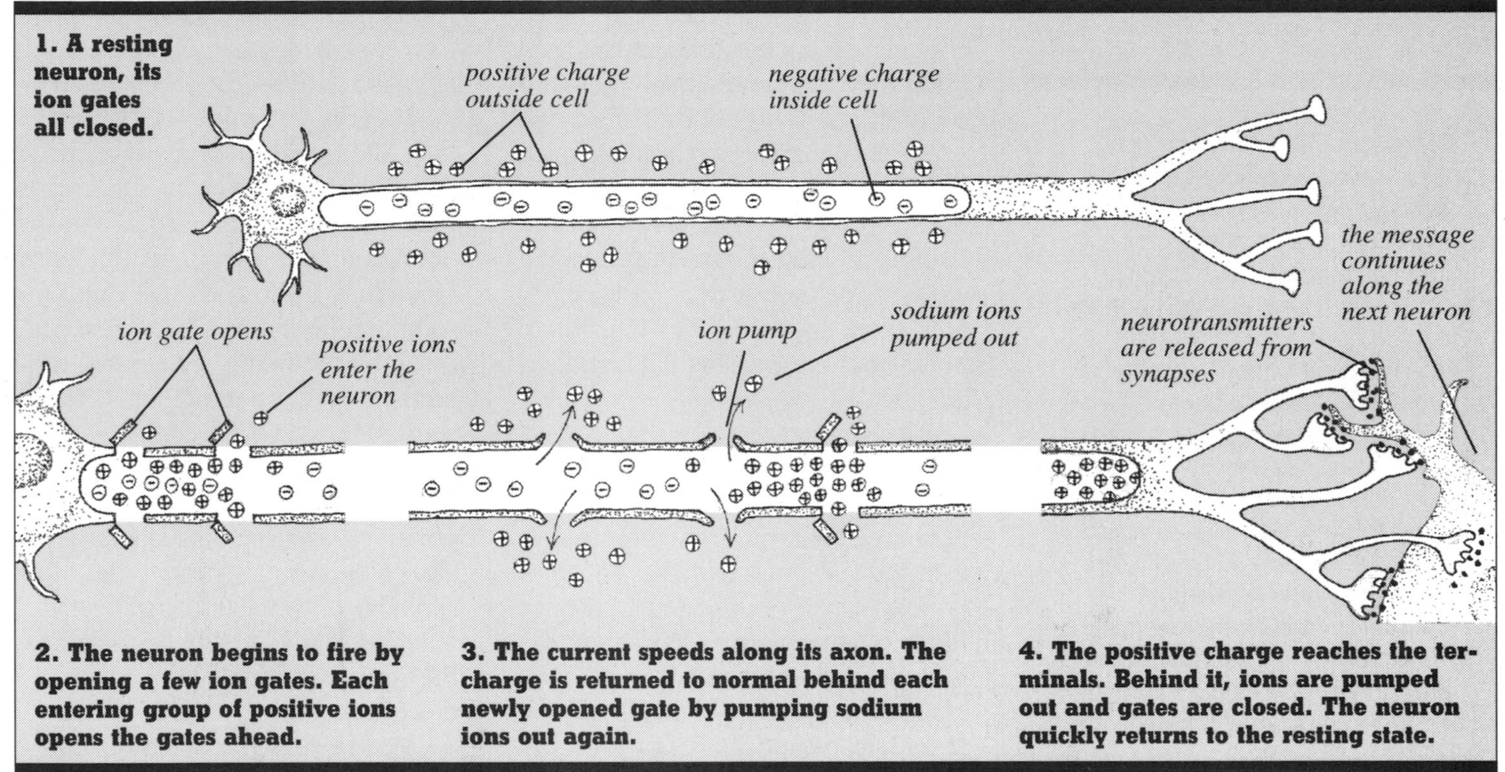

2. The neuron begins to fire by opening a few ion gates. Each entering group of positive ions opens the gates ahead.

3. The current speeds along its axon. The charge is returned to normal behind each newly opened gate by pumping sodium ions out again.

4. The positive charge reaches the terminals. Behind it, ions are pumped out and gates are closed. The neuron quickly returns to the resting state.

Your brain weighs about three pounds. Eighty percent of its weight is water: Without a skull to hold it, it would sag like a lump of jelly. Yet that furrowed, grayish, watery lump contains 10 billion neurons which send signals to one another across 100 trillion terminals. Each can signal hundreds of times a second, and at speeds approaching 250 miles per hour. This signaling is your intelligence, and it can be used for an astounding feat: a brain considering itself.

In relation to the size of the body it serves, the human brain is the biggest brain in the world. If our body were rat-size, our brain would be hundreds of times larger than a rat's brain. If we were ape-size, our brain would be at least five times larger than a chimpanzee's. And our intelligence is not just due to the number of neurons we have in our skulls: A greater proportion of those neurons have nothing else to do but think.

The part of the brain you think with is the outer layer, called the cortex. In most other mammals, the cortex is largely devoted to processing incoming sensory information, and to controlling movement. These are specialized tasks: Feature detectors compute, they don't think; the motor map controls movement, but doesn't understand it. A rat has only a tiny portion of brain that isn't committed to such things as processing smells or working paws, and that little bit is the only portion free to serve as the rat's IQ. In us, the cor-

Zap!

Insecticides kill insects in a cunning way: They sabotage their nervous system. Neurons produce at their receiving end enzymes that digest neurotransmitters each time they are spurted into the synapse. Without that enzyme, each spurt of neurotransmitter would make a neuron fire over and over again, even though no new message was being sent. Insecticides block the production of one of those enzymes. The result is nervous chaos, and death. The reason for all the cautions on insecticide labels is that we make the same enzyme, and for the same reason: We, too, can die a twitching, paralyzing, insecticidal death.

tex grows into a great bulge in front, giving us a huge area of brain freed from the responsibilities of running the body. It also gives us one of the strangest skulls in the animal kingdom: We are the only creatures in the world with foreheads.

An Electric Situation

A typical neuron resembles a very long, skinny tree. The bushy cell body, which contains the nucleus and the usual cell machinery, receives messages and sends them along its thin stem, the axon, into numerous rootlike tips which communicate with the cell bodies of other neurons. Thinking is neurons signaling one another, carrying the signal electrically through their own length, and, at the tips where they transmit to other neurons, passing the signal on chemically.

A current is a moving charge. Current in a wire is moving electrons, which have a negative charge. Handier charged particles for cells are salt. Common table salt is made up of chlorine and sodium ions—atoms that have lost or gained electrons. A chlorine ion has gained an electron, and so it is negatively charged. A sodium ion has lost an electron, and so it is positively charged. When salt dissolves, the ions come apart. Current in a neuron is moving, positively charged sodium ions.

Normally sodium ions are pumped out of cells, and neurons in your brain that are not involved with your thoughts at the moment are surrounded by crowds of sodium. That makes the outside of the cell membrane more positively charged than the inside of the cell membrane, and keeps an inactive neuron in an electric situation: Sodium ions outside its membrane are attracted to negative ions inside its membrane. The neuron keeps them out with positively charged electric gates, which repel them, and which are pulled shut by the negative ions.

But now you think RED. Gates in the cell body of neurons involved in that thought spring open. Sodium ions rush in. Their positive charge pushes open other gates from inside, letting more ions in. At each opening more sodium spills in, spreads out, and pushes with repellent force against other gates, which, opening, let still more sodium in.

This is the electrical signal. What rushes along a neuron is this surge of positively charged ions opening gate after gate, letting in troop after troop, spreading a switch in charge from negative to positive over and over again all the way from the cell body to the very tips of its axon.

When a surge of switching charge reaches the end of an axon, thousands of pockets in each tip, each containing as many as 10,000 molecules of neurotransmitter, plop their chemical out. The transmitter chemical diffuses across a gap to the next neuron, and is picked up by receptors in the receiving neuron's membrane. The filled receptors open their ion gates. Now the whole process is repeated: The receiver undergoes a surge of switching charge along its body, down its axon, to its tips, and the signal continues across the next gap to the next neuron in that transmission line.

Meanwhile the first neuron has pumped out the flood of sodium, and is ready to signal again. The receiver has destroyed the neurotransmitter that opened its gates, and is ready to receive again. You could have thought RED during the whole time it took to read these paragraphs, because each neuron giving you that thought can refire within half a millisecond or less, over and over again, without tiring.

An Audience of Multitudes

But you would not have found it easy to think one thing for that long. Thoughts wander.

The roundish cell body of a neuron, where signals are received, is bushy with short branches called dendrites, after the Greek word for tree, *dendron*. Messages can be received on the dendrites, or on the cell body itself. Although a neuron's axon is usually unbranched for most of its length, its end branches, and each branch sprouts out into numerous buttonlike terminals that secrete neurotransmitter. Each terminal nearly, but not quite, touches the cell body or dendrite of a receiving cell. Chemical messages are sent across the gap, called a synapse.

This sounds straightforward until you realize how many terminals, from how many different senders, may be

Not All Alike

These are just some of the shapes of neurons in your brain and body. They all have cell bodies in which the nucleus is kept, but one here has no dendrites on its body. Another sprouts most of its dendrites at the end of an arm almost as long as its axon. The neuron without dendrites on its cell body has two axons; so does the neuron below it. The dendrites on the nerve cells to the far left and far right are almost as elaborate as the rooty ends of axons. These various architectures allow a greater variety of wiring schemes than would be possible if all neurons had the "typical" shape.

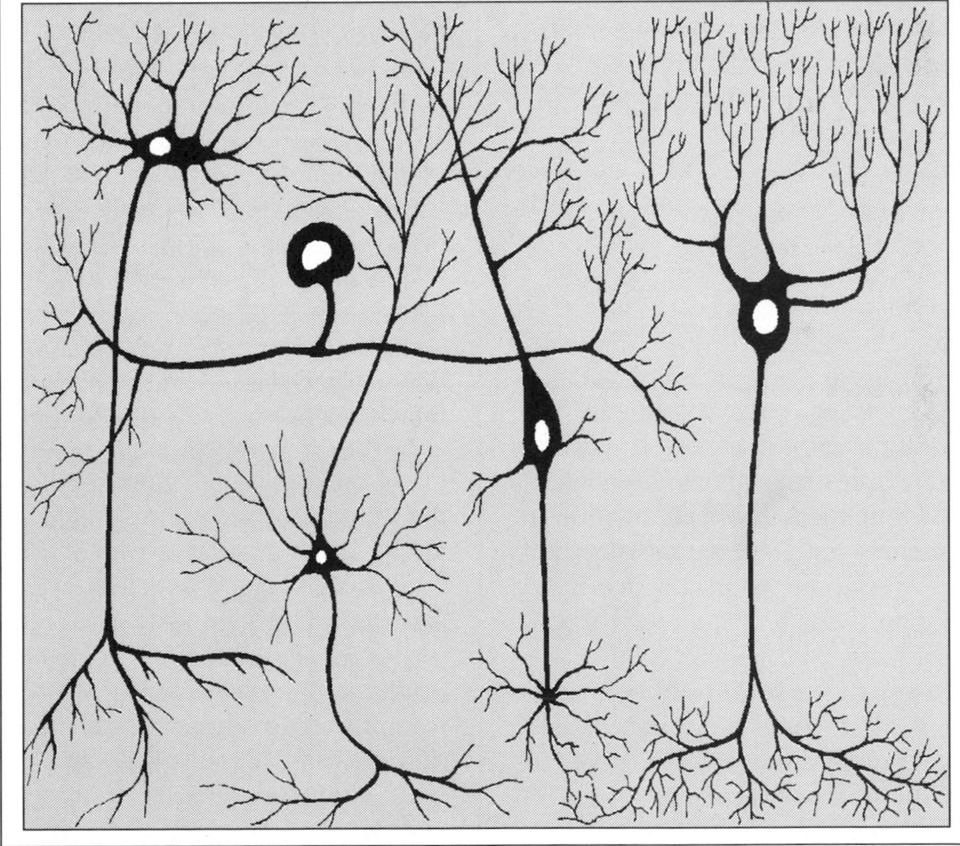

signaling at any moment to a single receiver and—the other way around—through how many terminals a single sender may be signaling to as many different receivers. An axon may branch into thousands of terminals. When the neuron fires, the signal may reach thousands of receivers. Each receiver's body may be covered with thousands of other neurons' terminals, like an old-fashioned central switchboard plugged into a multitude of conversations. And these wires go on and on, reach from skin to skull, plug in to one another throughout the brain, pry everywhere tapping information like spies bugging the computer network of a nation. Each neuron receives signals from, and sends signals to, such a multitude of others, that a thought may start at RED, and end up almost anywhere.

Old movies show scenes in which a switchboard lights up like a Christmas tree with so many incoming calls that the operator is overwhelmed. Obviously, the nervous network can't work like simple wiring. Every neuron in you is in some way connected within the total network. If each time a neuron lit up, every other neuron with which it synapsed also fired, and each of those in turn triggered their targets, every single one of the billions of neurons in your body would fire at once like the explosion of a fireworks factory—and all for the thought of RED.

A Fly Goes By

An event as simple as the brush of a fly may well fire a million neurons, but signaling is exquisitely controlled. Take the response of an interneuron (one that carries messages within the spine or brain, rather than to and from them) receiving news of the fly's alighting. Plugged to the interneuron's body and dendrites are, say, 2,001 terminals, only one of which reports a tickle. The other 2,000 are either silent, or saying something else. If many are silent, the small amount of neurotransmitter received by the interneuron will open too few ion gates to fire it, and the fly report will go no further.

Perhaps, though, quite a few other neurons are also reporting "fly," some because a buzz was heard, some because a bug was seen, some because an ear was touched, some because a bite was felt, some because a memory of black flies in the woods in June lit up a whole network of uneasiness. Then the interneuron, saturated with transmitter, will open up a slew of gates pronto, and it will fire.

On the other hand, it may not. There are different classes of neurons, and different neurotransmitters that each class secretes. Some open up chlorine ion gates instead of sodium ones. Chlorine ions are negative. They pull sodium gates tighter shut than ever. In spite of all the other messages an interneuron is receiving, a heavy dose of inhibition will force it to stay quiet.

Neurons also have a way of intercepting signals, and either turning up or turning down their volume. If you have a genuine crisis on your hands, an emergency announcement may interrupt the ordinary news. This announcement is axon to axon, from the emergency speaker directly to terminals about to spill their message. The neurotransmitter in this case is inhibitory: It jams terminals, preventing them from releasing their own transmitting chemical. Jamming may prevent you from even feeling that fly.

But what if some interneurons have reason to believe the fly is actually a bee? In this case the axon-to-axon emergency announcement is broadcast by stimulating neurons: Flood gates wide open, the news spills loudly out in a burst of juice.

The "news"—your awareness that a bee is buzzing you—is not the report of a single neuron. No neuron stands for "bee"; in fact no neuron knows anything. Your recognition of "bee" is like your recognition of the smell of plain vanilla: many firings in a distinctive pattern that always forms when a bee is present.

Touch Base, or Die

A newborn baby knows nothing of flies and bees. If a fly alights on him, he can't

Rigor Mortis

Dead bodies are at first limp; then they stiffen with rigor mortis. The stiffness of rigor mortis is contracted muscles: The corpse has actually moved! When neurons signal living muscle fibers to contract, they do so with a neurotransmitter that is received at the surface of the muscle fiber. The signal makes the fiber open calcium ion channels, and it is the calcium that actually causes the contraction. The muscle then gets rid of the calcium in two ways: It stores some in its mitochondria, and pumps the rest out. When a body dies, stored calcium leaks, and calcium pumps break down. The excess calcium makes the telescoping assemblies in muscle fibers shorten, stiffening the whole body. The strength of muscle tension in a corpse is greater than the animal's living strength because all fibers everywhere are at maximum contraction.

even localize the tickle, know if it came from right or left, arm or leg. This is not because he isn't brainy: He has all the billions of brain cells he will ever have. But they are not yet well connected.

The basic organization of neurons in your brain and body was roughed out well before you were born. The process is fiercely competitive, and many neurons die during it.

Take a neuron, born in the spinal cord when an embryo still has a curling tail, that will one day receive signals from the motor map in the brain, and transmit the signals to a muscle fiber in a thumb. This neuron emerges from the embryo's spinal cord into a bud of flesh that is growing into an arm. Its regulatory genes instruct it to grow its axon, and to synapse with a muscle fiber. Hundreds of thousands of sister neurons also emerge from the spinal cord at that spot, all with the same instructions. However, there is not nearly enough muscle to go around. Each muscle fiber requires contact with just one axon branch, and a single motor neuron can handle several hundred fibers by sprouting a branch for each. As swarms of neurons grow probing axons into the arm, every muscle fiber is found, and found again, until the surface of each is a babble of synapses.

These neurons are competing not only for a place, but for their lives. Muscles secrete nerve growth factor. The substance attracts axons, makes them grow, makes them branch, and keeps the branch alive. If few or no axon branches receive nerve growth factor, the whole neuron dies.

Each muscle fiber declares the winning branch by secreting to the one that signals it most clearly and most often. Axon branches that have synapsed at the wrong place shrivel up and die; those that rarely signal perish. Neurons that have not received connections at the spine are killed off altogether for their failure to fire. In the end, every muscle fiber twitches for the neuron that served it best, and none are jerked by misfits.

Competition for life-saving connections is the rule throughout the nervous system. Each neuron learns, clue by clue according to its time and place, which chemicals it must give, and which it must receive. Motor interneurons in the spine must receive the right neurotransmitter from neurons in the motor map in the brain, and give the right neurotransmitter to motor neurons in the arm. And the same is true for sensory neurons, their relays in the spine, and their map in the brain. Those that fail to make the right connections perish within days. Altogether, 50 percent of the neurons you had while you were an embryo were punished by death for failing to reach out and taste someone.

School Days for Brain Cells

The fate of neurons born in the spine is settled by the time a baby's born, but for most born in the brain, their struggle is not yet over, and for those with which you think, it never will be. Learning is a lifelong competition among brain cells.

A fly's tickle reported by a sensor in a baby's toe may be spread by eagerly branching interneurons over a large area of the sensory map in the brain, to neurons that have been swarmed over just as eagerly by axons bearing signals from other toes, and heels, soles, ankles, knees. In other words, this is not yet a map with clear-cut boundaries. It is confused, overlapped, blurry. The baby feels the tickle, but can't locate the toe. For him to learn where it is, his neurons have to make the right connections.

Receivers of touch information in the sensory map select their proper signalers by obeying a rule similar to the one muscle fibers use to select their best twitcher: They nourish those axons that signal to them at the same time, or within a few seconds of one another. Little by little, tickle after tickle, the spot on the map that will be "toe" rids itself of connections to interneurons that have nothing to say when that toe reports. Neighboring neurons do the same, pruning from their bodies axons that fail to speak in unison. The map becomes accurate through its own experience as the baby, touched and touching, speaks to it in synchrony.

This is not just a matter of touch. All through the brain, interneurons jumbled with synapses reporting all sorts of sights and sounds and touches favor those connections that signal together. Look of fly, sound of fly, feel of fly in this way become represented in circuitry that, when a fly arrives, recognizes it. This is a memory. This is learning. And, by no coincidence, it reflects the connectedness among events in the outside world, black to buzz to bug to bite.

Such wonders do not happen suddenly, or even soon. Neurons in the newborn brain have made only the most essential and programmed connections. Their axons will branch according to use: The more often neurons are fired, the twiggier they grow, and the more synapses they seek. The more connections they make, the more they are pruned into memories, synchronized into sense. And the smarter the child will be.

Learning is scary because it is real. Math struggled with is axons eagerly branching. Math learned is new connections made. Math recalled is old connections fortified. Math put to a new use is novel patterns of connections, inventive thoughts that had never been possible before.

Baby Games

Numerous traditional games that parents play with babies seem designed to teach neurons their proper connections. "This Little Piggy," "Show Me Your Nose," "Pat-a-Cake," and "Soooooo Big!" all help to shape a baby's body image. "Peek-a-Boo" practices facial memory: The baby holds the face in mind until it reappears. In a more advanced version of Peek-a-Boo, the baby covers his own face. In the course of this game, and the later one of "Hide-and-Seek," he becomes able to imagine himself from the other player's point of view, first hidden, then reappearing. The very sense of self that we tend to take for granted has in fact been painstakingly constructed through many kinds of experience, including the ancient baby games we don't know why we play.

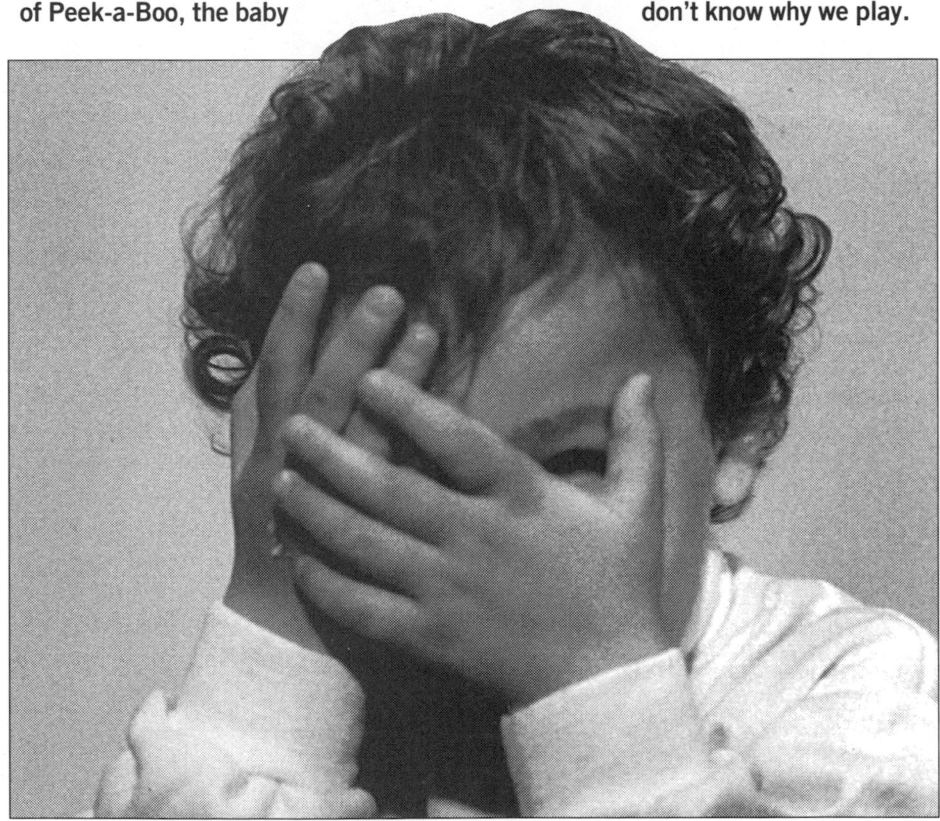

Unused neurons become useless. If they are not fired, their axon fails to branch, and so they cannot teach. If they are not signaled to, they become deaf, dumb, disconnected, dead.

School days for nerve cells are your school days, from the first lessons in jerk and twitch that taught motor neurons the basics of survival when you were an embryo, to your first view of the world that encouraged the curious sprouting of spot and feature detectors, through all the incredible connections that were made as you came to crawl, walk, talk, argue, read, paint, play, plan, and, finally, understand: Intelligence is physical; you make it happen, through chemistry.

Remember?

Remember the fly? The one that tickled the baby's toe? What color were the fly's eyes?

You never really saw a fly in this book; you saw only the word, "fly." Yet you remember it as an image, not a word. The image is not flat like a picture. You can look at it from all sides; you can make it move; you can zoom in to see the color of its eyes.

Maybe you protest that this is an exercise in imagination, not memory. There may be no difference. Anything that you can think about you have constructed in your brain as a pattern of interconnecting neurons.

Curiouser and Curiouser

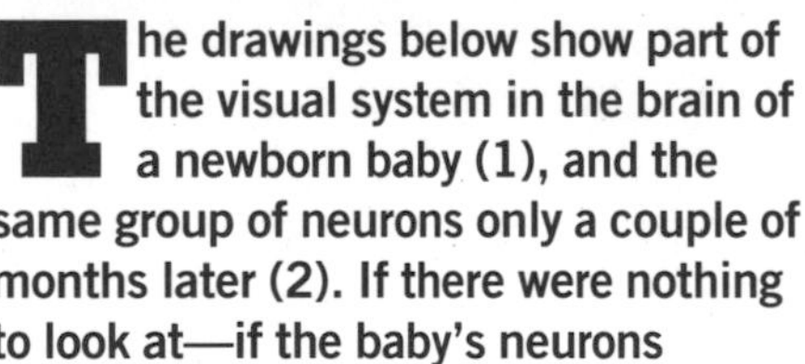

The drawings below show part of the visual system in the brain of a newborn baby (1), and the same group of neurons only a couple of months later (2). If there were nothing to look at—if the baby's neurons weren't signaled to—axons attempting to make contact would fail to survive, and this part of the brain would not develop. Although neurons have innate curiosity in that they actively seek for new connections, the organism as a whole must provide them with experiences to keep them branching. Toddlers, who try anything and get into everything, stimulate their neurons to make more connections then they ever will again. This is what makes kids at that age seem so "creative." As children learn more about reality—that buckets aren't hats, for instance—improbable connections disintegrate from disuse. Compared to the two-year-old's wild bush of a brain, that of a six-year-old is a sensibly pruned shrub.

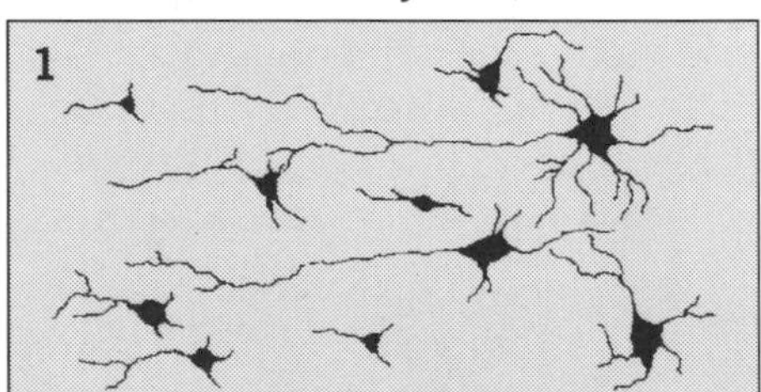

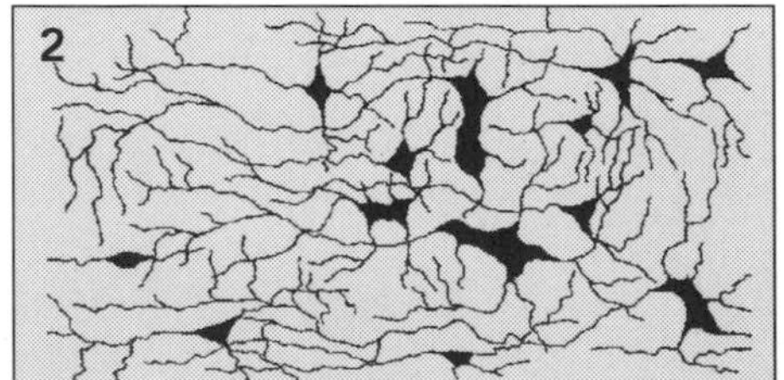

Even the simplest mental image—an egg, say—is assembled out of countless neuron firings that, experienced simultaneously, are the memory. The complexity of these networks is what gives a memory its peculiar fluidity, its tendency to self-transform as you examine it, fading, flickering in and out of view, turning from white to brown to Easter colors, or chocolate, or changing into jellybeans. The millions of neurons that, each summoning others, dish up egg images have a rambling way of doing so because the memory networks you have woven for years and years follow numerous paths and byways, and there's no telling which turn your mind might take among them. But you can also choose the paths—turn your thoughts from fly to egg, from egg to fly, and imagine eggs you've never seen, or turn the fly around to see the color of its eyes.

When you play such mental games, you are aware of the images, but not of the processes by which they form. In fact, 99 percent of mental activity is beyond awareness. To be aware of anything going on around you right this second requires that your brain transform the raw data of sights and sounds into short-term memories. Short-term memory is what lets you read from the beginning of this sentence to the end without losing the first words before you've reached the last ones. But now that you've read the sentence, do you recall the exact words? Not likely, although the sense remains. The sentence was just squiggles (not even sounds); you made the squiggles into words, gave them meaning, and "recalled" them in a form entirely different from the raw data delivered from your eyes.

We can never know what raw data are like. They are held briefly in a buffer zone, from which they make it into short-term memory only through interpretation that cooks some sense into them. Most sounds, sights, and touches fade out in buffer zones before they can be processed, and therefore you don't see, hear, or feel them. That's why you haven't been aware of the pressure on your elbows, the number of

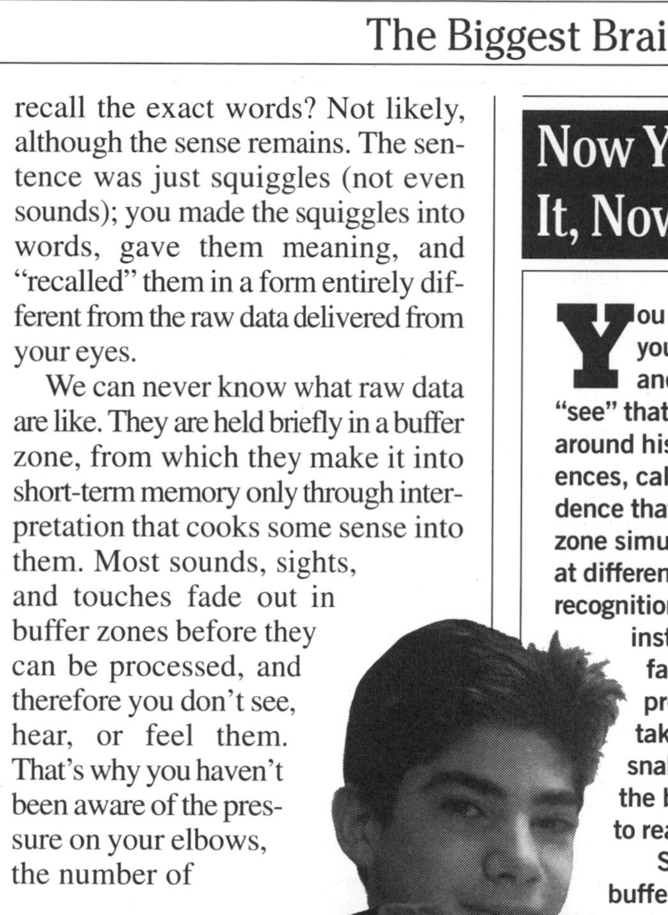

Now You Don't See It, Now You Do

You say "Hi" to a friend as you pass him in the hall, and, a second later you "see" that he was wearing a snake around his neck. Such experiences, called double takes, are evidence that data arriving in a buffer zone simultaneously may emerge at different times. The first take—recognition of a friend—seems instantaneous because such familiar data are quickly processed. The second take—recognition of the snake—lags behind because the brain has to work longer to realize the unexpected.

Sounds may be kept in a buffer for even longer than sights. While you're watching the end of a mystery, somebody says, "When are you going to do the dishes?" The buffer zone holds that sound pattern long enough for you to listen to the mystery's closing lines. Then you "hear" the question.

Aha! Oh Oh

When, after studying something for a period of time, you suddenly see the light, that great feeling is neurons bubbling at their synapses, making new connections that they had never made before. Pity, in contrast, the neurons that you cram. Without time to poke among many possible connections, they stay sparse, isolated, and too far from the beaten path to ever find the meaning of it all.

this page, the sound of traffic on the street, although these sensations all are held in buffers from which, by processing them into memory, you can become aware of them. You have probably had the experience of rescuing something from the buffer zone before it fades, but many seconds after it occurred—for example, your name called while you were busy with another thought, and only heard after that thought was finished.

Even when an item makes it into short-term memory, it is held for less than 20 seconds unless it is continually repeated, or thought about. That's why you have to repeat a telephone number, or notice something special about it, to keep it in mind long enough to reach a telephone. If experience is to remain available for future thinking, it must be processed into long-term memory, the kind that you retrieve when you recall your own number.

The Rhythm of Remembering

Short-term memories aren't transported into long-term storage. The circuitry involved is, instead, sensitized so that it fires more easily, and is connected up with other circuits so that it can be reached from other memories. This is done through the act of thinking.

As you think, a small bit of brain—a sort of memory enabler—sends carefully-timed pairs of signals to the active circuits. That special signaling rhythm acts as a volume control. It amplifies neuron signaling by either increasing the amount of neurotransmitter the cell secretes, or by tuning up the sensitivity of its receptors for other neurons' transmissions. The rhythm also helps a neuron broadcast and receive over a larger area, for it makes it sprout new branches at both ends. These changes are long-lasting; often they are permanent. A circuit that has been amplified has become a long-term memory.

The permanence of the memory will depend on how thoroughly you weave it within memory networks along pathways previously laid down, and along new paths that you, by thinking, provide its eager sprouts. The more you know, the more you learn, the more you think, the more you remember.

Thinking is creative. Think about what happens when you think about a memory. Remember the fly? However it first appeared to your mind, it has now changed: It has, for instance, colored eyes. The brain is not like an encyclopedia to which any number of new items can be added without altering previous ones. Rather, each additional thought or experience changes the network itself, as though the brain were a weird computer in which each bit entered subtly alters the programming, and so changes its mind and memory.

Mysteries of Sleep

As far as any scientist has been able to discover, neurons do not tire. The same is true for most other cells in the body. Livers work around the clock; fibroblasts spin all their lives; phagocytes don't rest. Muscles do tire out, but they recover easily, with rest, not sleep, and in much less than eight hours. As for brains, they are as active during the night as they are during the day. Then what is sleep, and why?

There are two completely different kinds of sleep. The first is the sleep you enter through drowsiness, the "drifting off" in which you gradually become less aware of your surroundings. Breathing and heartbeat are the same

Knot, Knit, Type, Bike

Do you remember how to tie a shoe? Try it—in your head, not with your hands. Probably you can manage to imagine the motions, but only slowly, and with considerable mental effort. Yet you can tie a shoe effortlessly, in a moment, and apparently without thinking about it at all. Skill memory is different from other kinds of memory. While a person is learning to knot, knit, write, type, or drive the motions are laborious and the learner is painstakingly aware of them. With practice, the firing sequences begin to function smoothly, and awareness fades. The action is eventually put on automatic pilot. From then on, awareness tends to interfere with both the speed and accuracy of the skill. Ask a fast typist to think where each finger should strike next, and see what a mess awareness makes! Unlike other memories, skill memories are indelible, possibly because they have been removed from the thinking that tinkers with our other recollections.

as when you're awake, and muscles remain ready for action. If you're uncomfortable, you move; if your name is called, you wake up. You may even continue to think, although the thoughts are blurry.

Then, very abruptly, after a half-hour or so of this regular sleep, you enter the dream sleep state. Dream sleep is bizarre: The muscles that move your body become paralyzed; breathing and heartbeat are irregular; but the brain zips into action, signaling as intensely as when you are wide awake and thinking hard.

The most active portion is the visual center at the back of the brain: It creates the visual imagery of a dream, and throughout a dream the eyes move rapidly back and forth as though they were watching it. Other portions of the brain are also active. People run and leap, punch and fly in their dreams, even though they cannot actually move the muscles of their arms and legs (and have never flown!). Certainly the sleeper remains aware, for not only do people "see"—and sometimes "hear," "smell," and "touch"—dream images, they also provide a story line that seems logical at the time. You may even have experienced the upsetting event of realizing a dream is a dream (and a bad one at that) and trying to awaken from it, only to discover that you can't move a muscle. That's the paralysis. Without paralysis, dreamers might act upon their dreams, and that would be unwise.

People are much harder to wake up during dream sleep than during regular sleep. Rather than awaken, the brain will incorporate into the dream disturbing sensations such as a full bladder or a ringing alarm clock. But then, after about 10 or 15 minutes, sleep changes again to the drowsing kind, the dream is over, breathing again becomes regular, and the sleeper can move. The two kinds of sleep alternate during the night, with about 80 percent of the time spent in regular sleep, and the rest spent dreaming.

Some people remember most of their dreams; others don't remember, and think they don't dream. In fact, everyone dreams for about the same amount of time each night—unless they are babies, who dream a great deal more. When a person is deprived of dreams (by being awakened every time she begins to slip into the dream state), she dreams much more often than usual for the next several nights until the total amount of lost dream time is made up. The brain *needs* to dream, and insists on doing so.

The reasons aren't yet clear, but some scientists think the dreaming brain is sorting out the day's experience, discarding trivia, strengthening important connections, and relating new thoughts to older ones. That would explain at least a few things. It would explain why babies, who pile in new experiences at

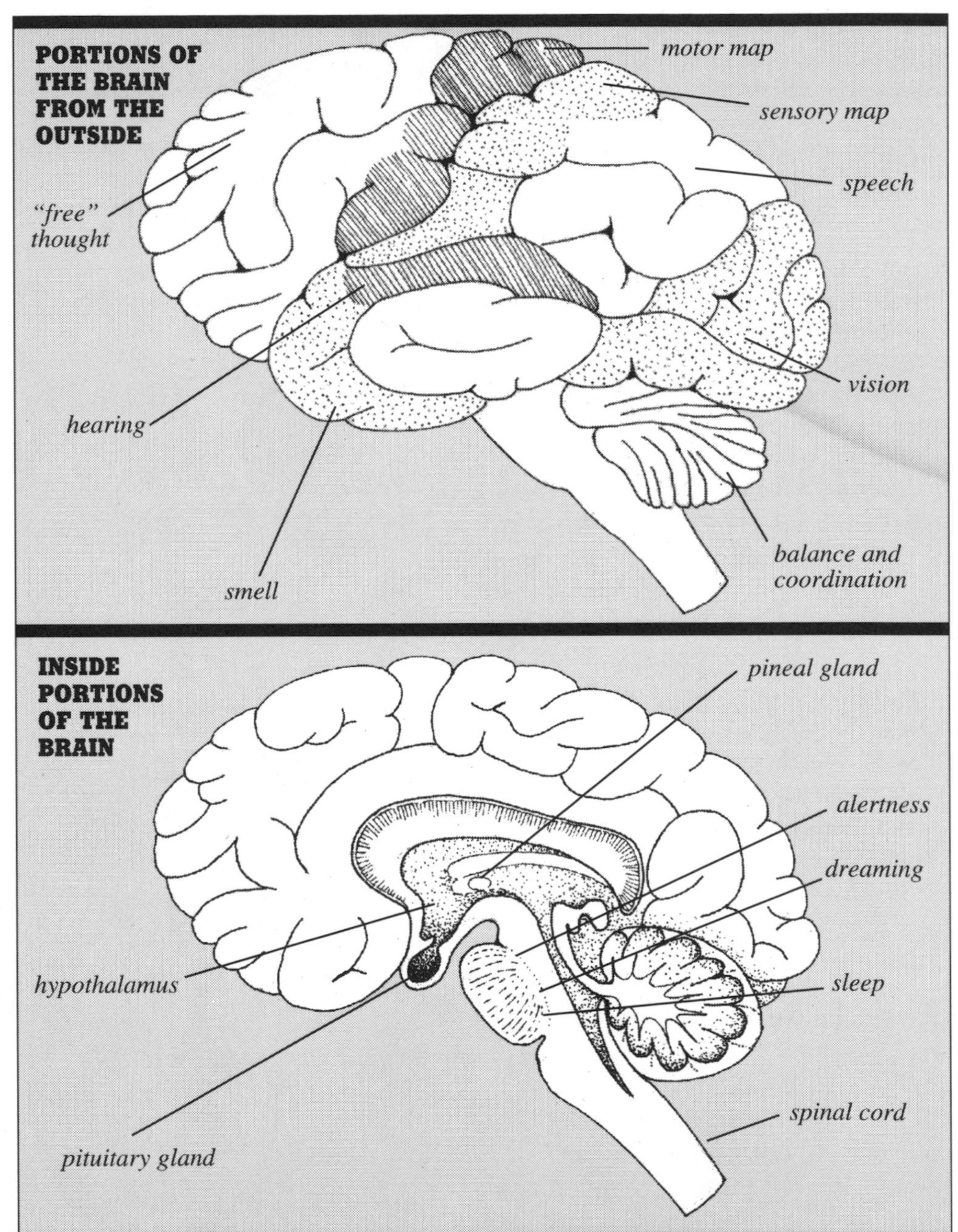

a rapid rate, need more dreaming time to sort things out. It might also explain why psychiatrists often find childhood experiences woven into people's dreams, as though a recent happening were being tied by the brain into much earlier memory networks. Sometimes people talking about their dreams recall something they had forgotten for many years, but which the dream had found a pathway to. Maybe our sense of having always been the same person, even though our views have changed considerably, is because, during the night, our brain knits up the raveled strands of all our years' experience.

The least active portion of the brain during a dream is the reasonable cortex which, upon awakening, may think the dream crazy, or shameful. There's a lot of stuff in dreams that people don't like to admit to others, or even to think about themselves. The waking cortex can censor such thoughts. Maybe the dreaming brain has to shut it up so that it can, for a while, think freely.

But why the plain old regular kind of sleep? No one knows.

Deep Down in Ancient Places

Sleeping and waking are regulated by two control centers deep within the brain, just above where it connects to the spinal cord. The alertness center is

Dragon Brains

There's little difference between the core of a reptile's brain and the core of ours. There is therefore no reason to believe that this lizard doesn't feel the same emotions that people feel, or that it doesn't dream. Our cortex can contradict our feelings, and find our dreams unreasonable. Lizards probably lack that aptitude for self-criticism.

Bad Luck, Good Luck

When researchers first discovered that the brain has opiate receptors, and makes its own opiate to fill them, they thought they had found the perfect painkiller, for how could a natural body drug be addictive? Unfortunately, they were wrong: Endorphins are as addictive as heroin or morphine. If they weren't, we'd be in trouble. Addicts are willing to put forth a great deal of effort for a dose of good feelings. People learn from experience what releases their own endorphins, and whatever it is that does it, they'll work to do it again. If they do something well, and are praised for it, they receive the shot of brain opiate that praise releases, so they strive to do well again. The intellectual connections that people call "positive self-image" most likely are encouraged by an addiction to endorphins.

firing now, keeping you awake. But while it is keeping you awake, the sleep control center below it is secreting an inhibiting neurotransmitter, a kind of sleep drug. As the sleep drug accumulates, alertness fades. You feel drowsy; you sleep.

How do you wake up again? Strangely enough, it's dreams that cause you to wake up each morning. The dream control center lies between the alertness and the sleep centers. It needs the sleep drug in order to turn on dreaming, but its activity, in turn, uses up the drug. By morning, there is not enough left to inhibit the alertness center, and so you just naturally wake up.

These control centers are in a part of the brain that evolved very early. Dinosaurs, whose brains lacked our reasonable cortex, slept, and maybe dreamed. They must have felt rage, fear, and some dinosaurian version of delight: Such emotions are created in this old, deep portion of the brain.

As brains evolved, layer after layer of neurons piled up around and on top of the old reptile core, but without ever losing connections with it. These newer layers—especially those that form the bulging cortex in the human brain—exercise some control over the dragon depths: They can, at least, talk sense to it, tell it that a nightmare isn't real, explain that there's no reason to be angry at the cat that scratched you by mistake.

But the core remains in an interesting position. It intercepts painful messages of the cat's scratch on the way up from the spinal cord to the cortex; it intercepts signals of your intention to strike back on the way down from the cortex to the spinal cord; and through its many connections, it can make you feel furious at the cat in a split second, before you have had time to tell it otherwise. The core flavors your inner world with emotion.

These flavors are essential. Why would you eat if food gave you no pleasure, and a full belly no satisfaction? Or, for that matter, if hunger were not unpleasant? Why would you defend yourself if a punch didn't make you angry, and why would you get out of the way of a careening car if you weren't afraid? Emotions are part of an animal's basic survival kit. They are to us what swimming toward sweet, and tumbling away from sour are to a bacterium: the value judgments that make us act to meet our body's needs.

The hypothalamus is part of the brain's core, and it works together with the parts that create emotion to make you take care of yourself. The hypothalamus directs hunger, thirst, salt appetite, and other cravings necessary to maintain the environment inside you, but it doesn't supply the punishment of unpleasant feelings if a craving isn't satisfied, or the reward of pleasant feelings if it is. The hypothalamus makes you shiver when you're cold; the emotion-makers say being cold feels awful, and so force you to get up and get a blanket. The hypothalamus then stops the shivering, while the emotion-makers reward your effort with a snuggly sense of comfort.

What's Fun?

Cravings dictated by the hypothalamus are ancient ones, and are the same in other animals that, like us, must eat, drink, and keep their temperature right. But whether an animal gets good feelings from munching grass or catching mice is not up to the hypothalamus. The emotional core of the brain is hooked up to all sorts of other circuits that differ from species to species. The circuits define what an animal can do; the hookups say whether it's fun or not. What's fun for an animal turns out to be what it needs to do in order to survive.

A baby monkey *can* walk on two legs, but doesn't get a thrill from it, and so doesn't do it much. It gets a kick from climbing, so that is what it practices, and that is what it needs to learn to survive up in the trees. A monkey needs to learn to keep away from snakes. A built-in visual circuit recognizes sinuous shapes; a hookup to the core flavors the shape with horror. You can terrify a monkey with a coiled length of hose.

Researchers have discovered quite a few built-in learning systems in our babies besides those for human voices and human faces. Babies are rewarded by good feelings when they taste something sweet; they are punished by bad feelings when they taste something bitter. As they learn the look and smell of sweet and bitter foods, those new connections get hooked up to the original, built-in ones. They reach for cookies, but turn away from grapefruit. Babies even come prepared to like the look of ripe fruits in particular: Their favorite colors—those their brain rewards them most for seeing—are red and yellow.

You no longer smile at a nodding oval with a line for a mouth and dots for eyes that you would have smiled at readily as an infant. These early, automatic hookups were just to get you started. Now your pleasure is in the relationships that grew from the smiles exchanged—in what smiles mean, not what they look like. This is a most efficient learning system. A baby need know only that sharing smiles feels good: Whatever new connections come his way through actual experience will be rewarded by joy juice from the core.

Joy Juice and Other Brain Drugs

Don't laugh (or rather, do—you'll get a spurt from it): Joy juice is real. When you're delirious with joy, your neurons are drunk on neurotransmitters called endorphins.

The word "endorphin" means roughly "inner morphine": Endorphins are opiates, chemical relatives of morphine, codeine, heroin, and opium, all of which are made from the juice of

"I Will Please"

Can a sugar pill cure a headache? Yes, if the person believes it is real medicine.

Doctors have known for hundreds of years that they can help people feel better with pink sugar pills so long as the patient does not know they're fake. They call such "medicines" placebos, from the Latin for "I will please." The comfort one feels when a kind doctor offers a potion to ease one's suffering releases endorphins in the brain, and turns down the flow of stress hormones. Pain is eased by endorphins. Tension is relieved as adrenalin levels fall. The immune system that battles infection works better with less cortisone.

The medical effects of placebos are so real that they are used to measure the effectiveness of new medicines. The new medicine is tested with two groups of patients, one of which is given the genuine drug, the other is given a look-alike placebo. Researchers tell neither patients nor their doctors who got which. Only if those patients who received the real thing show more improvement than those who received the placebo is the medicine considered to have passed the test.

No Measure of Success

IQ tests are designed so that the average scores of both sexes are the same. Girls usually do better in the verbal portions, boys in the math. However, they are also designed to measure a very narrow range of intelligence. They don't measure intuition. They don't measure leadership. They don't measure gentleness, nimbleness, charm, or courage. Other tests are even narrower. S.A.T.s are designed to predict only how well a person might do in academic subjects. They often fail even at that, and success in academic work doesn't anyway predict how smart people will be in other kinds of work. The more that is found out about the workings of the brain, the less it seems possible to measure the varieties of thought that, altogether, are intelligence. How smart are you? No test can tell. So take the tests you must, but don't take the results as a measure of your mind.

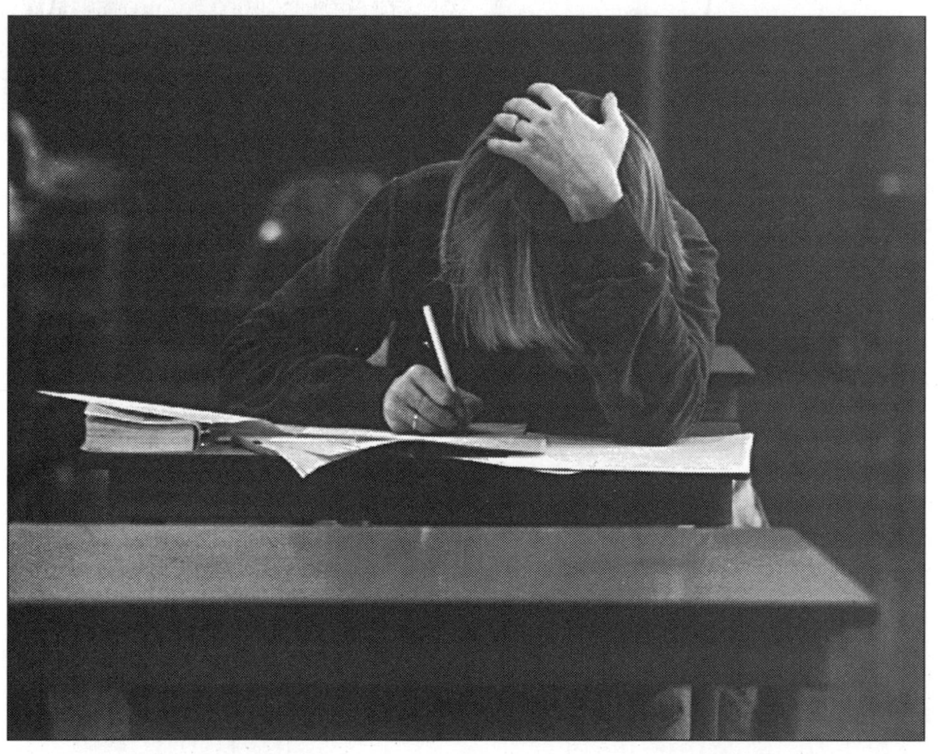

opium poppies. Doctors use opiates to soothe sick people, and to relieve their pain. The brain uses its own opiates in the same way. One prescription soothes you with good moods. Other doses give you a more excited kind of happiness—an all-A's, birthday-present, first-day-of-vacation sort of feeling. The brain uses its most potent mix as medicine. The runner's "high" is a shot of endorphins that keeps her going in spite of exhaustion. An injured athlete may feel no pain until the game is over, a wounded soldier until safely back at camp. Endorphins are powerful painkillers that the brain prescribes in large doses during imagined or real emergencies.

You may wonder why, if the brain can prescribe joy juice to itself, it doesn't always do so. Why not be happy all the time? Why ever feel pain? Temporary painlessness is meant to be the lesser of two evils: bad for the wound, but best for survival. The brain is actually making a mistake when it relieves pain during a game. However competitive athletes may feel, winning is not really a matter of life and death, and continuing to play makes the unfelt injury worse.

Happiness can also be too much of a good thing. You *ought* to feel miserable when you flunk a course. The punishment may prevent you from flunking again. Feeling bad is supposed to push you around, make you do something to ease your pain, avoid a threat, solve the problem. So the brain makes misery chemicals, too.

Altogether, some 30 neurotransmitters have been identified so far. Many are involved in one way or another with how you feel, and all of these work simultaneously, making you feel a little this way, a little that way, but rarely totally depressed, or insanely happy. The various mixes of neurotransmitters, and their doses, and the specific neuron networks that respond to each kind, account for the uncounted shades of feelings people feel. Think of all the words you know to describe just shades of sadness!

The purpose of this pharmacy is to tune one's mood to the realities of the moment. Reality for humans can be very complicated: Just the slightest quirk in the hundred muscles that bring us smiles can twist a smile to a sneer, or express insincerity, sexual interest, or the threat of violence. Just think of the difference between someone laughing with you, and at you! The brain's pharmacy has to mix flavors deftly to make your feelings fit, and so guide your actions wisely.

Bad News on Drugs

Drug control in the brain is not exclusive to humans. Guppies, garter snakes, robins and rhinoceroses tune their moods to reality in just the same way, and even bee-brained insects adjust their behavior chemically. Plants have used this fact in their own defense. They have evolved mind-bending drugs to protect themselves from chewing insects, gnawing rodents, and grazing cows. These drugs work in small doses to sabotage the eater's behavior—to make it stuporous when it should be alert, frenzied when it should be calm. Large doses simply kill.

In the course of evolution, individuals with a fatal attraction to such plants have rarely survived to hand their tastes on to their descendants. If they don't die of overdose, frenzied insects and stuporous mice are nevertheless easy prey for predators, and either way the individual, along with its taste for that plant, is eliminated from the population. The upshot is that over time the population of that species is more and more made up of individuals who dislike the smell and taste of these poisonous plants, and so avoid eating them. We, the cleverest of all animals, are the only ones who purposely harvest mind-bending plants to chew, smoke, sniff, or inject ourselves into dangerous unreality.

Any drug that acts to alter mood, thoughts, or sensations acts in the brain either by mimicking a neurotransmitter, by destroying a neurotransmitter, or by making neurons produce their own drugs in abnormal doses. The more powerful drugs distort connections between thought and reality. That is, they make you crazy.

Heroin is an example. It is an opiate similar in shape to the brain's own endorphins, and so it fits the same receptors. A person taking heroin feels happy. What's crazy is that there may be nothing to feel happy about.

Worse yet, this artificial joy juice soon causes genuine misery. The amount of natural opiates produced in the brain is controlled by a feedback system in which the drug acts to inhibit its own production. A person taking heroin shuts down the manufacture of his own endorphins. After the initial "high" has worn off, he is left feeling unusually low. Again, there may be nothing really to feel miserable about, and therefore nothing the person can do to make himself feel better—except take another dose of heroin. Finally, he must take the drug continually to even feel normal. That's addiction.

Many kinds of drugs alter alertness, and they, too, are addictive. Tranquilizers—"downers"—block receptors in the alertness center. They literally turn you off. Stimulants do the opposite: They mimic the neurotransmitter used by the alerting system to keep you awake and active. Caffeine in coffee, tea, and cola drinks (all of which are made from plants) works that way, and so does the nicotine in tobacco. A little caffeine can help in late-night cramming for a test, but a little more causes restless jitters in which one is alert to everything, but can't keep one's mind on anything.

Amphetamines—"uppers"—and cocaine and crack are more powerful stimulants. They raise alertness to such a pitch that the brain assumes there is an emergency: something to run from, something to fight. Crack addicts don't just *feel* the fear and rage appropriate to an emergency. They make up thoughts to match their feelings. They imagine that people are out to get them, and they act upon these imaginings. That's delusion; that's really crazy.

Dreams are crazy too, but the brain is careful to keep the sleeper still while dreams are happening. The drugs called hallucinogens sabotage that safeguard. LSD, for instance, so deranges the whole sleep-wake system that "trippers" have wide-awake dreams called hallucinations—but without the safety of paralysis, and without either the guarantee that the hallucination will end soon, or that it will not be a nightmare. Marijuana—pot, hash, grass, weed—is less powerful, but still warps one's sense of reality. The drug gives events a dreamy distance, and, as during dreams, shuts up the cortex's criticism and judgment. A person high on pot is slow to grasp the meaning of what is going on, and the muscles that might be needed to do something about it become sluggish too. Pot continues to affect the brain between highs. It dulls reality until, in time, nothing seems to matter very much. You know what that's called: dropping out.

Alcohol is the one mind-bending drug that doesn't act at neuron synapses in the brain: It acts on the whole cell. Alcohol disrupts a neuron's membrane, gets inside, messes up its inner chemistry. And alcohol doesn't select just one section of the brain. A person who is drunk can't talk straight, walk straight, drive straight, or think straight. She may get high and silly, sad and tearful, enraged and violent—and can't control these feelings, or the exaggerated thoughts that go with them, or her behavior.

Alcohol is downright poison. Liver cells attempt to detoxify it, but many are killed in the process. Brain cells are killed, too, and with them, intelligence. Alcoholics become sick, and they become stupid.

The Future

So it's smart to let your brain conduct its own chemical business. It took more than 3 billion years for intelligence to evolve from the sweet-and-sour judgments of bacteria to the level of the human IQ. It's taken us a million years more to begin to understand how that intelligence works. Among the most startling discoveries is that 50 percent of our genes—a full half of all the genetic knowledge inherited over the course of human evolution—is read only in the brain. Your brain weighs a mere three pounds: To fuel its thoughts, it uses 20 percent of the glucose you provide. So you are aware of just a hundredth of what is going on in there: That's all the more reason not to meddle.

Your brain has surprises in store for you as time goes by. Sooner or later it will make you fall in love. Little kids can't do that; a clock controls the timing. Sooner or later you'll mate with the one you love. Both the want-to and the how-to of sex are there in your circuitry, awaiting juicing up. If you have sons and daughters, you'll notice that the sexes are not alike—not even in the brain, not even as babies. Testosterone sees to that by influencing the development of the brain in male embryos. Even now, by noticing carefully how your parents parent, you'll see that fathering and mothering are as different as boys are from girls. If you can remember way back when, you'll recollect that already by nursery school you were practicing for adulthood just as, before memory began, you practiced for your birth.

It's all there in the brain, the whole cycle of life even to the gradual gentling of old grandparents who, when your parents were little, withheld the cookies until the peas were eaten, and now are much more kind. In the end, even the biggest brain in the world is in the service of the next generation.

NO END

Where are you going? Very likely you're going the way your parents and all your ancestors before them have gone: growing up, pairing up, caring for the next generation so that it, too, can grow up, pair up, and continue to hand on its genes into the future. From the genes' point of view, that's the only purpose of a body, or of life.

But there are side effects of living that go beyond the selfish interests of genes. Living forces bacteria, whether they are interested in plants or not, to nevertheless supply their minerals. Living forces plants, whether they are interested in you or not, to nevertheless supply your vitamins. If bacteria can be gardeners, and gardens can feed humans, what might you not do?

There's really no telling. The side effects of human living have created new species of organisms, and destroyed others. We've changed the very surface of this planet. We've raised it's temperature. We've altered its atmosphere. We've left its atmosphere. We've touched the moon. We've sent our extraterrestrial sensors all the way to the edge of the solar system, and beyond.

Some of these effects have been as mindless—and as harmful—as those caused by infectious bacteria which, after all, are only going about their business of living. We didn't intend to harm Earth's atmosphere by burning coal and oil, the fossil remains of life that came before us. A bacterium, however, has no choice. It can only change its genes, not its mind, and only by accident, not on purpose. We, with the biggest brain in the world, can choose to change our mind.

We can learn. We can understand. We can decide. The sheer number of neurons in our skulls, and the countless connections among them, give us free will: the capacity to select from among the myriad paths our thoughts might take those on which we will act.

More than that, we have a collective intelligence made up of all 5 billion of our individual brains. A bacterium can inject a partner with only a small portion of its individual wisdom, a scrap of genes. We can communicate among ourselves all that we have stored in the circuitry of our brains. With words and deeds we have influenced each other to form societies that have invented computers, created the Constitution. Through such inventions we have achieved a global society, in which our words and deeds spread at the speed of light, bounce off satellites, beam into television sets, buzz onto paper at the terminals of telephone lines. Our bodies lack magnetic sense; our eyes don't see ultraviolet. But by using our collective brain we have made sensors for everything than any animal senses, and more besides. We have X-ray vision. We can see atoms.

Reading this book has altered your brain. Telling friends how neurons work will alter their neurons. You change people. No matter what you do in your life, you will affect how others think, and therefore the choices they make, the kind of society that grows out of those choices, and the lives of all the other creatures that, like us, evolved from stardust. Even if your genes were never to make it into the next generation, the changes that you cause by living, thinking, learning, and communicating will cause changes in generations to come, and far into the future.

Where are you going? Wherever it is, there may be no end to the journey you've begun.

GLOSSARY

ADENINE
One of four molecules that constitute the genetic code of DNA; see also cytosine, guanine, and thymine.

ADENOSINE DIPHOSPHATE (ADP)
A molecule of ATP after one phosphate group has been removed to release energy.

ADENOSINE TRIPHOSPHATE (ATP)
An energy storage molecule containing three phosphate groups, one of which is removed to release energy for chemical work within a cell, such as protein manufacture.

ADRENALIN
A hormone produced by the adrenal gland and responsible for symptoms of worry and fear such as trembling, paleness, rapid heartbeat, and "butterflies in the stomach."

ALLERGENS
Substances that cause allergic reactions such as wheezing, itchy eyes, runny nose, or rash.

ALVEOLI(US)
Minute air pockets in the lung through which oxygen diffuses into the bloodstream.

AMINO ACIDS
Any of 20 short molecules that are the building blocks of proteins.

AMPERE
A unit of electric current.

ANDROGENS
A group of hormones, including testosterone, responsible for the development of male sex characteristics.

ANTIBODIES
T-shaped molecules produced by B-lymphocytes to grasp foreign germs or substances and mark them for destruction.

ANTIGEN
Any molecule that can be recognized by an antibody.

AXON
The long extension of a neuron (nerve cell) through which electrical signals are conducted from the receiving to the transmitting end of the cell.

B-CELL
Immune cells that secrete antibodies during an infection.

BACTERIOPHAGES
Viruses that infect bacteria.

BASAL CELLS
Cells at the base of skin that divide to replace old skin cells as they die and flake away.

CANCER
A disease in which a mass of cells grows out of control, invading and damaging surrounding tissues.

CANINES
Sharp, pointed teeth in the upper jaw used usually for puncturing and tearing flesh, but too small for that use in humans.

CAPILLARIES
The smallest blood vessels, through which blood circulates from arteries into veins.

CARBOHYDRATES
Simple, chainlike molecules of sugars and starches.

CELLULOSE
A tough starch that encloses and supports plant cells.

CHLOROPLASTS
Organelles in plant cells that contain green pigment and in which photosynthesis takes place.

CHOLESTEROL
An animal fat that stiffens cell membranes.

CHROMOSOME
A strand of genetic material containing a molecule of DNA surrounded by a protective protein coat.

CHONDROBLAST
A cell that manufactures cartilage.

CILIA
Threadlike or tentaclelike projections of a cell that are capable of coordinated whipping motions.

CIRCADIAN RHYTHMS
Physiologic events, such as sleep, which recur at intervals of about a day.

COLLAGEN
A strong, white, shiny protein that is the major fiber in cartilage, ligaments, and tendons.

CONE CELLS
Cone-shaped cells in the eye's retina that are responsible for color vision.

CONNECTIVE TISSUE
Tissue that is secreted, such as bone, tendon, ligament, and dermis.

CORNEA
The transparent surface layer of the eye.

CORTEX
The outer portion of the brain that, in humans, bulges at the forehead and is responsible for conscious thought.

CYTOSINE
One of four molecules that constitute the genetic code of DNA; see also adenine, guanine, and thymine.

DENDRITES
Short branches extending from the cell body of a neuron that receive signals from other neurons.

DENTINE
The bony material of teeth.

DERMIS
A fibrous material that forms the underlayer of skin.

DIAPHRAGM
A thick, flat muscle separating chest from belly and used to inflate the lungs.

DNA (DEOXYRIBONUCLEIC ACID)
A molecule shaped like a twisted ladder and containing genetic instructions for how proteins are to be assembled.

EGG
A female sex cell from which, when joined by a male sex cell, a new individual can grow.

ELASTIN
Loosely coiled fiber molecules that form a stretchy material in dermis.

ELECTRONS
Extremely small charged particles that orbit the nucleus of an atom.

ENDOCRINE SYSTEM
The glands that secrete hormones into the bloodstream.

ENDORPHINS
Neurotransmitters produced in the brain that have soothing or elating effects.

ENDOSKELETON
A skeleton that is embedded inside the animal, such as the one humans have.

ENZYMES
Proteins that enable chemical reactions by holding, bending, or otherwise manipulating the molecules involved.

ESCHERICHIA COLI (E. COLI)
A common rod-shaped bacterium that inhabits the gut.

ESTROGEN
A hormone produced in the ovaries that is responsible for the development of female sex characteristics.

EXONS
Sections of genetic material that are spliced together to construct a complete gene.

EXOSKELETON
A skeleton that is on the outside of an animal, such as the shell of a crab.

FERTILIZATION
The joining of genetic material from a sperm cell with the genetic material of an egg cell.

FERTILIZED
Made capable of growing, as when a sperm has joined its genes with those of an egg and so made the egg capable of growing into a baby.

FIBROBLASTS
Cells that specialize in manufacturing and secreting fibers.

FIBRONECTIN
A molecule that acts as a glue to attach cells to one another and to surrounding materials.

FLAGELLA
Very long cilia, such as the "tail" with which sperm swim.

FOLLICLE
The deep pit in the skin from which a hair grows.

FUNGUS
Any of a group of related organisms that include mushrooms, yeasts, and molds.

GENE(S)
The unit of inheritance; a section of a DNA molecule containing instructions for assembling a protein.

GLYCOLYSIS
A chemical process by which cells obtain energy by partially disassembling molecules of sugar.

GRISTLE
Sheets of tendon that hold one muscle to another

GUANINE
One of four molecules that constitute the genetic code of DNA; see also adenine, cytosine, and thymine.

HALLUCINOGENS
Drugs that cause hallucinations—vivid visions or voices that seem real but are not.

HEMOCYANIN
A pigment containing copper that is used for oxygen capture by some mollusks, and that color their blood blue.

HEMOGLOBIN
A pigment containing iron that is used for oxygen capture by vertebrates, and that colors our blood red.

HISTAMINE
A substance released by mast cells that causes skin to itch and swell.

HORMONE
A substance released into the bloodstream that acts as a chemical signal to cells elsewhere in the body to change their behavior in a specific way.

HYDROSTATIC SKELETON
A fluid-filled chamber, such as the body cavity of a worm, against which muscles exert force to move the animal.

HYPOTHALAMUS
A small area within the core of the brain that monitors and controls temperature and other critical aspects of the body's interior environment.

IMMUNOGLOBULINS (IGS)
Antibodies.

INCISORS
Chisel-shaped teeth at the front of the upper and lower jaw used as a cutting edge when biting.

INSULIN
A hormone secreted by the pancreas that increases cells' ability to take in sugar and to rebuild it into fat and starch for storage.

INTERNEURONS
Short neurons that relay messages within the brain.

IONS
Atoms that have lost or gained electrons, and that are therefore positively or negatively charged.

IRIS
The circular mechanism in front of the eye's lens that widens or narrows the pupil to control the amount of light reaching the retina.

LIGAMENTS
Bands of connective tissue that attach bones to one another.

LYMPH NODE
A chamber within the lymphatic system inhabited by phagocytes and lymphocytes that cleanse body fluid of debris and germs.

LYMPHOCYTE
An immune cell, either a B-cell or a T-cell.

MAGAININS
Powerful antibiotics found in frogs that protect them from infection.

MAST CELLS
Cells in the dermis whose secretions cause itching and inflammation.

MELANIN
The black-brown pigment that colors skin.

MELANOCYTE
A cell that manufactures melanin and injects it into skin cells to color them.

MELATONIN
A hormone made in the pineal gland that may coordinate body responses to daily and seasonal changes.

MEMBRANE
A thin, pliable layer, such as the covering of a cell.

MENSTRUATION
The period during a woman's monthly egg-ripening cycle during which, if the egg has not been fertilized, her uterine lining is shed.

MICROBE
Any very small organism such as a bacterium, virus, or microscopic fungus.

MITOCHONDRIA
Cell organelles in both plants and animals where respiration takes place.

MOLARS
Flat teeth in the back of the mouth used for grinding food.

MOLECULE(S)
A group of atoms bonded to one another.

MUCOUS MEMBRANE
Interior lining skin, such as in the respiratory and digestive tracts, that contains numerous mucus-secreting glands.

MUCUS
A slippery substance secreted by glands in mucous membranes that moistens, lubricates, and cleanses delicate tissues.

MUTANT
An organism that differs from the normal type due to an accidental change in its genetic instructions.

NEURONS (NERVE CELLS)
Cells, usually very elongated, that transmit nerve signals electrically and chemically throughout the body.

NEUROTRANSMITTER
A substance secreted by a neuron to transmit a chemical signal.

NUCLEUS
A spherical area, usually in the center of a cell, that contains the cell's chromosomes.

OPTIC NERVE
A thick bundle of neurons that transmits visual information from the eye to the brain.

OSSIFICATION
The hardening of bone with calcium phosphate crystals.

OSTEOBLASTS
Cells that secrete the collagen matrix of bone.

OSTEOCLASTS
Cells that erode old bone in preparation for rebuilding by osteoblasts.

OVARIES
Female reproductive glands where eggs are stored and ripened.

OVIDUCTS
A pair of tubes opening near the ovaries through which eggs are conducted into the womb.

OXIDIZING
A chemical reaction in which oxygen, by pulling electrons from a molecule, causes it to fall apart and release energy.

PENIS
The male reproductive organ that delivers sperm to the female during sexual intercourse, and through which urine also is excreted.

PERISTALSIS
Waves of muscular contraction by which food is squeezed through the digestive tract.

PHAGOCYTES
Large white blood cells that scavenge debris and engulf germs.

PHEROMONES
Scent molecules by which animals convey messages to one another through the air.

PHOTOSYNTHESIS
The chemical process by which plants capture the sun's energy and use it to build carbohydrates from carbon dioxide and water.

PIGMENT
A colored molecule, such as the brown melanin in skin or the green chlorophyll in leaves.

PINEAL
A small gland in the head that responds to light and dark via nerve connections to the eye.

PITUITARY
A gland in the brain that secretes important regulatory hormones especially involving growth and maturation.

PLACENTA
An organ embedded in the mother's uterus through which the developing fetus obtains nourishment and disposes of wastes before birth.

PLAQUE
A fuzzy coating on the teeth made up of communities of bacteria and their sticky secretions.

POLAR MOLECULES
Molecules with an uneven distribution of electric charge such that one area may be negatively charged, and another positively charged.

PORE(S)
An opening such as a hole through a cell membrane through which materials may enter the cell, or the opening through skin from which sweat oozes from a sweat gland.

PROGESTERONE
A hormone secreted in the female ovary that is involved in a woman's monthly reproductive cycle.

PROSTAGLANDIN
A hormone made in the uterus (and elsewhere) that causes pain and contractions.

PROSTATE
A small gland in the male reproductive tract that produces an acid-neutralizing component of semen.

PROTEINS
Very large molecules made up of long strings of amino acids coiled, pleated, bent, and folded into extremely complex shapes.

PROTONS
Positively charged particles that, along with neutrons, make up the nucleus of an atom.

REDUCTION DIVISION
A series of divisions by which reproductive cells create daughters (eggs or sperm) that have only half the usual number of chromosomes.

RESPIRATION
The chemical process by which mitochondria obtain energy for a cell's use by disassembling molecules stepwise, and storing the energy released at each step in molecules of ATP.

RETINA
The rear surface of the eyeball that is lined with light-sensitive rod and cone cells.

RIBOSOME
A large, two-part molecule that, using a copy of a gene as a template, assembles the protein for which the gene codes.

ROD CELLS
Rod-shaped neurons on the eye's retina that are responsible for black and white vision.

SCROTUM
The sac that holds a male's testes.

SELF-MARKER
Any molecule embedded in a cell membrane by which the immune system recognizes that cell as part of its own body.

SEMEN
A milky fluid made in the male reproductive tract in which sperm are nourished and protected.

SKELETAL MUSCLE
Muscle that moves the skeleton, such as that which works the limbs and back.

SPERM
The very small, mobile male reproductive cell that, when it fertilizes the egg, enables it to grow into a baby.

SQUAMES
Old, dead, flat skin cells that flake from the skin surface.

SUNSCREEN
A skin lotion that blocks harmful ultraviolet light from the sun, and so prevents sunburn.

SYNAPSE
The space across which a neuron transmits a chemical message to another neuron or to a muscle.

T-CELL
Immune cells that conduct chemical warfare at the site of an infection.

TENDONS
Sheets and bands of connective tissue that sheath muscles and attach them to bones and to each other.

TESTES
Male reproductive glands in which sperm are made.

TESTICLES
Testes; but also commonly used to mean the testes and the scrotum (sac) that holds them.

TESTOSTERONE
A hormone produced in the testes that is the most powerful of the androgens responsible for the development of male sex characteristics.

THYMINE
One of four molecules that constitute the genetic code of DNA; see also adenine, cytosine, and guanine.

THYROID
A gland in the neck that secretes hormones influencing basic life processes, such as growth rate.

ULTRAVIOLET PHOTONS
Invisible, high-energy light particles that cause cell damage such as sunburn.

UMBILICAL CORD
The cord that attaches the unborn baby to its placenta, and through which run blood vessels that bring the baby nutrients and remove its wastes.

URETHRA
The tube from the bladder through which urine is excreted.

UTERUS
Womb; the female's hollow, muscular, pear-shaped organ richly supplied with blood in which her baby develops for the nine months before birth.

VACCINE
A preparation of antigens taken by mouth or injection to immunize a person against a disease.

VAGINA
The entry into a female's body through which sperm reach the womb and the egg to be fertilized, and through which babies are born.

VERTEBRAE
The individual, interlocking bones that make up the backbone.

VIRUS
A scrap of DNA, sometimes containing only a few genes encased in a protein jacket, capable of entering a cell and forcing it to make multiple copies of the virus.

VULVA
The external parts of female genitals, including the clitoris, protective flaps and the opening to the vagina.

WOMB
See Uterus.

INDEX

A

B

D

E

F

H

I

J,K

L

M

N

P

Q,R

S

T

W

X,Y,Z

PHOTOGRAPHY CREDITS

Page v: (left) Donnelly Marks, (right) Peter Arnold, Inc. © David Scharf; Page vi: Howard Earl Simmons; Page vii: (left) Peter Arnold, Inc. © David Scharf, (right) Donnelly Marks; Page viii: (left to right) Donnelly Marks, Donnelly Marks, Sheilah Scully-Daly, Howard Earl Simmons; Page ix: (left and right) Donnelly Marks; Page 2: Astronomical Society of the Pacific; Page 6: Peter Arnold, Inc. © SIU; Page 10: Photo Researchers, Inc. © Barbara Ries; Page 12: Peter Arnold, Inc. © David Scharf; Page 18: Julia Beame; Page 19: (top) Photo Researchers, Inc. © Petit Format/ Nestle, (bottom) Dr. M.A. Ansary/ Science Photo Library; Page 21: Photo Researchers, Inc. © Hella Hammid; Page 22: Photo Researchers, Inc., J. Stevenson; Page 23: Sheilah Scully-Daly; Page 26: Superstock; Page 28: Rona Beame; Page 33: Julia Beame; Pages 34-35: Rona Beame; Page 38: Peter Arnold, Inc. © David Scharf; Page 40: Superstock; Page 41: Sheilah Scully-Daly; Page 42: Donnelly Marks; Page 43: Peter Arnold, Inc. © David Scharf; Page 44: Courtesy of Nora Martinez and Katie Cahill, photo by Ervin Simon Photo Studios; Page 46: Photo Researchers, Inc. © Jack Dermid; Page 49: (left) Dr. Rosalind King/Science Photo Library, (right top) Peter Arnold, Inc. © Mandred Kage, (right bottom) Photo Researchers, Inc. © K.R. Porter; Page 50: USDA Photo; Page 52: Photo Researchers, Inc. © Biophoto Assoc.; Page 54: Donnelly Marks; Page 55: Photo Researchers, Inc. © Scott Camazine; Page 56: Hand Surgery Associates; Page 59: Rona Beame, Hand Surgery Associates; Page 61: Dr. Marvin L. Kessler; Page 62: CNRI/Science Photo Library; Page 63: Howard Earl Simmons; page 64: Julia Beame; Page 68: (left) Science Photo Library, James Stevenson, (center) Peter Arnold, Inc. © Manfred Kage, (right top) Photo Researchers, Inc. © 1986 SIU, (right bottom) Peter Arnold, Inc.; Page 70: Agence Stock Photo, Jean-Francois Leblanc; Page 75: Howard Earl Simmons; Page 76: Superstock Four by Five; Page 79: (left) Photo Researchers, Inc. © 1982 Susan Rothenberg, (right) National Association of Anorexia Nervosa and Associated Disorders; Pages 82-93: Julia Beame; Page 88: (left top and bottom and right bottom) Chemical Design Ltd./Science Photo Library, (center and right top) Peter Arnold, Inc. © Leonard Lessin; Page 90: Scott & Pam Manson; Page 91: Sheilah Scully-Daly; Page 92: Howard Earl Simmons; Page 94: Sheilah Scully-Daly; Page 95: Julia Beame; Page 100: Sharon Guynap; Page 102: Rona Beame; Page 103: Donnelly Marks; Page 106: Bonnie Moors; Pages 108-109: Donnelly Marks; Page 110: Lia Di Stefano; Page 111: Donnelly Marks; Pages 112 and 114: Rona Beame; Page 117: Donnelly Marks; Page 120: Sheilah Scully-Daly; Page 121: National Cancer Institute; Page 126: American Academy of Pediatrics; Page 130: AP/World Wide Photos; Page 135: American Academy of Pediatrics; Page 136: Julia Beame; Page 137: Dr. Tony Brain/Science Photo Library; Page 141: Donnelly Marks; Page 145: Photo Researchers, Inc. © Chuck Brown; Page 146: Howard Earl Simmons; Page 150: Ellen Fisher Turk; Page 152: Sheilah Scully-Daly; Page 154: Julia Beame; Page 155: Lia Di Stefano; Page 156: Photo Researchers, Inc. © 1982 Ed Lettau; Page 166: Julia Beame; Page 169: Howard Earl Simmons; Page 170: Donnelly Marks; Page 171: Photo Researchers, Inc. © Alan Carey; Page 176: Donnelly Marks; Page 178: American Academy of Pediatrics; Page 179: Peter Arnold, Inc. © Matt Meadows; Pages 180 and 183: Julia Beame; Page 185: Johannes Hofmann/OKAPIA 1988; Page 187: Donnelly Marks; Page 190: (left top) Photo Researchers, Inc. © Marshall Sklar 1979, (left bottom) © Eric Hummel, (center) Dr. M. Phelps & Dr. J. Mazziotta et al/Neurology/ Science Photo Library, (right top) Laurence Weil, D.D.S., (right bottom) Photo Researchers, Inc. © M.W.F. Tweedie; Page 193: (left to right) Donnelly Marks, Donnelly Marks, Sheilah Scully-Daly, Howard Earl Simmons; Page 194: Julia Beame; Page 197: Photo Researchers, Inc. © Blair Seitz; Page 198: Darrell Rideout/La Leche League Int'l.; Page 202: Julia Beame; Page 205: Photo Researchers, Inc. © Alice Kandell; Page 207: Sheilah Scully-Daly; Page 210: Julia Beame; Page 213: Professor Oscar Miller/Science Photo Library; Page 216: Photo Researchers, Inc. © Akira Uchiyama; Page 218: © 1991 STAR TRIBUNE/Minneapolis-St. Paul; Page 219: Custom Medical Stock © R. Becker; Page 228: Armed Forces Institute of Pathology; Page 229: Medichrome/Tom Raymond; Page 230: Photo Researchers, Inc. © Stan Levy; Page 231: Photo Researchers, Inc. Science Source; Page 233: Julia Beame; Page 234 Photo Researchers, Inc. © Grapes/Michaud; Page 236: Courtesy of Damminix; Page 237: Julia Beame; Page 241: Photo Researchers, Inc. © George E. Jones III; Page 243: Peter Arnold, Inc. © David Scharf; Page 244: USDA Photo; Page 246: Rona Beame; Page 251: Julia Beame; Pages 253-255 Howard Earl Simmons; Page 257: Photo Researchers, Inc. © Barbara Ries; Page 259 Photo Researchers, Inc. © '87 Lawrence Migdale; Page 262: Photo Researchers, Inc. © Joseph Szabo; Page 265: Photo Researchers, Inc. © Ursula Markus; Page 266: NASA